CPCO.

A History of Pastoral Care

A History of Pastoral Care

Edited by

G. R. Evans

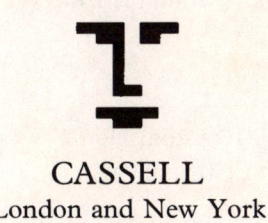

CASSELL
London and New York

Cassell
Wellington House, 125 Strand, London WC2R 0BB
370 Lexington Avenue, New York, NY 10017-6550

© The editor and contributors 2000

All rights reserved. No part of this publication may be reproduced or transmitted in any form or by any means, electronic or mechanical, including photocopying, recording or any information storage or retrieval system, without prior permission in writing from the publishers.

First published 2000

Acknowledgements
The Publishers acknowledge permission to reproduce the following copyright material in this book: (a) Excerpt from XXIII 'The Sacraments of Healing', in *Catholicism, Completely Revised and Updated*, by Richard P. McBrien. Copyright © 1994 by Richard P. McBrien. Reprinted by permission of HarperCollins Publishers Inc. (see pp. 400–13 of this volume); (b) Excerpt from *Introduction to Ecumenism*, by Jeffrey Gros, FSC, Eamon McManus and Ann Riggs. Copyright © 1998 by Paulist Press Inc. Used by permission of Paulist Press Inc. (see pp. 433–45 of this volume)

British Library Cataloguing-in-Publication Data
A catalogue for this book is available from the British Library.

ISBN   0-225-66840-8

Typeset by BookEns Ltd, Royston, Herts.
Printed and bound in Great Britain by
Cromwell Press, Trowbridge.

Contents

Contributors vii
Preface ix

Introduction 1
G.R. Evans

PART I The Biblical Foundations
1 The Old Testament 15
   J.W. Rogerson
2 The New Testament 30
   David Graham

PART II The Early Christian World
3 The Fathers and the early Councils 59
   G.R. Evans
4 Pastoral care and the monks: 'Whose feet do you wash?' 77
   Benedicta Ward

PART III The Middle Ages
5 Penitentials and pastoral care 93
   Thomas O'Loughlin
6 Pastoral care: the Fourth Lateran Council of 1215 112
   Norman Tanner
7 A ministry of preachers and confessors: the pastoral impact
   of the friars 126
   Michael Robson
8 The charitable and medical activities of the Hospitallers
   and Templars 148
   Malcolm Barber
9 'Since the pestilence time': pastoral care in the later
   Middle Ages 169
   William J. Dohar

| 10 | Catechesis in East and West
Lambros Kamperidis | 201 |

PART IV The Early Modern Period
11	The Reformation crisis in pastoral care *David Cornick*	223
12	The ministry to outsiders: the Jesuits *John O'Malley*	252
13	The family and pastoral care *Ralph Houlbrooke*	262
14	George Herbert and *The Country Parson* *Philip Sheldrake*	294
15	Pastoral care in England: Perkins, Baxter and Burnet *David Cornick*	313
16	The twentieth-century Anglican Franciscans *Petà Dunstan*	328
17	The growth of the soul in Charles Kingsley *G. R. Evans*	345
18	Post-Enlightenment pastoral care: into the twentieth century *David Cornick*	362

PART V The Modern World
19	Pastoral care at the end of the twentieth century *Ian Bunting*	383
20	The sacraments of healing: penance and anointing of the sick *Richard P. McBrien*	400
21	Justice: pastoral care and the ecclesiastical law *Rupert Bursell*	414
22	Ecumenism and ecclesial and pastoral proclamation *Jeffrey Gros, Eamon McManus and Ann Riggs*	433
23	Sects and new religious movements *Martyn Percy*	446
22	The pastoral care of people of other faiths *Christopher Lamb*	454

| Conclusion | 465 |
| Index | 467 |

Contributors

Malcolm Barber, Professor of Medieval History in the Department of History, University of Reading.

Ian Bunting, Research Officer to the Bishop of Southwell.

His Honour Judge **Rupert Bursell QC**, Circuit Judge, Bristol; Priest, Chancellor of the Dioceses of Durham and St Albans.

David Cornick, Principal of Westminster College, Cambridge and Fellow and Director of Studies in Theology at Robinson College, Cambridge.

William J. Dohar, Department of History, University of San Francisco.

Petà Dunstan, Librarian, Divinity School, Cambridge and Fellow of St Edmund's College, Cambridge.

G. R. Evans, Faculty of History, University of Cambridge.

David Graham, Minister of the Church of Scotland, Parish of North Berwick, Lothian.

Brother Jeffrey Gros, Associate Director of Ecumenical and Interreligious Affairs for the National Conference of Catholic Bishops in Washington, D.C.

Ralph Houlbrooke, Department of History, University of Reading.

Lambros Kamperidis, Department of Philosophy, Ethics and Theology, Université de Sherbrooke, Canada.

Christopher Lamb, Anglican priest in the diocese of Coventry.

Thomas O'Loughlin, lecturer in the Department of Theology and Religious Studies in the University of Wales, Lampeter.

John O'Malley SJ, Professor of Church History at Weston Jesuit School of Theology, Cambridge, Mass. and Past President of the Renaissance Society of America.

Richard P. McBrien, Crowley-O'Brien-Walter Professor of Theology, University of Notre Dame in Indiana.

Eamon McManus, Church of St Matthias the Apostle, Lanham, Maryland.

Martyn Percy, Director, Lincoln Theological Institute for the Study of Religion and Society, University of Sheffield.

Ann Riggs, National Conference of Catholic Bishops.

Michael Robson, Dean, St Edmund's College, Cambridge.

J. W. Rogerson, Professor Emeritus of Biblical Studies, University of Sheffield.

Philip Sheldrake, Vice-Principal, Sarum College, Salisbury and Honorary Professor, University of Wales, Lampeter.

Norman Tanner SJ, University Research Lecturer, Oxford University, and Visiting Professor of Ecumenical Councils in many places. Editor of *Decrees of the Ecumenical Councils* (1990).

Benedicta Ward SLG, Reader in the History of Christian Spriituality, Harris-Manchester College, Oxford and author of twelve books in this and related areas.

Preface

A history of pastoral care is a history of the Christian Church in action. But if we are to make sense of the work and effort of so many over so many centuries who have been fired with the love of Christ, we ought to look not only at the practicalities of making the message of the gospel a reality on earth, but also at the ideas which have informed the attempt, century by century.

The notion of 'shepherding' has not always been the same. Sometimes shepherds have gone in front of their flocks, sometimes behind; sometimes they have walked beside them. Sometimes the sheep have done their own shepherding. But it is striking that pastoral ministry has never been so controversial an issue as sacerdotal ministry. Christ is the Good Shepherd and also the one High Priest. In both he is unique. But while the question whether any human minister can 'be a priest' as his representative has divided the Church, there has never been any real difficulty with the pastoral ministry. That may be because it is a lower-key role. But it is no less important in the balance of the teachings of Jesus. For he was insistent that his disciples should not only love God, but also love their neighbours as themselves.

This is the history of 2000 years. Until comparatively late in that story the bulk of the formative thinking about pastoral care took place in Europe. Modern worldwide concerns have inevitably been formed by that earlier endeavour, sometimes in reaction against it. Much of this book is concerned with the background against which the modern issues have to be set if we are looking at a *history* of pastoral care.

Introduction

G. R. Evans

Pastoral care and society

The foundation text of the theology of pastoral care is Jesus' summary of the commandments in the form of the exhortation to love God with all one's heart and mind and soul; and to love one's neighbour as oneself (Matthew 5.43; Mark 12.31; Luke 10.27).

That places at the heart of the pastoral role of the Church the understanding that Christians stand in a relation not only to God but also to one another. Christ is the head of a body made up of all the members of the Church. There has been a return in the last decades of the twentieth century to an understanding of the centrality of the New Testament idea of community or *koinonia*. So pastoral care is *social*. But societies have taken many forms through the Christian centuries and the Christian 'social duties' of pastoral care have been varied according to the needs of the context. For example, there has always been a sense of the need to address the problem of 'slavery to sin'; yet in practical terms there is no responsibility to slaves in a society which does not know slavery, although there may be a pastoral duty to look after those who are 'enslaved' in other ways which deny them fullness of life, for example by addiction to drugs or alcohol or gambling.

In the Christian tradition *sin* stands at the head of the story. Throughout Christian history it has been taken that all human beings are spiritually in the wrong with God. If that is the starting-point, it follows that there is something to put right in every human soul. Pastoral care then becomes a matter of healing and restoration.

Pastoral care might on the face of it also seem to have a natural *missionary* dimension. Christ sent his disciples out to win others to faith in him. But the call to mission has not always been straightforward or uncontroversial. Sometimes Christianity itself has been divided, with missionaries from different denominations in competition with one another for the same souls. There has been grave misunderstanding, even ignorance. For example, when Russia again opened to the West in the 1990s, and ordinary Orthodox worship was possible once more, the faithful, many of whom had gone on practising their religion quietly, returned to their old ways, which were very ancient ways, rooted in the first centuries of the Christian tradition. But Baptist and other missionaries from the United States (and elsewhere) sometimes seem to have arrived under the impression that Russia had never heard about Jesus. They brought a gospel which had in fact been in that land for many centuries, and from which it had gone out into a wider Orthodox community.

Often, especially since the missionary period of the nineteenth century sowed small Christian communities all over the world, Christianity has been only one of many religions in a given country. There have been uncomfortable transitions during the twentieth century, away from the confident assumption that Christian missionaries had a duty to convert those of other faiths to their own, to bring to 'the heathen' a way of life which was not only better for them spiritually but also better for them economically and in other secular ways. There was imposition of Western learning and Western ways, and resentment about that has not been quick to fade.

All these aspects have their place in the chapters of this book. It is unavoidably a book with a great deal in it about the West, for the early Christian centuries had a mainly European scene and that continued to be the case for 1500 years. The ground-rules were laid in that arena. The contributors have looked for the most part at that mainstream story of the history and theology of pastoral care, because it has been the foundation for the explorations of the pastoral role in other parts of the world and later centuries. But as the tale rolls on into our own century the contributors have taken a broader canvas and tried to set the pastoral task in its world context.

Where Christianity has been the state or 'official' religion, there has arisen the question how far that gives the state a licence to consider itself a moral 'nanny' and to intrude into people's lives 'for their own good' or for the common good. Another way of putting this is in terms of the question whether a sin ought to be a crime. Should the state impose sanctions and guarantee protection to ensure that Christians toe the line not only as citizens but as Christians?

Membership of the secular community was, during most of the Middle Ages in the West, dependent upon and coextensive with membership of the Church marked by baptism of all infants immediately after birth. Civil disabilities might attend upon not being a member of the Christian Church in that way, or (later) upon not being a member of that branch of it which the state approved. That was the case in England for several centuries after Royal Supremacy was established over the Church of England. The spiritual and the social outcast might thus become one.

There were paradoxes everywhere arising from this uncomfortable coupling of social and spiritual acceptability. Mediaeval Christendom took it for granted that it was God's will that some should be socially inferior to others, and it had no difficulty with the New Testament and patristic notion that, spiritually, it was a positive advantage to be poor and socially disadvantaged. At the same time the poor were frequently suspected of being responsible for their own condition and so 'culpable', as the English Poor Law long supposed (unless they were known locally, so that it was clear that they were respectable and hardworking and that their poverty was no fault of their own). Vagrants were outlawed. There are examples throughout the essays in this volume of the confusions which could arise out of such overlap of social and spiritual categories.

It is only in the late twentieth century that the leading responsibility for taking care of people has shifted to the state, and then not on religious grounds but, once more paradoxically, with the secularization of society.

Individualism and the individual soul

By asking about the spiritual 'community' in which Christians live and work and its relation to the secular community, we risk losing sight of the individual. From an early period there has been a twin allegorical interpretation of the Song of Songs, in which the presumption has been both that the individual *soul* is the bride of Christ and also that the *Church* is the bride of Christ.

The New Testament approves of diversity. It is clear that there are different gifts of the Spirit. So it is acceptable for people to be themselves.

But that is not the same thing as approving eccentricity, or departures from the norm beyond a certain level. 'Individuality' in the sense of 'distinctiveness of individuals' has been treated with caution by the Church and it is a relatively modern ideal to value it and foster such 'personal development'. Christianity has characteristically sought in the pastoral ministry to value each soul while not taking all souls to be equal in their hopes of heaven.

Pastoral care and the family

There has always been a lingering sense that Paul was right when he gave only a reluctant permission for Christians to marry, on the grounds that it is better to marry than to burn. Ralph Houlbrooke describes the family in early modern England. The family in the form in which it exists in the modern West is not the only model, or indeed the most common model. For much of the Middle Ages and in much of the world today, families have been composed of large kin-groups, not small units of a father and mother and two or three children.

Nor has there always been the intimacy of prolonged contact between parents and children. A baby sent away to a wet-nurse might not see its parents until it was a toddler. Jane Austen's family had that experience in early eighteenth-century England. Because the structural relationship was often more important, family ties did not need to be emotionally close to involve close commitment and responsibility. A man's son was his heir, and his daughter his to give away in marriage, even if he was not emotionally close to either.

The early Christian centuries were more familiar with the *familia*, the Roman household which contained slaves as well as members of the family related by blood and marriage. Christian pastoral wisdom has generally encouraged slaves to obey their masters and masters to be kind to their slaves, and neither to disrupt the social hierarchy. It did not seem pastorally necessary to work for the emancipation of slaves until the eighteenth century, when the Evangelical William Wilberforce worked for the freedom of the African slaves who had been taken to America to work in the cotton plantations.

Similarly, in most times and places it has been natural for Christians to encourage wives to obey their husbands. Even in the novels of Trollope in nineteenth-century England it is taken for granted that a woman needs a strong man to lean on and that it is her role in life to be a clinging vine, although Trollope seems sometimes to have his tongue in his cheek when he says so.

The late-twentieth-century family in the West has taken a variety of forms in which two parents living together with their children is far from being the standard or only model. There is deep confusion in the churches about their pastoral duty in this situation. On the one hand there is a sense of the need to uphold the sanctity of marriage. Roman Catholicism still sets its face against divorce, taking sexual intercourse to be permissible only within marriage, while Anglicanism agonizes. On the other hand, there is an ancient duty to protect the helpless. One-parent families are perhaps the modern Western counterpart of the widows and orphans of the New Testament.

Who are the pastors?

In James 5.16 it seems to be assumed that Christians will help and support one another, talking to one another and 'forgiving' one another in love. This sounds very much like modern 'counselling', or simply common-sense resort to a friend in time of trouble. It does not imply that there exists a class of Christian specially set apart for such work with responsibilities different from those every Christian shares, because every Christian has a duty to love his or her neighbour.

But the pattern throughout the life of the Church has been to have such a special category. Some Christians have had ministerial responsibility, and commonly that has been understood to be a pastoral responsibility. So the first question is, in what respect and to what extent are those with pastoral care set apart? There is authority in Scripture for thinking in terms of a 'priesthood of all believers'. But that is a collective priesthood, not an individual entrusting to each person of a personal ministerial responsibility. Jesus spoke of the Good Shepherd who looks after his sheep. This is the model of all pastoral care in the Christian Church, but it has proved to be capable of great development and variation.

When Jesus sent out his disciples to preach the gospel he began a process of 'making ministers' who were to win people over to faith and also to care for them once they became Christians. From the beginning there was dispute about the character he intended this ministry to have, and its authority. But in New Testament times there was already a recognition that there were at least two main tasks: one of administering the sacraments, preaching and teaching and educating souls; and the practical one of making sure that widows and orphans did not go hungry. These two facets of the shepherd's task were exemplified in Jesus' own life and work, and they have remained clear throughout the history of the Church.

Jesus spoke of the Good Shepherd (John 10.14), and in other religions, too, there are gurus. This has tended to create patterns in thinking about pastoral care in which the learner sits at the feet of someone older, wiser, more experienced, a parent in the spiritual life. Although they may be of infinite value to him, the sheep are not the equal of the shepherd, and they can never become so. This 'parental' motif has been strong in the Christian theology of ministry. Calling a priest 'Father' remains a natural usage in the Roman Catholic Church and elsewhere, and the Church is traditionally 'Mother'.

The episcopal system which evolved from the period of the early Church gradually developed a 'ladder' structure, with those called to the ministry becoming first deacons, then priests and finally bishops. The sense of hierarchy was strong, with an obligation of canonical obedience to their bishop heavy upon the lower orders of ordained ministers. Gregory the Great emphasizes the role of bishops as *rectores*, rulers of the Church, and *episcopos* itself means 'overseer'. The bishop became 'the *Lord* bishop'.

By the twelfth century in the West this pattern was beginning to encounter some resistance among anti-establishment dissidents such as the Waldensians, or 'Poor Men of Lyons'. They questioned the appropriateness of according respect to such spiritual 'rulers' of men when some of them were visibly corrupt. They asked whether it was really true that the sacraments over which the priestly classes had complete control were necessary for salvation. They even asked whether it was necessary for the priestly classes to enjoy that complete control. From such movements Lollards and others derived, who felt free to set up ministries of their own, on a quite different basis. Some allowed women to minister. Others emphasized the brotherhood and sisterhood of all Christians with their inbuilt equality. In the sixteenth century, sects following this line of teaching appointed and dismissed their own ministers, rotating the ministerial tasks among members of the community and moving away in many respects from the 'parental' model.

Nevertheless, in Christian history there has been a consistent pattern of encouraging the individual to follow the examples of those who are spiritually their seniors. Hagiography was written in the Middle Ages chiefly for that purpose, and Bernard of Clairvaux describes features of the life of St Malachi which he intends his listeners to seek to emulate.

According to this way of thinking, one individual might come to be regarded as better or higher than another (though paradoxically usually also as more humble, for Christianity has taken humility to be a spiritual virtue) and this habit encouraged a cult of the 'expert', the 'specialist' in the spiritual life. Such were the Desert Fathers in Christianity's earliest centuries, and, as Gregory the Great describes as late as the sixth century, they attracted people in search of the benefits of propinquity, and the spectacle of a wonder. People came to those awaiting martyrdom treating them as confessors and seeking to get absolution.

Holiness is powerfully attractive, although the holy man or woman may not be directly helpful to one seeking what he or she has to offer. The holy person does not necessarily behave like a guru, advising or counselling. Indeed, in some of the stories of the Desert Fathers the holy person is often found to be silent, remote, brusque, even unreasonable. However, as failure to respond can be as educative as willingness to respond, this does not mean he or she cannot be a teacher. When Augustine of Hippo (354–430) went to Bishop Ambrose of Milan to ask for clarification of some theological points which had been troubling him, he found him preoccupied, reading, with a patient queue waiting to see him. Augustine learned something.

Do-it-yourself pastoral care

For most of the history of the Church the principal shepherd was normally the bishop, and he appointed priests as his 'vicars', to look after the people of each area of his diocese. The principle that pastoral care remains with the bishop was clear, but the day-to-day work and personal knowledge of the members of the 'flock' passed to the priest. The forum in which this type of ministerial pastoral care is exercised has ranged from the universal to the intimate, where the sinner meets the confessor in the privacy of the confessional.

The model of equals, companions on a journey, is less common in Christian history. Yet even in the centuries when an ordained pastoral ministry was the norm everywhere, as it was in both East and West until the sixteenth century, lay people and dissidents of various sorts formed groups for mutual pastoral help. The confraternities of the later Middle Ages were such 'brotherhoods'. In the eighteenth century Methodists formed 'little churches', *ecclesiolae*, 'classes' which met regularly. The members kept a vigilant eye on one another's conduct, with a sanction of possible exclusion if standards of conduct and devotion were not maintained.

A rather different pastoral need has been met by 'Bible study groups'. These were already taking place in Lollard England in the early fifteenth century, and the intellectual level of Bible commentary they achieved was sometimes surprisingly high. Such study groups remain popular in the twentieth century, especially among Evangelicals. They afford both an opportunity for prayer and an educational vehicle. They provide mutual support for their members in a pastoral situation where Christians exercise a form of 'pastoral' care for one another.

The private and shared journey: going apart

There is a persistent motif of 'journeying' in Christianity, which is found in other religions too, and which clearly answers a need for a sense of spiritual growth and development. The soul goes on a pilgrimage to God; literally, in the stories of actual pilgrimages, but also inwardly. Sometimes the theme is one of return to a home from which the soul has been cast out, sometimes of a voyage of pioneering discovery in which the soul grows in its hunger for God from its spiritual infancy; until it becomes capable first of bearing the shattering glory of his presence, and eventually of enjoying it. The picture of heaven in Augustine's mind was of an eternal intellectual communion with God in unimaginable love. In the brief raptures experienced by some mystics there is a foretaste of that. In *The Book of Margery Kempe*, the fifteenth-century English mystic, Christ says to her:

> As suddenly as the lightning cometh from Heaven, so suddenly come I into thy soul, and illuminate it with the light of grace and of understanding, and set it all on fire with love, and make the fire of love to burn there-in, and purge it full clear from all earthly filth. And sometimes, daughter, I make earthquakes to frighten the people, so that they should dread me.
>
> And so, daughter, ghostly have I done with thee, and with other chosen souls that shall be saved, for I turn the earth of their hearts upside down and make them sore afraid, so that they dread vengeance should fall upon them for their sins.

And so didst thou, daughter, when thou turnedst first to me, and it is needful that young beginners do so; but now, daughter, thou has great cause to love Me well, for the perfect charity that I give thee putteth away all dread from thee.[1]

A conscious undertaking to find God involves concentration upon an inner life. This, as Margery Kempe's experience shows, is both spiritual and intellectual. It is a rational reflection upon what is happening, as well as an affective experience, and has bred a literature of mysticism.

This undertaking has created pressures in the outward and visible lives of individuals. Someone who seeks God must find time and space for the task, and some have responded by retreating in some way to concentrate upon it. Religious orders have had a variety of distinctive visions of their purposes but they have all had in common a perception that their members stood in a special relationship to the world. Benedictines have taken a contemplative route, working for the world by praying for it, and growing their own souls in that work of prayer. The mendicant orders had a special vocation to preach, and to do that they returned into the world; indeed, they wandered about in it. But they remained dedicated and separate.

Testing the system: the problems of pastoral care at the end of the twentieth century

In the modern world the canvas is broader and the assumption is now, for many, not that there is a need to 'bring back into the fold' but that Christian ought to meet non-Christian in mutual respect and mutual support.

Ecumenism is at a precarious stage of its development, and although local ecumenical projects flourish in many parts of the world, in such contexts practical conflicts can arise over the models and methodologies of pastoral care with which different ecclesial communities have been used to working. Modern Orthodoxy in Russia bears the marks of its survival under communism; elsewhere, too, there are pastoral care problems because of the after-effects of trauma at the hands of communist regimes which sought to outlaw the practice of the Christian religion. Interfaith dialogue has aspects in which problems of pastoral care arise. For example, that young Islamic girls born in Britain are sent to Pakistan to be married without their consent raises delicate questions because of the conflict between what the West sees as fundamental human rights and what the Islamic community may well see as interference with its customs.

World mission and pastoral care are linked in the 'peace and justice' struggles across the globe, for example in the 'liberation theology' of Latin America.

Some will remain outside all pastoral networks, however informal. The 'outcasts', the 'underclass', those who live rough in the streets, those whose withdrawal is voluntary and those who are involuntarily excluded by the society of the day. What is the pastoral duty of the Church in the situations Martyn Percy describes? What is its duty to the excluded and the bullied and the ineffectual and the idle and the shiftless? Are there some who do not deserve to be helped? Would such an attitude be Christlike?

Then there are problems without precedent which arise as a result of scientific development, or new medical technology. If a child is created to the stage of being a fertilized embryo and 'stored', it may eventually be born as the younger brother of an identical twin sibling implanted some years earlier. Or there may be destruction of such embryos, after a period in storage, without any clear moral or legal resolution of their status as human beings with putative rights.

Perhaps the best way to embrace all this is by returning to the New Testament notion of a 'diaconal' ministry. There has always been a *diakonia*, a ministry of practical service, which was at first charged with looking after widows and orphans. Those who have give to those who have not: food or shelter or advice.

Eighteenth-century English Sunday schools set out to teach poor children to read and write. Friendly societies, burial societies and sodalities are descendants of the late mediaeval religious fraternities, and they have continued in practical social purposes. Provisions for child care, orphanages, the rescuing of street children, protection societies again have social purposes, although the early orphanages certainly sought to inculcate a Christian faith. Temperance societies were set up for a social good, so were the Samaritans. There is an element of pastoral care in each. There are aspects of pastoral care which are supremely practical, and in which the spiritual element may lie deeper than conscious access.

The chapters which follow seek to bring together not only the classic issues in the history of pastoral care in the Christian system and beyond, but also new things which challenge the old assumptions.

In the preparation of this book it became plain at every stage of the planning and discussion with prospective contributors that this is a subject full of interconnections. It is important to exploit them. One value of a comprehensive account is that it can throw up new juxtapositions. We hope we have succeeded not only in providing a reference-book, but also in saying something new about a subject whose coherence speaks for itself.

Conclusion: applying the work of Christ

> I fled him, down the nights and down the days;
> I fled him, down the arches of the years;
> I fled him, down the labyrinthine way
> Of my own mind; and in the midst of tears
> I hid from him ...
>   Halts by me that footfall:
>   Is my gloom, after all,
> Shade of his hand, outstretched caressingly?
> 'Ah, fondest, blindest, weakest,
> I am he whom thou seekest!
> Thou dravest love from thee who dravest Me.'[2]

For many people there is no dramatic change of mind at all, but merely a steady growth of conviction. But for all those who become Christians there is a time of spiritual growth and learning. Christ's saving work has to be applied to each individual. Evil deeds go on being committed, and inside each man and woman there is a continuing experience of the warfare between good and evil. The pastoral role changes in new contexts. But the central task is the same.

It has been the work of the Church down the ages to assist the work of grace in this personal journey of salvation – or some would say rather to tend it, like a gardener watching over a plant as it grows – through various provisions for taking care of struggling souls.

We shall be looking in these essays at the practical and also the theological ideas the Church and the Churches have brought to bear on this task.

Notes

1. Ch. 77.
2. Francis Thompson, 'The Hound of Heaven'.

PART I

The Biblical Foundations

1

The Old Testament

J. W. Rogerson

Shepherd and saviour

If pastoral care is understood as the exercise of a ministry towards individuals to help them appropriate the benefits of the saving work of Jesus Christ, then there is no pastoral care in the Old Testament. This may seem a surprising statement. The obvious 'ground' for this assertion, that it is anachronistic to look for Christian salvation in the Old Testament, can be countered by pointing out that Christian theologians of all generations have found 'types' or anticipations of the gospel in the Old Testament. It can also be argued, in favour of the Old Testament as a proper starting-place for a history of pastoral care, that the fundamental model for pastoral care, that of the sheep and the shepherd, comes from Ezekiel 34, and that although ancient Israel was a nation, it was also a community of faith with an established priesthood. The purpose of this chapter will be to point out the differences between ancient Israel as portrayed in the Old Testament and the Christian Church, when considered in the context of pastoral care.

Dietrich Bonhoeffer wrote that the faith of the Old Testament is not a religion of salvation.[1] By this he meant that it did not promise a deliverance from the cares, anxieties and sins of this world into a better world beyond the grave. This fact, that separates historical Christianity from the religion of the Old Testament, is fundamental when considering pastoral care. According to the Old Testament there were institutions in ancient Israel that enabled individuals to seek help in time of need. There were also customs of instruction and support within the family network, as well as formal judicial arrangements for settling disputes. There were elaborate arrangements for procuring the forgiveness of sins – sins largely understood as infringements of ritual and purity laws. But all of these functioned within the horizon of life that had to be lived here and now. In Christian devotion, a psalm such as Psalm 84 could be understood to describe the pilgrimage of the soul through life to a heavenly Jerusalem. This possibility was not available to users of the psalm in the Old Testament period, and this fundamental difference of perspective must be borne in mind in what follows. The chapter will fall into two main parts: first, an examination of passages in the Old Testament that deal with the support of individuals; second, an attempt to sketch what little is known about the social development of ancient Israel towards something that might resemble pastoral care.

Pastoral care and the support of individuals in Old Testament passages

Genesis 14

The story of Abram's military mission to rescue his nephew Lot from abduction by an alliance of four kings is an indication of the importance of the kin group in the protection and support of members of a family. Although families, as depicted in the Old Testament, could witness rivalry between brothers and between wives of the same husband, and although there are instances of fratricide and rape within families, intrusion into the kin group from outside would unite a family in support of a wronged member. This aspect of social organization probably survived all the other changes in ancient Israelite society.

Exodus 18.13–27

As with Genesis 14, it is not necessary to suppose that this chapter is historically true. What it nevertheless does is to express something that would make sense in the experience of the intended readers/hearers of the story. In it, Moses is persuaded by his father-in-law not to try to be the sole arbitrator in disputes between individuals. Moses is to select people who will deal with minor disputes, and who will refer difficult cases to him. The story reflects two aspects of individual support – that of support within the family network and the support that individuals looked for when in dispute with each other. Needless to say, we are in the realm of secular, not religious guidance.

Leviticus 13

The regulations about the examination of people suffering from skin complaints implies that priests had at least rudimentary medical knowledge. Whether this was used to effect cures of illnesses as well as to diagnose them is not stated. However, as will be seen later, prophets and holy men were believed to be able to assist those who were ill.

1 Samuel 9.3–10

In this passage Saul and a servant are sent to find some lost asses. As a last resort they decide to consult a man of God who, they hope, will be able to tell them where the animals can be found. The man of God, Samuel, tells them that the asses have now been found. It is clear from the narrative that the lost asses have been used by God to bring Saul and Samuel together, so that Samuel can anoint Saul as prince over Israel (1 Sam. 10.1). The narrative thus expresses the idea of God's pastoral care for Israel.

1 Samuel 16.1–13

The theme of God's pastoral care for Israel continues in the story of the anointing of David by Samuel. So as not to arouse Saul's suspicion, Samuel is told by God to invite Jesse and his sons to a sacrifice at Bethlehem. This brings David and Samuel into contact. God's pastoral care for Israel is to be exercised through David.

1 Kings 17.8–24

During the drought announced by Elijah, the prophet is sent to the widow in Zarephath in Sidon. He provides her miraculously with food and brings her son to life when the boy dies. This is an instance of the initiative being taken by God and a prophet in support of an individual, who happens in this case to be a non-Israelite.

1 Kings 22.1–23

This important passage expresses the relationship between kingship and shepherding, which is at the root of a Christian model of pastoral care. On the eve of the battle of Ramoth-gilead between Israel and its allies and Syria, the prophet Micaiah foresees the defeat of Israel and the death of the king. His vision is described in the graphic words

> I saw all Israel scattered upon the mountains, as sheep that have no shepherd; and the Lord said, 'These have no master; let each return to his home in peace.' (v. 17)

The connection between kingship and shepherding is very old in the ancient Near East, and can be found in Egypt and Mesopotamia. Thus Gudea (c.2141–2122), the *Ensi* (governor) of Lagash, recalled in a description of a dream, 'I am a shepherd; the princeliness of a shepherd has been entrusted to me.'[2] Later in the account, the god Ningirsu addresses Gudea as follows:

> When, O trusty shepherd Gudea
> Thou shalt have started for me [work] on Eninnu, my royal abode ...[3]

Hammurabi, king of Babylon (1792–1759) described himself in the preface to his laws

> Hammurabi, the shepherd, called by Enlil am I;
> the one who makes affluence and plenty abound.[4]

H.W.F. Saggs quotes the address of an official to a first-millennium king:

> All the people rely on you, O Shepherd, in connection with the propitious utterance of your mouth.[5]

There are many other examples.[6] For Egypt, there are not only references to rulers such as Amenhotep III (1386–1349) and Seti I (1291–1278) as shepherds; the shepherd's crook was a symbol of royalty, and is shown, for example, on the black granite seated statue of Rameses II (1279–1212) in the Turin Museum, and the depiction of Rameses III (1182–1151) in the Great Harris Papyrus in the British Museum in London.

The understanding of kingship in the Old Testament in terms of shepherding was thus part of Israel's share of its cultural milieu. It is noteworthy that 1 Kings 22.17 is implied in the New Testament as expressing the compassion of Jesus for the people who came to seek him in lonely places, and immediately prior to the feeding of the five thousand (Mark 6.30–44, esp. v. 34).

2 Kings 4

Among the many miracle stories surrounding Elisha are several that repeat Elijah's feats, including miraculously providing oil for a woman in debt (vv. 1–7), and providing and restoring to life a son (vv. 11–37). Additional miracles in this chapter are the neutralizing of poisonous food (vv. 38–41) and the feeding of a hundred men with twenty barley loaves (vv. 42–4). The overall thrust is that of the way in which God cares materially for the prophetic groups that serve him, through the miraculous gifts of Elisha.

2 Kings 19.1–7 = Isaiah 37.1–7

This is an instance of a king, Hezekiah, seeking guidance from a prophet, Isaiah, during a time of crisis. The setting is the Assyrian invasion of Judah in 701 BCE. The king does not go to Isaiah in person. Nevertheless, the prophet sends a word of reassurance to Hezekiah. The Assyrian king will hear a rumour that will cause him to return to his own land.

The Book of Job

The book of Job is the only text in the Old Testament that records an explicit attempt to give pastoral support. Job, having been deprived of his children and his possessions as a result of God's wager with the Satan, is visited by three friends, Eliphaz, Bildad and Zophar. Their initial reaction is to share in his grief by tearing their garments and sprinkling dust on their heads. They sit with him in silence for seven days and nights (Job 2.12–13).

The interpretation of this silence is bound up with questions about the relationship between the prose and poetic parts of the book of Job. The prose prologue is the necessary backdrop to the dialogues that form the bulk of the book, and given the unsympathetic way that Job is treated by his friends in the dialogues, it is possible, on a 'final form' reading of the book, to regard the initial silent sympathy of the friends as cynical, insincere or merely conventional. It is possible, however, to approach the matter from a different angle. The main concern of the writer of Job was to explore certain theological themes by way of the dialogues put into the mouths of Job and the three (later four) friends. To do this it was necessary to set up the dialogue situation, and this was done by drawing upon a custom that would have been familiar to the intended readers/hearers of the book. This was the custom of silent companionship with a suffering person, the silence being broken only by the sufferer himself (perhaps, in women's circles, by the sufferer herself). There is thus no need, for the purposes of this chapter, to speculate upon the motives of the characters in the book of Job read as a piece of literature. It can be treated as an instance of a pastoral care that was by now customary.[7]

The dialogues, if they are considered in the context of pastoral care, do not appear to be examples of good practice. The initial three friends never address Job by name and their purpose is to convince Job of the wrongness of his position and the rightness of theirs. There is little attempt to address Job's arguments directly. Nor do the friends address God directly; he seems to be the abstract guarantor of their rigid beliefs. Job, on the other hand, if thwarted in seeking to confront God (Job 23.3–7), at least addresses God and believes that God would listen to him and reason with him if only Job had this opportunity:

> Oh, that I knew where I might find him, that I might come even to his seat!
> I would lay my case before him and fill my mouth with arguments.
> I would learn what he would answer me, and understand what he would say to me.
> Would he contend with me in the greatness of his power?
> No; he would give heed to me.
> There an upright man could reason with him,
> and I should be acquitted for ever by my judge.
>
> (Job 23.3–7)

One of the themes of the book of Job, then, is that human pastoral care has its limitations and that only God can be trusted to deal with individuals fairly. It is fitting that the climax of the book should be a direct address of God to Job out of a whirlwind – an address which does not answer Job's intellectual questions but which enables him to make sense of his predicament by experiencing a transcendence directed personally to him. It may not be too far-fetched to employ this fact for reflection on Christian pastoral care. The latter is grounded in the incarnation of God and it is effective to the extent that it enables individuals to experience a transcendence that is specifically directed to them.

Psalms

By far the greater proportion of psalms are what form-critical scholarship has identified as individual or national laments. Their typical structure is that of a complaint followed by an assertion of confidence.

Psalm 6 is a typical individual lament. It opens with an appeal to God to be gracious in the face of the psalmist's physical illness and his oppression by 'workers of evil'. It ends with an assertion of confidence:

> Depart from me, all you workers of evil;
> for the Lord has heard the sound of my weeping.
> The Lord has heard my supplication; the Lord accepts my prayer.
> All my enemies shall be ashamed and sorely troubled;
> they shall turn back, and be put to shame in a moment.
>   (Psalm 6.8–10)

How has the change from lament to confidence come about? One view is that laments such as this were part of a liturgy for the individual used in the presence of a priest or a cultic prophet. Once the worshipper had made his complaint the cultic official gave a blessing or a prophetic oracle, and it was this that gave the worshipper confidence to express thanks to God for hearing the complaint.[8] If this theory is correct, it is evidence for a particular kind of pastoral care in the context of a sanctuary.

The psalms contain references to God as shepherd, of which Psalm 23 is the best-known instance. Other examples are Psalm 77.20

> Thou didst lead thy people like a flock
> by the hand of Moses and Aaron,

Psalm 80.1

> Give ear, O Shepherd of Israel,
> thou who leadest Joseph like a flock!

And Psalm 100.3b (cf. also Psalm 95.7)

>   we are his people, and the sheep of his pasture.

Such forms of address in the latter examples are typical of how gods were understood in the ancient Near East.[9] The interpretation of Psalm 23 is uncertain. It could be seen as a royal psalm, spoken by a royal representative of the community and expressing his special relationship to God as shepherd; it could be the utterance of an individual Israelite concerning his experience of God's goodness.[10] In either case the image of God as shepherd is unaffected.

Proverbs

A recurrent phrase in the book of Proverbs is 'my son' followed by an exhortation to listen to or observe a father's teaching. Typical are 1.8

> Hear, my son, your father's instruction,
> and reject not your mother's teaching,

and 2.1

> My son, if you receive my words and treasure up my commandments with you ...

Because of this, it is not surprising that the origin of some of the material in the book has been sought in instruction given by parents to children, most likely in aristocratic families (cf. Prov. 4.3). This is another aspect of the way in which kin networks within society offered support and guidance to individuals.

Ezekiel 34 (Jeremiah 23.1–4)

In moving from Proverbs to Ezekiel a number of references to God or to the king as shepherd have been passed over. These include Isaiah 40.11, 'He will feed his flock'; Jeremiah 3.15, 'I will give you shepherds [i.e. rulers] after my own heart'; 10.21, 'For the shepherds are stupid'; and 22.22, 'The wind shall shepherd all your shepherds'.

Ezekiel 34 is the most extended treatment of God and of rulers as shepherds in the Old Testament, and it is the passage on which John 10.1–29 is based; but it also has close affinities with Jeremiah 23.1–4. The latter passage condemns shepherds who destroy and scatter the sheep, and who have not cared for them. It promises that God will gather his flock from the lands where they have been scattered and will set over them shepherds that will care for them. Whether the Jeremiah passage is earlier than that in Ezekiel is a moot point.[11]

The Ezekiel passage spells out the duties of shepherds, duties that have been neglected in the case of those condemned by Ezekiel:

> You do not feed the sheep. The weak you have not strengthened, the sick you have not healed, the crippled you have not bound up, the strayed you have not brought back, the lost you have not sought.
> (vv. 3b–4)

Doubtless these accusations are based upon accepted conventions of the duties of actual shepherds who looked after sheep; but it is not difficult to apply them generally to the obligations of leaders, especially if read in the light of a passage such as Psalm 72:

> May he [the King] judge thy people with righteousness,
> and thy poor with justice!
> May he defend the cause of the poor of the people,
> give deliverance to the needy, and crush the oppressor!
> For he delivers the needy when he calls,
> the poor and him who has no helper.
> He has pity on the weak and the needy, and saves the lives of the needy.
> From oppression and violence he redeems their life;
> and precious is their blood in his sight.
> (vv. 2, 4, 12–14)

In turn, these words in the psalm can be seen as part of a wider understanding of the duties of kings in the ancient Near East. In the Ugaritic legend of King Keret, the king's son Yassib addresses his sick father and reproves him because of his failing powers. Among his charges are

> thou canst not judge the cause of the widow, canst not try the case of the wretched, canst not put down them that despoil the child(ren) of the poor, canst not feed the orphan before thy face (and) the widow behind thy back.[12]

Ezekiel 34 handles the imagery of shepherds in several different ways. Initially (vv. 1–16) it condemns the shepherds, who are probably to be understood as the rulers of Judah, for not caring for the sheep, the result of which was that the sheep were scattered and found themselves at the mercy of wild beasts. This scattering is probably an allusion to the deportations of 597 and 587. God then promises that he will become the shepherd and will gather them together from where they have been scattered. Verses 17–24 introduce a new theme, that of condemnation of the strong sheep and goats within the flock that thrust aside the weaker animals and trample the pasture and foul the drinking water. The reference would seem to be to the anarchy that prevails in the absence of a ruler who upholds justice, and God promises that he will set up his servant David as their shepherd. This contrasts with the first section of the chapter in which God himself will perform the duties of the shepherd.

The final section (vv. 25–31) develops the imagery in a third direction – that of establishing a covenant of peace. Wild beasts will be banished from the land, rainfall will be reliable and the land will be fruitful. All will have plenty to eat, and there will be no danger from invasions of the land by foreigners. Thus, while firmly anchored in the conventions of shepherding and of the duties of kings in the ancient Near East, Ezekiel 34 develops these images in a distinctly Israelite way and in the context of the destruction of Jerusalem in 587 and the Babylonian exile.

Micah 5.2–4 (Heb. 4.14–5.3)

This well-known passage, famous for its reference to Bethlehem as the place from which a ruler for Israel is to come forth, can be read as the original continuation of Micah 3.12.[13] Micah 3 contains one of the most brutal condemnations in the Old Testament of behaviour by those in religious and political authority. The rulers are likened to cannibals who tear the flesh and cook the bones of people called, significantly, 'my people' (i.e. God's people). The prophets lead the people astray as do the seers and diviners. Justice is corrupted by bribery, and all these unsavoury activities are gilded by the hypocrisy of the belief that no evil will come upon the nation because people say 'Is not the Lord in the midst of us?' Micah's judgement upon Jerusalem is that it will be destroyed and never rebuilt. It will become a wooded height.

The post-exilic editing of Micah has followed this condemnation immediately with the oracle also found at Isaiah 2.2–4 about the nations going up to Jerusalem in the latter days to learn God's ways. If, however, 5.12–14 originally followed 3.12, the rejection of Jerusalem and the corrupt (in Micah's view) line of David is followed by the promise of a new beginning centred upon Bethlehem. Although David is not explicitly mentioned, the oracle looks forward to a ruler from Bethlehem who will 'stand and feed his flock in the strength of the Lord' (Micah 5.4).

The sociology of pastoral care in ancient Israel

The only source of information about pastoral care in ancient Israel is the Old Testament, and this is the literature of a religious movement or movements in Israel which has left strong traces of the diversities that existed among the people and the rulers, and which were opposed by the circles that produced the Old Testament. It will be convenient to begin by considering forms of pastoral care of which the official religion of Israel disapproved.

The strongest condemnation of unacceptable forms of pastoral care occurs in Deuteronomy 18.10–12:

> There shall not be found among you ... anyone who practises divination, a soothsayer, or an augur, or a sorcerer, or a charmer, or a medium, or a wizard, or a necromancer. For whoever does these things is an abomination to the Lord.

Although the exact meanings of these terms and the functions of their practitioners may be uncertain, they broadly cover activities designed to discover or influence the future course of events. This is attempted by contact with the dead, by inspecting objects or their configurations, and by performing symbolic actions. If it is asked why this should be thought necessary, two narratives in the Old Testament provide an answer. The first is 1 Samuel 28.3–19, in which Saul enquires of a medium at En-dor how to conduct his imminent battle with the Philistines. Significantly, we are told that Saul 'had put the mediums and the wizards out of the land' (v. 3), and the reason why he needed guidance from a medium was because God had not answered his request 'either by dreams, or by Urim, or by prophets' (v. 6). In the narrative, the medium conjures up Samuel, who refuses to advise Saul and who tells him that he and his army will be defeated by the Philistines. The other narrative is at 2 Kings 1.2–18, where King Ahaziah sends messengers to enquire of Baal-zebub the god of Ekron whether he will recover from a serious injury resulting from a fall.

Guidance and support, therefore, were sought in boundary situations, when individuals faced crises such as imminent battles or serious injuries; and there existed in ancient Israel various types of specialist who could be consulted. The En-dor incident is interesting because it shows that the Old Testament religion was not opposed to seeking guidance or reassurance, as long as it was sought from God by what official Old Testament religion regarded as legitimate means.

This raises the question why the official religion of the Old Testament wanted to suppress the specialists mentioned in Deuteronomy 18.10–11. One answer would be that the move towards suppression was part of the move for greater control in general over the lives of ordinary Israelites. There is undoubtedly truth in this. There is no good reason for dissociating the book of Deuteronomy from Josiah's reformation of 622 onwards; and that reformation was undoubtedly an attempt to establish control over the religion of Judah by closing local sanctuaries and declaring Jerusalem to be the sole legitimate sanctuary (see also 2 Kings 23.24).

Granted this, the crucial question is whether the whole process should be understood in terms of the surveillance over the lives of ordinary people that is associated with the emergence of the modern state.[14] If this view is taken, a somewhat sombre, if not cynical, account of the Old Testament view of pastoral care can be developed, in which care becomes control, and the instrument of control is the limiting of access to specialists who are approved by those in command. However, if the conclusions of Giddens are followed, and it is accepted that ancient Judah, as a traditional state, did not achieve the measure of control and surveillance of the modern state, a different approach is needed; and it is the one that will be followed here.

If the reforms of Josiah did not establish centralized control over Judah – and according to the evidence of 2 Kings 23.31–7 his reforms did not survive after his death – then what we have in texts such as Deuteronomy 18.10–11 are the expression of ideals rather than material that permits us to conclude that mediums, sorcerers and necromancers were actually suppressed in Judah as part of the establishment of control over the lives of ordinary people. This in turn raises the question why these particular ideals were expressed, and what lay behind them. It could be objected to my line of argument that whether control was actually established or only desired to be established is immaterial, and that the fact remains that pastoral care in Israel and Judah was an attempt to make people conform to a particular type of religion; that people needed to be prevented from turning to traditional sources of guidance and comfort and made to turn to channels that were officially approved.

It cannot be denied that there is truth in this objection. The representatives of official religion in Judah believed that God was offended if people sought guidance from sources that excluded God (cf. the narratives discussed above – 1 Samuel 28 and 2 Kings 1). However, it is also important to draw attention to that material in the Old Testament which resists the idea that the goal of pastoral care was the complete control of ordinary people. The book of Job is a powerful document of determined resistance to efforts to control what is to be believed. If what is argued above about the book of Micah is correct, then it, too, is evidence of an alternative viewpoint, one condemning Jerusalem and its abuse of power and looking for a new beginning elsewhere. Paradoxically, the book of Deuteronomy itself contains material about restricting the power of monarchy (Deuteronomy 17.14–20); and if the book of Proverbs seeks to define the ideal character of an 'upper-class' Israelite, Ecclesiastes goes out of its way to undermine the achievements of wisdom and to classify them as vanity.

There is a strong element of protest and nonconformity running through the material in the Old Testament so that any account of pastoral care in the perspective of Old Testament religion that portrays it as simply a matter of seeking to exercise control and to impose uniformity of belief and behaviour, is inadequate. Although the understanding of what it meant to be a person in ancient Israel was much less individualistic than in modern Western society and more bound up with membership of a group, there were provisions for meeting individual needs, and rulers were to be sensitive to the distinctive needs of individual groups. Deuteronomy can be seen as a sincere attempt to legislate upon the nation the need to care, and Job as articulating the need to avoid the caring that kills.

Notes

1. D. Bonhoeffer, *Widerstand und Ergebung. Briefe und Aufzeichnungen aus der Haft*, ed. E. Bethge (Munich: Christian Kaiser Verlag, 1951), p. 225. ET by R. H. Fuller, *Letters and Papers from Prison* (London: SCM Press, 1953), p. 153.

2. Quoted in H. Frankfort, *Kingship and the Gods: A Study of Ancient Near Eastern Religion as the Integration of Society and Nature* (Chicago: University of Chicago Press, 1948), p. 256.
3. Frankfort, *Kingship*, p. 257.
4. *Ancient Near Eastern Texts Relating to the Old Testament*, 2nd edn, ed. J. B. Pritchard (Princeton, N.J.: Princeton University Press, 1955), p. 164.
5. H. W. F. Saggs, *The Greatness that was Babylon* (London: Sidgwick and Jackson, 1962), p. 371.
6. See especially the article 'Sheep, Shepherds', in *The Anchor Bible Dictionary*, ed. D. N. Freedman (New York: Doubleday, 1992), vol. V, pp. 1187–90.
7. For a detailed discussion of Job 2.12–13 see D. J. A. Clines, *Job 1–20*, Word Biblical Commentary, 17 (Dallas: Word Books, 1989), pp. 63–4.
8. S. Mowinckel, *The Psalms in Israel's Worship*, trans. by D. R. Ap-Thomas (Oxford: Basil Blackwell, 1962), vol. 2, p. 11. E. S. Gerstenberger, *Psalms Part 1 with an Introduction to Cultic Poetry*, The Forms of Old Testament Literature, (Grand Rapids: Eerdmans, 1988), pp. 62–3, goes even further in suggesting that Psalm 6 is part of a liturgy for a sick person which included a sacrifice or offering as in Mesopotamian practice.
9. See the article 'Sheep, Shepherds', in *ABD*, n. 6 above.
10. See further A. A. Anderson, *Psalms*, New Century Bible (London: Oliphants, 1972), vol. 1, pp. 195–6.
11. See W. McKane, *Jeremiah*, vol. 1: *I–XXV*, International Critical Commentary (Edinburgh: T. & T. Clark, 1986), pp. 553–9 for convincing arguments that the passage in its final form is exilic or post-exilic.
12. Translation in G. R. Driver, *Canaanite Myths and Legends*, Old Testament Studies, (Edinburgh: T. & T. Clark, 1956), p. 47.
13. The criticism of Micah is complex, and many interpreters ascribe much of chapters 4–7 to a period later than that of the 8th-century elder from Moreshet-gath in Judah. For more details see E. M. Meyers and J. Rogerson, 'The Old Testament World', in H. C. Kee, E. M. Meyers, J. Rogerson and A. J. Saldarini, *The Cambridge Companion to the Bible* (Cambridge: Cambridge University Press, 1997), p. 211.
14. The modern attempt is described by Z. Bauman, *Legislators and Interpreters: On Modernity, Post-Modernity and Intellectuals* (Cambridge: Polity Press, 1987), ch. 4. See A. Giddens, *The Nation State and Violence*, vol. 2 of *A Contemporary Critique of Historical Materialism* (Cambridge: Polity Press, 1985), p. 52 for the view that traditional states did not achieve the degree of surveillance characteristic of modern states.

Bibliography

A. A. Anderson, *Psalms*, New Century Bible (London: Oliphants, 1972)

Z. Bauman, *Legislators and Interpreters: On Modernity, Post-Modernity and Intellectuals* (Cambridge: Polity Press, 1987)

D. Bonhoeffer, *Widerstand und Ergebung. Briefe und Aufzeichnungen aus der Haft*, ed. E. Bethge (Munich: Christian Kaiser Verlag, 1951). ET by R. H. Fuller, *Letters and Papers from Prison* (London: SCM Press, 1953)

D. J. A. Clines, *Job 1–20*, Word Biblical Commentary, 17 (Dallas: Word Books, 1989)

G. R. Driver, *Canaanite Myths and Legends*, Old Testament Studies, 3 (Edinburgh: T. & T. Clark, 1956)

H. Frankfort, *Kingship and the Gods: A Study of Ancient Near Eastern Religion as the Integration of Society and Nature* (Chicago: University of Chicago Press, 1948)

D. N. Freedman (ed.), *The Anchor Bible Dictionary* (New York: Doubleday, 1992)

E. S. Gerstenberger, *Psalms Part 1 with an Introduction to Cultic Poetry*, The Forms of Old Testament Literature, 14 (Grand Rapids: Eerdmans, 1988)

A. Giddens, *The Nation State and Violence*, vol. 2 of *A Contemporary Critique of Historical Materialism* (Cambridge: Polity Press, 1985)

W. McKane, *Jeremiah, vol. 1: I–XXV*, International Critical Commentary (Edinburgh: T. & T. Clark, 1986)

E. M. Meyers and J. Rogerson, 'The Old Testament World', in H. C. Kee, E. M. Meyers, J. Rogerson and A. J. Saldarini, *The Cambridge Companion to the Bible* (Cambridge: Cambridge University Press, 1997), pp. 32–287

S. Mowinckel, *The Psalms in Israel's Worship*, trans. D. R. Ap-Thomas (Oxford: Blackwell, 1962)

J. B. Pritchard (ed.), *Ancient Near Eastern Texts Relating to the Old Testament*, 2nd edn (Princeton, N.J.: Princeton University Press, 1955)

H. W. F. Saggs, *The Greatness that was Babylon* (London: Sidgwick and Jackson, 1962)

2

The New Testament

David Graham

Just as there is no commonly agreed definition of 'spirituality', so definitions of pastoral care also differ. This chapter attempts to identify those aspects of the care or cure of souls which are apparent in the varying strands of the New Testament canon. In so doing, we will, a priori, recognize the diversity which the different witnesses contribute to the topic. There will be no attempt to harmonize these, but rather to allow them to speak with their own diverse voices.

The Gospels

It has long been a scholarly device to differentiate between the first three or 'synoptic' Gospels (traditionally named Matthew, Mark and Luke), and the fourth (traditionally, John).

The Fourth Gospel was recognized by the early church Fathers as a 'spiritual' Gospel, and that (sometimes popular) understanding has lasted down the centuries. It might be seen to imply that 'John' has more to say about spiritual and pastoral issues than the synoptics, but this distinction can be over-emphasized. With the help of the Gospels in parallel columns in a synopsis, it is in fact easy to compare the similarities and differences between the four traditions. It emerges that Mark is the common link between all three synoptics in most cases, and the arguments from common order and vocabulary suggest that Mark was prior to the other two. Also, while Matthew may agree with Mark against Luke, or Luke with Mark against Matthew, there are very few occasions when Matthew and Luke agree against Mark.

These facts (and others, such as stylistic 'improvements', and theological factors) suggest that Mark was probably written first (so-called 'Markan priority'). Given that, there is a lot of material found in both Matthew and Luke which is not in Mark, mainly sayings of Jesus; although it is in both Gospels, it is not always identical in wording. Scholarship suggests that this was a separate source of material used by both Matthew and Luke, usually called 'Q' (which may be from the German for 'source', namely *Quelle*). Finally, both Matthew and Luke each have material unique to themselves, found nowhere else. This is generally called 'M' and 'L' respectively.

These relationships are called the 'synoptic problem', and the solution given above is the so-called two- (or four-)source solution. Other solutions have been offered, but the one accepted by the vast majority of scholars is the one above, sometimes with individual refinements.

The main areas of debate are whether Q, M and L were originally written documents, or some other sort of oral traditions; the relationship of Matthew to Luke, especially with respect to their use of Q; and how far oral tradition continued to shape the process.

Let us now consider the individual Gospel accounts.

Matthew

Eusebius of Caesarea, the early historian of the Church, records Bishop Papias of Hierapolis as stating that 'Matthew wrote the sayings in the Hebrew [or Aramaic] language [or perhaps style?], and everyone interpreted [or translated] them as they were able.' This testimony to Matthew's authorship is the earliest, but its reliability is open to question. Whatever the differing interpretations of it (and we have indicated some of the possible ways of translating or interpreting it in brackets above), what it certainly does is to show the unambiguous link between the early Church's Gospel tradition and the Jewish matrix and milieu of earliest Christianity. This is an important clue to any search for the New Testament tradition of pastoral care: the Jewish tradition is its most important context. Others have written about this, however; here it is perhaps enough to note the importance of the community and family aspects of pastoral relationships. Within early Christianity, the family model is reinterpreted as the family of God, the community itself. Personal family relationships are understood in a new light, shed by Jesus' teaching on personal relationships.

Many accept Antioch (in Syria) as a suitable place of writing for Matthew, but opinion is divided as to whether it had an urban or a rural setting. The majority view is that an urban context is most likely as the place of composition of the Gospel, but some (e.g. E. Schweizer) suggest a rural setting, linking Matthew with the later monastic movement. Certainly, some of the traditions in the Gospel (e.g. Matt. 19.12) were foundational for the monastic movement. Yet its later use, the history of interpretation, need not force us to conclusions about its origins (*pace* the work of Ulrich Luz on this aspect).

Matthew has a number of unique features. Early in the twentieth century, a five-fold binary pattern was identified in it: chapters 3–4 and 5–7; 8–9 and 10; 11–12 and 13; 14–17 and 18; 19–22 and 23–5. This was related to the Jewish tradition of publishing books in five sections or volumes, as in the Torah, the Psalms and the Pirqe Aboth of the Mishnah. If this is correct (although it has to overlook the infancy and passion narratives in order for the pattern to work), then once again it underscores the Jewish influences on the literature of the early Church.

This 'Jewishness' of Matthew is of interest. Recent work suggests the Gospel arose at (or after?) a time of intense conflict between Christians and Jews, perhaps related to the synagogue ban on Christians or heretics, the so-called *birkat ha minim* (the 'blessing', which was in reality a curse, on the *minim*, probably heretics or deviants). This was the twelfth of the eighteen benedictions in the synagogue liturgy (the *amidah* prayer), perhaps formulated during the Jamnian period of Jewish reconstruction after the Jewish War, late in the first century CE. Perhaps Matthew is a sort of Christian response to Judaism, which argues for Christianity's superiority and lays claim to the true interpretation of Torah. The 'antitheses' (Matt. 5.21–48) and 'formula quotations' (e.g. Matt. 1.22f., 2.5f., 15, 17f., 23) are also important in this regard.[1]

If such an interpretation is at all valid, then we might expect two things of this Gospel: first, that it will be pejorative towards Judaism, and second, that it will draw tight boundaries around its own community. This is the sort of world-view which in other contexts might develop into a sectarian view of the world. At the same time, it concentrates pastoral relationships in ways which may support the disenfranchised and outsiders in society, especially in its original context: those who have transferred allegiance from one religion to another.

Mark

This is widely regarded as the earliest Gospel (though not the earliest New Testament writing), tradition linking it with Peter in Rome (the earliest testimony once again being Papias, recorded by Eusebius).

This Gospel concentrates on Jesus' passion (suffering and death) more than the others, and this ties in with the call for disciples to suffer. Reasons for this may be several. Suggestions range from seeing Mark as an attempt to correct an overemphasis on Jesus as a 'divine man', to seeing it as a help for persecuted Christians (perhaps in Rome?). One recent writer has, however, suggested its origin as Syria at the outbreak of the Jewish War. Thus, if Matthew's pastoral concern arises from the emergence of 'Christianity' as a religious tradition distinct from Judaism, Mark's arises from the beginning of suspicion and persecution in the Graeco-Roman world (whether in the Roman or Judaean context).

The passion of Jesus ('the son of man must suffer') is a prominent theme, perhaps *the* theme, of the Gospel. In Mark, although there is a strong tradition of Jesus as an exorcist and miracle-worker, as the story unfolds and the messiahship of Jesus is gradually, and sometimes suddenly, revealed (the 'messianic secret'), the Gospel also quickly propels the reader into Jesus' ministry and conflict. A story which begins with its hero as one who expels demons and rebukes the evil forces of nature, ends in weakness and fear. The ending of the Gospel is uncertain, with a longer ending in some later manuscripts; this is less likely to be authentic, since it undermines the whole structure of the Gospel; rather, Mark offers no easy answers to the problems of the Christian disciple. Even for Jesus, the Lord, there is suffering and death. The admonition to take up the cross (as Jesus himself had to do) involves imitation of Jesus in resolute facing up to suffering, but not escape from it.

Luke (and Acts)

As with the other synoptics, it is Church tradition beginning in the second century which links this Gospel with the name Luke (see also Colossians 4.14; 2 Timothy 4.11). The Gospel and the Acts have the same author, as seen from Luke 1.3/Acts 1.1 and Luke 24.50–3/Acts 1.3–9.

The addressee, 'Theophilus', may have been a wealthy patron (though some suggest the name, which means 'lover of God' may be a pseudonym). Does the prologue to Luke suggest a catechetical motive in writing? Just as we have seen the other Gospels provide rich material for the Church to quarry in later generations, in formulating and developing its pastoral care, Luke too provides a model for the catechumenate. That itself would become a very important part of the Church's pastoral activity.

The 'narrative' which Luke writes may, therefore, be intended as descriptive rather than prescriptive. Nevertheless, the story of Jesus and the early Christians must have been quickly taken as normative for the Church's life, in particular, the cameo pictures of 'life in the early Church'. Luke is written in 'Biblical' (i.e. septuagintal) Greek, and as such its style, like the early tradition about Matthew, links it with the Jewish tradition, although mediated through the history of the diaspora. The popular view that Luke was a gentile (usually based on Colossians 4.11) may indeed be correct. Certainly, the Gospel has a 'universalistic' thrust, as also does Acts.

A number of distinct themes emerge from the Gospel: themes such as an interest in prayer, in wealth and the poor, in the Spirit. Those who are blessed as the 'poor in spirit' in Matthew are simply 'the poor' in Luke. There is an interest in the marginalized in society, in the outcasts, and in the piety of ordinary people, which is seen as exemplary. The remedy for the poverty and woes of life is seen in the joy of the Spirit, which is an anticipation of the eschatological joy. This might be criticized as a 'pie-in-the-sky' theology, but for Luke it is very real in a world before the Christianizing of the empire, and in which Christians are a minority group. The concentration of teaching parables in Luke, as in Matthew, sets the life and worship of the Church in the context of its catechism and doctrine. Thus, the axiom that right living is right doctrine begins to develop, and Church dogma becomes vital in the development of the concept of 'ministry' in the Church.

Many of Luke's themes continue in the Acts, and the Gospel stories anticipate them. However, issues arising from Acts are complex, and, as with the Gospels, it is useful to consider what its purpose may have been, in order to get a clearer picture of its relevance to pastoral care. A missionary story, an apologetic for Roman readers, or a defence brief for Paul's trial have all been suggested. Paul certainly emerges as a figure towering over the early Church, but whether this was to rehabilitate his reputation after the time of his death, to bear historical verisimilitude, or to point towards (perhaps in a third volume?) the apostle completing his plan to spread the message to Spain, cannot be known with certainty. In this debate, the speeches have played a major part: to what extent are they verbatim reports (even when the author could not have been there?), and to what extent are they composed for theological purposes? Without doubt, even given the historical and literary complexities of the literature, and although in the past a great deal of scholarly attention was directed to the differences between the Acts and the Pauline corpus in the New Testament, the figure of Paul in both groups of writing is remembered in the literature of earliest Christianity as the pastor *par excellence*. Acts portrays him more as a preaching figure, establishing churches and revisiting to nurture them as they grow.

It may be, as tradition suggests, that Luke was the medical companion of Paul, following Colossians 4.14; 2 Timothy 4.11; Philemon 24 and the 'anti-Marcionite' prologue *c*.160–80 CE:

> Luke a physician of Antioch in Syria ... companion of Paul until his martyrdom ... moved by the Holy Spirit, composed his gospel in the parts of Achaia, and after also wrote the Acts of the Apostles ... he served the Lord without distraction, without wife or children, and fell asleep in Boeotia at the age of 84, full of the Holy Spirit.

We could look to Irenaeus, *c*.180 CE: 'Luke the follower of Paul wrote the gospel'; the Muratorian 'canon', *c*.200 CE: 'the gospel of Luke the physician ... companion of Paul ... he did not himself see the Lord in the flesh' and many of the Church Fathers. We have – at least in the tradition – a close interest in the story of Paul and his communities, even if the 'evidence' of medical language alleged (by Hobart, and Harnack) was shown by H. J. Cadbury to be dubious. Certainly, the internal evidence of the Gospel could support that: in (Luke–)Acts, the 'we' passages indicate the author was at times a traveller with Paul (Acts 16.10–17; 20.5–15; 21.1–18; 27.1—28.16).

A few selective comments on Luke may help us to see some of the above points. For example, John the Baptist (Luke 3.1–20), who was obviously an important historical figure (mentioned also in Josephus, and see Acts 19.1–3), is portrayed as a prophetic figure, with the background of 1 and 2 Kings and Malachi in mind. Luke quotes from Isaiah 40, and sets John firmly in the mould of the desert ascetic. John's message is one of eschatological judgement, like that of the Old Testament prophets; he undercuts Jewish notions of privilege and election, and gives an ethical test instead. Luke alone emphasizes this with the examples of people coming for baptism.

In the story of the baptism of Jesus (3.21–2), Luke's account is brief and is placed after the baptisms of others (compare Matt. and Mark). The scene is typical of Jewish apocalyptic (the heavens opening, a vision, a heavenly voice), which serves to emphasize the eschatological theology of Luke. And the prayer is typically thematic of Luke: for this evangelist, prayer is the appropriate response to all the experiences of life, and a vital ingredient in spiritual growth and development.

In Luke's genealogy (3.23–38), by taking the ancestry back to Adam, and not just to Abraham, as in Matthew, Luke portrays Jesus as the man for all: representative of humanity, and perhaps hinting at the 'new/last Adam' theme (cf. Paul's theology in Rom. 5.14–19; 1 Cor. 15.45).

The temptation story in Luke (4.1–13) is important as a window into his understanding of spiritual growth. It is introduced by the phrases 'Full of the Holy Spirit ... led by the Spirit') which are typically Lukan, and in the whole temptation narrative, Jesus is presented as (new) Israel (cf. Matt. 2.15). The test with which Jesus is confronted is to forsake the messianic way of suffering, for a way of miracle and glory. He refuses. This story would soon become important among the early Christians as they faced persecution, and the temptation to deny Christ and forsake the way of the Messiah in the face of persecution.

However, as a complement to that, there is the supernatural aspect of Jesus' ministry. Miracles, especially healings and exorcisms, were essential in Jesus' proclamation of the reign ('Kingdom') of God. In antiquity, many illnesses were thought to be caused by evil spirits (even the fever in Luke 4.39 is 'rebuked'!). In healing and exorcizing, Jesus is bringing in the reign of God (see Luke 11.20). Healing was also looked on as a sign of the messianic age (7.18–22).

Jesus is seen as the 'great physician', who is obedient to the Jewish law (5.14), and often found in prayer (5.16). The healing of the paralysed man (5.17–26) raises the question of forgiving sins. Healing and forgiveness were associated with each other in Judaism and early Christianity (James 5.16), and healing the lame was seen as part of the messianic era (Is. 35.6). In Matthew 9.8, 'Son of Man' and the power to pronounce forgiveness is understood as referring to the community (cf. John 20.23).

In Luke 5.33–9 there is a debate on fasting, which was a normal part of Jewish piety (see Matt. 6.16), as also of early Christianity. John the baptizer appears as an ascetic, compared to Jesus, who enjoyed food and drink (Matt. 11.18f.). Luke's view of the joy of the Kingdom, mediated through the Holy Spirit, however, precludes fasting at least during the time of Jesus' ministry. This story may not only be taken as an explanation for the non-ascetic practices of Jesus' followers (in contrast to Judaism), but as a foundational story for the regular practice of fasting in early Christianity. The dissimilarity between Christianity and its Jewish hinterland is also found in the sabbath controversies (e.g. Luke 6.1–11). Just as Torah observance was central in Judaism, including sabbath, so its observance was a point of conflict between Jesus and Jews. In this case, as often, the controversy ranges round interpretation of the law (Luke seems to have deliberately omitted the ambiguous reference found in a parallel in Mark 2.26).

In the so-called sermon on the plain (Luke 6.17–49), the Lukan beatitudes promise an eschatological reversal of values in the Kingdom of God. They are less 'spiritualized' than in Matthew (who has 'poor in spirit', 'hunger and thirst for righteousness'). The sermon also gives the ethical values of the Kingdom: love for enemies, non-retaliation, and the 'golden rule' of verse 31. The prophetic message of justice, mercy and humility comes to mind (cf. Hosea 6.8).

Reflections on the synoptic tradition

The teaching of Jesus was foundational for the development of the tradition of pastoral care in the Church. We have seen quite wide contrasts between the different synoptic Gospels, the material which became the building-blocks for the Church's community. We will discuss Paul in more detail below. As pastor *par excellence*, Jesus gives the example of one who, though Son of God, suffers and prays through times of conflict and trial. The ascetic tradition, and the suffering Church, would draw on this in future years. In contrast, the eschatological joy and charismatic aspects of the Gospel of Luke (10.21) provide a model of victorious, even triumphalist, religion. The *deus ex machina* of Matthew 28.16–20 anticipates the universalism, imperialism and triumphalism of later 'Christian' states and empires. This, however, is in stark contrast to Jesus as the meek and lowly one who will not even break a reed (Matt. 12.18–21), and in contrast to the patient, repeated attempts to bring back one who has strayed from the Christian fold (Matt. 18.12–17). This latter passage has often been interpreted with the emphasis on excommunication, and the power of the Church or its officials to cast out offenders or dissidents. However, from the way in which it is constructed, this appears very much as a last resort, after other efforts at reconciliation have failed (cf. Matt. 18.35). This is a salutory example of how a text can be used in different ways, and can even be abused in the hands of those with power, to oppress the powerless.

Apart only from Jesus, Peter occupies a unique role in the Gospels, particularly in Matthew. His character is mixed in Matthew; for example, compare these texts: 14.28-31; 16.17; 16.18, 19; 16.23. Peter's fortunes in the Gospel fluctuate, like the proverbial yo-yo! He is the recipient of a heavenly revelation, and also rebuked by Jesus as 'Satan'. He walks on water, but begins to sink because of lack of faith. Peter occupies a unique place in the early Church. Indeed, an early tradition links him with the material in Mark's Gospel. But let us look at the crucial text, at Matthew 16.16-19, the confession, followed by the 'rock' and the 'keys' sayings.

In Matthew 16.16, 17, Peter's confession of Jesus as the Messiah is a watershed in the Gospel (but compare Martha's similar confession in John 11.27).

There have been various interpretations of Matthew 16.18 in the history of the Church: seeing Peter as a representative or typical disciple (i.e. not unique); interpreting Peter's confession of faith as the 'rock'; regarding the 'rock' as Christ himself (cf. Eph. 2.20); or understanding this as the foundation of the primacy of Peter and the beginning of the papacy.

Isaiah 22.22 may be the background to Matthew 16.19, but the language used by Matthew, of 'binding and loosing', is identical to later Rabbinic terminology for forbidding or permitting certain behaviour (including infringements of the Torah, such as purity, food or sabbath). Is this, then, permission to decide on issues of Christian behaviour? It has been taken this way, for example by later Church 'courts' and councils.

But was this authority unique to Peter? If we look at Matthew 18.18, the same language is used, except this time in the plural, and the context shows that it is applied to the whole Church community. The 'keys' saying and the 'binding and loosing' saying are probably an example of parallelism: that is, saying the same thing in two different ways (a very common device in Jewish writings and in Jesus' teaching, e.g. the Lord's prayer). We do know that by the early second century, we have a developed system of 'hierarchical' Church leadership, with bishops, elders and deacons. These words to Peter encouraged the development of a 'monarchical' system of church government.

Leadership and organization

Several years ago there was a meeting of the British New Testament Society. It included several papers on Matthew's Gospel, and happened to coincide with St Matthew's Day in the Church year. After some of the papers had been delivered, during the plenary discussion, the question arose as to what sort of 'churchmanship' Matthew may have had. One academic present – an Anglican – suggested that Matthew would have been an Anglican. Another proposed that Matthew would be at home in a Congregational setting (the speaker was a nonconformist). Yet a third said that both the previous opinions were wrong, and that Matthew was, of course, a Presbyterian: you have probably already guessed his background; in fact, he was a former Moderator of the General Assembly of the Church of Scotland.

We have already noted that the second-century Church had a system of episcopacy which was monarchical, consisting of the bishop with other lesser offices beneath him. How the early, charismatic situation developed into a more structured system of offices, is not fully known. But some see Matthew as a sort of transition: there are prophets (Matt. 10.41), although admittedly some of them are false and dangerous (Matt. 7.15–23) and apparently itinerant. There may also have been some who pursued a more ascetic, 'monastic' life of discipleship, perhaps with vows of chastity (Matt. 19.10–12). There may also have been people who belonged to the classes of scribes or sages, well known in Judaism (Matt. 23.34). But passages such as the words to Peter also give indications of at least the beginning of a more institutionalized structure.

Pastoral care and discipline

Chapter 18 of Matthew's Gospel deserves special attention. It has been compared to the Community Rule of the Dead Sea Scrolls. Let us summarize some of the points in it.

> 18.1–6. The example of the child. The example of humility seems to be uppermost here.
> 18.7–11. Not causing others to stumble (i.e. pastoral care for others in the community). Who are the 'little ones' mentioned? Is this the young, or rather a way of describing all disciples?
> 18.15–20. Patiently attempting to restore a sinner. Is there a warrant here for 'excommunication'? There are three attempts to win someone

back. Notice that the community is to be the final arbiter, with the approval of God and the presence of Christ.

18.21–35. Forgiveness is the hallmark of the Church. This speaks for itself.

Jesus as a teacher

The Gospel of Matthew is probably best known for its great Sermon on the Mount (chs. 5–7), including famous passages such as the beatitudes and the Lord's prayer. We have considered some parts of this before, such as the 'antitheses' and the section on false prophets.

A key concept in Matthew is that of 'righteousness' (Greek *dikaiosune*): Matthew's use of this word is different from Paul's, who uses it in a legal sense of being acquitted. Matthew is more like the letter of James, who describes an upright life before God, in obedience to the law (see, for example, Matthew 1.19, in different translations).

Interestingly, Matthew follows the Jewish pattern of piety: almsgiving, prayer and fasting (6.1–18), yet with a different emphasis. Christian piety is to be personal, spiritual, and not ostentatious. Yet Jesus' commendation of peacemaking (5.9) also implies a communal and public dimension. The end result is a 'higher' righteousness (5.20) which is unimpeachable (5.48) and focuses on God's Kingdom (6.32).

In Matthew, Jesus does not dispense with the Torah (5.17–19): –

Look at Matthew 15.17, and compare Mark 7.19. What does Mark include which Matthew does not?

As we see in Matthew 23.3, the Gospel does not simply do away with Jewish teachings, but is concerned with the essentials.

Look at Matthew 23.23, and pay special attention to the end of the verse. The great prophetic Old Testament principles of justice, mercy and truthfulness are enshrined here (compare, for example, Amos 5.24; Hosea 1.7; Micah 6.8).

In short, Jesus is the all-powerful teacher and miracle-worker in Matthew. His teaching, unlike that of the Jewish scribes, is authoritative (7.29), and all authority is delegated to him (28.19) – an astonishing statement, and one which would be used to vindicate the wielding of power by the leadership of the Church in later centuries.

What has been seen in the synoptic Gospels (and Acts) is also true in the rest of the New Testament, as we shall now see. There is no single tradition, but the narratives and discourse materials, descriptive of how

Jesus' life was recalled by the early Church, and prescriptive for its life, led to differing trajectories as the gospel spread in the empire.

The Fourth Gospel

Several influential scholars (notably J. L. Martyn and R. E. Brown) see the Fourth Gospel as the product of a period after the separation of church and synagogue (9.22; 16.2). John's community has its own history, part of which involved Jewish elements, and also a strong Baptist influence. When the Gospel was written, the community was increasingly separated from Judaism, and more Hellenistic-Christian. If this is so, then, like Matthew, we might expect to find polemical material within it. That is the case, for example in the references quoted above, and the controversies with 'the Jews'. However, other aspects of the Gospel also serve to balance this emphasis, and make John the pre-eminently important Gospel in the history of pastoral care.

Clement of Alexandria (*c.*180) stated that John wrote a 'spiritual Gospel', and John 21.24 identifies the 'beloved disciple' as the evangelist, yet never reveals his identity (John 13.23; 18.15; 19.26; 19.35; 20.2; 21.7). It may be that the Johannine tradition links John with the beloved disciple. In any case, the tradition of the disciple whom Jesus loved has been an important one as a model of pastoral relationships. So, too, is the Johannine metaphor of the 'good shepherd'. This may have some connection with the parable of the shepherd in Matthew and Luke, but is certainly developed much more fully in John. The reputation of John, then, as a spiritual Gospel with pastoral emphases, would be important for the later Church.

In the prologue, many of the later themes of the Gospel are anticipated, and others are mentioned there uniquely. Using the dualistic language of antithetic pairs, we are introduced to grace, light and life. In many ways, the theology of John is a realized eschatology, with what is only anticipated in the synoptics and the main Pauline letters being a present reality in John (cf. chapter 17). This 'heavenly' perspective (which we have already noted to a lesser extent in the synoptics, and which appears in the later, deutero-Pauline writings) serves to challenge and counteract the present reality of the Johannine Christians.

The important concept of Wisdom, through whom everything is made (cf. Prov. 8.22f.) lies behind much of what John's prologue mentions. The feminine aspect of Wisdom personified in Judaism, which also recalls God speaking in creation and revelation, might be a very important gender-specific metaphor for the New Testament.

The dualism of light versus darkness, and the contrast of spiritual birth, illumination, and darkness, revealed to those with faith, are very important to John, but perhaps because of an other-worldly perspective. This can inform a spirituality which is private, or even sectarian. The spiritualizing use of metaphor in the Gospel even extends to narrative incidents in the story of Jesus. The interpretation of the event in the Temple (John 2.14ff.) differs from the synoptics. Jewish hopes that the Temple would be renewed/restored (e.g. Zech. 14.21 and intertestamental writings) lie behind this, as do the prophetic actions of the Old Testament prophets (e.g. Jer. 7; 13; 18; 19; Isa. 20.2f.). The evangelist ('John') interprets Jesus' action as foreshadowing the resurrection (2.21f.). It probably also hints at the point of the conversation in 4.21, with the spiritual worship of an omnipresent God.

The Fourth Gospel, then, has become a model for a certain tradition of spirituality and pastoral relationship. It is simple, yet intense. Jesus, as God's wisdom, is the one who loves his people and has an intimate relationship with them. There is a close personal, one-to-one relationship with much less awareness of the wider world. It has been described as sectarian; perhaps proto-sectarian is more accurate. Such views can be supportive of people in pastoral situations where external pressures are strongly in competition with their religion, as many people in situations of persecution have found. But they can also lead to an unhealthy, 'hothouse' spiritual practice with all its inherent dangers, as groups such as the modern 'shepherding' movement, and cult and sectarian groups, testify. The Gospel materials can always be used as a two-edged sword.

The apostle Paul

All of Paul's letters were probably written before any of the Gospels, and they are therefore the earliest evidence we have for Christianity. His missionary and pastoral strategy is an interesting one. He first visited places familiar to him (Cyprus, Cilicia); he went to synagogues; he targeted large population centres; he spent some time in some of them; he revisited them; he kept contact through letter; he had a team with which to work; he returned periodically to his base; and he had plans for his future ministry. Because of the selective nature of the New Testament documents, we have in Paul the most documented and systematic example of pastoral care in the New Testament. Working within these parameters (there are no others for this period), we gain some fascinating insights about Paul as a pastor.

In Christian history, Paul's letter to the Romans has been the most influential of the letters. Written from Greece (16.1) before Paul went to Jerusalem, the letter fits into the space in Acts 18.2, the three-month's winter in Corinth. Paul's work in the eastern Mediterranean was drawing to a close, and he planned to go west (15.19, 23). The collection for the saints (1.10–15; 15.19ff.) fits best after 1 Corinthians 16.3f.; 2 Corinthians 8–9. See also Acts 19.21; 20.3 (Rom. 15.31); 24.17.

How did Paul know so many people (26, most not Jewish) in Rome, when he had never been there? Some scholars have suggested that either Romans 16 or all of the letter was for Ephesus. It seems likely, however, that this is simply an example of Paul's wide contacts with the early Christians, made possible by his and their travel in the Roman world.

The letter has often been taken to be Paul's 'systematic theology'. But it lacks several important ideas, such as eschatology, the Church, the Lord's Supper. If it is a summary of his theology (e.g. to explain his gospel to the Romans), it is selective. More broadly, is it an introductory letter from Paul to Rome, before he visits them to be cheered on his way? It was written at a turning-point in his life. But it deals with specific issues. The question of the Jews in God's plan (9–11 are not an 'aside'!); the 'weak and strong' (14) as well as other moral issues (12, 13). These must be added into the equation. The social problems in Rome: the Emperor Claudius had expelled the Jews in 49 CE for riots – possibly these were Jewish-Christian problems? Tensions between Jews and Christians were inevitable; but probably also between Jewish and gentile Christians, over issues such as the (food) law.[2]

Whatever the details, Paul seems to be addressing specific problems in the Roman Church, while grappling with more general issues of the identity of the people of God: has God brought to birth a new people, and if so, what now of the Jews? Or is the Church part of Israel?

Paul may also be explaining his mission to the gentiles to Jerusalem; word (copies of the letter?) would reach there.[3]

Paul, often seen in hindsight as the great systematic theologian, in fact turns out to be very much a pragmatist, whose main aim is unity in the factional Christian Church, and between it and its Jewish neighbours. Rather than coming with *a priori* theological ideas to the churches and their problems, he approaches the problems with a pragmatist mindset, and his theology develops very much in the context of these concerns. His thinking is situational, and his theology is contextual. Paul the pastor is also very much Paul the pragmatist.

The first letter to the Corinthians was written in response to news or a letter from Corinth (1 Cor. 1.11; 5.1; 7.1). It is an 'occasional' letter, responding to a particular situation. The problems become clear as we read through the text. Many of them are the result of the infant Church in a pagan society; Jewish and (even more) pagan influences can be detected. Social divisions can be seen. Issues of belief and ethics are problematic.[4]

Much of the letter responds to problems of divisions in the Church. The fellowship of Christ has been broken (1.13) by factions: followers of Paul, of Apollos, of Cephas and of Christ (1.12; 3.4). Were the Corinthians perhaps treating the Church like a pagan guild or association? The factions may also have been caused/aggravated by social divisions (1.14, 26; Acts 18.8; Rom. 16.23; 'households' and, later, food problems).

The Corinthians put great store on wisdom (*sophia*), knowledge (*gnosis*) and eloquent speech; these were highly valued in paganism (1.20), and may have been the cause of some of the problems. Paul himself denied that he had any of these qualities; we might wonder how true this was to reality. He claimed to draw his authority from God and Christ. But at the same time, he was well able to come down with a very heavy hand of judgement. And in the very letter where he denies gifts of eloquence (2 Corinthians), he produces the most powerful purple passages of rhetoric. Will the real Paul please stand up? His relationship to them seems to be different, according to whether he is there in person or not, and whether speaking or writing to them. Perhaps this is the first example of a heavy-handed pastoral letter from someone who found it easier to be harsh by letter than in person.

Many of the specific problems in Corinth concerned how new Christians should live when they were converted from paganism, and how much of their religious and cultural 'baggage' could be transposed into their Christian community. The Church had to be seen to be distinct; boundary markers were vital. Thus, sexual ethical standards were to be high (ch. 5). Some pagans believed in the religious value of sex (e.g. sacred prostitution).

How do you react to Paul's advice to shun such people and throw them out (5.11–13)? Would this be Jesus' attitude? Why does Paul say this?

The Church's power to excommunicate is followed in chapter 6 with the Church settling legal cases. It is to be used, not the state system. The Church is here in the process of defining itself, its boundaries and its powers. The question of 'church and state' begins here, but would not go away after this. The power of the Church to judge moral issues (compare the discussion on Matthew 18, above) focuses on the negative aspects of this, and opens the way for such power to be abused. Also, by separating the religious from the secular powers, accountability is kept as an internal issue, with no external controls. Again, this is a system which, if worked with fairness, could be good, but could also be open to abuse. And although in places he distinguishes his own 'I say' from 'the Lord' (e.g. 7.10), one gets the impression that to disagree with Paul is to argue with God himself. Paul's apostolic authority is something which he has to argue vigorously for on several occasions, and it would be interesting to be able to hear the other side of the arguments, from his opponents, as to why they denied his apostleship. Did they, perhaps, see him as self-appointed, lacking credentials? He appeals to his commission by the risen Christ, but one wonders how much ice that cut with others. They may have thought (as people always do) that it is all too easy to claim a personal revelation for oneself, as the basis of doing whatever one wishes.

Galatians, in comparison, deals with the issue of how 'Jewish' Christianity should be. The Jewish law, especially circumcision, is a major issue in this. It is not so much a question of 'law versus grace', but of whether, having become followers of Christ, people also need to keep the Torah. Paul bases his argument in the letter on his personal experience, with a spiritual 'autobiography' saying that his call to the gentiles was from God himself.

This was very important for Paul's pastoral relationships with his churches, and gave him a self-styled authority. This was an example of delegated authority, and sets up Paul as an intermediary between God and his churches, with his vision and ideas being conveyed as those of God, so that any of his opponents are anathematized by him (Gal. 1.8).

Paul's rhetoric also appeals to the scriptures of the Old Testament (as he almost always does). To his readers, whether sympathetic or opponents, this would seem to be almost irrefutable logic. Using the story of Abraham, no less, and also bringing the experience of the gift of the Spirit to bear on this, he argues against the need for keeping the Torah; and against charges of lawlessness ('antinomianism'), he appeals to the Spirit as the motive for ethics.

From a later period in Paul's ministry comes Ephesians, a captivity epistle (see 6.20), with similarities to Colossians (cf. Eph. 6.21f. and Col. 4.7f.).

While its contents are reasonably clear, its purpose is not. Why was it written? Is it 'an epistle in search of a life-setting'? The theme of Christ and the Church is prominent. However, it is more a prayer or meditation than a letter. The issue of unity of Jew and gentile is prominent, but this is true throughout the entire New Testament, and it is difficult to relate it to the history of Christianity in Asia Minor, about which we know little. It has been suggested that the language of light, etc., and the doxological, prayerful style, point to it being a baptismal liturgy. But this is only one suggestion.

One important issue is its relation to other Paulines. What explanation can be given for the common material with Colossians? More significant, detailed work suggests great differences in language, style and vocabulary from the main Pauline letters. For example, the Greek constructions, long sentences, unique vocabulary, words used with different meanings (e.g. 'mystery', 'economy'), a more developed church order. This has led many scholars to suggest that Ephesians (and other letters) are pseudonymous; that they were written by another author, using a pseudonym. It is usually said that this was after Paul's time, perhaps by an admirer or disciple of his. Is Ephesians then the 'crown of Paulinism', or part of the 'deutero-Pauline' corpus? The more critical of scholars would assign Ephesians, Colossians, (some also 2 Thessalonians) and the pastorals to pseudonymous authors.

But whatever its original origins and authorship, it has been included within the canonical Pauline corpus, and takes the form of an epistle, although it is really an example of exhortation. The household codes which it contains (5.22–6.9) were no doubt part of a common genre of ethical admonition, and appeal to a commonly accepted tradition of similar bodies of material. Here, of course, they have been Christianized by the inclusion of phrases mentioning Christ, God and the Lord, and also by the extended metaphor of the body of Christ. But beneath this, the pastoral admonition which Paul gives is drawing on 'secular' parallels, but using Christian motivation for obeying the instruction. In a similar way, modern Christian counselling often uses secular techniques and therapies, sometimes with little or no religious 'overlay'.

Philippians is another of the captivity epistles, with the theme of suffering prominent throughout. The letter is basically a thanks for a gift sent to

Paul (2.25, 27; 4.10, 14). Containing touching personal comments, it also warns the readers about 'circumcisers' (cf. Galatians). Tensions between Christians and those advocating the law are high. Who are the troublemakers whom Paul warns about? Some have seen gnostic elements, but this is unlikely. Jewish features are prominent. There may also be an element of triumphalism and/or pneumaticism: Paul emphasizes suffering in the Christian life.

There is also the important passage in 2.6–11. It is a hymn, which some think is pre-Pauline because of its uncharacteristic language. The background of thought is Adam and Wisdom in the Old Testament and intertestamental writings.

Colossians is unusual among the Pauline letters, in that it is written to a church which Paul had probably never visited (but see Acts 19.10). Paul certainly seems to know about the situation there, but whether he knew the Christians cannot be said for certain (see Col. 4.15–17). It deals with a particular problem or heresy, the details of which can be put together from the letter, and which contains elements which are Jewish, pagan and 'gnostic'.

The letter emphasizes the pre-eminence of Christ (1.15–19, a Christological hymn). Did the heresy compromise this? – it also had Jewish and philosophical elements: see 2.4–23; 3.5–7. We can detect astrology and angel worship, asceticism, sexual licence, all in all suggesting a heavily paganized and syncretistic form of Judaeo-Christianity. However, others (e.g. M. D. Hooker) have suggested there was no specific heresy involved. Recently, N. T. Wright makes a case for the letter being a satirical attack on heterodox and syncretistic Judaism.

Philemon, often associated with Colossians, is another unusual letter, unlike the other Paulines. It deals with a slave-owner from Colossae, and his runaway slave (Onesimus), who has come to Paul. Containing superb rhetoric and irony, Paul writes to explain the situation and offer a solution. The letter is a unique insight into the social effect of Christianity in the Roman world.

What, in fact, does Paul say about the situation of Onesimus? What literary/rhetorical devices does he employ in the process? What wider issues does the letter raise about slave ownership in antiquity?

Several themes emerge from the Thessalonian letters of relevance to our topic, among them the problems of persecution, and Christian morality. But perhaps the most intriguing is Paul's use of the theological understanding of the parousia in his moral exhortation. Eschatological fervour pervades the letters, especially 1 Thessalonians. Two issues are tackled: first, the place of believers not still alive when Christ returns. What will happen to them? Second, the timing of the return. Apparently, some in Thessalonica were expecting the parousia at any moment, and hence stopped working. Paul urges them to be ready (1 Thess. 5.6), but says that the parousia will be preceded by various events. Here we have an unashamed use of a theological motif, as encouragement or threat to idle members of the community. The implications of this are immense, not least in the ways it might be used or abused by others. For example, 2 Thessalonians 3.10 was quoted by Mrs (now Baroness) Margaret Thatcher, when she infamously addressed the General Assembly of the Church of Scotland, as a legitimation of her particular brand of capitalism. Would Paul have agreed?

The Christian movement is becoming a self-conscious community, with issues of leadership and pastoral care prominent. 1 Thessalonians 2 is particularly interesting, with its mixture of rich metaphors describing Paul's pastoral relationship with the congregation. This relationship has been likened to that of ancient philosophical traditions, between the philosopher-teacher and his/her pupils. Once again, we see Paul's use of common non-Christian models for his own self-understanding.

We might expect to find in the letters of Timothy and Titus, the so-called 'pastoral epistles', material particularly rich for our topic, and in a sense that is so. Although these letters were recognized for their material on church order in the early Christian centuries, it was only in the eighteenth century that this group of three letters were called 'pastoral'. The name has stuck! While it is right to think of them as forming a self-contained group within the Paulines, we must not overlook the differences which there are between them. Several themes emerge from a reading of the letters.

Throughout, there are warnings about dangerous teaching which stressed knowledge, genealogies, asceticism and moral licence. It also seems to have had some unusual eschatology. Some see it as early gnosticism, though there are also similarities to the problems in Colossians (and Corinthians), and it is combated by emphasis on the faithful tradition, apostolic teaching and faithful sayings. There are regulations about church 'offices', and the qualities of those who fill them. This is different from the 'charismatic' system of, say, 1 Corinthians. Here, offices within the Church are recognized, and people fill these who have particular qualities to match.

The letters are from a senior to junior Christian leaders. We get the impression of Paul as the 'senior pastor', with a wide remit both geographically and spiritually. Godly living and Christian virtue are stressed, some seeing in this teaching a 'middle-class' Christianity with minimal challenge to the surrounding society. Instead, the Church is to blend in peacefully with the surrounding culture. Their 'bourgeois' value system, the theological tone of the letters and social organization (so-called 'early catholicism'), combined with the possible heresy warned against, suggest to some scholars that they are late works. But the dating of them is less immediately important than the teaching which they contain about the place of the Church in society. Christians are to blend in and, by honesty and good living, cause no disturbance to society: easier to do when that society poses no threat or challenge, perhaps. The leaders of the churches are to obey Paul's teaching, and presumably on the basis of his perceived authority. He had founded churches, been instrumental in the conversion and nurture of many church leaders, and suffered for his faith. Thus, he commanded respect. And while he gives teaching and instruction about the offices in the Church (bishops, elders, deacons), he himself is given no such title. What he might be called by others, either in his day or ours, is anyone's guess.

Other New Testament writings

The Letter to the Hebrews is surely the most rhetorical of New Testament books, and also one of the longest (despite 13.22!). As its style is rhetorical, so its theology is typological, and similar to (e.g.) Philo and later Alexandrian exegesis. Using Platonic thought, the 'reality' is seen as heavenly (and Christological); the 'earthly' (Temple and tabernacle) are only temporary and pale shadows of those.

Christological concerns loom large, especially the supremacy of Christ over angels, Moses and the Levitical priesthood (contrasted with Christ's Melchizedekian priesthood). The Old Testament is quoted liberally to show this (as also for the other arguments in the letter).

Hebrew does not have the formal characteristics of a letter (epistle), and is better understood as a homily (or sermon); indeed, the author calls it a 'word of exhortation' (13.22). Perhaps it should be seen as one of the earliest examples of a bishop's pastoral letter, as it draws heavily on Old Testament Scripture, and non-Christian rhetorical devices, to make its points. It encourages perseverance among those second-generation Christians who are in danger of falling away from their faith, or falling (back, as the writer would understand it) into Judaism.

Its sheer rhetorical flourish makes it effective, even where its scriptural arguments may fail to convince. Homiletic therefore wins over hermeneutics: which is no less true for many a modern pastor, preacher and counsellor.

Among the several people named James in the New Testament, the 'pillar' apostle (Gal. 1.19) and brother of Jesus, prominent in the early Church (1 Cor. 15.7; Acts 12.17; 15.13; 21.18) is the most likely author of the Epistle of James (not the James of Acts 12.2, killed in 44 CE). Later tradition, such as in Eusebius, portrays him as 'the just', a man of prayer and piety, and the first bishop of Jerusalem, stoned to death in 62 CE (Eusebius, *HE* 2.23; Josephus, *Ant.* 20.197–203).

The letter has several interesting features, notably its Jewishness (many see it as a document of Jewish Christianity) and its relation to Paul's letters, especially the 'faith and works' debate (2.14–26). Is James in dialogue with Paul; even critical of his views (compare Jas. 2.24 with, for example, Rom. 3.28; 4; Gal. 3.6–9)? Or perhaps of a distorted Paulinism which James seek to correct?

It was long ago described as an example of Christian paraenesis, with the unstructured nature of the 'letter', with its pithy sayings reminiscent of the Jewish wisdom traditions.

The First Letter of John, as it is known, is not epistolatory in style, but an exhortation or tract. The main problem in the background are people (heretics/schismatics/secessionists) who have split from the Johannine community and gone their own way (1 John 2.19; 4.1). Their faults were Christological and moral: they denied the incarnation (1.1; 2.22; 4.2, 15; 5.5, 10), claimed superior knowledge (2.3, 4), claimed a monopoly of truth (2.20, 28; 4.17), had visions and prophecy (4.1; 5.9 cf. 2.27), lacked love (2.6, 9) and showed moral faults while claiming 'sinlessness' (1.8, 10; 3.9, 10; 4.14). Were they dualistic (1.5)?

R. E. Brown[5] sees 1 John as a correction of a misunderstanding of John's Gospel, especially the prologue. The Gospel was popular with gnostics. G. M. Burge[6] sees a 'classic charismatic crisis' happening between John and 1 John. Some see the start of sectarian attitudes in 1 John.

Sects often do write tracts, and the dogmatism, the polemical tone of 1 John, and emphasis on the internal community ('the brothers') may fit the tract to a sociological model of a sect. However, are the community or the heretics the more sectarian?[7]

John combines theology with ethics: emphasis on 'doing' the truth, 'obeying' etc. The practical consequences of God's love (seen most supremely in the Cross) are to love one another. How universal is this? Is it confined to 'the brother' (and sister)? Love is to be self-sacrificial and unselfish. This comes of 'abiding' in God, having fellowship with him. This also creates fellowship with others.

Many of the ideas and much of the language in the letter can be traced to the Old Testament but they would also appeal to Hellenized readers:

> John no doubt has in mind ... those from a Greek background who denied the reality of the Incarnation and the Atonement, and also believed that right conduct was immaterial. In his insistence on the true Sonship of Jesus, however, the writer would also have furnished a response to those who had emerged from a Jewish background, and whose understanding of Christ's divinity was impoverished.[8]

Judaism in the diaspora (and Judaea) was heavily influenced by Hellenistic thought.

John's moral exhortation illustrates how doctrinal error can often be accompanied by moral error.

The 'problem of sin(s)' in 1 John concerns how the author regards sin. Note first how John uses 'sin' and 'sins'. What is the difference? Then compare 1.8, 10; 2.1; 3.6, 9; 5.18. Can a believer not sin? Verses 3.6 and 5.18 may be present continuous ('goes on/keeps on sinning', e.g. NIV), but 3.9 and 5.16 contradict this. Is there a distinction between different kinds of sin? – 5.16 may suggest so, but which is which type, and why does 1 John mention it near the end of the letter? This is the ideal situation. John aims high, hoping believers will aim for this. (Jesus also gives high targets: Matt. 5.48). It is exaggerated language because of the polemic of the letter. (Again, compare Jesus: Matt. 5.29f.)

John is perhaps giving a counsel of perfection here, and the reality may have been different. Yet, such an approach may be self-defeating, since setting high ideals may in fact drive people more to despair than hope. One wonders, when looking at the Second and Third Letters of John, whether the approach in 1 John was at all successful. But since the chronological sequence of the Johannine letters (and Gospel) is open to question, this enters the realm of speculation. What is a surer opinion is that John tends to paint the opponents in black tones, almost to demonize them. Once again, this raises questions of how historically or theologically accurate this is. It is a common device to use, especially to sharpen boundaries and give a community a greater sense of cohesion and self-identity.

The First Letter of Peter was sent to diaspora Christians, whose faith was resulting in persecutions (1.6, 7; 3.13–17; 4.12–19). Is this like the situation in Bithynia in the early decades of the second century, as evidenced by Pliny's letters to Trajan? It has been suggested that the readers were suffering, not so much official persecutions, but social estrangement. This could involve sporadic mob violence, discrimination, and confiscation of goods. There is no reference to formal accusations, imprisonment or execution. Does it fit better in Rome in the late 60s? Yet such attitudes might have occurred at different times and places, and 5.13 suggests Rome.

What purpose did 1 Peter have? As Christian paraenesis, to encourage those under pressure? Or perhaps a more specific *Sitz im Leben* (life-setting)? The imagery used in the letter, and its hymnic sections, suggest to some that it originated in the context of early Church baptisms, as either a baptismal liturgy or homily (3.20, 21). But its epistolatory form suggests a simpler explanation, as a letter of encouragement, explaining the contents of the faith with reference to Christ and the Old Testament. The reference in 3.18–22 is probably to Jewish apocalyptic, especially 1 Enoch.

The Second Letter of Peter shares common material with Jude (compare 2 Peter 2.1—3.3 with Jude), and most think that 2 Peter depends on Jude. Authorship is a much-debated, complex issue: there are elements in these letters of a more structured, organized Church with faith as a deposit to be passed on, over against later heresy – elements of 'early catholicism', more like the Church of the second century than of the apostolic age. 2 Peter 3.16 also assumes a Pauline corpus of letters.

False prophets and heresies are warned against (2.1), and 2 Peter uses Noah, Lot and Balaam as examples of God's judgement and salvation. In the discussion about judgement, the delay of the parousia is an issue (3.3–9). Here, as in all the catholic letters, the importance of scriptures (the Old Testament and some intertestamental writings), the rising threat of heresy, and the dangers of moral laxity, are the main issues.

Jude, a 'brother of James' (is this James the brother of Jesus or another one?) gives us an example of paraenesis (exhortation). It is critical of immoral behaviour (e.g. v. 12), rather than false doctrine. Like 2 Peter, it is dependent on Jewish intertestamental writings; 1 Enoch (vv. 5, 14), Assumption of Moses (v. 9), and possibly the Testaments of the Twelve Patriarchs (vv. 6, 8), and these are used to bolster the anti-worldly ethic it espouses. The contrast between this, and the deutero-Pauline emphasis on leading a quiet life in society and preserving orthodoxy, is interesting.

We have already seen the emphases in the other 'Johannine' literature in the New Testament. John's apocalypse is the same, writ large. Its genre is important for interpreting it. Is it apocalypse (i.e. a 'revelation': 1.1; 22.6)? And/or a prophecy (1.3; 22.7–19, etc.)? And where do the letters of chapters 2–3 and 22.6–21 fit in to this? It seems to share some features of apocalyptic (e.g. bizarre imagery, numerology, symbolism, and 'a well-stocked apocalyptic menagerie' (L. T. Johnson), but not all of them. Some of these have been the inspiration for art and poetry. Apocalyptic was a common genre in Judaism, perhaps beginning with Ezekiel ('the father of apocalyptic'), in Daniel, and parts of other prophets, e.g. Zechariah, and then in intertestamental literature.

Apocalypses were often the literature of oppressed, persecuted or marginalized groups, and there is certainly persecution and the danger of martyrdom here. The view of Irenaeus that it was written near the end of the reign of Domitian is likely (i.e. *c.*96 CE). Domitian's claim of worship as 'our Lord and God' (according to the Roman historian Suetonius) would produce conflict in Christians, and he was responsible for the first official persecution. Possible references to Vesuvius (8.8) and Nero (11.7; 13; 17) may support this date. The state is pictured as a beast (contrast this with Paul's letters).

Moreover, the letters to the seven churches depict problems, especially with regard to compromise between Christians and paganism. There is a danger of apostasy. Christians themselves are described as 'saints', 'prophets' and 'witnesses'. The Church in Revelation is a community of prophetic witness, testifying to Christ amidst a world of persecution but which, nevertheless, will come through tribulation to triumph and glory.

54   David Graham

The great message of John's apocalypse (as also in others) is that God controls the world: the chaos and dangers of the present are to be seen in contrast to God's heavenly victory. The Christology of the book is among the highest in the New Testament: the lamb sits on the throne with God, and is to be equally worshipped.

Interpreters of the book have varied widely; from millenarians like the Montanists to David Koresh of Waco. Calvin, perhaps wisely, wrote commentaries on every New Testament book except this. For our purposes, we can see encouragement to perseverance, even in the face of martyrdom, and the glorified saints are depicted as victors over the fierce beasts of the world's powers. Once again, the 'heavenly' perspective prevails, something which we also noted in the Gospels and Paul. The ultimate cure – and curer – of souls is the heavenly one.

In conclusion, the sheer variety of pastoral methods in the New Testament is breathtaking, using models and metaphors at home in ancient Judaism and the Hebrew scriptures, as well as from society at large. It certainly provides rich veins of material which the Church was to mine for centuries to come, in ways which would prove to be at times both beneficial and harmful. The primary concern in the pages of the New Testament was to form a cohesive community, in the face of problems and divisions outside and within. The concern of the later Church would be to retain this.

Notes

1. Useful recent work includes H. C. Kee, 'The Transformation of the Synagogue after 70 CE', *New Testament Studies* 36, 1–24; A. Overman, *Matthew's Gospel and Formative Judaism. The Social World of the Matthean Community*, Minneapolis: Fortress; G. N. Stanton, 1992 *A Gospel for a New People; Studies in Matthew*, Edinburgh: T. & T. Clark 1990.
2. See A. J. M. Wedderburn, *The Reasons for Romans*; K. P. Donfried, *The Romans Debate*.
3. J. Ziesler, J. D. G. Dunn, C. K. Barrett, C. Cranfield, F. F. Bruce, M. Black all have excellent comments on these points.
4. For the social setting of the letter, refer to Howard Kee, *Christian Origins in Sociological Perspective* (SCM, 1980), pp. 93–8; Gerd Theissen, *The Social Setting of Pauline Christianity* (Fortress, 1982), pp. 69–110, 121–40, 145–68; Derek Tidball, *Introduction to the Sociology of the NT* (Paternoster, 1983), pp. 90–103.
5. *The Community of the Beloved Disciple.*
6. *The Anointed Community.*

7. Good discussion of these issues can be found in the commentaries of I. H. Marshall (NICNT); S. S. Smalley (Word); J. Stott (Tyndale); R. E. Brown (Anchor).
8. S. Smalley, Word *Commentary*, p. 26.

Bibliography

Bartlett, David L. (1993) *Ministry in the New Testament*, Fortress

Barton, Stephen C. (1992) *The Spirituality of the Gospels*, SPCK

Bennet, David W. (1993) *Metaphors of Ministry: Biblical Images for Leaders and Followers*, Paternoster (Regnum/Lynx)

Best, Ernest (1988) *Paul and his Converts*, T. & T. Clark

Johnson, Luke T. (1996) *Scripture and Discernment: Decision Making in the Church*, Abingdon

Longenecker, Richard N. (1996) *Patterns of Discipleship in the New Testament*, Eerdmans

Malherbe, Abraham J. (1987) *Paul and the Thessalonians: The Philosophic Tradition of Pastoral Care*, Fortress

Osborn, Lawrence, and Walker, Andrew (1997) *Harmful Religion: An Exploration of Religious Abuse*, SPCK

Percy, Martyn (1998) *Power and the Church: Ecclesiology in an Age of Transition*, Cassell

Theissen, Gerd (1992) *Social Reality and the Early Christians*, Fortress

PART II

The Early Christian World

3

The Fathers and the early Councils

G. R. Evans

The Christian community and the wider community

The second-century *Epistle to Diognetus* describes Christians as lending a certain character to the daily life of the communities in which they find themselves. The Christians, it explains, live among other citizens and obey the laws. They are a city within a city. They are like the soul in each body, diffused through the physical world and spread among its peoples, invisible but profoundly influential.

But that was not necessarily how others saw Christians. They, like the Jews, stuck out in late Roman society because they would not mingle their God with the gods of the pagans. There was a conflict between the Christian's duty to recognize no other God and his civil duty to worship the emperor as a divinity .

There were centuries of persecution of Christians, and in those periods when they were an oppressed minority their pastoral needs were largely inwardly directed, to mutual support and the care of their own widows and orphans. There was much resentment and suspicion of what was widely seen as a secret society, and stories were spread about infant sacrifice and other sinister rituals. To try to scotch such rumours Justin Martyr (*c.*100–*c.*165)[1] painstakingly describes what actually happens in the administration of the sacraments.

When Constantine the Great became a Christian and the Empire adopted Christianity as its official religion, a great deal had to change.

The arena of Christian pastoral care opened out. The Christians officially ceased to be a 'minority'. The love of neighbour embraced a far wider range of people. And the oppression stopped. Christians who had been persecuted, enslaved, exiled for their faith, were now to be freed; and the families of those who had been martyred were to possess their goods and inheritances in peace. That did not mean that pagans were now to be persecuted instead. There was to be freedom of conscience for them, too.

But it was bound to make a difference that Christians now basked in imperial approval. There were signs of the new status of the Christian religion in the building of churches in the new imperial capital of Constantinople (Istanbul).

This physical marking of the world with tokens of the new acceptance of Christianity was not confined to Constantinople. Constantine's mother, Helena, and his mother-in-law, Eutropia, encouraged pilgrimage. The key sites in the Holy Land were identified, so that people could visit the actual place of the crucifixion, the tomb of Christ, the place from which he ascended into heaven. They could also go to Bethlehem to see where he was born. These holy places were marked with fine buildings.

There were also new laws in favour of the clergy and the Christian Church and its social norms. Constantine gave the Church an official place in the judicial structure of society, with rights of jurisdiction for bishops.[2] From 333 CE slaves could be freed by a declaration in a church in the presence of priests. Sunday was made an official holiday, with an obligation to observe it. Sexual rules were tightened for all citizens, with, for example, sanctions against concubinage, which had formerly been tolerated.[3]

The Christian had always had the obligation to 'render to Caesar what was Caesar's' (Matt. 22.21; Mark 12.17; Luke 20.25). That was Christ's directive. The difference it made was that he was now a citizen of a Christian state. The slave religion became a state religion. At the same time, the new status posed new challenges. Christianity had to give an account of itself to a category of fellow citizens made up of the highly educated adherents of pagan philosophical systems.

Membership

Baptism is pastorally as well as spiritually important. In the course of the Middle Ages it became the case that membership of society was coterminous with visible membership of the Church. That is to say, everyone in the West except Jews was baptized. It was far from being the case in the reign of Constantine that all citizens of the Empire were baptized. Once that became the usual pattern for the whole population, it became relatively easy to define the 'flock' and to make provision for their pastoral care.

Even in Christian families, baptism of infants was not at first the norm. It became the normal practice in the West only at the end of the fourth century. One prompter appears to have been the debate with the Pelagians. Pelagius was a fashionable preacher in Rome who had been persuasively arguing that it was possible to be a good Christian merely by making an effort to imitate Christ. That undermined the doctrine of original sin and of the helplessness of the sinful human will to do good by its own efforts. It also implied that there was no need to rely on the sacraments as vehicles for grace, which was recognized to be the 'free' action of God assisting the soul. It could even be taken to imply that the work of grace was not essential. Augustine countered that by strongly emphasizing the dependency of the human soul upon the work of grace. The normal channel for the operation of grace in the forgiveness of sin was baptism. A stronger doctrine of baptism – and Augustine was not the only one to urge it – makes it seem more dangerous to risk leaving baptism until late in life. If, as Augustine held, an unbaptized infant will not be able to enter heaven, parents will want their children baptized as soon as they are born. Infant mortality was high.

Until Augustine's day, it was usual for adult converts to spend considerable periods of time as catechumens, and baptism might take place quite late in life. This approach places a strong emphasis upon the importance of an 'instructed' faith in the economy of salvation. That is a different matter from the sixteenth-century Lutheran notion of 'justification by faith'. It does not say that the mere act of trust and commitment is enough. It says that a believer must *believe*, and believe in something of which he can give account.

The deferment of baptism until the new Christian understood the faith and could put his faith in Christ intelligently and knowledgeably was not the only factor in encouraging late baptisms. Baptism could take place only once. Only once did Christians have an opportunity to have the guilt and the penalty of their sin lifted from them. It was not universally accepted that it was possible to find any remedy if one fell back into sin after baptism. So the later in life one was washed from one's sins the better.

All this had various pastoral ramifications. The need for education in the faith had to be met pastorally and that was done in various ways. There was, for a few, the possibility of self-education. Augustine himself spent a period of time after his conversion living with a group of friends at Cassiciacum on Lake Como in north Italy, reflecting on his new faith in the light of his previous philosophical and religious beliefs. Only after that did he offer himself for baptism. But he was unusual in being professionally and intellectually equipped for this sort of study. The pastoral care of such sophisticated and highly educated individuals was a challenge of a high order, and new recruits to the faith of the calibre of Augustine might soon find themselves actively pressed into episcopal office.

Most of those who wanted to become Christians in the early Christian centuries had a more commonplace path mapped for them. They were to begin by becoming 'hearers', until they had been taught about the faith and could make a commitment of faith with a clear understanding of what they were doing. Augustine's *De catechizandis rudibus* gives a picture of the mode of this instruction in his own day. He describes 'adult education' teaching sessions in which bystanders may join in with questions and in which the catechist will have to be capable of discussing with the convert his difficulties in adjusting what he formerly believed to what he is now asked to hold.

Origen, writing against the pagan philosopher Celsus,[4] explains that the Christian communities appoint proven Christians to enquire into the lives and conduct of the hearers to ensure that they are not secret sinners but are living up to the standards of their new faith. This was a necessary precaution. In the late fourth and early fifth centuries, Augustine wrote a number of books on the relationship between faith and good works, to emphasize that holiness of life ought to go with faith. In his day it was not uncommon for a new believer to come to the instruction classes but to put off changing his manner of life until he was actually baptized.

The dispute with the Pelagians not only made Augustine sharpen his own thinking on the role of human will; it set him on the road to the development of a doctrine of predestination which was to have huge pastoral consequences for the Church. To believe in predestination is to believe that no action or omission in this life will alter the outcome. God knows who are to be saved and he will not change his decision. Augustine did not think that those who are to be saved are themselves conscious of the fact. That was Calvin's opinion, but not his. The pastoral consequences of the Calvinist view are different, for it means that those who believe themselves to be saved may be tempted to rest on their laurels while those without that confidence may despair and also cease to make any effort to live a good Christian life. Augustine's conviction, that it is not until the life to come that anyone will know where he is to spend it, leaves room for the exhortation to live a virtuous life. The mediaeval Church was to make much of that pastorally.

The threshold passed at baptism made the Christian a member of the visible Church. It was not clear to Augustine or others whether it necessarily made him a member of the invisible Church. If baptism guaranteed entry to heaven it could not be true that no-one knew who was to be saved. Moreover, if God, as he undoubtedly could, chose to intervene, might not the act of grace be sufficient to ensure that a person who was not baptized could enter heaven? That seemed entirely plausible in the case of individuals who desired baptism but who, for some reason which was not their fault, could not receive it.

Schism

One of the effects of the consolidation of the Church into a body in some respects coterminous with the state was that it became much more conscious of itself as the *catholica*, the universal Church, one, holy and apostolic. There were various ways in which this unity could fail or be fragmented, with pastoral consequences for those for whom it became broken.

The first was by schism, the breakdown of structural unity which seemed to Augustine to be itself a heresy, for it divided the one body of Christ. The most notable of the schisms of the early Christian centuries was that of the Donatists. During the period of persecution under the Emperor Diocletian, Felix, bishop of Aptunga had been a *traditor* (traitor). Under threat, he had given up the books of Scripture. Later (311) he consecrated Caecilian as bishop of Carthage. An indignant group maintained that that consecration could not be valid because the consecrating bishop no longer had authority to conduct it. A rival to Caecilian was consecrated and he was succeeded by Donatus. His followers began to maintain that it alone was the true Church and that the episcopal succession from Caecilian and its people was no Church at all. The pastoral consequences were considerable. The Donatist party had strong support from local African nationalists and they became involved with marauding bands of thugs known as the *circumcelliones*. These were gangs of disaffected peasants, with social grievances, who would surround the houses of the 'catholic' Christians and attack them. They called themselves 'soldiers of Christ', crying 'praise be to God' as they went in to the attack. The authorities tried to win them round by argument, and they tried force, but this pattern of behaviour continued into the fifth century, with all the breakdown of peace it entailed.

Heresy

Heresy does not consist merely in getting some point of faith wrong, but in persisting in error when the fault is pointed out. But the question whether a given idea was right or wrong was not always easily answered in the early Christian centuries. There were many questions which had to be answered for the first time. The clauses of the Nicene Creed of 325 embody one after the other the resolutions of these disputed questions.

The pastoral problem was the danger that the faithful would be confused and misled. Cyril of Alexandria wrote to the heretic Nestorius at the time of the Council of Ephesus in 431. He reminded him that it was a great offence to God to place a stumbling-block in the way of one of Christ's 'little ones' (Matt. 18.6). He expresses concern at the number of individuals who are disturbed by Nestorius' teaching. That is why the Council has set out the definition of the faith.

Lapsing

Some Christians simply lost interest and ceased to be active members of the Church. At times of persecution some gave up the faith out of fear. Christ had said that anyone who put hand to plough and then turned back was not fit for the Kingdom of Heaven (Luke 9.62). Apostasy was ranked with murder and adultery as serious sin for which the punishment was excommunication.

The lapsed and the apostates posed a pastoral problem if they repented and wished to return to the Church. One school of thought was rigorist, and said that there could be no forgiveness for those who had set their hands to the plough and looked back. Another emphasized the divine mercy and said that restoration to the community was possible, at least for the laity. This was a theme on which Origen had something to say in his book against the pagan Celsus (*Against Celsus* 3.51). He speaks of the sorrow with which Christians mourn the loss of the lapsed, thinking of those who have fallen into serious sin as if they were dead men. He says that if they show real conversion and sorrow, and keep up their repentance for a long time, they may eventually be readmitted to the community, but that those who have been clergy may not subsequently hold any clerical office. The eleventh canon of Nicaea, 325, allowed the penitent to return at last, after a total of twelve years from the time of repentance. The same canon rules that for priests there could be no return to the priesthood, and none of the lapsed who had returned could subsequently be made priests.[5]

Superstition

There was a further possibility of falling away from the faith, and one likely to be far more common. That was the muddled continuance or resort to old habits alongside Christian adherence. It was a serious continuing difficulty in the early Church that converts, especially the simple and uneducated, found it difficult to leave their old practices behind and sometimes went on worshipping the old gods alongside the one God to whom Christ bore witness. It was entirely understandable that they should do so. In theory the Christians and the Jews stood apart from this process as monotheists, and insisted that their God was not simply Jupiter by another name. But that did not mean that at the level of popular superstition there was not a lingering reluctance to abandon the security and familiarity of the old, smaller gods. There was the additional complication of the danger that saints would somehow 'replace' them, being treated as though they were themselves gods and being worshipped at their shrines.

Augustine's mother was a Christian and not given to the worship of the old gods. But her behaviour exemplifies a related pattern of difficulty. She had that devotion to the saints and their shrines which could be hard in some respects to distinguish from the continuing worship of pagan gods. It had the look of polytheism. Late Roman religion was syncretist. That is to say, it took in the pantheons of the conquered races and states and matched them where possible with Roman deities. The Greek Zeus was equated with the Roman Jupiter, Athene with Minerva, and so on.

Augustine of Hippo fully realized the pastoral difficulty of insisting that simple people abandoned these comforts. He discusses in *The City of God* the hypothesis that the small old pagan gods are real spirits. They are in fact the demons, he says. They are fallen angels, and just as the virtuous angels are real forces for good in the universe, working at God's behest, so their fallen brethren are real forces of evil. It is possible to be sure that the gods are such fallen spiritual beings, Augustine argues, because of their behaviour. They can be bribed and angered and have to be mollified. They are attracted by base gifts, by decadent theatrical performances. They show none of that high spiritual dignity which marks the unfallen angelic creation.

Connected with this problem of the need to have a small, local 'deity' to hand was the enthusiasm of the simple for relics and icons. The understanding here was that the spiritual and holy could have a local habitation in objects and places associated with a holy man or woman. The idea is rather like that of the 'treasury of merits' which was to be outlined in the thirteenth century by Bonaventure. Saints might be thought more than holy enough to ensure their own salvation, so it might be possible to envisage a surplus of virtue or merit which could be applied to someone else's spiritual needs. This was a highly quantitative view of the nature of holiness, and among the simple faithful there was a correspondingly crude physical sense of the storage of this surplus. Those who visited the shrines of saints in search of spiritual benefit were hoping to come away with something of this holiness attaching to themselves.

Other things might come of such a visit, which would not be at odds with true Christian faith. The power of a holy place to evoke an intensity of spiritual experience, the stimulus to prayer, was a quite different thing and potentially of value. But the dangers were real.

The good Christian life: the value of suffering

Christianity is not only a belief-system. It is a way of life whose parameters were set out in the teaching of Jesus; and that had pastoral aspects. One of the most obvious was the duty to help the poor and needy and afflicted, to visit those in prison. To love one's neighbour as oneself imples an equality; it was a proper equality to become humble and poor oneself, to share the suffering of others. The second-century *Epistle to Diognetus* says that the soul thrives on poverty and punishment. Those well-fed and at their ease do not think much about spiritual things. So Christians ought to accept that they will be better Christians without the distractions of worldly goods. Among the three main penitential penalties – almsgiving, fasting, prayer – there is a certain balance of these elements.

The penitent gives to others and he denies himself; and he does both in an offering to God.

About 200 CE Clement of Alexandria wrote about the problem of the rich man's attaining salvation, in the face of an uncertainty which was beginning to arise as members of the wealthier classes joined the slaves and the generally socially humble earliest adherents of the faith. Ought a rich man to give away all his goods when he became a Christian? Clement says no, only what will stand in the way of his salvation. That means that what he depends on he loves too much. Worldly goods can be rightly used. They may even assist the believer on the road to salvation (*Stromateis* 15.1–6; 24.1.24).

But the more widespread Christian view was that it was best to be poor. For it was clear that Jesus loved the poor. Christianity began as a minority religion whose followers were frequently persecuted and commonly of lowly and disadvantaged social class. There was a strong sense of the value and nobility of enduring such suffering for the faith. There was a clear and consistent assumption in the early Christian centuries that suffering sanctifies, that those who suffer through no fault of their own are blessed and that the right way was for Christians to accept suffering, to embrace it, even actively to pursue it (the more so if they suffer for the faith as martyrs).

Clement, bishop of Rome, says in his First Epistle to the Corinthians at the end of the first century AD that by being exiled, stoned, persecuted, Christians set an example and draw others to the faith. There are lively accounts of the horrors which were suffered and of the effect upon the bystanders of the sight of the courageous bearing of the martyrs. Martyrdom not ending in death left those who suffered it as living heroes to others. It was even believed that they could grant penitents absolution. Cyprian speaks (*De Lapsis*, CCSL 3) of the ambiguous position of martyrs who had been tortured and who were granting dispensation from penance and readmitting the excommunicated to communion as though they were in holy orders and had the authority to bind and loose. Cyprian's view was that this was permissible only in an emergency, that is, if the penitent was fatally ill. Justin says in his second-century *Apology* 1.16 that Christian patience and forbearance even in less testing circumstances is a great winner of converts.

The pastoral tension here is between helping those who suffer and pointing to them as setting a good example to others who suffer. A balanced Christian life is not a life of moderation.

One rational Christian response to the perception that it is best not to become too enamoured of the world is to leave it, and there were various ways of withdrawing.

One was spiritually, in prayer.

One was by going apart to live a life of special dedication, the 'religious life' of a monk or hermit. During the first Christian centuries there were a number of experiments in this direction. Some placed the stress on the solitary life and were eremitical. The 'desert fathers' were particularly important here, and some of them are described in a series of short stories by Gregory the Great in his sixth-century *Dialogues*; others we know of through their surviving 'sayings'. Both ways of making an impact on the world influence by example. The woman who tries to tempt a hermit is outwitted; a hermit gives spoken guidance to someone who comes to him for advice, and that is preserved and passed on with reverence.

There was a good deal of resort to such hermits and holy men. They were seen as a focus of holiness, a place of resort for those in search of spiritual assistance. They were therefore discharging a pastoral function, not in any formal way but in the broader sense of providing help and support and counselling and setting an example of a strong and sacrificial religious devotion.

There were also nascent forms of communal religious life. These varied in form in the early Christian centuries, but they had in common an ideal of community. Some communities lived closely together, others consisted of groups of monks living separate lives in their cells but meeting from time to time for meals or for worship. The Rule of St Basil in the East seeks to curb the more extreme austerities of the desert fathers. He prefers a community life under obedience with a routine of liturgical prayer and manual work – the balanced life of poverty and chastity. Children were to be taught in classes attached to the monasteries.

In the West, Augustine's Rule had some importance in setting parameters for those intent on a less formalized monastic life or intellectual companionship in the Spirit. It was not until the sixth century that Benedict of Nursia created the Rule by which almost all monks in the West were to live for many centuries. Within these communities there was a burden of mutual pastoral care. They all practised hospitality, but they did not have a duty of care towards those who lived outside their walls.

Another way of withdrawing from the world was by fixing one's hope and interest on the life to come. This is the rationale of asceticism. The ascetic life could be lived at home as well as in the desert, and a number of letters survive from Jerome to various Roman ladies living as widows or virgins in Rome. He encourages them to remain in their celibate state and to live under a strict discipline in their domestic environment, fasting and praying. The underlying idea here is that what is good for the body, by way of comfort and indulgence, is bad for the soul.

This was not by twentieth-century pastoral standards a balanced life. But moderation was not the ideal to which those who sought to leave the world for God were looking. They were making an extreme choice and it was one which could be better fulfilled by severity and self-discipline.

Apocalypse

It follows logically from the notion that one improves one's chances of salvation by turning from the world, that the advent of the world to come is something to look for eagerly and to seek out. There were always apocalyptic movements in the Church: the first generation of Christians expected to see the second coming of Christ before they died, and that expectation survived the first generation surprisingly well. There was an apocalyptic movement among the Montanists in the late second century, which still expected the second coming imminently and an outpouring of the Holy Spirit to precede it. This sort of pentecostalism has certain customary accompaniments. Prophets speak of the old age of the world (*senectus mundi*), the decay of things in these last times. Such a movement inclines to be very rigorist because time is short: no second marriages are allowed; strict fasting is enjoined; people are to bear persecution with courage and not to run away; a primitive fervour is visible.

The sense of imminence and urgency which pervades the literature of apocalypse had its own pastoral effects. One of them was to create in the late antique world a strong interest in a complex of questions to do with the prediction of the future and whether or not there was any way of changing it: providence, fate and fortune, divine foreknowledge, predestination, the freedom of choice of rational creatures.

In the first book of his *The City of God* Augustine was obliged to discuss this matter because as a bishop in north Africa he was being confronted with angry exiles from an Italy which was falling to the barbarian invasions. They were asking him why, if the Christian God was the only true God, omnipotent and with a plan for the ultimate good of his creation, the Christian Roman empire was being allowed to fall to the barbarians. Augustine's eventual answer was that it was necessary to take a sufficiently large view of that purpose to make the Roman empire and its fate shrink into its proper proportions. Catastrophic though it seemed to those driven into exile in north Africa, within the divine plan this was but a small episode.

Boethius, too, writing his *Consolation of Philosophy* in the sixth century in the context of the personal crisis of his political house-arrest and imminent execution, addressed himself to the question of the purpose of life and the degree to which any human being could alter his destiny by his own efforts. He looked outside the Christian tradition at fortune and fate, at a world from which there was missing the comforting assurance that a good and all-powerful God is in charge and that all will be well in the end. Here, too, there were pastoral issues. Christians might not feel safe in this life, but it was important for them to be able to feel safe in the next.

The shepherd and his 'cure'

The role of the ordained minister developed in the early Church from the starting-points provided by the key texts of the New Testament, but not without active debate on the roles involved. It is not a simple matter to say that they were 'pastoral'. Jesus had commissioned his disciples first and foremost to preach the gospel. He had sanctified baptism by being himself baptized. He had instituted the Lord's Supper, exhorting his disciples to celebrate it in memory of him. He had also given a power to bind and loose (Matt. 16.19; 18.18). So there were clear pathways for the growth of a ministry of the Word and for a ministry of the sacraments, although the details were to take many centuries of discussion and controversy in the unfolding. One of the results of these shifts in the organizational patterns of the young Church was to create a strong sense that it was right that there should be shepherds and sheep, clergy and laity.

The ministry of all believers was seen as a collective ministry, within which it was appropriate for there to be a special ministry. Less clear was the structure within which ministry was to be *organized*. The models of the early communities were experimental.

There was a tension between charism and order: institutional patterns were repeatedly challenged by individuals believing themselves to move under the direction of the Holy Spirit. There was a further tension within the order of the Church between collegiality and hierarchy, and it was this which became the most important formative influence structurally. Jesus' disciples had had a leader. The Acts of the Apostles shows them working out ways of governing themselves and making decisions when he was no longer physically present with them. It was natural for them to find human leaders, in Peter and Paul. But there was a continuing sense that the *koinonia*, the communion or community, should think and act cooperatively and as of one mind. This theme of the need to seek a *consensus fidelium* has remained strong, but during the patristic period it was hierarchy which came to dominate.

Gradually the ministry evolved into a ladder. Bishops became senior to priests and priests to deacons. Only bishops had authority to ordain and to confirm. In the first Christian centuries, they stood at the head of the penitential system, excommunicating serious sinners and restoring them to the community if they showed themselves sincerely repentant. Priests as well as bishops had authority to administer the sacraments, and the presidency of the Eucharist became increasingly important as the defining mark of priesthood. Deacons, who had begun as a separate order of minister with practical responsibilities (see below) began to be regarded as beginners on a road which led in due course to the priesthood and sometimes the episcopate.

All this placed the bishop more and more conspicuously at the top of a hierarchy. Augustine had to emphasize more than once that he did not regard himself as a bishop over his people so much as a bishop 'with and among' them. By the time of Gregory the Great at the end of the sixth century, the bishop was *rector*, ruler. Gregory himself became bishop of Rome and he was influential in moving onward a tendency to elevate patriarchs even higher, and even to reach for a primacy. Here he encountered resistance from the patriarchs of the East, in Constantinople, Antioch, Jerusalem and Alexandria, to whom it was by no means clear that the patriarch of the West had a claim to be primate over them all, merely because he was heir to St Peter.

Gregory the Great meant by *rector* something much richer than 'ruler'. His *rectores* were exercising a ministry of oversight both in the sense that they watched over the community and in the sense that they were deemed to see further into spiritual realities and could thus teach their people.

This was not, however, a lordship held by the priest or bishop in his own right. It was his in and through the gift of the Holy Spirit. Although that was easily lost sight of in later mediaeval centuries, at the outset the principle was clear.

Ambrose, bishop of Milan and contemporary of Augustine, describes a priestly ministry of prayer. He conceives it in terms of the priest's acting as a channel for the Holy Spirit. 'The office of a priest is a gift of the Holy Spirit, and it is the Holy's Spirit's law which binds and looses.'[6] He examines in his *De Sacramentis* the idea of the athlete anointed to run the race for the crown of eternal life. This race takes huge effort; there is pain now but the inestimable gain of eternal life to come. Because it is so difficult, the soul needs the help of the sacraments and a priest to administer the sacraments.[7] The priest prays for his people.[8] When he speaks, for example, in preaching, he touches the ears of his people with his words and their ears are opened.[9]

Christ was 'priest' and 'shepherd', and these two roles, the sacramental and the 'caring', ran for the most part in parallel in the roles of the ministry of bishops and priests. They were not necessarily separated in the people's minds.

Cyprian and Ambrose are among those who explore the 'lost sheep' motif of Christ's teaching. The shepherd has a responsibility to go and find his sheep if they are lost, for he must make sure they do not perish. And the shepherd must go further: Augustine stresses that he must find them pasture.[10] He ought to be willing if necessary to lay down his life for his sheep and to take it up again according to their need, argues Augustine.[11]

Because of his distinctive gift of the Spirit the priest is held to be stronger than his people. He is their protector. The sheep do not fear the wolf when their shepherd is there, says Jerome, another contemporary of Augustine.[12] With his strength goes gentleness. The Good Shepherd himself was meek and gentle and so should his priests be.[13]

It was considered pastorally undesirable that very recent converts should be baptized and then at the same time made priests or even bishops. It may seem surprising that they were. But social pressures and the shortage of priests led to physical capturing and forcible ordination of talented individuals.

Christ was the one shepherd of one flock.[14] Augustine points out that the shepherds who are human priests are themselves the sheep of the Good Shepherd.[15] But each priest or bishop has a smaller flock, a microcosm or a part of the whole. The label *pastoralis cura* is local and specific. Priests do not have a general duty but a pastoral charge of a particular group of sheep. *Pastoralis cura* appears to be principally a mediaeval term, but it is already in Gregory the Great's letters.[16]

Rules for priests and people

The rules governing the priest's life, and *a fortiori* that of the bishop, are strictly referenced to his high pastoral and sacramental duties. Self-discipline was the keynote.

Priests were expected to be whole. Those who had become eunuchs through no fault of their own – for example, by being castrated at the hands of barbarians or through surgery when they were ill – might remain among the ranks of the clergy. But no-one who had castrated himself could continue to be a priest (Canon 1, Nicaea 325).

Priests were also expected to lead lives of sexual continence. The calling to ministry was early understood to require a special and sacrificial commitment. The priest needed to be free to give all his time and energies to God's service. That might make it inappropriate for him to be a married man with family responsibilities. It was also a commonplace of the first Christian centuries that sexual abstinence was a higher calling than marriage and that a celibate priest was choosing the better part. Canon 16 of the Council of Chalcedon provides for the excommunication of those who make a commitment to celibacy and then marry. But there is provision for the local bishop to handle the matter 'humanely' and be merciful.

Clerical celibacy was not in the end required in the Eastern half of the Roman empire, and Orthodox clergy are still able to be married. The Church in the West from the eleventh century firmly forbade priests to marry, with a number of pastoral consequences.

Priests given to usury were to have their names taken from the official roll (Nicaea 325, Canon 17). Nor should any priest manage property or otherwise engage himself in worldly business (Chalcedon 451, Canon 4). No bishop should perform an ordination for money (Chalcedon, 451, Canon 2).

In the early Christian centuries, priests had to be discouraged from wandering from city to city because that tended to foster factionalism, the formation of parties of personal adherents. That was done by requiring any travelling priest to carry letters of commendation from his bishop (Nicaea 325, Canon 15; Chalcedon 451, Canon 13). There is a further stricture in the Canon 18 of Chalcedon 451, against the forming of secret associations among clerics, who were then as in other periods given to plot against one another. Monks were also to be found wandering the Empire and causing trouble (Chalcedon 451, Canon 23). Wandering was discouraged among the laity too. Paupers and the needy are to travel with ecclesiastical letters of peace, but they are not to be given letters of commendation. Letters of commendation are proper for persons of good reputation only (Chalcedon 451, Canon 11). The wanderer is, by definition, outside the pastoral arena and that, in an ordered ecclesial community, is a bad thing.

Do deacons have a pastoral function in the early Christian centuries? If 'pastoral' is taken as a synonym for 'caring' the answer must be yes. If pastoral is taken to imply a leadership function, having charge of a flock of sheep, then by definition, deacons do not have a pastoral ministry.

The ministry of deacons is clearly distinguished in the New Testament from that of preaching and the ministry of the sacraments. The early Church had found that it needed to appoint a distinct group of individuals to look after the practical needs of widows and orphans. For this task, women were at first held to be as well-fitted as men. It was only when the diaconate gradually became a stepping-stone to the priesthood that that changed.

It was necessary to ensure that the women who were chosen for diaconal work were sober, mature and respectable. The Council of Chalcedon of 451, Canon 15, says, in accord with Canon 19 of Nicaea 325, that women under 40 years of age may not be made deacons. And if a woman who has been made a deacon 'despises God's grace and gets married' she is to be anathematized together with her husband.

Some roles were not considered appropriate for priests, though they might be for their sheep. The early Church did not stand in the way of Christians becoming soldiers. The metaphor of the soldier of Christ was taken literally too. But there were reservations. Priests were not allowed to fight. Origen, *Against Celsus* 8.73, says that the best way to help a righteous cause is by prayer. Intercession is a stronger support to the emperor than the wielding of a sword.

On the other hand, manual labour was acceptable for those with pastoral responsibility, but not if it got in the way of their pastoral duties.

Study was acceptable, even appropriate, even necessary for the discharge of the pastoral function of teaching the faith. But because the first Christians were unlettered men and women there was a certain unease in the early Church about the place of learning. The most sophisticated of contemporary pagans had a philosophical education and much of the thought and energy of the leaders of the first Christian centuries was occupied with the question of the attitude they ought to take to this sort of learning. In the end Christianity absorbed and adapted much of what it had to offer. Origen writes in his *Homilies on the Psalms* 36.5.1 to exhort his listeners not to be hostile to those who devote themselves to study. Study is not incompatible with simplicity. Jerome's concern is explicitly with the potential for conflict between the 'Ciceronian' and the 'Christian', the educated man who knows secular subjects and the Christian who may have to turn his back intellectually on some of what the world teaches him if he is not to be false to his faith.

That concerns Augustine, too, especially in the *De Doctrina Christiana*. On the other hand, it is only too easy to confuse simplicity with ignorance. The idea of a 'learned ignorance' is found in Augustine. He sees it in terms of an ignorance repaired by the Holy Spirit coming to the aid of human weakness. This is a learning more profound than anything which can be taught by human tutors, and independent of any such instruction. The principle is that the Holy Spirit does not make those he teaches knowledgeable; he makes them wise.

The parameters of pastoral care were comprehensively set out in the developments of the early Christian centuries. When Gregory the Great wrote his *Regula Pastoralis* for the guidance of prelates, a number of principles seemed clear to him. Those who were set in positions of authority in the Church as bishops were to exercise a ministry of oversight. They were above all *rectores*, rulers, and preachers or teachers. Their primary responsibility was for the maintenance of the faith and of good order in the Church. But Gregory's own voluminous correspondence gives the lie to any suggestion that he had no pastoral instincts in the milder and more caring sense. He is endlessly concerned for the welfare of those to and about whom he writes, for fair and appropriate outcomes to disputes.

Gregory wrote for the circumstances of the world he lived in. That will be the pattern page after page in this study, as we travel through the scenes and preoccupations of later ages. But we see in the vicissitudes of the theology of pastoral care the steady Christlike concern which shines in recognizable form in every age.

Notes

1. *Apology* 1.61–7.
2. *Theodosian Code*, 23 June 318, 1.26.1.
3. *Codex Justinianus* 5.36.1, law of 326.

4. Origen, *Against Celsus*, 3.51.
5. Canon 10, Nicaea, 325.
6. Ambrose, *De Paenitentia*, CSEL 73, 1.2.8.
7. Ibid., 1.2.4.
8. Ibid., 4.4.14.
9. Ibid., 1.1.2.
10. *In Johannis Evangelium*, Tract. 45.15.
11. *De Consensu Evangelistarum* 4.10.18, p. 412.
12. Jerome, *In Isaiam*, CCSL 73, 7.17.2.
13. Jerome, *In Sophoniam*, CCSL 76A, 3.
14. Augustine, *On the Psalms*, CCSL 39, Ps. 78.3.45 and CCSL 40, Ps. 117.3.
15. *In Johannis Evangelium Tractatus*, 123.5, line 101.
16. And his comments on 1 Kings 4.

Bibliography

Augustine, *Confessions*, trans. Henry Chadwick (Oxford, 1991)
Blair, John, and Sharpe, Richard (eds), *Pastoral Care before the Parish* (Leicester, 1992)
Chadwick, Henry, *The Early Church* (Penguin, 1967)
Krupp, R. A., *Shepherding the Flock of God: The Pastoral Theology of John Chrysostom* (New York, 1991)
Lawless, George, *Augustine of Hippo and his Monastic Rule* (Oxford, 1987)
Poschmann, B., *Penance and the Anointing of the Sick* (ET, Freiburg, 1964)
Straw, Carole, *Gregory the Great* (California, 1988)
Volz, Carl A., *Pastoral Life and Practice in the Early Church* (Minneapolis, 1990)

4

Pastoral care and the monks

'Whose feet do you wash?'

Benedicta Ward

Monastic life supplied pastoral care in all its forms to Christian Europe for over a thousand years. While the abbot was first of all a 'father' (*abba*) to his own monks (later on the friars had similar leaders), he and they also taught and preached, heard confessions, administered parishes, dioceses and estates, gave food to the hungry, medicine to the sick, care to the needy, education to the unlettered, and advice of all kinds to the poor as well as to potentates and princes. They were an essential part of the way in which Christians understood the two-fold command of the gospel to love God and one's neighbour as oneself. But monastic life was not primarily concerned with the 'love of neighbour' which was later to be so obvious a part of monastic life among the barbarian cultures of northern Europe. To discover the basis of monastic service to others it is necessary to look at the beginnings of the Christian forms of monasticism in Egypt and Palestine in the early fourth century[1] whose tradition supplied all monks with the primary understanding of their vocation.

It must be said at once that these early monks were not concerned with external ministry at all. They understood that the command and promise of the Lord to love one another applied to the relationships among themselves: 'my life and my death is with my neighbour'[2] was one of their comments. Towards newcomers, they were courteous and showed them some basic ways of desert survival; if the new monks wanted spiritual advice, they were reluctant to give it but would prefer to allow disciples to see what their own way of prayer and life was like, and to learn what they could from their example. Their concern for each other was conditioned by the fact that they met rarely, and also by a profound respect for the choice that each one had made of silence and solitude; but when they saw a brother in any difficulty, however trivial, they responded not with fuss and interference but not with rebuke either:

> Some old men came to see Abba Poemen and said to him, 'When we see brothers who are dozing during the services, shall we rouse them so that they can be vigilant?' He said to them, 'For my part, when I see a brother who is dozing, I put his head on my knees and let him rest.'[3]

But what about their care for those who were not their immediate neighbours? Is there anything in the records of their lives to clarify our own thoughts about external ministry? And if not, why write about ministry at all in relation to those who were by definition alone, *monos*, outside the normal boundaries of society? Monks, moreover, in the deserts of Roman Egypt, who had fled their own society and who have been dead for 1600 years? Their interests and their situation seem remote from modern concerns. Few readers (though no doubt there are some) are preparing to depart into the desert, and on the other hand, many may be expecting to be involved in some way in ministry. These first monks were not clergymen, teachers, social workers, or married laymen, they were not even interested in church services, theology or sacraments. Some of them were not even baptized until after they had lived as monks for years; few of them could actually read the Scriptures, though they knew a great deal of them by heart; the hermits who lived in Nitria and Scetis could attend the liturgy on Sundays[4] but the solitary hermits might be without the eucharist for years; Mary of Egypt, for instance, received communion only twice in her life, with a gap of 47 years between those occasions.[5] Even the recitation of the regular round of psalmody was regarded as rather secular: they said that if you only prayed at those hours, you are not really praying: 'a true monk has prayer always in his heart'.[6]

> Abba Lot went to see Abba Joseph and he said to him, 'Abba, as far as I can, I say my little office, I fast a little, I pray and meditate, I live in peace and as far as I can, I purify my thoughts. What else can I do?' Then the old man stood up and stretched his hands towards

heaven; his fingers became like ten lamps of fire and he said to him, 'If you will, you can become all flame.'[7]

The institutional Church did not create monasticism but was aware of the monks and recognized their contribution. Most of the monks were not from the sophisticated and educated classes in the Church, but when Athanasius (c.296–373) wrote the life of one of them, Antony the Great (c.251–356),[8] some great churchmen were inspired to withdraw to the desert also. Their example triggered famous conversions of men who were to become bishops, such as that of Augustine of Hippo (354–430). Another effect of this literature from the desert was that the bishops began to shape the lifestyle of their clergy along the lines of celibate monks. There were also occasions when the monks were sadly misused by the Church: they were made unwillingly into bishops, and aroused the monks against heresy and paganism so that their zeal could be turned into fanaticism. The first Christian monks were at once an ambiguous sign, heroes, but marginal; they were not 'tame'.

The few who followed this special way of living out the call of God to a life of solitude could do so because they were part of a larger whole. This relates to the 'many mansions' (John 14.2) in the house of the Lord and the 'diversity of gifts' (1 Cor. 12.4). There were monks of the city, grouped around the bishops, expressing love by their liturgies, their hospitals for the sick, schools for the ignorant and alms for the poor, and with their keen analysis of doctrine for the faithful. The solitaries were aware of this and considered that the gospel was being preached in the cities quite well without them. They put it in these terms: the eucharist is now celebrated in the towns so the devils have been driven out; they have only the wilderness to go to; so it is there that the monk must go to defeat them. This may have seemed an odd conviction for those who actually knew the wicked cities of Alexandria and Antioch, but perhaps what they meant is that there was in the established round of Christian life and prayer in the towns of late antiquity an awareness of the promise of redemption. It was to the places without any Christian presence that the devil, overcome by Christ in his members, had fled, to the places the gospel still had not reached; that desolation was without and within. In this conviction they were also aware that it was not a nice, orderly, good, well-behaved city that God promised upon earth, but the presence of the redeeming work of Christ in mercy among all the desolations of all times.

The 'town monks', such as those grouped around Basil in Caesarea

(330–79), had themselves been inspired by the desert model of total love and dedication to God, and they expressed that commitment by the work they saw was needed in the body of Christ 'which is the Church'. They had therefore a question for those who remained in solitude, outside the normal Christian community; they asked them how could they, while living alone, fulfil the service laid on all Christians, that of love of the brother? They asked it in the form of a question: whose feet do you wash? That is to say, what is your charity towards your neighbour? What is your part in the true service of a Christian towards others? It is the question which is always being put by those involved in service, to others who are concerned solely with prayer. The answer has to do with the nature of prayer and of vocation but there has to be also an answer on a less profound level. The hermit-monks were Christians and a part of the Church; their neighbours therefore were their fellow Christians. Their work was not primarily the actual service of other people, even Christians, but when they did meet need, how did they deal with it? Can their records tell us something useful?

First of all, it would be possible to consider the use made of the monks by their actual neighbours in the desert. Even in a desert there are other people – for instance, the wandering bedouin, the refugees from taxation and from conscription into the army – there were also the villagers living beside the Nile; how did the monks love these actual neighbours? The local people used them as medicine men for the rising of the Nile, for making peace between factions where they were the outsiders, as a refuge from tax collectors and army conscription. Faced with immediate need, they responded with practical compassion, doing what was asked of them for individuals.

But the main place of contact with non-monks was through visitors, and this in two ways. First, there were the actual visitors to the desert. Second, there were the accounts the visitors gave of the desert. The latter formed one of the main ways in which knowledge of the desert spread and it is there that the admiration for monks is found in what is essentially a view from the outside. The monks lived 'outside society' in the desert; they formed a frontier between the towns of the valley with their domestic limitations and the vast ocean of the desert, an image of those ages of infinity that surround all life. The valley impinged on them most of all in the form of visitors; some of whom were seekers after God, some of whom were inquisitive tourists. All were met with the washing of the feet in its most practical and obvious meaning. Foot-washing had become in the gospel the paradigm of Christian service, by which Christ, who humbled himself by incarnation, showed by practical service of the humblest kind how much he loved and how much his disciples should love one another. In the desert it was also a commonplace of courtesy: guests were received by washing their dusty hot feet, and the action of Christ gave this a sacramental value. The guests, the visitors, provided the obvious way in which the hermit came into practical contact with the world and they were first served by individual and practical courtesy. But those who came out of curiosity were not given the same welcome as those who were really seeking God; there was a severe limitation about such contacts.

Who else did they serve? 'No-one', they said. The first fact about any service they did or did not do was a profound and sincere humility. The hermits agreed that the monks of the city were better than they were because of their service of others; they saw themselves in the desert as sinners, less than anyone, not even able to live according to the gospel. The great ones, they said, were those in the city who were able to keep peace of heart as well as serve others. But they were all called to the primary work of the monk, which was repentance. To do that according to their calling was their real service to the world. They were not claiming any great insight or ability; again and again stories were told among them of those in the cities who were closer to God than they were:

> It was revealed to Abba Antony in his desert that there was one who was his equal in the city. He was a doctor by profession and whatever he had beyond his needs he gave to the poor and every day he sang the Sanctus with the angels.[9]

So, for God's sake, they occasionally served their brothers and disciples and their neighbours in the desert, and visitors who came there: always therefore they had some kind of immediate service of their neighbours. How did they serve? They did not explain directly, but in the records about them, in their examples, perhaps there is more to be said and it is a part of their continuing service to take notice of the basis of their actions. Five aspects from this tradition illustrate their attitude to service of others in a practical way through the stories they told themselves. Given total absorption in God, loving the Lord God with all one's might, what was the result in loving the neighbour?

First and basic: for the monk, it was no use serving others at the expense of destroying his own relationship with God. Actual physical need always brought an immediate response, but it was always dealt with within the reality of the context of the monastic life. Receiving guests meant acting with discernment. They did not see themselves as being required to provide social services or medical care centres or hostels for wayfarers. Their work was interior and solitary, unless God sent them opportunities for service. For instance, in times of famine, the monks would send what food they could to the city; there was always, however, discernment about whether they were really being asked to help, when a genuine request was seen as a call of God not as breach of rule:

> A brother came to see a certain hermit and as he was leaving he said, 'Forgive me, abba, for preventing you from keeping your rule.' The hermit replied, 'My rule is to welcome you with hospitality and to send you away in peace.'[10]

The opportunity of service of this occasional kind was welcomed with a passionate humility. The habitual austerity of the monks was not to stand in the way of either giving or receiving such service:

> It was said of an old man that he dwelt in Syria on the way to the desert. This was his work: whenever a monk came from the desert, he gave him refreshment with all his heart. Now one day a hermit came and he offered him refreshment. The other did not want to accept it, saying he was fasting. Filled with sorrow, the old man said to him, 'Do not despise your servant, I beg you, do not despise me, but let us pray together. Look at the tree which is here; we will follow the way of whichever of us causes it to bend when he kneels on the ground and prays.' So the hermit knelt down to pray and nothing happened. Then the hospitable one knelt down and at once the tree bent towards him. Taught by this, they gave thanks to God.[11]

Second, their service was always individual and shaped by circumstances:

> A brother asked an old man, 'What thing is there so good that I may do it and live?' And the old man said, 'God alone knows what is good ... the scriptures say that Abraham was hospitable and God was with him; and Elias loved quiet and God was with him; and

David was humble and God was with him. Therefore what you find your soul desires in following God, do it and keep your heart set on Him.'[12]

Abba Poemen said that Abba John had said that the saints are like a group of trees, each bearing different fruit, but watered from the same source. The practices of one saint differ from those of another, but it is the same Spirit that works in all of them.[13]

Third, a fundamental theme of their life towards others was never to judge others, but always to be alongside the sinner:

> A brother in Scetis committed a fault. A council was called to which Abba Moses was invited, but he refused to go. Then they sent someone to him saying, 'Come, everyone is waiting for you.' So he got up and went. He took a leaking jug filled with water and carried it with him. The others came out to meet him and said, 'What is this, father?' The old man said to them, 'My sins run out behind me, and today I am coming to judge the errors of another.' When they heard this they forgave the brother and said no more to him.[14]

They were always concerned with this attitude, so that they never judged those they might help, as if from a position of higher power, since all are faced with death and the eyes of the Lord are over each one. It was clear to them that people have enough sorrow and guilt without making it worse. This long and positive perspective is not a refusal to recognize evil; it was rather to know that discerning and locating evil in others was in no circumstances their concern. The violence of evil must not be given new life by long discussion and new condemnation; the monks would 'cover' the faults of others, since there is only One who judges. Immediate condemnation was also inappropriate since no-one knows the whole picture, either for themselves or anyone else. There was enough judgement, condemnation and guilt already without the monks adding to it.

> They said of Abba Macarius that he became as it is written a god upon earth, because just as God protects the world, so Abba Macarius would cover the faults that he saw as though he did not see them, and those which he heard as though he did not hear them.[15]

Fourth, this attitude of non-judgement was not blind, but in fact deepened mutual understanding, since it avoided the inner temptations of power and authority. Then as now there were enough people ready to organize and tell people what they ought to do and how to do it, to improve people according to a pattern; but for the monks this was not even an option. They did not lecture others and put them right from their own powerful and correct position, even if the others were novices or disciples: their conviction was that there was only one spiritual father, Christ, for all alike:

> A brother asked Abba Poemen, 'Some brothers live with me; do you want me to be in charge of them?' The old man said to him, 'No, just work first and foremost and if they want to live like you, they will see about it for themselves.' The brother said to him, 'But it is they themselves, father, who want me to be in charge of them.' The old man replied, 'No, be their example, not their legislator.'[16]

There is One who is served and who is servant of all; that was their only rule of counselling and care. It was not their way to organize a long-term response to need; out of their own awareness of themselves as needy and sinners they simply did what was asked, and that self-effacing service, being one with those in need, was offered as a friendship which both reflects the love of God and conveys it. The story of Agathon and the cripple is a paradigm of the monk's attitude to service:

> Going into town one day to sell some small articles, Abba Agathon met a cripple on the roadside, paralysed in his legs, who asked him where he was going. Abba Agathon replied, 'To the town to sell some things.' The other said, 'Oblige me by carrying me there.' So he carried him to the town. The cripple said to him, 'Put me down.' So he did. When he had sold an article, the cripple asked him, 'What did you sell it for?' Agathon told him the price. The cripple said, 'Buy me a cake,' so he bought it. When Abba Agathon had sold a second article, the cripple asked, 'How much did you sell it for?' and he told him the price. The cripple said, 'Buy me this,' and he bought it. When Agathon had sold all his wares and wanted to go home, the cripple said, 'Are you going back?' Agathon replied 'Yes.' So he said, 'Oblige me by carrying me back to the place where you found me.' So he picked him up again and carried him to that place. Then

the cripple said, 'Agathon, you are filled with the blessing of God, in heaven and on earth.' Raising his eyes, Agathon saw no man; it was an angel of the Lord.[17]

One of the features of our age is the great institution, the big impersonal machine of help; perhaps the hermits demonstrate another way, in which the Christian minister 'understands' by 'standing under'. Sacramental ministry as well as social service can be seen as, at least in part, an exercise of power. With the best will in the world, a priest may see himself as the expert in giving the sacraments and thus be involved in a kind of exersion of power, at a distance, creating a barrier between 'helper' and 'helped'. The hermits show humble service above all, in which love is exchanged not out of needs and desires, but through the love that is Christ. As sinners before the saviour, broken men before God, the monks asked God daily to have mercy upon them, to create love in them as a new creation, not as a self-centred illusion. Of central importance in this way is solitude and silence of the heart. The minister, the carer, like the monk, is not just another expert: he is on the same level as the most broken person and therefore available to all. There is always the temptation to be an expert, to have a special role for oneself, either in counselling or even in liturgy, as the only one who celebrates the Eucharist or gives absolution; this can be seen and used as an expertise, gratifying to the one who feels himself to be one who gives to others; this is quite other than the monks' view of all prayer as an overflowing of the love of God as much to themselves as to others.

Throughout history monks have done very great and extensive work in all spheres, from agriculture to education, but the priority for the monk is always that of prayer and humility before God. From this, the love of God can be released for the healing of the world, beyond and through the immediate situation of need. In the desert of Egypt, the hermits could specialize in this inner stillness because they were part of an educated Christian world, with plenty of reflection on Scripture and doctrine elsewhere, plenty of literacy, and care for the needy. In other places and times, the solitary monks had to undertake other pastoral concerns as well, though always with the same priorities; and their stillness was never apart from service:

> There were three friends who were not afraid of hard work. The first chose to reconcile those who were fighting each other as it is said,

'blessed are the peace-makers'. The second chose to visit the sick. The third went to live in prayer and stillness in the desert. Now in spite of all his labours the first could not make peace in all men's quarrels and in his sorrow he went to him who was serving the sick and found him also disheartened for he could not fulfil the commandment either. So they went together to see him who was living in the stillness of prayer. They told him their difficulties and begged him to tell them what to do. After a short silence he poured some water into a bowl and said to them 'Look at the water' and it was disturbed. After a little while he said to them again. 'Look how still the water is now' and as they looked into the water, they saw their own faces reflected in it as in a mirror. Then he said to them, 'It is the same for those who are living among men, disturbances prevent them from seeing their faults; but when a man is still, especially in the desert, then he sees his failings.[18]

In the desert, the primary place of Christian monasticism, they served Christ only, who washed their own feet and through them those of whoever they were near: that is, their brothers, those who visited them, those who persecuted them, those they met, and so the whole world. But what they *were* was more central than what they *did*. Just as trees make oxygen to purify the atmosphere, so the monks were trees of the spirit; and no more, and no less:

> It is clear to all who dwell in Egypt that it is through the monks that the world is kept in being and that through them also human life is preserved and honoured by God ... There is no town or village in Egypt that is not surrounded by hermitages as if by walls and all the people depend on the prayers of the monks as if on God himself.[19]

Fifth and finally, was there more than this to the 'pastoral outreach' of the hermits on a spiritual level? It is sometimes said that the monk is there to pray for the world, to be an expert in prayer to be appealed to, especially in crisis. If this is so, it is not in the magical sense of a mysterious figure who will make things happen for the rest of us if we ask him; he is not a beaver:

> There was also a Beaver, that paced on the deck,
> Or would sit making lace in the bow;

And often (the Bellman said) saved them from wreck
Though none of the sailors knew how.[20]

The early monks were not this kind of remote medicine men. They were sailors also. They lived among people who were not particularly religious in a 'churchy' way; just humans, created by God, redeemed by Christ, indwelt by the Spirit, not churchgoers or at least not much. The desert fathers were on the margins of the institutional Church, not because they despised or distrusted the Church, but first because many of them had had little contact with the establishment and also because they were convinced that their life in the body of Christ was to be interiorized; it was in the place of solitude that reality was faced within. What they faced in solitude was of course themselves, that central battleground of all the passions, and much of their literature was about this fight with the demons in themselves. Recognizing and dealing with their own failure, despair and sense of non-identity was their central work; it was because they were ready to open themselves to this work of God that they could be used by God for others. It is in this sense of being part of the muddle of humanity that they were intercessors. And this ordinariness linked them as closely to the rest of creation as their response to God linked them into the redeeming work of God in Christ. The work of intercession was the whole life of the monk, and surely this is the calling of each Christian, to pray without ceasing; the monks did not themselves claim to be great intercessors for others; it was others who claimed it for them:

> Palladius said, 'One day when I was suffering from boredom I went to Abba Macarius and said, "What shall I do? My thoughts afflict me saying, you are not making any progress, go away from here." He said to me, "Tell them, for Christ's sake, I am guarding the walls." '[21]

This most vital work of prayer was done by facing brokenness, not by power and ability but by failure and non-success; the model for the monks was Christ who emptied himself, and became the servant of all; and so they found that at the same moment as their sorrow, love issued in true joy and tenderness and unity:

> This place was called Cellia because of the number of cells there, scattered about the desert. Those who have already begun their

training in Nitria and want to live a more remote life, stripped of external things, withdraw there. For this is the utter desert, and the cells are divided from one another by so great a distance that no-one can see his neighbour nor can any voice be heard. They live alone in their cells; there is a huge silence and a great quiet there. Only on Saturday and Sunday do they meet in church and then they see each other face to face as men restored to heaven.[22]

This sense of being united in love to others through deeper knowledge of Christ in solitude remained at the heart of monastic life in both East and West. In the centuries after the devastation of Scetis and the invasions of northern Europe by the barbarians, the work of conversion of non-Christian peoples fell largely to the monks. The *Rule of St Benedict*, (*c*.480–550), which became after 800 the paradigm for Western monks, relied explicitly on the traditions of the desert. It was not a change in the essential commitment of the monastic life but the new demands of society that caused monks to become priests and leaders, bishops and even popes, to take a share in literacy and education, and in the exploration of theology and the Bible. In the East, a more obvious continuity with the desert is discernible, in the greater isolation of monks from the usual concerns of society, though there also the monks have continued the essential monastic outreach of hospitality, whether in the great monasteries, the hermitages, or in idiorhythmic patterns of life. Behind them all, West as well as East, in the fourth century and today, is the basic Christian sense of martyrdom as a life wholly united with Christ on the Cross for the salvation of all creation. The monastic life has been well described as a 'white martyrdom', not because of suffering but because of the love that overflows from such total giving of the self to Christ: as Antony of Egypt said: 'I no longer fear God; I love Him.'

Notes

1. The sources used here are translations of Greek and Latin texts of the fourth century: *Sayings of the Desert Fathers*, trans. Benedicta Ward (London and Kalamazoo, 1975–) (*Sayings*); *Wisdom of the Desert Fathers*, trans. Benedicta Ward, (Oxford, 1976) (*Wisdom*); *Lives of the Desert Fathers*, trans. N. Russell with monograph by B. Ward (London and Kalamazoo, 1981) (*Lives*).
2. *Sayings*, Antony 9.
3. *Sayings*, Poemen 92.
4. *Lives*, pp. 148–94.

5. B. Ward, *Harlots of the Desert* (London and Kalamazoo, 1987), pp. 26–54.
6. *Sayings*, Epiphanius 3.
7. Ibid., Joseph 7.
8. Athanasius, *Life of St Antony*, trans. R. T. Meyer, (London, 1950).
9. *Sayings* Antony 24.
10. *PL* 73, col. 943 (this text is part of a Latin version of the *Sayings*, quoted here from a new translation by B. Ward, to be published by Penguin Classics, 2002).
11. *Wisdom*, 151, p. 42.
12. *PL* 73, col. 956.
13. *Sayings*, John the Dwarf 34.
14. Ibid., Moses 2.
15. Ibid., Macarius 32.
16. Ibid., Poemen 174.
17. Ibid., Agathon 30.
18. *Wisdom*, 1.
19. *Lives*, Prologue, p. 50.
20. Lewis Carroll, *The Hunting of the Snark*.
21. Palladius, *The Lausiac History*, trans. W. K. Louther Clark (London, 1918), 18.29, p. 86.
22. *Lives*, pp. 148–9.

Bibliography

Athanasius, *Life of St Anthony*, trans. R. T. Meyer (London, 1950)
Chitty, Derwas, *The Desert a City* (Basil Blackwell and Mott Ltd., London, 1966)
Lives of the Desert Fathers, trans. N. Russell (London and Kalamazoo, 1981)
Sayings of the Desert Fathers, trans. Benedicta Ward (London and Kalamazoo, 1975–)
Ward, B., *Harlots of the Desert* (London 1987)
Wisdom of the Desert Fathers, trans. Benedicta Ward (SLG Press, Oxford 1995)

PART III

The Middle Ages

5

Penitentials and pastoral care

Thomas O'Loughlin

A Christian dilemma

One of the underlying tensions in early Christianity was between the notion of Jesus as ushering in the perfect life with God, and as the one who welcomed sinners. While a preacher might argue that there was no conflict between these two notions – Jesus welcomed sinners and by forgiving them allowed them to share in divine life – pastors and practice knew otherwise. It was clear to all that new Christian life involved a moral aspect, so the articulation of sin was a pillar of preaching.[1] But it was equally clear that Christians continued to sin after their baptism.

On the one hand the evil of sin could not be explained away, and as notions of asceticism developed such 'going soft' was seen as a sinful compromise in itself. To 'downplay' sin was seen to undermine preaching and sell Christ short. An elegant indicator of this concern was the hesitation over the story of the woman about to be stoned for adultery, now in John 7.53–8.11; sometimes it was found there, sometimes elsewhere in the Gospels, sometimes omitted altogether,[2] and it was always a difficult text for the preacher – it could too easily be seen as Jesus mitigating a lawful sentence for adultery.[3]

On the other hand, Christians sinned. This was a fact that would not go away. So unless the Church consisted only of those who never sinned after baptism, there had to be some means of reconciliation. This concern can be seen explicitly already in a second-century text, significantly named the *Pastor*, linked to one 'Hermas'.[4] Those seeking a means of forgiveness could point to the phrase in the Lord's Prayer 'forgive us ... as we forgive,'[5] or references to leaving the ninety-nine sheep to search for the stray which signified the rejoicing over the repentant sinner,[6] or the text 'For I came not to call the righteous, but sinners.'[7] These two positions arose relative to one another, but if there was any attempt in the early Christian period to integrate them, it has not come down to us.

And it is as an attempt to overcome this basic opposition in the actual life of the Church that we must view the development of 'penitentials' in Celtic-speaking lands in the early mediaeval period.[8] These were lists of sins and the fixed penances needed for their forgiveness, which were intended to help the sinner recover from his/her sin. They possibly appeared first in Wales, but they developed their characteristic form in Ireland. From Ireland they spread to the Anglo-Saxons and the Franks, and eventually became common throughout Latin Christendom. While they arose as part of pastoral praxis, their basis lay in the theology of asceticism rather than in the disputes about sin after baptism, and they changed not only Western practice but its whole moral theology. They initiated a new way of looking at sins, sinning and reconciliation; introduced new links between penance and the process of the Christian life, and brought new rituals into common use. The penitentials mark a departure which finally led to individual private confession as a quasi-judicial sacrament which took place between a contrite penitent and a priest. So this sketch of the origins of penitentials and their pastoral context is really but an introduction to a longer and more complex history.

The crisis of public penance

By the mid-fifth century, about the time that Christianity was spreading in Ireland, sin in the life of Christians was a concern in the Latin Church in two, virtually discrete, spheres. In the dioceses the question was one of restoring someone after a lapse from baptismal regeneration through a once-off severe public penance; meanwhile in the expanding monasteries sin was being seen as what hindered perfection, the overcoming of sin was, therefore, an integral part of conversion and discipleship based on the command: *paenitentiam agite* ('Do penance!'),[9] and so perfection involved a life of penitence.

Structurally, public penance was one of the best-regulated parts of church life. The questions surrounding it had been treated extensively by theological writers from Cyprian (mid-third century) onwards, and every major Latin figure (Ambrose, Jerome, Augustine) had contributed opinions. Equally, it was regulated in law as synod repeated synod prescribing its conditions and methods; and as public act it had a formal liturgical expression. Starting with the assumption that it was an act to restore the baptismal state after a lapse which had destroyed the new life of grace, certain features of public penance followed almost logically. First, it was concerned with those crimes which were seen as significant enough to constitute a complete breakdown of Christian life. While lists of sins could be found from the times of the earliest Christian documents,[10] a trio of capital sins based on Acts 15.29 came to be seen as requiring the full rite of public penance. These were apostasy, homicide, and fornication.[11] Second, it was seen as a restoration of baptism, and as it was unrepeatable, so too was penance. Penance was a 'laborious baptism', the second chance and 'the plank after shipwreck'; and it could only be availed of once in life. While these strictures were seen as safeguards against being seen to make light of the demands of Christ and to rebut groups such as the Donatists that the Catholics were soft on sin and took lapsation lightly, they were, despite the words of all the great preachers of the fourth and fifth centuries, pastorally disastrous: the system just did not work. The all-or-nothing nature of public penance and the public humiliation it involved meant that it was seen as a last resort. In effect it meant that for many baptism was postponed until late in life and people remained on the edge of the Church. In the case of those who were baptized, then penance was postponed until the last possible moment. Moreover, when penance is reserved for the worst sins, then the lesser faults in the Christian life – those which were seen to be remitted through the petition 'forgive us as we forgive' in the Lord's Prayer and through the normal course of fasting and almsgiving – were correspondingly reduced to being of negligible importance. While this impasse was recognized, very few bishops in the West proposed alternatives; those who did, such as Caesarius of Arles, wished to see a limited repetition of penance and to provide a private means by which everyday sins could be addressed.[12]

Pastors and physicians

The theological keys that would unlock the problem of public penance both came from the East. John Cassian in his series of works on monasticism addressed in detail the question of what impeded the perfect life. In cataloguing the sins of monks his aim was not primarily a code of crimes, but an analysis of the nature of afflictions of the soul by analogy with a physician's knowledge of bodily diseases. And if sin is a disease then the overcoming of sins must be understood medicinally, and, adapting a medical basic principal of 'contraries are healed by contraries', he propounded a model of penance as a set a remedies congruent with a set of maladies. Just as a bodily disease such as fever is healed by applying cold, so the damage of a spiritual disease such as gluttony is repaired by fasting.[13] Although often underestimated, Cassian more than anyone else deserves the credit for the sophistication of the post-patristic theology of sin. By studying sin as that part of the ongoing life of the monk which had to be examined and removed as an ailment, he shifted the view of penance in several significant ways.

First, it was not punishment but medicine: penance was to make good damage done and so was a reparation and repayment rather than the cost of being saved after disaster. Second, there was a new emphasis on the individual, as sin was a sickness needing diagnosis rather than a crime needing prosecution. This put a value on spiritual self-knowledge in place of the need for public declaration within the Church; equally, the one who announced the nature of sins was not necessarily the bishop acting as a judge in the forum, but rather the one who had the care of the souls of the monks, and his decisions were those of physician or trainer with the patient or trainee. Third, since it was designed to deal with the range of sins that afflicted the monk's life it was by nature a sliding scale capable of dealing with minor as well as major diseases, and so it was an ongoing lifelong process. Thus the question of repeating penance ceased to be of importance, and the distinction between those who needed formal penance and those who did not disappeared. Cassian's work became widely available from the middle of the fifth century, yet on the Continent the major development he inspired in relation to sin was the reformulation from his work of the list of Eight Principal Vices by Gregory the Great.[14]

Another Eastern development addressing the problem of public penance was that which in Greek was referred to as 'the baptism of tears'.[15] Building on a series of biblical images of repentance, a number of fourth-century writers, most notably Gregory Nazianzen, had stressed that the essential element in forgiveness after baptism was that the sinner was truly sad for his or her sins. This sadness was expressed in their tearfulness day-after-day and night-after-night at the thought of their offences. If a sinner were truly sorry, then the pain of that sadness and the waters of those tears would wash away sins as surely as the waters of baptism had done. So a key to penance was contrition, compunction and tearfulness. We are not sure how widespread this theme became in the West in the fifth and sixth centuries, but we know that one of Gregory Nazianzen's homilies on the theme was translated by Rufinus; we see the notion of compunction appear as part of penitential thought of Cassian and Caesarius of Arles; and later again we know that Isidore of Seville was familiar with the notion from Rufinus. When these two themes of penance as medicine and as contrition are combined in a pastoral context, the result is our penitentials.

The earliest insular evidence

The first evidence for Irish practices regarding penances comes from Patrick's *Epistola ad Coroticum*.[16] Patrick presents himself as a judge publicly condemning Coroticus and his men as guilty of the capital sins of apostasy and shedding blood,[17] and they are excluded as they will not submit to penance. The background is, as we should expect for the fifth century, that of public penance, although curiously he adds that the penance those soldiers should undergo is 'tearful penance'.[18] That said, we now enter a dark period until we arrive at the fully developed *Penitential of Finnian* (usually dated to the late sixth century[19]). In the interim, a series of crucial developments must have taken place, yet we have but a few indirect glimpses in documents where a consensus as to dating and sequence is lacking among scholars.

Perhaps the most significant development in Western Christianity in the fifth century was the growth of monasticism, and we know from Patrick that a form of monasticism for both men and women was present from the start of his mission.[20] Moreover, monasticism's impact on the life of ordinary Christians increased, as we see in the number of monks who became bishops, for instance Eucherius of Lyons and others connected with Lérins.[21] We presume that the earliest ecclesiastical structures in Ireland were somehow diocesan. However, in the absence of the urban environment in which such structures were obviously apposite, church structures easily yielded to those which were focused on monasteries. At the very least we can say that in Ireland, without counterbalance of diocesan bishops, Christianity took on a primarily monastic aspect and that the primary agents of pastoral care were monks linked to an abbot rather than non-monastic clergy linked to a governing bishop. The office of bishop remained the cornerstone of the Church's ministry, but a practical separation of functions took place between the bishop and the head of the monastery that anticipated the later canonical distinction between the power of order and the power of jurisdiction. This 'monasticization' certainly took place in Ireland, and a similar process probably took place in Wales, or at least in those areas which were in close association with Ireland at the time. In that situation the theological vision and pastoral practice came to reflect the values and outlook of monasteries, and so the understanding of sin reflected Cassian.[22] Equally, in such a monastic-dominated environment the tendency to focus on the bishop as the source of spiritual authority with regard to discipline was reduced.

Another cultural factor which may have inspired the penitentials is Old Irish law. While the law texts which survive are not only later than the penitentials, and indeed show the influence of Latin canon law, it does appear that a central native feature is that crimes, from the smallest trespass by an animal to homicide, can be punished by the payment of a fine between the two parties involved.[23] In this system a crime is an offence committed against a person and his/her family group. The offence is made good by the payment of an honour price by the guilty party or by the guilty party's family. That fine varies with the nature of the offence, and in a society of complex social ranks it also varied with the status of the one offended, and the status of the offender. If this aspect of native law was already present in the fifth/sixth centuries, then an extension of it to the religious realm – where a sin is an offence against God's dignity which carries a price if the offence is to be removed – would explain how the monastic notion of ascetic reparation could so easily be extended to the whole society as a way of understanding and overcoming sin. Each offence has a particular price, and when that is paid in penance, then the harmony between the parties is restored; moreover, the price should vary with the status and culpability of the offender, and we see this in the incipient casuistry of the penitentials.

Documents that claim to come from the fifth and sixth centuries are notorious among historians of Celtic history for the difficulty of dating them, and so they are referred to here with that caution. For my purposes it is sufficient to note that they are most probably older than the *Penitential of Finnian*; while they are not penitentials but collections of canons on ecclesiastical discipline, they do show signs of an understanding of sin similar to that found in the earliest extant penitential. The first text is the *Synodus episcoporum* ('First Synod of Patrick'),[24] which is 35 prescriptions about discipline (e.g. the length of fast before baptism[25]) or canonical practice (e.g. clerical credentials[26]), where the standard punishment for the offence is excommunication.[27] The basic argument for its antiquity is that while monks and nuns are mentioned, most of the clergy appear to be secular (i.e. they are married and answerable to a bishop[28]) and pagans are still a distinct group in the society.[29] However, we have this canon, clearly modelled on the 'Three Great Sins' of public penance based on Acts 15.29:

> A Christian (*Christianus*) who has killed or committed fornication or who has sworn an oath to a soothsayer ([h]*aruspex*) according to the customs of the nations[30] let him do a year's penance for each crime; that done let him come with witnesses and then be loosed by the priest. (12 (14), p. 10)[31]

There are echoes here of public penance, but also a new note. Instead of someone being in a condition of having through lapsation lost grace which then must be restored, here we see a set of distinct crimes with specific punishments attached: if a Christian then commits any of them, let him pay the price and the problem is solved. Indeed, it is explicit that if one had committed two or all three of these crimes, then one would just need witnesses that one had done the necessary cumulative amount of penance. If this document is fifth or sixth century, then it is a world away from contemporary Gaul or Spain, where calls to maintain the rigour of the earlier system had the shrill tone of law in desuetude. The *Synodus* has a few other prescriptions where the remedy for sin is a fixed penitential tariff: for example, theft requires restitution of the stolen goods (if possible) and a quota of penance (six months with twenty days on bread alone) before returning to the Christian community;[32] while someone who gives credit to pagan forces (one of the Great Sins) must not only verbally renounce them but do penance.[33]

Equally difficult to date are texts associated with Wales, but which claim to be of sixth-century origin.[34] I shall mention just three of them: the *Preface of Gildas on Penance*;[35] the *Synod of the Grove of Victory*[36] and the *Synod of North Britain*.[37] In the *Preface*, among many regulations and penances for crimes, are some features that indicate a major break with the patristic period and a new pastoral practice about sins. Its opening regulation is about a presbyter or deacon who commits fornication, and it gives the culinary restrictions of the three-year fast in the greatest detail.

That there is a fixed tariff is surprising enough, but the significance of 'presbyter or deacon' becomes clear in the subsequent prescriptions: it is less for a monk who is not also a cleric, and so on (n. 2, and n. 3), and also there is a distinction made between intention and fact (n. 4). Culpability is essential to the understanding of the offence, and it explicitly notes that the punishment is to be seen as a heavenly medicine (n. 1), for offence is indicative of a sickness, while one who points out an offence is to see himself not as an accuser but as one engaged in medicine (n. 18). This theology of sin is derived from Cassian as the document supposes that the whole process is one carried out by an abbot caring for his disciples (nn. 4 and 27), but the document seems to suppose a community that is larger than that of a monastery. There is only one mention of a bishop (n. 24), and this has no connection with penance. We should note that the compilers were aware that their penances were lighter than those of the 'ancient fathers', but significantly they assumed, or pretended, that their method was in line with ancient practice: the 'ancients' demanded a tariff of twelve years' fasting from a fornicating presbyter and seven from a deacon (n. 5).

The *Synod of the Grove of Victory* and that of *North Britain* can be seen as complementary in that the first is explicitly concerned with society at large while the second is narrowly focused on monks (some of whom are clerics), but both assume the same practice for reconciling sinners by tariffs of fasting or pilgrimage. In the *Grove of Victory* adultery is punished by three years' penance (n. 3), theft is obviously a lesser crime with one year's penance (n. 1), while killing another Christian is mitigated if not premeditated and in an outburst of anger, and in seriousness is on a par with adultery: three years (n. 2). In the *Synod of North Britain* the penance for fornication among clergy is, in contrast to Gildas, carefully related to rank, and so presumably culpability, with one year for deacons, three for presbyters and seven for bishops or abbots (n. 1). But significantly these are prescribed on the judgement of the teacher (*doctoris iudicio*), which shows that the realm of discourse is not that of the forum where someone has canonical jurisdiction, but rather that of caring for the growth of disciples. The world of Cassian seems to be just below the horizon. In these early documents, not yet formal penitentials, all the theological and pastoral structures that developed with the growth of the penitentials can already be seen; and, perhaps more importantly, the key break with the practice, and so the pastoral impasse, of public penance has been made.

The Irish penitentials

With the *Penitential of Finnian* we have a short handbook for pastoral use in dealing with sins.[38] The fifty or more situations envisaged as requiring penance cover the whole range of sins, and assume that the one judging the required penance – and there is no hint as to his status in terms of Holy Order – will meet people from the whole of society, lay, monastic, clerical, men and women. To each crime it prescribes a specific 'penitential remedy'[39] of a fixed quantity. There is a tradition of deriding such works as Finnian's as an encounter with the worst aspects of the mediaeval Church as 'reducing the mercy of God to a quid pro quo' or making sin into a matter of a 'laundry list' of automatic fines and 'mechanical forgiveness'.[40] While there is no human institution that has not been perverted from its ideals by the demands of following 'the standard procedure', it should be remembered that such mechanization had no place in the mind of the compilers of these documents. Finnian's first prescription is this:

> If anyone has sinned in his heart through thought, and then at once has repented, let him strike his breast, and ask God for pardon, and make satisfaction, and thus he will become well [*sanus*].[41]

For Finnian sin is always an internal matter between the conscience of the individual and God who is offended. This is a locus of sin whether or not there is a corresponding external act. Thus the primary element in reconciliation is what later would be termed 'contrition': the first step is sorrow to God for the offence: manifested in the gesture of striking one's breast at once, accepting responsibility and expressing regret. Then comes the next stage which is the petition to God for pardon, and then the actual payment of the fine which satisfies the demands of justice between the offender and the One offended. The basis of the possibility of being able to repay the offence with a fixed penance – the most obvious part of the whole system of penitentials – is that the offender is already sorry. And that this sadness for sin is central is made even more clear later in the text where it speaks of 'weeping and crying for sin both day and night' (n. 29) and of the necessity for 'compunction' (n. 31). The text stands in the tradition of Cassian's emphasis on compunction and conversion of heart and combines that with the notion of 'the baptism of tears'.

If in its background it has these themes that forgiveness must begin within and must involve sadness for the offence, we can also see Finnian's work as part of the background for future developments in Latin theology. Most obviously Finnian sees reconciliation as a process (the later *processus iustificationis*) rather than as a single momentary act. The task of overcoming sin is the continual presence of penitence in the Christian life, and the awareness that as one departs so one must seek at once to return. On the practical level this process expresses itself in the sequence of sin, then sorrow, then penance, and then health. In that the starting-point of the return to God after sin is sorrow for sin and petition for mercy, we have an inkling of the debate that raged from at least the time of Abelard as to the essence of forgiveness: is it the moment of contrite internal conversion or the moment of sacerdotal absolution or some combination of these?[42] And in the very act of noting a sequence beginning with the sense of contrition, Finnian is assuming a complexity in the process that allows one to see foreshadowings of later scholastic distinctions such as that of the 'Two Debts' (the *reatus culpae* which is for the offence to God, and the *reatus poenae* which repays the penalty imposed by God as the just reward of sin). Likewise when later canonists and theologians would write of the 'Four Parts' of penance, they would probably find that Finnian is closer to their view than someone such as Augustine.

The penances that Finnian laid down in his *Penitential* vary not only with the rank and status of the offender, but with their intention, state of mind, and the immediacy of their sorrow for their offences. All this reflects a genuine awareness built up in actual practice that 'situations alter cases'. Such a casuistry, while abstracted and generalized in a manual, indicates that Finnian's expertise was not limited to the scriptures – which he invokes as his authority – but based in actual pastoral care. And while in common with most church documents of the period there is a great deal of emphasis on sexual sins and a tendency to see women as the source of such sins,[43] the most consistent image is that of caring. There are references to health, to curing sins as if they were ailments, and to remedies. Moreover, Finnian sees his own work in producing the manual as the paternal work of caring for his children. In several places the text says that the sinner must 'ask pardon or help of God' (e.g. nn. 1, 2, 5, 29) or that they have access to 'the mercy of God' (e.g. nn. 8, 12, 22, 29) or it mentions the heart as the place of the offence between the sinner and God (e.g. nn. 3, 6, 17, 45), and so it produces an image of God as One who is always ready to forgive and who is standing close to the situations in which people find themselves with help and mercy.

Probably the first penitential used in continental Europe was that of Columbanus.[44] More cut-and-dried than Finnian, it lists the sins and their penances in a staccato fashion. However, its theoretical understanding of sin as sickness needing various remedies is even more explicit:

> A variety of offences makes for a variety of penances. And as physicians have to make a variety of medicines [for different ailments], so spiritual doctors (*spiritales medici*) must have different cures for the different wounds, ailments, pains, weaknesses of the soul. But since few know all the correct treatments to cure and bring back the soul to complete health, these are a few [instructions] for that purpose gathered from the tradition of the elders ....[45]

As with Finnian, while its origins are monastic – Cassian's notion of 'contraries are to be healed by contraries' is far more clearly stated ('A' 12) – it was intended for use with ordinary people (specified as *laicus*, etc.). However, unlike Finnian's work it does not give the impression of having a wide base in pastoral practice, almost all the 'lay sins' are either sexual or concern church ritual and discipline. Its view of serious sins seems to be based on an extension of a concern for the sins of monks. One feature, in the 'B' recension of the text that does stand out is the notion of 'capital crimes' (*De capitalibus ... criminibus*) ('B' *ante* 1), but this covers all the material except the 'minor crimes of monks'. It is possible, however, that there were other category divisions which have not survived. In support of this contention is the fact that the first crimes dealt with are murder ('B' 1), then fornication (nn. 2–4), and then perjury, false oaths and magic (nn. 5–6): this may reflect an evolution from the 'Three Great Sins' of public penance.

The final Irish text I shall mention is the *Penitential of Cummian*.[46] It is interesting not for the specific penances it gives for sins or the range of people whose failings it covers (in this it stands close to Finnian), but, primarily, for the depth of pastoral concern; and, second, for its careful explication of the notion of Christian forgiveness. Cassian's influence is paramount. Most of its content is formally arranged using Cassian's eight-fold scheme (the *ogdoas*)[47] of vices.[48] These vices are seen as the sources of sinfulness in all Christians, the difference being the way sin is manifested in different ways of life. Reading the prescriptions about greed (pt. III) or drunkenness (pt. I) one has the impression that this document was forged in real experience rather than looking outwards from the cloister.

If Cassian's works provided most of the architecture of this penitential, his view of sin as an ailment needing therapy introduces it: it is medicine for the health/salvation (*medicinae salutaris*) of souls, it is the fathers' remedies for wounds (Incipit). Moreover, it provided a detailed explanation of the principle of 'contraries healed by contraries' as the basis of Christian hope (n. 14). However, the most original element in the whole work is its list of the twelve ways by which sin is remitted: baptism, charity, alms, tears, confession, affliction of heart and body, amendment of morals, the intercession of the saints, mercy and faith, the conversion of others, offering forgiveness to others, and martyrdom.[49] It is thus within a synoptic presentation of the Christian life as the interaction of the mercy of God and human effort that Cummian situated his actual prescriptions. The practice regulated by the penitentials was but one of the many ways by which Christians were brought to their destination.

The spread of the penitentials

That the penitentials as a way of dealing with sin became popular first in those areas with the closest contacts with Ireland, Anglo-Saxon England and Brittany, is not surprising. Not only did they present a developed moral theology, but they worked in actual pastoral situations. Convenient for use, they could be a means of passing on Christian moral/spiritual instruction, and they were not intimidating in the way the rules of public penance were. From the preacher's point of view they not only prevented penance being ignored by being linked to moral extremes, but put penitence as a daily struggle for perfection at the heart of life. In preaching, the approach to sin of the penitentials dovetailed with the celebration of the liturgical year and gave concrete remedies to link to warnings of the coming judgement.[50]

It appears that once clergy became aware of the practice presumed by the penitentials, they wished to adopt it. However, those who recalled the earlier legislation on public penance – and exhortations to it were still common in seventh-century synods in France and Spain – or else did not welcome Welsh or Irish approaches, raised questions or objections to their introduction. Two of these cases of hesitation about penitentials are especially enlightening. The first concerns Theodore of Canterbury towards the end of the seventh century; the second, Theodulf of Orléans in the first quarter of the ninth century.

Around the time of Theodore's arrival in England the use of the penitentials was causing concern among some of the clergy even though it is clear from Theodore's own writing that the ancient discipline of public penance had not even a vestigial existence in England.[51] A cleric showed him a *libellus scottorum* (little Irish book) on penance and sought to know if Theodore approved of it. Theodore did approve, and declared that it was the work of 'a man of the Church'. What appears to have happened is that Theodore recognized that whether or not this practice was that of the ancient discipline, it was built upon the notion of the 'baptism of tears' with which he was already familiar from his time in the East; and upon the same basis of the 'baptism of tears' he composed his own penitential.[52]

The second case comes from France when a series of councils in the first decade of the ninth century under the guidance of Theodulf attempted to curtail the use of penitentials and legislate a return to public penance.[53] The penitentials were seen as being an innovation that was not sanctioned by tradition and were popular because they minimized the horror of sin. However, these condemnations and their plea for the pure rigour of an idealized antiquity have to be seen against the actual spread of penitentials in France at the time. Not only were new penitentials appearing, but the older Irish and Anglo-Saxon ones were being copied – indeed if it were not for the ninth-century French and German copies our knowledge of these insular texts would be minimal. It is possible to dismiss the action of Theodulf as one more case of his known dislike of things Irish, but it equally could only have found support because of the recurring fear, generated by granting decisive authority to the patristic sources which produced the pastoral impasse, that divine forgiveness must always be difficult to obtain after baptism lest sin lose its seriousness. These hesitations were not answered theologically during the mediaeval period, but practically: the penitentials worked and so were used. To the pastor they provided a private and frequent means by which ordinary people could examine their lives and seek forgiveness. They answered the basic need of people to be able to express their sinfulness and then to put the past behind them: this pastoral effectiveness set the pace, as it would do until the Reformation, in everything to do with penance. Practice was then followed by canon law, and law by theology.

The legacy of the penitentials

As church life became more legally consistent with the steady growth of canon law in the period between the tenth century and the 'classical period of canon law' with Gratian, so it was inevitable that the penitentials would become more legally precise. Public penance had been in the hands of the bishop, but the early penitentials do not specify the nature of the one who administered them (only in the ninth century was the presence of a priest deliberately mentioned). Most of the early evidence points to someone with responsibility in the monastery, undoubtedly often a cleric and presumably often a presbyter [priest]. In the pastoral situation outside the monastery it was even more likely that the penitentials would have been used by the religious leader of the community, namely, the local priest who offered Mass and preached. In becoming part of the work of the local clergy the penitentials became part of the very fabric of pastoral life everywhere in the West, and as such they are the immediate antecedents to 'confession'. Moreover, as pastoral textbooks they continued to evolve until we arrive at the *summae confessorum* in the twelfth century.[54]

More complex penances, combined with the problem of collecting penances according to the number of times a sin was committed, brought its own problems: one could collect more years of penance than one could carry out or even consider. Such a pastoral impasse would render the penitentials as ineffective as public penance, and for much the same reasons. This problem was recognized in Ireland, possibly as early as the eighth century, in that we possess a document known as *The Old-Irish Table of Commutations*.[55] In effect it equiparated longer punishments with those which could be fulfilled by prayer in a shorter time-span. For example, seven years' penance equals, and so can be substituted by, a hundred Masses, the recitation of the whole Psalter, a hundred recitations of the *Beati* (the Canticle of Daniel (Dan. 3.56–88)), the Creed, and the Lord's Prayer, along with a hundred hymns (n. 14). With this development the way to the growth of indulgences in close connection with penitential satisfaction was wide open. And, as was noted above, the awareness that the offence to God was not simply to be identified with a fine – a mark of the subtlety of the theology of those who developed penitentials – left open the distinction of the *reatus culpae* and the *reatus poenae* which would become the theological 'explanation' for the existence of indulgences.

The penitentials focused on the link between the conscience of the Christian and the mercy of God, and as such they highlighted for the West the notion of contrition in the restoration of the harmony destroyed by sin. In so far as contrition became central to the scholastic theology of penance, this development can be seen as the major contribution of the practice to formal theological reflection. But perhaps the most significant effect was in Christian understanding of the notions of sin and penance. In the patristic period sins were instances which produced a state/condition in the life of the baptized person; penance, on the other hand, was an event/act in that life. For those who used the penitentials, sins were individual acts that occurred in specific contexts, but penance, by contrast, became an ongoing condition of the Christian life which was instanced in moments with a confessor.

Notes

1. See the first part, especially ch. 1, of the *Didache*.
2. See B. M. Metzger, *A Textual Commentary on the Greek New Testament*, 2nd edn (London, 1975), pp. 219–23.
3. See T. O'Loughlin, 'The Woman Taken in Adultery: Patristic Considerations', in L. J. Kreitzer (ed.), *Scribblings in the Sand: Interpretations of the Adulterous Woman (John 7:53–8:11)* (forthcoming).
4. This is particularly evident in its first part, 'The Visions'; see G. F. Snyder, *The Shepherd of Hermas* (Camden, 1968).
5. Matt. 6.12 and Luke 11.2.
6. Luke 15.4–7 (and cf. Matt. 18.12–14).
7. Mark 9.13.
8. Since the work of F. W. Hermann Wasserschleben (*Die Bussordnungen der abendländischen Kirche nebst einer rechtsgeschichtlichen Einleitung*, Halle, 1851) the penitentials have been the subject of intense study. However, the following English-language works survey the state of scholarship: still the largest collection of texts, along with a fine historical introduction, is J. T. McNeill and H. M. Gamer, *Medieval Handbooks of Penance* (New York, 1938), but for a more up-to-date edition of the earliest stratum of material from Ireland see L. Bieler (ed.), *The Irish Penitentials* (Dublin, 1975); the 'classic' analysis of them in relation to the history of sacramental theology is B. Poschmann, *Penance and the Anointing of the Sick*, trans. F. Courtney (London, 1963), pp. 122–38, and they have been presented within a more contemporary theological context by K. B. Osborne, *Reconciliation and Justification: The Sacrament and its Theology* (Mahwah, N.J., 1990), pp. 84–94; there also have been two recent monographs, and while each is limited in its perspective, together they note most of the recent discussions: P. J. Payer, *Sex and the Penitentials: The Development of a Sexual Code 550–1150* (Toronto, 1984), and H. Connolly, *The Irish Penitentials and their Significance for the Sacrament of Penance Today* (Dublin, 1995).
9. Matt. 4.17; however, this command was not read as an isolated text but as part of a biblical mosaic of texts which used *paenitentia* in the Vulgate: Jesus is in line with the command of John the Baptist (Matt. 3.2) and the prophets

(e.g. Ezek. 18.30); it fits into the larger scheme of his mission as saviour (e.g. Luke 5.32; 13.3; 15.7); and this theme was continued in the Church: e.g. Peter preaching in Acts 2.38.
10. E.g. 'The Way of Death' in the *Didache*; Gal. 5.19–21; Mark 7.21–2; or Rev. 21.8.
11. Acts says 'from what is offered to idols, from strangled blood, and from fornication'; the first element was interpreted to cover reversion to paganism and idolatry, the second to cover bloodshed, and the third to cover a range of sexual sins.
12. See H. G. J. Beck, *The Pastoral Care of Souls in South-East France During the Sixth Century* (Rome, 1950), pp. 187–222, esp. 216–22.
13. For an account of Cassian's monastic vision see C. Stewart, *Cassian the Monk* (Oxford, 1998), esp. pp. 62–84. For the medical theory underlying Cassian's approach, see J. T. McNeill, 'Medicine for Sin as Prescribed in the Penitentials', *Church History* 1 (1932), 14–26.
14. On Gregory and penance, see C. Straw, *Gregory the Great: Perfection in Imperfection* (Berkeley, 1988), pp. 213–35.
15. T. O'Loughlin and H. Conrad-O'Briain, 'The "Baptism of Tears" in Early Anglo-Saxon Sources', *Anglo-Saxon England* 22 (1993), 65–83.
16. This aspect of Patrick's writing is dealt with in the running notes to my translation of this letter in *St Patrick: The Man and his Works* (London, 1999).
17. *Epistola* 2.
18. *Epistola* 7.
19. For convenience I shall take, unless otherwise noted, the dates found in M. Lapidge and R. Sharpe, *A Bibliography of Celtic-Latin Literature 400–1200* (Dublin, 1985) as the commonly accepted date; the *Penitential of Finnian* is n. 598 in Lapidge and Sharpe.
20. *Confessio* 42 and *Epistola* 12.
21. Cf. T. O'Loughlin, 'The Symbol Gives Life: Eucherius of Lyons Formula for Exegesis', in T. Finan and V. Twomey (eds), *Scriptural Interpretation in the Fathers: Letter and Spirit* (Dublin, 1995), pp. 221–52 at 221–5.
22. It has become a commonplace to note parallels between 'Celtic' and 'Eastern' monks (and on occasion to postulate intricate hypotheses to explain 'the links' between them). However, to point to such parallels is really no more than to identify the extent of Cassian's influence. For a summary of Cassian's legacy to Latin monasticism, cf. Stewart, *Cassian the Monk*, pp 24–5; and for his connection to the monasticism of fifth-century Gaul, see O'Loughlin, 'The Symbol Gives Life'.
23. The essential introduction is F. Kelly, *A Guide to Early Irish Law* (Dublin, 1988); on the relationship between native law and canon law, see L. Breatnach, 'Canon Law and Secular Law in Early Ireland: The Significance of *Bretha Nemed*', *Peritia* 3 (1984), 439–59; for a window into the society reflected in early Irish law tracts, see F. Kelly, *Early Irish Farming* (Dublin, 1997) in conjunction with T. P. Oakley, 'The Penitentials as Sources for Medieval History', *Speculum* 15 (1940), 210–23; for the *status quaestionis* of

early Irish law, cf. L. Breatnach, 'Law', in K. McCone and K. Simms (eds), *Progress in Medieval Irish Studies* (Maynooth, 1996), pp. 107–21.
24. For a bibliography see Lapidge and Sharpe, *Bibliography*, n. 599; the text is found in Bieler, *Penitentials*, pp. 54–8; but a more recent edition and study will be used here: D. N. Dumville, *Councils and Synods of the Gaelic Early and Central Middle Ages* (Cambridge, 1997).
25. 26 (29), p. 14.
26. 24 (27), p. 14; 30 (33), p. 16.
27. Excommunication is mentioned in fourteen of the canons: 1a; 4 (6); 5 (7); 6 (8); 8 (10); 9 (11); 10 (12); 14 (16); 15 (17); 23 (25–6); 24 (27); 25 (28); 28 (31); and 29 (32).
28. 1b (4–5); 2; 3; 4 (6); 5 (7); 6 (8); 8 (10); 9 (11); 21 (23)—25 (28); 27 (30)—32 (35).
29. 6 (8); 11 (13); and 18 (20).
30. A pagan oath is equivalent to making an offering to idols and tantamount to reversion to paganism.
31. All translations, unless otherwise noted, in this paper are by the present author.
32. 13 (15), p. 10.
33. 14 (16), p. 10.
34. For the general background to these texts see W. Davies, *Wales in the Early Middle Ages* (Leicester, 1982).
35. See Lapidge and Sharpe, *Bibliography*, n. 147; the text is in Bieler, *Penitentials*, pp. 60–4.
36. See Lapidge and Sharpe, *ibid.*, n. 145; the text is in Bieler, *ibid.*, pp. 68.
37. See Lapidge and Sharpe, *ibid.*, n. 146; the text is in Bieler, *ibid.*, pp. 66.
38. See Lapidge and Sharpe, *ibid.*, n. 598; the text is in Bieler, *ibid.*, pp. 74–95.
39. Cf. the conclusion of the penitential, it is worth remembering that *remedium* belongs first and foremost to the language of medicine.
40. This statement is a compound of criticism that I have seen or heard over the years; for one of the most trenchant, and widely quoted, negative judgements of the penitentials see C. Plummer's edition of Bede's *Historia ecclesiastica gentis anglorum* (Oxford, 1896), vol. 1, pp. clvii–clviii; and cf. K. Hughes, *Early Christian Ireland: An Introduction to the Sources* (Cambridge, 1972), p. 84. In recent years there has been a growing impatience on the part of several scholars with general accounts of mediaeval theology which dismiss the penitentials as either peripheral or bizarre, cf. D. Billy, 'The Penitentials and "The Making of Moral Theology"', *Louvain Studies* 14 (1989), 143–51; and an increasing interest in noting the intellectual contribution of the penitentials to European culture; cf., for instance, P. J. Payer, 'The Humanism of the Penitentials and the Continuity of the Penitential Tradition', *Mediaeval Studies* 46 (1984), 340–54.
41. n. 1. Finnian claims that his work draws from the scriptures. While there are few direct quotations, right through the text there are echoes and allusions to Scripture as here: for *et sanus sit*, cf. John 5.6–14 and Luke 8.36. A proper study of the use of Scripture in this penitential is overdue.

42. For a convenient summary see Osborne, *Reconciliation and Justification*, pp. 106–8.
43. See Payer, *Sex and the Penitentials*; and cf. T. O'Loughlin, 'Marriage and Sexuality in the *Hibernensis*', *Peritia* 11 (1997), 188–206.
44. See Lapidge and Sharpe, *Bibliography*, n. 640; the text is in Bieler, *Penitentials*, pp. 96–106.
45. [Prologue] B, p. 96.
46. See Lapidge and Sharpe, *Bibliography*, n. 601; the text is in Bieler, *Penitentials*, pp. 108–134.
47. Cf. *Institutiones* 5.1 and *Conlationes* 5.18.
48. They are gluttony, fornication, greed, anger, dejection, sloth, vainglory, pride. This scheme can be found in many places in early mediaeval Latin writing on penance, but rarely is it so consciously employed as a guide in actual practice. On the theme in the penitentials, cf. T. P. Oakley, 'Cultural Affiliations of Early Ireland in the Penitentials', *Speculum* 8 (1933), 489–500; and on its larger context, cf. U. Voll, 'Sins, Capital', in the *New Catholic Encyclopaedia*, vol. 13, pp. 253–4.
49. This list of the means of forgiveness, each supported by scriptural testimonies, does not appear to have any parallels in mediaeval theology.
50. Cf. T. O'Loughlin, 'The Celtic Homily: Creeds and Eschatology', *Milltown Studies* 41 (1998), 99–115.
51. Cf. *Poenitentiale Theodori* 1.13.4, in A. W. Haddan and W. Stubbs (eds), *Councils and Ecclesiastical Documents relating to Great Britain and Ireland*, (Oxford, 1878), vol. 3, p. 187; despite the more recent, but incomplete, work of P. W. Finsterwalder, *Die Canones Theodori Cantuariensis und ihre Uberlieferungsformen* (Weimar, 1929), the edition of Haddan and Stubbs is to be preferred on balance (on the continuing value of that edition, see R. Kottye, 'Paenitentiale Theodori', in *Handwörterbuch zur deutschen Rechtsgeschichte* 3 (1982), pp. 1413–16. For translation, see McNeill and Gamer, *Medieval Handbooks*, pp. 179–215 (and for the damning judgement on Finsterwalder's edition, see pp. 54–5). The most complete introduction to the theology, work and impact of Theodore is the introduction by M. Lapidge to B. Bischoff and M. Lapidge (eds), *Biblical Commentaries from the Canterbury School of Theodore and Hadrian* (Cambridge, 1994); and for a fuller account of the material presented here, see O'Loughlin and Conrad-O'Briain, 'The "Baptism of Tears"'.
52. Finsterwalder, *Die Canones*, pp. 201–3, proposed that the most likely Irish text to be offered to Theodore was that of Cummian – and this proposal is now often treated as fact. While Cummian lists tears, as noted above, as one of the means of the remission of sins, the case is far less clear than Finsterwalder imagined, for all the extant Irish penitentials show a dependence on the theology of the baptism of tears.
53. This material was surveyed by R. Pierce, 'The "Frankish" Penitentials', in D. Baker (ed), *The Materials, Sources and Methods of Ecclesiastical History* (Oxford, 1975), pp. 31–9, who concluded, rather amazingly, that the new synodal calls for public penance indicated that the penitentials were by then

'old-fashioned' and that they were left behind! The article was replied to by A. J. Frantzen, 'The Significance of the Frankish Penitentials', *Journal of Ecclesiastical History* 30 (1979), 409–21, who showed that far from being out of date, the calls of those councils show just how significant was their impact at the pastoral level. The most important recent study of these ninth-century penitentials is F. B. Asbach, *Das Poenitentiale Remeense und der sogen. Excarpsus Cummeani: Überlieferung, Quellen und Entwicklung zweier kontinentaler Bussbücher aus der 1. Hälfte des 8. Jahrhunderts* (Regensburg, 1975).
54. Cf. P. J. Payer, 'The Humanism of the Penitentials and the Continuity of the Penitential Tradition', *Mediaeval Studies* 46 (1984), 340–54; and L. E. Boyle, *The Setting of the* Summa theologiae *of Saint Thomas* (Toronto, 1982).
55. There is an edition and translation by D. A. Binchy, 'The Old-Irish Table of Penitential Commutations', *Ériu* 19 (1962), 47–72; he republished the translation in Bieler, *Penitentials*, pp. 277–83.

Bibliography

F. B. Asbach, *Das Poenitentiale Remense und der sogen. Excarpsus Cummeani: Überlieferung, Quellen und Entwicklung zweier kontinentaler Bussbücher aus der 1. Hälfte des 8. Jahrhunderts* (Regensburg, 1975)

L. Bieler (ed.), *The Irish Penitentials* (Dublin, 1975)

J. T. McNeill and H. M. Gamer, *Medieval Handbooks of Penance* (New York, 1938)

K. B. Osborne, *Reconciliation and Justification: The Sacrament and its Theology* (Mahwah, N.I., 1990)

P. J. Payer, *Sex and the Penitentials: The Development of a Sexual Code 550–1150* (Toronto, 1984)

B. Poschmann, *Penance and the Anointing of the Sick*, trans. F. Courtney (London, 1963)

6

Pastoral care

The Fourth Lateran Council of 1215

Norman Tanner

The Fourth Lateran Council of 1215 opens a unique window onto pastoral care in the Middle Ages.[1] Summoned by Pope Innocent III and meeting in the Lateran basilica in Rome during the month of November 1215, the assembly of several hundred bishops and other prelates from all over Western Christendom enacted in its 71 decrees the most impressive and influential legislation of all mediaeval councils.

Regarding the preparation for the council, the balance between papal input and that of other contributors is difficult to weigh precisely. Most of the decrees appear to have been drafted by Pope Innocent and the Roman Curia before the beginning of the council, so the task of the latter was largely to rubber-stamp the prepared legislation. More detailed information about possible amendments introduced by individuals is hard to come by on account of lack of evidence about the council's proceedings. On the other hand, the decrees were not invented out of nothing. Several of them are traceable to decrees of earlier councils and in the letters sent out in April 1213 to announce the forthcoming council, bishops were invited to suggest topics for the council. In the next two and a half years, moreover, many local councils were held in preparation, at the Pope's express wish, and it seems likely that these local councils had some influence upon the decrees that were drafted for Lateran IV. In short, while the principal impetus for the decrees came from the Pope and the Roman Curia, they certainly reflect a wider constituency within the Church.

The purpose of the council was set forth by Innocent in his letter of summons: 'To eradicate vices and plant virtues, to correct faults and reform morals, to remove heresies and strengthen faith, to settle discords and establish peace, to get rid of oppression and foster liberty, to induce princes and Christian people to succour the Holy Land.' A broad programme of what we can recognize as pastoral care is intended and this is reflected in the decrees of the council.

The first decree is a creed, entitled 'The Catholic faith'. Coming first, it is a forceful reminder that a correct presentation of Christian doctrine was regarded as the most important pastoral care that could be offered to people. Salvation came through a right understanding and acceptance of God's saving work in Jesus Christ, and salvation surpassed everything else in importance. The creed begins in the plural, 'We firmly believe', not the singular 'I believe', reminding us of the communitarian nature of Christian faith and practice in the Middle Ages: the Church and Christian society formed a community of believers, not just a collection of individuals. The teachings about the Trinity that follow speak about God's plan of salvation for us. Notable, too, is the stress on the goodness of creation. The context here is Catharism, the most prominent heresy of the time and teaching a dualism that portrayed the material world, including our bodies, as intrinsically evil. God is 'the creator of all things invisible and visible, spiritual and corporeal' and 'created human beings composed of both spirit and body in common'. The emphasis is worth noting because the mediaeval Church is often regarded as negative towards creation and human achievement: on the contrary, it was often defending our worth against those who denied or minimized it. Sin and evil come afterwards, not before: 'The devil and other demons were created by God naturally good but they became evil by their own doing. Men and women sinned at the prompting of the devil.'

The last section of the creed concerns the role of the Church in pastoral care and it is printed at the end of this chapter in the Appendix. Its opening words, 'There is indeed one universal Church of the faithful outside of which nobody at all is saved,' emphasize the importance attached to belonging to the Church; though who is a member of the Church is not defined precisely. Teaching about the sacraments, as the normal means of salvation, is also prominent. The Eucharist is spoken of as a 'mystery of unity' in which 'we receive from God what he received from us' and the role of the priest is emphasized in that 'nobody can effect this sacrament except a priest'. Baptism 'brings salvation to both children and adults' and penance – described as 'penitence' rather than explicitly as a sacrament – is available to those who fall subsequently into sin. Finally, marriage is given support with the statement that 'married people find favour with God by right faith and good actions and deserve to attain to eternal blessedness'.

This first decree provides a doctrinal and spiritual justification for pastoral care. The second decree will not detain us since it concerns a rather abstruse controversy about the Trinity, connected with the writings of Joachim of Fiore. The third decree 'On heretics', however, although it makes hard reading for us today, is essential for understanding the practicalities of pastoral care in the Middle Ages. Its main sentences are printed in the Appendix. The most important key to understanding the decree is the idea of a Christian society. Membership of the Church was regarded as vital for salvation, as mentioned above, and being part of a Christian society was normally a corollary to membership of the Church: Christian society was an aspect of the Church. Another key is the sense that the Christian message is self-evidently true so that anyone who has seen the light and then rejects it must be gravely at fault. That is why the decree says that 'heretics have different faces but their tails are tied together inasmuch as they are alike in their pride'.

We are speaking about a society, Western Christendom, that was largely Christian. There were also Jews and Muslims living within it, but the former, although influential and widely dispersed, were relatively few in numbers and the latter were largely confined to its borderlands, mainly its eastern edge and southern Spain. Christianity dominated as the official religion. The feel is closer to an Islamic country today, far removed from the pluralist society that we almost take for granted as the norm in the West. All this could and did lead to intolerance, which we may rightly deplore, and the decree is a good example of it. On the other hand the decree was trying to protect what was considered important and precious and we may appreciate this aspect of pastoral care. The protection, moreover, was the responsibility of lay people – the secular authorities mentioned in the decree – as much as the clergy.

The fourth decree, 'On the pride of Greeks towards Latins', is another that grates today. Western crusaders had sacked Constantinople only a decade earlier, in 1204, and yet there is no remorse or apology, only placing the blame for the schism between the two churches on the Greeks. The mediaeval West had a passionate concern for truth and right living, usually in justification of its own teaching and behaviour. The dark side was intolerance and self-righteousness, but the brighter side was creativity. Much of the inventiveness of the mediaeval West in religion, as in other areas of life, arose out of this concern for the truth and right living and without it much of the originality would have been lost. A fundamental function of pastoral care was to make creativity – especially creativity in religious affairs – possible and to protect it.

Another undercurrent is the inferiority complex of the West. From the sixteenth century onwards Christianity developed into a world religion with an accompanying confidence and often arrogance. The Middle Ages precede that development: Christianity, more particularly Western Christendom, then occupied a small corner of the globe and in many ways was a shrinking religion. Islam and the Tartars threatened its very existence, as the Second Council of Lyons, taking place in 1245, just four years after the city of Budapest (in Hungary) had been captured and sacked by the Tartars, bemoaned in its decree 'On the Tartars': 'When – God forbid! – the world is bereaved of the faithful, faith may turn aside from the world to lament its followers destroyed by the barbarity of this people.'[2] Besides the physical threats, four civilizations were felt in various ways to be superior to Christendom: the classical world of ancient Greece and Rome, with which the mediaeval West had in many ways never really caught up in terms of material and intellectual achievement; Byzantium, which considered itself to be the true heir of the ancient world much more than its upstart barbarian neighbours in the West; Islam with its spectacular religious and material successes; and Judaism, a much older religion than Christianity and whose adherents excelled Christians in many walks of life.

The fourth decree of Lateran IV directs attention to the second of these perceived cultural threats, Byzantium. But it provides an opportunity to consider the wider question of the West's defensiveness at this time, which lies just below the surface of various other decrees: hence the above semi-digression. The relevant point is that pastoral care at this time meant care of people and institutions that were perceived to be vulnerable or fragile, the Christian religion and Christian society. Many decrees of the council appear aggressive and uncaring but they should also be seen as the rather clumsy instincts or panic reactions of people who felt threatened, of people who cared for and wished to preserve what was precious to them.

The fifth and sixth decrees, 'The dignity of patriarchs' and 'Provincial councils' are concerned with ecclesiastical organization rather than immediate pastoral care. However, they remind us that the mediaeval

Church was in many respects more democratic and more given to legitimate pluralism, including in its pastoral approach, than at least the Roman Catholic Church is today. Thus the fifth decree renewed 'the ancient privileges of the patriarchal sees' – the pentarchy of Rome, Constantinople, Alexandria, Antioch and Jerusalem – and the sixth decree insisted on the regular holding of synods in each diocese and province.

The seventh and eighth decrees, 'Correction of offences' and 'Inquests', introduce us to the importance of law and correction in pastoral care. 'Prelates of Churches', says the former, 'should prudently and diligently attend to the correction of their subjects' offences, especially of clerics, and to the reform of morals. Otherwise the blood of these persons will be required at their hands.' The latter is a general decree on 'How a prelate ought to inquire into and punish the offences of his subjects'. Canon law was seen as an essential dimension of pastoral care, and many other decrees of the council, as we shall see, were devoted to its implementation.

The ninth decree, 'On different rites within the same faith', reminds us of the legitimate diversity within the Church that has been mentioned already. 'Since in many places peoples of different languages live within the same city or diocese, having one faith but different rites and customs, we order bishops of these cities and dioceses to provide suitable men who will, in the various rites and languages, celebrate the divine services for them, administer the Church's sacraments, and instruct them by word and example.' The decree, on the other hand, in seeking unity and order, says that normally there should be only one bishop for each city or diocese.

The tenth and eleventh decrees, entitled 'Preachers' and 'Schoolmasters', show that proclamation of God's word and communicating an intelligent and intelligible faith to people were central concerns of the Church's pastoral care. 'Among the various things that are conducive to the salvation of the Christian people, the nourishment of God's word is recognized to be specially necessary', begins the former decree and it goes on to instruct bishops 'to appoint suitable men to carry out this duty of sacred preaching, who are powerful in word and deed'. The other decree renewed that of the Third Lateran Council of 1189, which had enacted that 'in each cathedral Church there should be ... a master to instruct without charge the clerics and other poor scholars'[3] and added that each metropolitan church 'shall have a theologian to teach Scripture to priests and others and especially to instruct them in matters pertaining to the care of souls'. The approach may be too clerical for modern tastes – mostly the clergy instructing the laity – but at least the scriptural and intellectual aspects of Christian faith and pastoral care are taken seriously.

The next two decrees, 'General chapters of monks' and 'Prohibition against new religious orders', show the importance attached to religious orders and their proper ordering and at the same time a suspicion of novelty: the tension between charism and institution, innovation and conservation, in the Church and its pastoral care. The second of the two decrees may appear heavy-handed and negative, but the background is the extraordinary vitality of Christians at the time, in this particular context the foundation of the four orders of friars – Franciscans, Dominicans, Carmelites and Augustinians. Pastoral care was not so much directing people from above, rather keeping some check on and channelling properly their enormous religious energy and creativity.

Decrees 14–19 concern the personal lives of the clergy. The titles of the decrees give a good idea of their contents: 'Punishing clerical incontinence', 'Preventing drunkenness among the clergy', 'Dress of clerics', 'Prelates' feasts and their negligence at divine services', and 'Sentences involving the shedding of blood or a duel are forbidden to clerics'. It is not possible here to enter into the details of the kind of priest or cleric envisaged but the general point is clear, that the behaviour and probity of the clergy were regarded as crucial for pastoral care.

Church buildings, especially parish churches, were the topic of the next two decrees, entitled: 'Profane objects may not be introduced into churches', and 'Keeping chrism and the eucharist under lock and key'. For most people, especially in rural areas, the parish church was the most important large building in the neighbourhood and there were many secular purposes for which it might be used: a warehouse, a market-place, a theatre, a village hall, even a fortress in time of war. The two decrees are concerned to maintain the religious functions of churches, to the exclusion of secular ones, and to preserve decorum inside them. They show the central place that was accorded to the parish church in pastoral care, though as with so many other decrees, the first of them, in prescribing against what were seen as abuses, provides also a glimpse into what may have been the rather different attitudes of the laity!

Decree 21 on annual confession and communion was probably the council's most influential decree of a pastoral nature. It is printed in the Appendix. While confession and communion were recommended to people before this time, the obligation 'after they have reached the age of discernment' was created by the decree. There was a loophole regarding communion if 'they think, for a good reason and on the advice of their own priest, that they should abstain from receiving it for a time'; and regarding 'their own priest' in confession, friars were soon given permission to take the place of parish priests, often to the irritation of the latter. Richard Helmslay, a witty English Dominican friar from Newcastle-upon-Tyne, argued from the opening words of the decree, 'All the faithful of both sexes' (*Omnis utriusque sexus*), that it applied only to hermaphrodites but he was roundly condemned![4]

The pastoral intent of the decree is clear and is spelled out well in the instructions given to the priest in confession in the second half of the decree. Nevertheless the decree proved irksome to many people and it was a cause of tension between laity and clergy. The penalties were severe: 'They shall be barred from entering a church during their lifetime and they shall be denied a Christian burial at death.' The decree is a reminder that Lateran IV gives official or clerical approaches to pastoral care and it would be wrong to assume that everyone else agreed with them.

Decree 22 is also both indicative of official attitudes and suggestive of other approaches 'from below'. Entitled 'That the sick should provide for the soul before the body', it tells doctors and other medics ('physicians of the body'), 'when they are called to the sick, to warn and persuade them first to call in physicians of the soul so that after their spiritual health has been seen to they may respond better to medicine for their bodies; for when the cause ceases so does the effect' – acknowledging the reasoning given earlier in the decree that 'sickness of the body may sometimes be the result of sin'. The paramountcy of the spiritual over the bodily is reinforced in the final sentence: 'Moreover, since the soul is much more precious than the body, we forbid any physician, under pain of anathema, to prescribe anything for the bodily health of a sick person that may endanger his soul.' The supposed dangers to the soul are not spelled out but the use by physicians of astrology, charms, magical potents and such like may have been in mind. Many of the best doctors, moreover, were Jews, and there was suspicion of them in some quarters. Another reason was given later by Boniface Ferrer, former prior-general of the Carthusians and brother of St Vincent Ferrer. He thought that doctors were urging greater and irregular indulgence in sex as a cure for bodily ailments.[5]

The next ten decrees, 23 to 32, are all concerned, in one way or another, with the provision of suitable pastors in the Church. Bishoprics and other benefices must not remain vacant for more than three months after the death or resignation of the previous incumbent (23); elections to benefices must be made freely and be properly confirmed, without undue pressure from kings and other secular lords (24–6); ordinands for the priesthood must be properly trained, and only suitable persons should be promoted to offices in the Church (27, 30–1); parish priests, in return, should be given a proper income (32). An incumbent who agrees to resign his benefice cannot change his mind (28). Nobody may hold more than one benefice involving the cure of souls (29), though at the end of the decree comes an amazing exception: 'As for exalted and lettered persons, however, who should be honoured with greater benefices, it is possible for them to be dispensed by the apostolic see when reason demands it.' The reasons for the importance of priests in pastoral care are given clearly in decree 27, 'On the instruction of ordinands', which is printed in the Appendix.

Decrees 33 and 34 forbid bishops and other prelates to demand excessive taxes from their subjects. Then follow many decrees on canon law, mostly concerning technical points of the law. They are not immediately relevant to our concern though they show the value that was given to canon law in pastoral care, as means to the end. On the one hand, there was an obvious danger of the Church becoming too preoccupied with the law, a criticism that was indeed often made at the time. On the other hand, many of the decrees are quite pastoral in their formulation and phrasing, and a number of them are concerned to protect the rights of subjects against those in authority in the Church, of the laity against the clergy.

In the middle of these points of canon law are five decrees on the relationship between the two 'swords' of spiritual and temporal authority (42–6). A correct balance between them was regarded as very important for pastoral care in a Christian society. On the one hand, 'we wish clerics not to lay claim to the rights of the laity ... and not to extend their jurisdiction, under pretext of ecclesiastical freedom, to the prejudice of secular justice'. On the other hand, the clergy were not to allow themselves to become mere puppets of secular lords by taking oaths of fealty to them where this was inappropriate. Lay rulers, moreover, were not to enact laws that were prejudicial to the Church or to impose unjust taxes on it. The underlying principle was Christ's words, 'Render unto Caesar the things of Caesar, and to God the things of God.' The principle is easy to state and yet it is so difficult to know – as mediaeval people were well aware – where in practice the dividing line lies.

The fundamental goodness of marriage had been stated in the first decree, as mentioned earlier. Decrees 50–2 address three particular issues. In the first, the number of degrees of consanguinity and affinity within which marriage was prohibited was reduced from seven to four. The reasons for the reduction are interesting. The decree admits that human laws can be changed 'when urgent necessity or evident advantage demands it, since God changed in the New Testament some of the commandments of the Old Testament'. It admits implicitly, moreover, that the former rules were not being observed: a reminder in general perhaps that laws should not be taken too seriously and that the whole pastoral framework of Lateran IV, indeed that of the whole mediaeval Church, 'came about' rather than was simply enacted from above. The number four, for the prohibited degrees in future, was chosen because 'there are four humours in the body, which is composed of the four elements' (earth, air, fire and water), an intriguing line of thought that is not expanded upon!

The second of the three decree tries to prohibit secret (or 'clandestine') marriages: 'When marriages are to be contracted they shall be publicly announced in the churches by priests, with a suitable time being fixed beforehand within which whoever wishes and is able to may adduce a lawful impediment.' The advantages of knowing clearly who were, and who were not, married were obvious to both Church and state, even though many people preferred cohabitation or a somewhat ambiguous marital status. The third decree gives procedures for disputed cases about the impediments of consanguinity and affinity.

All three decrees are generally supportive of marriage, an institution that was itself perhaps the most important of all forms of pastoral care – though the decrees do not focus on this aspect – and the indispensable framework for many other forms. Indeed, the second decree ends with the warning, 'Anybody who maliciously proposes an impediment to prevent a legitimate marriage will not escape the Church's vengeance.' And the third ends on a tolerant and pastoral note: 'It is better to leave alone some people who have been united contrary to human decrees than to separate, contrary to the Lord's decrees, persons who have been joined together legitimately.'

Decrees 53 to 56 and 61 turn to the delicate issue of tithes, the payment of a tenth of a person's income to the Church. Reaching back to the Old Testament, tithes were a reverse of the normal form of pastoral care: financial care for pastors, rather than pastors caring for other people.

They could be oppressive and unpopular but the main aim of the four decrees is to close various loopholes so that the tithes were duly paid and reached the persons for whom they were primarily intended, namely parish priests, and were not siphoned off by monasteries or secular lords.

Saints' relics, alms-collectors and indulgences are the topics of decree 62. The decree is concerned mainly to purge various abuses. Relics are to be displayed in reliquaries and may not be sold. New relics, moreover, require authorization from the papacy before they can be venerated. Alms-collectors, too, must be authorized by the papacy or by the diocesan bishop. They are to be 'modest and discreet and let them not stay in taverns or other unsuitable places or incur useless or excessive expenses, being careful above all not to wear the garb of false religion'. Regarding indulgences, 'because the keys of the Church are brought into contempt, and satisfaction through penances loses its force through indiscriminate and excessive indulgences, which some prelates of churches do not fear to grant, we decree that for the dedication of a basilica the indulgence shall not exceed one year, and forty days for the anniversary of the dedication'. The whole panoply of mediaeval popular religion is conjured up before us, from Chaucer's pardoner to the preacher of indulgences denounced by Martin Luther, John Tetzel. Lateran IV supported popular devotions but it was well aware of possible abuses.

The abuse of simony is the topic of the next four decrees, 63 to 66. Taking its name from Simon Magus in the Acts of the Apostles, who tried to purchase with money the power of the Holy Spirit, the abuse meant in the Middle Ages primarily the buying and selling of benefices and ministries in the Church. It was very damaging of pastoral care and difficult to eradicate inasmuch as it gave the opportunity to unsuitable men to obtain positions in the Church and then to exploit them for financial gain or for the advancement of their families and friends. The dividing line between the simony of demanding payment and the legitimate acceptance of a gift was fine, and the four decrees try to regulate some border areas.

The four decrees on Jews that follow (67–70) are among the most difficult for us to understand today. The titles alone indicate a hostile tone: 'Usury of Jews', 'Jews must be distinguished from Christians in their dress', 'Jews may not hold public offices', 'Converts to the faith among the Jews may not retain their old rite'. Jewish money-lending is called a 'perfidy' by which Christians are 'savagely oppressed'. Jews are ordered to wear distinctive dress and they are forbidden to enter marriages with

Christians, which are described as a 'damnable mixing'. They were forbidden to hold public offices since 'it is absurd for a blasphemer of Christ to exercise power over Christians', and Jewish converts to Christianity were to be prevented by a 'salutary and necessary coercion' from returning to Judaism. The decrees were certainly regarded as an important aspect of pastoral care, mainly to protect Christians from Jews, and this has to be faced. The desire for protection resulted partly from the sense of unease and inferiority towards Judaism that has been mentioned. There was too the belief in Christian society, also mentioned above. Still, it is reasonable to see the decrees as a sad deviation and to recognize that pastoral care can go badly wrong when it becomes over-zealous.

The council's last decree, 71, on the crusade to the Holy Land, is also difficult for us to accept today. Yet as the final decree it was intended to be the climax of all the other decrees, the culmination of the reforms initiated by them: a reformed Church in a united Christendom would be able to undertake the crusade to recapture Jerusalem and other parts of the Holy Land that had fallen to Islam. 'It is our ardent desire to liberate the Holy Land from infidel hands', the decree begins, and it goes on to describe the enterprise as 'this work of Jesus Christ'. The crusade, therefore, was regarded as the crowning achievement of successful pastoral care.

All 71 decrees have now been surveyed, warts and all. There is much that we may find distasteful and it is reasonable that we should be critical: we need not be neutral in matters of pastoral care. Nevertheless, it would be a pity if the limitations lead us to ignore the strengths and points of interest in the decrees. The legislation expresses official attitudes – those of the Pope, the Roman Curia and the bishops of the council – rather than those of the people: though it would be wrong to contrast their outlooks too sharply. The decrees, moreover, were not intended as a systematic treatise on pastoral care in a modern sense: their order is somewhat haphazard and some topics are not treated at all. Still, taken together, they form a remarkably comprehensive programme. Indeed, the concern for reform and better pastoral care is perhaps the most impressive feature of the council. There is, certainly, a passion for the salvation of souls – that we humans reach our final destiny and fulfilment – and the means to this end are given careful attention: spiritual, intellectual and material.

How influential were the decrees? Was the council the motor of developments in the Church in the thirteenth century – often regarded as the golden age of the Western Church in the Middle Ages – or was it merely an onlooker? No doubt the answer lies somewhere in between.

What is certain is that in almost all the areas of Christian life in which the century saw spectacular achievements, as well as deviations and disasters, the council issued a decree of some relevance: famous saints such as Francis and Clare of Assisi or King Louis IX of France; the four orders of friars – Franciscans, Dominicans, Carmelites and Augustinians – and the beguine movement for women; the universities, pre-eminently Bologna, Paris and Oxford, and theologians of the stature of Thomas Aquinas and Duns Scotus; mystical writers such as Mechtild of Magdeburg and Gertrude of Helfta; parish churches, cathedrals and works of art; the Christianity of countless individuals, largely unknown; as well as the Inquisition, crusades, continuing schism with the Eastern Church, the expulsion of Jews. The council did not produce the results single-handed but at least it was a guide, not just a spectator.

Appendix: Texts of the decrees

The catholic faith (last paragraph of decree 1)

There is indeed one universal Church of the faithful, outside of which nobody at all is saved, in which Jesus Christ is both priest and sacrifice. His body and blood are truly contained in the sacrament of the altar under the forms of bread and wine, the bread and wine having been changed in substance, by God's power, into his body and blood, so that in order to achieve this mystery of unity we receive from God what he received from us. Nobody can effect this sacrament except a priest who has been properly ordained according to the Church's keys, which Jesus Christ himself gave to the apostles and their successors. But the sacrament of baptism is consecrated in water at the invocation of the undivided Trinity – namely Father, Son and Holy Spirit – and brings salvation to both children and adults when it is correctly carried out by anyone in the form laid down by the Church. If someone falls into sin after having received baptism, he or she can always be restored through true penitence. Not only virgins and the continent but also married persons find favour with God by right faith and good actions and deserve to attain to eternal blessedness.

On heretics (extracts from decree 3)

We excommunicate and anathematize every heresy raising itself up against this holy, orthodox and catholic faith which we have expounded above. We condemn all heretics, whatever names they may go under. They have different faces indeed but their tails are tied together inasmuch as they are alike in their pride. Let those condemned be handed over to the secular authorities present, or to their bailiffs, for due punishment. Clerics are first to be degraded from their orders. The goods of the condemned are to be confiscated, if they are lay persons, and if clerics they are to be applied to the churches from which they received their stipends ... Let secular authorities, whatever offices they may be discharging, be advised and urged and if necessary be compelled by ecclesiastical censure, if they wish to be reputed and held to be faithful, to take publicly an oath for the defence of the faith to the effect that they will seek, in so far as they can, to expel from the lands subject to their jurisdiction all heretics designated by the Church in good faith ... Catholics who take the cross and gird themselves up for the expulsion of heretics shall enjoy the same indulgence, and be strengthened by the same holy privilege, as is granted to those who go to the aid of the Holy Land. Moreover, we determine to subject to excommunication believers who receive, defend or support heretics.

Annual confession and communion (extracts from decree 21)

All the faithful of both sexes, after they have reached the age of discernment, should individually confess all their sins in a faithful manner to their own priest at least once a year, and let them take care to perform the penance imposed on them. Let them reverently receive the sacrament of the eucharist at least at Easter unless they think, for a good reason and on the advice of their own priest, that they should abstain from receiving it for a time. Otherwise they shall be barred from entering a church during their lifetime and they shall be denied a Christian burial at death.

The priest shall be discerning and prudent, so that like a skilled doctor he may pour wine and oil over the wounds of the injured one. Let him carefully enquire about the circumstances of both the sinner and the sin, so that he may prudently discern what sort of advice he ought to give and what remedy to apply, using various means to heal the sick person. Let him take the utmost care, however, not to betray the sinner at all by word or sign or in any other way. For if anyone presumes to reveal a sin disclosed to him in confession, we decree that he is not only to be deposed from his priestly office but also to be confined to a strict monastery to do perpetual penance.

Instruction of ordinands (decree 27)

To guide souls is the supreme art. We therefore strictly order bishops carefully to prepare those who are to be promoted to the priesthood and to instruct them, either by themselves or through other suitable persons, in the divine services and the sacraments of the Church, so that they may be able to celebrate them correctly. But if they presume henceforth to ordain the ignorant and unformed, which can indeed easily be detected, we decree that both the ordainers and those ordained are to be subject to severe punishment. For it is preferable, especially in the ordination of priests, to have a few good ministers than many bad ones, for 'if one blind man leads another, both will fall into the pit'.

Notes

1. The decrees of the council (in English translation as well as in the Latin original) and other references in this chapter, unless otherwise stated, are to be found in N. P. Tanner (ed.), *Decrees of the Ecumenical Councils* (1990) (hereafter, Tanner, *Decrees*), vol. 1, pp. 227–71. The phrase 'pastoral care' (*cura pastoralis*) does not appear in the decrees. This poses an obvious problem of definition. Still, there is quite sufficient overlap between the modern understanding of pastoral care and the concerns of the council for the phrase to be used meaningfully.
2. Tanner, *Decrees*, vol. 1, p. 297.
3. Ibid., vol. 1, p. 220.
4. Quoted in W. Pantin, *The English Church in the Fourteenth Century* (Cambridge, 1955), pp. 164-5.
5. *Tractatus pro defensione Benedicti XIII*, ch 26, quoted in E. Martène and U. Durand, *Thesaurus novus anecdotum* (Paris, 1717), vol. 2, p. 1457.

Bibliography

R. Foreville, *Latran I, II, III et Latran IV*, Histoire des Conciles, 6 (Paris, 1965)
J. Sayers, *Innocent III* (London, 1994), pp. 95–101: 'The Fourth Lateran Council'
S. Kuttner and A. García y García, 'A New Eyewitness Account of the Fourth Lateran Council', *Traditio* 20 (1964), pp. 115–78
M. Gibbs and J. Lang, *Bishops and Reform 1215–1272, with Special Reference to the Lateran Council of 1215* (Oxford, 1934)
Norman P. Tanner (ed.), *Decrees of the Ecumenical Councils* (London and Georgetown, 1990), vol. 1, pp. 227–71, contains the Latin original and an English translation of the decrees

7

A ministry of preachers and confessors

The pastoral impact of the friars

Michael Robson

The urgent need for renewal within the Church was articulated by Innocent III in a letter of 17 November 1206, when he called for reliable men whose lives would mirror Jesus Christ's poverty to the poor.[1] While the context of this plea was the campaign against heresy in the south of France, it had a broader application. Saints Dominic (1173/5–1221) and Francis (1181/2–1226), natives of Caleruega in Castile and Assisi in Umbria, responded to this thirst for a revitalization of the Church based on a return to the vigour and simplicity of the apostolic life. Both saints experienced a personal call to proclaim the gospel and this was communicated to their disciples. The increase in the number of friars coincided with the Fourth Lateran Council in 1215, which sought to renew the life of the Church through a programme of evangelization. The Dominicans and the Franciscans found their vocations outside the cloister of the monastic orders. Their pastoral instincts took them into the heart of urban communities and they regarded themselves as orders sent to help those in need of salvation.[2] Unlike the secular clergy who ministered within a particular parish or a specified geographical area, friars worked within a broader perspective. Their pastoral mandate was global, prompting one contemporary to observe that the whole earth was their cell and the ocean their cloister.[3] Members of an international order, they were on occasion sent from one province or country to another for the exercise of a particular ministry. One expression of this universal fraternity was their relationship with Popes who used their talents for the promotion of missions, the crusades and other specialized apostolates. This study focuses on the founders of the two orders; on the friars as preachers with their related roles as confessors and theologians; on their urban ministry; and on their work in the service of Popes and the global mission.

The founders

On the completion of his studies in Palencia in Spain, Dominic entered the Canons Regular, and by January 1201 he had been appointed as sub-prior of the Osma chapter. Between 1203 and 1206 he twice accompanied Diego de Azebes, his former prior and then bishop of Osma, to northern Germany on a matrimonial mission for Alfonso VIII, king of Castile. In the course of his journey he underwent a profound change as a result of meeting Albigensians, who flourished in the south of France. At Toulouse he was drawn into disputation with his host, who subscribed to heretical beliefs, and the discussions continued deep into the night before Dominic finally convinced him to turn his back on error. On the advice of Bishop Diego the three Cistercian abbots, sent by Innocent III to combat heresy, adopted a simpler lifestyle, more consonant with the Gospel. Diego and Dominic thus embraced the apostolic life, becoming itinerant preachers, in their resolve to curb the spread of heresy.[4] This combination of preaching and personal poverty was to become a hallmark of the order which later gathered around Dominic. After an absence of two years Diego was obliged to return to his diocese, leaving Dominic behind in Toulouse, where he vigorously opposed Albigensian propaganda by preaching and disputing.

Dominic continued his ministry in Languedoc, where he gained the support of Fulk, bishop of Toulouse. He received his first recruits and began to realize his dream of forming a group of preachers. In the summer of 1215 Fulk, a stout supporter of Dominic's ministry, bestowed his approval upon the nascent order devoted to preaching and the eradication of heresy.[5] Dominic attended the Lateran Council with Fulk and asked Innocent III to confirm his order. The following summer Dominic and his new companions adopted the Rule of Saint Augustine with their own constitutions. Following the deterioration in the fortunes of Simon de

Montfort, Dominic decided to switch the focus of his ministry from Toulouse to Bologna, whence his disciples spread throughout western Europe. The new community was confirmed on 21 January 1217 by a mandate from Honorius III, who referred to the work already begun, that of preaching the word of God.[6] On 26 April 1218 he urged prelates to make use of the Dominicans, styled as an order of preachers, and to encourage them in their office.[7] C. H. Lawrence believes that the community was called into existence to reinforce the orthodox clergy of the area in their struggle with the Cathars.[8]

While Dominic was already a priest before his visit to Langeudoc, Francis of Assisi was a layman who later joined the clerical ranks. The son of a merchant, he swapped the values of the market-place for a more authentic form of Christian life in 1206. After a lengthy period of searching for guidance and direction, he came to realize that he was called to disseminate the gospel in a literal manner. Immediately he returned to Assisi and exhorted the people to observe the gospel more fully. He became an itinerant preacher, reviving the conduct of the apostles who travelled from town to town, communicating the Good News which they had received from their divine teacher. His first recruits were men of Assisi and, with the encouragement of Guido II, bishop of that city, he took his first steps towards securing the blessing of Innocent III. In the corridors of the papal court Guido proved himself to be Francis's most powerful friend and ally, introducing him to the reform-minded John of Saint Paul, cardinal bishop of Santa Sabina.

Conferring his blessing upon the fledgling fraternity, Innocent authorized the friars to preach repentance,[9] admitting them to the clerical state; the band of twelve friars received the minor order of tonsure from John of Saint Paul.[10] This may have been the occasion when Francis was ordained to the diaconate and Guido may have provided him with a title for his ordination. On his return to his native city, Francis found that the city's pulpits were opened to him and he continued to work closely with Guido; a profound reverence for bishops and priests was one of the hallmarks of the fraternity. From 1217 the fraternity began to expand rapidly and admitted priests and laymen alike. The general chapter of that year established new provinces in France, Germany, the Holy Land, Hungary, Spain and the remaining parts of Italy.[11] The experience of these and subsequent missions stimulated the movement towards the theological studies needed to equip friars for their diverse ministries. Just as Dominic responded to the dearth of theologically articulate preachers,

Francis wished to supplement the preaching of the secular clergy as he wandered from parish to parish preaching fervently and skilfully. His insistence that his friars should assist priests and bishops, rather than offering competition to them, was reiterated in the early hagiography[12] and constitutions of the order.[13]

Dominic was hailed as a man intent on wisdom and Francis as a man filled with seraphic ardour.[14] While the two orders of friars saw themselves as having different emphases,[15] they both developed close relations with the papacy. Innocent III was a pivotal figure in the early history of the two orders, which he saw as potential champions of his own programme of reform. His insight was confirmed by their remarkable expansion, quickly establishing themselves in the cities and larger towns. His dream about the collapse of the Lateran basilica symbolized their role in maintaining and sustaining the life of the Church. In the middle of the 1240s mendicant hagiographers claimed that the dream involved Rome's cathedral being supported on the shoulders of their founder. The *Vita secunda* by Thomas of Celano[16] and the *Legenda* by Constantine of Orvieto[17] were both written between 1246 and 1248 in response to appeals for stories about the two founders in the Franciscan general chapter of 1244 and the Dominican general chapter of 1245. Some manuscripts of the chronicle of Gerald de Frachet identify Cardinal Rainerio Capocci as the source of the Dominican version of the story. The cardinal would probably have been in a position to know anything that was being said about Innocent's dreams in 1215. It is possible that in the 1240s he was telling a story about the Pope's dream; as a supporter of both orders of friars he may have felt that the dream was being fulfilled in either or both of the saints.[18] An early artistic illustration of this is the work of Nicola Pisano and his assistants in San Domenico at Bologna on the occasion of the second translation of the founder on 5 June 1267. J. Sayers reports that the scene of Francis propping up the Lateran basilica was depicted in mosaic in the church of Santa Maria in Aracoeli in Rome and associated with Nicholas IV, the first Franciscan Pope (1288–92). In a long mosaic inscription in the Lateran, Nicholas explicitly connected his restoration of that basilica with Innocent III's dream of Francis sustaining the Church.[19] J. Gardner argues that this propaganda suited both the papacy and the Franciscans,[20] who subsequently immortalized the scene in the upper church of the basilica of San Francesco in Assisi.

The spur behind the mendicant claims to the dream may have been their increasingly strained relations with the secular clergy at parochial and university level. Sustained by Capocci's reminiscence, the friars turned this dream to their advantage in the propaganda war about their pastoral role. This was a powerful weapon for the friars, who had to deal with a mounting chorus of criticism from both prelates and parish priests. The friars' vocation was not to be primarily within the parochial structures; they were not founded as parochial clergy. Neither was their ministry to be circumscribed by parochial boundaries, which they were required to respect. Instead, they were to supplement the work of the parochial clergy and to be missionaries, a term with both local and international connotations, as the experience of the two saints confirms: when Francis heard the priest read that Jesus Christ had sent out the apostles to preach, he realized that a similar mandate was entrusted to him[21] and as Dominic prayed in the basilica of Saint Peter, Rome, he had a vision in which he saw his friars scattered throughout the world in pairs to preach the word of God.[22]

The preaching mission of the friars

The friars claimed that there had been little preaching before their foundation,[23] an assertion which was not contested by some reforming bishops.[24] Friars attributed this lack of preaching to the personal failings and ignorance of the secular clergy. They argued that because the secular clergy were incapable of exercising the office of preaching the duty had passed to them, especially because they, the friars, had made the people accustomed to hearing preachers whose sermons were based on sound theology and the search for evangelical perfection.[25] Preaching, moreover, stood at the heart of their mission. Humbert of Romans maintained that the Dominicans, from their inception, were specially concerned with preaching and saving souls.[26] Bonaventure argued that the Rule of Saint Francis expressly imposed the authority and office of preaching; he adds that he had not found such an explicit directive in any other religious rule.[27] The friars' preaching was inextricably connected with the ministries of hearing confessions and study, the three elements springing from the decrees of the Fourth Lateran Council, particularly canons 10 and 11.

The friars' pastoral influence was seemingly ubiquitous and was symbolized by their sermons in the market-places and other urban locations. When John of Vicenza preached at Verona in 1233, the city's officials made special arrangements to accommodate the large crowds which came to hear the Dominican. They constructed two bridges and a

60-foot tower from which he would preach.[28] Berthold of Regensburg was accustomed to preach in the fields from a wooden tower, constructed like a bell tower. On the top of the tower he had constructed a wind-indicator, so that those present knew where to sit in order to hear the Franciscan.[29] The friars' ministry of preaching was exercised in diverse areas: an unnamed Dominican preached ten sermons to the nuns of Elstow Abbey, near Bedford, between 1275 and 1283;[30] mendicants preached 37 of the 84 university sermons at Paris between 8 September 1230 and 29 August 1231;[31] Jordan of Saxony, master general of the Dominicans, preached at Oxford on 11 November 1229 and challenged the assembled prelates to save the souls of the people throughout England;[32] friars of both orders accompanied Robert Grosseteste, bishop of Lincoln (1235–53), on his visitations to archdeaconries, where they preached to the people and heard their confessions;[33] John de la Rochelle preached before the papal court in the Dominican church at Lyons on 4 December 1244;[34] four years later Stephen, a Franciscan at Genoa, preached at a synod convened by the archbishop of the city;[35] Bonaventure preached in the chapel royal at Paris before Louis IX at least 19 times between 1257 and 1269.[36]

Despite these examples of mendicant preaching on a broader front, friars were drawn to the parish churches where they initially attended the liturgical celebrations. They began a programme of preaching in the parishes, promoting the decrees of the recent council, and their emphasis on eucharistic piety was long remembered.[37] On Easter day 1224 or 1225 Haymo of Faversham preached in the church which the Franciscans attended in Paris, and for three days he heard the confessions of the people.[38] Matthew Paris was a witness to the friars' practice of preaching in parish churches on Sundays and holy days.[39] The friars' ministry in England was sometimes mentioned in the reports of various civic and ecclesiastical officials:[40] during a visitation of the church of Snaith on 7 October 1275 Alexander, the chaplain, testified that the parish had no vicar and that the Franciscans and Dominicans often visited it and preached there;[41] the Cistercians were in conflict with the mendicants at Scarborough in the 1280s and 1290s, provoking the intervention of the archbishop of York. On 14 July 1284 the monks were rebuked for preventing the Franciscans from preaching in the parish church at Scarborough[42] and about 12 February 1290 steps were taken to ensure that the monks did not impede the Dominicans' preaching.[43] The practice of friars preaching in parish churches, even in cities where they had their own friaries, continued into the fourteenth century, as the experience of

Bernard Délicieux reveals. Resident in the Franciscan friary at Carcassonne, he preached in the parishes of Saints Michael and Vincent.[44]

The friars, like their canonized founders, embarked upon preaching tours. While they were accustomed to preach throughout the year, they seem to have been particularly in demand during Advent and Lent, when people were preparing for the celebration of the major festivals. Humbert of Romans notes that Advent and Lent were the busy preaching seasons, when the friars were absent from the friaries.[45] The synodal constitutions of Winchester in 1295 decreed that the Dominicans and Franciscans, when they passed through the parishes in Lent or at other times to hear confessions, should not be hindered since their preaching and words bore much fruit; they should be received with hospitality and respect.[46] These annual visits by friars were mentioned in contemporary literature.[47] Throughout western Europe the friars' ministry was largely focused on the urban centres. Humbert of Romans, however, admonished friars not only to preach in cities and *villae magnae*, but also *in loca minus populosa*.[48] While the friars in Ireland established themselves in all the chief towns of the English colony and penetrated the Gaelic world,[49] they also ministered in the less-populated Gaelic regions, such as Ulster and Connacht.[50]

The mendicant chronicles and *exempla* collections provide an invaluable insight into the ministry and experience of the mendicant preachers. With the approach of Christmas in 1281 the guardian at Dumfries sent out friars to preach. The author of the *Lanercost Chronicle* met two of them travelling to the region of Annandale, to the south of the friary.[51] When Humile of Milan was at the Franciscan friary at Fano, the people dwelling in the mountains invited him to preach. Accompanied by his *socius*, he spent many days preaching and hearing confessions.[52] A Dominican friar, probably at Cambridge and licensed as a general preacher throughout the province, refers to his visits to several cities and towns, including Bath, Bury Saint Edmunds, Leicester, March, Norwich, Oxford, Winchester and York.[53] Tomás O Cuinn, Franciscan bishop of Clonmacnoise from 1252, had earlier served as a preacher in Connacht and recounted his experiences in the diocese of Clonfert. Large crowds followed his confrère, Duncan, and another unnamed preacher. As these friars travelled through Ulster about 1270 their preaching and indulgences attracted crowds and a multitude followed them from day to day and from place to place.[54] The preaching tours of Berthold of Regensburg covered large distances, as he travelled throughout Bavaria, Switzerland and other parts of Germany. In 1262 he undertook a preaching tour through Hungary and Czechoslovakia, and the following year he was commissioned to preach against heresy in France.[55]

From the 1240s the friars had shown signs of greater permanence within the cities, where they began to construct churches. By the end of that century enormous mendicant churches began to adorn the cities of western Europe. Perhaps the best-known examples are Santa Maria Novella and Santa Croce, the Dominican and Franciscan churches at Florence. At the same time there was a similar building drive in the Tuscan cities of Lucca, Pisa, Pistoia, Prato and Siena, where the mendicant churches, frequently dedicated to San Domenico and San Francesco, generally rivalled the cathedrals in size; these churches were built in the same style and dimensions. A special feature was the vast nave in which the pulpit was prominent. The friars celebrated the liturgy with a fervour and dignity which attracted the laity.[56] The practice of the clergy and laity assembling in mendicant churches is demonstrated by the sermon of Eustace of Arras to the clergy and laity on the second Sunday in Advent in the Franciscan church of Arras.[57] During Advent and Lent the friars arranged special services, generally featuring a homily. In some churches the friars preached each evening in Lent.[58]

The friars' pastoral ministry was sustained by their network of schools, which were attached to each community, with more specialized centres at custodial and international level. These schools had a strong pastoral outlook and were established to prepare friars for their ministry as preachers and confessors. In addition to following the normal scholastic exercises the lectors in these schools supported their confrères' ministry in three major ways: the compilation of model sermons, sometimes with advice on addressing particular groups; commentaries and concordances on the Bible; and pastoral manuals. First, Anthony of Padua compiled a series of model sermons for Sundays and the major feasts for the benefit of itinerant preachers.[59] In the course of the thirteenth century several friars compiled similar collections, including Humbert of Romans[60] and Guibert of Tournai.[61] Guy of Evreux's collection of 74 sermons was completed in 1293. His intention was to aid preachers, including those who might be fairly ignorant of theology, by providing them with sermons for all occasions. An alphabetical index of key terms was prepared and advice was dispensed on the best use of the sermons.[62] Second, friars wished to root their teaching on a firm understanding of the sacred text. Hugh of Saint Cher compiled a commentary of the whole Bible, and he and a group of friars at Saint-Jacques in Paris prepared a concordance on the Bible.[63] Third, the way in which the pastoral manuals contained a distillation of both theological and canonical teaching is exemplified by John of Freiburg's *Summa confessorum*, which was completed in 1297/8. John wished to provide his confrères with a summary of the theological riches available to the friars in the *studia generalia*.[64]

Response to urban problems

Dominic's experience in Toulouse had persuaded him that the gospel should preferably be preached by those who had voluntarily espoused a life of evangelical simplicity and poverty. Francis's evangelical poverty was clothed in an eschatological dimension by John Pecham, who maintained that the saint was combating avarice in these latter days.[65] The friars were pledged to support their ministry of preaching with a lifestyle based on a return to the gospel, and their sermons were addressed to different groups of citizens, with the intention of guiding their members towards a fuller and more generous response to the gospel. Their witness to evangelical poverty lived alongside the merchants' struggle for ever greater profits from their trade. The way in which the Dominicans and Franciscans at Florence offered guidance on the conduct of business at the end of the thirteenth century and the beginning of the fourteenth has been examined by D. R. Lesnick. While there were many tensions between the norms of the gospel and those of the market-place, there were two particular scourges faced by the mendicants working in cities: one, discord in communities; the other, usury.

The tensions within the cities of mediaeval Italy are well documented. The friction between the Guelfs and the Ghibellines formed the context for Dante's *Divine Comedy*. The turbulent state of some Italian cities in the early 1220s merited the attention of the papal legates, who were busy re-establishing peace among the northern cities of Lombardy and the March of Treviso.[66] Living in their own religious communities, the friars promoted harmony and mutual tolerance in the growing urban centres and served as mediators. Francis, who had earlier fought in Assisi's civil war, was accustomed to begin his sermons by praying for peace, and he announced peace to all people. One of the first-fruits of his early preaching was that many who had hated peace and salvation also embraced peace.[67] His reputation as a promoter of peace reached England, where Matthew Paris records the tradition that for many years the saint had preached the gospel of peace.[68]

A salient feature of Francis's sermon in the piazza at Bologna on 15 August 1222 was his emphasis upon urban conciliation and his capacity to heal the wounds of suspicion, division and bloodshed. Such results were interpreted as a manifestation of the power which God bestowed upon Francis's words in a fragmented society. He spoke of the duty of putting an end to hatred and of arranging a new peace treaty; his words restored peace in many a seignorial family which had been torn apart by old, cruel and furious hatreds, even to the point of assassinations.[69] The peace movement of 1233, known as the Alleluia, began spontaneously at Parma in the Easter season and spread quickly and enthusiastically throughout Italy. In April 1233 the bishop of Bologna and the city council approved the appointment of John of Vicenza as a mediator of long-standing disputes over jurisdiction. A few days later the whole population of Faenza came to hear him and followed him with banners. John preached penance and peace and railed against the practice of imprisoning debtors. At the same time throughout north central Italy Dominicans and Franciscans held similar authority in cities such as Milan, Parma, Modena, Piacenza and Cremona. In these cities they reformed the statutes, reconciled quarrelling factions, freed debtors from prison and returned exiles. They could count on the will of a people weary of war to support their calls for penance and peace.[70]

Dominic and Francis were determined to carry the gospel to the piazza, applying Jesus' words to the market-place; for some years Francis had worked as a merchant and was well placed to know the temptations associated with that profession. The two orders paid particular attention to the ethics of commerce, and this enterprise was shaped and sustained by the debates held in the mendicant schools during the thirteenth century. L. K. Little draws attention to the range of ethical questions, impinging upon commerce, which were debated by the early masters in the mendicant schools.[71] One of the negative aspects of this drive for wealth and security was the scourge of usury, which was roundly condemned by the mediaeval Church. The Third Council of the Lateran in 1179, canon 25, and the Second Council of Lyons in 1274, canons 26 and 27, forbade the practice and invoked penalties against its practitioners.

Attacks on usury remained a principal theme of Dominican and Franciscan preachers[72] and confessors,[73] and this was symbolized in a miniature in a manuscript about 1250 depicting a friar of each order rejecting offerings from usurers.[74] The first biographer of Anthony of

Padua drew attention to this aspect of his teaching: the saint commanded that whatever was taken by usury or violence was to be restored. This reached the point that many, having mortgaged houses and fields, placed the money at the feet of Anthony, and, with his advice, restored them to those whom they had cheated through extortion and bribery.[75] John of Vincenza, who fulminated against usurers in his sermons,[76] declared that through the preaching of the Dominicans more than 100,000 had been brought back to the Catholic Church in Lombardy. One of the fruits of these conversions was the way in which the penitents had subdued usury and arranged for repayments.[77] When a Franciscan of Padua was preaching on a feast day at Como in 1233, he was disturbed by the excessive noise made by workmen busily engaged in constructing a tower for a local usurer. He predicted that the tower – a symbol of wealth and prestige – would fall within a short time. When this prediction came true, many regarded it as a miracle.[78]

The conversion of usurers and their subsequent religious vocations as friars living in apostolic poverty were carefully chronicled. One of the miracles attributed to Anthony was the conversion of Jacopino of Cartura, a small town in the province of Padua, who had been an unrestrained usurer before entering the Franciscan order.[79] The public display of penitence by Lord Bernard Bafulo of Parma, a usurer before he became a friar, seems to have been instrumental in the conversion of two others usurers, Illuminato and Bernardo, who also sought admission to the fraternity. They restored all their ill-gotten gains and gave clothing to 200 poor people. They also gave 200 pounds imperial to the Franciscans to help pay for the construction of their friary at Parma, which was then being built in a field of the city. Inspired by the divine love and the example of Bafulo, Illuminato had himself scourged through the city with a purse of coins tied around his neck.[80] The order's general chapter at Paris in 1292 urged friars to exercise caution in granting absolution to usurers, who failed to make adequate restitution;[81] more than once the Franciscans were accused of absolving wealthy usurers without requiring them to make restitution to the victims of their malpractice. It was claimed that they were benefiting improperly from usurers' payments.[82]

Guibert of Tournai exhorted men exercising political and judicial power in the cities not to countenance and nourish usurers, an activity which he deemed both dishonest and illicit.[83] Usury was important enough to be included in the series of cases assembled about 1260 by a

Dominican lector, probably at Pontefract.[84] This question was examined in the schools, and one of the more developed expositions was provided by Thomas Aquinas. Addressing the problem in the context of social justice, he declares that making a charge for lending money is usury in itself.[85] Giles of Lessines, who had studied under Albert the Great at Paris and Thomas Aquinas at Paris, wrote a *Tractatus de usuris* about 1280 in reply to severe criticism of the friars and their teachings by Henry of Ghent, a master at Paris. Giles's treatise was the first theological tract devoted entirely to the problems surrounding the handling of money, and he gave a comprehensive survey of what he had learned from his famous masters. Alexander Lombard, a Franciscan, produced a *Tractatus de usuris* early in the fourteenth century.[86] Giordano da Pisa argued for modest aspirations as a corrective to the excesses of the merchant bankers, discussing usury and a just price. The celebrated Dominican reflected that Florence was full of wealth, especially from usury. These were the worst riches and to acquire them men became shameful, malicious, traitorous and corrupted.[87]

Friars in the service of the Popes and the global mission

The inception, approval and development of the two orders of friars would not have occurred without the insight and strong support of Innocent III. From the outset the two orders enjoyed close relations with the Popes, who, in turn, protected them and bestowed a range of permissions and privileges upon them. The policy of encouraging the two orders was continued by Honorius III and Gregory IX. Prior to his election to the chair of St Peter, Gregory had worked closely with both Dominic and Francis, serving as cardinal protector for the Franciscan order from 1220. On 18 January 1221 Honorius III recommended the Dominicans to the bishops in his letter *Quoniam abundavit iniquitas* and expressed his conviction that the friars were a providential response to the lethargy which had gripped the world. God, he explained, had raised up the friars, who were not seeking their own advantage, but that of Jesus Christ as they laboured to halt the spread of heresy. The friars gave themselves to the dissemination of the word of God through their ministry of preaching in voluntary poverty. Gregory issued a letter with the same title and largely the same contents concerning the Franciscans on 6 April 1237 with the additional reference to the friars' ministry as confessors; sections of the letter are repeated almost verbatim,[88] offering an invaluable insight into the way in which Gregory considered the two orders to be conducting similar apostolates.

A succession of Popes, beginning with Gregory IX, brought mendicants into the Curia as chaplains, penitentiaries, confessors and lectors of theology. The Spanish Dominican, Raymond of Peñafort, a papal chaplain and penitentiary,[89] was employed by Gregory to compile the great collection of decretals or papal judgements to supplement the work of Gratian. Hugh of Saint Cher served as master in the Dominican school at Paris and as prior provincial of France before becoming the first mendicant cardinal as bishop of Santa Sabina in 1244.[90] Nicholas Carbio (Calvi) was the confessor of Innocent IV[91] before becoming bishop of Assisi in 1250 and subsequently the biographer of that Pope. Innocent established a Curial university to provide instruction in theology and law at the papal palace, and the school followed the migrations of the Curia. The school was staffed mainly by a succession of friars, who were styled as lectors at the sacred palace. While the friars did not monopolize this office, their dominance is a reflection of their influence in the faculties of theology in the universities. Thomas Aquinas served as lector there in 1267/8, when the papal court was at Viterbo.[92] The friars' close relations with the papal court enabled Popes to exercise their own influence on the development of the mendicant orders, enabling them to draft friars into areas where their special zeal, competence and knowledge were required.

The two orders had a strong missionary impulse which manifested itself in the early experiences of their founders. Dominic was intent on accompanying Bishop Diego on his mission to preach to the Cumans in eastern Hungary.[93] He also shared his contemporaries' high regard for martyrdom and believed that he was unworthy of such a death at the hands of the heretics.[94] He was determined to halt the number of people in Languedoc from leaving the Church to join the Albigensians and regarded his own work as missionary. In 1217 he dispatched four friars to preach in Spain.[95] Francis sent friars to Morocco,[96] where five of them became the protomartyrs of the fraternity on 16 January 1220.[97] One of the areas which both orders regarded as missionary was the Holy Land. Francis wished to go there as a pilgrim and a preacher; he also sought martyrdom. His first two attempts were thwarted.[98] His Rule makes provision for friars whom God had inspired to work among unbelievers[99] and he launched a mission to the Holy Land under the leadership of Elias of Cortona in 1217,[100] the year in which both Dominicans and Franciscans were at Acre and Damietta.[101] By 1228 the Dominicans had established a province in the Holy Land.[102] The customary recruitment was at a more modest level and frequently involved Europeans, such as Conrad of Speyer, who joined the Franciscans in the Holy Land and was then appointed to lead the mission to Germany in 1221.[103] The friars in the Holy Land were reinforced by recruits from several provinces in western Europe and the launching of subsequent crusades brought additional friars there between 1240 and 1270. Another distinctive feature of the province was the papal provision of friars to bishoprics in the Holy Land. J. Riley-Smith notes that some of the friars serving as papal chaplains were appointed as bishops.[104] Among the English Dominicans appointed to dioceses in the crusading states were William, bishop of Antaradus in Syria, in 1247; William of Fresney, archbishop of Edessa, in 1263, and Geoffrey, bishop of Hebron, in 1268.[105] In the course of the thirteenth century the friars ministering in the Holy Land shared in the vicissitudes experienced by the crusaders. As cities and camps fell to the resurgent Arabic forces, several friars went to their deaths and were hailed as martyrs. In 1256 the master general of the Dominicans announced to the order that two friars had been killed by the pagans and two more had been beheaded in the Holy Land by the Saracens.[106] Ricoldo di Monte Croce, a Dominican missionary in Baghdad, wrote to Nicholas, the patriarch of Jerusalem, about the death of their confrères at Acre, which was taken on 18 May 1291; the entire Dominican community was martyred inside their own priory along with 14 Franciscans and the community of Poor Clares.[107]

The leaders of western Europe viewed Mongol incursions into Poland with mounting anxiety. When Innocent IV summoned the Council of Lyons in June 1245, he sought a remedy for this menace and decided to draw upon the mendicants' services, initially as envoys and later as missionaries. But even before the council assembled he had despatched to the Mongol world no fewer than three separate embassies. Each party was authorized to have dealings with non-Latin churches of the East.[108] Innocent sent John of Piano Carpini to the Tartars in 1245, and on his return the Franciscan wrote an account of his travels.[109] Carpini's mission was soon followed by the legation of three Dominicans, Simon of Tournai, Ascelin and three others. Andrew of Longjumeau and two other Dominicans were in the next party.[110] In 1253 William of Rubruck announced that he was embarking upon a ministry among the Tartars in accordance with the Rule of Saint Francis.[111] He met Dominican missionaries at Naxaun in January 1255[112] and at Aini on 2 February

1255.[113] He himself baptized the three sons of a poor German.[114] Perhaps the most audacious missionary enterprise of the Western Church in the thirteenth century was the decision to launch a mission to China. Nicholas IV, appointed John of Montecorvino, his confrère, to make one last attempt to convert the Great Khan. The party set out in July 1289. Before leaving Italy John recruited Nicholas of Pistoia, a Dominican, and Peter of Lucalongo, a merchant. From the Persian Gulf their perilous journey took them through southern India, where John baptized about a hundred people in different places. Nicholas died in India en route and it was not until 1293 that John reached Beijing, where he built a church. He reported that he had baptized some 6,000 people; the malevolence of the Nestorians, he claimed, prevented others from seeking baptism. For many years he worked in China without the assistance of another priest, until the arrival of a friar from the province of Cologne in 1306. In a letter written to the ministers of the Franciscans and Dominicans in February of that year John complained about his isolation. The following year Clement V appointed Montecorvino as the first archbishop of Beijing.[115]

Conclusion

While the twelfth century had seen little preaching in parish churches, the friars embarked upon an intensive programme of preaching throughout Europe. Their pastoral care sprang from an imperative to present the gospel to everyone. Their apostolic ministry breathed new life into the Church in the thirteenth century and they were perceived as a providential response to the urgent need of supplying fitting pastoral care for the expanding urban centres; they brought the gospel from the tranquillity of the cloister to the bustle of the market-place, where they applied the ethics of the New Testament. They spread rapidly throughout western Europe and settled in the major centres of population, where they eventually erected their own churches which attracted crowds to hear the friars' homilies. They provided the papacy with a pool of zealous missionaries, imaginative preachers, skilful confessors and gifted theologians who could be employed in the pursuit of various objectives. One of the specialized tasks delegated to them was the promotion of reconciliation with the Eastern Christians. Between 1232 and the Second Council of Lyons in 1274 there were various legations to promote dialogue with the Eastern Church. The first of these was arranged by Gregory IX, who on 18 May 1233 commissioned four friars, Peter of Sézanne and Hugh, Dominicans, and Haymo of Faversham and Ralph of Rheims, Franciscans, to enter into dialogue with theologians from the Eastern Church.[116] For John Pecham it was a matter of pride that no winter had ever prevented his barefooted confrères from making long journeys among the Tartars, Greeks and Saracens.[117] From 1234 friars were recruited to preach the crusade and to raise funds for it,[118] an activity which brought them much criticism.[119]

Both orders of friars were anxious to ensure that their development was consistent with the vision and heritage of their founders. They generated reforms and continue to play a prominent part in the life of the contemporary Church. The ecumenical appeal of Saint Francis influenced the new forms of religious life within the Anglican Church, culminating in the establishment of the Society of Saint Francis, as Dr Dunstan demonstrates.

Notes

I am indebted to Professor J. A. Watt, who kindly read an advanced draft of this paper and made many helpful observations. Abbreviations: *AFH* = *Archivum Franciscanum Historicum*; *AFP* = *Archivum Fratrum Praedicatorum*; *MOPH* = *Monumenta Ordinis Fratrum Praedicatorum*; RS = Rolls Series.

1. V. Koudelka, *Dominic* (German *Dominikus*), trans. S. Tugwell (London, 1997), pp. 27, 133.
2. Salimbene de Adam, *Cronica*, ed. G. Scalia, Scrittori d'Italia, 232 (Bari, 1966), p. 639.
3. Matthew Paris, *Chronica majora*, ed. H. R. Luard, RS 57v (London, 1880), p. 529.
4. Cf. J. B. Freed, *The Friars and German Society in the Thirteenth Century*, The Mediaeval Academy of America (Cambridge, Mass., 1977), pp. 142–5; A. Dondaine, 'Saint Pierre Martyr', in *AFP* 23 (1953), pp. 66–162; M. d'Alatri, *Eretici e inquisitori*, 1, Bibliotheca Seraphico-Capuccina, 31 (Rome, 1986).
5. Koudelka and R. J. Loenertz (eds), *Monumenta diplomatica S. Dominici*, MOPH 25 (Rome, 1966), no. 63, pp. 56–8.
6. Ibid., no. 79, pp. 78–9.
7. Ibid., no. 91, p. 94.
8. C. H. Lawrence, *The Friars: The Impact of the Early Mendicant Movement on Western Society* (London, 1994), p. 71.
9. Thomas of Celano, 'Vita prima S. Francisci', in *Legendae S. Francisci Assisiensis saeculis XIII et XIV conscriptae*, Analecta Franciscana, 10, (Quaracchi, Florence, 1926–41), nos. 32–4, pp. 1–115, 25–8.
10. T. Desbonnets, 'Legenda trium Sociorum Edition critique', no. 52, in *AFH*, 67 (1974), pp. 38–144, 128.

11. *Chronica Fratris Jordani*, ed. H. Boehmer, Collection d'études et de documents sur l'histoire religieuse et littéraire du moyen âge, 6 (Paris, 1908), no. 3, pp. 3–4.
12. R. Brooke (ed.), *The Writings of Leo, Rufino and Angelo, Companions of St. Francis*, Oxford Medieval Texts (1970, reprinted 1990), no. 15, pp. 112–15.
13. M. Bihl, 'Statuta generalia Ordinis edita in Capitulis generalibus celebratis Narbonnae an. 1260', ch. 1, no. 3, in *AFH* 34 (1941), pp. 13–94, 284–358, 39.
14. Dante Alighieri, *The Divine Comedy: Paradiso*, trans. J. D. Sinclair (Oxford, 1971), ch. 11, vv. 37–9, pp. 164–5.
15. *Doctoris Seraphici S. Bonaventurae Opera Omnia ed. studio et cura PP. Collegii a S. Bonaventura ad plurimos codices mss.emendata, anecdotis aucta, prolegomenis scholiis notis illustrata*, 5 (Quaracchi, Florence, 1891), p. 440.
16. Thomas of Celano, 'Vita secunda S. Francisci', ch.17, in *Legendae S. Francisci Assisiensis saeculis XIII et XIV conscriptae*, pp. 127–260, 141.
17. Constantine of Orvieto,'Legenda Sancti Dominici', no. 25, in *Monumenta Historica Sancti Patris Nostri Dominici*, ed. M. H. Laurent, MOPH 16 (Rome, 1935), pp. 261–352, 301–2.
18. S. Tugwell, 'Notes on the life of St Dominic', in *AFP* 65 (1995), pp. 5–169, 10–11.
19. J. Sayers, *Innocent III: Leader of Europe 1198–1216* (London, 1994), p. 126.
20. J. Gardner, 'Patterns of Papal Patronage circa 1260–circa 1300', in C. Ryan (ed.), *The Religious Roles of the Papacy: Ideals and Realities, 1150–1300*, Pontifical Institute of Mediaeval Studies, Papers in Mediaeval Studies, 8 (Toronto, 1989), pp. 439–56, 442–4, 449.
21. Thomas of Celano, 'Vita prima S. Francisci', nos. 21–2, pp. 18–19.
22. Constantine of Orvieto, 'Legenda Sancti Dominici', no. 25, p. 304.
23. *Doctoris Seraphici S. Bonaventurae Opera Omnia*, 8 (Quaracchi, Florence, 1898), pp. 318–9.
24. S. Gieben, 'Robert Grosseteste on Preaching, with the Edition of the Sermon "Ex rerum initiatarum" on redemption', in *Collectanea Franciscana*, 37 (1967), pp. 100–41, 112.
25. Salimbene, *Cronica*, pp. 596, 614.
26. J. J. Berthier (ed.), *Opera beati Jordanis de Saxonia*, vol. 2 (Fribourg, 1891), pp. 38–9.
27. F. M. Delorme, 'Textes franciscains', in *Archivo italiano per la storia della pietà*, 1, (1951), pp. 179–218, 214.
28. D. A. Brown, 'The Alleluia: A Thirteenth Century Peace Movement', in *AFH*, 81 (1988), pp. 3–16, 13.
29. Salimbene, *Cronica*, pp. 813–9.
30. M. O'Carroll, 'Two Versions of a Sermon by Richard Fishacre OP for the Fourth Sunday of Lent on the theme: "Non enim heres erit filius ancille cum filio libere" ', in *AFP* 54 (1984), pp. 113–41, 113–14.
31. M. M. Davy, *Les sermons universitaires Parisiens de 1230–1231*, (Études de philosophie médiévale, 15 (Paris, 1931), pp. 3–6.
32. A. G. Little and D. L. Douie, 'Three Sermons of Friar Jordan of Saxony,

Successor of St Dominic, Preached in England, A.D. 1229', *English Historical Review* 54 (1939), pp. 1–19.
33. S. Gieben, 'Robert Grosseteste at the Papal Curia, Lyons 1250: Edition of the Documents', in *Collectanea Franciscana*, 41 (1971), pp. 340–93, 375–6.
34. J. Bougerol, 'Sermons de maîtres franciscains du XIIIe siècle', in *AFH* 81 (1988), pp. 17–49, 47–8.
35. Salimbene, *Cronica*, pp. 460–1.
36. L. K. Little, 'Saint Louis's involvement with the friars', *Church History*, 33 (1964), pp. 125–48, 130. Cf. J. Bougerol, 'Saint Bonaventure et le roi saint Louis', in *S. Bonaventura 1274–1974*, vol.2, ed. J. Bougerol *et al.* (Grottaferrata, 1973), pp. 469–93.
37. A. G. Little (ed.), *Fratris Thomae vulgo dicti de Eccleston Tractatus de adventu Fratrum Minorum in Angliam* (Manchester, 1951), pp. 94–7.
38. Ibid., p. 28.
39. Matthew Paris, Historia Anglorum, ed. F. Madden, RS 44ii (London, 1866), pp. 109–10.
40. *Calendar of Inquisitions post mortem. Edward III*, vol. 7 (London, 1909), no. 253, pp. 194–5, which records that a Dominican was preaching at Ashby Mears, near Northampton, in December 1307.
41. *The Register of Walter Giffard, lord archbishop of York, 1266–1279*, ed. W. Brown, Surtees Society, 109 (1904), no. 918, pp. 322–4.
42. *Historical Papers and Letters from the Northern Registers*, ed. J. Raine, RS 61, (London, 1873), p. 79.
43. *The Register of John le Romeyn, lord archbishop of York, 1286–1296*, vol. 1, ed. W. Brown, Surtees Society, 123 (1913), no. 594, p. 211.
44. A. Friedlander, *Processus Bernardi Delitiosi: The trial of Fr. Bernard Délicieux, 3 September–8 December 1319*, Transactions of the American Philosophical Society, 86 (Philadelphia, 1996), pp. 233, 290, 292, 297.
45. Humbert de Romanis, 'Instructiones de officiis', in *Opera II*, pp. 254–61.
46. C. Deeds (ed.), *Registrum Johannis de Pontissaria, episcopi Wyntoniensis, A.D.MCCLXXXII–MCCCIV*, Canterbury and York Society, 19 (1915), p. 222.
47. G. Boccaccio, *The Decameron*, trans. G. H. McWilliam, 2nd. edn (1972; 1995, Penguin Books), pp. 469–70, 842–3, where Friar Cipolla, a Hospitaller of Saint Anthony, made an annual visit to Certaldo on a Sunday in August.
48. Humbert of Romans, *Opera de vita regulari*, vol. 2, ed. J. J. Berthier (Turin, 1956), pp. 428–9.
49. J. A. Watt, *The Church in Medieval Ireland* (Dublin, 1972; 2nd edn, 1998), pp. 62–71.
50. F. J. Cotter, *The Friars Minor in Ireland: From their Arrival to 1400*, Franciscan Institute Publications, History Series, 7 (New York, 1994), p. 77.
51. *Chronicon de Lanercost M.CC.I.–M.CCC.XLVI*, ed. J. Stevenson (Edinburgh, 1839), p. 107.
52. Salimbene, *Cronica*, pp. 594–5.
53. S. L. Forte, 'A Cambridge Dominican Collector of *Exempla* in the Thirteenth Century', in *AFP* 28 (1958), pp. 115–48, 116.

54. A. G. Little (ed.), *Liber exemplorum ad usum praedicantium*, British Society of Franciscan Studies, 1 (Aberdeen, 1908), pp. 85, 98–9.
55. L. K. Little, *Religious Poverty and the Profit Economy in Medieval Europe* (London, 1978), p. 186.
56. Salimbene, *Cronica*, pp. 607–8.
57. J. Bougerol, 'Sermons de maîtres franciscains du XIIIe siècle', pp. 33–4.
58. I. Origo, *The Merchant of Prato* (London, 1957), pp. 188, 345. Margaret and Lapa, the wife and sister of Francesco di Marco Datini, the celebrated merchant of Prato, attended San Francesco, Prato, each evening in Lent 1385. The merchant, who died on 16 August 1410, was buried in the same church.
59. Anthony of Padua, *Sermones Dominicales et Festivi*, vols. 1–3, ed. B. Costa, L. Frasson, J. Luisetto and P. Marangon (Padua, 1979).
60. S. Tugwell, *Early Dominicans: Selected Writings*, The Classics of Western Spirituality (London, 1982), pp. 326–70, assembles and translates a series of model sermons.
61. D. L. d'Avray, 'Sermons to the Upper Bourgeoisie by a Thirteenth Century Franciscan', in *The Church in Town and Countryside*, Studies in Church History, 16 (Oxford, 1979), pp. 187–99.
62. P. Michaud-Quantin, 'Guy d'Évreux, O. P., technicien du sermonnaire médiéval', in *AFP* 20 (1950), pp. 213–33.
63. Salimbene, *Cronica*, p. 253.
64. L. Boyle, 'Notes on the Education of the Fratres Communes in the Dominican Order in the Thirteenth Century', in R. Creytens and P. Künzle (eds.), *Xenia Medii Aevi Historiam Illustrantia, oblata Thomae Kaeppeli O. P.*, Storia e Letteratura raccolta di Studi e Testi, 141 (Rome, 1978), pp. 249–67, 253.
65. John Pecham, 'Expositio super regulam Fratrum Minorum', ch. 4, no. 2, ch.6, no. 7, in *Doctoris Seraphici S. Bonaventurae Opera Omnia*, 8, pp. 391–437, 412, 421.
66. *Vita prima o Assidua*, ed. V. Gamboso, Fonti Agiografiche Antoniane, 1, (Padua, 1981), ch. 27, n. 15, pp. 422–5.
67. Thomas of Celano, 'Vita prima S. Francisci', no. 23, pp. 19–20.
68. Matthew Paris, *Chronica majora*, ed. H. R. Luard, RS 57iii (London, 1876), p. 134.
69. *Historia pontificum Salonitanorum et Spalatensium*, Monumenta Germaniae Historica, 29 (1892), p. 580.
70. D. A. Brown, 'The Alleluia', pp. 10–11.
71. L. K. Little, *Religious Poverty and the Profit Economy in Medieval Europe*, pp. 175–83.
72. A. Vauchez, 'Une campagne de pacification en Lombardie autour de 1233: L'action politique des Ordres Mendiants d'après la réforme des statuts communaux et les accords de paix', *Mélanges d'Archéologie et d'Histoire* 78 (1966), pp. 503–49, 534.
73. R. Davidsohn, *Forschungen zur Geschichte von Florenz*, 4 (Berlin, 1908), pp. 85–6.
74. MS. Paris, Bibliothèque nationale, lat. 11560, f. 138.

75. Assidua, ch. 13, n. 11, pp. 344–5.
76. D. A. Brown, 'The Alleluia', p. 10.
77. 'Acta canonizationis S. Dominici', no. 39, in *Monumenta Historica Sancti Patris Nostri Dominici*, pp. 89–194, 158–9.
78. Salimbene, *Cronica*, pp. 105–6.
79. *Vita del 'Dialogus' e 'Benignitas'*, ch. 23, no. 12, ed. Gamboso, Fonti Agiografiche Antoniane, 3 (Padua, 1986), pp. 586–7.
80. Salimbene, *Cronica*, pp. 891–2.
81. Bihl, 'Statuta generalia', ch.6, n. 4a, pp. 74–5.
82. B. J. Nelson, 'The Usurer and the Merchant Prince: Italian Businessmen and the Ecclesiastical Law of Restitution, 1100–1550', *Journal of Economic History*, 7 (1947), supplement, pp. 104–22, 112.
83. d'Avray, 'Sermons to the Upper Bourgeoisie', p. 196 n. 42.
84. Boyle, 'Notes', p. 263.
85. Thomas Aquinas, *Summa Theologiae*, 2a2ae, q. 78, a. 1–4.
86. L. K. Little, *Religious Poverty and the Profit Economy in Medieval Europe*, pp. 181–2, where there is a summary of Giles's teaching.
87. D. R. Lesnick, *Preaching in Medieval Florence: The Social World of Franciscan and Dominican Spirituality* (Georgia, 1989), pp. 117–20. Giordano's sermon on 14 February 1307 was devoted entirely to usury. He affirms that the sin of a usurer is that of loving himself inordinately and this defect drives him to seek usurious money from his neighbour. The usurer's moral perspective is blurred and he does not realize the gravity of his sin; he argues that he takes usury on account of a contract. He lends 100 lire and seeks 110 in return.
88. *Monumenta diplomatica S. Dominici*, no. 140, p. 143; J. Bougerol, 'Le origini e la finalità dello studio nell'ordine francescano', in *Antonianum*, 53 (1978), pp. 405–22, 406–7.
89. *Chronica et Chronicorum Excerpta historiam Ordinis Praedicatorum illustrantia*, ed. B. M. Reichert, *MOPH* 7 (Rome, 1904), p. 7.
90. Gerald de Frachet, *Vitae Fratrum Ordinis Praedicatorum*, ed. B. M. Reichert, MOPH 1 (Rome, 1897), p. 332.
91. Eccleston, p. 88.
92. Creytans, 'Le "Studium Romanae Curiae" et le Mâitre du Sacré Palais', in *AFP*, 12 (1942), pp. 5–83.
93. Jordan of Saxony, 'Libellus de principiis ordinis Praedicatorum', no. 17, in *Monumenta Historica Sancti Patris Nostri Dominici*, pp. 3–88, 34–5.
94. Ibid., no. 34, pp. 41–2.
95. Ibid., no. 49, p. 48.
96. *Chronica XXIV Generalium Ordinis Minorum*, Analecta Franciscana, 3 (Quaracchi, Florence, 1897), pp. 15–19.
97. Jordan of Giano, nos. 7–8, p. 7.
98. Thomas of Celano, 'Vita prima S. Francisci', nos. 55–6, pp. 42–3.
99. *Opuscula Sancti Patris Francisci Assisiensis*, ed. C. Esser, (Bibliotheca Franciscana Ascetica Medii Aevi 12), Grottaferrata, Rome, 1978, pp. 237, 268–9.

100. Jordan of Giano, no. 9, pp. 7–8.
101. Stephen de'Lusignano, *Chorografia et breve historia de Cipro* (Bolgna, 1573), f. 51r, cited in G. Golubovich, *Biblioteca Bio-Bibliografica della Terra Santa e dell'Oriente Francescano*, vol. 1 (Quaracchi, Florence, 1906), pp. 92–3.
102. W. A. Hinnebusch, *The History of the Dominican Order: Origins and Growth to 1500*, vol. 1 (New York, 1965), p. 173.
103. Jordan of Giano, nos. 9, 14–15, 18, 23, pp. 7–8, 13–15, 19–21, 27–8.
104. J. Riley-Smith, 'Latin Titular Bishops in Palestine and Syria, 1137–1291', *Catholic Historical Record* 64 (1978), pp. 1–15, 6–7, 14, 15.
105. W. A. Hinnebusch, *The Early English Friars Preachers*, Institutum Historicum FF.Praedicatorum Romae ad S. Sabinae, 14 (1951), p. 426.
106. *Chronica et Chronicorum Excerpta historiam Ordinis Praedicatorum illustrantia*, p. 14.
107. Golubovich, *Biblioteca*, pp. 350–3.
108. P. Jackson and D. Morgan, eds., *The mission of Friar William of Rubruck : His Journey to the Court of the Great Khan M'ngke 1253–1255*, (Hakluyt Society, second series 173), London, 1990, p. 28.
109. John of Piano Carpini, 'Ystoria Mongalorum', in *Sinica Franciscana*, vol. 1, ed. A. Van den Wyngaert (Quaracchi, Florence, 1929), pp. 1–130.
110. C. Dawson, *The Mongol Mission: Narratives and Letters of the Franciscan Missionaries in Mongolia and China in the Thirteenth and Fourteenth Centuries* (London, 1955), pp. xviii–xxi.
111. 'Itinerarium Willelmi de Rubruc', ch. 1, no. 6, in *Sinica Franciscana*, 1, pp. 145–332, 168.
112. Ibid., ch. 38, no. 5, p. 324.
113. Ibid., ch. 38, no. 10, p. 326.
114. Ibid., ch. 36, no. 1, pp. 305–6.
115. 'Fr. Iohannes de Monte Corvino', in *Sinica Franciscana*, vol. 1, pp. 333–55. Cf. J. Richard, *La papauté et les missions d'Orient au moyen-âge (XIIIe–XVe siècles)*, Collection de l'École Française de Rome, 33 (Rome, 1977), pp. 145–66.
116. H. Golubovich, 'Disputatio Latinorum et Graecorum seu Relatio Apocrisariorum Gregorii IX de gestis Nicaeae in Bithynia et Nymphaeae in Lydia 1234', in *AFH* 12 (1919), pp. 418–70.
117. *Fratris Johannis Pecham quondam archiepiscopi Cantuariensis Tractatus tres de Paupertate*, ed. C. L. Kingsford, A. G. Little and F. Tocco, with a bibliography, British Society of Franciscan Studies, 2 (Aberdeen, 1910), pp. 112, 129.
118. Cf. C. T. Maier, *Preaching the Crusades: Mendicant Friars and the Cross in the Thirteenth Century*, Cambridge Studies in Medieval Life and Thought (1994).
119. W. R. Thomson, 'The Image of the Mendicants in the Chronicles of Matthew Paris', in *AFH* 70 (1977), pp. 3–34, 17–22.

Bibliography

R. Brooke (ed.) *The Writings of Leo, Rufino and Angelo, Companions of St. Francis*, Oxford Medieval Texts (1970, reprinted 1990)

C. Dawson, *The Mongol Mission: Narratives and Letters of the Franciscan Missionaries in Mongolia and China in the Thirteenth and Fourteenth Centuries* (London, 1955)

P. Jackson and D. Morgan (eds), *The Mission of Friar William of Rubruck: His Journey to the Court of the Great Khan Möngke 1253–1255*, Hakluyt Society, 2nd series, 173 (London, 1990)

V. Koudelka, *Dominic* (German *Dominikus*), trans. S. Tugwell (London, 1997)

C. H. Lawrence, *The Friars: The Impact of the Early Mendicant Movement on Western Society* (London, 1994)

D. R. Lesnick, *Preaching in Medieval Florence: The Social World of Franciscan and Dominican Spirituality* (Georgia, 1989)

L. K. Little, *Religious Poverty and the Profit Economy in Medieval Europe* (London, 1978)

C. T. Maier, *Preaching the Crusades: Mendicant Friars and the Cross in the Thirteenth Century*, Cambridge Studies in Medieval Life and Thought (1994)

S. Tugwell, *Early Dominicans: Selected Writings*, Classics of Western Spirituality (London, 1982).

8

The charitable and medical activities of the Hospitallers and Templars

Malcolm Barber

The Order of the Hospitallers was founded upon hospitality and beyond this exercises military functions and makes many gifts ... the Templars were founded particularly as a knighthood and in all their *bailliages*, three times a week, they make a general gift to all those wishing to receive it and to the poor they give continuously a tenth of all their bread.[1]

In 1306 or early 1307, James of Molay, as yet unaware that he was the last master of the Order of the Temple, arrived in France from Cyprus, bringing with him two *mémoires* on the subject of the crusade, which had been requested by the Pope, Clement V. The theme of one of these was the current question of whether the two great military orders of the Temple and the Hospital should be united, much discussed since at least the Council of Lyons in 1274. Molay himself was strongly opposed to the idea, but nevertheless he dutifully set out the arguments, carefully weighting his material to demonstrate how disadvantageous such a union would be. As he saw it:

When pilgrims of the Lord, whoever they are, great or small, come to the Holy Land, they always find refreshment, comfort, help or succour from either one or other of the orders. And if there had been only one religion, perhaps they would not have found so much comfort or such comprehensive help.

Although the arguments which the master put forward were basically self-interested, since he clearly saw a threat to his own authority in such a union, his view of the respective functions of the orders was in fact a fair reflection of their differing origins. These had grown out of the success of the First Crusade, which had taken Jerusalem in 1099. In the following decade, three Latin states – Jerusalem, Tripoli and Antioch – were added to the lordship carved out by Baldwin of Boulogne at Edessa in 1098. This meant that the Latins held all the places which, according to an anonymous guide of the mid-fourteenth century, should be visited by the conscientious pilgrim: that is, Jerusalem and the immediate vicinity, especially Mount Sion and the Mount of Olives, and Bethany; Bethlehem and Hebron to the south; Nazareth and the Sea of Galilee to the north; and the River Jordan to the east.[2] Immediately after the capture of Jerusalem such pilgrims began to arrive in unprecedented numbers, and they continued to do so over the nearly two centuries of the Western occupation of the Palestinian mainland. However, in the early twelfth century there was almost no infrastructure to cope with them; demand had been stimulated, but appropriate facilities were lacking. In these circumstances the secular and ecclesiastical authorities strove to utilize to the full the few possibilities which did exist, so that within a generation the Hospitallers, who already ran a small hospice before the crusaders' arrival, had transformed this into a major 'palace of the sick', while the Templars had been persuaded that the protection of pilgrims travelling to the holy places was a charitable goal of equal importance.

Interest in pilgrimage in the West had been growing well before the Latin conquest, and a hospice had been established in Jerusalem sometime before 1071 as part of St Mary of the Latins, a Benedictine monastery situated south-west of the Church of the Holy Sepulchre. The monastery had been endowed by Amalfitan merchants, who were then the leading Italian traders in the Muslim East, and appear to have been able to acquire the necessary permission from the Fatimid rulers. By c.1081 two other hospices linked to St Mary had been built, one run by female Benedictines for women pilgrims in honour of St Mary Magdalene, the other exclusively for men.[3] According to William, archbishop of Tyre – who, although he wrote in the 1170s, was a well-informed observer, born in the East – the latter had been set up because 'there was no one to offer a roof to our unfortunate people, ground down and ill to the limits of their endurance'. As a consequence,

> the most holy men who lived in the monastery of the Latins arranged for a hospital to be built within the area assigned to them, mercifully providing food and shelter for the needs of such people. Here they brought both the healthy and the sick in case they were found on the roads at night and killed. In that place, they administered whatever there was from the remains of the fragments derived from both monasteries, the male and the female, for their daily sustenance.[4]

Later evidence suggests that they took in women as well as men, although it is not clear if this was the case at the beginning.

King, patriarch and visiting pilgrims quickly appreciated its value, especially given the otherwise ruined state of Jerusalem in the early twelfth century. King Baldwin's confirmation of their possessions in 1110 summed up his anxieties: 'I wish that they might always exist for the feeding and needs of the poor', while two years later, the patriarch, Arnulf of Chocques, quoted from the Psalms, 'Blessed is he who considers the needy and the poor'. Similarly, pilgrims saw and benefited from their activities and often made donations, especially *in extremis*. In 1126 two witnesses testified that they were present 'when Bernard William, who is said to be from Fraxino, undertaking a pilgrimage to Jerusalem, and detained at Tripoli by an illness from which he died', had granted 'to God and St John and the Hospital at Jerusalem established in the service of the sick', all that he possessed at Oliana (near Lerida) in Catalonia.[5] Led by a south Italian or Provençal called Gerard, who had looked after the hospital before the crusader era, it therefore began to attract donations on a sufficient scale for it to end its dependence upon the monastic way of life of St Mary of the Latins in favour of closer links with the canons of the Holy Sepulchre. Originally it had been dedicated to the Cypriot holy man, St John the Almoner – appropriately, in William of Tyre's view, since he was 'a man particularly excelling in works of piety, whose pious zeal and liberal almsgiving will be recalled for ever in every church of the saints'. However, in 1102–3, the acquisition of its own church nearby, a fifth-century Byzantine building dedicated to St John the Baptist, seems to have led to a change of allegiance. In 1113 Pope Paschal II recognized the Hospital's importance as an entity in its own right when, in *Pie postulatio voluntatis*, he took it directly under papal protection, confirmed its possessions, granted exemption from tithes and allowed the brothers the right to elect their own master. These privileges were so that they could support what the Pope describes as their *xenodochium* 'for the sustenance of pilgrims and the needs of the poor'.[6]

Sometime between *c*.1130 and 1153, during the mastership of Raymond du Puy, a Rule containing nineteen clauses was put together; the strong Augustinian influence suggests that it reflects earlier practices, however, since the canons of the Holy Sepulchre, with which the Hospitallers were associated, had followed the Augustinian Rule since 1114. Here, in clause 16, was expressed the key concept of the order, that of 'our lords the sick', a phrase that was to become common in the rules of the local hospitals which multiplied very rapidly in Latin Christendom during the twelfth and thirteenth centuries:

> when the sick man shall come there, let him be received thus, let him partake of the Holy Sacrament, first having confessed his sins to the priest, and afterwards let him be carried to bed, and there as if he were a Lord, each day before the brethren go to eat, let him be refreshed charitably according to the ability of the House; also on every Sunday let the Epistle and the Gospel be chanted in that House, and let the House be sprinkled with holy water at the procession.[7]

The concept was institutionalized through the recitation of a special prayer each evening after compline (that is, at about eight o'clock) in the great hall of the sick in the Hospital. The earliest surviving version dates from *c*.1197, but it must have been in use well before this. A second version, dating from *c*.1305, was still recited in the hospital at Limassol, built after the fall of Acre in 1291. It consisted of a series of invocations to pray for peace, for the fruit of the earth, for the hierarchy of the Church, for kings, counts and barons on both sides of the sea, for pilgrims who travel by sea and by land, for those who give alms to the order, for those held captive by the Saracens, for the sick themselves and all the sick of the world, for the master and brothers of the Hospital, and for the souls of deceased relatives and all the departed.[8]

According to William of Tyre, until the arrival of the Latins in 1099,

> there were neither revenues nor possessions in this venerable place which in this way charitably stretched out its hand to mankind, but

that each year the Amalfitans, both those at home and those away engaged in trade, made a monetary collection which those who went to Jerusalem offered to the abbot of the time. Consequently the brothers and sisters could provide food and shelter and, from the remainder, bring other kindnesses to the Christians coming to the hospital.

Such an unsophisticated approach could not survive for long in the new circumstances. Even though the confirmation of Hospitaller guest-houses in the bull of 1113 in seven key places along the Mediterrenean pilgrimage routes – Bari, Otranto, Taranto, Messina, Pisa, Asti and St Gilles – cannot be authenticated by other documents, it is clear that, from 1099 onwards, the Hospital began to acquire substantial endowments in the West. It is indeed possible that Pope Urban II had seen the potential value of the Hospital as early as 1095 and that Daimbert of Pisa, papal legate and patriarch of Jerusalem between 1099 and 1101, had begun to put this into practice.[9] By 1121 at the latest, for example, the order was using its extensive establishment at St Gilles as its administrative centre in the West. It has been argued that the Popes quite consciously set out to ensure that the Hospital was well provided for in the West, having recognized the potential of its role in the crusader states. Certainly this was how William of Tyre saw it: in his opinion, both the Hospital and the Temple outgrew their modest beginnings, largely as a result of papal privilege, a development of which he did not approve.

But the archbishop was not being realistic; the Hospital needed its Western possessions to support its charitable activities in the East, at the heart of which stood its great hospital complex, laid out in the area south of the Holy Sepulchre now known as the Muristan, probably in the northwestern part, west of the church of St Mary Major. This appears to have been enlarged in the 1150s, so that about a decade later the German pilgrim, John of Würzburg, saw various buildings in which 'a very great multitude of sick people is collected', both men and women, numbering, he was told by attendants, in the region of 2,000. Their care and feeding was a 'vast expense'. Beyond these, many poor were fed at the door by stewards and dispensers of the order.[10] This is a huge figure, well beyond the capacity of any hospital in the West at this time and, it has been suggested, may have been inflated by short-term crisis; Theoderich, a German monk on a pilgrimage to Jerusalem in 1169, shortly after John of Würzburg's visit, saw a thousand beds in the main hospital.[11] An anonymous cleric, who stayed in the Hospital for a period in the early

1180s, described the *palacium infirmorum*, in which he said there were eleven wards, as well as a separate *palacium* for women. However, he maintained that there were 'many times' when this was not sufficient for the numbers requiring help, and on these occasions the brothers themselves would give over their own dormitory to provide the extra space.[12] The main hall, which Theoderich seems to have been describing, was a large rectangle about 70 metres long by about 36.5 metres wide, divided by three rows of piers supporting arches about 5.5 metres high. This was probably part of the mid-century enlargement, still unfinished when the city fell in 1187. A lane led east to the church of Saint Mary of the Latins, passing numerous smaller buildings which might have been those referred to by John of Würzburg. The Hospitallers themselves seem to have lived to the south-east of this where they also had their stables. Numerous cisterns, many of which long predated the crusaders, were needed to cope with the evidently massive demand for water.[13]

Simultaneously, the Hospitallers had built another great complex inside the north wall of the main port of the kingdom of Jerusalem at Acre which, after the loss of Jerusalem in 1187, became the new headquarters. Extensive archaeological work has uncovered parts of this complex, the buildings of which were largely grouped around a courtyard with what may be a refectory and kitchen to the south, a large dormitory to the east, warehouses to the west, and a set of seven halls to the north. This compound had five towers, one on each corner and one in the centre; after 1187 the south-west tower seems to have been the residence of the master.[14] The dormitory was probably for the brothers, although it may have been used for pilgrims as well, but the location of the main infirmary remains a matter of conjecture. It was thought that this was a separate building near the south-east corner, converted from an Arab caravanserai, but recent excavations have suggested that there was a very large two-storeyed building on the west side of the courtyard. The upper hall could have formed the main hospital accommodation, while the basement may have been used for storage. To the north was a latrine tower connected to a cess-pit and a large drain.

Overseas visitors were awed by the great hospitals at Jerusalem and Acre, as indeed they were meant to be. Theoderich was deeply impressed by the manner in which, he said, it expended its wealth for the relief of the poor and the sustenance of the destitute. Back home in the West, donors therefore could be sure that their gifts were being put to their intended use. Moreover, the order had a spread of lesser hospices in the East, which included a smaller hospital in Jerusalem run by Germans for pilgrims from their own country, but ultimately responsible to the Hospital; in Nablus and Toron elsewhere in the Kingdom of Jerusalem; Mount Pilgrim in the County of Tripoli; Turbessel in the County of Edessa; and in the city of Antioch.[15] One of these was at Abu Ghosh, about eight miles to the north-west of Jerusalem, on one of the roads to Ramla. Contemporaries identified this as the biblical Emmaus, where, as Theoderich says, 'The Lord appeared to the two disciples on the actual day of his resurrection', the story told in chapter 24 of Luke's Gospel. The church built over the spring at Abu Ghosh was therefore an important place of pilgrimage, and the Hospitallers, who held this place from at least the 1160s, provided shelter and care in the converted caravanserai connected to the church beyond the east end.[16]

Both the Templars and the Hospitallers were innovatory institutions and, as such, neither had exact models to follow. Both therefore added to their regulations as circumstances demanded, and a further set of statutes promulgated in 1182 under the mastership of Roger des Moulins (1177–87) gives some idea how the Hospital ran this huge operation. For the hospital at Jerusalem, four doctors should be engaged 'who are qualified to examine urine, and to diagnose different diseases, and are able to administer appropriate medicines'. In addition sergeants were used as nursing staff: 'in every ward (*rue*) and place in the hospital, nine sergeants should be kept at their service, who should wash their feet gently, and change their sheets, and make their beds, and administer to the weak necessary and strengthening food'. The patients were to be provided with beds long enough and wide enough to be convenient for rest; each bed was to have its own coverlet and sheets, each sick person was to have a sheepskin cloak and woollen cap and boots 'for going to and coming from the latrine'. Cradles for babies of female pilgrims born in the hospital were to be provided by the bed, so that there was no danger of the baby being smothered by the mother. The sick must have fresh meat three days per week (pork or mutton), or chicken if they were unable to eat other kinds of meat. Impoverished couples who wished to marry were to be given food and provisions with which to celebrate the marriage.[17]

As well as describing the way that the sick and poor should be cared for, the Rule of 1182 also laid down that abandoned children should be received and nourished. The description given by the anonymous cleric implies that the Hospitallers expected to receive such children quite regularly, either brought in by those who found them or left secretly by mothers who could not cope. Nurses were employed at a salary of 12 talents a year to look after these infants in their own homes. The quality of care was regularly checked:

> in case they are negligent in looking after the little ones, as is usual with that which belongs to others, the nurses are held to bring them frequently to the hospital, so that the sisters of the house can see each one as if giving maternal care and commit those badly looked after to the custody of other nurses. For there are in the hospital sisters who are matrons of advanced years, continent widows, honest, religious women.

This was a description of the hospital at Jerusalem, but it seems to have been general policy. In Edessa, Count Joscelin II's grant to the hospital established at Turbessel in 1134 had stated that 'the poor and sick, widows and orphans' should be cherished and protected from want and poverty and molestation by the infidel. By 1190 Pope Clement III found it necessary to issue permission for the Hospitallers to baptize children 'often left at your gate, or born in the Hospital, who, as happens many times, die without the sacrament of baptism'.[18]

All this was to be supported by the payment of responsions from the order's priories in both East and West. Most were required to send set quantities of cotton or fustian cloth for coverlets, but the prior of Mount Pilgrim 'should send to Jerusalem two quintals of sugar for the syrups, and the medicines and electuaries of the sick'. A statute of 1176 or 1177 ordered that the grain produced on the two *casalia* of Sainte Marie and Caphaer (north of Jerusalem) should be supplied to brother Stephen, the *hospitalarius*, and his successors, to make white bread for the poor and the sick of the hospital. Nor were they to suffer from any failure of the crops, for in these circumstances the treasurer was required to provide the money to buy them elsewhere. Individual donors also contributed. A royal confirmation of 1182 shows that Joscelin III, titular Count of Edessa, continued his family's support with a grant of one quintal of sugar each Easter 'for the use of the sick' at the hospital in Acre.[19]

The attitudes which lay behind these regulations can be discerned in an Anglo-Norman rhymed version of the Rule of Raymond du Puy, translated and glossed by an anonymous chaplain of the order, and probably reflecting practices at the order's English headquarters at Clerkenwell. It dates from the decade or so before 1187. As the author saw it, nobody should be turned away from the Hospital's doors, for to do so would be the equivalent of acting like Dives in the famous story in Luke 16, where Lazarus, the beggar covered in sores, is refused the leftovers from the rich man's feast. 'If they have little and we excess, it is not a good thing; in fact it is a bad thing. For all is theirs; let us give to them all except what we use ourselves.'[20] In the parable, it is Dives who is dragged to hell, while Lazarus is carried to heaven by Abraham. This story was vividly depicted in romanesque sculpture, mostly notably on the north door of the cathedral at Autun in Burgundy and on the south door of the abbey-church of Moissac on the River Tarn. Significantly, both were situated at key points on the pilgrim routes. For the chaplain therefore there can be no holding back. 'If the house is under the patronage of St John, then it must be wide open and welcoming; let those who dwell there make a fair countenace to strangers.' According to the clerical witness of the early 1180s, the Hospitallers at Jerusalem took this open-door policy quite literally. Quoting Acts 10.34, '*God is not a respecter of persons*', they admitted Muslims and Jews as well as Christians, 'wishing no one to perish'. The only exclusion was that of lepers, who were, in fact, already provided for by the Order of St Lazarus, an offshoot of the Temple.

James of Molay, therefore, was quite correct in his perception of the fundamental mission of the Hospital, and of the ways in which this differed from that of the Templars; nevertheless, it does seem that the charitable impulses of the two orders were originally connected. Indeed, the development of the Hospital may have inspired the co-founders of the Temple, the French knights, Hugh of Payns and Godfrey of St Omer, to dedicate themselves to help pilgrims. In 1119 or 1120, King Baldwin II, acutely aware of the military deficiencies of the military establishment of the Latin East, seems to have convinced these men and their companions to take an oath to provide a military escort for pilgrims en route to the holy places, in particular on the road from the port of Jaffa up to Jerusalem. The early Templars therefore seem to have been a lay confraternity not dissimilar from the early Hospitallers, performing complementary charitable services for pilgrims, a role confirmed by the official recognition they received from the papal representative at the Council of Troyes in 1129. In this context, the famous will of Alfonso I of Aragon of 1131, in which the childless king left his lands to be divided between the canons of the Holy Sepulchre, who served and guarded the Sepulchre, the Hospital of the poor in Jerusalem, and the Templars, who defended the Christian name there, makes better sense than historians have usually believed, for the three elements of liturgical, charitable and military functions all stem from the same root, and thus offer the balanced rule of the true Christian kingdom.[21]

Once the resources were available, protection of the pilgrim routes developed quite naturally into a much larger military role for the Templars. In the course of the twelfth century, the order was able to take control of a number of major castles in Jerusalem, Tripoli, and Antioch, encompassing the entire length of the Latin settlements from Baghras in the north to Gaza in the south, while its knights and sergeants were present in all the important military campaigns. By the 1180s therefore the Order of the Temple looked very different from the small group formed by Hugh of Payns; even so, the protection of pilgrims remained central to the order's activities and ethos. Two examples, separated by almost a century, emphasize the continuity of this role. Inspired by the vision of Christ's baptism and the 'Spirit of God descending like a dove', many pilgrims wished to bathe in the Jordan, an ambition which could only be achieved by crossing the rocky desert of Judaea. By the 1170s at the latest the Templars had established fortresses along this route specifically for the care of pilgrims. About halfway between Jerusalem and Jericho stood Adummim, 'the Red Cistern', a spacious rectangular enclosure with a tower and cistern, large enough to accommodate both pilgrims and a garrison, while another 6.5 kilometres to the east, the Templars had built a tower at Bait Jubr at-Taktari which, as it was much smaller than the Red Cistern enclosure, was presumably for the Templars' own knights, ten of whom were permanently assigned to patrol the road. At the end of the route, the Templars had refortified the enclosure at the foot of the Mount Quarantene, at a place known as 'the Gardens of Abraham', where many pilgrims were able to spend the night before descending to the Jordan. Theoderich describes this place as a well-watered refuge, protected on three sides, with the fourth patrolled by the knights of the two orders. At the river itself the Templars had another tower, intended to guard against sudden raids at the place of baptism.[22] On a much grander scale was the fortress of Safad, rebuilt by the Templars in the early 1240s to dominate the Galilean Plain. The anonymous account of this work (dating from the early 1260s) extols the military importance of the castle in the conflict with Damascus, but at the same time shows how an equally important part of its function was to reopen the pilgrim sites of Galilee to the Latins. 'Now the famous places which are in the district of the castle of Safad can be visited.'[23]

On the other hand, King Alfonso's will in 1131 makes no mention of the Hospitallers as fighting knights, yet in the 1160s John of Würzburg saw a military role as integral to the order. 'And apart from all these expenses to do with sick people and the other poor, the same house has many men instructed in every martial art, for the defence of the land of the Christians against Saracen attacks, and keeps men in its castles everywhere.' Although the chronology and extent remain matters of controversy, the Hospitallers probably took on a military role during the 1130s. Their first known castle in the East was that of Beit-Jibrin, near Ascalon, given to them by King Fulk in 1136, while in the early 1140s Count Raymond II of Tripoli ceded them Crac des Chevaliers among other properties on the borders of the county. By the 1160s they were in a position to supply as many as 500 knights for King Amalric's campaigns in Egypt, although they are unlikely all to have been professed brethren.[24] These developments were evidently controversial, for the Egyptian campaign burdened the order with heavy debts, and for a time weakened its ability to carry out its original functions. Pope Alexander III more than once ordered the Hospitallers to keep a sense of proportion: in c.1178, for example, he warned Roger des Moulins to take care 'lest on account of [the practice of] arms, the care of the poor should in some way be diminished'.[25] Most historians have seen Alexander as percipient. The sets of statutes enacted by the Hospital between 1203 and 1310 pay less attention to the needs of the sick than to military affairs. The statutes of 1203-6 are the first to mention 'brother knights'; in 1182 there were only 'clerical and lay brethren', although a brief reference to 'armed brothers' acknowledges their existence.[26] It may be significant that the main addition to the complex at Acre in the first half of the thirteenth century was the vaulted west wing, which has been identified as a chapter hall rather than a refuge for pilgrims.

Although it is probable that the order was influenced in this by the success of the overtly military Templars in attracting support, it is equally likely that the Hospital's own needs provided some of the original impetus, for as its establishments increased in number and scope they obviously needed protecting. Abu Ghosh, for instance, was within the territories controlled by the order's castle at Belmont, which also encompassed another hospital at Aqua Bella for the order's own sick and elderly brethren. In the County of Tripoli, Crac des Chevaliers, granted to the Hospitallers as part of a package of rights in 1144, provided security for the so-called 'baptismal chapel', situated about 40 metres beyond the north-east wall, and apparently intended for the use of the Christian peasant dependants of the order. Fragments of frescoes found here show that the west wall was decorated with the Virgin and Child and St Pantaleon, the Christian physician martyred for the faith in *c*.305. The acquisition (and later development) of Crac des Chevaliers is the most famous manifestation of the militarization of the order, but the message of the chapel is equally clear, for St Pantaleon was famous in the East as the holy man who treated the sick without payment.[27] Indeed, for the Hospitallers, their medical and military roles were evidently interrelated. The anonymous account of the early 1180s describes their field hospitals, tents in which emergency treatment could be given to battle casualties by the order's surgeons before the wounded men were moved either to Jerusalem or to one of their other permanent hospitals. Some casualties were, of course, beyond help, and both orders also collected bodies after battles. The Toulousain cleric, William of Puylaurens, describes how after the death of Peter II, King of Aragon, at the battle of Muret in September 1213, when the king's forces had been defeated by Simon de Montfort's crusaders, the Hospitallers 'asked for and were conceded the body of the king, which they found naked on the field, and took it away'. The Templars provided a similar service for the other side in the Albigensian conflict for, in the following year, after Baldwin, the brother of Count Raymond VI of Toulouse, had been hanged as an alleged traitor to the southern cause, they were allowed to take the body down from the tree and bury it in the cloister of their preceptory of Lavilledieu. As his will of 1218 shows, Raymond VI himself wanted to be buried in Hospitaller ground and when he lay dying four years later, the brothers placed their mantle on him. After his death they took his body back to their house at Toulouse, but they were never able to give him ecclesiastical burial as he was an excommunicate.[28]

The care of captives was a logical extension of this: under the Hospitaller statutes of 1182 the Almoner was obliged to give captives twelve *denarii* on their release, recognition of the difficulties faced by many, often after long years in Muslim prisons. Ransoming seems to have been less common, although in times of emergency such as in the aftermath of the disasters of 1187 the order helped redeem some of the mass of poor captives, while sometimes it was also involved in negotiations for the release of individuals. In the latter case the Hospital could usually rely on grateful relatives to show their appreciation, even though circumstances sometimes frustrated their efforts. In 1227, William of Queivilliers (near Péronne in northern France) travelled to the East in an effort to obtain the release of his father, Peter, held prisoner by the Muslims in the castle of Saône in Syria. Through the Hospitaller prior in France he had arranged for the master, Garin of Montaigu, to act for him, 'but when we were negotiating, it happened that my father paid the debt of the flesh; who, had he lived a little longer, would without doubt have been liberated with the help of the master'. He therefore confirmed the grant he had already agreed to make, because of the 'immense charity' of the Hospital in this matter. Families were equally grateful for the order's services when it was known that their relative was already dead. Early in 1229, Hartmann IV together with Hartmann V, his nephew, Counts of Kyburg (in Swabia), made a grant to the order, 'since the Hospitallers have celebrated worthy obsequies in the funeral of my brother [Werner], and afterwards, when peace had been made between the Christians and the Gentiles, they buried his bones, as befitted their devotion, honourably in the holy city of Jerusalem'.[29] Indeed, since 1143, the Hospitallers had maintained a cemetery for the burial of pilgrims at Akeldama, south of the city, just beyond the Pool of Siloam.[30]

When the Latin states in Palestine and Syria fell to the Mamluks in 1291, the brethren of both orders retreated to Cyprus together with the other Christian survivors. They already had a presence there and they attempted to continue to function within the spirit of their foundation and traditions, the Templars by organizing raids on the Egyptian and Syrian coasts and by an abortive attempt to garrison the island of Ruad off the Tortosa in 1302; the Hospitallers by beginning to build a new pilgrim hospital at Limassol in 1297, which was operative by 1301 at the latest. However, neither found their activities in Cyprus to be a long-term solution to the loss of Palestine and Syria. In 1307 the Templars in France were arrested by officials of King Philip IV and accused of blasphemy and obscenity. Although the resulting trial had more to do with the financial needs of the government on the one hand and the superstitions of King Philip on the other than with any offences committed by the Templars, the damage had been done. A beleaguered Pope Clement V tried to take control of the situation by ordering the general arrest of the brethren, but was able to do nothing to save the order once the French government had extracted a multiplicity of confessions, mostly by force. Although a spirited defence by some Templars prolonged the trial, in 1312 the Pope felt obliged to suppress the order, transferring its lands to the Hospitallers since that seemed to accord best with the wishes of the original donors. As for the Hospitallers, the settlement in Cyprus has been rightly described as an 'interlude'.[31] It is not clear how much progress had been made with a new hospital by 1306 when the Hospitallers began the conquest of Rhodes, held by the Byzantines. Success in taking the city itself was achieved in August, 1309, although the island was not fully under the order's control until 1310. A hospital began to function almost immediately, although initially by making use of existing structures. In 1314 an annual sum of 30,000 besants – drawn from designated estates on the island – was allocated for new buildings and, by the mastership of Roger of Pins (1355–65), the order had a fully functioning, purpose-built hospital. This continued in use until 1483, even though a completely new hospital was started in 1440.[32]

Building new hospitals was for both prestige and practical purposes. It was intended that, as in the past, travellers and patients should spread news of this work in the West, so that donations towards the war with the Ottomans would continue to flow. At the same time this may also have been a response to growing demand, perhaps because of the promotion of Rhodes as a pilgrimage centre in its own right. The second new hospital was projected by the grand master, Antoni Fluvi, in 1437 and completed by 1489. The decision to build was reinforced by the issue of a new set of statutes in 1440, which returned to the medical traditions of 1182. The hospital was built around a courtyard in a style ultimately derived from the infirmaries of Benedictine monasteries, but more immediately in the order's own manner as seen at Jerusalem and Acre in the twelfth century. The central feature was the great hall on the first floor on the eastern side, which was 51 metres long by 12.25 metres in width, divided down the middle by a range of octagonal pillars, their capitals decorated alternately with the cross of the order and the arms of Pierre Aubusson, the reigning grand master at the time of its completion. This formed a huge hospital ward, complete with curtained beds and privies built into the wall. The chapel was the very centre of the ward, above the main entrance, and there was a refectory adjacent to the southern end. Along the northern wall of the courtyard were private rooms, presumably for high-status visitors or even for the order's own officers. Around the courtyard at ground level were the service rooms and next to these an auxiliary courtyard leading to gardens used for growing medicinal herbs and vegetables.[33]

Niccolò da Martoni, a notary from the small town of Carinola, just to the north of Naples, was among those who admired the new building and the services it offered. Niccolò visited Rhodes in July 1394 and January 1395, on his way to and from his pilgrimage to Jerusalem. The hospital, he says, 'had a great number of beds for pilgrims and the sick, in which there are great alms, with doctors always prepared and other things necessary for the sick'. Fourteen paupers were fed and served at table in the hall of the knights three days each week, while on the other three days outdoor relief was provided for those who came to the hospital, some of whom, he thought, borrowed other people's children to carry in their arms in the hope of obtaining more bread.[34] A century later, a Czech pilgrim, John of Lobkowicz, was equally impressed by the new hospital. He saw a high-quality building clad in dressed stone and decorated internally with fine painting. All Christians who were ill, whatever their social status, were provided with a comfortable bed, access to a balcony and privies, and fed on a diet specially prescribed by the doctors. The resident doctors had the support of a pharmacy, also endowed by the Hospitallers. 'And none need pay anything for his stay there, except he freely of his goodwill gives anything to the servant that has waited upon him.' The knights made sure that he retained this favourable image of them: on the return journey he and his companion were given the exceptional privilege of two rooms in the infirmary itself, followed by an audience with Pierre Aubusson and his councillors.[35]

The continuity of Hospitaller tradition is evident, for the statutes of 1440 echo those of the mid-twelfth century, laying down that, on entry, the sick should confess their sins, take communion, and make their wills in the presence of the prior and the notary. The prior and the chaplain were responsible for hearing Mass in the chapel each morning, for administering the sacraments to the sick, and for burying the dead and celebrating the offices for them. Based on figures derived from evidence in 1314 and 1478 it has been calculated that the Rhodes hospital on its own absorbed about 7.5 per cent of the convent's budget at Rhodes.[36] The Rhodes infirmary though, appears to have been mainly for the sick and convalescent; by the 1390s the admiral Domenico d'Allemagna had endowed the hospice of Sainte Catherine just behind the sea-wall, where high-status pilgrims travelling to and from Jerusalem were accommodated. There does not, however, seem to have been a specific house for poorer pilgrims, who often found difficulty in obtaining lodgings, a circumstance which suggests that the propaganda value of institutions designed to impress the wealthy and influential remained a priority for the order.[37]

Despite the increased military emphasis from the second half of the twelfth century, therefore, the Hospital always tried to maintain a great hospital at its headquarters, whether at Jerusalem, Acre, Limassol, Rhodes or, after 1530, Malta. Even though it is apparent that in Rhodes at least, the medical staff and the military brethren had become quite distinct and separate elements, this central hospital remained the most striking symbol of the order's commitment as well as a practical means of helping the sick and poor. However, the hospital and the military and naval operations were massively expensive and could only be maintained through the system of responsions, sent by the commanderies in the West. Although the papacy and the early Hospitallers may have intended to establish hospitals at important points along the pilgrim routes to Compostella and Rome, and at the ports of embarkation for the East, it soon became evident that the primary function of the Western houses had to be that of supply rather than care, or at least that care had to be provided with an eye to income as well. When Henry II, count of Champagne, was about to set sail from Marseille on crusade in the spring of 1190, he was approached by Ogier, prior of nearby St Gilles, with a request for a donation. The prior knew the susceptible state of mind of those in Henry's position, and the consequence was a grant of a chapel and cemetery at Bar-sur-Aube, the village of Courcelles, and a vineyard at Roivos.[38]

The Hospital's commandery at Toulouse offers a good example of the way the order in the West functioned. The city had to cope with the needs of a population which had risen to about 25–30,000 by the mid-thirteenth century, as well as large numbers of pilgrims on the way to and from Compostella. The order had been granted a former hospital at Saint Rémézy in *c.*1114–16 and it became one of the larger providers with perhaps sixty or more beds. The acquisition of the Templar house after the suppression added considerably to this capacity: in 1446 the former Temple had 'almost one hundred beds, as well as many other utensils necessary for the hospital'. Nevertheless, it was only one of the fifteen known hospitals in the city in 1246, apart from the more specialist houses such as those for lepers, and therefore did not play the key role that it did in Jerusalem, Acre or Rhodes. Its presence was important, though, because it served a focus for what might be called 'social services', many of which were profitable to the order. A range of grants reflect this role, which was of great social value, but by definition was of little relevance to the poor. Most commonly, grantors sought a kind of insurance, which would ensure that they would be kept in their old age, or if that proved not to be necessary, that they would be taken into the house on the verge of death and buried in the order's ground. Others made provision for widows or offspring to be cared for should they themselves die prematurely. Even so, some displayed a distinct reluctance to enter the religious life, even stipulating that 'if they died as seculars they should be buried in the cemetery of the Hospital'.[39] It may well be that the house at Toulouse provided for the needy both inside and at the gates in the way envisaged by the author of the Anglo-Norman translation of the Rule, but it is equally clear that the socio-economic role of the Hospitallers' Western houses was much more complex than that.

The enterprise shown by the Prior of St Gilles and the multi-faceted relationships with the local community seen at Toulouse enabled the Hospital to build up a formidable structure of commanderies in the West in the twelfth and thirteenth centuries. Often these appear little different from more conventional monastic orders. In 1231, Walter, Count of Brienne, granted the Hospital 500 arpents of woodland in his forest at Bateis in order to construct a chapel and associated buildings, 'where they will cause to be celebrated the divine offices for myself and my ancestors'. At times the Hospitallers seem to have been too obliging in acceding to requests from seculars, being several times reproved by the papacy for interring alleged heretics and excommunicates in their cemeteries.[40] There were, too, a limited number of houses for women, not for nursing staff as might be thought, but for female contemplatives who had joined the order.[41] They do not seem to have undertaken an active role in the charitable work of the Hospital. Nevertheless, the Toulouse hospital shows that some Western commanderies continued to provide for the sick while, because of the nature of the order, it tended to acquire other houses established for charitable purposes, either because this had been the donor's wish, or because the house would have failed otherwise. The geographical spread of these hospitals was impressive. In *c*.1159, for instance, Wladislaus II, king of Bohemia, endowed the order with a church and hospital near the bridge at Prague. The charters of the order show that hospitals were taken over in places as far apart as Poggibonsi in Tuscany (1191), Würzburg in Franconia (1215), Boxerols in Aragon (1227), and Gramat in the Lot region (1259).[42] Moreover, most of the leper houses under the Hospital's wing were acquired in this way rather than being Hospitaller in origin. The evidence suggests that in the later Middle Ages the order was less active in adding to its network, partly because of the financial crises it had to face in the second half of the fourteenth century. Nevertheless, new hospices were built, often on the initiative of wealthy individual Hospitallers or groups of brethren: at Aix-en-Provence in 1325, at Santa Caterina at Venice, based on the former Templar house there, from 1358, at Toulouse in 1408 and at Puente la Reina in Navarre in c.1445.[43]

Like the Hospitallers, the economic strength of the Temple was founded upon its houses in the West. According to the Rule, the order's Western provinces were divided into seven provinces as early as the 1160s, encompassing France, England, Poitou, Aragon, Portugal, Apulia and Hungary (which probably meant Dalmatia).[44] By the thirteenth century Provence and northern and central Italy had become key elements in the system. Inevitably, the primary purpose of these Western preceptories was to supply the almost limitless demands of warfare against the Muslims, but they too contributed to an infrastructure which enabled pilgrims and crusaders to overcome the formidable problems of travel to the East. While medical care remained largely in the hands of the Hospitallers or other specialist institutions, the Templars were able to offer finance, shipping and shelter for pilgrims. Although the many other needs of the order as well as the uneven pattern of donations made it impossible to create a structure entirely geared towards pilgrims (even had the Templars so desired), the order nevertheless succeeded in planting preceptories along the important pilgrimage routes. In the thirteenth century they took particular interest in developing their Italian possessions, for the Adriatic ports were becoming increasingly important for contact with the Holy Land. Therefore, despite the accusations that they had failed in their mission which followed the loss of Palestine and Syria in 1291, the Templars continued to expand this provision for pilgrims. One such example comes from the north-east of the peninsula. In April 1305, Boniface, bishop of Parenzo, taking account as he said of the fact that the order had no houses in Istria, granted the Templars the possession of the monastery of San Michele in Lemmo, which had been neglected, so that they could build a complex there for pilgrims setting out for and returning from the Holy Land.[45]

Although this was the most obvious charitable role of the Templars, they also understood their obligations to the poor as a whole. The Latin Rule of 1129 sets this down: 'Although without doubt the reward of poverty, namely the Kingdom of Heaven, is due to the poor, we order you, to whom the Christian faith speaks clearly about them, to give a tenth of all your daily bread in alms.' At the same time food provided for the brothers themselves was deemed sufficient for a surplus to be left for distribution to the poor.[46] Templar witnesses in the early fourteenth century testify that this almsgiving was maintained throughout the order's existence: Western preceptories handed out food three times a week on a regular basis, while in times of crisis, such as famine, much larger quantities were distributed. In 1307, Ramon Sa Guardia, Preceptor of Mas Deu in Roussillon, reminded King James II of Aragon that at various times the Templars of Gardeny, Huesca, Monzon, Miravet and Mas Deu had fed thousands of the needy.[47]

The Hospitallers and the Templars are best known for their key military role in the defence of Latin Christendom in the eastern Mediterranean, a role maintained by the Hospitallers in Malta down to 1798. Yet both were, as Pope Innocent II said of the Templars, 'kindled by the flame of charity', and many thousands of crusaders and pilgrims and their relatives had cause to be grateful for their hospitality, protection, medical care, negotiating skills, and spiritual comfort.

Notes

1. *Le Dossier de l'Affaire des Templiers*, ed. and trans. G. Lizerand, Les Classiques de l'Histoire de France au Moyen Age (Paris, 1964), 2–15.
2. *Guide-Book to Palestine*, trans. J. H. Bernard, Palestine Pilgrims' Text Society, 6 (London, 1894).
3. See A. Luttrell, 'The Earliest Hospitallers', in B. Z. Kedar, J. Riley-Smith and R. Hiestand (eds), *Montjoie: Studies in Crusade History in Honour of Hans Eberhard Mayer* (Aldershot, 1997), 37–54; and R. Hiestand, 'Die Anfäng der Johanniter', in J. Fleckenstein and M. Hellman (eds), *Die geistlichen Ritterorden Europas*, Vorträge und Forschungen, 26 (Sigmaringen, 1980), 31–80.
4. Guillaume de Tyr, *Chronique*, ed. R. B. C. Huygens, Corpus Christianorum, Continuatio Mediaevalis, 63/63A, 2 vols. (Turnhout, 1986), 816–17.
5. *Cartulaire général de l'Ordre des Hospitaliers de S. Jean de Jerusalem, 1100–1310*, ed. J. Delaville Le Roulx (Paris, 1894–1906), vol. 1, nos. 20, 25, 75, pp. 22, 26, 72.
6. Ibid., no. 30, pp. 29–30.
7. Ibid., no. 70, pp. 62–8. Translations from *The Rule, Statutes and Customs of the Hospitallers, 1099–1310*, trans. E. J. King (London, 1934).
8. L. Le Grand, 'La Prière des Malades dans les Hôpitaux de l'Ordre de Saint-Jean de Jérusalem', *Bibliothèque de l'Ecole des Chartes* 57 (1896), 325–38.
9. See M. Matzke, 'De origine Hospitalariorum Hierosolymitanorum – Vom klösterlichen Pilgerhospital zur internationalen Organisation', *Journal of Medieval History* 22 (1996), 1–23.
10. *Peregrinationes tres. Saewulf, John of Würzburg, Theodericus*, ed. R. B. C.

Huygens, Corpus Christianorum, Continuatio Mediaevalis, 139 (Turnhout, 1994), 131.
11. Ibid., 157–8.
12. B. Z. Kedar, 'A Twelfth-Century Description of the Jerusalem Hospital', in H. J. Nicholson (ed), *The Military Orders*, vol. 2; *Welfare and Warfare* (Aldershot, 1998), 3–26 (text 13–26).
13. C. Schick, 'The Muristan, or the Site of the Hospital of St. John of Jerusalem', *Palestine Exploration Fund. Quarterly Statement* (1902) 42–56.
14. See Z. Goldman, *Akko at the Time of the Crusades. The Convent of the Order of St. John* (Akko, 1987).
15. *Cartulaire général*, vol. 1, nos. 5, 79, 104, 244, 258, pp. 9, 74–5, 89–90, 183–4, 195–6.
16. *Peregrinationes tres*, 184; D. Pringle, *The Churches of the Crusader Kingdom of Jerusalem: A Corpus*, vol.1: *A-K* (excluding Acre and Jerusalem) (Cambridge, 1993), 7–17.
17. *Cartulaire général*, vol. 1, no. 627, pp. 425–9. See, too, a further set of statutes, recently discovered, which probably date from after 1206, A. Luttrell, 'The Hospitallers' Medical Tradition: 1291–1530', in M. Barber (ed.), *The Military Orders: Fighting for the Faith and Caring for the Sick* (Aldershot, 1994), 67.
18. *Cartulaire général*, vol. 1, nos. 104, 898, pp. 90, 570.
19. Ibid., vol. 1, nos. 494, 625, pp. 339–40, 424.
20. K. V. Sinclair, 'New Light on Early Hospitaller Practices', *Revue Bénédictine* 96 (1986), 118–24.
21. *Cartulaire général*, vol. 1, no. 95, pp. 85–6. See J. Richard, 'Hospitals and Hospital Congregations in the Latin Kingdom during the First Period of the Frankish Conquest', in B. Z Kedar, H. E. Mayer, and R. C. Smail (eds), *Outremer: Studies in the History of the Crusading Kingdom of Jerusalem Presented to Joshua Prawer* (Jerusalem, 1982), 89–100.
22. *Peregrinationes tres*, 175–7. See D. Pringle, 'Templar Castles on the Road to the Jordan', in M. Barber (ed.), *The Military Orders: Fighting for the Faith and Caring for the Sick* (Aldershot, 1994), 148–66.
23. 'De constructione castri Saphet', ed. R. B. C. Huygens, *Studi Medievali*, series 3, 6 (1965), 355–87.
24. See J. Riley-Smith, *The Knights of St John in Jerusalem and Cyprus, c.1050–1310* (London, 1967), 71–3.
25. *Cartulaire général*, vol. 1, no. 527, pp. 360–1.
26. Ibid., vol. 2, no. 1193, p. 37.
27. See J. Folda, 'Crusader Frescoes at Crac des Chevaliers and Margat Castle', *Dumbarton Oaks Papers* 36 (1982), 192–6.
28. Guillaume de Puylaurens, *Chronique 1203–1275*, ed. and trans. J. Duvernoy (Paris, 1976), 84–5, 88–9, 112–13; *Cartulaire générale*, vol. 2, no. 1617, p. 246, for the will of Raymond VI.
29. *Cartulaire général*, vol. 2, nos. 1861, 1937, pp. 363–4, 394–5.
30. Ibid., vol. 1, no. 150, pp. 121–2.
31. Riley-Smith, *Knights of St John*, ch. 7.

32. A. Gabriel, *La Cité de Rhodes: MCCCX-MDXXII* (Paris, 1921–3), vol. 2, pièces justificatives, nos. 1, 6, pp. 221, 223–4.
33. Ibid., vol. 2, 13–36, pièces justificatives, nos. 2, 3, 4, pp. 221–2. See F. Karassava-Tsilingiri, 'The Fifteenth-Century Hospital at Rhodes: Tradition and Innovation', in M. Barber (ed.), *The Military Orders: Fighting for the Faith and Caring for the Sick*, 89–96.
34. E. Legrand, 'Relation du Pèlerinage à Jérusalem de Nicolas de Martoni, notaire italien: 1394–1395', *Revue de l'Orient latin* 3 (1895), 584–5, 640.
35. John of Lobkowicz, 'What a Pilgrim saw at Rhodes', trans. C. von Schwarzenberg, *Annales de l'Ordre Souverain Militaire de Malte* 26 (1968), 103–6.
36. See Luttrell, 'The Hospitallers' Medical Tradition', 73.
37. Gabriel, *Cité de Rhodes*, vol. 2, 102–6.
38. *Cartulaire général*, vol. 1, no. 888, p. 564.
39. See J. Mundy, 'Charity and Social Work in Toulouse, 1100–1250', *Traditio* 22 (1966), 203–87.
40. *Cartulaire général*, vol. 2, no. 1985, p. 420; vol. 1, no. 572, p. 388; vol. 2, no. 1392, pp. 146–7.
41. See A. J. Forey, 'Women and Military Orders in the Twelfth and Thirteenth Centuries', *Studia Monastica* 29 (1987), 67–77.
42. *Cartulaire général*, vol. 1, no. 278, p. 208; vol. 2, nos. 1445, 1857, 2923, pp. 177–8, 361, 872–4.
43. See Luttrell, 'Medical Tradition', 78–9, and 'The Hospitallers' Hospice of Santa Caterina at Venice: 1358–1451', *Studi Veneziani* 12 (1970), 369–83.
44. *La Règle du Temple*, ed. H. de Curzon, Société de l'Histoire de France (Paris, 1896), 80.
45. F. Bramato, *Storia dell'Ordine dei Templari in Italia*, vol. 2: *Le Inquisizioni. Le Fonti* (Rome, 1994), no. 470, p. 180.
46. *La Règle du Temple*, 37.
47. H. Finke, *Papsttum und Untergang des Templerordens*, (Münster, 1907), vol. 2, p. 72.

Bibliography

M. Barber, *The New Knighthood. A History of the Order of the Temple* (Cambridge, 1994)

M. Barber (ed.), *The Military Orders: Fighting for the Faith and Caring for the Sick* (Aldershot, 1994)

J. Riley-Smith, *The Knights of St John in Jerusalem and Cyprus, c. 1050–1310* (London, 1967)

9

'Since the pestilence time'
Pastoral care in the later Middle Ages

William J. Dohar

Late in July 1348, Archbishop William Zouche of York issued a pastoral letter to the clergy and people of the northern province warning them of a plague which had already devastated parts of the continent and was threatening England. His letter was meant to convey a spirit of hope against the coming plague but it was laden with admonition:

> As human life on earth is warfare, there is little wonder that those who wage war on the miseries of this world are sometimes disturbed by uncertain events, at times favourable, at other times adverse. For Almighty God occasionally allows those he loves to be chastised since, accompanied by grace, strength is made perfect in infirmity. Therefore, who does not know what great death, pestilence and infection of the air hang about various parts of the world and especially England these days. This indeed is caused by the sins of people who, caught up in the delights of their prosperity, neglect to remember the gifts of the Supreme Giver.[1]

These images of spiritual warfare and the chastening manner of God's love were commonplace in pastoral letters such as these. So too was the assertion from prelates and preachers that brooding over planetary causes of plague was wasted time; it was human sinfulness, not the discordant alignment of planets that tested God's patience and provoked such a hard judgement. As sin was the cause, penance was the only solution. Thus the archbishop attempted by the letter to animate the faithful toward repentance and the small hope that God's wrath might yet be averted. He ordered that processions be held every Wednesday and Friday at the cathedral as well as in every parish church in the diocese, that the litany be chanted and a special prayer against the pestilence be recited every day.

The letter illustrates a number of important aspects of pastoral care in the mid-fourteenth century. It implies an already established tradition in parish churches of public processions and penitential actions invoked against threats to the peace of the kingdom and Church. It relied upon a complex of pastoral and administrative structures to implement the archbishop's command; it was addressed to the archdeacons and deans of the diocese, who would publish its contents in the expected and usual manner through some hasty local convocation and alert the parish clergy, who would, in turn, announce the news from York to the people and arrange the customary processions and prayers. Most significantly, the letter appealed to a tradition long-established by the fourteenth century which associated physical maladies with the condition of the soul. Well over a century before, the Fourth Lateran Council (1215) had prohibited sick people from retaining a physician for any longer than three days unless a priest had been summoned to hear the person's confession. Sin was regarded as the root cause of physical illness much as any other factor and 'when the cause is removed the effect will pass away'.[2] Thus, the archbishop's letter was not perceived as a last, desperate measure of defence against approaching death. Its prescribed antidote of prayer and penance was the only defence that Christians should invoke and if a penitential spirit could restore by God's mercy a sick person to health, then perhaps the movement of an entire Church might sway the judgement of the Most High.

By the time Zouche's letter had been issued in the north, the first incidents of plague in England had been reported in the south. There the archbishop of York was joined by other church leaders who read as well the evil of the times and issued similar pastoral mandates for penance and prayer. The bishop of Lincoln anticipated Zouche by a few days with his own *ad orandum pro pestilentia*. A fortnight later, Ralph of Shrewsbury, bishop of Bath and Wells, ordered his own people to fast and pray.[3] William Edington of Winchester ordered the cathedral chapter to recite special prayers, especially 'the great litany instituted by the fathers of the Church for use against the pestilence'. The custom called for the monks of the cathedral to organize penitential processions, leading the people barefoot and with heads bowed through the market-place of the cathedral city, fasting and reciting as often as possible the *Pater* and *Ave*.[4] The procession ended with Mass at the cathedral and all in attendance were mildly warned to remain there through the entire service. As the other bishops had done, Edington attached an indulgence of 40 days as added encouragement to the pious execution of his mandate. To the west in Exeter, Bishop Grandisson issued his own orders for prayers on 30 October and John Trillek of Hereford ordered customary liturgies sometime earlier that month for the churches of his diocese.[5]

Within weeks and months of these letters, and following the parish rites they prescribed, the plague would move through England as it had other places causing an upheaval that was unprecedented in the mediaeval world. Because of its close association with God's judgement, the plague's religious significance was unquestioned in the minds of most who witnessed its devastation. The spiritual aid which the Church held out as people's only hope was at the same time severely checked as the plague carried off countless priests and shook the foundations of pastoral care. The Black Death of 1347–50 was to alter the pastoral landscape along with every other facet of fourteenth-century society as long as its impact and effects endured. And because it was not a singular incident but a series of epidemic plagues that would recur throughout the remainder of the Middle Ages and into the seventeenth century, plague would become a force of change in late mediaeval society. The intention of this chapter is to observe this force of change within pastoral care in two stages: the immediate and violent impact of the Black Death on parishes and their pastors, and then the fanning out of those first changes into lingering and chronic challenges to pastoral care over the century and a half that followed.

Pastoral care is our main concern here, and while mediaeval parishioners defined the contours of pastoral care they are often an elusive presence in the documents and records that survive from the time. Thus, our emphasis will fall mainly on the agents of pastoral care, the parish clergy who represented the expectations of pastoral care in the ministries they provided. Also, for the sake of a sharper focus in a subject that occupies a vast place in late mediaeval history, our discussion will be limited to the experience of plague and pastoral care in England. What happened there is emblematic of the events and reactions the plague drew from other churches in other lands. Before we can appreciate the upheaval caused by the plague and its attendant effects on pastoral care, it is necessary to provide a very general view of pastoral care in the relatively calmer thirteenth century, an age that gave considerable and significant shape to the very pastoral structures, conventions and institutions that weathered the changes of the fourteenth century.

Penance and pastoral care

Pastoral care in the later Middle Ages, as in every age, entailed many activities, ranging from the breadth of sacramental ministry, to leading the people in prayer, to preaching and feeding the poor. But by the fourteenth century if pastoral care was defined along any particular ministry it was the healing gained through the sacrament of penance. Pope Innocent III, that architect of mediaeval pastoral care, asserted that of the many things comprising the cure of souls absolution was the most salutary.[6] In the famous decree from Lateran IV, *Omnis utriusque sexus*, priests were described as *medici animarum*, physicians of the soul, who in the sacrament of penance were to make careful and discreet enquiries regarding the nature and circumstances of sin and sinner in order to prescribe the most effective spiritual medication in the forms of counsel and penance.[7] Other pastoralists took up the metaphor and all that it implied in the daily activities of the cure of souls. In the preface to statutes for the diocese of Exeter in 1287, Bishop Peter Quivel challenged priests to be like Jesus, the best physician of souls

> who gives us relief from our pain through contrition, and through confession we receive a purgative; he recommends a healthful diet through our keeping of fasts; he orders therapeutic baths through our outpouring of tears; he prescribes bloodletting through our recollection of Christ's passion. But what is this medicine? – Penance.[8]

The belief that grave sin threatened salvation was at the heart of pastoral care in the thirteenth century and endured through the rest of the Middle Ages and beyond as descriptive of the pastoral challenge. In a very real sense it marked a turning-point in the history of pastoral care. As it encouraged the parish priest to be a physician of souls, it elevated him to the status of pastor, the one from whom people should typically seek the ministry of the Church. The schools of religious foundations, hospitals and almshouses would continue to provide other forms of pastoral care, but the sacraments were increasingly the ministry of the parish priest. This movement also regarded the laity as parishioners whose activities with respect to the Church were ordered within this identity. They were bound, according to the same decree that regarded the local curate as a spiritual physician, to attend to the sacrament of penance at least once a year and receive from their own parish priest (*proprius sacerdos*) penance and absolution.

In a way, all other ministries in the parish took place with this conversion in mind: preaching, rituals, blessings and prayers were prologue to confession. Afterwards, there were other activities in prayer, sacraments and works of mercy that aided the soul in a life of holiness and service. For the benefit of the parish priest there were instructional aids to his ministry in the sacrament of penance, a new literary genre of pastoral *summae* (handbooks) that flourished from the thirteenth century to the end of the Middle Ages. Pastoralists and church leaders steadily reiterated the importance of the sacrament of penance and the need for parish priests to be worthy of this and related ministries. Thus also, from the thirteenth century, higher standards of education and expectations in moral behaviour were applied to priesthood: how they should dress, the condition of their tonsure, their absence from secular business and entertainments, the preservation of their chastity and moral rectitude.[9]

Institutions were required to sustain this pastoral identity along with laws and effective sanctions protecting those institutions. If pastors were given a higher calling in the sacrament of penance and other forms of ministry, educational opportunities were needed to support these ambitions. The thirteenth century witnessed significant developments in clerical education and instruction for pastoral care. Support for theological instruction was added to the arts in grammar and cathedral schools. Bishops like Quivel of Exeter and John Pecham of Canterbury issued diocesan statutes as pastoral syllabi for essential learning in parish cures.[10] At the end of the century Pope Boniface VIII issued a decree, *Cum ex eo*, to encourage pastoral education among beneficed clergy through provisions for leaves of absence and the use of parish revenues for scholastic support.[11] The availability of pastoral *summae* augmented the resources for the instruction of parish clergy.

It was also necessary for ecclesiastical superiors to oversee more thoroughly the examination and ordination of parish clergy. The late thirteenth and early fourteenth centuries witnessed the highest levels of clerical recruitment in the mediaeval church and leaders had to take greater precaution in scrutinizing the many candidates who presented themselves for orders.[12] The bishop was meant to be the principal examiner of clerical candidates, but he was more often than not assisted by members of his administrative household who themselves were witness to the expanding responsibilities of the bishop for all things pertaining to pastoral care. Thus, he was steadily accompanied in his tours of the diocese by scribes and notaries, advisors, commissaries and advocates in his employ. The pastoral impetus of the thirteenth century also included in a special way the regular pastoral visitation of the diocese by the bishop and others, like the archdeacon, who had specific duties relative to parishes and the cure of souls. Bishops were expected to make triennial visits of the clergy and people of their diocese, enquiring into the pastoral practices of their priests, the moral lives of the people and the physical condition of churches and churchyards and of the vessels, vestments and books needed for the worthy exercise of pastoral care.

Parishes were the centres of pastoral care, but they were also sources of revenue, hence their varied regard by persons of authority, clerical and secular. Most parishes in the thirteenth century had a parson, a curate or a rector who had been instituted to that church as the spiritual and temporal administrator of the parish. He could be joined by other clergy, assistant chaplains who were paid an annual wage out of the freewill offerings and seasonal tithes required of parishioners. They might live in the rectorial manse or find suitable and affordable lodging on their own. There were likely to be younger men in minor orders, acolytes, subdeacons and deacons to assist the local clergy in the celebration of daily Mass or in visitations to the sick or relief of the poor. If the rector had to be away from his parish for any length of time and with the leave of the bishop he would employ a vicar to oversee the spiritual needs of his parishioners. Finally, the practice of appropriating parish revenues to some religious foundation with an expressed and recognized need grew in the later Middle Ages. In this case, a monastery or a convent would become the rector of a church and enjoy the fruits of the benefice without prejudice to the pastoral life of the parish through the employment of clergy necessary for the management of the cure.

All of this merely suggests the complexity and diversity of pastoral care and the structures that grew in defining it through the course of the thirteenth century. But we need to see even in this sketchy manner how parishes functioned in order to understand more clearly the impact which a force as broad and far-reaching as the plague was to have. The sickness and deaths of clergy and people on such a scale would alter the conventions of pastoral care. Social dislocation, fear and massive grief would strain the traditions of parish communities. The local and often modest economic systems that supported the cure of souls would in some places be entirely destroyed and in many others severely crippled.

The effects of plague

By conservative estimates at least a third of England's population succumbed to the Black Death; some historians place the rate of death at 50 per cent or two-thirds of the overall population.[13] Among some of the better-off parishioners, one out of every four tenants who held land directly of the king died during 1348 and 1349. The facts of their deaths are noted in the inquisitions *post mortem*, royal records of inquests held in the wake of a tenant's death to determine the rightful inheritance of the property and the feudal relief owed the king. An examination of these inquests reveals a mortality rate of 27 per cent among these landowners.[14] The people who worked their lands suffered in greater numbers. For example, records show that at least half the peasants who worked Crowland Abbey's estates died during the plague. Elsewhere in the Lincoln diocese, at Tilgarsley, the entire village was depopulated as a result of the plague.[15] Two-thirds of the bishop of Winchester's tenants died at Bishop's Waltham with similar reports of death at other manors at Downton, Witney and Cuxham. By the end of 1349 the village of Durrington was desolate and the bishop's manor at Farnham had lost at least 20 per cent of its inhabitants.[16] In Worcester diocese, on the bishop's manor at Hanbury, the population declined from 61 tenants at the beginning of the fourteenth century to only four after the plague and there was at least a 36 per cent decline in the tenant population at fourteen other episcopal manors in the diocese during 1349.[17] Exchequer accounts for the deanery of Amounderness in Lancashire report the startling and no doubt exaggerated figure of 13,180 persons dying in ten parishes between 8 September 1349 and 11 January 1350.[18] But even a fraction of these deaths would have been devastating.

Most parishes in later mediaeval England served rural communities where the plague moved with uneven effect. Some places were barely touched while others were depopulated. Mortality in the cities was bound to be higher where the plague moved effectively through denser populations and was facilitated by the generally unsanitary conditions of the time. A few years after the plague, in a supplication made to the Holy See, a London courtier claimed a staggering 60,000 deaths in London alone. While the figure has to be astronomically incorrect, it is possible that at least a third of that figure – staggering nonetheless – died during the plague.[19] Norwich was said to have lost nearly half its population, and about a third of the citizens of York died.[20] According to Henry Knighton, parishes in the town of Leicester were hard hit by the plague: in 'the small parish of St. Leonard's more than 380 people died, in the parish of Holy Cross, 400, in the parish of St. Margaret's, Leicester, 700 and so in every parish'.[21]

We have marginally better estimates of mortality among the pastors of these people, especially those men who had received appointments as rectors or vicars of parish churches, a fact that was especially noted in the bishop's register. It was standard practice to enter the circumstances for the vacancy that preceded the institution of a new rector or vicar, and during the plague years death was more often than not the principal factor behind the change. In a dated study of the institution lists for ten English dioceses, between 39 and 49 per cent of these clergy died during the Black Death, with Exeter, Winchester and Norwich at the higher end of recorded clerical mortality.[22] Other studies have tended to support these findings. For instance, in York just under half of the 535 benefices that fell vacant during the Black Death were due to the deaths of previous incumbents, though the actual figure is probably even higher.[23] Lincoln's toll was nearly as high, with an overall level of 40 per cent mortality among the higher clergy.[24] In Coventry and Lichfield just over 208 beneficed clerics died during the plague year, nearly 40 per cent of the total for the diocese. That figure represents a mortality rate of 33 per cent among the rectors in the diocese and 46 for the vicars whose duties more specifically entailed residence and pastoral care in the parishes.[25] In Hereford diocese at least one in three beneficed clerics died during the plague year, though the number must have been higher given the large rate of churches whose circumstances of vacancy were never recorded.[26] There are similar figures for neighbouring Worcester diocese, where in Gloucestershire 80 vacancies occurred during the plague from the deaths of incumbents.[27] Ely and Bath and Wells fared much worse, both reporting 48 per cent mortality rates. But by far the most troubled were Exeter, Winchester and Norwich, where nearly half of the beneficed clergy died. The parishes of Kenn deanery in Exeter were probably the worst-affected in all of England: in the seventeen benefices of the deanery 86 incumbents died during the plague.[28] Winchester suffered badly as well. There were ten times as many institutions as normal during the years 1349 and 1350, most of those attributed to the deaths of incumbents. The city of Winchester itself may have lost nearly 4,000 people at this time.[29] The plague was at its height in eastern England during the summer of 1349; in that year alone 800 benefices fell vacant, 83 of them twice and ten of them three times. Two-thirds of the benefices in the diocese of Norwich had received new incumbents by the end of 1349, though not all could be said to be death-vacancies.[30]

These figures become mind-numbing after a little while and we are likely to glaze over the very important fact that the pastoral care of a parish or chapel was greatly disturbed by the sudden death of its incumbent. It indicated in rough measure the presence of mortality among his parishioners, but it also told of the disruption, even temporary, of the parish's pastoral care, especially at a critical time. Given the high rate of death among the beneficed clergy, there is little doubt that their assistant chaplains died in similar numbers if not higher. Unlike the incumbent, they were not canonically bound to reside in the cure; their presence was an economic necessity with their livelihood dependent upon the often meagre wage paid them by the parish rector or vicar. In many cases it was not death that reduced the number of clergy in a parish but rather fear of contagion and flight in advance of the plague. The parish leadership was especially chastized for leaving the cure to which they were bound as if in marriage. A Canterbury chronicler reported that 'parish churches remained altogether unserved, and beneficed persons turned away from the care of their benefices for fear of death ...'[31] Later, William Langland would add greed to the fear of contagion: 'Parsons and parish priests complained to their bishops that since the pestilence time their parishes were poor and so they asked leave to live in London and sing for their money for silver is sweet.'[32] The lure of London chantries and the singing of Masses for the dead were inducements to beneficed clerics who were presiding over diminishing parishes and income.[33] What happened at that level of parish administration occurred elsewhere in the pastoral care of churches: the stipendiary clergy were also reported as deserters from their cures who had found themselves in high demand in a considerably altered market. As the king had attempted to keep labourers in their traditional places of employment according to the same pay scale as before the plague, bishops issued decrees ordering stipendiary clergy to remain in their churches and require no more than they had in previous years for their pastoral labour.[34] At the height of the plague, the bishop of Rochester ordered all hired chaplains in his diocese to remain in their churches and accept what they were paid in past years. Edington of Winchester did much the same in early April 1350. Churches in that diocese had been left empty, the bishop said, so that birds and other animals were nesting in their sanctuaries. All clergy were ordered to return within the month.[35] In spite of their decrees, the bishops were little more effective in their realm than the king was in his.

While parishes had long been established as the usual and normative places of pastoral care, there were many foundations at the time that exercised various other ministries than those of the altar. Hospitals and the religious communities that served them suffered special hardship during the plague. Not only did their administration suffer in the loss of lives among the brothers or nuns that served the hospitals, but death was rife among those weakened by infirmity and old age. In the summer of 1349 Bishop Edington of Winchester petitioned the Pope on behalf of Walter de Marlawe, a brother at St Thomas Martyr hospital in Southwark. The hospital, which was run by brothers and sisters, had lost its prior and a number of the religious who tended the sick. Walter was the only fit candidate for prior, but his illegitimacy, pending the Pope's approval of the dispensation, barred him from leading the house through difficult times. Leper houses in England witnessed as well a sharp decline among inmates and those who laboured in their care.[36] St Giles at Stamford in Northamptonshire had a chaplain to care for the lepers; the Lazar house disappears from the records at the time of the Black Death. St James hospital in Westminster had been founded before the Conquest to care for women lepers. After the plague only a single inmate survived.[37]

Mortality was the first and most impressive effect of the epidemic, but from that flowed other crises that compounded its overall impact. It was the tendency of all institutions including pastoral ones to adhere to established conventions against the strong undertow of sudden change, but this was rarely possible, especially in the moment of the plague where the usual religious activities of a community were slowed, suspended or ceased altogether. As the contagion spread, groups were far less likely to gather, in either the market-place or the nave. Few sacraments were administered with their usual regularity or ceremony. Though we lack the records to prove it, there was little likelihood that many couples met at the church porch to exchange vows during the course of an epidemic.

Families were too preoccupied with grasping after their own stability to ponder new alliances. Often the disposition of victims' properties remained in doubt until the usual procedures that clarified possession, probate and inheritance had been restored. Midwives baptized newborns quickly who might be received in a more formal manner at a later time if there was a priest to solemnize the baptism. The sacrament of confirmation, occasional at best in the later Middle Ages and occurring usually when the bishop was touring his diocese on visitation, could wait another season. The bishop probably had his mind on more urgent matters, like the ordination of clergy to fill the vacancies in the pastoral workforce. The sacraments that surrounded death – confession, and extreme unction with its eucharistic viaticum – were the pastoral matters of the moment. In the Mass, too, one would remember the souls of the dead and pray for their release from purgatory.

The changes that had gone on in parishes amounted to more than a shift in liturgical emphasis. The sheer volume of death had created a crisis in pastoral care. In some communities death was a daily reality through the months when the plague was at its height. The demands which came to be placed on local pastors were immense. If they kept to their cures (and some did not) and survived (as more did not) their pastoral work was a constant ministry to the dying and the dead. In some parishes the passing bell was an unceasing, daily reminder of the strength of this plague and the weakness of the earthly body. In most places, visitation of the sick on Sundays and feast-days was a normal part of the local curate's duties. But there were also times of need when the priest might be summoned day or night to visit the sick-bed of one of his parishioners. He was meant to take the Blessed Sacrament in procession to the house, accompanied by a cleric who would carry a candle and ring a bell to announce the Lord's coming and, if required, hear the confession of the infirmed.[38] During plague time this duty was all the more required and all the more fearsome for the contagion that threatened. There was always the danger that ministry would be abrupt and perfunctory when it happened at all in a house infected by the pestilence. Even so, the more devoted pastors would console the dying and the mourners as best they might in a season when hope in God's mercy was sorely tried.

The increased general mortality and the scarcity of parish clergy meant that traditional ways of burying the dead and grieving were less available to communities and families. Customs surrounding the preparations of bodies for the funeral and burial were hastily carried out or dismissed altogether. Only the most devoted or those infected themselves would wash and wake the body of one who had died of plague. The traditions of mourning, the support of the community for the family that had lost one of its members, the more patient ministrations of the Church in ritual and human consolation, were abbreviated or gathered together for the many who faced death at the same time. Common funerals were held to relieve the parish of the dead and commit the bodies of victims to the earth as quickly as possible. Whether it was because his parish was overwhelmed with funerals or because he was an enterprising businessman, one parishioner in Everton in York diocese used his own home as a place where the dead could be brought and prayed over before burial.[39]

In little time churchyards became choked with victims of the plague and some places had to resort to the ignominy of common burials and graves. Old cemeteries had to be expanded and new ground blessed to make way for the dead. Some bishops on their own initiative consecrated plots for this use; others had to be badgered by their parishioners before they would concede a grant usually associated with the rights and revenues of a mother church. Wealthy individuals like Walter Manny provided a place for the dead as an act of piety. His cemetery at Smithfield near London had filled rapidly during the plague with the remains of Londoners.[40] Bishop Northburgh of Coventry and Lichfield approved the expansion of a churchyard at Astlebury late in the summer of 1349, and by 1352 had to commission one of his officials to dedicate a new cemetery at Diddlebury chapel in the parish of Manchester.[41] The brothers at St Oswald's Hospital in Worcester were asked to inter the bodies of plague victims there in April 1349, as the cathedral cemetery had already exceeded its capacity.[42] The small parish of Templeton in Exeter diocese had no cemetery in which to bury their dead; victims of the plague were piled on carts during the night and taken to the churchyard in neighbouring Witheridge.[43] William de Dene, chronicler of the Rochester diocese at this time, mentioned that 'men and women carried their own children on their shoulders to the church and threw them into a common pit. From these pits such an appalling stench was given off that scarcely anyone dared even to walk beside the cemeteries.'[44]

With the heightened need and the diminished resources for pastoral care, the essential ministries of confession and the Eucharist were in far greater demand. Pastors encouraged their people to seek the consolation of these sacraments in any way that they could. A few weeks after he had issued his mandate for prayers and processions against the plague, Bishop

Edington of Winchester reminded his flock that 'sickness and premature death often come from sin; and that by the healing of souls this kind of sickness is known to cease'.[45] To that end, he granted faculties to clerics in his diocese to hear confessions and absolve sins, even ones usually reserved to the bishop. The heads of religious houses in the diocese were similarly allowed to appoint priests to hear the confessions of nuns. At about the same time as this decree was issued, the bishop appealed to Pope Clement VI for an indulgence that would offer comfort and further incentive to the people of his diocese for the sacrament of penance. On 19 January 1349 Edington ordered his official to announce that 'the most holy father in Christ, our lord the Supreme Pontiff, had ... on account of the imminent and great mortality, granted to all the people of the diocese ... who should confess their sins with sincere repentance to any priest they might choose a plenary indulgence at the hour of death if they departed in the true faith, in unity with the holy Roman Church and in obedience and devotion to our lord the Supreme Pontiff and his successors the Roman Bishops'. Edington ordered the news to be broadcast through the diocese at once.[46] The indulgence was originally meant to last only until Easter, but on account of the plague's duration, Edington petitioned for and received an extension until the following Michaelmas. Also, for the course of the grant the customary obligation of parishioners to confess their sins to their own parish priests was, in this time of emergency, suspended.

In other dioceses the sacrament of penance was encouraged through the appointment of penitentiaries, clerics of usually high reputation who were granted special faculties by the bishop to hear confessions and absolve even in cases of reserved sins. In Coventry and Lichfield as well as Hereford the bishops appointed canons from the cathedral as well as mendicant friars to hear confessions in specified regions of the dioceses.[47] The bishop of Bath and Wells did not have the time to make such appointments which were meant to accompany, not replace, the ongoing activity of confessors in their parishes. In January 1349 when the plague was at its height in his diocese, he issued a mandate to his clergy and people which epitomizes the pastoral crisis caused by the epidemic. Too suddenly there were too few priests in their parishes, some on account of death, others through fear of the same. As a result parishioners in the diocese were discouraged from confessing their sins because of the common belief that confession could be made only to a priest. The bishop ordered the remaining clergy to 'publicly command and persuade all people, especially those currently sick or who should fall sick in the future' that if on the point of death and without recourse to a priest, they should confess their sins to one another, man or woman, 'as is permitted in the teaching of the Apostles'.[48] Absolution was implied in this grant, but the bishop bound anyone who heard a neighbour's confession according to the seal of the sacrament or suffer the wrath of God and the entire Church.

The scarcity of priests further threatened the regular celebrations of the Eucharist and other sacraments as well as the numerous Masses for the dead now brought to local parish priests. In the same letter on the sacrament of penance, Ralph of Shrewsbury urged deacons to distribute the Blessed Sacrament where priests were unavailable. But the sacramental concessions stopped there; if someone dying was in need of extreme unction and there was no priest to provide it, 'as in other matters, faith must suffice'.[49] In many parishes and larger churches a special Mass for deliverance from the pestilence was sung in place of the regular liturgy. Pope Clement VI had formally approved the Mass in 1348, when the plague had taken hold of most of the continent, and applied an indulgence of 260 days for any who would attend it. If the faithful carried a burning candle in their hands for five days following the celebration of this Mass, the plague would not touch them. Special readings and prayers were assigned to the Mass, which told of God's power to send and stay his wrath as the sins of the people merited.[50]

Not only were priests called upon to shrive penitents, celebrate Masses, visit the sick and bury the dead, but they were needed to administer the churches in times more violent than usual. The devastation in certain places had brought with it reactions that ranged from cowered piety to explosions of violence against any authority, religious or secular. After the death of the bishop of Worcester in August 1349, looters raided his lands carrying off livestock and other goods belonging to the bishop's estate.[51] In Rochester, William de Dene commented on the violent actions committed by people in the wake of the plague. People 'became so rebellious that neither the king nor the law and their judges who enforced it were able to correct them, and more or less the whole population turned to evil courses, became addicted to all forms of vice and stooped to more than usually base behaviour, thinking not at all of death or of the recently-experienced plague, nor of how they were hazarding their own salvation'.[52]

Though England was spared the more frenzied expressions of public piety and demonstrations witnessed on the continent of Europe, there were occasions when religious acts bordered on madness. We have no idea what London pastors made of the parades of flagellants recorded by Robert of Avesbury in his chronicle, but they and their parishioners must have marvelled at the exotic scenes of penitents scourging themselves and one another. Robert says that about six hundred of these men came to England from Zeeland and Holland and reached London around the feast of St Michael in late September 1349. They made public appearances twice daily in the area around St Paul's, where they 'marched naked in a file one behind the other and whipped themselves with these scourges on their naked and bleeding bodies. Four of them would chant in their native tongue and another four would chant in response like a litany.'[53] Though such exotic displays of self-mortification were rare among Englishmen during and after the plague, the foreigners incited fear and dread, admiration and repulsion in the minds of their less excessive observers. Onlookers must have questioned their own piety and penitential fervour in the face of mortality and beseeched their already beleaguered pastors for insight and guidance.

Recovery and pastoral needs

The grim future that processions such as these tended to forecast proved premature by late 1349 and early 1350 when the plague, at least in England, was beginning to abate. But against the hopes of many people, the absence of plague and its disruptions did not result in either the immediate restoration of traditional ways of life or the ready availability of new elements with which to repair the weakened social fabric. In matters of pastoral care, parish communities had suffered from the violent and sudden changes of the plague not only in the moment of the epidemic but for years to follow. Some of these were permanent changes, as in the merging of parishes required for lack of parishioners and resources to support separate cures. The bishop of Ely approved such a petition from the clergy and people of All Saints and St Giles churches, and in Hereford Bishop Trillek allowed two churches to be united, Great and Little Collington, due to the number of deceased parishioners from the last plague and the impoverishment of their survivors.[54] In most cases, people wanted to find in the ruin of the present the order that had preceded the plague, but as they applied themselves to efforts along these lines the nature of the plague was to reveal itself with dramatic force. A second outbreak of plague in the early 1360s broke the relative calm; this plague was called the 'children's plague' because of the mortality among those born since the Black Death and who had acquired no immunity.[55] Subsequent epidemics would hit in the later fourteenth and early fifteenth centuries with repeated impact in 1369, 1375, 1390, 1399–1400 and 1405–6, and most of these occurred on a national scale.[56] While they were not as devastating in the toll of lives as were the plagues of the mid-fourteenth century, their regular visitations were to have accumulative effects that could not but alter outlooks and institutions in the later Middle Ages. Their effects joined with other incidents and movements in the period that prompted new challenges to pastoral care, events such as the prolonged and scandalous schism in the papacy and challenges to religious and civil authorities in heretical movements and peasant uprisings. But by far the most critical challenge to pastoral care was the profound fact that there were far fewer pastors to serve the parishes and, as some had opined, fewer still who were qualified in learning and morality to manage a cure of souls.

Pastoral institutions had been defined as places for sacramental ministry and, as was indicated earlier, the emphasis on penance as one of the most important, if not the central aspect of piety in the lives of parishioners made the presence of priests indispensable. Much of pastoral leadership in the second half of the fourteenth century lay in providing priests adequate in number and quality to the parishes for this and other ministries in the cure of souls. This meant finding ways of shoring up the diminished clerical workforce, chief among which was the holding of ordination ceremonies. Also, the presence of a cleric in a cure did not mean that the parish was necessarily in good hands; the more vigilant bishops of previous centuries had this concern before them always, but in the decades following the Black Death there was the possibility that whatever standards of clerical learning and behaviour had obtained in the old days had declined against the need to fill cures at any cost. In a very real sense, the greatest pastoral challenge was not in the desperate moment of the plague, but in the years that followed when the immediate decline in numbers of clergy met the unremitting downward trends in the general population.

There were enough problems keeping priests in their cures through times of radical change and upheaval, and raising up new ones from the diminished population proved a challenge for a full century following the Black Death. There was indeed a smaller population pool from which future priests could be drawn, but there were other dissuasive factors as well. However unstable the economy was in the decades following the plague of 1348/49, there was a more diversified labour market to which anyone could apply who might otherwise have considered a clerical life.[57] Furthermore, the restrictive measures on the part of bishops to turn clerical wages back to what they had been before the *prima pestilentia* (first plague) were hardly encouragement for men whose pastoral zeal was tempered by more pragmatic interests in a dependable livelihood. There was also a gathering sense of disappointment over the Church and its clergy, some of it traditional but much of it in the wake of the apparent impotence of pastors to lift the hand of God in these repeated epidemics. In the plague Mass which Pope Clement VI urged be prayed all over the world during the Black Death, the offertory prayer reads: 'The priest stood between the living and the dead, with a gold censer in his hand, and offering the sacrifice of incense he appeased the anger of the Lord, and the plague ceased from the house and people of Israel.'[58] The failure of that appeasement raised doubts in the minds of people that priesthood was indeed what church leaders claimed it was. The aura of the office was no doubt tarnished and sullied even further by the new wave of anti-clericalism that characterized the late fourteenth century, with oafish priests, religious hypocrites and bumbling pastors moving about the literary landscapes of Chaucer's pilgrimage and Piers Plowman's dream. Many of the suspicions harboured in such characters were confirmed in the official records of their real counterparts appearing shamefaced in the discoveries of episcopal visitations and in court documents regarding criminous clerics.

None of these factors aided bishops in finding men worthy and willing to serve the parishes of their dioceses. General trends in clerical recruitment after the Black Death were downward, and often unremittingly so, until the late fifteenth century. For the better part of those decades parishes had to cope with a diminished pastoral workforce and often care of a diminished quality. The shift in recruitment was immediate. For example, the bishop of Rochester ordained 83 clerics in 1347, and 144 at ordinations in 1348, but during the year that followed less than half those numbers sought admission to orders.[59] From 1344 to 1346 in Winchester the annual average of priests ordained was 111; from 1349 to 1365, the year Bishop Edington died, that average had dropped to twenty. By the pontificate of William Waynflete in the mid-fifteenth century fewer than a dozen priests were ordained each year for the diocese.[60] In Ely the numbers were just as bleak. In the 1340s nearly one hundred men were ordained to the various ranks of order each year, but in 1349 there were no ordinations at all and between 1350 and 1356 the annual average had dropped to forty.[61] In York recruitment levels had been high in the years preceding the plague, with an annual average of 315 acolytes from 1343 to 1346. Acolyte levels are important barometers for the clerical workforce as they anticipate the size of the clerical population from which the higher orders are drawn. During the plague year in York the number of acolytes ordained soared to twice its pre-plague levels, suggesting a large influx of candidates who came out of piety or the prospect of work as plague threatened the north. Those trends peaked in 1350 when 436 acolytes were ordained. With the passing of the plague the number dropped to 175 in 1351. A similar pattern occurred in candidates for the priesthood in York. In 1348 there had been 185 priest-ordinands, the following year 299 and in 1350, as vacancies increased throughout the diocese, 724 men were ordained to the priesthood. But the same attrition witnessed in the acolytes in 1351 occurred as well in the higher orders: only 183 men were priested in York that year.[62] This overall direction in decline took place in Hereford as well: ordinations peaked in 1349, after which they fell sharply, tapering off to far lower annual numbers of ordinands than in the past century. In the early 1400s there were fewer than ten priests ordained each year for a diocese that through the ten years before the Black Death had averaged annually nearly a hundred men ordained to the priesthood.[63]

Once clergy were available for service in the churches and ordained properly to that end, bishops had to contend with the chronic challenge of keeping them in their cures. There were provisions for a beneficed cleric to resign his cure, but in any case it had to be cleared by the bishop or one of his officials. Study leaves were available to rectors and vicars according to the terms set by Boniface VIII's decree *Cum ex eo*, or a cleric might seek a temporary leave from his church to wait on some local noble. Finally, it was possible to exchange one's benefice for another, an act that by its very nature involved the resignation of one cure and the taking up of the other. In general, bishops resisted granting many resignations during and immediately following the plague. It was too important that parishes have some stability and leadership in these times. Still, there were exceptions. Some clerics insisted that their churches had become too poor to support them, and they contrived through resignation to acquire a more profitable benefice. In Coventry and Lichfield there had been only four resignations of priests from cures in the year prior to the Black Death. From April to

October 1349 there were 35 resignations and during the following year as many as 42.[64] Often the church had become so poor that curates chose to look elsewhere rather than serve a cure with diminishing revenues.

The greater problem seemed to lie with the non-beneficed clergy, those priests who had been hired for a set wage to assist in the pastoral care of parishes. There is no doubt that their livings were generally poor. Because of the relative abundance of clergy and too few livings in the years before the Black Death, assistant priests could be had for small wages. But in the priest-scarce times of the plague, when their services were needed more urgently then ever before, some of these priests bartered their ministry of the sacraments for a more liveable wage, an advantage that bishops like Hethe of Rochester and Edington of Winchester found deplorable. Their outrage was joined to the archbishop's in a decree carrying full metropolitan authority. In the decree *Effrenata* issued 28 May 1350, Archbishop Simon Islip ordered the wages of all stipendiaries to be fixed in conformity with the minimum set by the Council of Oxford in 1222.[65] The archbishop further rebuked those priests, evidently great in number, who were exacting more money than was customary for spiritual services such as burials and Masses for the dead. Not only were their tactics self-seeking and scandalous for the avarice that was manifest, but the clergy were offering a dangerous example to other labourers who had begun to weary of their lot in life.[66]

The decrees of bishops like Islip, Edington and Hethe against clerical opportunists were difficult to enforce, and the tendency for the clergy to take advantage of desperate situations would provoke subsequent pronouncements from their superiors. Chantry chaplains who had been employed for the service of an altar and the daily singing of Masses *pro defunctis* (for the dead) found a steady market for part-time ministry in the post-plague Church and, in opposition to the intent of *Effrenata*, often charged whatever they could get away with. Others simply refused to involve themselves in the daily activities of a cure of souls. After the plague of 1361, Archbishop Thoresby of York ordered a chantry chaplain to comply with the wishes of his rector that he help shoulder the burden of the cure in these desperate times. The chaplain had been promised a fair wage by the rector of Hotham but still refused to assist in services other than the ones that strictly pertained to his chantry.[67] There were clerics who thought little of searching the rubble of the post-plague Church for advantage, promotion and gain, but it was hardly a time of prosperity for most clergy. The expectations of their pastoral labour were unchanged:

though congregations were smaller in size, the need of the few for ministry, leadership in prayer and the many other daily activities that comprised the pastoral care were still as great if not more so in the years that followed the plague. And there were fewer clergy to carry out these duties, fewer available from the thinned ranks of the clerical proletariat, fewer who would work for poor wages. There were almost universal complaints that parishes that were once modest curacies had fallen into poverty. In the years that followed the plague curates would petition local authorities for canonical changes in the status of their churches or for augmentation of their revenues. Those with fixed incomes, like most rectors and vicars, often fared worse in the years after the plague than some of their wage-earning associates. As tithe-offerings declined in the years when the crops failed or in time of plague, so too did parish revenues. In some places parishes were united as there were too few parishioners and too little income to support the necessities of one curate, let alone two. Vicars whose portions were small in the years before the plague suffered even more acutely in the economic troubles that followed. As a curate's income was less from the offerings of fewer or poorer parishioners, the portion or revenues of the place were accordingly smaller. Less could be done in many churches, less in terms of feeding the poor and offering hospitality to travellers, less in renewing and enhancing the church, less even in keeping the church fabric in simple repair.

What happened in the parishes also occurred in the larger institutions of the diocese. Monastic houses applied for church appropriations in order to augment their income; bishops did the same for households and estates that had suffered the depredations of the plague.[68] After 1350 plague was a regular factor in the petitions of parishes and monasteries seeking an increase in their revenues. And since they relied on parish revenues as the means for their financial improvement, the plight of those parishes could not have been much lessened, thereby increasing the anxieties of parish communities to the advantage of higher authorities. Thus, what was in some ways a merely financial relationship between a monastery or the bishop and a parish church became in some cases a cause of further tension and resentment.

Even chantries which had drawn a number of parish priests away from their cures were beginning to decline in value after 1350. Those that were attached to endowments of land or tenements suffered the same encroaching poverty that troubled other landowners.[69] In 1377, after the accumulated effects of three national epidemics, Bishop John Gilbert of Hereford formally united two chantries in the church of Ross 'on account of the plagues'. One of the chantries had been established by John of Ross, the other by a parish guild or confraternity, but by the mid-1370s the lands attached to both chantries had so declined in their value that the two had to be consolidated into a single chantry.[70] It was the lack of available and competent priests rather than economics that forced Bishop Stretton of Coventry and Lichfield to revise the statutes for a chantry in Chesterfield in 1365. Chaplains were so scarce that it was 'not easy to find an honest, circumspect and literate person in priest's orders to whom the cure and rule of the aforesaid chantry might be committed'. So the bishop reduced the requirements for residency, ceremonial attendance, financial management of the chantry and routines governing prayer. So needed was a priest for the chantry that the old stipulation that he should not be seen at all in taverns was relaxed to the encouragement that he not visit them on a regular basis.[71]

Due to the economic flux of those decades, poverty was a chronic concern in pastoral care and parochial administration. The economic bases on which parishes were built shifted to some degree in the readjustments of local communities to changing markets. Parishes simply could not afford to hire as many clergy as they once had or build up the church fabric as most parishioners wanted. And there were always the cases of a more wilful neglect and indifference where available resources were hoarded or diverted from their intended places like chancel and nave.

In a Church where there were simply far fewer priests than in previous decades, minor clerics and what service they could provide were in steady demand. By long tradition, parishes were encouraged to have an acolyte on his way through orders, a holy-water clerk, often called in the records of the time *aquabajulus*, who was to assist the curate in a variety of ways – bearing holy water as his title implied, but also candles in processions and ringing church bells as required. Late in the fourteenth century William Courtenay, the archbishop of Canterbury, urged the restoration of this office and the stipend attached to it. The matter was spiritual as well as vocational. Holy water, the archbishop wrote, 'is the Christian's armour against the wiles and deceits of demons' and the diminishment of clerks who assisted in this spiritual campaign was a matter of grave concern.[72] Parishioners bemoaned the loss as well. An episcopal visitation in Hereford in 1397 turned up a few complaints about the absence of minor clerics in parish churches. Parishioners in Leominster asked for a cleric who would ring the bells and carry a lit candle before the priest on his house calls to the sick. The rector of Wistanstow was derelict in his duty to provide for a deacon at his church and the pastor at Pontesbury was similarly at fault for not hiring a deacon or a clerk to read the lessons at Mass and ring the church bells.[73]

This dearth of clerics to provide services promised by the Church or requested by the people brings us to the question of how able were those men who did seek orders and positions in pastoral cures. There were certainly witnesses in the later Middle Ages to the generally disappointing quality of parish clergy. A Leicestershire canon of the late fourteenth century, Henry Knighton, complained about the lack of competent clergy. He pointed to the easy influx of men at the time of the Black Death whose only qualification seemed to be their availability. These were widowers who lacked learning, and even if they showed some basic competence in letters, they could not possess the pastoral sense that comes with a clerical education and parish experience.[74] Langland's laughable portrait of the parish priest as Sloth seems to confirm his contemporary's judgement: 'I'd rather hear a racy tale, or about the summer sports of cobblers, Or laugh at lies about my neighbour, Than anything that Mark, Matthew, John, or Luke wrote.'[75] John Gower was reminiscent of better pastors from a bygone era in contrast to the uninspiring preachers of his own day.[76] Church leaders less inclined to wistful recollections did see the pressing need for better-educated clergy in the world of the late fourteenth and fifteenth centuries. Bishops Bateman of Norwich, Wykeham of Winchester and Islip of Canterbury all tried to address the problem with their foundations at Oxford and Cambridge. Their efforts were directed at offsetting the intellectual poverty that had come with the deaths of 'learned and wise men' after the plagues of 1349, 1361 and 1369.[77]

There can be little doubt that the sea-change which occurred in Church and society after the Black Death affected the quality as well as the number of clergy in pastoral cures. But it is also tempting to assign the criticisms implicit in the above writers to all parish clergy. Certainly, there were inept pastors in Langland's day, and Gower's appeal to better preaching was not baseless. But one can also say with a measure of confidence, thus it has always been. Before we offer conclusions about the quality of pastors in the later Middle Ages, we need to acknowledge a few important aspects of what comprised standards of pastoral preparation and execution in the later Middle Ages.

Clerical standards were always difficult to enforce in the Middle Ages because they were difficult to define in any universal way. With respect to preparation for the cure of souls, the canonical tradition was consistent: for a man to be ordained to the priesthood he had to be of sufficient age and learning, morally upright and free from any impediment, physical or spiritual, that would interfere with his ministry.[78] What was meant by sufficient learning was never really articulated in the law, but it was up to the examining prelate at ordination to determine how learned his future pastors needed to be in the churches they were likely to govern. There is a further point regarding pastoral literacy: the candidate had to be *diligens*, not *exquisita* in learning, which meant that he needed a certain basis on which to build. Canonists like the late-fourteenth-century Cambridge chancellor John de Burgh described this foundation as a two-fold knowledge, the *scientia* of letters required for a priest to read and understand the Latin of the Mass, the teachings of the Church and the statutes of his diocese, and the *virtus* of his own Christian faith. He had to have a proper moral life that would enable him to grow spiritually and to preach as much in the manner of his living as in the words he may have offered from the pulpit.[79]

Thus Henry Knighton may not have been exaggerating when he commented on an influx of unlearned men after the Black Death. While there are no references in bishops' registers to exceptions being made to the general standards of literacy in examinations for orders, there were plenty of occasions when indults from minority of age or illegitimacy were sought from the papacy by ecclesiastical authorities.[80] With the immediate and pressing need for parish clergy in the wake of the plague, bishops may have made acts of faith regarding the men they were ordaining or appropriated a blunt pragmatism that regarded the placement of priests in parishes as a prior claim on their pastoral leadership. If there was a conscious decision to moderate conventional standards of learning, it does not figure in the memoranda or official records of the time. And if the introduction of less able men was viewed as an unfortunate necessity in the hasty requirements of the moment, a change had been initiated which the subsequent and repeated outbreaks of plague would make difficult to reverse. Institutionally speaking, until the mid-fourteenth century bishops were constantly faced with a deficit of clergy in most of the parishes in their dioceses, especially the poorer benefices.

Compounding this situation was the fact that traditional means of acquiring that *scientia* needed for sound pastoral leadership were less available after the mid-fourteenth century. The modest scholarship that once accompanied the parish office of holy-water clerk had all but disappeared as an educational opportunity for aspiring clerical candidates by the late fourteenth century. Cathedral schools like the one in Hereford, once lustrous for its reputation in the sciences, suffered from the lack of vigilance and leadership on the part of the cathedral chapter.[81] The lofty designs behind Boniface VIII's educational reform decree *Cum ex eo* had diminished to the basic needs for clerical residency in parish churches. The terms of the decree had required the rector who anticipated a study leave to find and hire a vicar for the period of his leave. But both suitable vicars and the means to support them were less easy to come by after 1350. Bishops were also less inclined to grant leaves of absence at this time.[82] Pastors were more likely to benefit from the expanding library of pastoral literature in the fourteenth and fifteenth centuries. Heftier and broadly inclusive *summae* like William of Pagula's *Oculus sacerdotis* (*c.*1320–3) and John de Burgh's *Pupilla oculi* (1384) were popular sources of pastoral lore through the end of the period. But there were also the lesser handbooks that provided summaries of what a pastor should know and what his people should learn from him. In the thirteenth century these had been exemplified by Bishop Quivel's *summula* or Archbishop Pecham's syllabus of essential pastoral learning. By the fifteenth century these were increasingly available and often in vernacular translations for the readier reference of parish priests.[83]

Whether the clergy read those texts or availed themselves of whatever educational opportunity was within reach is impossible to say. While there are no indications in official records of the time that standards in testing literacy or assessing what was meant by moral uprightness were lowered, it is likely that there was a gradual accommodation on the part of ecclesiastical superiors to the changes in pastoral institutions and anticipated groups of clerical candidates. For all of this, the language of pastoral ministry and the worthiness of the priest remained lofty throughout the period. In a vernacular sermon of the late fourteenth or early fifteenth century, one preacher offered Basil the Great's image of the priesthood as pertinent for his own age:

> A priest's office contains great dignity. It is performed on earth but its minister is heavenly. This office of priesthood can be performed by no ordinary man, nor even by an angel or an archangel; no other creature can do it unless by the infinite goodness of Almighty God himself. He made the office of priesthood so perfect that no angel ever attained such a high, perfect office.[84]

It is significant to the state of pastoral care in the later Middle Ages that this sermon with its fantastic language about the priesthood might have been preached near the time when another priest John Ball was rallying the peasants to rebellion or Wycliffite preachers were describing an egalitarian priesthood of all believers. At no time in the Middle Ages was pastoral care uniformly exercised or its ministers drawn from a single type. Indeed, there were plenty of references in late mediaeval records to unlearned clerics who fumbled at their Latin or were notorious loiterers at village taverns. But it was also the nature of these records to note problems to be solved rather than commendable actions to be praised.[85] This is not an appeal from the indicting images of poets and ecclesiastics – there were plenty of occasions in the later Middle Ages when men who had found their way to pastoral cures were shown as patently unqualified for the work they did or did not do. And much of this can be attributable to a gradual erosion of pastoral excellence, perhaps as much on the part of those men who presided at clerical examinations and ordinations as those who passed through the widening filters of scrutiny.

From the perspective of the early thirteenth century there was much to be done in the reform of the Church and much of this required careful attention to pastoral care. The Fourth Lateran Council drew up an agenda which, if completed, would have approached the kind of reform longed for by men like Innocent III and Robert Grosseteste. But they and their contemporaries were also aware of the realities in the Church of their age: universalist appeals could only be approximated in their local implementation. For decades after the council, the English Church convened in synods and assemblies to hammer out in meaningful ways the general designs of Lateran IV. The statutes and decrees that followed touched upon every aspect of pastoral care – the education of the clergy, the nature of the parish, the rights and obligations of the clergy and laity alike, and the jurisdictional claims of church courts, to name but a few. Clearly, some of these measures were less contested or more realized or even more necessary than others, but the general movement in pastoral developments in the thirteenth century was forward.

By the middle of the fourteenth century, that impetus was interrupted and perhaps changed forever in the range of effects radiating from the Black Death and subsequent epidemics. It was not that reform was completely forgotten; the fourteenth and fifteenth centuries had their own animating force in this respect. But there was an obvious deterioration of traditional structures and institutions that contemporaries realized had to be confronted. As David Herlihy wrote of this decline, it 'was never so deep as to stifle awareness of decline'.[86]

At the same time, it is tempting to see a radical departure from pastoral traditions after the mid-fourteenth century. To be sure, there were monumental changes in that century and a half. The institutions, customs and conventions of pastoral care had all been stunned in the course of the Black Death, and in its wake had been hampered by the unsuccessful attempts to regain lost stability. The same disruptions caused by the first plague were to be borne over and over again. Patterns of recruitment to the clerical life and pastoral care had declined through the rest of the century and would not regain something of their pre-plague levels until later in the fifteenth century. And those who did appear for ordination and subsequently sought placement in a church were not always, according to their contemporaries, fit for the pastoral office. But the movement was not all in one direction; there were changes in Church and society, some of them initiated by the first or far-ranging effects of the plagues, that revealed some degree of growth, even vigour, in spiritual and pastoral concerns. The mystical literature of the later fourteenth century and the widely popular guides to dying well (*ars bene moriendi*) in the fifteenth gave voice to a potent spirituality among the clergy and laity of the later Middle Ages. The rise of lay confraternities and parish guilds at this time also indicated a material and spiritual investment in chantry foundations, the pastoral care that accompanied them and the devotional activities of the collective that reached into the communities around them.[87]

Despite the many changes required of it, the Church in the later Middle Ages clung to traditional notions of pastoral care. As long as there was sin a priest would be needed to absolve people of their transgressions. The pastoral literature through the end of the Middle Ages maintained a traditionally strong emphasis on this reality. Indeed, it is interesting to mark how little change occurs within the pastoral literature regarding descriptions of what a priest should know and do. As for the consistently unpredictable quality of clerical candidates and the pastors many of them became, this was attributed in large measure to the basically local character of the late mediaeval Church. What was expected of curates in London did not always apply to pastors in remotest Cornwall. Bishops were given considerable latitude in determining what was needed for the churches and people of their own dioceses. This was evident in the local perspectives that often governed the examination of clergy at ordination and subsequent enquiries at an institution to a pastoral benefice. Until the sixteenth century when a more distinctly clerical culture emerged from the seminaries, the mediaeval practitioners of the art of arts would always be men diverse in background, education, learning and life. And that diversity was bound to affect the cure of souls for better and for worse.

Notes

1. J. Raine (ed.), *Historical Papers from the Northern Registers*, Rolls Series, 61 (London, 1873), pp. 395–7.
2. Lateran IV, c. 22 in Norman P. Tanner (ed.), *Decrees of the Ecumenical Councils* (London and Washington, 1990), vol. 1, p. 246; Richard Palmer, 'The Church, Leprosy and Plague in Medieval and Early Modern Europe', in W.J. Shiels (ed.), *The Church and Healing*, Studies in Church History, 19 (Oxford, 1982), pp. 79–99.
3. A. H. Thompson, 'The Registers of John Gynewell, Bishop of Lincoln, for the years 1347–1350', *Archaeological Journal* 68 (1911), pp. 309–10; Philip Ziegler, *The Black Death* (London, 1969), pp. 123–4.
4. Rosemary Horrox (ed.), *The Black Death* (Manchester, 1994), p. 117.
5. *The Register of John de Grandisson, Bishop of Exeter (A.D. 1327–1369)*, ed. F. C. Hingeston-Randolph, pt. 2: *1331–1360* (London and Exeter, 1897), p. 1069; *Reqistrum Johannis de Trillek, episcopi Herefordensis, 1344–1361*, ed. J. H. Parry, Canterbury and York Society, 8 (1912), p. 139.
6. *Cum satis*, X (= Decretals of Gregory IX) 1.23.4; G. Franzen, 'The Tradition of Medieval Canon Law' in *The Sacrament of Holy Orders. Some Papers and Discussions concerning Holy Orders at a Session of the Centre de Pastorale Liturgique, 1955* (London, 1962), p. 211.
7. Lateran IV, c. 21; Tanner, *Decrees*, vol. 1, p. 245. See also Leonard E. Boyle, 'Aspects of Clerical Education in Fourteenth-Century England', in Paul E. Szarmach and Bernard S. Levy (eds), *The Fourteenth Century* (Binghamton, N.Y. 1977), pp. 19–32.
8. The *Summula* for the diocese of Exeter (1240 and 1287); F. M. Powicke and C. R. Cheney (eds), *Councils and Synods With Other Documents Relating to the English Church*, vol. 2. (Oxford, 1964), pp. 1060–77; for a translation of the *Summula* and further description of Quivel's authorship, see John R. Shinners and William Dohar (eds), *Pastors and the Care of Souls in Medieval England*, (Notre Dame, Ind., 1998), pp. 170–85. In his manual for inquisitors, Bernard Gui OP echoed the tradition when he urged the inquisitor to be 'like a prudent physician of souls' enquiring into all the circumstances regarding the person being questioned. See the excerpt from Gui's *Practica inquisitionis heretice pravitatis* in W. L. Wakefield, *Heresies of the High Middle Ages* (New York, 1969), p. 378. For the earlier tradition of the *Christus medicus*, see Carole Rawcliffe, *Medicine and Society in Later Medieval England* (Stroud, 1995), pp. 17–21.

196 William J. Dohar

9. Joseph Goering, 'The Changing Face of the Village Parish: The Thirteenth Century', in J. Ambrose Raftis (ed.), *Pathways to Medieval Peasants* (Toronto, 1981). See also the requirements for clerical attire outlined in Archbishop John Stratford's constitutions from 1342 in E. Cutts, *Parish Priests and their People in the Middle Ages in England* (London, 1898), pp. 164–6.
10. Archbishop Pecham's *Ignorantia sacerdotum* (1281) was a compilation of pastoral lore which every curate should know in order to teach his parishioners the essentials of the faith. Powicke and Cheney, *Councils and Synods*, vol. 2, pp. 900–5.
11. For some earlier evidence of the decree's use, see John R. Shinners, 'University Study Licences and Clerical Education in the Diocese of Norwich, 1327–35', *History of Education Quarterly* 28 (1988), pp. 387–410.
12. The Legatine Council of London (1237) required that official lists of approved candidates be kept among the bishop's records. See Powicke and Cheney, *Councils and Synods*, vol. 2, p. 248 and William J. Dohar, 'Medieval Ordination Lists: The Origins of a Record', *Archives* 20 (1992), pp. 17–35.
13. See, for example, T. H. Hollingworth's calculations for plague mortality in *Historical Demography* (London, 1964), p. 385, and John Hatcher, *Plague, Population and the English Economy, 1348–1530* (London, 1977), ch. 2.
14. J. C. Russell, *British Medieval Population* (Albuquerque, 1948), p. 216; J. Z. Titow, *English Rural Society 1200–1350* (London, 1969), pp. 66–73, believes Russell's figures are far too low.
15. F. M. Page, *The Estates of Crowland Abbey* (Cambridge, 1934), p. 121; M. Beresford, *The Lost Villages of England* (London, 1954), p. 159.
16. P. Ziegler, *The Black Death* (London, 1969), pp. 144, 153–4; *Victoria County History* Wiltshire, iv, p. 39.
17. E. Fryde, 'The Tenants of the Bishops of Coventry and Lichfield and of Worcester After the Plague of 1348–9', in R. Hunisett and J. B. Post (eds), *Medieval Legal Records* (London, 1978), pp. 229, 230.
18. A. G. Little, 'The Black Death in Lancashire', *English Historical Review* 5 (1890), p. 525.
19. *Calendar of Entries in the Papal Registers relating to Great Britain and Ireland: Petitions to the Pope A.D. 1342–1419*, ed. W. H. Bliss (London, 1896), vol. 1, 234; E. M. Thompson, *The Carthusian Order in England* (London, 1897), pp. 167–75. Robert of Avesbury stated that nearly 200 people were buried daily from the chapel at Smithfield from early February to early April 1349. Robert of Avesbury, *De gestis*, ed. E. M. Thompson, Rolls Series (London, 1889), p. 407. Cf. Ziegler, *Black Death*, pp. 162–4.
20. Ziegler, *Black Death*, pp. 176–7, 188.
21. *Chronicon Henrici Knighton*, ed. J. R. Lumby, Rolls Series, 92 (London, 1889–95), vol. 2, p. 61.
22. The original study by J. Lunn, 'The Black Death in the Bishops' Registers' (Cambridge, Ph.D. thesis, 1937) was lost years ago, but its figures are often used as a general guide to clerical mortality during the Black Death. The salient parts of Lunn's work were summarized by G. G. Coulton in *Medieval*

Panorama: The English Scene from Conquest to Reformation (Cambridge, 1938), pp. 495–500, 747–50 and, later, debated by J. F. D. Shrewsbury, *A History of the Bubonic Plague in the British Isles* (Cambridge, 1970), pp. 54–125.

23. A. H. Thompson, 'The Pestilence of the Fourteenth Century in the Diocese of York', *Archaeological Journal* 71 (1914), p. 152.
24. A. H. Thompson, 'Registers of Gynewell', p. 322. It should be kept in mind that mortality occurred unevenly in the various regions of a diocese. For instance, there was only a 15 per cent recorded rate of mortality in Lincoln's Hitchin deanery while 60 per cent of the beneficed clergy died in Wycombe.
25. R. A. Davies, 'The Effect of the Black Death on the Parish Priests of the Medieval Diocese of Coventry and Lichfield', *Historical Research* 62 (1989), pp. 86–7.
26. W. J. Dohar, *The Black Death and Pastoral Leadership: the Diocese of Hereford in the Fourteenth Century* (Philadelphia, 1995), pp. 45–9.
27. Between 1 April and 6 August 1349, 139 beneficed clerics are known to have died, at least one-third of all beneficed clerics in the diocese: R. M. Haines, 'Wolstan de Bransford, Prior and Bishop of Worcester, *c.*1280–1349', *University of Birmingham Historical Journal* 8 (1962), p. 111. For Gloucester, see *Victoria County History*, Gloucestershire, ii, p. 19.
28. Ziegler, *Black Death*, p. 140.
29. Shrewsbury, *Bubonic Plague*, p. 90; Ziegler, *Black Death*, p. 151.
30. F. A. Gasquet, *The Black Death of 1348 and 1349* (London, 1897, 1908), p. 149; A. A. Jessop, *The Coming of the Friars and Other Historic Essays* (London, 1895; repr. 1908), pp. 166–261.
31. From Stephen Birchington's *Vitae Archiepiscoporum Cantuariensium* as in Ziegler, *Black Death*, p. 164.
32. *The Vision of William concerning 'Piers the Plowman'*, ed. Walter Skeat, EETS o.s., 38 (Oxford, 1869), vol. 1, p. 4 (B-text, 11. 83–6) modernized here.
33. A. K. McHardy (ed.), *The Church in London 1375–1392*, London Record Society, 13 (London, 1977), p. ix.
34. Ada E. Levett, 'A Note on the Statute of Labourers', *Economic History Review* 4 (1932), pp. 77–80.
35. Coulton, *Medieval Panorama*, pp. 497–8.
36. R. M. Clay, *The Medieval Hospitals of England* (London, 1909), pp. 24, 42–3.
37. David Knowles and R. Neville Hadcock (eds.), *Medieval Religious Houses, England and Wales* (London, 1953), pp. 309, 313.
38. John Myrk, *Instructions for Parish Priests*, ed. E. Peacock, EETS o.s., 31 (London, 1868), pp. 53–4, 57–9.
39. R. S. France, 'A History of Plague in Lancashire', *Transactions of the Historical Society of Lancashire and Cheshire* 90 (1938), p. 24.
40. *Calendar*, vol. 1, p. 234; Thompson, *Carthusian Order*, pp. 167–75. Robert of Avesbury stated that nearly two hundred people were buried daily from the chapel at Smithfield from early February to April in 1349: Avesbury, *De gestis*, p. 407.
41. *Register of Roger de Norbury, Bishop of Lichfield and Coventry, 1322–58*, ed.

Bishop E. Hobhouse, William Salt Archaeological Society, *Collections*, 1 (Birmingham, 1880), pp. 277–8.
42. T. R. Nash, *Collections for the History of Worcestershire* (London, 1871–2), vol. 1, p. 226.
43. W. G. Hoskins, *Devon* (London, 1954), p. 169.
44. William de Dene, *Historia Rossensis* (1314–50 with continuation to 1540) ed. Henry Wharton, *Anglia sacra sive collectio historiarum de archiepiscopis et episcopis Angliae ad annum 1540* (London 1691), vol. i, p. 376.
45. *Req. Edyndon*, vol. 2, ff. 17b–18; Gasquet, *The Black Death*, p. 126.
46. *Req. Edington*, vol. 2, f. 19; Gasquet, *The Black Death*, p. 127.
47. *Victoria County History*, Staffordshire, vol. 2, p. 39; *Req. Trillek*, pp. 19–21.
48. David Wilkins, *Concilia Magnae Brittaniae et Hiberniae* (London, 1737), vol. 2, pp. 745–6.
49. Ziegler, *The Black Death*, p. 129.
50. J. Viard (ed.), 'La mess pour la peste', *Bibliothèque de l'Ecole des Chartes* 61 (1900), pp. 334–8.
51. Fryde, 'Tenants of Coventry and Lichfield', p. 228.
52. William de Dene, *Historia Roffensis* as in Horrox, *The Black Death*, p. 72.
53. R. A. Browne, *British Latin Selections AD 500–1400* (Oxford, 1954), p. 127.
54. Gasquet, *The Black Death*, p. 157; *Req. Trillek*, pp. 174–6.
55. *Anonimalle Chronicle*, ed. V. H. Galbraith (Manchester, 1927), p. 50; Shrewsbury, *Bubonic Plague*, p. 128.
56. Robert Gottfried, *The Black Death: Natural and Human Disaster in Medieval Europe* (New York, 1983), pp. 131-3. 'Such national outbreaks are, in any case, far from being the whole story. Work is accumulating to show that many manors and religious houses experienced abnormal mortality levels about once every decade in the two centuries after the plague's arrival – although plague may not have been the culprit in every case' (Horrox, *The Black Death*, pp. 11–12).
57. R. L. Storey, 'Recruitment of English Clergy in the Period of the Conciliar Movement', *Annuarium Historiae Conciliorum* 7 (1975), p. 304. See also R. K. Rose, 'Priests and Patrons in the Fourteenth Century Diocese of Carlisle', in *The Church in Town and Countryside*, Studies in Church History, 16 (Oxford, 1979), pp. 207–18 and JoAnn Hoeppner Moran, 'Clerical Recruitment in the Diocese of York, 1340–1530: Data and Commentary', *Journal of Ecclesiastical History* 34 (1983), pp. 19–54.
58. 'Masses to be Said in Time of Plague', in Horrox, *The Black Death*, p. 123.
59. *Registrum Hamonis Hethe*, vol. 2, pp. 1044–50.
60. Virginia Davis, 'Rivals for Ministry? Ordinations of Secular and Regular Clergy in Southern England *c.*1300–1500', *Studies in Church History* 26 (1989), pp. 101–3. Davis also finds rising trends in the ordinations of regular clergy as those for seculars diminish. See also by the same author, *William Waynflete: Bishop and Educationalist* (Woodbridge, 1993), p. 25.
61. Gasquet, *The Black Death*, pp. 241–2.
62. Moran, 'Clerical Recruitment', pp. 22–3.
63. Dohar, *The Black Death*, pp. 91–103.

64. Coulton, *Medieval Panorama*, p. 499.
65. Wilkins, *Concilia*, vol. 3, pp. 1–2.
66. The text of the decree was copied into Trillek's register: *Req. Trillek*, pp. 157–9.
67. *Req. Thoresby*, BI, Reg. 11, f. 204b. See also, A. H. Thompson, *The English Clergy* (Oxford, 1947) p. 144.
68. R. A. R. Hartridge, *A History of Vicarages in the Middle Ages* (Cambridge, 1930), pp. 108–10. See also the various petitions from bishops and monastic heads in petitions to the Pope: *Calendar*, vol. 1, pp. 228 (Lincoln diocese), 195 (Worcester diocese), 282 (Reading Abbey).
69. K. Wood-Legh, *Perpetual Chantries* (Cambridge, 1965), pp. 93–129.
70. *Req. Gilbert*, p. 2.
71. Amendment of statutes governing a chantry, 1365, in Horrox, *The Black Death*, pp. 304–6.
72. 'Decretum ... contra male decimantes', Wilkins, *Concilia*, vol. 3, p. 220.
73. A. T. Bannister, 'Visitation Returns in the Diocese of Hereford in 1397', *EHR* (1930), pp. 99, 452, 462.
74. *Chronicon Henrici Knighton*, vol. 1, pp. 61–4.
75. *The Vision of William concerning Piers the Plowman*, p. 166, modernized here by John Shinners in Shinners and Dohar, *Pastors*, p. 26.
76. G. R. Owst, *Preaching in Medieval England* (Cambridge, 1926), p. 26.
77. W. A. Pantin, *Canterbury College, Oxford*, Oxford Historical Society n.s., 8 (1950), vol. 3, p. 159; Ziegler, *Black Death*, pp. 262–3. Lucas Wadding made similar complaints about declining standards of admission among mendicant friaries from the fourteenth century. L. Wadding, *Annales Minorum*, vol. 8: 1347–1376 (Florence), p. 25.
78. *Distinctio* 24, c. 5.
79. John de Burgh, *Pupilla Oculi* (London, edn of 1516), lib. 7, ch. 4.
80. See, for instance *Calendar*, vol. 1, 178, 179 for petitions from Archbishops Islip of Canterbury and Zouche of York to dispense clerical candidates in their dioceses from minority of age and illegitimacy.
81. Dohar, *The Black Death*, pp. 122–3.
82. Ibid., pp. 120–6.
83. See, for example, John Myrk's *Instructions*, a rhymed vernacular translation of a portion of William of Pagula's *summa*, and 'A York Priest's Notebook', a brief Latin collection of priest-lore from the north of England in Roy M. Haines (ed.), *Ecclesia Anglicana: Studies in the English Church in the Later Middle Ages* (Toronto, 1989), pp. 163–77. For the circulation of these texts among parish priests, see John R. Shinners, 'Parish Libraries in Medieval England', in Jacqueline Brown and William P. Stoneman (eds), *A Distinct Voice: Medieval Studies in Honor of Leonard E. Boyle* (Notre Dame, Ind., 1977), pp. 207–30.
84. Woodburn O. Ross (ed.), *Middle English Sermons*, EETS o.s., 209 (1940), p. 280, modernized by J. Shinners, in Shinners and Dohar, *Pastors*, p. 15.
85. See for example the many unflattering references to inept pastors in Bannister, 'Visitation Returns', *passim*, and the visitations of 1391 and 1394

in *The Register of John Waltham. Bishop of Salisbury 1388–1395*, ed. T. C. B. Timmins, The Canterbury and York Society, 80 (Woodbridge, 1994), pp. 113–68.
86. David Herlihy, *The Black Death and the Transformation of the West* (Cambridge, Mass., 1977), p. 59.
87. Clive Burgess, 'For the Increase of Divine Service: Chantries in the Parish in Late Medieval Bristol', *Journal of Ecclesiastical History* 36 (1985), pp. 46–65; C. Barron, 'The Parish Fraternities of Medieval London', in C. Barron and C. Harper-Bill (eds), *The Church in Pre-Reformation Society: Essays in Honour of E. R. H. Du Boulay* (Woodbridge, 1985), pp. 13–17.

Bibliography

Barron, C. and C. Harper-Bill, *The Church in Pre-Reformation Society: Essays in Honour of E. R. H. DuBoulay* (Woodbridge, 1985)

Boyle, Leonard E, *Pastoral Care, Clerical Education and Canon Law, 1200–1400* (London, 1981)

Davis, Virginia, 'Rivals for Ministry? Ordinations of Secular and Regular Clergy in Southern England c.1300–1500', *Studies in Church History*, 26, ed. W. J. Shiels and Diana Wood (Oxford, 1989), pp. 99–109

Haines, Roy M., *Ecclesia Anglicana: Studies in the English Church in the Later Middle Ages* (Toronto, 1989)

Pantin, W. A., *The English Church in the Fourteenth Century* (Cambridge, 1955)

Shinners, John and William J. Dohar, *Pastors and the Care of Souls in Medieval England* (Notre Dame, Ind., 1998)

Swanson, R. N., *Catholic England: Faith, Religion, and Observance before the Reformation* (Manchester, 1993)

10

Catechesis in East and West

Lambros Kamperidis

In the Greek part of Christendom catechesis was understood and practised as a stage of initiation into the mysteries of the Church. Its oral nature was very much tied to its aural qualities. Etymologically *catechesis* has a direct reference to *echos*, or sound, and implies the transformation of a catechumen into a receptacle receiving the sounds that are deposited in his soul through the words of the catechist. The catechumen is, literally, a sounding-board resonating and vibrating not only with the words of his instructor-catechist, but with the *logos* of the unique instructor, the Word of God. In the Greek sources the words *catechesis* and *logos* are inseparable.[1] John Chrysostom describes the catechumen who has not yet been baptized as an empty receptacle to be restored to its function by the instructors,[2] and immediately he quotes the relevant passage from the Gospel where the one who is building his house upon a rock is likened to a wise man who has *heard* Christ's words and has acted accordingly. All this, of course, is the result of the auditory nature of teaching, to which Chrysostom, in his *Baptismal Catechesis*, refers frequently when he urges his audience to lend their ears to what he is saying; to hear,[3] that is, in the same way that Christ exhorted his listeners to do when he concluded his teaching with the proverbial 'He who has ears to hear, let him hear.'[4]

All teaching in antiquity was 'acousmatic' ('for the hearing'), and the audience was anything but passive. There were live exchanges between the speaker and the hearer; the participatory mood of the audience, the vivid interventions coming from the public, the spontaneous applause and loud cheering, all constituted a valid measure of the public's appreciation regarding the message being received.

Catechesis and baptism

In the Greek part of the world catechesis was also understood as a mystagogical experience. It led to the mystery of baptism.

The process of catechesis, from a Greek perspective, may be summed up as follows: God spoke; creation was the catechesis, that is, the resonance of his Word. God revealed his hidden mystery; mystagogical catechesis leading to the mystery of fulfilment was the resonance of God's Word in his creature. The creature's response, the fulfilment of the mystery, now through sacramental initiation, is the fulfilment of God's salvific plan for the world.

Cyril of Jerusalem calls those who are undergoing initiation *photizomenoi*, illumined, and those who have been baptized *neophotistoi*, newly illumined. There is no other area, either of darkness or of twilight, for God's creatures to live, except this resplendent area, in this state of being illumined in the light of God's presence. All that is required, in the catechetical context, is to attune one's inner life to that resonating principle, to allow oneself to assume a truly hearing disposition, open to the Word of God.

For this mystery to be truly effective Cyril of Jerusalem demands from the catechumens two conditions: that their decision to be catechized is one of free will and that it is done for an authentic, true motive. If these conditions are not met the Holy Spirit does not act and the grace of the sacrament remains ineffective.[5]

According to Cyril of Jerusalem, this is the ultimate will of God worked in humanity through the agency of the catechist, who initiates the catechumen into the mysteries of Christ. The catechist's role is to bring into play the synergy that potentially exists between the three participants:

> to me belongs the act of saying, to you the deliberate choice, to God the completion and fulfilment. Let us activate boldly the intellect, exert and strain the soul, prepare the heart. We run the race for the sake of our souls; we set our hopes on things eternal.[6]

Catechetical instruction, through its liturgical and didactic character, acquires a pastoral significance guiding the spiritual life of the faithful. It is for this reason that Cyril gives to his *Catecheses* the attribute 'mystagogical'; they truly 'lead' the adept 'to the mysteries' of the Church through the gate of baptism, the first sacrament in the transformed life of 'the new creature'.

One of the important works of early Christianity, offering some uncommon views on the 'pedagogical' nature of catechism, is the *Pedagogue* of Clement of Alexandria, director of the catechetical school of the same city. The true mission of the unique Pedagogue, Christ the incarnate Logos, is revealed by Clement to be that of a teacher (*didaskalos*), who is leading his unformed pupils from ignorance, associated with tender age, to the knowledge of his wisdom.

In our pedagogical relation to our teacher and instructor we are like children. God is concealing this life-giving knowledge from the wise and prudent and reveals it unto babes (Luke 10.21). A first stage of catechesis is the nourishing milk (1 Cor. 3.3) of kerygma leading to the true knowledge, which comes with the solid food of eucharist, that is, faith based on the foundation of catechesis.

In the Eastern Church the scope of catechism as an initiatory stage in the life of the new Christian was gradually abandoned as infant baptism became widespread in the fourth and fifth centuries. This does not imply that the mystagogical nature of the catechetical experience diminished in importance or intensity; rather, it was incorporated in the ecclesiastical offices and found a new expression in the theological nature of the Orthodox liturgy. Catechetical instruction, in the form that was practised in the West, was not introduced in the Orthodox Church until the seventeenth century and only gained acceptance by the end of the eighteenth century. There is a strong link connecting the atrophy, or even the abandonment, of formal catechetical instruction of adults with infant baptism, and with the consolidation of liturgical forms in the Orthodox Church.

The liturgy was modelled on the much-loved ritual of the ancient theatre. The choir replaced the ancient 'chorus' and it was called by that very name, *choros*, in the liturgical setting. The *templum*, or chancel, which later evolved into the elaborate *iconostasis*, with its royal doors and the deacon's entrance on both sides serving as *ingressus* and *exitus*, clearly evoked the *proscenium* and the *parascenia*. The elevated ambo from which the word of God was proclaimed was surely the substitute of the raised *logeion* – *pulpitum* in the Roman theatre – from which the actors addressed the audience. An even more elevated platform in the upper part of the *scene* of the ancient theatre, on which appeared gods, was appropriately called the *theologeion*. The deacon replaced the *angelos* as the messenger who united the celestial realm of the sanctuary behind the *templum* with the earthly domain of the nave. With his constant comings and goings between the two he took the celestial message to the people who, in turn, addressed it back to God.

The liturgy, with its obvious references to ancient Greek practices, retained its character of public service performed by free citizens. What distinguished the citizens of the new assembly of God, of the Christian *ekklesia*, from the old *ekklesia*-assembly of the city-state, was their citizenship of the kingdom of God in which they participated as members of the ecclesial community. Liturgical life implied the full, communal participation of the people in the cultic service rendered to God.[7]

The Church *koine*, or common language, was the vernacular spoken and understood by all. This contributed enormously to the strengthening of the cultural homogeneity of the Byzantine world; it united the catechetical experience of the Church by incorporating it in the *koine*, that is, the common, public liturgical *praxis*. Thus, catechism and catechesis became indistinguishable in the collective ecclesial consciousness. Catechesis, very much like the printed word in the Reformation, was widely diffused in the homiletic, hymnographic, architectural, linguistic, and iconographic tradition of the Church. Hymnography must be singled out as an especially popular medium for the dissemination of subtle theological messages chanted in folk-tune type melodies. All of the above went into the making and development of the liturgical *praxis* as a popular expression of traditional theology and formed the new catechetical tradition.

Catechism estranged from liturgical experience in the West

The development of liturgical *praxis* was quite different in the Western part of Christendom. The spread of Christianity in the West was accomplished through missionary activity. After the end of the Roman Empire the West attacked the urban sophistication of the East and did not share the same standards of intellectual life and culture. The gospel was preached to isolated tribes in remote areas. The Roman Church spoke an increasingly unintelligible tongue, as Latin ceased to be a vernacular, and, in most cases, represented a foreign element associated with conquest and oppression. Entire tribes were converted *en masse*, following the conversion of their chieftain, receiving little or no catechetical instruction. Their liturgical experience was very different from the one lived by their Eastern brethren. They participated in offices conducted in a language other than their own. They came in contact with a ritual that was entirely new to them, accompanied by art forms which had first to be understood before being appropriated.

The language-barrier had to be surmounted. One of the earliest references to catechetical practice in the West is the homily addressed by John, bishop of Constance, (d. 646) to his congregation, on the day of his consecration. In all probability this occasion presented him with an opportune moment to deliver a catechetical lesson to the bishop's flock in their own language. A century later, the Council of Cloveshow in 747 decreed that bishops would have to make sure that priests knew by rote the Lord's Prayer and the Creed and that they would explain them to their parishioners in their language. A similar decree was promulgated at the Council of Frankfurt in 794. Charlemagne himself ruled on the catechetical needs of the dioceses of the Carolingian kingdom. Some of the scholars of his court produced works of catechetical tenor destined for the use of the aristocratic members of his entourage.

The acquisition of virtues perceived as complementary catechesis

Undoubtedly, the catechetical needs in both parts of the Christian world differed 'as far as the east is from the west' (Psalms 103.12) and were necessarily addressed in distinctly differing terms. From an early period Latin catechism acquired its own particular characteristics. Great emphasis was laid on the instructional and moral rather than on the mystagogical nature of catechism. Definitive instructions were given to the elect concerning their purification from a sinful condition. A great part of Ambrose's homilies to the catechumenate of Milan, among whom one could have detected the young Augustine, dealt with basic moral principles reinforced with concrete *exempla* drawn from the Scriptures.

Teaching virtuous living

Before his elevation to the episcopal throne of Milan in 374, Saint Ambrose was consular prefect of Liguria and Emilia. One can imagine him having the same dream as Saint Jerome, in which Christ had reproached Jerome for being more Ciceronian than Christian, for Saint Ambrose's 'On duty', *De officiis*, is clearly modelled on Cicero's *De officiis*, a work addressed to his son Marcus, which is basically an elaborate copy of the *Peri Kathikonton* of the Stoic Panaetius of Rhodes. To set himself apart from any possible pagan influences, Saint Ambrose infused his work with exhortations to his spiritual sons – his diocese's ministers – to practise the Christian virtues of modesty (*verecundia*), beneficence (*beneficentia*), generosity (*liberalitas*), chastity (*castimonia*). He mentions these among other virtues as a variation of the four cardinal Platonic virtues: prudence (*prudentia*), justice (*iustitia*), fortitude (*fortitudo*) and moderation (*temperantia*). It was Cicero who had defined the four virtues as sources of moral duties (*De Officiis* 1, 4–5), and the Stoic doctrine of duties and virtues was so firmly fixed in the accepted ideas of that time that Saint Augustine, with all his opposition to pagan learning, borrowed one of his definitions of virtue straight from Cicero.[8] Even one and a half centuries later the Bishop of Braga, known as Martin of Bracara, was inspired by Seneca in the compositions of his moral treatises on the four virtues and the virtuous life.

Both Saint Jerome[9] and Saint Gregory the Great acknowledged the primacy of the four cardinal virtues. The early Latin fathers legitimized the Christian adaptation of the Platonic virtues by placing them in paradise; Saint Ambrose compared them to the four rivers of Eden and Saint Augustine repeated his mentor's original claim.[10] Saint Gregory the Great brought together the four cardinal virtues with the three 'sapiential' virtues of faith, hope and charity (1 Cor. 13.2, 13).

Good acts lead to salvation

It was uncontroversial in the Middle Ages that the acquisition of the virtues paves the way to the good life. The *vita honesta*, the virtuous life, is regulated by definite rules of conduct. The good life ensures happiness, the *summum bonum*, since it is associated with love of wisdom, pursuit of virtue, enjoyment of good health and shunning of vice, which, in their sum (*summum*), constitute the implementation of one's duties to oneself, to the other, and to God. In the twelfth century John of Salisbury's perception, 'philosophy assigns the virtues according to which one proceeds in particular duties ... for no one advances towards happiness except by way of virtue ... And these are the greatest goods [*summa bona*].'[11]

In the fifteenth century, Jean Gerson, in addition to the corpus of his theological works, also wrote on a number of popular subjects, ranging in scope from the evils of masturbation, *De confessione mollicei*, to a book of good conduct, the *Règles de bien vivre*. This treatise does not limit its message to the acquisition of virtue but examines in their minutest details inconsequential incidents of daily life, from the toilet of women to table manners, the absence of which may be characterized as manifestations of the vice of vanity or gluttony. He wrote on the Creed and the Decalogue, and gave a guide to sins, for use at confession, and to the 'art of dying well'. Gerson, as part of his catechetical programme, had also composed a vernacular work, which was used for the acquisition of literacy skills, as well as for catechism, the *L'ABC des simples gens, de très grande utilité et proufit*.[12]

On the eve of the Renaissance, in the fifteenth century, we encounter several works which appeal to a wider public and specifically deal with questions concerning good conduct and correct social behaviour as a reflection of the virtues practised by the virtuous man or woman. The proverbial *bon vivant* character of the French or the Italian *virtuoso* and *virtuosa* denote men and women who are following the rules of good living – *règles de bien vivre* – and possess the necessary know-how, the *savoir-vivre* or *savoir-faire*, both indispensable qualities, which enable them to cultivate a virtuous reputation, to enter good society and to stay there.

Christine de Pisan's admonitions to ladies of rank, but also to the wives of artisans and labourers, to chambermaids and even to prostitutes, in her work *The Treasure of the City of Ladies*, or *The Book of the Three Virtues*, abound in good sense as to how a lady ought to behave in various circumstances, on how she ought to conduct herself towards her husband, towards his friends and relatives, on her behaviour as a widow, or 'of the behaviour that ought to be instilled into a young newly married princess'.[13] In the tenth chapter, elaborating on 'the moral doctrine that Worldly Prudence will teach the wise princess', she states unequivocally that good reputation and honour is all that one needs in life in order to be esteemed by other honourable members of the society to which one belongs. Even worldly riches are disregarded in favour of a good reputation and honour. 'But what things', the author's interlocutor demands, 'are necessary for genuine honour?' The reply is:

In truth they are good manners and behaviour ... Prudence will advise the wise princess about these things ... She will arrange her life principally in two areas. The first will be concerned with the manners and behaviour that she wishes to practise, and the second with the manner and order of living that she will wish to establish.

A detailed analysis of 'the behaviour ensuing from the above-mentioned virtues' follows, with an intricate description of the virtues of sobriety and chastity which will dictate the lady's normative behaviour at the table, in sleep, in her dress, jewellery, perfumes, tone of voice, control of her speech and laughter, her movements of the body or hands. To complete her moral way of living 'this lady will gladly read instructive books about good manners and behaviour and sometimes devotion'.

A few years before Christine de Pisan wrote her book on the three virtues, an older gentleman residing in the same city, the 'Householder of Paris' as he called himself, wrote a book of good manners and behaviour for his teenaged wife. The instructions of the Ménagier de Paris, although written by a man, do not differ in their content from Christine de Pisan's instructions to ladies. He accords the same primacy to honour and good reputation. He is untiringly advising his wife to shun the company of 'witless women, who have no care for their honour, nor for the honesty of their estate or of their husbands ... who know not how to maintain their own honourable fame....'.[14] And as if her honourable fame rests solely on her comportment in the street, and on how her gait, company, and manners will be perceived and interpreted by both her and his critics, he advises her on how to walk and where to look:

> And as you go bear your head upright and your eyelids low [an almost impossible task] and without fluttering, and look straight in front of you about four rods ahead, without looking round at any man or woman to the right or to the left, nor looking up, nor glancing from place to place, nor stopping to speak to anyone on the road.

To neglect to apply these rules to the daily occurrences of one's life will certainly lead one to the cultivation of vice and to eventual perdition. The totality of human life, even the mystery of life, is reduced to precise formulas of behaviour and manners, to rules and regulations that take into account the slightest possible contingency of lapsing into unacceptable behaviour which will imperil one's physical and metaphysical status.

The good person is formed and reformed by catechism

The assumption in all these manuals is that the intense cultivation of virtues and the application of duties activates the outpouring of grace upon the virtuous person. Saint Augustine had already asserted that faith is the result of grace and that there is no human merit that exists prior to grace,[15] but the formulation of the theological conviction, which has dominated our ideas about good actions, is due to Aquinas. He elaborated a theory of a grace entirely dependent on the will of God to help human nature accomplish good acts. Insofar as grace is 'created' by God, 'human nature needs the help of God as First Mover, to do or will any good whatsoever ... man by his natural endowments could will and do the good proportionate to his nature, such as the good of acquired virtue, but not surpassing good, as the good of infused virtue'.[16] The doctrine of created grace, the assistance of the infused virtues and the support of the seven sacraments are the solid foundations on which an *ex gratia* salvation is built.

For all these to be effectual a system of vigorous moral training must be implemented; a system which relegates the work of the Holy Spirit to a supporting role, whose function is to assist the person who is striving to acquire these moral virtues.

The theme is that the grace of the Holy Spirit is instilled in the person in proportion to his or her efforts to build up a system of moral perfection. This is a radical departure from the traditional Orthodox concept of *theosis*, 'deification', experienced as a human way of existence based on the communion of love, which is modelled on the communion of love as manifested and lived between the persons of the Holy Trinity. Within the Western mode of 'sanctification' one achieves sainthood by becoming a good person, by acquiring good habits, which will safeguard one's good conduct in the face of adversity. This is the reason why sanctification and not deification is the guiding principle in Western spirituality.

Catechism in Western Europe

It is probable that the twelfth-century French devotional work known as *The Lay Folk's Mass Book*, which was translated into English a century later, and which was popular in England, was circulating freely among village girls, women and mothers, who might have read it to each other or to their children.

The Lay Folk's Mass Book was not the only book of this kind to have enjoyed a wide appeal; a century later it was followed by Archbishop Thoresby's *Instructions*, a Latin catechism which was distributed in parishes with the intent of being expounded, in English, by parish priests throughout the diocese of York. In its commissioned verse translation into vernacular English, by the Benedictine John Gaytrick of St Mary's, York, it came to be known as the *Lay Folk's Catechism*. Much of its popularity could be ascribed to its short format and its versification, accounting for its ease of memorization; it was even made more attractive by the proviso attached to it guaranteeing a 40-days indulgence to those who would memorize it.[17] This popular catechism could be viewed as the precursor of all fourteenth-century catechisms emphasizing similar themes, namely, the Creed, the Lord's Prayer, the Decalogue, the seven sins, the seven virtues, and the seven sacraments.

It is also to be noted that popular devotional tracts were widely used as primers and as manuals for catechetical instruction.

Following the Fourth Lateran Council of 1215 the new element introduced into liturgical life is that preaching is not to be limited to the exposition of the scriptural passage of any given Sunday but shall henceforth include those elements of the faith which were previously received in a traditional but informal manner at home or in the monastic schools. Following the decree issued by Bishop Poore at Salisbury as a result of the canons promulgated by the Lateran Council, which was reissued at Durham between 1229 and 1237, another episcopal decree appeared in 1240 in the constitutions of Walter de Cantilupe, bishop of Worcester, which clearly defines the subject matter of the sermons to be preached on Sundays; these are to be commentaries on the Ten Commandments, the Creed, the Lord's Prayer, and the seven sins. These decrees, together with the instructions issued by Archbishop Pecham of Canterbury in 1281, are the precursors of the manuals for parish priests treating similar subjects for the instruction of priests and parishioners alike, which proliferated in the fourteenth century.[18]

The Church did not officially endorse any catechetical programme until the thirteenth century. The laity, not being able to comprehend the Gospel lessons read in Latin, relied on the priest's expositions and on a great amount of supporting material, mainly of iconographic and popular content, similar to what is described today as cultural landscape, to which they were exposed through a Christian culture permeating all facets of public and private life. These included a variegated array of folk material such as symbolic figures in embroideries, lace-work, paintings, woodcuts, tapestries and pottery-motifs, diffused in everyday common objects, mystery and morality plays, popular songs, nursery rhymes, fables and lays, and in an oral tradition handed down from one generation to the next by bards, storytellers and women, particularly mothers, who spent a great deal of time with their children and imbued them from a tender age with the rudiments of a simple faith. The iconographic content of such an emblematic imagery and symbolism formed the elements of a wide spectrum of pictographic material that was deciphered easily by all illiterate lay persons who recognized in this visual medium their own graphic scripture, the so-called *Biblia pauperum*, the poor man's Bible, which acted as the catechetical horizon of the *pauperum*, the common people of God.[19] There were certain crafts incorporating an intricate symbolism of complex imagery, such as embroidery and lace-work, which were entirely entrusted to women, but this specialization in popular forms of art did not exclude women from masculine occupations associated with the *scriptoria*, and their excellence in manuscript production is not an uncommon occurrence.[20] Nevertheless, one must bear in mind that these folk elements, strictly speaking, rarely found their way into the liturgical life of the Church; they retained, often at the insistence of ministers and prelates, their para-ecclesiastical, popular homely and cottage-industry character.

It is important not to lose sight of the informal role of women, especially mothers, in teaching the faith to children. The instruction Luther had received at home when a child, composed of rudiments of faith taken out of the Decalogue, the Creed, and the Lord's Prayer, was no different from the simple instruction in the faith received in any peasant's cottage or burgher's home throughout the Western Christian world. This was a vulgar-vernacular faith, as opposed to the 'learned' faith of the clerks, kept alive in families, propagated by mothers who, according to the reformer George von Anhalt, were 'the best priests and bishops of the family'.[21] This instruction was given in the local dialect, and easily understood by every child.

Any boy aspiring to be a clerk, however, had to begin his education with Latin grammar; he had to master this sacred language thoroughly, in order to be able to read the Scriptures. Yet although Latin was spoken exclusively by educated men, women also managed to get a smattering of reading and writing (more *reading* than writing), enough to express themselves clearly on a number of pastoral subjects. But the remarkable feature of women's involvement with learning and letters is that most, if not all, of their writing and reading was done in the vernacular, and there is ample evidence, from the late Middle Ages to the Reformation, to suggest that literature in the vernacular was largely the domain of women.

In this light the term 'mother tongue' acquires a deeper significance. Throughout the Middle Ages, the vernacular language, in all its simplicity and natural beauty, is likened to that simple faith kept, nurtured and passed on to children by their mothers. Catechetical works in the vernacular made it possible for the illiterate peasant, the burgher, even the knight, to be instructed orally by means of questions and answers committed to memory and learned by rote. It was this current that eventually led to the compilation of the *Small Catechism* by Luther (for the needs of children and the majority of Christians), an *Enchiridion*, a manual as he called it, well suited to a rudimentary instruction in the Christian faith.

The Western form of catechism is introduced in the East

The *Confession of Faith* of Peter Moghila, Metropolitan of Kiev, with its sequel, the *Shorter Catechism*, composed a little prior to 1640, is thought to be the first systematic attempt by an Orthodox to present the articles of faith of the Eastern Church in a format modelled on Western catechisms.

During the same period several Catholic catechisms, mainly commissioned from the papal office of the Propagation of the Faith, *De Propaganda Fide*, appeared in Greek, published in Rome, Paris, Vienna and Venice. To counteract their influence, a number of Protestant catechisms based on Luther's and Calvin's catechisms, including the integral text of the *Heidelberg Catechism*, were printed in Greek in Leipzig, Basle, Rostock, London, Leiden and Frankfurt. There was even a Protestant catechism published in Wittenberg in 1622, an original work written by a Greek, Zacharias Gerganos, who was a protégé of the Elector of Saxony.

However, the catechism *par excellence*, the only one that left lasting and indelible marks in the process of the Westernization of the Orthodox spirit in the eighteenth century, was written by Platon Levshin, Metropolitan of Moscow, in 1765, which he based on his catechetical lectures delivered in Moscow a few years earlier for the instruction of the Grand Duke Paul. It was first translated into Greek by a hieromonk named Matthew and published in 1776 in Petersburg. Six years later another translation by Diamandis (*sic*) Koraës was published in Leipzig and the same Matthew, who was now the chaplain of the Russian embassy in Paris, published a second edition of his translation in Venice; a third translation, made from the French by Vendotis, was published in Vienna by Lambanitziotis at the printing press of Josef Gerold. A second edition followed in 1783. The French translation was considered more accurate than Koraës's, which had been made from the German, since it had been approved by Platon himself, and Lambanitziotis had gone to great lengths to obtain this manuscript translation into Greek, having come across it on one of his travels to Hungary.[22]

A further edition of Platon's catechism appeared in Vienna in 1805, this time translated from the original Russian by Dimitrios Darvaris, an indefatigable educationist, to whose enthusiasm for the pedagogical ideas of the Enlightenment we owe several works written and published in Vienna, where he taught for over two decades at the schools of the Greek diaspora of the Austro-Hungarian empire.[23] At his death his brothers, who were wealthy merchants and bankers and had financially supported his numerous publications, donated 17,250 copies of his various works to the twelve schools scattered throughout the empire. Some 360 volumes, out of which 200 were copies of his catechetical works, were dispatched to his home town of Klisoura, in Macedonia. Upon the formation of the Greek state in 1829, his brother Peter forwarded four large boxes of Darvaris's works to the governor of Greece, John Kapodistrias.

Yet another version of Platon's catechism was elaborated by Constantine Oikonomos when he was teaching at the Gymnasium of Smyrna, and was printed in Vienna in 1813. By 1820 there was a third printing of this work, which was destined to be the official catechetical textbook of the independent Greek state. When Kapodistrias, in 1828, consulted Oikonomos on the curriculum of the Ecclesiastical Academy, which was to open in Poros, the latter was quick to suggest Platon's catechism as a standard textbook. George Gennadios, the first principal of the educational institution of the Greek state in Aigina, had also written a catechism based on Platon's work, as well as a treatise on the *Duties of Man*.

Whether in the Koraës, Vendotis, Darvaris or Oikonomos version, the catechism of Platon Levshin, despite its inaccuracies and its frequent deviations from Orthodox doctrine, came to be regarded as the official catechism of the Orthodox Church. It received praise from patriarchs, Holy Synods, statesmen, schoolmasters, and traditional monastics, as well as from progressive erudites and other luminaries of the spätaufklärung period. An indication of the appeal that the work exerted among the

Orthodox is attested by its translation into Turkish, printed at the Patriarchal Press of Constantinople in 1839 in *Karamanlidika*, that is, Turkish written with Greek characters, for the edification of the Karamanlides, the Turcophone Christians of Anatolia.

Indeed, the Greek translations became so popular that the original work was nearly eclipsed and it was not long before translations into English from the Koraës and the Darvaris versions appeared, first in Aberdeen and Edinburgh in 1846, then in London in 1857, and Cardiff in 1867. They were produced in order to demonstrate the similarities of doctrine between the Anglican and the Orthodox Churches, and to justify a theological *rapprochement*, which would spell out the principles on which the eventual union of the two Churches could be realized. It is not surprising to see in the Aberdeen edition, edited by William Palmer, the notice informing the reader that the endeavour was 'designed to shew that there is in the Anglican Communion generally, and more particularly and pre-eminently in the Scottish Church, an element of Orthodoxy, capable by a Synodical Act of declaring Unity and Identity with the Catholic Church of the East'. Indeed, anyone familiar with Protestant ideas would easily recognize them in this most Western type of catechism of the 'Catholic Church of the East', through which Orthodoxy becomes a *speculum ecclesiae occidentalis*.

Western-style 'good manners' are introduced in the East

When Koraës published his shorter catechism 'for the use of the public schools of the Greek nation' in Venice, in 1783, he appended a Preface addressed to 'pedagogues and to all the pious parents who desire the happiness of their children'. On page 12, elaborating on how children ought to be raised, he reproaches parents for not giving enough time to the proper upbringing of their offspring, then goes on to say that even when they do devote time to their upbringing it is usually limited to advice on how to present themselves and address their hosts when paying a visit and on how to appear coquettish, and in a footnote affirms:

> Truly, there is nothing more distressing, nowadays, than the way in which parents see to the upbringing of their own children. When they have mastered the manner of dressing and of mutual courtesies, when they have learned to put together a few words of compliment, which, frequently, produce an effect of nonsense, the parents not

only deem this more than sufficient, but think of their children as possessing more than their useful share of ethics.

In describing his code of ethics for children Koraës seeks to persuade parents not to confuse education in good manners with authentic education, that is instruction in the catechism of the Church, a synopsis of which is contained in his *Short Catechism*. That this work is to be used both as an instruction in the faith and as a primer is made clear by the instructions to pedagogues and the inclusion of a guide to the alphabet, spelling and elementary grammar presented in the Preface.

Saint Nicodemos (1749–1809) revisited the subject of good and bad manners at length by composing his own *Chrestoethia*, which was published in Venice in 1803. This work is addressed to the laity and brims with advice on how to behave both at home and in church. Following his affirmation that Christ never laughed and that God punishes those who laugh, he advises on how to refrain from laughing, from telling stories and jokes, and from reading humorous books, and generally on how to achieve the state of non-laughter, observing that the pagans praised the Christians for their ability not to laugh. He instructs on how and up to what point one may reject gloom and replace it with moderate joy. He lays down prohibitions against Christians playing musical instruments or singing (even at weddings) and elaborates on the evil caused by doing so, suggesting that as a result of the disorderliness associated with singing and dancing children may be born sick or handicapped. Similarly he exhorts Christians not to adorn themselves or use perfumes. Neither do the artisan classes escape his censure and he discusses at length the evil wrought by farmers, weavers, tailors and cobblers, and how easily fishermen are prone to lie under oath. He states that an artisan who sets his hopes on his craft is impure and how bad it is for craftsmen to kiss their hands (as a sign of respect for their craft), and culminates with a list of daily acts within which spiritual injury or benefit contributing to one's salvation or damnation may be lurking.

It is as if the princes' mirrors and the catechetical genres of the past, all of a sudden, had fused together to create the new Eastern chrestoethic code of manners.

The sophiological tradition was continued by La Fontaine, who turned Aesop's *Fables* into literary masterpieces which, beyond their moral value, served for the acquisition of an elegant manner of speaking and writing. As a preamble to the *Fables* he included the classical thirteenth century

Vita of Aesop by Maximos Planoudis, the same one that was included in all Greek primers. Aesop's *Fables* formed the indispensable complement to any primer as far back as documentary evidence is available. King Alfred translated them into Anglo-Saxon as an integral part of his educational programme. Marie de France used a twelfth-century English version from which she translated them into French under the title *Ysopet*.[24] Planoudis had also contributed to this sophiological tradition in teaching by translating into Greek Cato's *Distichs*, as had Luther in a similar manner with his translation of the *Fables* into German as part of his reforms in education. It would not be an exaggeration to say that Cato's *Distichs* together with the *Fables* of Aesop formed the moral outlook of the Western educated person from the early Middle Ages to the nineteenth century.

With Saint Nicodemos's work, however, we enter into a new domain where good manners and correct behaviour are seen in themselves as autonomous moral principles, detached from the cultivation of classical virtues, and capable of setting one on the right path to salvation without the aid of an ecclesiastical ethos to sustain or correct them. For Saint Nicodemos what is important is not so much to be a living member of the liturgical *praxis*, but rather to pay attention as to how to stand in church, where to sit, where to look, what to say and not to say, what to wear, and not to assume a 'barbaric posture and uncouth manners and conduct'. It is as if one's attitude and posture in church is not commensurate with the cosmic event that takes place during the liturgy, but rather, through an inverted kind of logic, one's attitude influences and gives meaning to the liturgical events 'because there is piety and tears brought about by the external attitude and posture of the body, such as praying with uncovered head'.[25]

Saint Nicodemos is by no means the sole representative of a romantic attitude to piety and repentance. The movement was widespread throughout the Orthodox world, and Saint Tikhon Zadonskii, with all his influence on Dostoevsky, may be seen as another variant of the same phenomenon. Both men influenced to a great degree monastic, ecclesiastical and popular forms of Orthodox piety. Both men are responsible for establishing and enshrining in the Orthodox ethos a moralistic attitude to life, an attitude which completes the long process of the infiltration of the theological ideas of the Reformation, which began with the introduction and the adoption of Western catechisms and concluded with the importation of codes of good manners and a romantic view of ecclesiology based on pious feelings of contrition and correct attitudes to everything.

The widespread, unquestioning and enthusiastic adoption of the catechetical genre by the Orthodox world in the eighteenth century inevitably points to certain conclusions regarding the predominance of Western ideas in the Orthodox Church in the nineteenth century and beyond. The consequences of the process which we have examined above deprived Orthodox spirituality of its lifeline with the patristic catechetical tradition. It also modified to a great degree the sophiological orientation of the educational programme. The ideological function conferred on the vernacular language (an unavoidable legacy of the Reformation ingrained in Western catechisms), introduced similar ideas about the idealized form of the Greek vernacular or demotic language, and its eventual adoption as the 'official' language of the Greek state, sanctioned in 1977 by a parliamentary Act. What had taken centuries of slow development in the Western world – this slow process which we have attempted to trace in the unfolding of the catechetical tradition in its progress from a sophiological to a moralistic genre with an accompanying well-defined system of ethical values – was adopted wholeheartedly in a matter of a few decades by the Orthodox world.

It is to this asymmetrical development of a moral system that the inadequacy and incompatibility of some basic Orthodox assumptions regarding modern ethics and pastoral care as practised and applied in the realities of the contemporary human condition can be attributed.

Notes

1. Luke 1.4; 1 Cor. 14.19.
2. Jean Chrysostome, *Trois catéchèses baptismales*, Introduction, critical text, notes and translation by Auguste Piédagnel, Sources Chrétiennes (Paris, 1990), p. 192.
3. Ibid., pp. 178, 202, 216.
4. Matt. 11.15; Mark 4.9, 23, and elsewhere.
5. Cyril of Jerusalem, *Procatechesis* 1, in *PG*, vol. 33, col. 333.
6. Ibid., 17. The translation is the author's.
7. For the transition of the sense of 'liturgy' in Greek from public service to the state, or discharge of specific services to the body politic, to cultic service to the gods and its passage to current use through its occurrence in the Septuagint, see Gerhard Kittel and Gerhard Friedrich (eds), *Theological Dictionary of the New Testament*, trans. Geoffrey W. Bromiley (Grand Rapids, Mich., 1964–76), vol. 4, pp. 216–31.

8. *De Inventione*, 1.2.53 in Saint Augustine's *De diversis quaestionibus*, in *PL*, vol. 40, 83, q. 31, col. 20. Alcuin, in his *Liber de virtutibus et vitiis*, writes of the four cardinal virtues as if they were the primal Christian virtues, and then goes on to define them with the very words taken from Cicero's *De officiis*.
9. In *Epistolae*, 52, n. 13, in *PL*, vol. 22, col. 538; and 66, n. 3, in *PL*, vol. 22, col. 640.
10. Saint Ambrose, *De Paradiso*, ch. 3, in *PL*, vol. 14, cols. 279–82. Pishon, flowing gold, is Prudence; Gihon washes Ethiopia – her name means impurity – and is identified with Temperance; Tigris is Fortitude; and Euphrates is Justice. Saint Augustine, *De Genesi contra Manichaeos*, 1.11, n. 13, in *PL*, vol. 34, cols. 203–4.
11. John of Salisbury, *Policraticus*, ed. and trans. C. J. Nederman (Cambridge, 1990), pp. 157, 160.
12. *The Oxford Encyclopedia of the Reformation*, ed. Hans J. Hillerbrand (1996), s.v. 'Catechism', p. 276.
13. Christine de Pisan wrote her works in vernacular French. The original title of the work mentioned is *Le Livre des trois vertus*, or *Le Trésor de la cité des dames*. All quotations above are from the only existing translation in English by Sarah Lawson (Penguin, 1987), pp. 55–6. A contemporary of Christine de Pisan, who was also attached to the court as royal notary and secretary to Charles VI, Alain Chartier, had written two books on the three virtues and the four ladies; their titles: *Livre des quatre dames*, and *L'Espérance ou Consolation des trois vertus*. His works are mentioned in P. Champion, *Histoire poétique du XVe siècle* (Paris, 1923), vol. 1, p. 135.
14. Eileen Power, *Medieval People* (New York, 1963), pp. 102–3.
15. *De praedestinatione sanctorum*, in *PL*, vol. 44, col. 961; and *De dono perseverantiae*, in *PL*, vol. 45, col. 1023.
16. Thomas Aquinas, *Summa Theologica*; the *Treatise on Grace*, Question 109, Art. 1, in *Great Books of the Western World*, vol. 20, p. 339.
17. W. A. Pantin, *The English Church in the Fourteenth Century* (Notre Dame, Ind., 1963), pp. 212, 233.
18. Ibid., pp. 193–4.
19. For an excellent discussion of 'popular' religion, cf. Eamon Duffy, *The Stripping of the Altars*, (New Haven, Conn., 1992).
20. B. Bischoff has identified a scriptorium in Chelles run entirely by nuns. Cf. 'Die Kölner Nonnenhandschriften und das Scriptorium von Chelles', *Medieval Studies* 36, pp. 16–33.
21. Joseph-André Jungmann, *Catéchèse. Objectifs et methodes de l'enseignement religieux* (Brussels, 1955), p. 18.
22. K. Sp. Staikos, *Die in Wien gedruckten Griechischen Bücher (1749–1800)*; (Athens, 1995), pp. 42–4.
23. For Darvaris's pedagogical work see Ariadna Camariano-Cioran, *Les académies princières de Bucarest et de Jassy et leurs professeurs* (Thessalonica, 1974), pp. 274–5.
24. For the sources used by Marie de France cf. K. Warnke, *Die Fabeln der*

Marie de France (Halle, 1898), and Marie de France, *Fables*, selected and ed. A. Ewert and R. C. Johnston (Oxford, 1942).
25. *Chrestoethia*, pp. 260, 263. Venice 1803 edition.

Bibliography

Adamson, J. W., 'Education', in C. G. Crump and E. F. Jacob (eds), *The Legacy of the Middle Ages* (Oxford, 1951)

Dictionnaire de théologie catholique, ed. A. Vacant, E. Mangeot *et al.*, 15 vols. in 18 (Paris, 1907–53)

Eisenstein, Elizabeth L., *The Printing Press as an Agent of Change* (Cambridge, 1979)

Smyth, Alfred P., *King Alfred the Great* (Oxford, 1995)

PART IV

The Early Modern Period

11

The Reformation crisis in pastoral care

David Cornick

The great reforming Fourth Lateran Council of 1215, presided over by Innocent III, decreed:

> On reaching the age of discernment, everyone of the faithful, of either sex, is faithfully at least once a year to confess all his sins in private to his own priest, and is to take care to fulfil according to his abilities the penance enjoined on him, reverently receiving the sacrament of the Eucharist at Easter ... Otherwise he is to be barred from entering the church in his lifetime and to be deprived of Christian burial at his death ... The priest is to be discerning and careful, so that like a skilful doctor he can apply wine and oil to the wounds of the injured person, diligently asking for the circumstances of the sinner and the sin, through which he can prudently understand what advice he ought to give, and what sort of remedy to apply, trying various things to heal the sick person.[1]

The rule of souls, the council concluded, quoting Gregory the Great, was the art of arts. Bishops were therefore commanded to train their priests in appropriate care of souls, lest the blind should lead the blind and both end up in a ditch. The art of pastoral care was to be crafted from the discipline of penance, the celebration of the Eucharist within the context of the rhythm of the Christian year and the skills of the confessor, a doctor of souls. The life of the soul before God, that most private and potent aspect of Christian living, is in all but a few well-documented cases properly hidden from the prying eyes of historians. It is a subject which has to be approached tangentially, the line of the tangent dictated by the availability of sources. The care of souls, however, is reflected in the way the Church instructs the laity, what it expects of the clergy, how it trains them, and how it orders the life of local communities. It is sources such as these that will open up the legacy of the Reformation in pastoral care.

The parameters set by the Lateran decree – the penitential cycle, the Eucharist, the Christian year, the work of the priest – circumscribe the landscape of popular religion, territory which was to play host to the fearsome battles of the reformations of the sixteenth century, for in the eyes of the reformers, the crisis brought about by Luther was pastoral. It had to do with the very essence of the faith – the nature of salvation.

However, some salient features of the landscape of 1500 remained in 1600. For example, the replacement of the penitential cycle by church discipline was but the exchange of one form of social control for another, and the transformation of parish priest into Reformed minister did little to change the distribution of authority – as Milton wryly commented, 'New presbyter is but old priest writ large.' In other ways, however, the reformations scorched the earth with such intensity that little remained of the devotional and pastoral structures that had sustained ordinary Christians for centuries. The Reformation legacy of pastoral care is therefore ambiguous. It laid waste a precious and loved landscape to build its brave new world.

The cartographers of popular religion have shown how orthodox doctrine, superstition and folk religion blended to produce a popular piety in a late mediaeval Church that was neither spiritually bankrupt nor ruined by abuse. In some places at least it was a vibrant and powerful force in the lives of ordinary parishioners. Late mediaeval culture was intensely visual and tactile rather than cerebral. Hence the crowds who flocked to the shrines of the saints at major pilgrimage centres. Hence the value of relics – holiness that could be touched, a bridge between heaven and earth. Hence too, of course, the disgraceful trade in manufactured relics. Significant and important though these were, popular religion was informed primarily by the sacramental cycle which began at baptism and ended with extreme unction at the point of death; and the most important part of the cycle was the repeated drama of the Eucharist.

'The first sacrament is God's body in the form of bread that the priest "sacret" at Mass. Yet every Christian man shall believe that it is verily God's body that was born of the maid Mary and hung on the cross.'[2] That quotation from a fourteenth-century English instruction manual takes us to the heart of late mediaeval popular religion. The central symbol of Western culture from $c.1200$ to $c.1600$ was the Eucharistic host. The belief that the ritual words of a priest turned a vulnerable and fragile wheaten disc into God was the fundamental intellectual and spiritual reality of European Christian life. For three hundred years intellectuals spent their lives trying to fathom its mysteries, and went in danger of death if they undermined its power. For three hundred years that symbol created human communities, from village parishes to empires. As the sacring bell rang, as the host was raised, heaven and earth were joined, the natural and the supernatural blended, and time and eternity were united. Here cosmic order and human community were united in a common religious language.

What mattered was not reception – the devout and seriously minded probably communicated no more than three times a year, most others annually at Easter. What mattered was seeing, the miracle of God made manifest. Church architecture was refined to make that possible – side chapels with their own altars proliferated, squint holes were bored in screens at kneeling height, and wherever possible a sight-line was created so that priests celebrating at side altars could see what their colleagues were doing at the high altar. 'Seeing' governed the timing of Masses so that the laity could see the host at several sacrings within a short space of time. Sometimes chaos ensued. In 1339 the bishop of Exeter tried to regulate the ringing of sacring bells in the private chapels of Ottery St Mary parish church to try and stop the choir rushing off in the middle of the office to adore the host.[3] A century and a half later Cranmer's bitter complaint testified to the same behaviour,

> What made the people to run from their seats to the altar, and from altar to altar, and from sacring (as they called it) to sacring, peeping, tooting and gazing at that thing which the priest held up in his hands, if they thought not to honour the things which they saw? What moved the priests to lift up the sacrament so high over their heads? Or the people to say to the priest 'Hold up! Hold up!'; or one man to say to another 'Stoop down before'; or to say 'This day I have seen my Maker'; and 'I cannot be quiet except I see my Maker once a day.'[4]

'Seeing' brought blessing. For mothers in labour, seeing could bring safe delivery. Travellers could be guaranteed safe arrival. The eyes of the blind might be opened.[5] Blessing flowed from the Mass. It was this belief that led to the founding of guilds and the endowments of lights to go before the sacrament as it was carried to the sick of the parish. Conversely stories abounded of thieves and sinners being convicted of their wrongdoing by a temporary blindness at the moment of elevation, and of doubters being miraculously convinced of the true nature of the sacrament. One theme which recurs again and again is of an unbeliever seeing a child in the place of the host. A version in an English source tells of a learned monk who had doubts about the Real Presence. He confided his doubts to two brothers, who prayed for him, and they were granted a vision at Mass. The priest broke the host after consecration and they saw in his hands a child being stabbed by an angel, so that the child's blood ran into the chalice.[6] Much earlier, just such a vision had been granted to King Edward the Confessor.[7] Images pile on each other – the presence of a real body, the historic Christ born to Mary, redemption through sacrifice, the death of a precious son, the sacrifice of Isaac, the presentation at the Temple, Christmas and Easter, birth and death.

Here was paradox and ineffable beauty. As an early English poem puts it:

> Hyt seems quite, and is red
> Hyt is quike, and seemes ded:
> Hyt is flesche and seemes brede
> Hyt is on and semes too;
> Hyt is God body and no more.[8]

So holy, so precious was the host that the laity were not normally allowed to communicate for fear that part of the body of the Lord might be lost, or his blood spilled. The restriction of communion caused the creation of substitute rituals – the pax-board and the holy loaf.[9] Both those rituals point to the fact that the Eucharist was a communal experience, not a privatized one. Here was a symbolic peace-making, a powerful form of social cohesion and control.

The Eucharist was the life-blood of popular religion, the weekly and daily re-enactment of the cosmic drama of salvation. It existed within a yearly liturgical rhythm that mirrored the ebb and flow of the seasons. Feasts and fasts, decorations and legitimized disorder, lights and processions, all worked to bring liturgical time and the rhythm of the seasons into holistic order.[10]

Under the framework laid down by the Fourth Lateran Council private confession to a priest at least once a year was regarded as an essential component of the Christian life. Confession and absolution were basic to the nature of forgiveness. Manuals for confessors enjoin priests to encourage honesty and completeness in confession. A common order shows the penitent beginning by making the sign of the cross, and then reciting the *confiteor*, breaking off at the *mea culpa* to give details of each individual sin, and then completing the recitation. The priest's questions followed. After that, instruction was given, a penance received, and absolution granted.[11] The form was traditional and clear. The penitent was guided through a check-list of the seven deadly sins, the Ten Commandments, the five senses, the seven works of mercy, the seven gifts of the Spirit, the seven sacraments and the eight beatitudes.

Most sixteenth-century Christians confessed once a year during Lent. The truly pious who were also wealthy could afford spiritual directors, and some of the professed religious like Luther, could afford the time and had the inclination for lengthy introspection. Most ordinary people brought their spiritual accounts up to date annually, and for most the actual practice of confession must have been short – 'in a time-honoured formula the penitent was to be brief, be brutal, be gone'.[12]

This landscape was to be irrevocably changed by the reformations. As 'justification by faith alone' laid waste the penitential system, the whole panoply of confession and works of satisfaction fell into disrepair, for they were no longer needed. Redefinitions of Eucharistic theology laid waste the bold symbolic statement that had held the world together for three hundred years, and the ritual year suffered grievous assault and died.

The speed of change could be truly astonishing. In a mere eighteen months in 1547 and 1548, the government of Edward Seymour, Earl of Somerset, Lord Protector of the precocious boy-king Edward, demolished the entire structure of popular religion in England. On 31 July 1547 the order went out that all shrines and pictures of the saints were to be destroyed, and the only candles allowed in church were those needed for illumination. Processions in church or outside were forbidden; palm crosses were banned. The injunction was enforced by visitation. In the September all images in churches to which the parish priest, the churchwardens, or the king's visitors objected, were to be removed. On

6 February 1548 Candlemas candles, Ash Wednesday ashing, Palm Sunday foliage and creeping to the cross were all prohibited. Cranmer quickly followed that by outlawing the three favourite Easter ceremonies – the sepulchre, the paschal candle and the hallowing of Easter fire. In the autumn communion in both kinds was instituted, and all institutions devoted to prayer for the dead and remission from purgatory were seized by the state. The speed and authority with which Cranmer acted was breathtaking. The guts of popular religion had been surgically removed. The mopping-up operation in 1548 saw St George (whom Edward VI loathed), Corpus Christi and Whitsun processions wiped off the liturgical map.

What brought about this dramatic change?

Martin Luther and the indulgence crisis

Some years ago Peter Newman Brooks posed the question, 'Although it ... remains the simplest possible interpretation to state that Martin Luther's original protest stemmed from concern lest the condition of the late mediaeval Church, and particularly the Roman Curia, obscure Christ's gospel to simple people, is the observation really so naïve?'[13] The force of that question is still considerable. However great Luther's debt to the nominalists (and it is large), whatever portion of his theology was prefigured in the works of such as Gabriel Biel and Gregory of Rimini, his reaction to the indulgence campaign of 1516/17 was that of a pastor. It was what his Wittenberg parishioners told him in the confessional of Tetzel's preaching and practice that led to the composition of the *Ninety-five Theses*.[14]

The theses encapsulated not just pastoral outrage, but the concerns of a professor of biblical studies who had been wrestling with the New Testament and the theology of repentance and righteousness for a number of years. Through those studies he had discovered that God was good, that he was a God who was for human beings, not against them, and that salvation was God's gift through the cross, no more, no less. God was not a tyrant who allowed only the fittest of spiritual athletes to attain the prize of salvation. No amount of fasting, praying and spiritual exercises could lead to salvation. It was rather a gift of divine largesse, and all that God required of the believer was faith that it was so. 'It was perhaps rather simple,' said Gordon Rupp, 'and perhaps one of the reasons why Luther towers above so many other Christian spiritual teachers is that he was, after all, a rather simple person.'[15] Over a decade after Luther's spiritual struggle Melanchthon elegantly (if dryly) encapsulated his doctrinal 'discovery' in the Augsburg confession (1530):

> Men cannot be justified before God by their own strength, merits or works, but are justified freely through Christ by faith, when they believe that they are received into grace and their sins forgiven through Christ, who made satisfaction by his death for our sins. This faith God imputes for righteousness before him.[16]

Given Luther's spiritual journey prior to 1517, it is unsurprising that the *Ninety-five Theses* were an incipient theology of righteousness rather than a simple condemnation of indulgences. The consequences of sin could not be removed by a mere cash transaction. The gospel alone was the remedy for sin. True repentance was nothing less than the gift of a loving response to God's love, and as such it encompassed the whole of the Christian life. As the first thesis stated, 'When our Lord and Master Jesus Christ said "Repent!" (Matt. 4.17), he willed the entire life of believers to be one of repentance.'

Luther's thinking was already moving beyond the immediate to the general, to the relationship between God's grace and the authority of the Church. All true Christians, he protests, have a 'share in all the benefits of Christ' (theses 36–7). The Pope's power is subject to proper limitation (5, 6, 25, 26). 'The true treasure of the church is the holy gospel' (62). Luther's *Sermon on Indulgence and Grace*, written at the same time as the *Ninety-Five Theses*, but not published until 1518, showed that a programme was developing. 'It is a grievous error to think that one could make amends for his sins, as God forgives sins without recompense, out of unlimited grace at all times, and demands nothing in return but living a proper life from then on.'[17] The grounds were set for the decisive debates and revolutionary tracts of 1517–21. Luther's rediscovery of justification by faith spelt the end of the penitential system within Western Protestantism, and as a consequence of that, a complete reordering of the way in which pastoral care was exercised.

Luther was no free-floating theologian. His feet were firmly on pastoral ground:

> Nobody can understand Virgil who has not been a shepherd or farmer for five years ... nobody can understand Cicero who has not

been a politician for twenty years – nobody can understand the Scriptures who has not looked after a congregation for a hundred years. We're beggars, that's the truth.[18]

It was because his feet were on pastoral ground that he saw with devastating clarity that a new church order was essential if his 'programme' of reform was to have any chance of taking root. His new understanding of the Christian faith – 'The sum of the gospel is this: who believes in Christ has forgiveness of sins' – implied a dramatic simplification of the Church. His emancipation from the chains of scholastic theology had coincided with a bitter critique of the hierarchy, whom he saw as misusing the gospel, exploiting spiritual privileges and turning the quest for salvation into a commercial activity. It is hardly surprising therefore that between 1517 and 1520 he appeared to turn his back on the Church as he knew it, and developed the concept of the priesthood of all believers in writings which are marked by a fervent anti-clericalism.[19] At first he thought the laity would be the springboard of the new evangelical movement. All Christians were priests, for all were justified by faith.

> Every Christian has the power the pope, bishops, priests and monks have, namely to forgive or not to forgive sins ... We all have this power to be sure, but no one shall dare exercise it publicly except he be elected to do so by the congregation.[20]

This was revolutionary indeed. Had Luther pursued his own logic, the clerical estate would have disappeared in favour of an egalitarian, mutually responsible Christian community. However, it did not take Luther long to back away from the implications of his own theology. The dangers of lay control were soon writ large in the events at Wittenberg whilst he was away in the Wartburg, in the Peasants' Revolt, and in the rapid development of apocalyptic radicalism. The parishes of Germany did not have a laity of sufficient maturity to handle the innovations and pressures of reform. So delicate and dangerous was the world in which Luther worked, he sought the co-operation of the secular authorities in creating the new church order. In the beginning he had assured congregations that they had the right to appoint their own pastors, but by 1520 he was appealing to the nobility to act as 'emergency-bishops', and expecting them to take responsibility for ecclesiastical change.

The 'Pure Gospel' had captured the mind of the German laity and they wanted preachers to expound it.[21] Providing for that was a huge supply-and-demand problem, but it was pastoral need that was to transform parish priest into Reformed minister. The Reformation could almost be subtitled 'the priority of preaching'. The imperative of every reformer was to allow the gospel free rein, for preaching was God's chosen means of bringing about salvation. A preacher, said Luther, ' ... is a very angel of God, a very bishop sent by God, a saviour of many people ... a light of the world'.[22] He called the church building a 'Mundhaus' (mouth-house). Preaching, the creation and conduct of liturgy and the exercise of proper ecclesiastical discipline dictated the need for a new ministerial order in Germany. As Luther put it, defending his decision to publish his 1526 German Mass,

> if one had the kind of people and persons who wanted to be Christians in earnest, the rules and regulations would soon be ready. But as yet I neither can nor desire to begin such a congregation or assembly or to make rules for it, nor do I see many who would want it ... to train the young and to call and attract others to faith, I shall, besides preaching – help to further such public services for the people, until Christians who earnestly love the Word find each other and join together. For if I should try to make it up out of my own need, it might turn into a sect. For we Germans are a rough, rude, reckless people, with whom it is hard to do anything, except in cases of dire need.[23]

The new Protestant ministry was therefore functional.

In the heady days of the 1520s all was in flux, and in matters of pastoral care, ministry and church order, Luther thought on his feet and took one pragmatic decision after another. The reformers never intended to destroy the unity of the Church but it was clear from the condemnation of Luther in 1521 onwards that reconciliation would be difficult if not impossible. However, for twenty years, up to the conference of Ratisbon (Regensburg) in 1541, reformers like Melanchthon and Bucer fervently hoped that the Church Universal might reform, and they devoted considerable energy to the quest for reconciliation. Hope continued to flicker until the defeat of the Catholic moderates in the Council of Trent and the election of the fearsome, despotic Pope Paul IV in 1555. Church order was not therefore at the top of their agenda. It was to be a second-generation concern, something which occupied the minds of Melanchthon and Bugenhagen, Bucer and especially Calvin rather than Luther and Zwingli.

Luther's early radicalism was tempered by later pragmatism. In some of his writings he appears to derive the ordained ministry from the universal priesthood of all believers. In others, he clearly distinguishes them and writes of the ministerial office as distinct and independent. It is also significant that he uses different words for the two concepts – 'sacerdotium' when he discusses the universal priesthood and 'ministerium' when he talks about the ordained ministry.[24] As he put it in *Concerning the Ministry* (1523), 'one is born a priest, one becomes a minister'.[25] Ministers were first and foremost preachers.

The vast majority of the first generation of evangelical preachers were drawn from the existing parochial clergy, and from religious who sympathized with the new movement. The standard of some of these ministers left much to be desired. In 1526 Melanchthon was part of a visitation team in Saxony. He enquired if one minister had taught his congregation the Ten Commandments, and received the unexpected reply, 'That book I have not been able to get.'[26] Martin Bucer's *De Censura* reveals the same need in England in the late 1540s. He pleaded for 'great exertions to see that the reform of the universities is complete and the spoliation of the churches finally stopped' so that clergy might be produced 'who are men so learned in the faithful word, which they are to impart in their teaching, and hold so fast to it, that they are able to give instruction in sound doctrine and refute those who contradict it'.[27] The parochial reformation was therefore inherently conservative, for the creation of a properly educated and equipped ministry was a universal requirement in the early decades of the Reformation, and it was not one which could be met easily or quickly. Until the mid-1550s (and in some cases later than that) across Reformed Europe, ideal church orders were tempered by simple practical problems, like the availability of personnel and what congregations wanted – which was sometimes not what church leaders thought they needed.

Luther wrote little about the specific office of the minister. He expected ministers to preach the Word and administer the sacraments. True elaboration of the Lutheran understanding of ministry, however, is really the work of Johannes Bugenhagen, the organizer of renewal in the north German churches in the 1520s and 1530s. He emphasized the nature of the ministry as a special spiritual office and developed a hierarchy of co-adjutors and superintendents. Emerging Lutheranism was to become increasingly hierarchical in the following decades.

In 1539 Luther listed the marks of the Church as the preaching of the Word, the administration of the sacraments and the exercise of discipline, and he added 'offices of the church', implying that he expected those duties to be part of the work of the Church's officers. These officers or ministers derived their authority in part from their local communities (by whom they were chosen), but also from God, for it was clear that such offices had scriptural mandate.[28] Discipline had previously been a function of the penitential system but Luther understood the power of the keys, of the binding and loosing of consciences, to be the responsibility of all Christians, for all were priests. He laid the theoretical foundations for Christians to unburden their consciences to each other and receive consolation and comfort from their fellow believers. Nonetheless, he was equally clear that only those authorized should perform that ministry in public, and pastoral care therefore remained a function of ministers, although they had no monopoly on it.

Luther was a widely experienced and able guide of souls, and his experience of the strengths of the mediaeval system led him to retain a high view of confession. He was maddeningly unsystematic, and his views on confession evolve. Initially he considered penance as one of the sacraments, although later he spoke simply of the two dominical sacraments. However, he sought to retain the pastoral power of confession, whilst freeing parishioners from the compulsion of the decree of the Fourth Lateran Council and its demand that all sins should be enumerated. That he considered unrealistic. Private confession remained an important part of the minister's armoury. However, the stress was on the educational task of explaining the true nature of contrition and faith for 'where there is not contrition and sorrow for sin, there is also no true faith' and equally 'true faith cannot exist where there is no true contrition and true fear and terror before God'.[29] The confessional was transposed into the relationship of pastor and people, and a pulpit ministry grounded in a genuine knowledge of the congregation. The healing of souls was taken into the home. Visitation became a significant part of the pastor's life – especially to the sick, the dying and those in prison. As sacrificing priest became preaching minister, visitation became the locus of pastoral care.

Later in the history of Lutheranism, particularly under the influence of Pietist leader Philip Spener (d. 1705), Luther's concept of the priesthood of all believers opened up the possibility of mutual care of souls by the laity. The size of some congregations had made confession as mechanical as it had ever been in mediaeval days. In 1688 John Winckler, the chief pastor in Hamburg, asked the Leipzig theology faculty how he could regard himself as the pastor of the 30,000 souls in his parish, most of whom he did not know. They pointed out that Jonah had ministered to four times that number and sought to reassure him that twenty confessions an hour was a perfectly acceptable way to go about this work. Spener was singularly unimpressed and suggested that the care of souls could also be expressed by the mutual friendship of Christian with Christian. That is still a facet of Lutheran life in some places.[30]

Although the dynamics of the Swiss reformations were different from those in Saxony and North Germany, the theology and practice of ministry and pastoral care which emerged were similar, not least because of the primacy of the Word. In Zurich, Strasbourg and Geneva, as in Wittenberg, the pastor was primarily a preacher. The Swiss reformers also experienced many of the same structural difficulties as their German counterparts such as an initial shortage of properly qualified preachers, and civil authorities anxious to retain control of the process of reform. Early Protestant conceptions of the ministry and pastoral care were forged on the anvil of rapid change, with no blueprint except Scripture and the fathers. They too had to steer between the Scylla of Rome and the Charybdis of the radicals. That helps explain both why there are so few treatises on ministry, despite its centrality to new visions of the way the Church should be, and why the pattern of local church leadership evolved pragmatically. That context determined the most significant early treatises on pastoral care, Zwingli's *The Shepherd (Der Hirt)* and *On the Preaching Office* (Vom Predigamt) and Bucer's *Concerning the True Cure of Souls*.

Huldrych Zwingli

Both of Zwingli's works were written in crisis. They are hasty polemics, not works of leisured systematics. *The Shepherd* was a (long) sermon preached to ministers during the second disputation in Zurich in 1523 and published some months later. It was written to secure the commitment of the parish priests to the reforming programme, contrasting the false Roman shepherd-priest with the true reformed shepherd. *On the Preaching Office* was a pamphlet fired in the battle on the other front, defending the reformed minister against the anabaptists.[31]

Zwingli's vision of the reformed ministry was deeply Christocentric. He must be 'pawned and spurned in himself, like a serf or a menial servant', looking only to God, and therefore begin his work at the foot of the cross. Emptied of himself, filled with God, in whom is all consolation and comfort, he can then begin his true work, which is the preaching of repentance.[32] For that, good humanist that he was, he expected a sound grounding in biblical studies. Yet the minister's work was not to be exhausted by preaching, for he must 'prevent the washed sheep falling into the excrement, that is, after the believers have come into a knowledge of their saviour and have experienced the friendly grace of God, they should thereafter lead a blameless life so that they no longer walk in death'. Pastoral sustenance and the exercise of discipline are part of the task, although Zwingli does not elaborate on this. Like all the reformers he expected a symmetry between preaching and practice, and called the 'true shepherds' to a prophetic stance. Sheep need a shepherd when they are in danger. So, they are to defend their sheep from idolatry and unrighteousness, and 'attack and destroy all buildings which have raised themselves against the heavenly Word', and do 'eternal battle with the powerful and the vices of this world'. The pastoral task necessitates a public ministry, which may well lead to death. All that is an outworking of divine love –

> It is apparent that nothing other than divine love can bring the shepherd to deny himself, to leave father and mother, to go forth without purse, knapsack and staff, to be dragged before the princes, beaten, falsely accused and killed and that love may not exist without the fundamental of undoubting trust.

If *The Shepherd* explored some of the inner structures of vocation, *The Preaching Office* emphasized the need for godly learning in ministers. Anabaptist preachers were infiltrating the parishes of Zurich in the early 1520s, promoting re-baptism. Zwingli wrote to defend the concept of a paid, educated ministry, sure in his conviction that labourers were worth their hire. He tells a story of an anabaptist weaver who announced that he would preach in his parish church one Sunday. The minister, to avoid disturbance, let him do so. He began to read from 1 Timothy, but when he came to the phrase 'whose consciences are branded' in 4.2, he stopped and said 'I do not understand this.'

> Whereupon the minister retorted, 'Stop then and I shall expound it for you.' When this happened the good people shouted, 'Bid him

come down.' The minister replied, 'Had I ordered him down on my account I would have aroused suspicion, therefore you bid him come down.' Thus he finally came down. Now let all Christians discern the spirit. First of all, he elevates himself without any regard for the whole church. Secondly, he claims to be a divine spirit, yet fails to understand, though he is able to read. But the divine spirit instructs even the ignorant of his meaning and intention. Therefore it is evident that it is not a divine mission but something that is rhymed together and a skill that puffs up.[33]

Vocation needs correlative support. The call of God in the individual's heart must be echoed in the authorization of the Church. Like Luther in his later writings, Zwingli differentiates between the priesthood in which all share, and the office of ministry, which he ties firmly to education, in the sense of a knowledge of the biblical languages.[34] Rounding once again on the anabaptists, he points to James 3.1 ('Not many of you should become teachers') – ' the godly, saintly apostle warns us not to take being a teacher too lightly, lest we set ourselves up, ill-prepared and poorly equipped'.[35] There is little directly said about pastoral care in this pamphlet, but that is unsurprising. Zwingli wrote about it nowhere at length, for all was subsumed into the work of the preacher. Preaching was not a rarified academic activity, although in his eyes it demanded the very best of scholarship. Applying the Word of God to the life of God's people, indeed of God's world, was at its heart a pastoral activity, just as it was for the Old Testament prophets in whose works he delights. It was all of a piece – public, prophetic, private, consoling, broken into the multiplicity of the minister's work, baptizing, administering the sacraments, visiting the sick, caring for the poor from the Church's resources, but above all teaching.[36]

Unlike Luther, Zwingli was clear from the first that penance was not a sacrament. Conviction of sin resulted from hearing the gospel, and confession was a matter for the believer and God. Much as he believed that auricular confession should be translated into private pastoral advice, he was, however, astute enough to see that 'there are still a number of people who place great value on confession and who would be greatly angered if they were to be done away with suddenly' and he therefore tolerated its continuance.[37] Binding and loosing, and the ultimate sanction of excommunication, was 'the sole prerogative' of the Church.[38]

Martin Bucer

Zwingli's short and turbulent ministry precluded him from more elaborate arguments. It was Martin Bucer, the Strasbourg reformer, who wrote the finest of the Reformed treatises on pastoral care, *Concerning the True Cure of Souls*. This was a work of measured reflection and maturity. It was written in 1538, over a decade after the establishment of reform in the free imperial city. By then Strasbourg had adopted a rudimentary reformed church order, established a public school system, devised a workable method of welfare, created courts to supervise both marriage and morals, and taken a firm stance against the anabaptists. Bucer's overriding theological passion was the vision of a true Christian society, where Church and state co-operated in the distinct yet complementary spheres. This was not a simple translation of the mediaeval 'corpus Christianum' but a nuanced attempt to provide a theology which allowed independence to the Church and a Christian foundation of citizenship. In an age of division Bucer was a tireless negotiator for unity. *Concerning the True Cure of Souls* was written to exhibit 'the essential means whereby we can escape from the present so deplorable and pernicious state of religious schism and division and return to true Christian unity and good Christian order in the churches'.[39] Consisting of twelve chapters and a summary, it is the most comprehensive and systematic pastoral theology of the Reformation era. Each chapter begins with citations from Scripture which are then carefully expounded. Bucer first affirms the unity of the Church, for Christians are 'one body, partaking of one spirit, of one calling as being called to one hope and awaiting one salvation, recognising one Lord, having one faith, all having passed through one baptism, indeed having died and being born again as children of God in Christ'.[40] The quality of that unity in Christ should be reflected in the life and witness of the fellowship. Christ provides for their upbuilding and exercises his heavenly rule over them through the work of various ministries – pastors, teachers and 'those commissioned by the whole church to care for those in need'.[41] He divides pastoral care into two functions – the care of souls, and the care of bodily needs. The latter was the work of deacons in the primitive Church, and Bucer argues for the reintroduction of that office, 'through which the Lord wishes to provide in his church for the bodily needs of his people'.[42] Bucer is profoundly Lutheran in his belief that the care of souls consists of 'the proclaiming of the whole word of God', which he breaks down into the component parts of teaching, exhorting, warning, disciplining, pardoning and reconciling. His striking originality lies in his perception that this is a plural ministry, not a conglomerate task for one minister of Word and sacraments. A careful survey of texts from Acts, 1 Corinthians, Ephesians, Titus and 1 Timothy leads him to conclude that each congregation should have 'as many [elders] as are required by the need of each church, depending on the number of people in it and the circumstances of the church'. There will be a 'bishop and chief pastor' drawn from their number.[43] They are to be such people as the congregation will trust and value, displaying the qualities outlined in the pastoral epistles, but Bucer adds perceptively, 'they are to be chosen from people of all classes and types; because the Lord desires to bring those of all classes and types to positions of honour and use them in this his ministry'.[44]

Bucer outlines a fivefold work for these carers for souls, based on Ezekiel 34.16.[45] They are to lead to Christ and the Church those still estranged from him, restore those who have fallen away 'through the affairs of the flesh or false doctrine', secure amendment of life for sinners within the Christian community, strengthen fainthearted Christians and protect and encourage the whole and strong in their Christian journey. The remaining five chapters explore in detail how that ministry is to be executed. The restoration of true church discipline was the vital component in Bucer's vision of pastoral care. He laments the absence of true penance from the mediaeval Church and expounds its biblical and patristic roots with insight and common sense. Here, he argues, is the medicine of Christ for the wounded soul.

In the case of serious errors – denial of the faith, adoption of false worship, deliberate blasphemy, murder, adultery and false witness – penance should be enforced. His concern is not with forgiveness – that is God's prerogative and his mercy is great – but with spiritual health. Penance is a genuine path to spiritual wholeness. Those under penitential discipline will be enabled the better to recognize, and therefore shun, their sins. It must, of course, be applied with diligence, wisdom and Christian gentleness, lest it frighten the sinner from the Church. However, if it is administered properly, so that 'people are caused, moved, brought and encouraged to exercise genuine child-like faith and amendment of life', it will be beneficial for the individual, the Church and the wider community. He underlines his point with the example of Ambrose and the emperor Theodosius, whose eight-month excommunication for the massacre in

Thessalonica led not only to the emperor's repentance but to a more humane and just legal system in the empire.

There was here a concept not just of a properly ordered (or controlled) Christian state, but of genuine concern for the integrity of the Christian community, coupled with shrewd perception about the work of such emotions as shame and acceptance in modifying moral and spiritual behaviour. *Concerning the True Care of Souls* is not a manual of moral theology, still less a Protestant confessor's guide. Yet it does display innate pastoral sensitivity in differentiating the encounters of pastoral carers with their parishioners. The weak in faith are to be 'lifted up ... not subjected to searching examination in their thoughts and consciences', the timid to be spoken to 'kindly and comfortably' that they may recognize and internalize God's fatherly intent, the strong in Christ to be encouraged that 'all their plans, decisions and actions stem from faith and a living knowledge of Christ'.[46]

Bucer's work marked the true recovery of the early-church discipline of pastoral theology amongst the churches of the Reformation.[47] However, theoretical ideals are rarely translated with ease into pastoral reality, as Bucer was to discover in Strasbourg. Corporate ministry and serious discipline had to contend with reluctant elders and an indifferent flock! Elders (or Kirchenpfleger) had been introduced into Strasbourg in 1531 as part of a process of decentralizing discipline into parishes, following the practice of Oecolampadius in Basel and Bucer himself in Ulm. There were three for each parish, one chosen by the magistrates, another from the 300 aldermen, and the third a parish member. They were expected to watch over the work of the clergy, but also to work with them in regulating parish life. The system clearly failed because the Senate reminded them of their authority again in 1539 after the pastors had asked that something should be done to hinder the multiplication of sects. Such documentary evidence as there is (a little from Bucer's own parish of St Thomas) suggests those who received summonses ignored them, and that the incipient anti-clericalism of the Senate worked against the scheme.[48]

This may well have been a contributory factor in one of the most remarkable developments in Bucer's ministry: the creation of small confessing 'Christian communities' in the parishes between 1547 and 1549 following the defeat of the forces of Protestantism in the Schmalkaldic War. They became the focus of the marks of the Church (unity, catholicity, holiness, and apostolicity) which he had fervently hoped would be characteristic of the entire Reformed world. It was a bitter irony that the apostle of unity should have been forced into what was (in spite of his fervent denials) a form of sectarianism and that he should leave the Strasbourg church in utter disarray when he left for exile in England in 1549.[49] However, his experience exemplified a problem that was to recur in countless ways in the later history of Protestantism: was the Church a confessing minority or the nation at prayer?

If Bucer may stake a claim to the title of 'Pastoral Theologian of Reformation', the accolade 'Ecclesiologist' should be granted to Calvin, his colleague in Strasbourg between 1531 and 1541. It was in the small, intimate city of Geneva that Bucer's insights were honed into a church order and discipline of lasting import. Under Calvin's watchful eye, guided by his pragmatic genius, *Kirchenpfleger* became elders, the corporate ministry a shared court of ruling and teaching elders, and discipline a force finely balanced between love and control.

John Calvin and Geneva

Calvin's work will be misunderstood unless it is appreciated that he was primarily a local minister, albeit one of prodigious ability and world reputation. He was not a professor of theology; indeed, he was a theologian only in so far as theology supported and grew out of his pastoral work. His life was circumscribed by the demands of the pulpit (preaching about 170 sermons a year), the pastoral needs of the small city and its endless influx of refugees, countless meetings and a voluminous correspondence which embraced the Protestant world. He gave of himself unstintingly, perhaps unhealthily so, for there is an almost neurotic compulsion about his unceasing activity. Part of the difficulty of writing about Calvin is that he was deliberately self-effacing. It was the Word of God that mattered, not its messenger. However, Calvin was a deeply respected director of souls. That was a ministry crafted from acquaintance with the joys and sadness of human living in the reflective context of the Word of God felt always on the pulses. He knew the pain of loss – of a beloved wife and a small baby. He knew the empathetic helplessness of a parent watching his (step)children's marriages fall apart, and for most of his working life he knew what it was to be slandered and pilloried by a section of the community for standing up for what he believed to be the truth.[50] His correspondence reveals the method of his spiritual counsel. It flows from Scripture. It is drenched in its imagery and he assumes his correspondents are as intimate with it as he is. He recommends them to meditate on Scripture and draw from it a certitude of faith which leaves no room for doubt. Within that context, there is evidence of deep humanity and understanding of the dilemmas and difficulties of life, whether he is writing to encourage the leaders of Reformed Europe in the struggle against the forces opposing reform, or consoling the bereaved, or sustaining those faced with the certainty of execution, or giving advice on matters of marriage, or exploring the moral maze of usury.[51]

If the heart of pastoral care is the interrelationship between pastor and people, Calvin was at its cutting edge throughout his career. There are clear points of continuity and discontinuity with the catholic tradition. As a 'spiritual director' he (like all early Protestants) saw himself as a physician for a soul in crisis rather than a permanent guide, and although he expected his advice to be considered thoughtfully, he never considered it authoritative. As a pastor he adopted the conventional Protestant view of confession, rejecting its obligatory nature but recognizing its pastoral value. He approved of mutual unburdening within the Christian community – 'we should lay our infirmities on one another's breasts, to receive among ourselves mutual counsel, mutual compassion, and mutual consolation'.[52] He believed that many would want to use their pastor in this role. Ministers appointed by God were given the power to correct and loose souls from sin, and the believer 'should not neglect what the Lord has offered by way of remedy'.[53] Indeed, he actively encouraged them to do so. In the section on the visitation of the sick in his liturgy Calvin wrote, 'The office of a true and faithful minister is not only publicly to teach the people over whom he is ordained pastor, but as far as may be, to admonish, exhort, rebuke and console each one in particular.'[54] He suggests that the pastor should hold an interview with each communicant before communion – which was all very well in a small town like Geneva served by a number of parishes. As in Lutheranism, the pastoral guidance which lies at the heart of confession turned into the work of pastoral visitation. He is equally clear that the power of the keys was given to ministers solely because it was through their preaching of the Word that 'the grace of the gospel is publicly and privately sealed in the hearts of the believers'.[55] The power of the keys is a function of the gospel and ministers are servants of the Word.

The grandeur of the Word, its encompassing of all that is necessary for salvation, dictated the work of the ministry and the exercise of discipline in the Church. Part of the distinctiveness of Calvin's ecclesiology was his distinction between the complementary jurisdictions of Church and state, doubtless in part a response to his observation of Bucer's struggle in Strasbourg. The spiritual jurisdiction of the Church was independent of that of the state. Calvin's elders were therefore different to Bucer's *Kirchenpfleger*. Bucer's teaching on discipline in *Concerning the True Cure of Souls* is much less clear-cut than Calvin's. There is a certain confusion between the roles of elders and pastors in Bucer. His elders at one point have a supervisory role over the pastors on behalf of the secular authorities, but at others they share in some of the pastoral functions of the pastors. Calvin's definition of the ministerial offices is far more precise, and he was more successful than Bucer in creating a lay office which was part of the jurisdiction of the Church rather than the state.[56]

The eldership must be seen within Calvin's total vision of a plural, fourfold ministry of pastors, doctors, elders and deacons. Few have had such a high view of ministers of the word and sacraments as Calvin – 'neither the light and heat of the sun, nor food and drink are so necessary to nourish and sustain the present life as the apostolic and pastoral office is necessary to preserve the church on earth'.[57] Their work was 'by the doctrine of Christ to instruct the people to true godliness, to administer the sacred mysteries and to keep and exercise upright discipline'.[58] Although the pastoral task involved teaching, Calvin (following a minority exegetical tradition) conceived of a distinct order of doctors whose work consisted solely of scriptural interpretation and keeping 'doctrine whole and pure amongst the believers'.[59] It was never to play a major part in the Reformed tradition. Deacons, all the reformers agreed, were responsible for the care of the poor. Calvin thought this should be a permanent office within the Church. These were relatively uncontentious conclusions.

Innovative, and determinative within the Reformed tradition, was the lay office of elder. As Elsie McKee has shown, Calvin derived the office essentially from his study of 1 Corinthians 12.28 and Romans 12.6–8. The Western exegetical tradition considered the *gubernationes* of 1 Corinthians 12.28 as those who had a pastoral or ruling function (bishops, priests, abbots, sometimes princes). Zwinglians saw their function as moral discipline, but they did not consider it a distinctly ecclesiastical office. Bucer considered the work of 'ruling' to be common to both secular and ecclesial offices. Calvin 'clarified' this insight by cross-referencing it with 1 Timothy 5.17, insisting that ecclesiastical elders were different animals from Christian magistrates.[60] Calvin, trained initially as a humanist lawyer, had a rare gift for clarity. By allowing Scripture to interpret Scripture he articulated the hints of earlier reformers about lay ministry into a coherent church order. What emerged was a lay ministry of ruling – discipline.

If the soul of the Church was Christ, Calvin suggested, discipline was its sinews, holding the body together. It was a 'bridle', a 'spur', and sometimes a 'father's rod to chastise mildly and with the gentleness of Christ's Spirit those who have more seriously lapsed'.[61] By judicious use of private admonition and public censure, the purity of the body will be maintained, the name of Christ protected from dishonour, the faithful protected and the sinner brought to repentance.[62]

Many assumptions have been made about the impact of Calvinist discipline in the compact city of Geneva. Much pastoral care and guidance was given privately. Only the most difficult cases reached the consistory, the court of pastors and elders set up under the *Ecclesiastical Ordinances* of 1541 to deal with matters of church discipline. There seems to be ample evidence to attest the negative aspects of the cultural revolution which Calvin brought to the city. The records of the consistory reveal a regime that objected to the playing of cards and dice, disciplined a barber for tonsuring a priest, and punished three young men for eating thirty-six pates! However, as Robert Kingdon has shown, such a reading is inadequate. The full records of the consistory have only recently been transcribed, and scholarly evaluation of them is still in progress. Historians have had perforce to rely on a partial nineteenth-century selection of material which gives undue emphasis to absurd and melodramatic cases. Kingdon's preliminary conclusion from an examination of the whole record reveals a gentler, wiser regime striving to bring a new Protestant world into being.

Far from being simply a court, the consistory seems also to have functioned as an educational institution and as a counselling service. Establishing Protestantism, a religion of vernacular words, demanded education, particularly for people whose religious world-view was visual, tactile and (when words were used) Latin. The consistory was an important element in this process, urging people to attend 'sermons' (a generic word for services, of which there were around 30 per week in the various parishes of Geneva, deliberately set at different times so that as many of the populace as possible could attend), and to learn the Lord's Prayer and the Creed and attend the catechism. At times the consistory could be quite harsh with those who stuck determinedly to the old ways. It could also be surprisingly gentle, as in its encouragement of the elderly widow Myaz Richardet, who could barely read, to memorize the Lord's Prayer and the Creed. For a period of a year in 1542/3 they gently guided her in the new ways, with quiet encouragement, until she was proficient.

At other times the consistory became a mechanism for resolving disputes between family members, business partners and neighbours. Once again the evidence suggests that the consistory had a genuine care for the individuals who came before it, seeking peace and reconciliation wherever possible. This was discipline as pastoral care. It was undoubtedly a remarkably instrusive agency, and a powerful force for social control, but the obverse of intrusion is loving concern. As Kingdon justly remarks, 'It really tried to assist everyone in its city-state to live the kind of life it thought God intended people to live. Nobody in Calvin's Geneva could complain of the kind of "anomie", or complete and hopeless anonymity, that is such a curse in so many big cities in today's world.'[63]

The early reformers created a new world. In place of the visual culture of late mediaeval catholicism with its central symbol of God made present in Eucharist host, they offered a God who had come in Jesus Christ, and spoke still through the words of Scripture and sermons in the language of every man and woman. It is hard after four centuries to capture the thrill of immediacy, the sense of involvement and participation which rippled through early Reformed Europe. Holiness was no longer the prerogative of the few, but the possession of all. All were priests. All the world resonated with the glory of God. The counting-house was as much a temple as the cathedral. Private confession and the penitential cycle, although probably not the source of mental anguish that some historians consider them to have been, were replaced by systems of care which made individuals valued members of spiritual and temporal communities. The profit and loss account of the Reformation was more equitably balanced than some suggest.

Establishing that world was far from easy, indeed it is a matter of open debate among historians if it was ever established. Some, like John Bossy, argue persuasively that the Catholic and Protestant Reformations should be seen as part of one process of Christianizing a pagan Europe.[64] Similarly the work of students of 'popular religion' in the early modern and modern periods reminds us that 'Christian orthodoxy' (however defined) was often the religion of a minority. The fundamental question raised by the Reformation – 'Who is a Christian?' – reverberates still. The history of Protestantism could therefore be read as the history of a range of pastoral strategies designed to Christianize local communities and help people grow in faith.

Bringing the new Protestant world to be entailed a massive educational task, both within parishes and in the training of clergy. The papers of the Genevan consistory, and visitation reports from varying countries, provide a glimpse into the difficulties of transforming devotional practices, and into the use of ecclesiastical and civil law to bring that about. The provision of a properly trained clergy was a headache for all Protestant church leaders in the sixteenth century. The Protestant minister was primarily a preacher who needed to be trained in the interpretation and exposition of Scripture. He was also responsible for the spiritual health of the Christian community, and expected to lead an exemplary life. Meeting those demands was far from easy. Almost all those appointed to the ministry in the early days in Geneva departed prematurely, and Bullinger soon realized that gentle management of under-educated rural clergy in the vast hinterland of Zurich was essential.[65]

Geneva provides an interesting but atypical case-study. Until 1545 the average tenure of ministers in Geneva was three years. Of the 31 ministers employed in Geneva between 1538 and 1546, only one remained in post throughout. Such instability was clearly counterproductive, and Calvin sought to improve the quality of ministry by hiring better qualified and more experienced Frenchmen, marked by 'education, proven religious zeal, noble birth, fiery preaching, and a measure of independent wealth'. This was part of his struggle for supremacy in Geneva. By 1546 things were improving, and the quality of the clergy was matched by the stability of the lay eldership serving on the consistory. At the same time programmes were instituted to provide care for the poor and education for all. Pastoral care, education and the quality of the clergy were interlinked. All were essential to the establishment of the new faith. After Calvin's eventual political victory in Geneva in 1555 the Senate turned its mind to the institution that would complete Calvin's reforming programme, the Genevan Academy.[66] Calvin had envisaged such an institution in his 1541 Ecclesiastical Ordinances.

It opened in 1559, under the rectorship of Theodore de Bèze, with the main aim of training men for the Reformed ministry. From the beginning there was conflict between the ministers, who thought of the Academy primarily as a seminary, and the magistrates who hankered after a more conventional institution of higher education which would embrace such subjects as civil law and medicine, bringing both much-needed income and welcome prestige to the city. It was part of the flowering of a Protestant network of universities and academies which spread across Europe as Catholic universities refused to accept Protestant students. The Academy's history raises sharply a question which has echoed across the centuries: How were ministers formed, by practical training or academic scholarship? The Academy, in co-operation with the Company of Pastors, provided a judicious blend. Academic standards were high, the teaching initially of a significantly impressive quality, rural pulpits provided preaching practice, and moral discipline was evident. The Academy made a significant contribution to the leadership of the new Reformed ministry, particularly in France, but also in the Low Countries, at least until the new University of Leiden was firmly established. In 1597 Jacob Anjorrant reported back to the Genevan authorities from the Netherlands that Geneva's reputation was still strong, and that ministers trained at the Academy were highly regarded for their learning and godly discipline in equal measure. The Reformed expected an integrated ministry. Sound learning in Greek, Hebrew, theology and the arts (the staple curriculum of the Academy) was of little worth unless allied to godly living.

The senders and recipients of ministers did not always share a common conviction about the skills necessary for ministry. In 1613 the church at Rouen wrote to the Company of Pastors pointing out that one candidate recommended to them could only remain in post for 18 months and had a large family – it was, they protested, barely worth the journey. Another caused anxiety because of his weak voice, and they doubted that he would be heard by 'the four to five thousand people who make up this church'. In the new aural culture such skills were important. The balance between theological competence, practical skills and godly living in candidates for ministry is a recurring theme in Protestantism. The correspondence of the churches to the Academy and the Company of Pastors in the late sixteenth century showed them to be preoccupied with practical concerns. While the magistrates pressed the Academy to transform itself into a pseudo-university, the churches expected a judicious measure of practical training. Ministry was as much an art as an academic discipline, so Genevan training relied on the good offices of the Company of Pastors as well as on the learning of the Academy's professors.[67]

The success of Calvin's entire system in Geneva was winsomely attractive, and became an ideal to the refugees and students from the Reformed world who were drawn to the city. It was not easily replicated.

Geneva was small, self-contained and relatively easily organized. Life was very different in other countries. In England and Scotland the Reformation was state-backed, and the choice of ministry determined by the available pool of talent (or lack of it). For a brief period in Elizabethan England almost anyone who presented himself was ordained. In Scotland great use was made of former notaries and schoolteachers. In France and the Netherlands where the Church was established in the teeth of state opposition, inner calling was more significant that higher education in the early decades.[68]

Different contexts demanded different strategies, and progress towards a graduate clergy was not uniform. Slowly (and in some places very slowly) the value of loyalty to the new regime was replaced by regulation and qualification. By the early seventeenth century the ministry had established itself as a significant and viable career option. Old priest had indeed become new presbyter. The clergy had survived the reformations.

The pastoral legacy of the reformations

The outline of the legacy of the Reformation in pastoral care is now clear. The forgiveness of sins was a function of the gospel, and the cycle of sin, guilt, conviction of sin and redemption became subsumed into the work of the pulpit and public liturgy – as seen in Calvin's insistence on the use of a general confession. Auricular confession was replaced with private pastoral advice. This was normally part of the relationship between minister and parishioner, but there was clear theological endorsement of the 'priesthood' of the faithful to each other, and as the traditions developed that took various forms. The purity of the community and the growth in faith and holiness of the elect was regulated by the use of church discipline. The way in which that discipline was exercised depended largely on the spectrum of ecclesiologies which developed within European Protestantism, and on the way in which reformation was fostered within nation-states.

The reformations of the sixteenth century shattered the unity of the Western Church. The Church Universal divided not just into national churches (in a longer perspective, that could be seen as continuing the trend of mediaeval Christendom), but into competing confessional bodies, some established, others dissenting. The nature of pastoral care in the seventeenth and eighteenth centuries was to be partly determined by those structural questions, but those patterns of continuity and discontinuity should not be allowed to detract from the coherence of a common inheritance.

Notes

1. Quoted in J. Mahoney, *The Making of Moral Theology* (Oxford, 1987), pp. 17-18.
2. An early 14th-century MS in Cambridge University Library, quoted in Miri Rubin, *Corpus Christi: The Eucharist in Late Medieval Culture* (Cambridge, 1991), p. 99 (my modernization).
3. Rubin, *Corpus Christi*, p. 60; Eamon Duffy, *Stripping the Altars* (London, 1992), p. 98.
4. Duffy, ibid., p. 98.
5. Ibid., p. 100.
6. Ibid., p. 103.
7. Rubin, *Corpus Christi*, p. 117.
8. Duffy, *Stripping the Altars*, p. 102.
9. Ibid., p. 125; Rubin, *Corpus Christi*, pp. 73–7.
10. Ronald Hutton, *The Rise and Fall of Merrie England: The Ritual Year 1400–1700* (London, 1994).
11. Thomas Tentler, 'Confession', in *The Oxford Encyclopedia of the Reformation*.
12. Duffy, *Stripping the Altars*, p. 60.
13. P. N. Brooks, 'Martin Luther and the pastoral dilemma', in P. N. Brooks (ed.), *Christian Spirituality: Essays in Honour of Gordon Rupp* (London, 1975), pp. 95–119.
14. Heiko Oberman, *Luther, Man between God and the Devil* (ET London, 1993), pp. 187–8.
15. Gordon Rupp, *The Righteousness of God* (London, 1953), p. 128.
16. G. Rupp and B. Drewery, *Martin Luther* (London, 1970), p. 145.
17. Ibid., p. 192.
18. Quoted in Rupp, *Righteousness of God*, p. 285; the references (which are not given in Rupp), are *Weimarer Ausgabe, Tischreden* 5677 and *Luther's Works* 54, p. 476. I am indebted to Dr Peter Brooks for these.
19. Andrew Pettegree, 'The clergy and the Reformation: from "devilish priesthood" to new professional elite', in Andrew Pettegree (ed.), *The reformation of the Parishes: The Ministry and the Reformation in Town and Country* (Manchester, 1993), pp. 1–22.
20. Wilhelm Pauck, 'The ministry in the time of the Continental Reformation', in H. Richard Niebuhr and Daniel D. Williams (eds), *The Ministry in Historical Perspective* (New York, 1956), pp. 110–49, p. 113 quoting *Church Postil* (1522).
21. Pettegree, 'Clergy and Reformation', p. 4.
22. Pauck, 'Ministry', p. 114, quoting *Weimarer Ausgabe* 30(2), p. 533, l. 20.
23. *Luther's Works*, 53, p. 63.

24. Bernhard Lohse, *Martin Luther: An Introduction to his Life and Thought* (ET Edinburgh, 1987), p. 184.
25. *Luther's Works* 40, p. 18.
26. Pauck, 'Ministry', p. 132.
27. E. C. Whitaker, *Martin Bucer and the Book of Common Prayer*, Alcuin Club collection, (Great Wakering, 1974), p. 46.
28. Euan Cameron, *The European Reformation* (Oxford, 1991), p. 149.
29. 'Instructions for the visitors of parish pastors', *Luther's Works* 40, p. 294.
30. J. T. McNeill, *A History of the Cure of Souls* (New York, 1951), p. 183.
31. W. P. Stephens, *The Theology of Huldrych Zwingli* (Oxford, 1986), pp. 276–81.
32. All quotations are from *The Shepherd*, trans. H. Wayne Pipkin, in *Selected Writings of Huldrych Zwingli*, vol. 2 (Pittsburgh, 1984), pp. 81–125.
33. *The Preaching Office*, in Pipkin, *Writings of Zwingli*, vol. 2, pp. 147–85, at p. 174.
34. Ibid., p. 173, 'all commentaries and teachers are as nothing when compared to the knowledge of languages'.
35. Ibid., p. 182.
36. Stephens, *Theology of Zwingli*, p. 281.
37. 'The defense of the Reformed faith', in *Selected writings of Huldrych Zwingli*, trans. E. J. Fursha, vol. 1 (Pittsburgh, 1984), pp. 118 and 319.
38. Ibid., p. 232.
39. *Concerning the True Cure of Souls and Genuine Pastoral Ministry*, trans. Peter Beale (1993, typescript in Westminster College Library), p. 1.
40. Ibid., p. 7.
41. Ibid., p. 17.
42. Ibid., p. 20.
43. Ibid., p. 23.
44. Ibid., p 34.
45. Bucer's version of Ezek. 34.16 reads differently to most modern translations. The phrase translated 'the fat and the strong I will destroy' in NRSV reads 'the sleek and the strong I will watch over'.
46. Bucer, *True Cure of Souls*, pp. 94–5.
47. Derek Tidball, *Skilful Shepherds: An Introduction to Pastoral Theology* (Leicester, 1986), p. 189.
48. Jean Rott, 'The Strasbourg Kirchenpfleger and parish discipline: theory and practice', in D. F. Wright (ed.), *Martin Bucer: Reforming Church and Community* (Cambridge, 1994), pp. 2–128.
49. See Gottfried Hamman, 'Ecclesiological motifs behind the creation of the "Christlichen Gemeinshaften"', and James Kittelson, 'Martin Bucer and the ministry of the Church', in D. F. Wright (ed.), *Martin Bucer*, pp. 129–44 and 83–95 respectively; for those views transposed into an English context, see Bucer's *De Censura* in Whitaker, *Bucer and the Book of Common Prayer*, p. 106.
50. For his family life see T. H. L. Parker, *John Calvin* (Berkhamstead, 1975), pp. 120–3 and William Bouwsma, *John Calvin: A Sixteenth Century Portrait* (Oxford, 1988), pp. 22–3.

51. For Calvin as spiritual director see McNeill, *History of the Cure of Souls*, pp. 203–9. He follows J. D. Benoit, *Calvin: Director of Souls* (1947).
52. *Institutes* III.iv.6.
53. *Institutes* III.iv.12.
54. McNeill, *History of the Cure of Souls*, p. 197.
55. *Institutes* III.iv.14.
56. The evolution of the office is traced in David Cornick, 'The Reformed elder', *Expository Times* 98/8 (May 1987), pp. 235–40; a detailed examination of the exegetical roots of Calvin's theory of eldership is E. A. McKee, *Elders and the Plural Ministry* (Geneva, 1988).
57. *Institutes* IV.iii.2.
58. *Institutes* IV.iii.6.
59. *Institutes* IV.iii.4; for the exegetical tradition see McKee, *Elders and Plural Ministry*, pp. 215–16.
60. Calvin's exegesis of 1 Tim. 5.17 seems more like eisegesis than exegesis to modern eyes, but the identification of a plurality of presbyteral ministries in the verse was unexceptional in both Roman Catholic and Protestant circles in the early sixteenth century. What was new was Calvin's use of that plurality to distinguish elders and pastors. McKee, *Elders and Plural Ministry*, pp. 87–100. This was to cause fierce debate later, particularly among Scottish presbyterians – Cornick, 'Reformed elder'.
61. *Institutes* IV.xii.1.
62. *Institutes* IV.xii.5.
63. These paragraphs rely on Robert M. Kingdon, 'The Geneva Consistory in the time of Calvin' in Andrew Pettegree, Alastair Duke and Gillian Lewis (eds), *Calvinism in Europe 1540–1620* (Cambridge, 1994), pp. 21–34. The quotation is from p. 34.
64. John Bossy, *Christianity in the West 1300–1700* (Oxford, 1985).
65. Pettegree, 'The clergy and the Reformation', p. 9.
66. William Naphy, 'The renovation of the ministry in Geneva', in Andrew Pettegree (ed.), *The Reformation of the Parishes* (Manchester, 1993), pp. 113–32. The quotation is from p. 124.
67. The Genevan Academy has received a good deal of recent scholarly attention – see Gillian Lewis, 'The Genevan Academy', in Pettegree, *et al.*, *Calvinism in Europe*, pp. 35–64 for matters of curriculum and politics; Karen Maag, 'Education and training: the Academy of Geneva', in Pettegree, *Reformation of the Parishes*, pp. 133–52; and *Seminary or University? The Genevan Academy and Reformed Higher Education 1560–1620* (Aldershot, 1995). Anjorrant's report is from the latter, p. 186.
68. Pettegree, 'The clergy and the Reformation', pp. 10–11.

Bibliography

John Bossy, *Christianity in the West 1300-1700* (Oxford, 1985)
P. N. Brooks, 'Martin Luther and the pastoral dilemma', in P. N. Brooks (ed.)

Christian Spirituality: Essays in Honour of Gordon Rupp (London, 1975), pp. 95–119
William A. Clebsch and Charles R. Jaeckle, *Pastoral Care in Historical Perspective* (New York, 1964)
Karen Maag, *Seminary or University? The Genevan Academy and Reformed Higher Education 1560–1620* (Aldershot, 1995)
J. T. McNeill, *A History of the Cure of Souls* (New York, 1951)
Andrew Pettegree, Alastair Duke and Gillian Lewis (eds), *Calvinism in Europe 1540–1620* (Cambridge, 1994)
Andrew Pettegree (ed.), *The Reformation of the Parishes: The Ministry and the Reformation in Town and Country* (Manchester, 1993)
Derek Tidball, *Skilful Shepherds: An Introduction to Pastoral Theology* (Leicester, 1986)
D. F. Wright (ed.), *Martin Bucer: Reforming Church and Community* (Cambridge, 1994)

12

The ministry to outsiders

The Jesuits

John O'Malley

Historians have so often depicted Jesuits as reformers, intellectuals, controversialists, schoolmasters and political connivers that they have obscured the fundamental fact that the Society of Jesus was founded 'to help souls', that is, for ministry. If we are to understand the Jesuits, we must look upon them first and foremost as ministers, for that is how they conceived themselves. Moreover, the Jesuits' pursuit of ministry had a number of special characteristics that make a study of it particularly fruitful for ministry today, partly because the Jesuits challenge on several levels the model of parochial 'care of souls' now prevalent in all mainline churches.

When the order was founded in 1540 by ten graduates of the University of Paris led by Ignatius of Loyola, it fitted naturally into the pattern of ministry created by the Dominicans, Franciscans and similar orders of friars in the thirteenth century. With those orders of friars, several corps of ministers had come into being with ecclesiastical (i.e. papal) approval, which were neither in theory nor in fact under the jurisdiction of bishops and which were distinct from the *local* or diocesan clergy. (Monks like the Benedictines were not, according to canon law, supposed to engage in ministry outside their monasteries.)

The ministry of the local clergy in parishes or their equivalent consisted for the most part in the conduct of local worship and the ministry of the sacraments, following rituals and rites according to a set calendar. The ministers might be 'local boys', usually and often inadequately 'trained' locally by being 'apprenticed' to a local priest. They might get their 'living' from a local magnate, or the town council, or from the bishop. They ministered to a predetermined local congregation.

The friars, in contrast, transcended diocesan boundaries, were moved about from place to place by their own elected superiors, developed elaborate systems of formal education for themselves, eschewed the parish as the locus of their ministry and, most important, saw preaching as their primary ministry – performed often in the open air and intended often to reach 'the sinner' who was an outcast or outsider, not the person already safely in the pews. This led them by the early years of the sixteenth century to becoming the missionaries to the newly discovered lands.

The early Jesuits built on these traditions and articulated them even more forcefully. While they of course worked with the faithful in Europe and elsewhere, from the beginning they took 'the other' as their special concern. As Jerome Nadal, one of their most influential spokesmen, said, 'The Society has the care of those souls for whom either there is nobody to care or, if somebody ought to care, for whom the care is negligent. This is the reason for the founding of the Society. This is its dignity in the Church.'

This orientation had a number of significant manifestations. First, the Jesuits foreswore the parish as a place where they would minister. By virtue of canon law the parish belonged to the local clergy, but, more fundamentally, by tradition it ministered to people already in its pews on the presumption that they were satisfied with what it offered. Second, by moving outside the standard rhythm of Word and sacrament as practised in the parish, the Jesuits were almost forced to devise new ministries or new forms of old ministries as they met people on new ground.

Third, they began to devise a new vocabulary to describe what they were about. They seem, for instance, to have given us the term 'mission' in our contemporary sense of being sent out (like the apostles) to do ministry. We use mission and missionary so easily today that it is difficult to imagine a time when it was not part of the Christian vocabulary, yet until the sixteenth century even the 'foreign missions' were spoken of as 'propagation of the faith' or 'journeying to the infidel'. The word is important, for it suggests an ideal of ministry based not on the pattern of resident bishops and pastors like Ignatius of Antioch, Irenaeus of Lyons and Augustine of Hippo, but upon the itinerant Paul or, more fundamentally, the itinerant Jesus. The Jesuits were explicit, in fact, that

Paul and the Jesus of itinerant preaching were their primary models for ministry.

Another of their special words about ministry is 'accommodation'. If the Jesuits were to operate outside the traditional rhythms of the parish and deal especially with 'the other' – whether pagan, heretic, sinner or the particularly fervent Catholic – the standard forms of ministry could not apply. What was needed was adaptation to time, places, circumstances and persons.

The idea that ministries needed to be adapted to circumstances was of course not new in the sixteenth century or peculiar to the early Jesuits. Indeed, it pervaded the mediaeval tradition of moral reasoning known as casuistry, and it was a fundamental principle in the classical tradition of rhetoric on which much of the ministry of preaching had long been based. Nonetheless, special to the Jesuits' recourse to 'accommodation' was its pervasiveness, the frequency with which it was inculcated and promoted, and its appearance at almost every conceivable juncture of action and reflection. The Jesuit *Constitutions,* authored by Loyola and filled with escape-clauses, are symptomatic – do such and such, *unless* under the circumstances something else seems better.

The significance of this emphasis becomes clearer when it is compared with the reform of ministry undertaken by the Council of Trent, where not 'accommodation' but 'discipline' was the operative word – the minister (i.e. the pastor of the parish) was to ensure that the discipline of regular attendance at Mass and proper reception of the sacraments be observed. This ideal was based on abstract norms and derived from them.

Jesuits espoused the discipline of regular observance of the sacraments, but their situation led them to some striking 'accommodations' within that framework. Among the natives of Brazil, for example, they resorted, much to the dismay of the bishop, to the use of women interpreters in order to hear confessions. As one of them wrote back to Lisbon about one of the women, 'I have to admit, she's a better confessor than I am.' The most striking instance of the application of the principle of accommodation was in the mission to China, where by the early seventeenth century the Jesuits were wearing Mandarin dress and trying to show how certain Confucian rites and beliefs were compatible with Christianity.

The Jesuits fit, then, in the tradition of non-diocesan corps of ministers first created in the thirteenth century, and they developed the implications of that tradition further.

Through the *Spiritual Exercises* of Loyola they were also alive to the importance of another mediaeval tradition, the cultivation of religious experience, and the process of articulation of it, as useful for others. They tried to integrate this tradition into their ideal and practice of ministry.

The persuasion that the truly effective minister was a virtuous minister was almost axiomatic among the devout by the sixteenth century, codified for instance in the mediaeval handbooks for preachers, the *Artes praedicandi*. The good example set by the preacher's life was his most powerful word. In the *Constitutions* Ignatius taught that the minister was effective to the degree he was united to God and thus able to be an instrument in God's hands.

But there was more to it than that. It is crucial to remember that Ignatius did not take up ministry as a consequence of his ordination but did so decades earlier as the immediate result of his great conversion experiences as a layman, in 1521–3, and that he engaged in 'helping souls' for another fifteen years before he was ordained. The origin of this turning to ministry was his personal spiritual experience, and this fact would greatly influence the ideal of ministry he proposed.

What he attained as a result of his inner experiences and struggles was a sense of divine presence as manifested in comfort, joy and serenity, which he generally described as 'consolation'. He set as the ultimate goal for persons being led through the *Spiritual Exercises* that God be able to communicate directly with them and they with God, from which consolation would sooner or later result. Implicitly, and sometimes explicitly, helping individuals reach this situation, with the resultant spiritual relish, became a goal in all the ministries the Jesuits engaged in.

While the Jesuits were not the only persons in the sixteenth century to espouse this goal for their ministries, they had the unique advantage as a group of having a handbook, the *Exercises*, to give them guidance in pursuing it. Their goal, in other words, was not simply to ensure proper performance of religious duties, which is a fair statement of the goals of the Council of Trent, but to help individuals to a deeper religious intimacy.

Another mediaeval tradition that the Jesuits adopted and modified and that gave some of their ministries a special modality was that of the confraternities, those voluntary associations of men and women which were the forum in many cities of Europe where most people learned and practised their religion. In Venice by 1500, for instance, there were some 120, ranging from a few large and rich *scuole* (schools) to much more humble institutions, which were ever more consistently turning their concern to what we would today call 'social ministries', such as care for the poor and orphans.

The Jesuits, who had themselves begun as a confraternity, immediately enlisted other confraternities as partners in ministry or as agents to continue ministries already begun. In 1543, for instance, Ignatius, in co-operation with some aristocratic matrons, founded in Rome the 'House of Saint Martha' as a kind of halfway house for courtesans and prostitutes who sought a new start in life. The women entered the house for about six months to break with their past. Meanwhile, dowries were collected for them, so that they might marry, which most wanted to do, or enter a convent. Within a few years, the Jesuits turned the whole operation over to a confraternity. The Jesuits used confraternities in some Italian cities to maintain the peace in the face of the frightful and bloody vendettas that raged in many localities. They also often found in them the source of a ready team of catechists.

The Jesuits wove into their ideal of ministry formal schooling according to the newly revived ideal of the Renaissance. They were the first large organized body of ministers explicitly and professedly to undertake *as ministry* the staffing and administration of schools. That in itself is a remarkable development in ministry, in effect the creation of a new ministry. The Jesuits' action is intelligible only when we understand that in the Renaissance the humanistic ideal of schooling saw the educational process as formative of character, as a process geared to produce virtuous and upright Christians, who had been trained for a life of service in Church, state or local community. The Renaissance borrowed the ideal from Greek and Roman antiquity, but thinkers like Erasmus had reformulated it to give it a specifically Christian interpretation.

When the Jesuits decided in 1547 to reverse their original intention of not undertaking any permanent teaching positions, and indeed to open a humanistic school in the Sicilian city of Messina, they could not have foreseen that within a few years such schools would become their primary ministry in most parts of the world. Neither could they have foreseen the immense and fundamentally determining impact the schools would have on them.

I will mention only three aspects of that impact pertinent to the Jesuits' ministries. First, the Jesuits conducted this ministry in what was essentially a secular space – or, if that is too strong, they were ministers who spent most of their time ministering outside the physical confines of a church or presbytery. The schools, though run under Jesuit auspices, were institutions of civic import that gave the Jesuits an access to civic life that their churches alone could never have provided.

Second, the Jesuits taught for the most part secular subjects – the literary classics of pagan antiquity and Greek scientific texts. Many Christians and many other Christian ministers did this, of course, but what was special about the Jesuits was that as a body they were trained not only in ecclesiastical subjects but also in secular subjects, and so trained with a view not merely to appropriating secular subjects but to a Christian ministry of teaching them. They were confident that when students properly studied these subjects, they would become more useful members of society and the Church.

Third, the schools set the Jesuits in a systemic relationship to the arts – especially music, dance and theatre – that they surely would not have had had they not conducted schools. With the schools came the large collegiate church, needed for the student body but opened to their parents and to others, which meant a systemic relationship to painting and architecture. This development further promoted and institutionally grounded in the Jesuits a remarkable use of the arts, especially music, as a means to success in many of their other ministries – a use of the arts that is worthy of note today when it is in most churches so restricted and unimaginative. Early on, for instance, the Jesuits adopted on a world-wide basis the practice learned in certain parts of Spain of setting the catechism to local tunes, so that children would enjoy learning it and enjoy teaching it to other children. Convinced of the power of pictures to move the soul, they established a painting academy in Japan in the sixteenth century.

I have described certain modalities of Jesuit ministry that made them somewhat different from the ministry in parishes that we tend to take as the norm. But the difference in modalities helped generate something that went further. It helped generate new ministries. One must be careful here, for in the Christian tradition some precedent can be found for almost everything that claims to be new. Nonetheless, I think that, with due qualification, 'new' is a word that can safely be used for some of the Jesuits' ministries in the sixteenth century.

I have already mentioned the most obvious and important one: formal schooling. This had of course Protestant counterparts, derived from the same origins, though I would question whether those counterparts were as consistently and professedly viewed as ministry on a corporate basis as they were with the Jesuits. Quite another, spectacular, phenomenon would be the impact the Jesuits' example had on women's orders in

France in the seventeenth century, where humanistic schools for girls sprang up in numbers that dwarfed what the Jesuits and now others were doing for boys. By the end of the century the Ursulines alone conducted over 300 such schools, and they were only one order among dozens.

For the Jesuits the schools became a great base out of which to operate a number of other ministries. The school vacations provided an occasion to allow the development of a new pastoral strategy that came to be known as 'missions', for it consisted in sending out – 'missioning' – a team of Jesuits to a given area for a week or many weeks of intense preaching and other ministry. The Jesuits seem to have been the first to develop this strategy, a forerunner of the 'revival' of later centuries.

Eventually these missions consisted in a carefully designed programme of preaching, catechesis, lecturing on the Bible, processions and other elaborate public rituals, hearing of confessions, and the establishment of confraternities to continue the work the missioners had begun. What made these missions into a new ministry was the marshalling of traditional ministries into an organized strategy of team ministry with clearly defined objectives. Originally directed to hamlets in the countryside, which was presumed to be pastorally the most needy area, by the beginning of the seventeenth century the missions began to target urban parishes or other districts within the cities.

Another ministry was 'lecturing'. The Jesuits, like many of their contemporaries, made a distinction between preaching and lecturing that has sometimes been lost sight of in subsequent generations. Preaching was roughly what we mean today by preaching, but 'lecturing' corresponded to what we would call adult education. The Jesuits considered this a distinct ministry, for it had its own goals, its own times and places. It consisted in a series of lectures on a given subject, usually a book of the Bible, that extended over the course of many weeks or months. Lectures would be given, for example, on the Letter to the Romans, verse by verse or section by section, several mornings or afternoons per week. Their primary purpose was instruction. The instruction was not, however, academic as in a university classroom but geared somehow to the practice of the Christian life.

While these lectures were usually delivered in church, they were not delivered from the pulpit. The lecturer usually sat in a chair somewhere in the body of the church and the listeners sat on benches near him, often with pen and paper in hand. Lecturers wore no liturgical vestments, whereas preachers always wore surplice and, when it was the local custom, a stole. Probably because when Jesuits preached in the pulpit they did so on passages from the four Gospels according to the liturgical texts of the Mass, they tended to choose other parts of the Bible for their lectures, showing a special preference for the Pauline epistles. The Jesuits gave such lectures an extraordinary prominence in their repertory of ministries, so that wherever they 'preached' they lectured almost more often.

The last 'new' ministry developed by the Jesuits is what came to be known as the 'retreat'. Although the practice of withdrawing from one's ordinary duties to spend time in reflection and contemplation is older than Christianity itself, there existed no widely recognized codification of it until the *Spiritual Exercises* of Ignatius of Loyola. The book not merely contained some of his more important ideas on the spiritual life but also provided a clear yet adaptable framework in which to consider one's situation and draw nearer to God.

For their ministry the Jesuits possessed no more distinctive instrument than the *Exercises*. No other group had a book like it. One of the world's most famous books, it is also one of the most misunderstood, partly because its most famous part, the 'Rules for Thinking with the Church', appear at the end of it, as if the purpose and culmination of the *Exercises* was to inculcate 'ecclesiastically correct' thinking. Those Rules are, in fact, an appendix, added years after the book was substantially finished, and they were little commented on by Jesuits in the sixteenth century. The real goal of the book was to help individuals get in touch with God's action in their lives, so that they turn their lives over to God's love and care, which is operative in all life's circumstances. The Jesuit who helps individuals during the retreat through conversation and instruction is instructed to do everything 'to permit the Creator to deal directly with the creature and the creature directly with his Creator and Lord' (Annotation 15). The *Exercises* can be looked upon as a distillation of spiritual wisdom to help towards conversion to a more devout life.

The basic principle of the book was that it be adapted – 'accommodated' – to different times, circumstances and purposes, as stated in the opening pages. This flexibility applied to its specific axioms and to the programme as a whole. In its fullness the *Exercises* were meant to be done apart from all one's normal duties for about a month, in conversation with a spiritual guide. This programme began with considerations of one's status as a forgiven sinner, then progressed through meditations on the life, death and resurrection of Christ, and culminated in a final contemplation on the love of God. Thus in a generic way the *Exercises* done in their fullness led individuals through the three traditional stages of the spiritual life – purgative, illuminative, unitive.

But the *Exercises* were from the beginning put into practice in a number of different ways. Frequently only the early parts on sin, forgiveness and conversion were used. Very early they began to be given to more than one person at a time, in groups of ten or fifteen, where the opportunities for private conversation with the Jesuit guide would obviously be reduced. Sometimes people continued in their regular occupations, but came to the Jesuits for guidance through the parts of the book over a period of many months. The programme of the *Exercises* was modified and adapted in a number of other ways. To provide a situation where more seclusion was possible, the Jesuits in 1553 constructed at Alcalá in Spain their first 'retreat house' for that purpose. They later built similar houses elsewhere.

One of the unintended results of this new ministry of retreats was a new prominence for the ancient ministry of spiritual counselling. The *Exercises* presupposed that individuals needed somebody with whom to converse about what was going on in their souls as they engaged in such an intense spiritual experience. This person soon came to be known as 'the director' and his function even outside the retreat as 'spiritual direction'.

To a large extent because of the important role attributed to the 'director' in the *Exercises*, the role of 'spiritual director' (or counsellor) developed in Catholic Europe with a new sophistication and became recognized as a distinctive ministry in its own right, consisting in a formalized and continuing relationship between the two persons involved. Of course, the Jesuits were in this regard symptomatic of a larger movement, promoted for instance by the writings of Teresa of Avila. Nonetheless, for the codification and intellectual refinement of this ministry, as it reached a new plateau in the seventeenth century, the Jesuits' role was crucial. In 1599, for instance, the head of the order, Claudio Aquaviva, published an instruction on the formation of spiritual directors within the Society, and the next year he published a small treatise on the matter that, while fundamentally based on the teaching from the ancient masters, combined it with some corporate wisdom derived from Jesuits acting as directors in the *Exercises*.

The sixteenth-century Jesuits were both special and symptomatic of their time. They had much success, and they had some spectacular failures. Above all, they were pragmatic, ready to try just about anything if it promised 'to help souls'. Perhaps we can still learn something from their efforts.

Bibliography

Bailey, Gauvin Alexander, *Art on the Jesuit Missions in Asia and Latin America, 1542–1773* (Toronto, 1999)
Ignatius of Loyola, *Ignatius of Loyola: The Spiritual Exercises and Selected Works* (New York, 1991)
Lucas, Thomas M., *Landmarking: City, Church and Jesuit Urban Strategy* (Chicago, 1997)
O'Malley, John W., *The First Jesuits* (Cambridge, Mass., 1993)
O'Malley, John W., et al. (eds), *The Jesuits: Cultures, Sciences and the Arts, 1540–1773* (Toronto, 1999)

13

The family and pastoral care

Ralph Houlbrooke

Introduction

The Protestant reformers of the sixteenth century, and particularly the more militant among them, are widely believed to have brought about profound changes in English family life. They are thought to have enhanced the status of marriage and the role of the family household as a centre of religious activity, including the instruction of children. Their teaching, it is agreed, also influenced marital relations and the balance of power between husband and wife, though there is some disagreement among scholars as to its precise effects. Some emphasize their assertion of husbandly authority, others the extent to which that authority was qualified by insistence on the duty of love, and the wife's own religious responsibilities.[1]

The most distinctive characteristics of the Christian family, founded on certain key passages in the Bible, had been established long before the Reformation. The family had for many centuries been regarded as the basic unit of Christian society, and the chief agency by which the ranks of the Church on earth were replenished with new members. Love and obedience, enjoined as duties, were the principal means by which the family was held together. Parents' responsibility of solicitous care for their children included teaching them the rudiments of religion. The Protestant Reformation must be viewed in a long perspective if its achievements and their limitations are to be properly appreciated. This essay will therefore begin with a brief glance at some of the most important New Testament passages about marriage and parenthood. Various emphases and concerns are apparent in these texts. These contrasts were later to be reflected in differences of opinion and interpretation among Christians, especially during the Reformation. The essay will next proceed to sketch some elements of the process by which the Church sought to shape European family life during the first millennium of its existence, and then home in on various aspects of pastoral care of the family in England during the later Middle Ages, before turning to the Reformation.

Marriage and parenthood in the New Testament: some key texts

On his way to Jerusalem, Jesus insisted that nobody could be a disciple of his without 'hating' his closest relatives (Luke 14.26). In practice he accepted the existence of the family, most fundamental of all social institutions, and had important things to say about marriage and children. Questioned about the possibility of divorce, Jesus recalled the words of Genesis 2.24: when a man left his parents and joined his wife, the two became one flesh. 'What therefore God hath joined together, let not man put asunder' (Matthew 19.6). These words of Jesus were the foundation of a new doctrine of indissoluble matrimony. His disciples, reflecting how much more challenging this command would make the marriage partnership, remarked that it was better not to marry at all. When Christ, in answering them, said that some had renounced marriage for the sake of the kingdom of heaven, he could have been thought to be encouraging celibacy. Paul's commendation of marriage to the Corinthians was distinctly grudging. It was better for those who could not control themselves to marry than to burn with vain desire (1 Corinthians 7.9). He was rather more positive when he reminded his fellow countrymen of God's judgements on sexual transgressors; marriage, on the other hand, was honourable, and the bed undefiled (Hebrews 13.4). Paul and his fellow apostle Peter had clear views about the principal duties of marriage partners: love and respect on the husband's part, and submission on that of the wife (Ephesians 5.22–33; Colossians 3.18–19; 1 Peter 3.1–7). Children are the most visible fruit of marriage. In passages immediately before and after the one setting out his teaching about marriage, Jesus is described as speaking of children in highly positive terms. He was angry when the disciples rebuked people who brought children for him to touch. 'Suffer the little children to come unto me', he told them, 'for of such is the kingdom of God' (Mark 10.14). Whoever did not accept the kingdom of God like a child, he continued, would never enter it. 'And he took them up in his arms, put his hands upon them, and blessed them.' Christ gave little children a kind and gentle welcome. But, Paul later made clear in writing to the Hebrews, echoing several passages in the Old Testament, God's love for his children also manifested itself in chastisement. The Lord scourged every child whom he received. 'But if ye be without chastisement, whereof all are partakers, then are ye bastards, and not sons' (Hebrews 12.8). In this context, Paul had persecution in mind. But God's correcting paternal hand could be seen behind all life's crosses. The image of a heavenly Father who, while loving his children, often punished them for their own good, influenced the pattern of earthly fatherhood.

The Christian Church and the Western European family

During late antiquity and the Middle Ages, the Church developed a body of laws and doctrines relating to the family which went far beyond the teaching of Christ and the apostles but which could nevertheless be defended as true to their spirit. It accepted marriage to the extent of formally bestowing its blessing on the marriages of individual Christians, while also insisting on their indissolubility. Wishing to prevent the excessive concentration of affection, and to encourage the formation of new ties outside existing circles of friendship or obligation, it gradually extended the degrees within which marriage was prohibited. The state of celibacy preferred by Paul was imposed on the 'priests and levites', those individuals who dedicated their lives to the closer service of God, and more specifically on all clergy from the rank of sub-deacon upwards in the eleventh century. Mindful of Paul's disapproval of 'lust' or 'inordinate affection' (Colossians 3.5), the Church sought to limit the frequency of sexual intercourse even within marriage. The procreation of children was the principal motive for carnal union. But, as Paul had insisted (1 Corinthians 7.1–5), each spouse's body belonged to the other: each had to give the other his or her due.[2]

Acting in the spirit of Christ's words, the Church welcomed children, and forbade infanticide and abortion. Anxious to increase the numbers of the faithful, it adopted the practice of infant baptism, placing upon the newly born the ineradicable stamp of membership. At baptism, the child's sponsors assumed responsibility for its religious upbringing. At first it was expected that the biological parents would normally be sponsors, but in course of time this duty was entrusted to separate godparents, thus providing an additional guarantee of the child's Christian education, and spreading the responsibility for it beyond the ranks of the nuclear family.[3]

The general thrust of the Church's teaching and action in relation to the family was clear. The overall aim was to support family bonds insofar as they contributed to the growth of Christian life, while also moderating excessive affection in such a way as to help human beings to be more receptive of God's grace. Among the effects was the weakening of ties between the nuclear or elementary family and the wider kindred. The nuclear family itself was opened to a measure of surveillance. The Church's encouragement of alms and other forms of pious gift or endowment, coupled with the discouragement of adoption, resulted in the alienation of substantial amounts of property from family ownership.[4]

The family and pastoral care in later medieval England

Marriage

Two of the sacraments, marriage and baptism, played a central part in family life, and served as foci for much of the Church's work of pastoral care in this field. In each of them the ordained minister had a special role. By mutual consent expressed in a suitable contract, couples could indeed enter into marriage without the participation of a priest. While conceding that such participation was not absolutely essential to a marriage's validity, the Church nevertheless encouraged it in the strongest possible terms. It was an offence to enter into full conjugal relations without ecclesiastical solemnization. In England the marriage service itself was preceded by banns thrice published in the parish of residence of each of the prospective spouses in order to bring to light any possible impediments or objections. The order for the solemnization of matrimony according to the rite of Sarum began at the church door with the reciprocal plighting of troth and the bridegroom's placing of the ring on the fourth finger of the bride's left hand. The priest recited the words to be spoken by each partner, blessed the ring, and sprinkled it with holy water. He then accompanied the couple to the altar step. A series of collects and benedictions included the prayer that God would sanctify and bless the couple's souls and bodies, and join them together in the union and love of true affection. The nuptial Mass followed. If both partners were marrying for the first time, they knelt under a pall to receive a special sacramental blessing. At the giving of the peace the bridegroom kissed the bride. The following night, the priest blessed their bed-chamber, the bed, and the couple in it. Despite all the dangers of inordinate affection, the sacrament of marriage was regarded as a powerful means of receiving grace.[5]

Baptism

Within this new family, children were born. The priest's normal part in the sacrament of their baptism was even more prominent and central, though the rite could be performed by a lay person in case of emergency. Before baptism itself took place, the priest carried out at the church door solemn exorcisms, repeatedly adjured the devil to depart from the child, and signed its forehead, breast and right hand with the cross. He put hallowed salt, signifying the Word of God, in the infant's mouth, and anointed its ears and nostrils with spittle in remembrance of the miracle by which Jesus had healed the deaf and dumb.

The baptism service itself began in the church with the officiant's interrogation of the godparents, who answered on the child's behalf his questions about its renunciation of the devil and all his works. He then anointed the infant's breast and back with holy oil. Assured by the godparents of the child's faith and desire for baptism, he baptized it in the name of the Father, the Son, and the Holy Ghost, immersing it in the font three times as he did so. After the child had been raised from the font, the priest smeared a cross of chrism (a special mixture of oil and balsam) on its forehead, wrapped it in the white chrisom cloth, 'holy and immaculate', and placed a candle in its hand. God had regenerated the child by water and the Holy Spirit, and given it remission of all its sins. Without baptism, it could not have entered heaven; afterwards, until it committed actual sin, its salvation was assured. The parents and godparents were to be enjoined to safeguard the child from fire and water and all other dangers until the age of seven, the godparents to teach it the Pater Noster, Ave Maria, and Creed. The service contained a reminder that the child was to be taken for confirmation as soon as the bishop next came into the neighbourhood.[6]

Not until some time had passed after the baptism of her child did the mother come to the church to render her customary thanks. After the saying of psalms and various prayers at the church door, the priest sprinkled the woman with holy water and led her by the right hand into the church. The rite was in many versions but not all termed 'purification'.[7]

Penance

Penance regularly played an important part in family life before the Reformation. It was through the confession which was the indispensable preliminary to the administration of the 'heavenly medicine' of penance that the confessor was sometimes admitted to intimate secrets of the domestic sphere. Delicate responsibilities might be involved. It was the confessor's duty, for example, to make sure that no penance which he assigned one spouse for secret infidelity should be such as to reveal the sin to the other partner and thereby cause hatred between the two.[8]

Preparation for death: the last rites

Confession and absolution preceded the reception of the sacrament of the altar. Regular reception was a Christian duty, but communion was also a recommended part of preparation for expected or possible death (as for example in childbirth). In terminal illness, the visitation of the sick (including the confession of sins), the administration of the sacrament of extreme unction, and the last communion or *viaticum*, might be performed separately or in one sequence. It was during these last rites that the Church entered domestic space in the most tangible and symbolically powerful fashion. In their solemnity and elaboration they stood in sharp contrast to the blessing of the couple and the matrimonial bed. In surplice and stole, preceded by bell and candle, the priest came into the house of sickness and invoked peace upon it and all who lived in it. During his visitation, he was supposed to exhort the sick person to perform works of charity by making satisfaction for wrongs he had done and by forgiving wrongs done to him.[9] Most late mediaeval testators seem to have made their wills shortly before death, and priests very often drafted these documents around the time of the administration of the last rites. Late mediaeval wills give the reader a vivid impression of the substantial amounts of money bestowed in 'pious uses', especially contributions to church fabrics, the maintenance of lights, the support of confraternities, and the celebration of intercessory Masses for the souls of the departed. Such bequests broadly speaking diverted resources from the family on earth – children and kinsfolk – to assist the spiritual wellbeing of the dead and those about to die – parents, ancestors, benefactors, and testators themselves.[10] The singing of intercessory Masses by the oft-stipulated 'honest priest' was presumably a source of comfort and satisfaction to many of the bereaved, the widowed in particular. Souls in purgatory were also members of the Church, ones towards whom the celebrant (especially if they had recently been members of his earthly flock) might feel a pastoral responsibility. The process of commending the soul to God's mercy began at the point of death and continued round the death-bed after it. Later the priest fetched the corpse from the dead person's house, sprinkled it with holy water, and accompanied it in procession to the church.[11]

Instruction as an element of pastoral care

Some idea of the extent of the clergy's responsibility for teaching their parishioners about their family duties may be gained from the copious diocesan legislation of the thirteenth century. Various bishops enjoined them to instruct the people concerning the forms of a binding matrimonial contract and of the words of baptism to be used in emergency. They were to warn mothers not to overlay their little children, and parents and heads of households to teach their children and other dependants the rudiments of religion, including the Creed, the Lord's Prayer and the angelic salutation. (The important 1281 provincial canon *Ignorantia sacerdotum* required priests to expound a fuller syllabus of religious texts to their people at least four times a year.) 'And married people should be taught the good things of marriage as well as how to bring up their little ones in the fear of the Lord', reads one of Bishop Walter de Cantilupe's 1240 statutes for the diocese of Worcester. Some statutes laid down that priests were to be present at the making of testaments and matrimonial contracts. Confessors needed to be able to expound the Ten Commandments and the seven deadly sins in English in order to do their job thoroughly. One example will show what sort of explication this entailed. In his *Summula* for their use (1287?) Bishop Quinel of Exeter pointed out in his comments on the fourth/fifth commandment that the honour due to parents included not merely refraining from laying hands on them, or injuring them by word or deed, but also helping them in poverty, and assisting them with alms and prayers after their deaths.[12]

Instructional literature for spouses and parents

The large number of vernacular religious treatises produced during the fourteenth and fifteenth centuries included several designed to instruct the clergy in their pastoral duties or provide them with sermon material. But an increasing proportion of this literature was intended for the laity.[13]

The growing readiness of some priests to address themselves directly to the literate laity in writing, temporarily inhibited by the campaign against those radical English heretics the Lollards, especially during the early fifteenth century, was to receive new impetus from the introduction of printing and the onset of the Reformation.

Two outstanding examples of pastoral literature printed not long before the Reformation give us some picture of what the conscientious literate layperson might learn about the Church's teaching on marriage at this time. *Dives and Pauper*, an anonymous tract probably written in Henry IV's reign, was printed in 1493 and 1496. It is a compendious exposition of the Ten Commandments in the form of a dialogue between a friar and a rich layman. *The Commendacions of Matrymony* was written by William Harrington LLD, prebendary of St Paul's, who had often addressed his own congregation on the subject, and printed by 1513 or 1515.[14]

Both authors agreed on the two principal ends of marriage: the procreation of children for the service of God, and the avoidance of sin. Harrington added a third: reciprocal solace and help, without coitus. Both writers pointed out that marriage was a sacrament which represented the unity between God and man, between Christ and the Church, and between Christ and the Christian soul. Harrington listed several other things which showed that it was a lawful and godly way of living in the world: instituted by God in paradise in the time of innocence before all other orders, and continuing since then among all branches of the human race, it had been the only order to be preserved in the Flood. The Virgin Mary had entered into it, and Christ had shown his approval of it both by attending the wedding at Cana in Galilee and by declaring that it was not to be dissolved.[15]

Harrington set out rules to be observed in matrimony, some of them adumbrated in *Dives and Pauper*. Each partner was to love the other above all other creatures. (Both authors remarked that the ring, made of precious metal, and, because circular, without end, aptly symbolized the character of married love.) The couple were to live together peaceably, not vexing each other by word or deed. The wife was to obey her husband in all lawful things. The husband might correct and punish his wife 'moderately' for a lawful cause. But if he beat her grievously for *any* cause he sinned greatly and deserved to be punished. (*Dives and Pauper* explained that Eve had been made of Adam's rib because that was next to his heart. She had not been made of his foot to be his thrall, nor of his head to be his master, but to be his fellow and helper. When she sinned, Eve had been made subject to Adam, but this subjection had its limits. The wife was to be ruled by her husband, and dread and serve him 'as felaw in loue & helper at nede & as nest solas in sorwe: nout as thral & bonde in vyleyn seruage'.) Both authors emphasized the partners' duty of reciprocal fidelity, and the need for moderation in the enjoyment of sexual intercourse. It was to be avoided during Lent and various holy days, during menstrual periods, and in later pregnancy. But neither husband nor wife could sin in satisfying the debt they owed the other. Both partners were to work together for their own livelihood and the support of their children (whose care in their early years belonged to the wife). They were to help each other in sickness, disease, adversity and poverty. All things were common between them; neither must waste or withdraw their shared goods. Finally, they were to bring up their children honestly and virtuously, with due correction and discipline, teaching them their religious and social duties as well as how to make a living. Harrington's acceptance of 'moderate' husbandly correction of wives offends modern sensibilities. It was, however, upheld by English law, and in Harrington's own eyes his emphatic condemnation of excessive punishment may have been his more important contribution. Both Harrington and the anonymous author of *Dives and Pauper* presented a picture of marriage which was on the whole both positive and sensibly practical.[16]

The author of *Dives and Pauper* stressed that religious instruction was the duty of natural parents as well as godparents. St Augustine had said that each man in his own household should fulfil the office of a bishop in teaching and correction. This responsibility belonged to every governor after his degree, including both the poor man and the rich man, the husband governing his wife, and the father and mother governing their children. Harrington's programme of religious education to be carried out by parents specifically included the articles of faith in the Creed, the Ten Commandments, the Lord's Prayer and angelic salutation, and the seven deadly sins 'wyth their braunches'.[17]

Writing some years after Harrington, Richard Whitford, monk of Syon, addressing himself to godly Catholics in his *A Werke for Housholders* (1530), set out a programme of domestic instruction which was to begin as soon as children could speak, and was designed to inculcate a thorough understanding. Whitford laid particular emphasis on the due observance of Sundays, when unfitting games were to be avoided, sermons attended, and godly books read. Heads of households were to see that all their dependants came to church with them. Children were to seek their parents' blessing, or their invocation of God's blessing, nightly before they went to bed, in a ceremony which underlined the parents' position as God's representatives within the household. They were also to learn to recite a rhyme in which they asked their mother or mistress to beat them if they misbehaved. Parents were, however, to administer the rod only when their minds were not disturbed by anger, and then tell the child that they did it unwillingly, compelled by conscience. The manipulative, hypocritical and sadistic child abuser has become such a bugbear in our generation that present-day readers are likely to feel a deep distaste for the rituals with which Whitford sought to invest punishment. But there is no reason to doubt the sincerity of the austere inmate of Syon (never of course a father himself). He regarded correction, ordained by Scripture, as helpful to salvation, a normal concomitant of education, and was concerned to build it into the domestic routine in such a way as to avoid insufficiency and excess, the results respectively of reluctance and passion.[18]

The Protestant Reformation

Marriage and celibacy

When Whitford wrote, the Protestant Reformation was already a looming threat to the devout Catholicism whose educational ideals he so clearly expressed. The Reformation brought significant changes in official teaching concerning marriage and the family, even though these were not as fundamental as has sometimes been supposed. Protestant thought about marriage was founded on Martin Luther's reappraisal, whose positive aspects closely resembled views already expressed by Erasmus in his *Encomium Matrimonii* (1518). On the one hand, Luther demoted matrimony from its previous status as a sacrament. It was common to both Christians and heathens, and he concluded that it did not transmit the grace of God as a means of obtaining salvation. On the other hand, he insisted that since the urge to procreate was an irresistible element of most people's nature, marriage was the ideal state for them. Only those who had received from God the special gift of chastity should choose celibacy. (Paul, while wishing that all were like him, had conceded that God had given different individuals different gifts.) Luther's fear and hatred of the consequences of enforced celibacy drove him to pronounce matrimony the worthier state.

The Protestant adoption of clerical marriage, officially permitted in England between 1549 and 1553, and again from 1559 onwards, was perhaps the most momentous consequence of Luther's teaching. From henceforth many, perhaps even most, of the English clergy who advised the laity concerning the duties and dangers of family life had themselves experienced it as husbands and parents. Lingering misgivings about some consequences of the marriage of priests were nevertheless evident in the 29th royal injunction of 1559, which complained of the 'lack of discreet and sober behaviour in many ministers of the church, both in choosing of their wives, and indiscreet living with them'. It laid down safeguards, including examination by the bishop and two justices of the peace. An undercurrent of popular hostility to married clergy, openly expressed in occasional ribald comment, continued for some time after the Elizabethan Settlement.[19]

Abolition of compulsory confession

Another development which radically altered the relationship between pastor and parishioner was the abolition of compulsory auricular confession, which vanished from the English orders of service in 1548–9. A procedure which had given the expert and sensitive confessor a window into the heart of the family, and a means of exercising an intimate influence over parents and spouses, was no longer available. Did this mean that some sins were more likely to go unpunished, while others, which might previously have been dealt with secretly, were more likely to be reported for judicial correction? Given the paucity of evidence of how confession functioned in practice, it is impossible to say. But it seems clear that the change must have enhanced the autonomy of the Christian family *vis-à-vis* the priest. Handbooks for the guidance of confessors and penitents, with their emphasis on sins to be avoided, disappeared from the repertoire of pastoral aids. But other works of Christian counsel, especially ones based on sermons, poured from the presses in increasing quantities.

The Books of Common Prayer

The first English Book of Common Prayer appeared in 1549. There was no wholesale rejection, but rather a comprehensive adaptation and revision, of the Sarum orders of service. Features common to all the new orders of service, besides translation into English, were the disappearance of a number of prayers, collects and ceremonies, and the inclusion of passages explaining to those present the significance of the rite being performed. *The Forme of the Solemnizacion of Matrimonie*, for example, contained a preliminary declaration of the purposes and dignity of marriage. It was a novel element in this context, but there was little in it that was original. The third purpose, 'the mutuall societie, helpe, and comfort, that the one oughte to haue of the other, both in prosperitie and aduersitie', was very similar to the one specified by Harrington, even though rather differently expressed. Also new was the inclusion, at the end of the service, of a selection of key passages from the epistles of Peter and Paul concerning the respective duties of husband and wife, for use when there was no sermon. The order reflected Protestant thought in that it nowhere called matrimony a sacrament, but it emphasized the dignity of this 'honourable estate' by bringing the whole service into the church and (following Luther's example) calling it '*holy* matrimony'. The crucial words of trothplight (betrothal) and wedding underwent comparatively little change. No special nuptial Mass followed the service, though the newly married couple were required to receive communion the same day.[20]

The declaration which preceded the *Administracion of Publyke Baptisme* explained that all men were born in sin, and that no-one could enter the Kingdom of God unless he were born anew of water and the Holy Spirit. The priest besought the congregation to pray God to grant the children who had been brought to be baptized that they might 'be Baptised with the holy ghost, and receyued into Christes holy churche, and be made lyuely membres of the same'. A drastically curtailed form of exorcism was included in the 1549 order, but disappeared thereafter. A 'briefe exhortacion' underlined the significance of Mark's account of how Jesus commanded the little children to be brought to him. Christ's warm welcome was ground for belief in God's good will towards the infants now brought to holy baptism and also for confidence that he looked favourably on the action of those responsible for bringing them. The heart of the service, the interrogation of the godparents and the immersion of the infant, was preserved. But the three immersions were reduced to one in 1552, and the chrisom cloth and the anointing of the baby's forehead disappeared at the same time.[21]

The order of baptism closed with an exhortation to the godparents to ensure that the newly baptized child was taught the significance of the vow made on its behalf, and the Creed, the Lord's Prayer, and the Ten

Commandments. Confirmation was to take place when he could recite these things, and was sufficiently instructed in the short Catechism included in the Prayer Book to be able to answer such questions as the bishop might put to him. The child was in principle expected to take a far more active part in the rite of confirmation than had hitherto been the case. This meant that the rite would not take place as soon as possible (as had previously been enjoined), but only after the attainment of the age of discretion. The responsibility for giving instruction in the Catechism once every six weeks was clearly placed on the shoulders of the priest who exercised the cure of souls. 'And all fathers, mothers, maisters, and dames, shall cause their children, seruauntes, and prentises ... to come to the churche at the daye appoynted, and obedientlye heare and be ordered by the curate, vntyll suche time as they haue learned all that is here appointed for them to learne.' The clergy's responsibility for the religious instruction of the young was thus much more clearly defined than it had been in mediaeval legislation. But at the same time the effectiveness of such instruction depended heavily upon the co-operation of parents and heads of families.[22]

The most significant change in the rite marking the newly delivered mother's return to church was perhaps that it all took place *inside* the church, so that she was not brought in by the priest only after being sprinkled with holy water. The name of the order was changed in 1552 to underline the fact that it was regarded as a 'Thanksgiving' not a 'Purification', though the framers of the 1552 Book added the clause 'commonly called the Churchynge of Women'.[23]

A long exhortation in the *Order for the Visitation of the Sicke* set out the possible reasons for the sick person's affliction: the trial of faith or the correction of sins. Repentance, patience, trust in God's mercy, gratitude for his fatherly visitation, and complete submission to his will, would help the invalid forward in the way to everlasting life. As St Paul had pointed out, chastisement was a manifestation of God's paternal love. There should be no greater comfort to Christian persons than to suffer as Christ had suffered before entering into eternal glory.There followed a rehearsal of the articles of faith for the invalid's assent, and an exhortation to forgiveness, reparation, the settlement of worldly affairs, and liberality to the poor. At this point the sick person had the opportunity of making a special confession if he felt his conscience 'troubled with any weightie matter', but this was not, on the face of it, a strictly enjoined and necessary duty, as it had been before the Reformation. Extreme unction, drastically curtailed in 1549, disappeared in 1552. The *viaticum* survived in the form of *The Communion of the Sick*, but the sick man was to be assured that, by true repentance and steadfast belief that Christ had died for him, he received the sacrament even if he did not do so with his mouth. After death, no rites took place in the deceased's home: commendations of the soul no longer had a place in the Protestant liturgy. Nor was the priest supposed to come to fetch the corpse from the house, but only to meet it at the churchyard gate.[24]

The changes in the orders of service were substantial, but they did not go far enough to satisfy the most militant English Protestants. Prayer Book ceremonies and their allegedly widespread misuse became prime bones of contention between the bishops and the 'precisians' or Puritans who wanted to eradicate all traces of 'popery' from the worship of the English Church. To Puritan eyes, such traces were all too evident in the prescribed forms of the rites which played so important a part in family life.

Articles and injunctions

In setting out the basic duties of the clergy, articles and injunctions issued in royal, episcopal and archidiaconal visitations reinforced or supplemented the requirements of the *Books of Common Prayer*. A major new responsibility, imposed in 1538, was that of keeping the parish register of marriages, baptisms and burials. This was a significant instrument of surveillance whose usefulness some zealous clergy enhanced by including details which they were not officially required to record, such as the names of godparents, the interval which elapsed between birth and baptism, or even respectful short tributes to departed parishioners of notable virtue.[25]

One use to which parish registers could be put was the policing of the observance of the now much reduced range of prohibited degrees. The interpretation of the degrees, the question which had led to the break with Rome, was settled in 1563 by Archbishop Parker's publication of a table which included all the ones specified in Leviticus 18 and their equivalents. The narrowing of the prohibited degrees lessened the likelihood of annulment of marriage. The only serious proposal of this period to introduce into English church law provision for the dissolution of marriages in case of adultery, cruelty or desertion, with the possibility of remarriage for the innocent party, died when Thomas Cranmer's plan to enact a new code of ecclesiastical law failed in 1553.[26]

The pastoral duty to teach children about the faith was emphasized in injunctions. The expected frequency of the religious instruction of the young was soon increased to every Sunday and holy day. In 1576 Archbishop Grindal required all those between seven and twenty who needed such instruction to attend, and this age span was the one most commonly specified thereafter. Parents and householders were expected to teach their children and servants the Lord's Prayer, the Creed and the Ten Commandments, as a royal injunction of 1547 made clear. (A number of zealous ministers later produced catechisms specially for domestic use to help householders in this task.) In 1591, Archbishop Whitgift tried to encourage the practice of catechizing children in the presence of their parents, 'whoe therby may take comforte and instruction alsoe'. A strongly worded royal injunction of 1547 made the clergy responsible for 'exhorting and counselling, and by all the ways and means they may, as well in their sermons and collations, as otherwise', persuading parents and employers 'diligently to provide and foresee that the youth be in no manner of wise brought up in idleness', but this requirement was less vigorously emphasized later on.[27]

After as before the Reformation, the clergy were expected to play their part in the never-ending struggle to confine sexual activity within the bounds of marriage. They now lacked the confessional as a means of supervision, but they were obliged not to turn a blind eye to open and notorious sin. Those guilty of it were not to be admitted to the Lord's Table without repentance. Ministers were repeatedly reminded that they must not allow the mothers of illegitimate children to be churched without having first performed penance or made public confession, and by the early seventeenth century some ordinaries were asking whether couples who had engaged in ante-nuptial fornication had also been punished. Such behaviour was very widespread: probably at least a quarter of those couples married in Elizabeth's reign had anticipated the ceremony in this way. It was widely associated with, and (at least in the eyes of the participants) largely legitimized by, secret contracts of marriage. Pressure to change behaviour may have borne some fruit: analysis of parish registers shows that the incidence of pre-nuptial pregnancy fell between the second half of the sixteenth century and the first half of the seventeenth, though not nearly as dramatically as pioneer studies once suggested. Irregular marriages, celebrated at the wrong time or in the wrong place, or without properly declared banns or parental consent were an increasingly important focus of concern.[28]

Royal injunctions of 1547 required all clergy to learn and have ready suitable scriptural texts with which to comfort sick parishioners tempted to despair when lying ill and in peril of death and to exhort their neighbours, especially when making their wills, to give generously to the poor rather than to 'blind devotions'. Many bishops subsequently enquired whether ministers had performed these duties, or visited the sick in accordance with the *Book of Common Prayer*. Bequests to the poor certainly increased markedly during and after the Reformation. The evidence of wills themselves, and of depositions describing how they were made, nevertheless suggests that clergymen were a less important source of help to testators after the Reformation than they had been beforehand. Will-makers, it appears, increasingly relied on other scribes. Puritan concern about 'private' death-bed communions and the claim by the separatist Henry Barrow that absolution was available for money to every 'prophane glutton and wicked atheist' at the hour of death suggests that demand for these ministrations continued, but there is not much evidence about them in visitation records or church court books.[29]

Many visitation articles and injunctions were concerned with the due and proper celebration of the sacraments and other services according to the *Book of Common Prayer*. They focused particularly on elements of the services which caused more or less widespread unease among Puritans: the part played by godparents in baptism, the signing of the child's forehead with a cross and the use of the wedding ring. All these were the subject of stinging attack in *An Admonition to the Parliament* (1572), and from time to time became matters of contention between ministers and parishioners. The baptism service (the *Admonition* complained) required of the godparents a promise which was not in their power to perform, and added (in the shape of the sign of the cross) a new sacrament to the one properly instituted by Christ; the wedding ring was a sacramental sign which recalled the popish designation of matrimony as a sacrament. Bishops had little sympathy with the militants' determination to differ over these matters of order. Questions concerning ceremonial nonconformity tended to become more precise and detailed as time passed, and especially during the early seventeenth century. It was then, for example, that women were in some jurisdictions officially required to wear the veil at churching, on the ground that it was an ancient custom of the Church, even though it was not one specified in the order of service.[30]

The importance of the underlying beliefs gave a special significance to the concerns about the conduct of baptism. Did it ensure salvation?

According to a rubric preceding the 1549 confirmation service it was certain by God's word 'that children being Baptised (yf they departe out of this lyfe in their infancye) are vndoubtedly saued'. But did this mean that the unbaptized child would *not* be saved, as the Catholic Church had taught? In 1577 Bishop Barnes of Durham enjoined his clergy to teach their parishioners that if any infant died without public baptism 'the same is not to be condemned or adjudged as a damned soul, but to be well hoped of, and the body to be interred in the churchyard'. God's grace was not tied to means, Protestants believed. Yet although the *Book of Common Prayer* called for baptism to be deferred till the next Sunday or holy day after birth, so that the infant might be welcomed by the congregation, it continued to provide for baptism at home in case of emergency. Not until 1604, indeed, did it exclude the possibility of the rite's performance by a midwife or other woman. Puritans regarded this as a scandalous anomaly stemming from superstitious misunderstanding.[31]

Printed instructional literature: homilies, sermons and tracts

The Protestant reformers attached the greatest importance to the creation of a preaching ministry to give the people effective instruction in their faith. Reforming bishops were nevertheless under no illusions about the daunting lack of preachers who were both doctrinally reliable and adequately qualified. It was for this reason that two books of homilies for reading on Sundays when there was no sermon were issued in 1547 and 1563.

An Homily of the State of Matrimony (1563) may have been, apart from the relevant passages of the marriage service itself, the discourse concerning the duties of husbands and wives which was most familiar to the parishioners of Elizabethan England. 'It is instituted of God, to the intent that man and woman should live lawfully in a perpetual friendly fellowship, to bring forth fruit, and to avoid fornication.' The reordering of the ends of marriage, so that 'friendly fellowship' appears first, foreshadows the emphasis of the homily as a whole, concerned as it was with the difficulty of preserving such fellowship. The enlargement of God's kingdom through the procreation of children is briefly touched on, and the dangers of 'filthiness' (the subject of a sulphurous triple salvo in the 1547 *Homily of Whoredom and Uncleanness*) at only slightly greater length. The main theme is the difficulty of maintaining matrimonial harmony, always threatened by stubborn will, self-love and the desire for dominance. The author remarked 'how few matrimonies there be without chidings, brawlings, tauntings, repentings, bitter cursings, and fightings'. Prayer to God for defence against the devil's wiles had to be seconded by diligent observance of the apostolic precepts. The chief responsibility for cherishing concord belonged to the husband, who was to yield in some things to the woman and show forbearance, making allowance for the fact that she was a 'weak creature, not endued with like strength and constancy of mind'. Gentle treatment and respect would the better enable the husband to have his wife's heart in his 'power and will'. It was the wife's responsibility to obey her husband without being too busy to remind him of his own duty. Wife-beating was quite intolerable.[32]

The first reasonably comprehensive Protestant work of advice about family life published in English was Miles Coverdale's *Christen State of Matrimonye* (1541), a translation of a treatise by Heinrich Bullinger of Zurich. It was to be followed in the later sixteenth and early seventeenth centuries by a large number of books on the subject by English ministers. By far the most copious, popular and best-known published works of this sort came from the pens of staunch Protestant clergymen who may be called 'moderate Puritans'. Some of these tracts had started life as sermons, or a series of sermons. Their authors dedicated their work to urban parishioners or to gentry who supported their labours. They were all actuated by a more or less urgent desire to promote the cause of godly Reformation which got some of them into trouble. There was comparatively little in what they wrote that was fundamentally new. The best of them are distinguished by a warmth and directness of pastoral tone which later led Richard Baxter to dub authors of their stamp 'affectionate practical English writers'.[33] As a group they were distinguished from their mediaeval predecessors by the fact that so many of them had personal experience of marriage and parenthood. The key biblical texts which have already been cited in this chapter continued to play a pivotal role in their discussion of family duties. But they drew on many others in their systematic and sometimes exhaustive expositions.

One significant difference between Protestant writers and their Catholic predecessors was that the Protestants no longer warned their readers that sexual activity was sin-free only under certain clearly defined circumstances, or called for abstinence during sacred seasons. The advice of William Whateley, vicar of Banbury (1583-1639) was fairly typical. Such activity was, he said, to be sanctified by prayer and thanksgiving, and temperate (because not chiefly ordained for pleasure, but for the increase of mankind and to quench lustful desires). It was to be used 'as seldome and sparingly, as may stand with the neede of the persons married: for excesse this way doth weaken the body, and shorten life: but a sparing enioyment would helpe the health, and preserue the body from diuers diseases in some constitutions'. Sleeping passions were not to be aroused for the sake of pleasure. Henry Smith (1550?–1591), preacher at St Clement Danes, described the marriage bed as 'the meanes of reconcilement' in the event of a quarrel between husband and wife.[34]

All the Protestant divines who wrote the most influential tracts on marriage duties built on the foundations of the apostolic texts. Their consistent message was that the relationship was an unequal one, and it was the wife's duty to obey her husband. This message had to be pressed home precisely because so many wives had failed to take it to heart. William Gouge (1578–1653), rector of St Anne's Blackfriars and author of one of the most exhaustive accounts *Of Domesticall Duties* (1622), observed how many wives were determined to have their own way and rule their husbands. 'Looke into families, obserue the estate and condition of many of them, and then tell me if these things be not so. If an husband be a man of courage, and seeke to stand vpon his right, and maintaine his authoritie by requiring obedience of his wife, strange it is to behold what an hurly burly she will make in the house: but if he be a milke-sop, and basely yeeld vnto his wife, and suffer her to rule, then, it may be, there shall be some outward quiet.' Among the reasons for such insubordination suggested by his colleague Thomas Gataker (1574–1654), rector of Rotherhithe, were the facts that some wives were 'of a greater spirit, and in some respect of better parts', or brought more material goods to the marriage.[35]

Yet although the wife's place was an inferior one, it was, according to William Gouge, the nearest to equality that might be. The wife was her husband's intimate counsellor. It was right that she should be consulted in all major family plans and ventures which were likely to affect her as much as her husband, remarked Daniel Rogers (1573–1652), lecturer at Wethersfield, in his *Matrimoniall Honour* (1642). It was up to the husband, these authors generally agreed, to exercise his rule with tact, tenderness, forbearance and discretion. He was to avoid meddling in the wife's own particular sphere of responsibility and irritating her with untimely commands. Since the wife was the weaker partner in intelligence and ability to master her passions, it was incumbent upon the husband to exercise self-restraint in face of any provocations which she offered him.

All the pain of childbirth and the exacting business of infant care fell on wives and mothers, and this was another reason for husbandly tenderness. Some of these writers refused to rule out altogether the possibility of the husband's striking his wife, especially in self-defence, but they all disapproved of it or hedged it with the strongest provisos. It should in theory have been easier for husbands to bear with their wives than vice-versa, according to some of these authors, because love was naturally stronger in the stronger and superior partner in a relationship: it flowed downwards from husbands to wives, and from parents to children. St Paul had directed his injunction concerning the duty of love to the partner who was (according to the ancient world's predominant assumptions about gender differences) better capable of fulfilling it.[36]

It was natural that the current of love should flow strongly downwards from parents to children. Parents loved and delighted in their children, not because they were fair, wise or witty but because they were *theirs*. When children were sickly, parents were the more tender towards them. Parental love increased with time: in this respect it was a model for marriage partners, whose affection was (allegedly) all too prone to wear thin. Yet there was one parental duty which was often neglected, especially in London and among the better off: that of maternal breast-feeding. The London minister William Gouge, whose familiarity with the practice enabled him to give a particularly full account of the reasons for it, opposed the use of wet-nurses especially strongly. The custom was thought by its opponents to be a possible source of danger both to the health and to the character of those entrusted to the nurses' care. An infant might imbibe something of its nurse's nature with her milk, adulterating or destroying characteristics inherited from its parents.[37]

'He that spareth his rod hateth his son: but he that loveth him chasteneth him betimes' (Proverbs 13.24). This ancient text, echoed in Paul's remarks about God's chastisement of his sons, was frequently cited in justification of a firmly corrective approach to upbringing both before and after the Reformation. The Protestant writers emphasized it not merely because of its hallowed scriptural authority but because they were deeply convinced by daily observation that parents were inclined by nature to indulge their children, failing to check the growth of evil habits which threatened their immortal souls. Many fathers either hated the task of correction, or undertook it only in the heat of their own anger. Such impulsive behaviour was to be avoided. Some Protestant writers warned of the dangers of paternal sourness and excessive severity. Had not Paul written 'Fathers, provoke not your children to anger, lest they be discouraged' (Colossians 3.21)? William Gouge saw corporal punishment as the last resort: it should always be preceded by rebukes, which were often sufficient. 'A reproof entereth more into a wise man than an hundred stripes into a fool' (Proverbs 17.10).[38]

Household religious duties

Protestant writers sought to extend and strengthen the process of household religious education. Thomas Becon (1512–67) recommended in his *Catechism*, written as early as Edward VI's reign, two of the practices later to be especially characteristic of the Puritan family: the children's rehearsal of sermon themes after their return from church, and their daily reading and discussion of a chapter from the Bible before dinner or supper. William Gouge wanted children to be catechized every day. The Bible was to be the first book they read. Conversations with them about the natural world could be used to reinforce religious doctrines.[39]

Ideally, the whole household was to be involved in the 'family duties' of prayer and Scripture reading; the married couple at its head were to pray together, and each partner was to set aside some time each day for prayer and reading. The Sabbath in particular was to be devoted to religious duties. The chief responsibility in all this was the husband's, but if he neglected it, the godly wife might remind him of his duty or even perform it herself, especially if he was unable to do so. William Gouge remarked that a husband was as a priest to his wife, and ought to be her mouth to God when they were together, but he had to admit that many women were better able to pray than their husbands. Joining together in private religious exercises was an important means of strengthening and refining conjugal love. By helping each partner see the magnitude of his or her own sins, William Whateley thought, it would prevent their blaming each other.[40]

This 'spiritualization of the household', its roots deep in the Middle Ages, was not in any way intended to weaken the family's participation in the religious life of the parish. Attendance at church remained the linchpin of religious observance. Godly ministers seeking to introduce local schemes of discipline, at Northampton in 1571, or Dedham in the 1580s, tried to increase it and make it more effective. At Dedham it was agreed that 'all gouernors of household' should do their best to come to their own churches before the start of divine service accompanied by their servants and whole family, excepting only those whose presence at home was required 'for necessary uses of children etc.' They were to cause 'their youth' to attend regular catechisms. Monthly communions were to be preceded by a series of examinations of all would-be communicants. (Separate sessions were to be organized for adults and young people.) All householders were to attend the two lectures read every week with some of their servants.[41]

Some personal experiences of the work of pastoral care

This sort of ideal scheme was probably realized in only a tiny minority of parishes, and there not for long. Meanwhile the conscientious clergy continued to labour among their people, breaking and tilling hard ground as best they might. In the case of a minority, these pastoral efforts are illuminated by their own writings, by biographical testimonies, and by surviving local records of various sorts. Daniel Rogers explained in the epistle dedicatory to his *Matrimoniall Honour* that he brought to his work as author much experience as counsellor to his flock: he had received many complaints from the married and daily questions from people intending marriage. In a later heartfelt complaint, he criticized those wives who imparted their marriage discontents to strangers, asking for their advice and thereby betraying their husbands to base report. Advising such women was fraught with danger. 'Oh, how many of these housewives have deceived both Minister, friends, and husbands by their subtilty? till afterward their sinne betray them, what mettall and stampe they are of!'[42]

In a few cases, we learn something of parishioners' reactions to the advice which godly ministers gave them. The 'silver tongued' Henry Smith spoke so eloquently at St Clement Danes of mothers' duty to suckle their own children that many fashionable women who had sent their babies to suburban wet-nurses had them brought back home. Very different was William Gouge's experience at St Anne's Blackfriars. When he first delivered his discourses of *Domesticall Duties* from the pulpit, 'much exception was taken against the application of a wiues subiection to the restraining of her from disposing the common goods of the family without, or against her husband's consent'. His recollection casts a fascinating sidelight on the readiness of wives in a well-off London parish to question what their minister told them, especially when it seemed to threaten the considerable autonomy which they enjoyed in household management. One of the earliest Puritan apostles, a man who had acted as Henry Smith's mentor, was Richard Greenham, rector of Dry Drayton (Cambs.), between 1570 and 1591. Despite his painful labours in preaching and catechizing, Greenham allegedly found his parishioners untractable and unteachable. Yet in one respect he seems to have left his stamp upon the parish. During his incumbency there was a striking but temporary increase in the number of biblical baptismal names recorded in the parish register.[43]

Funeral sermons

A medium which came to play an increasingly important part in the preaching ministry of many godly pastors between the Reformation and the civil wars was the funeral sermon. At first there was widespread mistrust among the more militant Protestants of this sort of discourse. They felt that the custom of including some personal reference to the dead had all too often been abused. Undeserved eulogies made unregenerate sinners seem good Christians, and gave their surviving friends a false assurance of their happy state in the next life. Yet many ministers overcame such misgivings so far as their own friends were concerned, and used the funeral sermon as a vehicle for the celebration of exemplary lives. Newly dead saints were set before the living as models for their imitation. The practice of the domestic virtues bulked large in these biographical accounts. Husbands and wives were praised for personal piety; living together in affection, harmony and fidelity; for bringing up their children and servants in the fear of God; and for maintaining household religion. Most of these sermons culminated in a description of the death-bed. Sometimes the preacher or one of his colleagues appeared in such descriptions as a physician of souls, armed with comfortable texts and ready to give good counsel. Yet the spotlight fell on the dying person and his or her ability to draw on inner resources of patience and faith. A steadily increasing number of funeral sermons found their way into print, and about 250 of them had been published by the outbreak of the first civil war.[44]

Conscientious ministers were soon included in the ranks of those who received funeral tributes, despite the fact that some of the men thus distinguished expressed their strong disapproval of such encomia. Their family lives were prominent themes of these accounts. The households of some of these men were described as a little church, or a little model of a church. William Gouge (d. 1654), perhaps the foremost of the godly Protestant writers on household duties, was said to have been indulgent towards the bodies of his children and servants, yet especially careful of their souls, as had been shown by his constant labour in catechizing them and the holy instructions he had given them each day. 'So amiable was the meeknesse of his carriage toward his wife, that for twenty two years (for so long they lived together) there was never heard any one word proceeding from him toward her, sounding like an angry one.'[45]

Non-Puritan advice and pastoral care: Cosin, Donne and Herbert

Most of the fullest and best-known works of advice on Christian family life written in England between Elizabeth's accession and the civil wars came from the pens of men who were either moderate Puritans or very close to the latter in their own churchmanship. Relatively little was written on the subject by divines who cherished a rival vision of the Church, expressed with increasing confidence from the later years of Elizabeth I's reign onwards. Differing in the extent to which they qualified or rejected Calvinist theology, and in their participation in the promotion of high-church policies, these men shared a respect for traditions, a reverence for the sacraments, and a love of order and formality in worship both public and private. It is probably going too far, however, to say that they sought 'to replace the spiritual autonomy of families with a clerically dominated, conformist religion'.[46] This is to exaggerate the contrast between conformists and Puritans, the extent to which the conformists shared a coherent and distinctive view of the place of the family within the Church, and the degree to which they wrote in conscious reaction against the Puritans.

Family life and duties were not prominent themes in the published sermons of the most active 'high-church' preachers. John Cosin (1594–1672), whose 'Popish innovations' were to anger the Long Parliament, delivered in 1624 a marriage sermon on John 2.1–2, describing Christ's invitation to the wedding at Cana in Galilee. Cosin's main theme was married people's need of Jesus' presence in their undertaking. Married life was so full of trouble that 'if Christ were not by to help them, and to comfort them with His presence, what joy could they take in such a state of life that had brought all these miseries upon them?' Had Christ not been present at Cana, men might have had cause to doubt whether it was good to marry at all. Jesus and his mother had been virgins 'and married life itself seems to be but an imperfect state, the state of perfection is virginity, so much commended by our Saviour, so highly esteemed by St. Paul'. Yet Christ's presence had confirmed that marriage was a state pleasing and acceptable to God, if undertaken according to his will and ordinance, excluding wantonness. Cosin himself married despite the somewhat pessimistic view of married life he expressed in this sermon.[47]

One of the most prolific court preachers of the early seventeenth century was John Donne (1571 or 2 to 1631). His spiritual and intellectual complexity defy any attempt at categorization, but his devotion to the sacraments, his comfortable acceptance of the Church's ceremonial requirements, and his delight in allegory, rhetorical conceit and ingeniously displayed patristic learning, set him clearly apart from even the moderate Puritans. Donne preached at churchings as well as christenings and marriages. Certain themes stand out in his marriage sermons. First, earthly marriage prefigures the perfect union of the soul with Christ in heaven, where there will be no marriage between men and women. Second, while marriage is honourable, and indeed an obligation for those who do not have the special gift of chastity, those who can contain themselves should remain single. Third, married people should behave with sober continency, avoiding excessive indulgence in sexual pleasure. Fourth, of the three ends of marriage, Donne spoke far more warmly of propagation (including the religious education of children) and mutual help (including bearing with each other's infirmities) than of the 'medicine' of sexual intercourse for the avoidance of fornication.[48] In his christening sermons, he dealt at length with the significance of the sacrament of baptism. It sealed election and was an instrument and conduit of sanctification. Not absolutely necessary, because God might use extraordinary means, it was nevertheless necessary by God's ordinary institution. Those who failed to provide duly for the baptism of their child had a heavier account to render to God if it died than if they had allowed it to starve.[49] In none of Donne's surviving sermons is there the sort of practical advice for spouses or parents confronting the daily problems of their station which so many Puritans loved to give.

George Herbert (1593–1633), a protégé of William Laud, notorious architect of high-church policies, nevertheless included in his *A Priest to the Temple* one of the period's most vivid accounts of an ideal pattern of pastoral care of families. Ensuring the observance of domestic religious duties both in his own household and in those of his parishioners was one of the most important responsibilities of Herbert's parson. Under his own roof the work would be shared with his wife, if he had one: Herbert thought virginity a higher state than matrimony, but nevertheless entered marriage himself. Such household religious duties included morning and evening prayers, catechizing, and reading of Scripture: Herbert's parson took a personal interest in the reading ability of his parishioners' children and servants. Herbert's vision of the godly household resembled that of the Puritans in certain important respects. He expected all parents to take a leading part in the religious education of their children, and his sketch of that education presupposed every family's possession of a Bible. Yet his parson, dispensing blessings upon households and children, hearing the particular confessions of the sick, intimating to them the virtue of the sacrament, and maintaining a close surveillance of each individual and household, was also a more sacerdotal figure than the typical Puritan minister.[50]

Conclusion

The sixteenth-century reformers' preference for marriage over enforced celibacy and their refusal to accord matrimony the status of a sacrament made very little difference to family life as most people experienced it. The Reformation did, however, bring important changes in the nature of pastoral support for the family. Open access to the vernacular Bible was a fundamental principle of the Reformation. The mediaeval Church's exposition of family responsibilities had rested on scriptural foundations, but the Bible itself had remained closed to most of the laity. Now it was made available in every church, and was soon to be more widely owned than any other single book. Nurturing faith by expounding the Word of God became the chief responsibility of the Protestant ministry. The orders of service, now also in the vernacular, were transformed into major vehicles of instruction, and their theatrical, ceremonial and sacramental elements were greatly reduced. Preaching, catechizing and homiletic exposition all had a bigger part to play; they were more systematically organized and monitored than ever before. Works of instruction addressed directly to the laity had begun to appear before the introduction of printing, which further stimulated their publication.[51] During and after the Reformation, however, the potential of this new technology was more vigorously exploited in the production of a vastly increased number of sermons, catechisms and advice books. Meanwhile

288 *Ralph Houlbrooke*

compulsory auricular confession was abolished, and priestly ceremonial or sacramental penetration of the domestic sphere declined. In the ideal Protestant community, the assembly of God's people for prayer, worship and instruction remained central. But the family Bible and catechism, printed advice literature, and the memorized sermon, all equipped the godly household for a fuller role.

How far were the reformers' aims achieved? First, a mass of testimony, notably in diaries, letters and funeral sermons, points to the realization of the ideal of the godly household by many individual families in the middling and upper ranks of society.[52] The new freedom to marry offered the clergy the opportunity of practising what they preached. It is much harder to assess the impact of the Reformation on the family lives of the population at large, or the extent to which godly ministers were successful in enlisting the support of householders and parents in their campaign of family evangelization. In 1588 the moderate Puritan divine Thomas Sparke believed that not one minister in twenty in England was catechizing, not one householder in a hundred.[53] The successes achieved by the godly ministers of the century after the Reformation outside the upper classes, the towns and those areas of the countryside where the industrious middling sort were thickest on the ground were patchy and limited. During the coming years of revolutionary upheaval, the reservoirs of unfulfilled desire for religious experience and action in the countryside, in the darker corners of the land, and among women and the less well educated, would be tapped more effectively by the proliferating sects. Of them all, the most formidably successful would be the Friends, for whom the Inner Light was superior even to the Scriptures, and who rejected sacraments, ministry and set forms of worship. Initially disruptive of family bonds, the sects would ultimately come to depend on them for their survival during the long decades of persecution and limited toleration.

Notes

1. The classic study is L. L. Schücking's *The Puritan Family: A Social Study from the Literary Sources* (London, 1969), originally published in German in 1929; cf. C. L. Powell, *English Domestic Relations, 1487–1653* (New York, 1917). The strong element of continuity between later mediaeval and Puritan advice on marriage duties was brought out by K. M. Davies, 'Continuity and Change in Literary Advice on Marriage', in R. B. Outhwaite (ed.), *Marriage and Society: Studies in the Social History of Marriage* (London, 1981), pp. 58–80; while M. Todd, *Christian Humanism and the Puritan Social Order*

(Cambridge, 1987), pp. 96–117, argued that the Puritans owed the most characteristic features of their view of the family to the Christian humanists. P. Collinson, 'The Protestant Family', in id., *The Birthpangs of Protestant England* (Basingstoke, 1988), pp. 60–93, and A. Fletcher, 'The Protestant Idea of Marriage in Early Modern England', in A. Fletcher and P. Roberts (eds), *Religion, Culture and Society in Early Modern Britain: Essays in Honour of Patrick Collinson* (Cambridge, 1994), pp. 161–81, discerned a more distinctive tone in English Protestant, and especially Puritan, advice about marriage. See also P. Crawford, *Women and Religion in England 1500–1720* (London and New York, 1993).

2. J. Goody, *The Development of the Family and Marriage in Europe* (Cambridge, 1983), pp. 56–9, 77–81, 190–1, 204–5, 210–12; F. Mount, *The Subversive Family: An Alternative History of Love and Marriage* (London, 1982), ch. 1, 'Marriage and the Church', pp. 15–28.

3. R. B. Lyman, Jr, 'Barbarism and Religion: Late Roman and Early Mediaeval Childhood', in L. deMause (ed.), *The History of Childhood* (London, 1976), pp. 84–91; R. Meens, 'Children and Confession in the Early Middle Ages', in D. Wood (ed.), *The Church and Childhood*, Studies in Church History, 31 (1994), pp. 55–61; Goody, *Development of Family and Marriage*, pp. 85, 194–6.

4. Goody, ibid., esp. pp. 68–75, 89–106, 123–5, 214–16.

5. *The Sarum Missal in English*, trans. F. E. Warren (London, 1911), vol.2, pp. 143–60.

6. *Manuale ad vsum percelebris ecclesie sarisburiensis*, ed. A. J. Collins, Henry Bradshaw Society, 91 (1960), pp. 25–31, 35–8; *The Rationale of Ceremonial 1540–1543*, ed. C. S. Cobb, Alcuin Club Collections, 18 (1910), pp. 6–12.

7. *Manuale*, pp. 43–4; D. Cressy, *Birth, Marriage and Death: Ritual, Religion, and the Life-Cycle in Tudor and Stuart England* (Oxford, 1997), p. 205.

8. *Councils and Synods, with Other Documents relating to the English Church*, vol. 2: *A.D. 1205–1313*, ed. F. M. Powicke and C.R. Cheney, (two parts, continuously paginated, Oxford, 1964), pp. 454–5, 593–4, 639, 705–6, 991–5.

9. *Manuale*, pp. 97–112.

10. M. M. Sheehan, *The Will in Medieval England* (Toronto, 1963). There are several studies of religious attitudes and practices in late mediaeval English communities and social groups which draw on the evidence contained in wills. One of the best is N. P. Tanner, *The Church in Late Medieval Norwich 1370–1532* (Toronto, 1984), esp. appendix 12, 'Analysis of Testamentary Bequests', pp. 222–3. The best short introduction is to be found in J. J. Scarisbrick, *The Reformation and the English People* (Oxford, 1984), ch. 1, 'Layfolk and the Pre-Reformation Church', pp. 1–18. For a survey which gives references to numerous recent studies see R. Houlbrooke, *Death, Religion and the Family in England, 1480–1750* (Oxford, 1998), pp. 110–16.

11. *Manuale*, pp. 114–24.

12. *Councils and Synods*, vol. 2, pp. 69, 87–8, 134, 228, 302, 405, 410, 423–4, 432, 443, 457, 520, 590, 643, 749, 900-5, 987–8, 996–9, 1046, 1063.

13. H. L. Spencer, *English Preaching in the Late Middle Ages* (Oxford, 1993), pp.

199–206; E. Duffy, *The Stripping of the Altars: Traditional Religion in England 1400–1580* (New Haven and London, 1992), pp. 53–63.
14. *Dives and Pauper,* vol. 1, ed. P. H. Barnum, Early English Text Society, 275, 280 (1976, 1980), W. Harrington, *In this Boke are conteyned the Commendacions of Matrymony* (n.d.). The date of this treatise is discussed by D. Ramage in *Durham Philobiblon* 1 (1949–55), 69.
15. *Dives and Pauper* 1, ii. 60–2; Harrington, *Commendacions*, sig. Aii^v–iv^r.
16. Harrington, ibid., sig. Cvi–Diii; *Dives and Pauper* 1, ii. 58–62, 67.
17. *Dives and Pauper* 1, i. 327–8; Harrington, *Commendacions*, sig. Diii.
18. R. Whitford, *A Werke for Housholders* (1530), sig. Bii^v–Ciiii^r; Diiii^v–Eiiii^v.
19. T. M. Safley, 'Marriage', in *The Oxford Encyclopaedia of the Reformation,* ed. H. J. Hillerbrand (New York and Oxford, 1996), vol. 3, p. 19; E. Tilney, *The Flower of Friendship: A Renaissance Dialogue contesting Marriage*, ed. V. Wayne (Ithaca and London, 1992), pp. 21–4; E. J. Carlson, *Marriage and the English Reformation* (Oxford, and Cambridge, Mass., 1994), pp. 3–4, 49–66 (the best short survey of clerical marriage in England). Professor Carlson points out that some Protestant clergy preferred to remain celibate. Cf. I. Morgan, *The Godly Preachers of the Elizabethan Church* (London, 1965), p. 150 (citing the view of William Perkins that a single life was superior for those who had the gift of continence).
20. F. E. Brightman, *The English Rite: being a Synopsis of the Sources and Revisions of the Book of Common Prayer* (London, 1915), vol. 2, pp. 800–17; Carlson, *Marriage and the English Reformation*, pp. 45–7.
21. Brightman, *English Rite*, vol. 2, pp. 724–47; H. Davies, *Worship and Theology in England from Cranmer to Hooker 1534–1603* (Princeton, 1970), p. 203.
22. Brightman, *English Rite,* vol. 2, pp. 744–7, 776–99.
23. Ibid., pp. 880–5.
24. Ibid., pp. 822–9, 834–6, 842–8.
25. *Documents of the English Reformation*, ed. G. Bray (Cambridge, 1994), p. 182; S. Smith-Bannister, *Names and Naming Patterns in England 1538–1700* (Oxford, 1997), pp. 34–7; B. M. Berry and R. S. Schofield, 'Age at Baptism in Pre-industrial England', *Population Studies* 25 (1971), 453–63; S. O. Addy, 'A Contribution towards a History of Norton, in Derbyshire', *Journal of the Derbyshire Archaeological and Natural History Society* 2 (1880), 12, 17.
26. *Documentary Annals of the Reformed Church of England*, ed. E. Cardwell (Oxford, 1844), vol. 1, pp. 316–20; Carlson, *Marriage and English Reformation*, pp. 74–7.
27. *Documentary Annals*, vol. 1, pp. 7–8, 92, 213–14, 227, 358–9, 370, 401–3; vol. 2, pp. 24, 42–3, 107–8; I. Green, *The Christian's ABC: Catechisms and Catechizing in England c.1530–1740* (Oxford, 1996), pp. 102, 114–15, 122, 132–3, 144-5, 204–13, 216–19.
28. Brightman, *English Rite*, vol. 2, pp. 638–9; *Documentary Annals*, vol. 1, pp. 221, 244, 245, 370, 402, 404; W. P. M. Kennedy, *Elizabethan Episcopal Administration: An Essay in Sociology and Politics,* 3 vols., Alcuin Club Collections, 26–7 (1924), vol. 2, pp. 15, 43–4, 50, 55, 71, 76, 94–5, 98, 114, 115, 121, 129, 131; vol. 3, pp. 142, 148, 151, 154, 166, 179, 180, 190, 194, 197,

202, 207, 212-13, 219–20, 224, 231-3, 259, 260, 263, 292, 321, 350; *Visitation Articles and Injunctions of the Early Stuart Church*, ed. K. Fincham, Church of England Record Society 1, 5 (1994, 1998), vol. 2, pp. 2, 5, 9, 12, 29, 40, 56, 60, 63–4, 74, 78, 82, 90, 103, 132, 135, 145, 164, 176, 180, 197, 201, 205, 208; P. E. H. Hair, 'Bridal Pregnancy in Rural England in Earlier Centuries', *Population Studies* 20 (1966–7), 233–43; id., 'Bridal Pregnancy in Earlier Rural England Further Examined', *Population Studies* 24 (1970), 59–70; M. Ingram, *Church Courts, Sex and Marriage in England, 1570–1640* (Cambridge, 1987), pp. 189–237; R. Adair, *Courtship, Illegitimacy and Marriage in Early Modern England* (Manchester, 1996), pp. 92–109.

29. *Documentary Annals*, vol. 1, pp. 14, 244–5; Kennedy, *Elizabethan Episcopal Administration*, vol. 1, pp. 56, 115; vol. 2, pp. 162, 213, 224, 259, 321, 337; Houlbrooke, *Death, Religion and Family*, pp. 95–104, 128–30; H. Barrow, *A Brief Discoverie of the False Church* (1590), in id., *The Writings of Henry Barrow 1587–1590*, ed. L. H. Carlson, Elizabethan Nonconformist Texts, 3 (1962), pp. 421, 458.

30. *An Admonition to the Parliament*, in *Puritan Manifestoes*, ed. W. H. Frere and C. E. Douglas (London, 1954), pp. 26–7; Cressy, *Birth, Marriage and Death*, pp. 124–34, 150–4, 216–22, 342–7.

31. Brightman, *English Rite*, vol. 2, p. 778 (the 1552 rubric omitted specific reference to death in infancy: ibid., p. 779); Kennedy, *Elizabethan Episcopal Administration*, vol. 2, p. 73; Cressy, *Birth, Marriage and Death*, pp. 105–6, 109–23; *The Catechism of Thomas Becon, S.T.P., ... with other pieces written by him in the reign of King Edward the Sixth*, ed. J. Ayre (Parker Society, 1844), pp. 208, 214–17.

32. *Certain Sermons or Homilies, appointed to be read in Churches* (Cambridge, 1850), pp. 118–34, 501–15, esp. 501–6, 508, 510–11.

33. R. Baxter, *A Christian Directory* (1673), quoted in W. Haller, *The Rise of Puritanism* (paperback edn, Philadelphia, 1984), p. 24.

34. W. Whateley, *A Bride-Bvsh. Or, A Direction for Married Persons, Plainely describing the duties common to both, and peculiar to each of them* (London, 1623 edn), pp. 15–20; H. Smith, *A Preparative to Marriage* (London, 1591), pp. 59–60.

35. W. Gouge, *Of Domesticall Dvties Eight Treatises* (London, 1622), p. 286; T. Gataker, *Marriage Dvties briefely covched togither; ovt of Colossians, 3. 18, 19* (London, 1620), p. 11.

36. Gouge, *Domesticall Dvties*, pp. 349–78, esp. 356; D. Rogers, *Matrimoniall Honovr: Or, The mutuall Crowne and comfort of godly, loyall, and chaste Marriage* (London, 1642), pp. 161, 264–5, 152–3; Whateley, *Bride-Bvsh*, pp. 106–8, 169–73; Davies, 'Literary Advice on Marriage', p. 68.

37. Gataker, *Marriage Dvties*, pp. 37–8, 41, 44; Gouge, *Domesticall Dvties*, pp. 149, 498–9, 507–18; Rogers, *Matrimoniall Honovr*, pp. 92–3.

38. R. C., *A Godlie Forme of Hovseholde Government* (London, 1600), pp. 50–9, 252-3, 290–7; Gouge, *Domesticall Dvties*, pp. 153–6, 550–8; Rogers, *Matrimoniall Honovr*, p. 299.

39. Becon, *Catechism*, p. 351; Gouge, *Domesticall Dvties*, pp. 539–41; R. C., *Godlie Forme*, pp. 251, 252, 254, 265.

40. Rogers, *Matrimoniall Honovr*, pp. 128–46; R. C., *Godlie Forme*, pp. 20–9; Gouge, *Domesticall Dvties*, pp. 235–7, 240, 243; Whateley, *Bride-Bvsh*, pp. 52–3.
41. Cf. C. Hill, 'The Spiritualization of the Household', in *Society and Puritanism in Pre-Revolutionary England* (London, 1964), pp. 443–81, a famous and influential essay which tends to overemphasize the contribution to this process of 'spiritualization' made by religious dissent and the industrious middling sort of people; R. C., *Godlie Forme*, p. 35; W. J. Sheils, 'Erecting the Discipline in Provincial England: The Order of Northampton, 1571', in J. Kirk (ed.), *Humanism and Reform: The Church in Europe, England and Scotland, 1400–1643. Essays in Honour of James K. Cameron*, Studies in Church History, Subsidia, 8 (Oxford, 1991), pp. 331–45, esp. 338–9; *The Presbyterian Movement in the Reign of Queen Elizabeth as illustrated by the Minute Book of the Dedham Classis, 1582–1589*, ed. R. G. Usher, Camden 3rd series 8 (1905), pp. 99–100.
42. Rogers, *Matrimoniall Honovr*, sig. A2, p. 136.
43. Haller, *Rise of Puritanism*, p. 30, citing *The sermons ... and the life of Mr Henry Smith*, ed. T. Fuller (1657); Gouge, *Domesticall Dvties*, epistle dedicatory; Carlson, *Marriage and the Reformation*, pp. 158–63.
44. F. B. Tromly, '"According to Sounde Religion": The Elizabethan Controversy over the Funeral Sermon', *Journal of Medieval and Renaissance Studies* 13 (1983), 293–312. Some examples: R. Pricke, *A Verie Godlie and Learned Sermon, treating of Mans mortalitie* (London, 1608), sig. E3 (Lady Lewkenor); C. FitzGeffrey, *Death's Sermon vnto the Living* (London, 1620), pp. 26–9 (Lady Rous); W. Miller, *A Sermon preached at the fvnerall of the Worshipfull Gilbert Davies Esquire* (London, 1621), sig. D1–D3; W. Stone, *A Curse become a Blessing* (London, 1623), pp. 53–6 (Paul Cleybrooke); W. Crompton, *A Lasting Iewel for Religious Woemen* (London, 1630), sig. E–F3 (Mrs Mary Crosse).
45. W. Jenkyn, *A Shock of Corn Coming in In its Season* (London, 1654), pp. 37, 40.
46. Todd, *Christian Humanism and Puritan Social Order*, pp. 234, 238.
47. 'Sermon III. Preached at Datchet near Windsor, on the second Sunday after Epiphany, A.D. MDCXXIV; at the Marriage of Mr. Abraham De Laune and Mrs. Mary Wheeler', in J. Cosin, *Works*, 5 vols (Library of Anglo-Catholic Theology, 1843–55), vol. 1, esp. pp. 54–7.
48. *The Sermons of John Donne*, ed. G. R. Potter and E. M. Simpson, 10 vols (Berkeley and Los Angeles, 1953–62), vol. 2, pp. 339–40, 345–6; vol. 3, pp. 244–55; vol. 8, pp. 99–109.
49. *Sermons of John Donne*, vol. 5, pp. 96–167, esp. 160–3.
50. G. Herbert, *The Country Parson, His Character, and Rule of Holy Life*, in *The Complete English Works*, ed. A. P. Slater (London, 1995), pp. 208–10, 217–20, 224–7.
51. Duffy, *Stripping of Altars*, pp. 53–87.
52. *Diary of Lady Margaret Hoby, 1599–1605*, ed. D. M. Meads (London, 1930); *The Diary of Bulstrode Whitelocke 1605–1675*, ed. R. Spalding, Records of

Social and Economic History, new series, 13 (1990); P. S. Seaver, *Wallington's World: A Puritan Artisan in Seventeenth-Century London* (London, 1985); J. Eales, *Puritans and Roundheads: The Harleys of Brampton Bryan and the Outbreak of the English Civil War* (Cambridge, 1990); J. T. Cliffe, *The Puritan Gentry: The Great Puritan Families of Early Stuart England* (London, 1984).
53. Cited in Green, *Christian's ABC*, p. 129.

Bibliography

Carlson, E. J., *Marriage and the English Reformation* (Oxford, and Cambridge, Mass., 1994)

Cressy, D., *Birth, Marriage and Death: Ritual, Religion, and the Life-cycle in Tudor and Stuart England* (Oxford, 1997)

Davies, K.M., 'Continuity and Change in Literary Advice on Marriage', in R. B. Outhwaite (ed.), *Marriage and Society: Studies in the Social History of Marriage* (London, 1981), pp. 58–80

Goody, J., *The Development of the Family and Marriage in Europe* (Cambridge, 1983)

Hill, C., 'The Spiritualization of the Household', in *Society and Puritanism in Pre-Revolutionary England* (London, 1964), pp. 443–81

Schücking, L. L., *The Puritan Family: A Social Study from the Literary Sources* (London, 1969)

14

George Herbert and *The Country Parson*

Philip Sheldrake

George Herbert (1593–1633) was a person of many parts, and it was this complexity, and perhaps an inward tension it produced, that made his spirituality so rich and what he wrote so memorable. Herbert has achieved classic status as arguably one of the greatest English poets. He was also one of the major seventeenth-century figures in the emergence of an Anglican spiritual tradition. Several of his poems were adopted as popular and profound hymns. To some people Herbert is an uncanonized saint, perhaps a mystic.

This essay concerns Herbert's understanding of the theory and practice of pastoral care. As the title suggests, what follows takes as its primary focus one of his two best-known works, the treatise on the priestly life entitled *A Priest to the Temple, Or, The Country Parson His Character, and Rule of Holy Life*. However, reference will also be made to Herbert's other great work, his collection of poems known as *The Temple, Sacred Poems and Private Ejaculations,* which also has a pastoral purpose.[1]

Herbert's life

George Herbert was born in 1593 into the aristocratic and powerful Pembroke family. He had an illustrious academic record as a pupil at Westminster School and then at Trinity College, Cambridge, where he eventually became a Fellow in 1614. Herbert seemed destined for a significant public career as he became first Public Orator of the University

(1620) and then a Member of Parliament (1624). Quite how and why Herbert settled on the Church as the context for his work remains a matter of conjecture.[2]

Herbert appears to have begun divinity studies as early as 1616. Yet he only became a deacon at the end of the 1624 Parliament when his ordination was hastily arranged with a special dispensation from the Archbishop of Canterbury. Once again the expected pattern was delayed. Although by 1626 Herbert had been made a (non-resident) canon of Lincoln Cathedral and given the living of Leighton Bromswold in Huntingdonshire, he was not ordained priest in Salisbury Cathedral until September 1630. By this time he had already taken up residence with his family as rector of the village of Bemerton just outside Salisbury. His ministry as parish priest lasted less than three years, for he died on 1 March 1633. The various delays make it reasonable to suppose that Herbert went through a period of struggle from 1616–24 and perhaps again after ordination as a deacon. Perhaps this concerned the contrary attractions of a public career and of vocation to the priesthood. However, the evidence of Herbert's writings suggests that it may have also involved a recurring sense of unworthiness in the face of God's love. This is certainly a thread running through much of his poetry.

'Protestant' or 'Catholic' sensibilities?

There has been some controversy about whether Herbert's works are to be interpreted in a 'Protestant' or a 'Catholic' sense. Some scholars have emphasized his place within the predominantly 'Catholic' structure and liturgy of the Church of England, based on a traditional threefold ministry and the Book of Common Prayer. The evidence adduced consists of mediaeval allusions or references in Herbert's works and his undoubtedly liturgical and sacramental spirituality. The 'Catholic' school of interpretation also tends to draw attention to the influences of post-Reformation Roman Catholic spiritual writers (such as Ignatius Loyola or Francis de Sales) on seventeenth-century Anglicans.[3]

Because this interpretation was one-sided, it was inevitably corrected by a 'Protestant' revisionism. This standpoint emphasized that the Church of England was essentially a Reformed Church even if there were continuities with the past. Thus Herbert's theology must have been unequivocally Protestant and specifically Calvinist.[4]

More recently there has been some attempt to mediate between the two poles of interpretation. First, there is the obvious fact that what is implied by the terms 'Catholic' and 'Protestant' is not as mutually exclusive as once thought. Members of the Church of England in Herbert's time, to whatever party they belonged, undoubtedly considered themselves Protestant. This did not mean that there was no sense of continuity with a Catholic past. Anglicanism (not a concept used by Herbert or his contemporaries) has a particularity which tended to be overlooked in the past but which contemporary scholars are more inclined to acknowledge.[5] There was a sense that the English Church in its ambiguities mediated between the two 'extremes' of Geneva and Rome. This sentiment is clearly expressed in Herbert's poem 'The British Church'.

There were undoubtedly some strict Calvinists within the Church of England. Indeed, during Herbert's period the Church as a whole was committed to a Calvinist doctrine of predestination, described as 'full of sweet, pleasant and unspeakable comfort' in Article 17 of the 39 Articles of Religion. However, the Church of England could not be labelled simply as Calvinist. Even Article 17 is ambiguous about the stricter Calvinist doctrine of double predestination.

George Herbert seems typical of most non-Puritan divines of his time in accepting aspects of Calvinist doctrine while not being a straightforward Calvinist. He was a friend of other contemporary spiritual figures such as Bishop Lancelot Andrewes and Nicholas Ferrar, whose theologies and spiritualities, like Herbert's own, were complex. Herbert would appear to be arguing in a simple way for loyalty to the established liturgy and formularies of the Church of England. In the context of the times, however, this was less irenical and more contentious than may now appear. Herbert's church connections, not least with Ferrar, his involvement in restoring and beautifying church buildings, as well as the defence in his writings of priestly blessings, confession, processions, the use of the sign of the Cross and, obliquely, of liturgical vesture, may be interpreted as a counter-blast to Puritanism. There is also some evidence in Herbert's poetic collection *The Temple* of a tension between the classical Reformed doctrines of predestination and justification by faith and a sense of people's freedom and responsibility. Herbert clearly believed that the Church to which he gave his loyalty made it possible to hold together the Reformation doctrines of grace, redemption and faith with a continued stress on liturgy, the sacramental life and personal holiness. The discussions about Herbert's 'Protestantism' or 'Catholicism' have, as we shall see, some relevance to our interpretation of his approach to pastoral care.

Writings: purpose and audience

The dating of Herbert's two great works and their precise purpose are also a matter of debate. Both works were published posthumously: the poems in 1633 with a preface by his friend Nicholas Ferrar, the founder of the community at Little Gidding, and the treatise as late as 1652. It used to be thought that Herbert wrote both works while at Bemerton. It is now accepted, however, that he probably edited and structured the works there but wrote a significant number of the poems at various points before 1630. Some scholars consider that his own remarks in the 1632 preface to *The Country Parson* that 'I have resolved to set down the form and character of a true pastor, that I may have a mark to aim at' suggest that the work was written in anticipation of taking up parochial ministry rather than as a description of his actual practice at Bemerton.[6]

Even if the main arguments of *The Country Parson* were largely completed prior to active ministry in Bemerton, the 1632 date of the preface indicates that Herbert did not wish to change the overall tone. It also suggests that Herbert had a didactic purpose even if the portrait of a parish priest in the Church of England was somewhat idealized. The most obvious conclusion to draw from the preface, entitled 'The Author to the Reader', is that the work was intended to offer a model for others rather than simply to be a personal *aide-memoire* of Herbert's own sense of duty. The concluding sentence of the preface runs 'The Lord prosper the intention to myself and others, who may not despise my poor labours, but add to those points which I have observed, until the book grow to a complete pastoral.' In the context, 'the others' would most likely be fellow ministers or those considering such a calling.

Is the work essentially a record of the priest's duties or a manual for the communication of practical information?[7] Such an approach to the work is undoubtedly too simple. A modern editor of Herbert's works points out the rhetorical style of his culture.[8] *The Country Parson* is a work of rhetoric in two senses. In the first place it is meant not simply to *instruct* but to *move* the reader to a deepening sense of call. In the second place the text portrays the priest as a rhetorician. That is, his fundamental task, in what he says, does and lives, is to move his parishioners to deeper faith and greater involvement.

Isaak Walton, the seventeenth-century author of Herbert's life, attributes a message from him to Nicholas Ferrar concerning the collection of poems known as *The Temple*. They are 'a picture of the many spiritual conflicts that have passed betwixt God and my soul before I could subject mine to the will of Jesus my Master: in which service I have now found perfect freedom'.[9] Even if the general tenor of these words is authentic, it is widely agreed that *The Temple* also has a conscious structure aimed at teaching the reader. It seems that the poems have as much of a pastoral purpose as *The Country Parson* while at the same time as they are a genuine expression of Herbert's own spiritual experience. Indeed it may be argued that the poems exemplify aspects of Herbert's approach to pastoral ministry that are less obvious in the prose treatise.

First, the scheme of the poems is closely ordered. They are gathered into a three-part structure, 'The Church Porch', 'The Church' and 'The Church Militant' of which the middle part is both the largest and spiritually the richest and most dynamic. The titles of the three sections correspond to the different meanings of 'Temple' or 'Church'. It is, first, a physical building, the architectural space within which God is praised in the liturgy. Some poems use features of the building as a framework for teaching ('The Altar', 'The Church Floor', 'The Windows'). In doing this, the poems subtly enhance the importance of order and beauty. The 'Temple' is also the Body of Christ, the Christian community. There are poems that express the Church's year or liturgical order (for example, 'Evensong', 'Mattins', 'Lent', 'Holy Communion'). Finally, the 'Temple' is the individual human soul, the 'temple of the Holy Spirit'.

This last emphasis points to a second aspect of pastoral ministry as exemplified in the poems. *The Temple* portrays a spiritual movement or process that is clearly meant to teach others something of the spiritual way.[10] Indeed, it seems that the poems were later put to a variety of instructional uses as spiritual reading alongside the Bible and collections of sermons and as a source of quotations for sermons.[11] This said, the way of teaching is not primarily instructional. It is true that there is something fairly didactic and morally exhortative about 'The Church Porch', the first of the three sections of *The Temple*. However, this is not typical of the famous lyrical poems in the large central section, 'The Church'. Stylistically, most are addressed to God and therefore take the form of meditation or familiar colloquy even if this prayer is conducted in public, as it were. Again, a rhetorical explanation seems appropriate. The poems 'teach' by moving the reader to a feeling response and therefore to a change of life. Equally, precisely because the poems deliberately lay bare Herbert's own spiritual life for the sake of other people, they suggest a sense of identification with the problems and aspirations of all Christians. This contrasts with the rather more detached approach to pastoral care communicated by *The Country Parson*.

Liturgical Foundations

The life and spirituality of the Church to which Herbert gave his love and loyalty was based firmly on corporate prayer. The key foundational document of the sixteenth-century reform was not a set of theological treatises or a catechism of belief but was the Book of Common Prayer. This was at the heart of Herbert's life and teaching. Archbishop Thomas Cranmer's second Prayer Book and its revisions was not simply a translation and reform of the Sarum Missal. It was also a manual of spiritual guidance intended to inculcate a certain spiritual temper and attitude of heart and mind.[12] Herbert understood well that in the Prayer Book, theology and faith were balanced with worship and spirituality, the sacred with the secular. The personal side of spirituality was to be shaped by living and worshipping as part of the people of God that is both ecclesial and civic. The Prayer Book encouraged a rhythmic approach to life – the rhythm of the liturgical year, the monthly recitation of the psalms and the daily twofold office.

Herbert's *The Country Parson* makes some reference to private prayer (for example, chapters 10, 'The Parson in his House', and 31, 'The Parson in Liberty') and even to individual spiritual guidance (chapters 15, 'The Parson Comforting', and 34, 'The Parson's Dexterity in applying of Remedies'). The overall emphasis, however, both in this work and the poems, is on common worship as *the* primary guide for the development of right belief, right attitudes and right action. The liturgy, particularly the daily offices, and the common life of Herbert's rather idealized country parish, were thought to be the real teachers of the Christian life. As we shall see, explicit instruction, catechesis and preaching were merely an expression of this broader understanding of teaching and learning.

> Though private prayer be a brave design,
> Yet public hath more promises, more love:
> And love's a weight to hearts, to eyes a sign.
> We all are but cold suitors; let us move

Where it is warmest. Leave thy six and seven;
Pray with the most: for where most pray, is heaven.
('Perirrhanterium', lines 396–402)

A didactic model

To describe Herbert's model of pastoral care as 'didactic' has some validity, but the description needs to be both explained and qualified. Some people find Herbert's prose work 'assertive', 'certain' and 'authoritarian'. However, this needs to be read alongside the poetry of *The Temple,* where the painful realities of inward spiritual struggle haunt the pages.[13]

First of all, it is clear that Herbert was a devoted servant of God's Word and it is reasonable to suggest that, in the context of the times, this reflected the 'Reformed' sensibilities of his Church. At the heart of the parson's knowledge and ministry lie the sacred Scriptures. For the Reformed minister these are a primary means both of divine communication and of moral transformation.

> The chief and top of his knowledge consists in the book of books, the storehouse and magazine of life and comfort, the holy Scriptures. There he sucks, and lives. In the Scriptures he finds four things; precepts for life, doctrines for knowledge, examples for illustration, and promises for comfort; these he hath digested severally.
> (ch. 4, 'The Parson's Knowledge')

Herbert believed in the power and potential of preaching and that preaching was fundamentally an exposition of the Scriptures. 'The country parson preacheth constantly, the pulpit is his joy and his throne' (ch. 7, 'The Parson Preaching').

Interestingly, Herbert's approach to the 'knowledge' of Scripture bears a striking resemblance to mediaeval monastic understandings of *lectio divina,* or the meditative–contemplative reading of Scripture. There is almost a sacramental quality to Scripture. The Word of God that has the power to transform human lives is present in the written words.

> Oh Book! infinite sweetness! let my heart
> Suck ev'ry letter, and a honey gain,
> Precious for any grief in any part;

To clear the breast, to mollify all pain.
>
> ('The Holy Scriptures', I)

This applies first of all to the parson's own knowledge. The means of knowledge is the heart which 'sucks' the words of Scripture in order to allow its 'honey' to sweeten, to heal and to enlighten.

> The second means [of understanding] is prayer, which if it be necessary even in temporal things, how much more in things of another world, where the well is deep, and we have nothing of ourselves to draw with?
>
> (ch. 4, 'The Parson's Knowledge')

The priest is to approach Scripture always in a spirit of prayer rather than of purely intellectual enquiry.

Apart from preaching, Herbert commended the importance of other forms of teaching, such as catechizing. 'Now catechizing being a work of singular and admirable benefit to the Church of God, and a thing required under canonical obedience, the expounding of our Catechism must needs be the most useful form' (ch. 5, 'The Parson's Accessory Knowledges'). The 'admirable benefit' consists of three things.

> The one, to infuse a competent knowledge of salvation in every one of his flock; the other, to multiply, and build up this knowledge, to a spiritual Temple; the third, to inflame this knowledge, to press and drive it to practice, turning it to reformation of life, by pithy and lively exhortations.
>
> (ch. 21, 'The Parson Catechizing')

The ecclesial context

Herbert's approach to preaching and teaching is always within an ecclesial context. The parson is 'the deputy of Christ' (ch. 1) and 'in God's stead' (ch. 20). Yet he is also and always the representative of the Church as Herbert indicates in his comments on the importance of using the official Catechism (chs. 5, 21). Equally, just as preaching should lead to prayer, so one important dimension of Herbert's teaching overall is preparation for the liturgy and sacraments, especially the celebration of the Eucharist.

The parson

> applies himself with catechizings, and lively exhortations, not on the Sunday of the Communion only (for then it is too late) but the Sunday, or Sundays, before the Communion, or on the Eves of all those days.
>
> (ch. 22, 'The Parson in Sacraments')

For Herbert, preaching and teaching in themselves have their limits. Herbert believed passionately that the purpose of words was to lead to prayer, to a kind of silence that is open to Presence. 'Resort to sermons, but to prayers most: / Praying's the end of preaching' ('Perirrhanterium', ll. 409–10). In Herbert's own words, in his famous poem 'Prayer' from *The Temple*, prayer is 'the soul's blood', the very source of life coursing through us and also 'the soul in paraphrase', the most perfect expression of our deepest self.

Herbert's country parson was more than simply a weaver of words. In the tradition of the Church of England, the priest's teaching role was expressed above all else in the leadership of worship, of public prayer. Within the spirituality implicit in the Book of Common Prayer public worship, whether the offices or the Holy Communion, was to be the main school of the Lord's service. The liturgy was both the foundation of and the privileged expression of the 'common life' of the parish as a human and religious community. For this reason, Herbert's parson was to give special attention to the dignity of public worship (ch. 6, 'The Parson Praying') and to the physical space, the church building and its furnishings, within which worship took place (ch. 13, 'The Parson's Church'). This was an essential element of the pastoral care to be exercised by the priest.

The priest's calling: a holy life

There is a totality to Herbert's portrayal of the priest, and the emphasis on holiness serves to underline that this is not merely a job but a way of life. It involves every moment and every aspect of life including how the priest manages his own household and family (ch. 10, 'The Parson in His House').

Herbert recommended that the parson should be fed by intellectual pursuits. 'The country parson hath read the Fathers also, and the schoolmen and the later writers, or a good proportion of all' (ch. 5, 'The Parson's Accessory Knowledges'). Yet at the heart of the parson's pastoral ministry lies holiness, or what we might term 'spirituality'. Without this nothing counts. So 'The Parson's Library' (ch. 33) is not in fact a reference to a collection of books. 'The country parson's library is a holy life.'

The notion that the roots of the priest's ministry lie in a holy life also applies to the parson's preaching. The attention of the listeners is gained

> first, by choosing texts of devotion, not controversy, moving and ravishing texts, whereof the Scriptures are full. Secondly, by dipping and seasoning all our words and sentences in our hearts, before they come into our mouths, truly affecting and cordially expressing all that we say; so that the auditors may plainly perceive that every word is heart-deep. (ch. 7, 'The Parson Preaching')

The priest's eloquence consists not so much in rhetorical devices as in 'holiness' in the sense of an experiential and transformative engagement with God and God's Word. Herbert's parson is effective as a preacher to the degree that his life is a window through which God's grace can pour.

> Lord, how can man preach thy eternal word?
> He is a brittle crazy glass:
> Yet in thy temple thou dost him afford
> This glorious and transcendent place,
> To be a window, through thy grace.
>
> But when thou dost anneal in glass thy story,
> Making thy life to shine within
> The holy preacher's; then the light and glory
> More rev'rend grows, and more doth win:
> Which else shows wat'rish, bleak and thin.
>
> ('The Windows')

The issue of how Herbert viewed the 'holiness' of the minister or priest is somewhat ambiguous. In general, a thoroughgoing Protestant viewpoint would tend to reject the mediaeval hierarchy of vocations – and especially the notion of a special priestly caste. However, in its search for balance, the Elizabethan Settlement left the Church of England with significant elements of the older model of a distinctive priesthood.

Herbert stresses the vocational nature of every human life under God.

Herbert's country parson is to respect and nurture the vocation of all. From creation, all humanity have had a 'calling' and that continues to remain true. 'All are either to have a calling, or prepare for it' (ch. 32). The parson is not to despise the 'holiness' of the most lowly of people or the most ordinary of places.

> He holds the rule, that nothing is little in God's service: If it once have the honour of that Name, it grows great instantly. Wherefore neither disdaineth he to enter into the poorest cottage, though he even creep into it, and though it smell never so loathsomely. For both God is there also, and those for whom God died.
> (ch. 14, 'The Parson in Circuit')

Whether in the parson's own life or in the life of parishioners, the ordinary daily round and the everyday world is the common context for God's presence and action.

> Teach me, my God and King,
> In all things thee to see,
> And what I do in any thing,
> To do it as for thee.
> ('The Elixir')

Yet, alongside an emphasis on the common Christian calling, Herbert also supported elements of what might be called a more pre-Reformation view of the particularity (and even higher nature) of the ministerial vocation.

Article 32 of the 1562 Articles of Religion made it clear that clergy might equally marry or remain single 'at their own discretion'. Herbert's personal view of the best possible lifestyle for the priest seems to have been somewhat different. He allows that for pragmatic reasons it may be best for the priest to marry, yet 'The country parson considering that virginity is a higher state than matrimony, and that the ministry requires the best and highest things, is rather unmarried, than married' (ch. 9, 'The Parson's State of Life'). Interestingly, this somewhat unreformed aspect of Herbert's idealized portrait of the priest is rarely if ever commented upon. The undoubted preference of the Queen for a celibate clergy at the time of the Elizabethan Settlement appears to have sustained sympathy for this viewpoint in parts of the Church of England until the end of the Stuart era.

For Herbert, there is a particular intimacy between God and those who preside at Holy Communion, and this lays a considerable burden upon them.

> The country parson being to administer the Sacraments, is at a stand with himself, how or what behaviour to assume for so holy things. Especially at Communion times he is in a great confusion, as being not only to receive God, but to break, and administer him.
> (ch. 22, 'The Parson in Sacraments')

The priesthood is a 'Blest Order, which in power dost so excel'.

> But th'holy men of God such vessels are,
> As serve him up, who all the world commands:
> When God vouchsafeth to become our fare,
> Their hands convey him who conveys their hands.
> Oh what pure things, most pure must those things be,
> Who bring my God to me!
> ('The Priesthood')

Yet the gap between this awesome calling and frail human nature, sin and failings, is vast. One can only respond to the call to priesthood in full knowledge of unworthiness. The poem 'Aaron' plays with the image of dress, inward and outer, no doubt with an eye to questions of priestly vestments. The true Aaron has 'Holiness on the head,/Light and perfections on the breast', and yet this is not so in the 'poor priest' (Herbert perhaps), who is naturally 'drest' in profaneness, defects and passions. The only answer is to 'put on Christ', for 'In him I am well drest.'

> Christ is my only head,
> My alone only heart and breast,
> My only music, striking me ev'n dead;
> That to the old man I may rest,
> And be in him new drest.

The priest as spiritual guide

As well as teacher and leader of worship, Herbert's parson is a spiritual guide to individuals. Before all else he 'digested all the points of consolation' (ch. 15, 'The Parson Comforting') and he seeks to alleviate scruples, particularly when advising people about their life of prayer, not least the problem of distractions (ch. 31, 'The Parson in Liberty'). In general he attends to the spiritual state of his parishioners, responding to each according to their need. Rather as St Ignatius Loyola, in his *Spiritual Exercises* (nos. 1–20)[14] offers advice to retreat-givers about how to teach spiritual discernment to retreatants, Herbert advises the parson to note the spiritual 'movements' within his parishioners and to react appropriately. So he advises vigilance to those who seem rather untroubled, and fortifies and strengthens those who are tempted (ch. 34, 'The Parson's Dexterity in Applying of Remedies'). Herbert is very much in the tradition of the Prayer Book[15] as well as other Caroline divines, such as Jeremy Taylor, when he recommends 'particular confession' as a comfort and remedy to those who are afflicted in any way.

> Besides this, in his visiting the sick, or otherwise afflicted, he followeth the Church's counsel, namely, in persuading them to particular confession, labouring to make them understand the great good of this ancient and pious ordinance.
>
> (ch. 15, 'The Parson Comforting')

Spiritual guidance (or 'spiritual direction') in the Anglican tradition as expressed by Herbert is something ordinary rather than extraordinary. There is a thread of pastoral or spiritual conversation that runs throughout the whole of *The Country Parson*. This takes place not only in church or on religious occasions but while entertaining in his own house (ch. 8) or visiting people's homes and on the occasions of their everyday work (ch. 14). The priest's household is to share in this ministry of spiritual conversation.

> And when they go abroad, his wife among her neighbours is the beginner of good discourses, his children among children, his servants among other servants; so that as in the house of those that are skilled in music, all are Musicians; so in the house of a preacher, all are preachers.
>
> (ch. 10, 'The Parson in His House')

The priest and healing

Apart from spiritual comfort and healing, Herbert shows a marked interest in physical healing. How this interest originated is uncertain. It may reflect what we know of Herbert's own history of poor health or it may have arisen from contact with country traditions of herbal remedies. Whatever the cause, physical healing is an interesting emphasis in a document on pastoral care.

Chapter 23, 'The Parson's Completeness', offers the most extensive treatment of physical healing. This is to be one of the parson's crucial tasks in the parish. The parson is to ensure the provision of basic medical care. Preferably he or his wife is to be a physician. Indeed, earlier in Chapter 10, 'The Parson in His House', skill in healing is one of the three basic qualities to be hoped for in a wife. Even the children are to have a modest healing role at least as visitors of the sick. Herbert lists other alternatives if the parson and his wife have no skill in medicine. He could keep a physician in his household if he can afford it or he could develop a friendly relationship with a nearby physician whom he can call into the parish when needed. In Chapter 14, 'The Parson in Circuit', Herbert even suggests that the parson should pass on some medicinal knowledge to parishioners during his visits.

Herbert seeks to persuade the aspiring parish priest that herbal medicine especially is not a difficult skill to learn. He recommends certain books and the development of a herb garden. A few examples of herbs and their uses are mentioned. Herbert argues that herbs are more natural and cheaper than drugs from an apothecary. Certainly 'home-bred' herbs are to be preferred to spices and 'outlandish gums', which he condemns as vanities!

The link between this concern for physical healing and spiritual ministry is to be maintained. Although the herb garden is a 'shop' of cures to replace the city apothecary, it may also become an extension of the Church. 'In curing of any, the parson and his family use to premise prayers, for this is to cure like a parson, and this raiseth the action from the shop to the church.'

The art of complete and adaptable care

From his interest in healing, it is clear that Herbert's notion of pastoral care is extremely broadly based. It expresses a sense of completeness and adaptability. First the parson seeks to be involved in every aspect of the life of the parish. To some modern readers this sounds oppressive, but to others it offers a holistic model of pastoral care. 'The country parson desires to be all to his parish, and not only a pastor, but a lawyer also, and a physician' (ch. 23, 'The Parson's Completeness'). As well as teacher, leader of worship and, as we have seen, herbal doctor, the parson is to offer a modest form of legal advice and arbitration. Clearly local knowledge is the bedrock of any effective pastoral response, and visiting is described as the most effective means.

> The country parson upon the afternoons in the weekdays, takes occasion sometimes to visit in person, now one quarter of his parish, now another. For there he shall find his flock most naturally as they are, wallowing in the midst of their affairs.
> (ch. 14, 'The Parson in Circuit')

In Herbert's mind, pastoral care must take thorough account of personalities and context. When the parson teaches he is to address specific needs and to adopt means that speak directly to the condition of the people to whom he ministers. Country folk, for example, were deemed to be better suited to stories and sayings than to anything more abstract (e.g. ch. 7, 'The Parson Preaching'). In a country context, the priest needs to take account not only of the nature of country people ('which are thick, and heavy'!) but also of their work. He places an emphasis on divine providence to counter an overemphasis on the natural order of things and a certain fatalism (ch. 30). He respects ancient country customs particularly those, such as processions or the blessing of lights, which have devotional origins (ch. 35, 'The Parson's Condescending'). The priest should also be familiar with the everyday life of agriculture. 'He condescends even to the knowledge of tillage, and pastorage, and makes great use of them in teaching, because people by what they understand, are best led to what they understand not' (ch. 4, 'The Parson's Knowledge').

The limitations of Herbert's model

It is obvious that George Herbert's vision of pastoral care is conditioned and limited by his historical, theological and social contexts. Contemporary readers of *The Country Parson* are often struck most forcibly by the social and ecclesiastical assumptions that are made and which appear, above all, to distance the text from our own times. We cannot ignore the fact that Herbert, for all the simplicity of his life in the parish (and recommendations of a simple life for parish priests), came from an aristocratic background. His Church, while affected by important aspects of Reformed doctrine, remained firmly hierarchical especially in its understanding of priesthood.

Herbert's country parson operates within a fixed social and ecclesial hierarchy and exists in an ambiguous relationship with his parish. On the one hand he is to mix freely with parishioners, to eat with them on occasion or to have them eat in his own house. He is to view unfeigned friendliness as a pastoral instrument. Yet the boundaries remain. The priest has an exclusive role in leading worship, dispensing sacraments and in the key aspects of pastoral care. It is not a collaborative model except, in a limited way, in relation to his wife and other members of his household. The parson and his household, however modestly they live and behave, are people with servants, with financial means and with knowledge. Their role in relationship to parishioners is parental – even the parson's children and servants are dispensers of charity and spiritual wisdom to others.

Insights that endure

However, it is important to place the poems of *The Temple* alongside *The Country Parson* as also exemplifying pastoral ministry. On its own, *The Country Parson* hardly suggests that the pastor shares the same spiritual concerns as everyone else. The approach of the prose treatise is more austerely didactic than the poetry. Taken on its own, the emotional reticence of the text can serve to emphasize detachment in pastoral care to such a degree that it becomes paternalistic. The honest self-exposure and spiritual depth of the poetic collection called *The Temple* rights the balance by revealing that passion and engagement also lay at the heart of Herbert's ministry.

The use of poetry itself was also a means of communicating certain values. Subjectively, Herbert understood the writing of poetry to be a form of prayer and many of the poems of the central part of *The Temple* (called 'The Church') are in the form of familiar conversations with God or Christ. As a means of teaching, poetry does not have as its primary aim the communication of information about faith or of instructions for a moral life. Compared to the language of *The Country Parson*, the language of Herbert's poetry has an evocative quality that more readily touches the emotions. It also has a particular capacity to unlock the imagination. Poetry is more readily able to speak of the mysterious, ambiguous and complex nature of faith. The pastoral value of the poetry, therefore, (and probably its conscious purpose) is to touch the reader in a more intimate way than the prose treatise and to provoke a richer and more complex response at a greater depth. If Herbert and his circle in the Church believed in the intimate relationship between beauty and holiness, the aesthetic power and imagery of the poetry made this connection real for the reader even at an unconscious level.

It is, therefore, possible to suggest underlying features of Herbert's model of pastoral care that continue to offer valuable material for contemporary reflection. First, pastoral care is not merely an activity but a way of life. What is offered to others is drawn from experience and from values that are lived out by the priest. Second, pastoral care at best is a difficult but necessary balance between detachment and passionate engagement. Third, true pastoral care is not merely a pale reflection of social work. It touches the human and spiritual depths and is inextricably linked with spirituality, prayer and worship. Fourth, pastoral care is linked with what we would call adult education and spiritual formation. For example, Herbert spends a great deal of time writing about the communication of adequate knowledge to parishioners both in terms of doctrine and of spiritual discernment. Yet, the use of poetry also suggests that there is a form of spiritual 'knowledge' to be found in aesthetic appreciation and the love of beauty that goes beyond the purely rational and conceptual. Fifth, pastoral care is not purely the care of individuals in isolation but the nurturing of a community of faith, worship and charity. Finally, pastoral care concerns all aspects of human life, not simply the obviously 'religious' dimensions. In contemporary terms this might be described as a holistic vision. In the end, Herbert attempts to describe a way of life and a set of relationships rather than a series of abstract theories. Consequently the image of pastoral care that emerges is flexible because it is inherently adapted to times, people and circumstances.

Notes

1. Two recent studies of both works are: L. Martz (ed.), *George Herbert and Henry Vaughan* (Oxford and New York, 1986) and J. N. Wall (ed.), *George*

Herbert: *The Country Parson, The Temple* (New York, 1981). Quotations and citations will refer to the Martz edition.
2. For discussions of this question see, for example, the still classic study of Herbert by J. H. Summers, *George Herbert: His Religion and Art,* Medieval and Renaissance Texts and Studies (Binghampton, NY, 1981 edn), ch. 2 'The Life'; and Wall, *Herbert,* pp. 6–26.
3. See for example, R.Tuve, *A Reading of George Herbert* (Chicago, 1952) and L. Martz, *The Poetry of Meditation: A Study of English Religious Literature of the Seventeenth Century* (New Haven, Conn., 1954).
4. See for example, B. Lewalski, *Protestant Poetics and the Seventeenth-Century Religious Lyric* (Princeton, N.J., 1979) and R. Strier, *Love Known: Theology and Experience in George Herbert's Poetry* (Chicago, 1983).
5. See for example the introduction by A. Raspa to his edition of John Donne's *Devotions Upon Emergent Occasions* (New York and Oxford, 1987). While G. Veith's important study, *Reformation Spirituality: The Religion of George Herbert* (London and Toronto, 1985) acknowledges that it is important to understand Herbert as 'Anglican', he adopts an excessively Calvinist interpretation of the Church of England.
6. For contrasting views on the dating of Herbert's works see, for example, Summers, *George Herbert: Religion and Art,* ch. 2, and Wall, *George Herbert: Country Parson, Temple,* Introduction, pp. 14–19.
7. See Summers, ibid., pp. 64, 99–100.
8. Wall, *George Herbert: Country Parson, Temple,* pp. 28–31.
9. Isaak Walton, *Lives* (Oxford, 1927), p. 314.
10. See for example D. Allen, 'The Christian Pilgrimage in George Herbert's *The Temple*', in B. Hanson (ed.), *Modern Christian Spirituality: Methodological and Historical Essays* (Atlanta, 1990).
11. E. Clarke, 'George Herbert's *The Temple*: the genius of Anglicanism and the inspiration for poetry', in G. Rowell (ed.), *The English Religious Tradition and the Genius of Anglicanism* (Wantage, 1993).
12. See G. Mursell, 'Traditions of Spiritual Guidance: The Book of Common Prayer', *The Way* (April 1991), pp. 163–71.
13. See for example the comments of J. Boyd White in *'This Book of Starres': Learning to Read George Herbert* (Ann Arbor, 1994), p. 72 n. 3.
14. For a recent English translation of the text of *The Spiritual Exercises,* see J. Munitiz and P. Endean (eds.), *Saint Ignatius Of Loyola: Personal Writings* (London, 1996). The numbers refer to the conventional sections in all modern editions.
15. For example the Exhortation before the reception of communion, and the Order for the Visitation of the Sick.

Bibliography

Louis Martz (ed.), *George Herbert and Henry Vaughan,* The Oxford Authors Series (Oxford, 1986)

Elizabeth Clarke, *Theory and Theology in George Herbert's Poetry,* Oxford Theological Monographs (Oxford, 1997)

R. Strier, *Love Known: Theology and Experience in George Herbert's Poetry* (Chicago, 1983)

J. H. Summers, *George Herbert: His Religion and Art,* Medieval and Renaissance Texts and Studies, Center for Medieval and Early Renaissance Studies (Binghampton, NY, 1981)

G. Veith, *Reformation Spirituality: The Religion of George Herbert* (London, 1985)

J. Boyd White, *'This Book of Starres': Learning to Read George Herbert* (Ann Arbor, 1994)

15

Pastoral care in England

Perkins, Baxter and Burnet

David Cornick

The history of the English Church from the accession of Elizabeth in 1558 to the eventual failure of comprehension in 1662 was one of tension and struggle as the principles of the Reformation were translated into a structure which retained much of its mediaeval shape. Part of that tension (not unnaturally) was the creation of a native English Protestant tradition of pastoral theology. It was to take on a wide palette of theological colour, from Perkins to Taylor, from Herbert to Baxter. The decisive significance of 1662 in shaping the nature of English religiosity should not blind us to the common ground shared by writers on pastoral care. What mattered as the seventeenth century drew to a close was the common Protestantism which held Taylor, Baxter and Burnet together, not the ecclesiological differences which sundered them. Anglicans devoured Baxter, dissenters honoured Burnet. The roll-call of the pastoral tradition is impressive – William Perkins, fellow of Christ's College, Cambridge; George Herbert, Public Orator of Cambridge University and failed politician, turned country priest; his friend Nicholas Ferrar at Little Gidding, experimenting in Christian community; Jeremy Taylor, Cambridge-born, Caius educated, bishop of Down and Connor from 1660, whose *Holy Living and Holy Dying* is one of the finest devotional works; Richard Baxter, the very model of a Reformed pastor; Gilbert Burnet, Church of Scotland divinity professor turned bishop of Salisbury, whose *Discourse of the Pastoral Care* was written 'to raise the sense of obligation of the clergy'.

As the relative merits of Calvinism and Arminianism (an intra-Reformed debate, be it noted) were being fought out in late-Elizabethan and early-Stuart England, the nature of human experience and moral conduct took on fresh significance. Justification by faith and theologies of election carried with them the ever-present danger of antinomianism. As Protestant theologians sought to navigate through these turbulent waters, they began to develop a body of 'practical divinity' which was to have considerable importance in the history of pastoral care. Whether their eventual theological destination was strict Calvinism (as in the cases of Perkins and Ames) or a modified version (as with Baxter), their method paid close attention to the nature of human experience. A strict Calvinist sought confirmation of elect status in the workings of the human heart, for predestination meant not only predestination to salvation, but predestination to the means of grace, which included good works and a relationship with Christ. Conscience was the touchstone of faith. 'Even the faintest sign of genuinely good works was a straw in the wind of providence that could only be wafted into sight by the grace of God.'[1] To those of a more liberal persuasion like Baxter who thought that such strict Calvinism was a denial of spiritual common sense and that Christ 'never intended to justifie or santifie us perfectly at first ... but to carry on proportionately and by degrees',[2] self-examination would lead to the discovery that the work of God was written in the progress of their souls.

Both routes led to a new introspection, to spiritual journalling and diarying, what Baxter once called 'a Book of Heart Accounts'. If the autobiography was to be the eventual fruit of this literary form, its midwife was a corpus of casuistical literature that was firmly grounded in the trials of the soul. The late-Elizabethan English church was fully aware of the need to improve the quality of pastoral ministry. Attempts were made to bridge the gap between the study of academic theology in the universities and what would now be termed pastoral practice. The prophesyings and classical movement both had a pastoral edge. Some university colleges, for example Christ's College, Cambridge, were virtually 'Puritan' seminaries. Conscientious pastors like Richard Greenham took in students for on-the-job training.[3] There were very few books that could offer guidance to new clergy.

William Perkins (1558–1602), 'the prince of Puritan theologians',[4] pupil of Chaderton's and a pastor of justifiable repute, both because of his ministry to the condemned in Cambridge gaol and his lectureship at St Andrews, was the first English Protestant theologian to try and supply the need. He wrote treatises on the ministry, and attempted to provide books of guidance for his fellow ministers, based on his own deep pastoral experience, and he was soon imitated, although none attained his systematic grandeur. The lack of a proper system of Reformed discipline within the Church of England meant that a heavier weight of guidance fell to the parish minister. As English Calvinism developed, the concept of the covenant which God made with humanity, and the consequent obedience due to God from men and women, lent prominence to the law (and in particular the Ten Commandments). Conscience was therefore a subject that preoccupied Perkins, and he provided the first extended English Protestant theology of conscience. It was, for Perkins, the vice-gerent of God, and he sought a correlation between conscience, action and the law of God as revealed in Scripture. 'Whatsoever we enterprise or take in hand, we must first search whether God gives us liberty in conscience and warrant to do it. For if we do otherwise conscience is bound presently to charge us of sin before God.'[5] Liberty of conscience was in Perkins' eyes freedom to do the will of God, and the will of God was revealed with axiomatic precision in Scripture under the guidance of the Spirit. The work of the pastor was therefore to guide his people to do the will of God, and Perkins provided them with paradigms of how a good conscience might be maintained.

The pastor was not just a preacher. He was a clinician of the soul, a surgeon of the conscience. Assurance of salvation was to be sought there, and eager attention was given to the tracing of the hand of God in cases of conscience. The people expected their ministers to have a clinical expertise in these matters. There was a ready market for works like Perkins' posthumous *Cases of Conscience* (1602), for lives of eminent divines, for funeral sermons (a good death was evidence of assurance), and eventually for the spiritual autobiography. By 1600, 1517 was long in the past, and, as Patrick Collinson has noted, 'for all practical purposes the puritan co-operated strenuously in his own salvation and took pains to hold himself upright in all his dealings'.[6] Angst in the confessional had become the angst of the diarist in pursuit of assurance.

During the seventeenth century works of casuistry and pastoral guidance flowed from the press, reaching maturity in three great studies of the mid-century – Joseph Hall's *Resolutions and Decisions of Divers Cases of Conscience in Continual Use Among Men* (1650), Jeremy Taylor's *Doctor Dubitantium* (1660) and Richard Baxter's vast, encyclopedic *A Christian Directory* (1673). Hall's work was sensible and modest. Taylor's was by far the most philosophical and scholarly, drawing on an impressively ecumenical range of sources. Baxter's was by far the longest and most comprehensive, containing a million words, twice the length of Taylor's.[7]

Baxter intended his book to be used, not read from cover to cover. His intended audience was inexperienced ministers who needed a 'promptuary ... for Practical Resolutions and Directions on the subjects that they have need to deal in', masters of families 'who may choose and read such parcels to their Families, as at any time the case requireth', and private Christians who may 'turn to such particulars as they most need'.[8] It was a breathtaking achievement, not least in the way it differed from its predecessors. Most English casuists argue from general principles to the particular, from the nature of conscience to illustrative cases. Baxter deliberately reversed that process. This is a case-book which was intended to cover all of life's eventualities, divided into four sections corresponding to the four spheres of duty of the Christian – private, family, Church and wider (i.e. duties to 'Rulers and Neighbours'). What is more, he stated baldly that they were all drawn from his own experience and memory.[9] Here, in other words, is the very texture of a ministry. No aspect of the work of a seventeenth-century minister is overlooked. There are directions for dealing with the melancholic, directions about handling the great sins of pride, humility, covetousness, the love of riches, sensuality and flesh-pleasing. The anxious and inexperienced minister will find here advice to be given to those who have sinful dreams, who fear the devil, or experience undue grief and overburdening despair, as well as strictures about stage-plays, gaming and dicing. The nature of Christian marriage, the duties of husbands to wives, masters to slaves, the art of the good death and the counsel to be provided at the sick bed are all covered in compendious detail. So too is every detail of church life – the role of the magistrate, the nature of baptism, ordination, catechizing, the sacrament of Holy Communion and the nature of prayer. Equally impressive is his treatment of the 'political' life of the Christian – here, as Weber and Charles Gore after him realized, is an entire Puritan ethics of economic behaviour.

One small example gives a flavour of Baxter's method. He devotes 8,000 words to the sin of 'sensuality, flesh-pleasing or voluptuousness'.[10] First he defines the meaning of flesh as 'the sensitive appetite itself', then he analyses the relationship of appetite, will and reason. Scriptural exegesis follows, accompanied by a brief comment about the misinterpretations of Libertines and Papists. The prolegomena complete, he outlines the importance of the 'flesh' in the divine economy, stressing that delighting the flesh is a natural good, but that when pleasing the flesh causes harm – and all intemperance breeds disease – it has become an idol. Then the God-given equilibrium of life is distorted because the higher end of all living, the glory of God, has been lost to sight –

> As the accustomed hand of a Musician can play a Lesson on his Lute, while he thinks of something else; so can a resolved Christian faithfully do such accustomed things as eating and drinking and cloathing him and labouring in his calling, to the good ends which he (first actually, and still habitually) resolved on without a distinct remembrance, and observable intention to that end.

Such pleasures as enjoying beauty, music, rest, the wearing of Sunday best and feasting on appropriate days can all promote spiritual service. However, the appetite can easily get out of control, for excessive flesh-pleasing is 'the Grand Idolatry of the world'.

There is a hard-headed pastoral realism about Baxter. He knows how human nature works – 'Men will part with Father and Mother and Brother and Sister and nearest friends, and all that is against it, for the pleasing of the flesh.' Having set out his argument he deals with common objections – 'but it doesn't hurt God'; 'but it is natural'; 'but Eve's experience shows us that appetite was present in Innocency'; 'why should God create humans in such a way as to bring Reason and Appetite into conflict?'

He then provides the pastor with a subtle diagnostic summary of the signs of sensuality – no referral to the higher end, more concern about prosperity than the soul, preferring gaming or getting a good bargain to living in faith and love, when the company of 'merry sensualists' is preferable to that of the Communion of Saints, and so on. However, pastors are not to be deceived by appearances. The over-scrupulous melancholic, or the sick who need a delicate diet (Baxter was a hypochondriac – he knew!) may appear sensualists when they are not. Conversely, the sensualist may appear in the lamb's clothing of temperance while his or her heart is captivated by pleasure. Diagnosis is followed by treatment, and the section concludes with seven directions (broken into subsections) – you will see 'Better things' with God, know yourself, monitor your appetites, keep Reason in its proper place of goveranance, 'Go to the grave and see there the end of sensual pleasure', and so on.

This is not the place to reconstruct the Puritan world-view, although Baxter's *Directory* is an ample source for that. What is significant here is the skill of the soul-doctor, the scrupulous attention to detail which is based on solid, earthy observation of human behaviour, and the fine discrimination of states of the soul which Baxter deploys. Thoughout its history the cure of souls has generated a literature which attends to the reality of the human condition and its dilemmas according to the intellectual and theological constraints of the age, from Gregory the Great's *On Pastoral Care* to Frank Lake's *Clinical Theology*. The work of the seventeenth century casuists should be seen in that tradition – and none is greater than Baxter's.

All Puritans placed the highest premium on the ministry of the pulpit – Baxter as much as any. And yet he knew how ineffectual even the finest preaching could be. The work of the pulpit was properly in a symbiotic relationship with knowing and understanding the people of God, through conversation, catechizing and awareness. If Protestantism sundered the division between sacred and secular, then Baxter was the finest exponent of engaged pastoring, for the whole panoply of life was invested with the stuff of eternity. His method was painstaking. In the introduction to *The Reformed Pastor* he explains how he spent Mondays and Tuesdays interviewing families in his house – fifteen or sixteen a week, so that each of the 800 families in his Kidderminster parish were given a spiritual review each year.[11] That he found to be of more effect than all his preaching, yet it was from this deep pastoral relationship that his preaching was shaped. His great achievement was the translation of theology into the minutiae and diversity of the human condition. It was truly practical divinity – 'all the flock, even each individual member of our charge must be taken heed of and watched over ... One word of seasonable prudent advice given by a Minister to persons in necessity, hath done that good that many Sermons would not have done.'

The parting of the ways between the Church of England and Dissent which occurred in Baxter's lifetime meant the creation of differing structures of pastoral care in England. The parish remained the basic legal community to which all belonged, and at least at rites of passages it was still the focus of the life of whole communities, Dissenters as well as members of the established Church. Alongside it the 'gathered' Church developed, until by the nineteenth century most villages and towns had multiple religious foci which were as expressive of social divisions as they were of religious convictions. This separation had serious consequences for pastoral care. The vicar or rector retained a legal responsibility for the lives of all within his parish, and all his parishioners had legitimate expectations of the services they might expect from him. The Dissenting minister related primarily to those who were voluntarily under his care, although pastoral zeal often directed his attention beyond that legal limit. Different models of church discipline emerged as Dissenting chapels rejoiced in being mini-Genevas. It would, however, be incorrect to see this as a division into the 'godly' and the 'ungodly'. Wheat and tares grew together in both communities, and eighteenth-century Anglican clergy were as anxious about the growth of holiness as Dissenting ministers.

The ejections of 1660–1662 dramatically realigned the theological pattern of the Church of England. The Reformed 'Puritan' tradition, which had been so significant a part of its life since the days of Elizabeth – even of Edward VI – fell into rapid decline, so that by 1730 the Calvinist minister was 'not merely an endangered, but an almost vanished, species'.[12] The vacuum, so Walsh and Taylor suggest, was to be filled by the Evangelical Revival, which brought to the Church of England a modified Calvinism, distinctly different from Wesley's evangelical 'universalism'. However, the broad outlines of the Reformation legacy of pastoral care can still be discerned within the Church of England, as well as in English Dissent, old and new, in the 'long' eighteenth century. Recent studies have called attention to the subtle shadings of the parties within eighteenth-century Anglicanism, and the taxonomic headaches which face historians in defining 'high', 'dry', 'latitudinarian' and 'catholic'! That is complemented by the fluidity of the terms 'Congregational' and 'Presbyterian', used almost to mean 'conservative' and 'liberal' until the emergence of denominationalism (which is an early-nineteenth-century construct). Chapels often switched allegiance at the change of a minister. Approaches to pastoral care cannot be reconstructed along party and denominational lines. More significant by far is the influence of wider intellectual and socio-economic changes, the emphasis on rational religion, the empiricism of experiential religion in the Evangelical Revival and the beginnings of industrialization and demographic shifts.

Gilbert Burnet belonged to a different world from Baxter. Baxter was a Puritan who refused a bishopric, Burnet a Scottish Presbyterian who became an outstanding bishop of Salisbury. Infuriatingly partisan, yet ecumenically generous in his friendships, he was a man of the post-

Restoration world who owed his preferment to the House of Orange. But if Baxter was the most conscientious of parish ministers, Burnet was a pastorally devoted bishop in a Church he believed to be in crisis. The post-Tridentine Roman Church was gaining ground on the continent, and the 'Depravations under which most Reformed churches are fallen', particularly in their neglect of discipline and pastoral care and the careless abuses of clergy (he has in mind pluralism and non-residence) meant that ground gained was now being lost. Equally perturbing was the growth across Europe of 'Atheism and Impiety'. His many discussions with sceptics had persuaded him that the root cause of decline was the laxity of the clergy; his *Discourse of the Pastoral Care* was therefore written to recall his clergy to their true vocation. It is a sensible, honourable, wise book although it lacks the spiritual resonance and power of Baxter at his best. It is a primer for clergy in a new, plural world – friendships with Romans and Dissenters are part of the Anglican priest's armoury, so that Romans may be regained by the use of 'Reason and Perswasion' and Dissenters by 'Perswasion and Kindness'.[13] Much as High Churchmen objected, there was a new realism here. The clock of toleration could not be turned back. England was legally pluralist, and that very pluralism encouraged some to think religious observation a matter of voluntary choice. The nation needed educating, if not converting.

Burnet was an historian to his fingernails (he is remembered primarily for his *History of the Reformation* and the delightfully gossipy *History of My Own Time,* which Macaulay plundered to great effect). His method is historical. He surveys the biblical, patristic and conciliar understandings of ministry, including the reforming decrees of Trent which he thought put the Church of England to shame. He stands firmly within the Reformation tradition, arguing that the two necessities of ministry are 'decency of behaviour' and sound learning – 'even a Proud and Passionate, a Wordly-Minded and covetous Priest, gives the Lye to his Discourses so palpably that he cannot expect they should have much weight'.[14] His model for ministry is drawn, in true Reformation style, from Scripture and patristic evidence. The clergyman must be willing to break with the world, wealth and pleasure, just as in the early Church those called to ministry were expected to show evidence of the spirit of martydom, and 'to look for nothing in this service but Labour and Persecution'.[15]

Burnet was formed by the Scottish tradition, not by the English universities. He lays down a scheme for training young clergy, outlining a two-year course of reading, and for a time tried to run his own seminary until opposition from the universities proved too powerful.

> I thought the greatest prejudice the Church was under was from ill-education of the clergy. In the Universities they for the most part lost the learning they brought with them from schools, and learned so very little in that that commonly they came from them less knowing than when they went to them ... I resolved to have a nursery, at Salisbury, of students in Divinity ... those at Oxford looked on this as a public affront to them, and to their way of education; so that they railed at me, not only in secret, but in their Acts, unmercifully for it.[16]

He expected those preparing for ministry to be reasonably proficient in Greek, to understand the Creed and 'Systems of Divinity', mastering the arguments of Calvinists, Arminians and followers of the Middle Way, to be able to combat atheism through gaining a working knowledge of natural religion, and to be able to state the grounds of Christian hope, the forms of salvation and show a clear view of the covenant with Christ. He looked for men whose characters were formed by a reading of Scripture and such classical moralists as Juvenal and Horace.

'Compleat' divines were formed only after ordination – and at that point he expected them to take a keen interest in church history, beginning with Josephus and Eusebius, the ancient historians and then the history of their own times. These lively-minded souls were expected to put down deep local roots. The parochial clergy should not farm or teach (as many did to make ends meet) because that was a distraction from their proper work – 'His Friends and his Garden ought to be his chief Diversions, as his Study and his Parish ought to be his chief Employments', and he recommended the study of physick to them, 'especially that which is safe and simple' as an admirable source of charitable works.[17] The parish priest should be a preacher. Preaching, Burnet thought, had advanced considerably since the Reformation. He looked for clarity, simplicity and forceful application, recommending his clergy when in the pulpit to think that they were in the home of the most unlearned man in the parish, and to preach accordingly for not more than half-an-hour. Preaching merits a separate chapter, but Reformed minister has by now turned 'Anglican' parish priest, for Burnet perceives the beauty of the 'Majesty' of the liturgy to be a means of grace.

That liturgical sense was allied to conventionally Reformed understandings of the pastor as educator and as the regulator of church discipline. Frequent catechizing, instruction of the young and those approaching confirmation, and admonishing 'anyone of his Parish guilty of eminent sins' before communion was the staple of clerical life. If public services were the tip of the iceberg of the clergy's work, private labours in the parish constituted the unseen expanse of the week – working for reconciliation between neighbours, admonishing those of rank who set ill examples (preferably by letter!), visiting the sick, preparing the dying for judgement, going from house to house to get to know his people.

Burnet expected his clergy to have an especial care for those with 'troubled minds', whom he considered more prevalent in towns than countryside. There were those weighed down with an enormity of sin who needed cherishing until they repented, and he laid down a system of discipline to bring about their return to spiritual health. Then there were the 'melancholic' who 'fall under dark and cloudy Apprehensions'. He suggests that they first be treated with medicine, and then diverted from thinking too much and being too much alone. The pastor must be particularly alert about those who feel God is angry with them. As in Baxter's *Christian Directory*, the best of contemporary scientific knowledge blends with the wisdom of the Christian ages –

> If then a Minister has occasion to treat any in this Condition, he must make them apprehend that the heat and coldness of their Brain, is the effect of Temper; and flows from the different States of the Animal Spirits, which have their Diseases, their hot and cold Fits as well as the Blood has; and therefore no measure can be taken from these, either to judge for or against themselves. They are to consider what are their Principles and Resolutions, and what's the settled Course of their Life; upon these they are to form sure Judgments, and not upon anything that is so fluctuating and inconsistent as Fits and Humours.[18]

The mere fact that Burnet felt that he needed to write his book suggests that his ideal of pastoral ministry was far from universal in the Church of England. The eighteenth century has long been a byword for negligence, but that assumption is under question. There were certainly abuses of pluralism and non-residence, and the financing of the parochial system (of which these abuses were symptoms) was a problem which had not been solved before the Reformation, and was not to be properly assuaged until the nineteenth century. However, Hogarth's cartoons of sleeping congregations and the impression of the clergy in picaresque novels do not tell the whole story. If Grimshaw of Howarth's pastoral zeal was unusual in mid-century, it also points to a continuity between the life of the eighteenth-century Church and the traditions of the Reformation – that of the pastor as teacher and educator. Evangelicals and dissenters shared a common tone and way of working, but the perception of many Anglican clergy was that their primary duty was to the godly, to those who came to church and sought to live holy lives. Bishop Butler advised an evangelical curate in 1835, 'if the inhabitants will not take the trouble to come ... far to hear your sermons, and much more the beautiful prayers of our Liturgy ... I am sure they do not deserve to have them brought to their doors'.[19] The laity had duties as well as the clergy. As Jeremy Gregory has suggested, post-Restoration Anglicanism owed more to the Puritan tradition than has sometimes been allowed. Catechizing, the formation of schools, the work of religious societies such as those ministered to by Horneck and Beveridge in London (so effectively hijacked later by Wesley), and the production of devotional books all point to a determined effort to continue the work of the Reformation as the Anglican clergy sought to make their age an age of faith.[20] They were educating the nation in the Protestant faith just as much as their Dissenting colleagues.

The rise and fall of church discipline

If the English Church went about its educational task with a will, the other main strand in the Reformation legacy of pastoral care, church discipline, was markedly less successful. The fight for the reformation of manners depended more on voluntary societies like the Society for the Reformation of Manners (f. 1691), and the SPCK (f. 1699) than church courts. Across the border in Scotland, and in the Dissenting chapels of England, the tradition was different. Post-1690 Scotland drew on the heritage of Calvin, mediated through Knox and Melville, and expressed its Presbyterianism through a classically Genevan structure of ministry and discipline. Discipline was the responsibility of the kirk session (i.e. the parish minister and elders), and higher courts only became involved in cases of appeal or in especially grave instances. Like all systems, it was subject to abuse. Intended to be an encouragement to godly living and reformation of the individual, it quickly became a matter of public punishment, concentrating unduly on sexual sins. Part of the reason for that was the intimacy of civil and ecclesiastical jurisdiction in sixteenth-century Scotland. In Glasgow and Perth in the early seventeenth century it was agreed that the provost and baillies should always be members of the Session, so close was the relationship between the civil magistracy and the eldership. Equally, the severity of ecclesiastical discipline, occasionally corporal, and usually serious psychological manipulation through public humiliation, needs to be seen in the context of the brutality of an age which exercised civil control through the use of judicial torture and execution.

Public repentance, barefoot and in sackcloth, was not the invention of Calvinists. Like so much else in the Reformation, it was an attempt to recreate the patristic Church, whose practice echoed in mediaeval Europe, as Henry IV knew to his cost. Scottish discipline was the responsibility of elders, and despite its worst excesses, was not unpopular. One writer in 1714 noted that discipline was willingly submitted to, 'being exercised by persons chosen from among themselves, appointed to represent them, to take care of their interests ... ruling elders are more conversant in the world, know better what the times will bear, and what allowances are necessary to be made in this or that case'. And there are instances of complaint that sessions were too lax in their exercise of discipline.[21] Sessions met for discipline weekly or fortnightly during the seventeenth century, but during the eighteenth century meetings became less frequent, and the exercise of discipline eventually fell into disuse in the nineteenth century. By the second half of the eighteenth century public appearances before the church were rare.

The practice of discipline amongst English Dissenting churches was a piebald affair. They could not be seen to be less stringent than the Church of England which until the end of the eighteenth century expected women found guilty of fornication to do public penance 'bareheaded, barefooted, and bare-legged' and draped in a white sheet. Michael Watts's survey of a variety of local congregational records shows huge variety. At the fashionable King's Weigh House in Little Eastcheap there is only one case of discipline recorded in the 47 years between 1695 and 1742. Conversely, during Richard Davis's controversial evangelical and expansionist ministry at Rothwell in Northamptonshire between 1690 and 1714, there were 199 excommunications. The theological stance of the minister, the composition of the congregation, its location and its attitude to evangelism all determine the severity of its discipline. Philip Doddridge declined the pastorate of the Independent/Baptist church at Pershore, Worcestershire in 1723 because 'their method of church discipline [is] so very severe, that I am afraid I should be a little uneasy with them'.[22] What mattered to Dissenting congregations was the purity of the fellowship and the repentance of the individual. The techniques they used were admonition and suspension from communion. Excommunication was a last resort, and even then the hope was expressed that the sinner would eventually return to the fellowship of the Church. An analysis of the minutes of the church meeting of the Independent church at Isleham in the Cambridgeshire Fens gives a moving sense of the way discipline was carried out. In this small, unprepossessing and remote church, discipline was exercised 28 times between 1700 and 1800. Five women were suspended, three for unnamed reasons, one for fornication and one for lying and sowing discord. Of the 22 suspensions of men, by far the largest proportion was for drunkenness. Other causes included conforming to the Established Church, theological differences, lying, non-attendance, fraud, dancing, swearing, being contentious and fornication. What is moving is the way in which the community admonished offenders, yet took every opportunity to bring them back into the life of the congregation. There were several recidivists amongst those suspended for drunkenness. One of those accused of fornication (which in that case meant a premarital pregnancy) was welcomed back warmly upon repentance. Here was a small, mainly working-class congregation striving to live a genuinely Christian life.[23]

There were significant continuities between the concepts of pastoral care that emerged from the Reformation and the strategies of pastoral care commended by both Anglicans and Dissenters in England and Presbyterians, both established and Dissenting, in Scotland in the eighteenth century, in the centrality of preaching, the role of the minister, expectations of the laity and the exercise of discipline. There were also notable discontinuities. The decline of discipline during the eighteenth century is a litmus test that gives clear evidence of changing pastoral patterns.

Notes

1. Ian Breward, 'Introduction' to *The Work of William Perkins,* The Courteney Library of Reformation Classics, 3 (Appleford, 1970), p. 95.

2. Quoted by N. H. Keeble, *Richard Baxter, Puritan Man of Letters* (Oxford, 1982), p. 72.
3. Breward, 'Introduction', p. 40; Patrick Collinson, *The Elizabethan Puritan Movement* (London, 1967), pp. 124–6.
4. Collinson, ibid.
5. Quoted by Breward, 'Introduction', p. 65; pp. 58–80 provide a telling analysis of both the originality and the shortcomings of Perkins's understanding of conscience.
6. Collinson, *Elizabethan Puritan Movement*, p. 434.
7. For a survey of the development of Puritan casuistry, see J. T. McNeill, 'Casuistry in the Puritan age', *Religion in Life* 12/2 (1942–3), pp. 76–89.
8. From the 'Advertisements' in *Chapters from A Christian Directory*, ed. Jeanette Tawney (London, 1925), pp. 5–6; see also Keeble, *Richard Baxter*, p. 78.
9. 'Advertisements', p. 4, and Keeble, *Richard Baxter*, p. 80.
10. Richard Baxter, *A Christian Directory, or a Summ of the Practical Theologie, and Cases of Conscience,* 2nd edn (London, 1678), pp. 222–30.
11. Richard Baxter, *Gildas Salvianus: The Reformed Pastor*, ed. J. T. Wilkinson (London, 1939), p. 59.
12. John Walsh and Stephen Taylor, 'Introduction: the Church and Anglicanism in the "long" eighteenth century', in John Walsh, Colin Haydon and Stephen Taylor (eds), *The Church of England c.1689–c.1833: From Toleration to Tractarianism* (Cambridge, 1993), pp. 1–67, p. 43.
13. *A discourse of the Pastoral Care* (London, 1692), p. 203–4.
14. Ibid., p. 143.
15. Ibid., p.154.
16. E. G. Rupp, *Religion in England 1688–1791* (Oxford, 1986), p. 87; the quotation is from T. E. S. Clarke and H. C. Foxcroft, *A Life of Gilbert Burnet, Bishop of Salisbury* (Cambridge, 1907), pp. 292–3.
17. Burnet, *A Discourse,* pp. 177 and 200–1.
18. Ibid., pp. 200–1.
19. Quoted in Walsh and Taylor, 'Introduction: the Church and Anglicanism', p. 13. This paragraph draws heavily from pp. 13–22.
20. Jeremy Gregory, 'The eighteenth century Reformation: the pastoral task of the Anglican clergy after 1689', in John Walsh, Colin Haydon and Stephen Taylor (eds), *The Church of England c.1689–c.1833: From Toleration to Tractarianism* (Cambridge, 1993), pp. 67–86.
21. G. D. Henderson, *The Scottish Ruling Elder* (London, 1935), pp. 105–6. Henderson's chapter on 'Kirk Session Discipline' remains a sane treatment of the subject. The standard work is I. M. Clark, *A History of Church Discipline in Scotland* (Aberdeen, 1929).
22. Michael Watts, *The Dissenters: From the Reformation to the French Revolution* (Oxford, 1978), pp. 321–5. The quotation from Doddridge is on p. 325.
23. My analysis is based on Kenneth Parsons (ed.) *The Church Book of the Independent Church (now Pound Lane Baptist) Isleham 1693–1805* (Cambridge, 1984).

Bibliography

Ian Breward (ed.), *The Work of William Perkins*, The Courteney Library of Reformation Classics, 3 (Appleford, 1970)

William A. Clebsch and Charles R. Jaeckle, *Pastoral Care in Historical Perspective* (New York, 1964)

G. D. Henderson, *The Scottish Ruling Elder* (London, 1935)

Michael MacDonald, 'Religion, social change and psychological healing in England 1600–1800', in W. J. Shiels (ed.), *The Church and Healing*, Studies in Church History, 19 (Oxford, 1982), pp. 101–25

E. A. McKee, *Elders and the Plural Ministry* (Geneva, 1988)

J. T. McNeill, 'Casuistry in the Puritan Age', *Religion in Life* 12/2 (1942–3), pp. 76–89

J. T. McNeill, *A History of the Cure of Souls* (New York, 1951)

Derek Tidball, *Skilful Shepherds: An Introduction to Pastoral Theology* (Leicester, 1986)

John Walsh, Colin Haydon and Stephen Taylor (eds), *The Church of England c.1689–c.1833: From Toleration to Tractarianism* (Cambridge, 1993)

16

The twentieth-century Anglican Franciscans

Petà Dunstan

Anglican religious in the service of the poor

In September 1897, James Adderley resigned his position as superior of the Society of the Divine Compassion (SDC), the Franciscan community which he had founded within the Church of England only a few years earlier. He did so because of a split within the small SDC as to the way forward for the community, an argument about how best to serve the poor. It was a division not over values or goals but over how best to achieve them. This dispute within SDC, and its dramatic consequence, might be viewed as a comparatively minor event among a small group of friars, of little importance beyond the chronology of the revival of religious life among nineteenth-century Anglicans. Yet, the arguments within SDC were an example of a much wider debate as to how best religious could serve the poor. It was a debate that continued for many years in the various branches of Anglican Franciscanism, with implications for religious life in a wider sense. These arguments and their consequences, therefore, have a greater significance than merely their immediate impact. They shed light on the development of models of pastoral care within Anglican religious life as a whole.

Pastoral care had been at the heart of the founding of communities in the Church of England from the 1840s onwards. Indeed, the suspicion that all things monastic were 'papist', and therefore inimical to the health of religion in Britain, was so widespread and deep-rooted that a revival of religious life had to have pastoral care as its public justification if it were to gain even tacit acceptance. The idea of a community life, lived under vows, as a good of itself within the Church had little claim then on the minds or hearts of most Anglicans. As a result, the founding of recognized cloistered contemplative communities had to wait until the end of the century.[1] However, the idea of sisters who cared for the poor and the sick was less alarming, mainly because it appeared one way of addressing the serious social problems with which the Church was faced. It is unsurprising therefore that many of the foundations of Anglican women's communities were initiated by parish priests, particularly in urban areas, who saw the need for sisterhoods to work among their parishioners, much as late-twentieth-century parishes might want 'pastoral assistants'. The sisters could be presented as local groups of 'parish workers' serving particular social needs in their area.

This perceived need was one response to the consequences of the Industrial Revolution and the rapid growth in population in early-nineteenth-century Britain, which had brought a new and visible urban poverty on a scale previously unimagined. Not only did this provide a moral challenge to Christians, but a growing class of economically deprived and suffering people was also a political threat. The value of the palliative care given to the sick and needy amongst the poor by Anglican sisters blunted the voices of those who saw their formation as a departure from Protestant norms. Gradually, the incidents of sisters being jeered at and attacked subsided, and hostility was replaced by respect for their achievements.

Most of these communities had been based on a particular parish or district, or else around the ministry of an institution, such as a hospital or school. They mostly remained within the power structures of the Church and under the control and guidance of the clergy. When, later in the century, sisterhoods tried to work more independently, outside the immediate jurisdiction of a bishop visitor or the local parish clergy, there was controversy.[2] Religious sisters were accepted as servants of the clergy, but came under pressure and disapprobation when the call to religious life pushed their communities into initiating projects and ministries outside male clerical authority. The clerical control also encouraged different communities to have little to do with each other, and they jealously guarded their own particular traditions and apostolates. In some cases, this pattern evolved into rivalries. Contact between sisterhoods was minimal.

For men called to religious life, the difficulties were equally restrictive. Priests were under the direct authority of their bishops and it was wellnigh impossible for them to pursue ministries to the poor outside parochial structures. From the very beginning of the Society of the Divine Compassion, this was the heart of the problem for James Adderley. The son of a Conservative MP, later a peer, Adderley was an example of a privileged young man who developed a conscience about the lower classes of society on whom his family's wealth was ultimately dependent. He was not a socialist in a party political sense, but part of the then fashionable 'Christian socialism', much of which was at root a paternalistic liberalism. Leading churchmen such as Bishop Westcott of Durham, following the theology of F. D. Maurice, believed in co-operation and 'brotherhood' between the classes. Yet, in practice, such men did not wish to threaten the status quo and overthrow the class structure of society. They wanted to create a unity between classes, where people looked after – and out for – each other, whilst tacitly accepting the social stratification maintained by a liberal capitalist economic system.

Adderley, however, went further than many of his Christian socialist contemporaries in wishing to live more literally alongside the poor. He saw the religious life of a friar as the way to achieve this. In St Francis, the thirteenth-century saint who had turned his back on wealth and privilege to embrace a mendicant lifestyle, Adderley saw the inspiration for founding the Society of the Divine Compassion.

The Franciscan ideal of the itinerant friar

The Franciscan ideal had been argued about for centuries and was open to different interpretations, but at its heart was a desire to take the religious life of prayer and community outside the confines of the monastery, and live out its values amongst the poor and the homeless. It was an evangelizing strategy, a witnessing to the gospel, more than a social policy. It was radical in its methods because it demanded that religious should live alongside the deprived and *share* their poverty, rather than minister from the comfort and security of the institutions of a Church which had grown rich and powerful. Amidst the desolation of the nineteenth-century landscape of Britains industrialized cities, this charism gripped Adderley's imagination and spirit. Wandering itinerant friars would serve the poor and be their voice.

It was a romantic concept, for whatever deprivations Adderley embraced, his education and background meant that he would always have the possibility of returning to a more secure way of life and standard of living, whereas the poor whom he longed to serve had no such option. His radical edge, however, came from his conviction that only friars free of official commitments could be a true voice for those who were disadvantaged. He felt that a Franciscanism which was established within the Church's structures would eventually be blunted and curbed, its witness contained by the pressures of running institutions, through which friars would eventually be liable to collude with the social system that tolerated poverty. He felt the parochial model of ministry would reduce Franciscans to palliative care and prevent any involvement with political campaigns or radical witness. The example of the Community of St Alban, a group of laymen living first in Paddington and then in Plaistow in the 1870s and 1880s, was instructive. The brothers worked for the parish of St Andrew's, but their appearance on political platforms during the 1880 election campaign had resulted in the withdrawal of much of the support of the Church, and the community rapidly declined. Most of the clergy of St Andrew's were prominent in this undermining of the community.[3] For Adderley, therefore, the prophet had to work from outside the system.

Adderley had gone on road missions, tramping with wayfarers, in the years before he founded SDC, and he saw this as an example of his principle that social questions need friars 'free from the narrow local interests' which consume parish clergy.[4] He wanted the base for friars to be a house of prayer in the country, a place apart where they could rest, and where they would be trained in disciplines of prayer. From the friary, they could go out to expedite whatever work they found was necessary amidst the poor. That might be teaching in elementary schools or mission work or helping wayfarers, but on a 'freelance' basis. There could be no question of being tied to a specific place or a specific 'work' as a group, and priests (like himself) would have no privileges over lay members of the community. The model for caring for the poor was one of flexibility and variety, responding to diverse calls primarily as an individual friar, with the community a product of the rest periods at the proposed rural friary, where the emphasis on prayer would provide the support for the demanding vocation. Thus, community life was reflected not in working together but in praying together. In Adderley's novel, *Stephen Remarx*, written to illustrate his ideas, the community which his hero founds is primarily made up of what would now be called Third Order members, people vowed to a rule of life but working in their own particular jobs in different localities. For Adderley, this Third Order model divorced the friar from being associated in the minds of the poor with any form of power or control. He believed this would mean fewer conflicts between the demands of obeying ecclesiastical authority and living out a Franciscan vocation.

The Franciscan ideal in the parish

Nevertheless, because of the necessity of providing an initial base and small income, Adderley accepted in 1894 the task of running a mission church, St Philip's, which was part of the parish of St Andrew's, Plaistow. Here, he was joined by Henry Chappel and Ernest Hardy, the latter taking the religious name of Andrew. Chappel was already a priest and Hardy was ordained soon after joining the fledgling SDC. However, in contrast to James Adderley, Fathers Henry and Andrew believed that Franciscans needed to work within the parochial system of the Church. Indeed, they could not see how else the Society could achieve definite goals in helping the poor. The purpose of being in community was to achieve collectively what would be less easy to achieve as individuals. They saw the mission church of St Philip's, Plaistow, as the ideal base for such a ministry: running a church but without the authority and power invested in the vicar of the parish as a whole. This meant the brothers stayed within the Church's structures, yet were more distant from the traditional social status of the Anglican clergyman than if one of them was appointed an incumbent. For the brothers, pastoral care was thereby distinct from ecclesiastical power, yet without the separation from the Church's authority structures advocated by Adderley. For Henry and Andrew, this was an opportunity to change attitudes towards the poor; by showing within one parish district a new kind of ministry, rooted in a shared poverty, Franciscans could show the Church as a whole a way forward in its witnessing to gospel values. It was being prophetic within the Church structures rather than outside them.

This approach was reflected in two practical policies. First, the brothers would not have any amenities denied to the majority of their parishioners, but live with similar conditions to those they served. One example of this commitment is that the SDC brothers did not have a bathroom installed in their house. Second, the concerns of the parishioners about jobs and other issues became those of the brothers.

Some of the lay brothers who joined SDC worked as local 'craftsmen', in mending clocks and printing, in addition to the priest brethren's more traditional parochial ministry. Both points are articulated in the Society's 1908 book, *A Franciscan Revival*.

> It [SDC] has its parish work, where it lives a neighbourly life, going out to the more active work of the ministry in preaching and missions; its workshops among the people, where it repairs clocks and watches, works its printing presses, decorates churches, and its members may belong to the same trade societies as the artizans among whom they live. It has had, in common with all Christians, its hours of darkness and temptation. It seeks to live a poor life, sharing the privation and discomfort of ordinary poor people.[5]

In so doing, they were providing a model of 'living alongside' which was stable and rooted in a local community.

Accordingly, when Fr William SDC marched with the unemployed to Hyde Park, London, in 1906, he felt able to do so because many of the marchers were his own 'flock'. He was not there as a Franciscan giving support to a political cause, but as a parish priest leading his own people in their fight for dignity. For example, the photograph of the marchers in the biography of Father William shows the banner they carried, which read: 'In the name of Christ we claim that all men should have the right to live.' At the head is a title: 'The Church in West Ham'. The emphasis was not on Franciscans bringing the plight of the poor to public attention, but Franciscans supporting the cause *on behalf of the Church*. Whereas Adderley wanted Franciscans individually to be prophets, his co-founders in SDC wanted Franciscans to be representatives of a prophetic Church. It was a crucial difference, which affected the chapter's choices as to both SDC's future location and the work it undertook.

His brothers' parochial vision of pastoral care could not hold Adderley. He pushed again and again for the implementation of his own vision. He was, he claimed, 'consistently opposed' by the rest of the SDC chapter and therefore felt compelled to resign. His attempt to form another community was short-lived and, ironically, he returned for the rest of his ministry to the work of a parish priest, which was a tacit admission of the failure to realize his own vision.

Ministry by withdrawal

Yet despite Adderley leaving SDC, the memory of his ideas still found a place in the community's deliberations. As their founder would have wished, in 1904, the SDC chapter decided to buy a house in the country at Stanford-le-Hope, in Essex, which became the centre for the SDC noviciate. Novices were there formed in a monastic setting of prayer and silence, before they were set to work in London's East End, so that,

> the life should be seen in its hardest, most monotonous aspects, and that the cost should be well counted before the irrevocable step is taken.

> Living in enclosure, with almost no intercourse with the outside world, there is not much fear of a man mistaking sentiment for vocation.[6]

But the work still remained defined by the parameters of parish and local community in Plaistow. The only exception to this was some brothers going to South Africa for a few years to teach in the mission field. However, the vision of Adderley still tugged at this model of pastoral care and did so in two very different ways.

The first was the result of the monastic style of the noviciate. Some novices became convinced of the value of contemplative life as a legitimate and necessary part of pastoral care. It was not merely a means of training and testing but was a significant ministry in its own right. To them, without the existence of contemplatives under vows, who would remain in the monastery and not seek outside work, the apostolic ministries would lack an important dimension. Amongst women religious in the Church of England, this trend had become strong in the first decade of the twentieth century. So, for example, the Servants of Christ, begun as an apostolic community in 1897, decided to become a cloistered contemplative order in 1905, adopting an essentially Cistercian spirituality. The following year, the Sisters of the Love of God were founded in Oxford, inspired by the Carmelite tradition. Among male religious the same impulse was surfacing. The Benedictines founded in the 1890s by Aelred Carlyle became increasingly contemplative, settling after ten years in the remote location of Caldey Island, off the South Wales coast. For SDC, the impulse proved all the more startling because it was the superior, Father William Sirr, who was among those who felt such a call.

Father William had expressed this desire on his standing down as superior in 1912, but his brothers in chapter were unsympathetic.[7] They could not see how a life of withdrawal at the novice house at Stanford-le-Hope was not sufficient for William. Yet he persisted in asking for release and, after much frustration, a new superior proved more understanding. In 1918, Father William was permitted to go and live in a disused stable block at Glasshampton in Worcestershire, and there he created the monastery of St Mary at the Cross. His spirituality was based on a Cistercian model (although there was no land to work) rather than a Franciscan one. There was no outside work, but the monk welcomed male guests, especially those who were in trouble or personal difficulty, and Glasshampton became a place of refuge. Here, Father William prayed for the world and for the poor among whom he had laboured during his years in Plaistow. Sadly for him, those who came to test such a vocation with him did not persevere. At his death in 1937, the contemplative community for which he had hoped had not emerged and he died still a member of SDC, a solitary Franciscan instead of a Cistercian monk. The importance of Father William in the subject of pastoral care amongst Franciscans was that he illustrated the need for a 'praying heart' to the community. His example was admired by many other Franciscan friars, even though they felt unable to emulate or join him. Despite his own looking towards Cistercian patterns of life and prayer, Father William can equally be claimed as part of the Franciscan eremitic tradition.

Ministry to the outcast

A second development within the SDC noviciate drew more definitive inspiration from James Adderley. The novice concerned was called Brother Giles, and, during his two years (1911–13) at Stanford-le-Hope, he became convinced that his ministry should be to those at the very margins of society: the wayfarers or 'men of the roads', who had lost families and self-respect as well as jobs and security. To fulfil this call, he wished to tramp, as Adderley had done, from doss house to doss house. But such an identification had little resonance for his superiors. In 1908, they had written,

> S. Francis embraced poverty literally. The need of this age is to emphasise the dignity of labour – not to beg with the beggar, but to work with the worker. Moreover, to do what can be done to ensure

that all have the opportunity to work, and to work under righteous conditions. Love for the poor – or rather the oppressed and starving – is best expressed in helping them to work ...[8]

Roaming around casual wards did not fall within this definition.

The SDC chapter could not, therefore, accept such a vocation and Giles had to leave the community. In turn, Bishop Charles Gore of Oxford refused Giles his protection or blessing. The Society of St John the Evangelist, the 'Cowley Fathers', gave him shelter in Oxford in his rest periods but would not give him official endorsement either. So Giles began in 1913 what might be termed a freelance ministry as a genuine itinerant, working outside any formal ecclesiastical structure. He was, however, more concerned than Adderley with building a religious community of friars for this ministry, not just a Third Order. It was not a time of public sympathy for the homeless, and Giles's way of life attracted little support – and no lasting companions. His vocation to community seemed far from realization.

Giles served in the armed forces during the First World War, but resumed his tramping as soon as he was able, early in 1919.[9] Public attitudes towards the destitute on the roads had now changed dramatically, as so many wayfarers were former soldiers. Their numbers grew steeply: there were nearly 2 million unemployed by the autumn of 1920. Giles found he now had support both from the Church hierarchy and from wealthy lay patrons. He was offered a location for a friary in the countryside by the Earl of Sandwich at a low rent so that he could create a 'home' for wayfarers. Most welcome of all was that he now also had several men willing to try their vocations with him. Late in 1921, Flowers Farm, near Hilfield in Dorset, became the friary of a new religious community, the Brotherhood of St Francis of Assisi (BSFA).

The idea behind the new friary was to create a labour colony, where the men of the roads could both rest and regain self-respect while at the same time working on the farm to earn their keep. These men were cut off from their roots, in terms of both locality and relationships, partly through the 'shame' of unemployment, which prevented them 'going home', where they felt they would be a burden to their families. They were condemned by the existing social legislation to tramp from casual ward to casual ward, often many miles, allowed to stay only two nights at each ward. The alternative of 'sleeping rough' was illegal until 1935; so they could only tramp – or else be liable to arrest and a prison sentence. From the stable base of the friary, however, these wayfarers could look for permanent work, helped by the brothers and their backers.

Giles had combined the Adderley and SDC visions. There was a base in the country (Flowers Farm), as Adderley had envisaged, but, unlike Adderley's ideal, it was not a base for withdrawal. Under Giles, it had become a place of both prayer and work, where wayfarers could be received for a period of rehabilitation. From SDC came the concept of parish, but the BSFA friary's parish was not the Dorset locality but the roads in general. The people of the parish were not those who lived around the friary but those who had no home and belonged nowhere. The new brotherhood was giving a parish to the parishless.

Giles was careful too to seek the backing of the Church. He had sought it in 1913. He gained it in 1919–22. If he wished to be prophetic within society, he also agreed with his former SDC brethren that he had to be prophetic from within the Church – not acting as a maverick but working on behalf of the whole community of the faithful. Therefore, his new community was established in line with the traditional arrangements of religious life, including having a bishop visitor and an agreed structure. The first novices were even given some basic training by the Cowley Fathers. So the ecclesiastical rootedness of SDC was mirrored in BSFA, while those who were served were the outcasts and so-called 'rejects' Adderley had desired to help.

But for Giles there was a heavy personal cost. After nine months in Dorset, stress and overwork brought him to a breakdown, which led to his leaving Dorset and the brotherhood for ever. Giles had moved the debate on, but in the end, like Adderley, he could not bring the vision to fruition. It is one of history's ironies that the man who did, Douglas Downes, was initially utterly hostile to the idea of becoming a friar. He was persuaded to leave his work as a chaplain in Oxford and take over the wardenless friary, so that the work would not have to cease. Yet at the beginning, he could not see the relevance of religious life to the ministry to wayfarers at all. Brother Douglas refused to be the superior of a friary or accept a 'rule' of life; instead he became the warden of a home. One witness remembered that Douglas's evangelical sensitivities made him think 'monks were people to be avoided'. So unsurprisingly Douglas refused at first to wear a habit and only the pleas of the Earl of Sandwich persuaded him to retain the patronage of St Francis.

Douglas Downes was no stranger to the problem of poverty.[10] As a curate before the First World War, he had moved out of his comfortable lodgings to live at the top of a working-class tenement, with orange boxes for furniture. Teaching in India in the years 1908–14, he had lived not in the staff quarters but with the Indian students in a hostel. As he would later write: 'How to preach the *Idea* of Poverty which has no visible expression I simply do not know. The Life must be the sermon.'[11]

He believed therefore that no-one could preach and demonstrate the gospel effectively to the poor without sharing the same hardships. In this sense he was like Giles. They had known each other in Oxford in the years 1919 to 1921 and it was Douglas who had encouraged Giles to accept Flowers Farm as a base for his work.

Being a voice for the outcast

Douglas was a contrast to Giles in that he saw little need for the trappings of community life. But as the 1920s progressed and Douglas went through many dark hours in his struggle to keep the friary financially viable, he began to grow into the religious life, seeing a community of brothers as a 'team' to do the job. By 1927, guided by the bishop of Salisbury and Father Barnabas SDC,[12] he accepted the habit and a traditional Rule. He saw that a priest acting as warden of a Home was akin to a charitable foundation or institution, whereas a religious community could more easily create the atmosphere of a home for the men they served.

By the late 1920s, the friary was freed from the debt incurred when it was first begun. Its work was praised in the House of Commons. The brothers tried to establish a Home for wayfarers in every county and about a dozen were founded in the years 1928–34. There had developed then a specific and settled ministry. It was a pattern which involved many helpers, as there were still fewer than half a dozen brothers. A Third Order began to develop, first through a loose group of 'associates' and then, more formally, as a traditional Third Order, whose members became novices and then took vows. These tertiaries were committed to sharing their resources and some went as far as living in a group on a poor housing estate, existing on only the same income as their neighbours. Through the work of Giles and then Douglas, Adderley's original idea was coming to fruition.

Just as Adderley would have hoped, the BSFA provided a voice for the wayfarers, taking their case to the public and to those in power. They did not do this by joining party political debates nor by lining up with the articulate leaders of the working class. Instead, they lent their weight to a broad (and successful) cross-party campaign to change the treatment wayfarers received in casual wards. The BSFA Homes showed how they could be given more dignity and support and he saw no reason why society as a whole could not adopt such methods. He accepted a round of preaching engagements in parishes and schools and conferences. He and his brothers went on road missions to gather reliable information to present to the relevant authorities. Douglas showed how a ministry to the poor was not only about care and support but about representation. Adderley and Giles's methods could be used as a means of presenting authentic information about a current social problem. It was not just protest, but an advocacy of how to put it right. This gave Douglas's campaign a moral authority.

Yet, there was a weakness in Douglas's leadership. As his idea of community was a team to do a job, he was unable to create community structures which would increase the bonds of support between his brothers. There was by the early 1930s no meaningful community life to which to draw novices, only a scheme of work. This in turn weakened the witness of the Third Order, who needed a First Order as their focus and inspiration. Douglas had no instinct for the religious life as such and his quip about BSFA being a 'group of social workers in brown dressing gowns' was an incisive judgement as well as a humorous comment. When Mark Kemp, a simply professed brother of SDC, was transferred to BSFA in 1933, he was made a novice, but in the following years profession was never even mentioned. Finally, he left. Another postulant remained so for four years and then left having never been made a novice. Such stories were not unusual under Douglas.

The witness of community

The Bishop of Salisbury intervened in 1934 and insisted the brothers must live a community life. Responsibility for the running of the Home was given to a committee, and a warden from outside the community then appointed. But Bishop Donaldson knew that another leader was needed, one with contrasting skills. He turned to Father Algy Robertson, the leader of another group of Franciscans based at the vicarage of St Ives in Huntingdonshire.[13] This group was an English offshoot of the *Christa Seva Sangha*, a Franciscan community at Pune in India, who witnessed both to a life of simplicity and one which mixed white and brown races, higher and lower castes, as a protest against the social divisions of the Raj. Father Algy had been invalided home in 1930 and, unable to return, he founded the CSS friary at St Ives. But Algy's talents and hopes could not be contained as a minor offshoot of a community thousands of miles away. His small group therefore sought ways to co-operate and eventually merge with Brother Douglas's Dorset friars. It was this aspiration which the bishop of Salisbury now strongly encouraged. The unity process evolved over a number years and by 1937 the new Society of St Francis came formally into being.

Father Algy started from the premise that the Franciscan witness to the world could only succeed if community was fostered. He introduced a programme of training and a more formal structure to the life, particularly for novices. But the significant contribution he made to the models of pastoral care was the concept of 'spiritual friendship'. Within the formality of structure, Algy created an opportunity for a more relaxed and personal approach than was found in most religious communities of the time. In an age when even good friends might not use each other's Christian names, he was not afraid to leap over social norms of deference. He regarded friendship as a tool of evangelism and pastoral care, once writing that 'It is in the atmosphere of friendliness that hearts may be most deeply touched.'[14] If this 'atmosphere' was to be used in the world to bring others to Christ, it had to be established within the community itself, and then taken out to those the Society served. He believed that it was not so much the Rule which was the 'school for sanctity' but its inner expression, what he termed 'sacramental friendship'. He wrote: 'Selfishness can be curbed there: growth in holiness (in 'christlikeness') is possible there – nowhere else is there such an opportunity.'[15]

There were two sources which shaped his Christian commitment into this particular form. One was India. He taught in Calcutta from 1917 to 1920 and then returned in 1927 to join the *Christa Seva Sangha* at Pune, staying for three years. Those six years shaped many of his attitudes towards community, for he found in Indian culture a mix of respect and informality which was a contradiction of the (then strong) British tradition of formal behaviour patterns. So, for example, contemporary British culture would have seen gestures of formal respect as boundaries in any interaction. In India, the initial gesture of respect was in order that one could subsequently enjoy a much more relaxed encounter. For Algy, this was a profound understanding of human relationships.

This influence was encouraged by a second, this time back in Britain. This was the Group Movement, or Moral Rearmament, founded by an

American Lutheran minister, Frank Buchman, in 1918, its aim being a revival in all churches. Its methods revolved around three concepts. First there was Guidance – in a Quiet Time of group prayer each morning in which the Holy Spirit's will would be sought. Then came Sharing – a time in which members of the group confessed their worries and their sins, and, shockingly for the time, this included frank exchanges about sex. The third element, perhaps predictably for an evangelical revivalist group, was Loyalty. In practice, this meant the Groupists followed what Buchman or his trusted acolytes decreed. After a few years, the movement faded and its long-term effects were minimal, but at its height, thousands flocked to its summer meetings held in Oxford colleges, the attendees including Brother Douglas, Father Algy and other Franciscans. Algy was enthusiastic at first, but eventually withdrew his support when he saw the authoritarianism of Buchman become more overt and the prospect of the Group Movement evolving into what amounted to a separate church.

However, Algy was nothing if not eclectic in constructing his vision for the Society. He took the lessons of sharing and intimacy he had learned from the Group Movement and put them into the safer context of spiritual direction. Here then was a further development in the Franciscan model of pastoral care. The quality of the relationships or friendships within a community were of direct relevance to the quality of ministry to the poor which that community then provided. Giles had united Adderley's freedom of work with SDC's belief in working from a friary. Douglas had added a political dimension to the prophetic witness. Now Algy had contributed a means of fostering the community spirit, on which the foundation of pastoral care would rest.

He also did not neglect to reintegrate Father William's Glasshampton legacy. Soon after the Second World War, the trustees of the monastery approached the Society of St Francis, asking them to take over care of it. Father Algy visited Glasshampton in April 1947 and was immediately impressed with its potential as a place of retreat for the friars, and a centre for those within the Society called to a contemplative vocation. The novice master, Father Francis, also convinced him that the novices should spend a 'term' there. Not the whole noviciate, as SDC's novices had spent at Stanford-le-Hope, but eight or nine months. This has proved a lasting decision and for fifty years this contemplative period has remained a requirement for all those who aspire to join SSF.

The Society of St Francis, therefore, not only united Anglican Franciscan friars but also brought together the different models of pastoral care which had emerged from the ideas of all its various founders. The Society of Divine Compassion did not take part in the merger which created SSF. However, in 1952, fifteen years later, after SDC membership had dwindled to two elderly friars, its work at Plaistow too was taken over by SSF.

One goal which united all the founders and runs like a thread through their history was the need for evangelism. SDC saw its Plaistow ministry to the poor as, 'to make Christ live again in their midst'.[16] Giles's life on the roads was essentially evangelical, as he wished to bring the love of Christ and the good news of the gospel to those whose lives he believed were spiritually impoverished as well as materially deprived. As for Douglas, he was frustrated by the time spent working on the land in the mid-1920s, bemoaning that, 'We must think more of the untilled garden in men's hearts than of the weeds in the orchard!'[17] Algy repeatedly urged the friars to give evangelism priority. In 1948, he wrote, 'our Franciscan community if it is to be true to its spirit must give itself to the preaching of the Gospel'.[18]

For them all, social injustice could not be combated by political campaigns or charitable works alone. There had to be a witness to society of a different set of attitudes, to foster a greater sense of fairness. Human failings of greed and selfishness could not be abolished, but Franciscans believed that the gospel offered a way in which they could be redeemed. Evangelism was therefore at the heart of pastoral care for Adderley and all those who followed him, because for them pastoral care was the gospel in action, the true following of Jesus Christ. This is not to say that pastoral care was a tool for the manipulation of the poor; rather that it demonstrated the love of Christ in human interactions and so was inevitably and inextricably linked to evangelism.

The principles of pastoral care in Anglican religious communities

The debates over the models for pastoral care within Anglican Franciscanism were therefore not divorced from the expression and commitment to the Christian faith which was the inner motivation for all these brothers. Looking back over their debates, there are five principles which emerge.

First came the imperative that Franciscans ought to embrace a freedom from *power,* particularly institutional power, in order to remain free to respond to a variety of calls. As this idea developed in the lives of his successors, this did not mean a freedom from *authority,* ecclesiastical or secular. Instead, it meant a detachment from positions which gave power over others, so that the community could retain an independence of thought and spirit, and be open to change when circumstances demanded.

Then came the necessity of being rooted in local communities, wherever friars served. This way, any ministry would not be something which appeared imposed from outside, but, in contrast, emerge as part of a solidarity with the poor in their struggles for justice. Friars would be acting out of their own experience of the same conditions instead of from a more intellectually conceived idea of 'what the poor wanted'.

Next came the principle of giving prayer a priority as a witness in itself. It was not merely an activity to keep a community together, but a valid expression of commitment to the poor. It had its place as a powerful tool in the work of those who sought to improve social conditions. Without the contemplative dimension, the active would be disarmed.

This, in turn, did not mean a refusal to engage in campaigns on issues vital to the wellbeing of the poor. Indeed, the need to represent in the political arena those who lacked the opportunity or the education or the confidence to speak out for themselves was a significant ministry.

Finally, there emerged the importance of relationships within a community. Working at, and through, such relationships was essential in order to create the spirit in which the various ministries could prosper. In doing so, friars would help create paradigms for relationships within society as a whole.

All these principles can be more closely associated with one of the founders more than the others. Yet, they were the fruit of the collaboration and interaction of a group of different men who, in response to the same social problems, contributed distinct visions. After fifty years, their ideas were all expressed within one community. The friars had found a strength out of the tensions and divisions within their movement. Although Adderley left SDC in 1897, a hundred years later the Franciscanism he had embraced inspired the largest of all Anglican religious communities.

Notes

1. However, there were some attempts. The Society of the Holy Trinity created a contemplative community within an apostolic one when it built Ascot Priory

in the late 1850s. The contemplative group would continue to receive vocations long after the 'active' sisters had died out.
2. For example, Mother Emily and the Sisters of the Church in Kilburn. Mother Emily maintained a strong objection to the community having a bishop visitor, even though it meant in the 1890s a long and public dispute with the archbishop of Canterbury. See *A Valiant Victorian*, (London, 1964), ch. 8.
3. A. Clifton Kelway (ed.), *A Franciscan Revival: The Story of the Society of the Divine Compassion* (Plaistow, 1908), p. 16.
4. James Adderley SDC to the SDC Chapter, 20 September 1897, Lambeth Palace Archives, SDC Papers, Box 1.
5. Kelway, *Franciscan Revival*, p. 3. The author of this quotation was Father Andrew SDC.
6. Ibid., p.12. The author of this quotation was Father Andrew SDC.
7. For a fuller treatment of Father William, see Geoffrey Curtis, *William of Glasshampton*, (London, 1947).
8. Kelway, *Franciscan Revival*, p. 10.
9. More background information on Brother Giles can be found in the relevant chapters of Petà Dunstan, *This Poor Sort*, (London, 1997).
10. More background information on Brother Douglas can be found in Father Francis, *Brother Douglas* (London, 1959), and the relevant chapters of Dunstan, *This Poor Sort*.
11. Douglas Downes to William Lash, 9 March 1930, Douglas box, Hilfield Archives.
12. The bishop (St Clair Donaldson) was BSFA's visitor and Father Barnabas was its spiritual adviser.
13. More background information on Father Algy can be found in Father Denis, *Father Algy* (London, 1964) and the relevant chapters of Dunstan, *This Poor Sort*.
14. *The Franciscan* (Winter 1948).
15. Father Algy SSF to Brother Michael SSF, 25 February [1945], Michael file, Hilfield Archives.
16. Kelway, *Franciscan Revival*, p. 4.
17. Brother Douglas to Charles Preston, 12 November 1924, Douglas box, Hilfield Archives.
18. *The Homes of St Francis Newsheet* (Autumn 1948).

Bibliography

Curtis, Geoffrey, *William of Glasshampton: Friar, Monk, Solitary, 1862–1937* (London, 1947)
Denis, Father, *Father Algy* (London, 1964)
Dunstan, Petà, *This Poor Sort: A History of the European Province of the Society of St Francis* (London, 1997)
Francis, Father, *Brother Douglas: Apostle of the Outcast* (London, 1959)
Kelway, A. Clifton (ed.), *A Franciscan Revival: The Story of the Society of the Divine Compassion* (Plaistow, 1908)

17

The growth of the soul in Charles Kingsley

G. R. Evans

Charles Kingsley's *The Water Babies* has within it a theology over which hang a number of questions. In her memoir of her husband's life Charles Kingsley's wife describes his early struggles with the orthodoxies of the Christian faith while he was preparing for ordination. 'From very insufficient and ambiguous grounds in the Bible, they seem unjustifiably to have built up a huge superstructure, whose details they have filled in according to their own fancies,' he remarked in 1840.[1] By 1842 he was reading the Fathers and mediaeval authors, and what he calls 'Popish books'.[2] He was drawn to two things: the beauty of what sometimes seemed a direct reflection of 'the life-blood of God's Spirit' in people and events,[3] and increasingly to 'the experimental religion of the Low Church School'. The attraction he felt was towards 'the depth and subtlety of knowledge of the human heart, which many of them display. It is so refreshing after the cold dogmatism of the High Church,' he comments.[4]

This attraction had a focus for him, in the belief that 'we must be holy'.[5] By 1842 he was consciously drawing upon the study of nature for prompters to moral reflections.[6] He thought it possible to grow in holiness by practice:

> Remember that habit, more than reason, will cure one both of mystifying subtlety and morbid fear; and remember that habits are a series of individual voluntary actions, continued until they become involuntary.[7]

> Our safe plan will be, as young and foolish children, first to learn the duties of daily life, the perfect ideal of humanity, from the Bible, and prayer, and God's earth; and thus to learn and practise love.[8]

All this is striking in a theologian of evangelical leanings, because it puts a heavy emphasis upon a 'sanctification' which, in the sixteenth-century debates, was frequently taken by reformers to be incompatible with 'justification by faith alone'.[9]

It would be forcing the evidence to seek to portray Kingsley as a theologian of strong intellectual consistency, and anyway he cannot have known the sixteenth-century debates as modern scholarship does. J.H. Rigg accused Kingsley of pantheism and also of being unsound on free will. It may be that he stumbled into the appearance of unorthodoxy by not thinking things through in a manner theologically consistent.[10] But we may reasonably ask him to provide us with a *moral* consistency and a fundamental coherence of thought in *The Water Babies*.

Kingsley recognized that need himself. He had a love of nature which was in many respects unsentimental. He wrote in 1956 to F. D. Maurice, about the conclusions to be drawn from:

> a universe in which everything is eternally *eating* everything else ...
> The study of nature can teach no *moral theology*. It may unteach it, if the roots of moral theology be not already healthy and deep in the mind ... I sometimes envy you, who are not distracted from work at the really *human* truths, by the number of joints in a grub's legs.[11]

This duality of an earthy realism and a tendency to draw moral lessons from his observations runs through his thinking. 'Why do fish take your caperer, spite of his ugliness, but because he looks the fattest one they ever saw yet?'[12]

Kingsley was extremely fond of fishing. This led him to spend a good deal of time gazing into water and contemplating its populations and drawing morals. To Tom Hughes he wrote in 1856:

> I can show him views ... which no mortal cockney knows, because, although the whole earth is given to the children of men, none but we jolly fishers get the plums and raisins of it, by the rivers which run among the hills, and the lakes which sit a-top thereof.

He describes the setting of one fishing stream and the lake with passion, something which will 'make you shiver, if you be sentimental – but *I* only think of the trouts – which the last I saw killed in Llyn Melch was 3½ pounds, and we'll kill his wife and family'. We need not believe him.

Kingsley undoubtedly had a social conscience,[13] and it is equally clear that he had a tender concern for children. One cannot do better than quote his wife. In her memorial volume, she says that:

> punishment was a thing little known in his house. Corporal punishment was never allowed. His own childish experience of the sense of degradation and unhealthy fear it produced, of the antagonism it called out between a child and its parents, a pupil and his teachers, gave him a horror of it. It had other evils, too, he considered, besides degrading both parties concerned. 'More than half the lying of children,' he said, 'is I believe, the result of fear, and the fear of punishment'. On these grounds, he made it a rule ... not to take a child suspected of a fault, at unawares, by sudden question or hasty accusation, the stronger thus taking an unfair advantage of the weaker and defenceless creature, who, in the mere confusion of the moment, might be tempted to deny or equivocate ... 'Shall we dare [he said] to confound our own children by sudden accusation or angry suspicion, making them give evidence against themselves, when we don't allow a criminal to do that in a court of law? The finer the nature the more easily is it confounded, whether it be of child, dog, or horse. Suspicion destroys confidence between parent and child.'[14]

'Do not train a child', he once said to a friend,

> 'as men train a horse, by letting anger and punishment be the *first* announcement of his having sinned. If you do, you induce two bad habits; first, the boy regards his parents with a kind of blind dread, as a being who may be offended by actions which to *him* are innocent, and whose wrath he expects to fall upon him any moment in his most pure and unselfish happiness ... Next, and worse still, the boy learns not to fear sin, but the *punishment* of it, and thus he learns to lie. At every first fault, and offence too, teach him the principle which makes it sinful – illustrate it by a familiar parable – and then, if he sins again it will be with his eyes open!'[15]

His wife adds:

> He was careful, too, not to confuse or 'confound' his children by a multiplicity of small rules. Certain broad, distinct laws of conduct were laid down ... This, combined with his equable rule, gave them a sense of utter confidence and perfect freedom with him. They knew what they were about and where to find him.[16]

As in the case of his thoughts about nature, all this is not mere homely common sense but theology too. It reappears *expressis verbis* in *The Water Babies*.

> Did she question him, hurry him, frighten him, threaten him, make him confess? Not a bit. ... No. She leaves that for anxious parents and teachers ... who, instead of giving children a fair trial, such as they would expect and demand for themselves, force them by fright to confess their faults ... ay, and even punish them to make them confess, which is so detestable a crime that it is never committed ... save by inquisitors.[17]

Providence, order and free choice

How far, then, can we extract a developed theology from Kingsley's pragmatic picture of the saving of a small chimney sweep in *The Water Babies*? There is an orderly and somewhat determinist universe here. Heaven in Kingsley's story is exemplified in the room of the little girl, which is 'all dressed in white', but 'the carpet was all over gay little flowers; and the walls were hung with pictures in gilt frames, which amused Tom very much' (23). The lady, too, is beautiful because she is white. 'Under the snow-white coverlet, upon the snow-white pillow, lay the most beautiful little girl that Tom had ever seen. Her cheeks were almost as white as the pillow, and her hair was like threads of gold spread all about over the bed' (25).

Heaven is above all a safe place, where sin and its consequences can no longer reach:

> A quiet, silent, rich, happy place; a narrow crack cut deep into the earth; so deep and so out of the way, that the bad bodies can hardly find it out. (48)

There is an 'everything in its place' character about Kingsley's sense of universal order:

> This is the reason why the rock-pools are always so neat and clean; because the water-babies come inshore after every storm to sweep them out, and comb them down, and put them all to rights again. (187)

More profoundly, a providence is in charge which cannot be thwarted. We learn of the fate of Mr Grimes, and it is the right fate for him. 'The fairies had carried him away, and put him, where they put everything which falls into the water, exactly where it ought to be' (133). The role of the Irishwoman is both to teach and to watch over Tom. When he ran away from the little girl's alarm the Irishwoman silently followed him 'wherever he went' (36, 40). 'And all the while he never saw the Irishwoman, not behind him this time, but before' (56). This is recognized to be a divine guidance.

> Why, God's guided the bairn, because he was innocent. Away from the Place, and over Hartover Fell, and down Lewthwaite Crag. Whoever heard the like, if God hadn't led him. (54)

In this mode the Irishwoman is perhaps a personification of divine grace. But if so, she does not force the free will of Tom, and neither do Bedonebyasyoudid and her sister. 'And all the while, close behind him,' as he stole the sweets, 'stood Mrs. Bedonebyasyoudid' (213). Why did she not keep the cupboard locked, asks Kingsley? But she never does. 'Everyone may go and taste for themselves and fare accordingly' (213).

There is an embracing generosity in Kingsley's theology of God's providential care: 'He's sick, and a bairn's a bairn, sweep or none' (53). He is reassuring:

> All the little children whom the good fairies take to, because their cruel mothers and fathers will not; all who are untaught and brought up heathens, and all who come to grief by ill-usage or ignorance or neglect; all the little children who are overlaid or given gin when they are young. (193)

Good works and the process of sanctification

Tom learns a great deal about how to be good by behaving wrongly or rightly and seeing the different consequences. This is in line with Kingsley's principle that salvation requires some effort on the part of the individual. 'It is not good for little boys to be told everything and never to be forced to use their own wits' (185). Tom is propelled out into the world to learn by his mistakes:

> She told him how he had been in the nursery long enough, and must go out now and see the world, if he intended ever to be a man; and how he must go all alone by himself, as every one else that ever was born has to go, and see with his own eyes, and smell with his own nose, and make his own bed and lie on it, and burn his own fingers if he put them into the fire. (227)

Mother Carey 'sits making old beasts into new all the year round' (270), though, as she tells Tom, she does not trouble herself with active construction. 'I sit here and let them make themselves' (273).

Again and again we meet the contention that good works count:

> Nobody can turn water-babies into sweeps, or hurt them at all, as long as they are good. (225)

> And she told him not to be afraid of anything he met, for nothing would harm him if he remembered all his lessons, and did what he knew was right. (227)

Kingsley's ideas about sanctification see it as a journey through a 'vale of soul-making'. And in turn the soul makes the body:

> 'I should like to cuddle you; but I cannot, you are so horny and prickly' ... Which was quite natural; for you must know and believe that people's souls make their bodies just as a snail makes its shell. (217)

Tom becomes a water baby but he is not to remain a water baby. It is an inchoate state, a learning stage, an apprenticeship for something better. That does not mean that he is de-formed when he becomes a water baby,[18] but it does mean that he has to 'grow in holiness':

People who make up their minds to go and see the world, as Tom did, must needs find it a weary journey. Lucky for them if they do not lose heart and stop half-way, instead of going on bravely to the end as Tom did. For then they will remain neither boys nor men, neither fish, flesh, nor good red herring. (135)

There is even a faint whiff of the influence of the hermetic tradition: 'He is but a savage now, and like the beasts which perish; and from the beasts which perish he must learn' (58).

Tom watches the transformation of a dragon-fly, and it is an object-lesson for him in the possibilities not only of change but of the making of something far more beautiful as a result:

And out of his inside came the most slender, elegant, soft creature, as soft and smooth as Tom: but very pale and weak, like a little child who has been ill a long time in a dark room ... And as the creature sat in the warm bright sun, a wonderful change came over it. It grew strong and firm; the most lovely colours began to show on its body, blue and yellow and black, spots and bars and rings; out of its back rose four great wings of bright brown gauze. (95)

The role of the Church, the role of grace

What are the agents of this transformation? For there are external assistants at least. It is not all done by Tom. All the authority and ministry figures in *The Water Babies* are female. Should we look for exactness in the personifications? Who are the fairies (angels?)? What is a water baby (the newly baptized human soul justified but in process of sanctification?)?

If the Irishwoman is the Church, then she has diaconal tasks in the forefront of her mind. She smooths the pillows of the sick, and thus helps the helpless, but she also cares for those who are their own worst enemies, 'turning women from the gin-shop door, and staying men's hands as they were going to strike their wives; doing all I can to help those who will not help themselves' (58).

There is a further ecclesiological hint, of the notion of the mutual help of neighbours, in what would be called a *koinonia* in the natural terminology of the late twentieth century. When Tom at last finds another water baby he is welcomed the moment he is recognized:

It ran to Tom, and Tom ran to it, and they hugged and kissed each other for ever so long, they did not know why. But they did not want any introductions there under the water. (185)

There seems an interactive process in which the Church assists:

'I hope ... you may have a stout staunch friend by you who is not beat; for, if you have not, you had best lie where you are, and wait for better times, as poor Tom did. (51)

What follows suggests that the Irishwoman is as likely to stand for divine grace.

Original sin and baptism

Kingsley suggests that the taint of sin is transmissible from one person to another, which is the first principle of the doctrine of original sin:

There have been more black beetles in Vendal since than ever were known before; all, of course, owing to Tom's having blacked the original papa of them all, with the dirt which flowed off him, just as he [the beetle] was setting off to be married, with a sky-blue coat and scarlet leggings, as smart as a gardener's dog with a polyanthus in his mouth. (50)

So there is not reason to suppose that he did not understand the need to be met by baptism in orthodox terms.

The link between the cleansing effects of water and the purging of sin is explicit in the opening passages of Kingsley's story, and it is of course essential to the validity of baptism that it is done with water:

> Cleansing my streams as I hurry along,
> To the golden sands and the leaping bar,
> And the taintless tide that awaits me afar.
> As I lost myself in the infinite main,
> Like a soul that has sinned and is pardoned again.
> Undefiled, for the undefiled,
> Play by me, bathe in me, mother and child. (44)

In *The Water Babies*, the theme of washing is introduced early in the story, and, ironically, with Grimes. When Tom saw Grimes 'actually wash, he stopped, quite astonished'. Grimes is quick to explain that ''Twasn't for cleanliness' he did it, 'but for coolness'. But Tom himself wants very badly to be *clean*, and he tries to follow Grimes's example and wash himself in the stream specifically for that purpose (12).

The Irishwoman who is watching makes it clear that what matters is the intention with which the washing is done, more even than that there should actually be washing. 'Those that wish to be clean, clean they will be; and those that wish to be foul, foul they will be' (13). That is the doctrine of the baptism of desire in a nutshell.

A little further on in the story, Tom is surprised to see so much apparatus for washing in the lady's bedroom, 'a washing-stand, with ewers and basins, and soap and brushes, and towels, and a large bath full of clean water – what a heap of things all for washing! "She must be a very dirty lady," thought Tom' (24). It is only when he has seen all these things which teach him what cleanliness is, and when he has gazed upon the whiteness of the lady, that he understands that he himself is dirty:

> Looking round, he suddenly saw, standing close to him, a little ugly, black, ragged figure, with bleared eyes and grinning white teeth ... And behold it was himself, reflected in a great mirror ... And Tom, for the first time in his life, found out that he was dirty. (26)

Thus the force of the metaphor is brought home to him.

It becomes linked in the course of the story with the understanding that baptism is not only a purification; it is also an entering into membership of the Church:

> He would go to church, and see what a church was like inside, for he had never been in one, poor little fellow, in all his life. But the people would never let him come in, all over soot and dirt like that. He must go to the river and wash first. And he said out loud again and again, though being half asleep he did not know it, 'I must be clean, I must be clean.' (55)

> 'I must be clean, I must be clean.' So he pulled off all his clothes in such haste that he tore some of them ... And the farther he went in, the more the church-bells rang in his head. (55)

There is a principle close to the view that there is no salvation outside the Church, *nulla salus extra ecclesiam*, in Tom's fear that unless he is quick and answers the invitation of the bells he will never be allowed in.

> 'Ah,' said Tom, 'I must be quick and wash myself; the bells are ringing quite loud now; and they will stop soon, and then the door will be shut and I shall never be able to get in at all.' (55)

Tom was mistaken. Kingsley takes the gateway to salvation to stand wide open:

> for in England the church doors are left open all service time, for everybody who likes to come in, Churchman or Dissenter; ay, even if he were a Turk or a Heathen; ... God's house ... belongs to all alike. (55)

What is the effect of baptism? There is a semi-philosophical discussion of the relationship between Tom the human child and Tom the water baby, which touches on the question. Is it helpful to talk of 'sea-lions' and 'sea-urchins' and to argue that Tom the water baby is just a 'sea' version of his 'land' self? That seems unsatisfactory, if 'the water things are not really akin to the land things'. No, says Kingsley, that is not right:

> They are, in millions of cases, not only of the same family, but actually the same individual creatures ... an alder-fly, and a dragon-fly, live under water till they change their skins, just as Tom changed his. (73)

He goes on to reason further that the analogy may actually be helpful in giving us a sense of the scale of the change:

> If the changes of the lower animals are so wonderful, and so difficult to discover, why should not there be changes in the higher animals far more wonderful, and far more difficult to discover? And may not man, the crown and flower of all things, undergo some change as much more wonderful than all the rest, as the Great Exhibition is more wonderful than a rabbit-burrow? (75)

The penitential process

Kingsley takes baptism to have made Tom free of two elements: 'Tom was now quite amphibious ... and what was better still, he was clean' (84). At the same time, it has taken away from him even the memory of his sinful condition. Indeed, 'he did not ever remember having ever been dirty' (83).

But forgetting that one has been dirty does not protect one against becoming dirty again. Penitential theology is built upon the presumption that that will happen if people are baptized as infants, because baptism takes away the guilt and penalty for sin, but not the tendency to sin. Tom finds out the truth of that:

I wish Tom had given up all his naughty tricks, and left off tormenting dumb animals now that he had plenty of playfellows to amuse him. Instead of that, I am sorry to say, he would meddle with the creatures, all but the water-snakes, for they would stand no nonsense. (193)

He discovers that there is no automatic transformation after he becomes 'clean':

Being quite comfortable is a very good thing; but it does not make people good. Indeed, it sometimes makes them naughty. (212)

If Tom was good he was given sea-sweets. But he grew too fond of them:

He was always longing for more, and wondering when the strange lady would come again and give him some, and what she would give him and how much, and whether she would give him more than the others. (212)

Tom falls into deception and deviousness:

He began to watch the lady to see where she kept the sweet things: and began hiding, and sneaking, and following her about, and pretending to be looking the other way ... till he found out that she kept them ... away in a deep crack of the rocks. (212)

Tom is torn. He greatly desires to steal the sweets, and yet he is afraid.

At last he plucks up his courage. But when he goes in search of the sweets, he finds that the cabinet among the rocks in which they are kept is open. The sight of the sweets frightens him, and he wishes he had never come. Then he touches one. 'Then he would only taste one, and he did; and then he would only eat one, and he did; and then he would only eat two, and three,' and so on. In the end he eats them all.

So, much of the latter half of Tom's story is taken up with the need for repentance and for learning from one's mistakes. Here Kingsley is not Tertullian. He is not rigorist. He does not insist that there can be no way back if the baptized fall into sin again. When Tom confesses he expects to be punished, but to his surprise, he is immediately forgiven. 'I always forgive every one the moment they tell me the truth of their own accord' (218). This sits a little uncomfortably with the doctrine of justification by works on which we found Kingsley so expansive earlier in this chapter.

The role of reward and punishment

The untutored children who are the newly baptized water babies need assistance. They are given it in the form of two allegorical moral monitors. Mrs Bedonebyasyoudid is 'a very tremendous lady'. The children instinctively respond to her by standing up straight 'very upright indeed', and smoothing down their bathing dresses and putting their hands behind them, 'just as if they were going to be examined by the inspector' (193). She knows without asking how each child has been behaving and she gives each its reward of sea-sweets and sea-fruits.

There is condign punishment as well as 'reward matched to effort'. To Tom she gives 'a nasty cold hard pebble'. He is tearfully indignant. She reproves him. He has been putting pebbles into the mouths of sea-anemones. 'As you did to them, so I must do to you' (195).

Tom pleads ignorance. He did not know that he was doing anything wrong. 'People continually say that to me,' remarks Mrs Dedonebyasyoudid. 'But I tell them, if you don't know that fire burns, that is no reason why it should not burn you' (196).

The retribution is mechanical:

'I am the best friend you ever had in all your life. But I will tell you; I cannot help punishing people when they do wrong. I like it no more than they do; I am often very, very sorry for them, poor things; but I cannot help it ... I work by machinery, just like an engine.' (196)

But it is also constructive. Mrs Doasyouwouldbedoneby will teach Tom how to behave, promises her sister. 'She understands that better than I do' (203).

Mrs Bedonebyasyoudid also gives condign punishment to all those who do harm to others out of ignorance or foolishness, such as ladies 'who pinch up their children's waists and toes', cramming their feet into 'the most dreadfully tight boots' and making them dance. Cruel schoolmasters have their ears boxed, and so on (199ff.). 'These people,' she explains, 'did not know that they were doing wrong: they were only stupid and impatient; and therefore I only punish them until they become patient and learn to use their common sense like reasonable beings' (202f.).

This retributive justice is not without mercy. When she explains to Tom that she is as old as eternity:

> there came over the lady's face a very curious expression – very solemn and sad; and yet very very sweet. And she looked up and away, as if she were gazing through the sea, and through the sky, at something far, far off; and as she did so, there came such a quiet, tender, patient, hopeful smile over her face that Tom thought for a moment she did not look ugly at all. (197)

Justice and mercy also merge in the pairing of the contrasting *personae* of the two allegorical figures:

> 'I am the ugliest fairy in the world [she says], and I shall be, till people behave themselves as they ought to do. And then I shall grow as handsome as my sister, who is the loveliest fairy in the world; and her name is Mrs. Doasyouwouldbedoneby. So she begins where I end and I begin where she ends; and those who will not listen to her must listen to me, as you will see.' (198)

> 'As for chimney-sweeps, and collier-boys, and nailer lads, my sister has set good people to stop all that sort of thing; and very much obliged to her I am; for if she could only stop the cruel masters from ill-using poor children, I should grow handsome at least a thousand years sooner.' (202f.)

Purgatory?

It is not obvious – and perhaps it is unnecessary to ask – whether Kingsley perceives all this as taking place in a purgatorial context. Kendall suggests that Kingsley's ideas about purgatory were developed in the follow-up to the controversy over everlasting punishment which led to the expulsion of F. D. Maurice from King's College, Cambridge.[19] But purgatory is technically a place beyond death, and it remains unclear whether Tom dies in becoming a water baby, or merely 'dies to sin' in baptism so that he can begin to 'grow in holiness' in this life. The soul in purgatory has its destiny fixed. It will come to heaven but not yet. It cannot go to hell.

Kingsley raises the question of successive rebirths, and perhaps it is forcing the evidence to seek too much clarification of the state in which Tom lingers while he is learning his lesson. He quotes Wordsworth's 'a sleep and a forgetting'. 'There, you can know no more than that,' he says:

> But if I was you, I would believe that. For then ... instead of fancying, with some people, that your body makes your soul, as if a steam-engine could make its own coke; or, with some people, that your soul has nothing to do with your body, but is only stuck into it like a pin into a pin-cushion, to fall out with the first shake; you will believe ... that your soul makes your body, just as a snail makes its shell. (85f.)

There is evidence that we are still 'in this life', during the unfolding of the story, in the fact that Grimes does in the end repent, and it is not too late. 'And he began crying and blubbering like a great baby, till his pipe dropped out of his mouth, and broke all to bits':

> 'I'm beat now, and beat I must be. I've made my bed, and I must lie on it. Foul I would be, and foul I am, as an Irishwoman said to me once; and little I heeded it. It's all my own fault: but it's too late.'
> ... 'Never too late,' said the fairy, in such a strange soft new voice that Tom looked up at her' ... No more was it too late. For, as poor Grimes cried and blubbered on, his own tears did what his mother's could not do, and Tom's could not do, and nobody's on earth could do for him; for they washed the soot off his face and off his clothes.

Grimes escapes from his prison, and although he has to spend a great length of time in penitential activity, sweeping out the crater of Etna, we are led to suppose that he will be happy at last. He recognizes the Irishwoman at the moment when he repents and she explains to him that he 'knew well enough that you were disobeying, though you did not know it was me' (320). So in his act of repentance, Grimes comes face to face with transforming grace.

The beauty of goodness

The attractiveness of goodness in the form of Mrs Doasyouwouldbedoneby is, Tom finds, far stronger than that of evil:

> And her delight was ... to play with the babies ... And therefore when the children saw her they naturally all caught hold of her, and pulled her till she sat down on a stone, and climbed into her lap ... And Tom stood staring at them; for he could not understand what it was all about. (204)

Goodness has a way of making each individual feel favoured without preferring any to anyone else:

> She took Tom in her arms, and laid him in the softest place of all, and kissed him, and patted him, and talked to him, tenderly and low, such things as he had never heard before in his life; and Tom looked up into her eyes and loved her ... till he fell fast asleep from pure love. (205)

The effect of Mrs Doasyouwouldbedoneby's caresses and teaching is to make Tom want to be good. 'So Tom really tried to be a good boy, and tormented no sea-beasts after that as long as he lived; and he is quite alive, I assure you, still' (208).

> And as for the pretty lady, I cannot tell you what the colour of her hair was, or of her eyes: no more could Tom; for, when any one looks at her, all they can think of is, that she has the sweetest, kindest, tenderest, funniest, merriest face they ever saw. (203)

This is to do with the attraction of *beauty* as well as that of goodness.

Conclusion

Kingsley wrote a comment on *The Water Babies* to F. D. Maurice:

> If I have wrapped up my parable in seeming Tom-fooleries, it is because so only could I get the pill swallowed by a generation who are not believing with anything like their whole heart, in the Living God.[20]

He was trying, in his allegory, to tell an orthodox Christian story:

> When he woke she was telling the children a story ... which begins every Christmas Eve, and yet never ends at all for ever and ever. (205)

But he left a number of dangerously loose ends in the realm of the theology of penance and the role of good works in the economy of salvation.

Notes

1. *Charles Kingsley, His Letters and Memories of His Life*, 2 vols, ed. F. Kingsley (London, 1901), vol. 1, p. 29. For bibliography, see further, S. E. Baldwin, *Charles Kingsley* (London, 1934); D. A. Downes, *The Temper of Victorian Belief; Studies in the Religious Novels of Pater, Kingsley and Newman* (New York, 1972); G. Kendall, *Charles Kingsley and His Ideas* (London, 1947); Q. D. Leavis, 'The Water Babies', *Children's Literature in Education* 23 (1976), 155–6.
2. *Letters and Memories*, vol. 1, p. 46.
3. Ibid., p. 47.
4. Ibid., p. 48.
5. Ibid., p. 50.
6. Ibid., p. 60.
7. Ibid., p. 62.
8. Ibid., p. 84.
9. See my *Problems of Authority in the Reformation Debates* (Cambridge, 1992).
10. Kendall, *Kingsley and His Ideas*, p. 124.
11. *Letters and Memories*, vol. 2, p. 20.
12. Ibid., pp. 21–2.
13. S. K. Sharma, *Charles Kingsley and the Victorian Compromise* (New Delhi, 1989), p. 130.
14. *Letters and Memories*, vol. 2, p. 33.

15. Ibid., p. 34.
16. Ibid.
17. Charles Kingsley, *The Water Babies* (1863; reprinted Penguin, 1995), p. 215. (Subsequent references in the text are to page numbers in this edition.)
18. As is suggested by Brian V. Street, *The Savage in Literature: Representations of 'Primitive' Society in English Fiction, 1858–1920,* (London, 1975), pp. 90–1, 99.
19. Kendall, *Kingsley and His Ideas*, p. 126.
20. *Letters and Memories*, vol. 2, p. 127.

Bibliography

Charles Kingsley, *The Water Babies* (1863; reprinted Penguin, 1995)
Charles Kingsley, *His Letters and Memories of His Life*, 2 vols, ed. F. Kingsley (London, 1901) (*Letters and Memories*)
S. E. Baldwin, *Charles Kingsley* (London, 1934)
D. A. Downes, *The Temper of Victorian Belief; Studies in the Religious Novels of Pater, Kingsley and Newman* (New York, 1972)

18

Post-Enlightenment pastoral care

Into the twentieth century

David Cornick

The severest dislocation in the history of pastoral care in the West came not at the Reformation but at the Enlightenment. The focus of care in mediaeval Christendom and in early modern Europe was on reconciliation. The penitential system and Reformed discipline shared a single aim – reconciliation with God. The gradual decline of discipline was indicative of a massive shift in intellectual history – the establishment of the primacy of reason, the autonomy of the human self, and the slow shrinking of the realm of the supernatural. The disentangling of religion and magic, the desacralizing of the world which had begun at the Reformation has been beautifully chronicled by historians like Keith Thomas. The transformation of the Christian cosmos into a natural, scientific, post-Christian universe was to take centuries. Burnet smelt atheism in the European air in 1692, but until 1870 most lay people in Britain still retained a popular Christian world-view, believing in the efficacy of prayer, the reality of judgement and the certainty of eternal life.[1] Pastoral carers, particularly the clergy who formed part of the educated elite, lived in the tension between the erosion of old certainties and the demands of a popular Christian culture.

It was a complex transition. The 'practical divinity' and fastings against demons that had featured so prominently in the pastoral work of pre-

Revolution Puritanism found new life in the enthusiasm and charismatic experience of Evangelical Revival. Simultaneously, however, the 'enlightened' scepticism of the governing elites in both Church and state was eventually to lead to the triumph of natural religion and natural science.[2] The last trial for witchcraft was held in 1715. Statutes against witches were repealed in both England and Scotland in 1735. The territory of the 'soul-doctor' began to shrink at precisely the same time that pietism and the 'enthusiasm' of the Evangelical Revival sharpened attention on the pathology of religious experience. That became an increasingly theological preserve, so much that, under the influence of Kant, Schleiermacher considered it the sole foundation for proper theological architecture. Concurrently, the wider workings of the human mind, territory which Baxter and Burnet considered legitimately shared between the minister and the physician, was fast becoming the preserve of medicine. The mapping of madness provides a telling insight into the confusion. Prayer, fasting and exorcism were giving way to the private asylum. The blurred edge between these worlds is reflected in the entry books of the Bedlam hospital, which record the admittance of 90 patients between 1772 and 1795, thought mad because of 'religion and Methodism'.[3] The clergy retreated from the ministry of healing, and their counselling of individuals became increasingly a matter of guiding the immortal soul on its earthly pilgrimage.[4] They were in danger of being herded into a religious ghetto, professional religionists for the professionally religious. The privatization of religion had begun.

If the process of intellectual secularization forced the Church to adapt the content of pastoral care to a new world, the impact of industrialization brought about a lasting impact on parochial structure and the systems by which it was provided. In England the dissenting 'denominations' were able to respond to the changes wrought by industrialization more rapidly and flexibly than the Church of England. That was because of two inherent advantages – they were financially and legally free, and they possessed a theology of lay ministry (expressed in many forms, from the strictly organized to the chaotically *laissez-faire*) which enabled them to liberate resources of plant and personnel with ease. Luther's doctrine of the priesthood of all believers, Bucer's experiments with a church within a Church, Calvin's creation of the eldership, and the value of a genuine lay leadership in the church meeting (in the Independent and Baptist traditions), all lay behind this. Ironically, it was an Anglican, John Wesley, who appreciated its value most acutely. 'Mr Wesley's preachers', the society, and the class meeting were all brilliant variations on established Reformation themes, some mediated through Moravian pietism, as well as superbly opportune methods of evangelism and pastoral support. The class meeting began as an administrative twinkle in the eye of Captain Foy of Bristol, a way of paying off the debt on the New Rooms, but Wesley immediately realized their pastoral potential. Under the authority of Wesley and his preachers, the leaders of the classes were able to sustain and nurture small numbers of Christians, and exercise discipline. The relationship between class, society and connexion was elegantly simple and infinitely flexible.[5] Pastorally the Methodist system was initially intended as complementary to that of the Church of England, not as a challenge to it, and well into the nineteenth century the local boundaries between the Methodist chapel and the parish church were blurred.

Urbanization and secularization solved the underlying ecclesiological question of the Reformation by default. In England Church and state were systematically uncoupled between 1828 and 1868, and although the vestiges of that relationship are still enshrined in the legal responsibilities of the parish priest at rites of passage, Anglican pastoral care became increasingly focused on the Eucharistic community as the national church became a denomination.[6] In practice, if not in theory, all churches became confessing churches and the clergy therefore became the providers of religion for the religious.

The huge range of tasks carried out by the clergy in earlier ages contracted significantly as the perception of what a 'professional' was changed. In the eighteenth century a 'professional' was an educated person of high social status living a leisured and cultured life. He was not expected to have specific skills, and indeed those who charged fees for professional services were not necessarily regarded as professionals. The increasing specialization brought about by industrialization led to a change from 'status' to 'occupational' professionalism.[7] That inevitably affected the clergy. They were no longer barefoot doctors, amateur lawyers and makeshift schoolteachers, for new professionals increasingly filled those roles. The clergy were therefore thrown back on their core religious responsibilities, which remained the same as they had been since the Reformation.

Brian Heeney's survey of the pastoral theology works of 40 Anglican clergy of all schools in the first part of Victoria's reign echoes almost exactly the concerns of the sixteenth-century reformers. These handbooks for the pastoral clergy concentrate on preaching, the catechetical preparation of confirmands, the establishment of groups of devout communicants for prayer and Scripture reading (had they read their Bucer?), rites of passage, care of the sick, preparation of the dying, and pastoral guidance growing out of a pastor's thorough knowledge of his people and community. The Tractarian reappropriation of confession was matched by the Evangelical's private encounter with the troubled soul, ending with an offered prayer.[8] The 'professional' pattern of the nineteenth-century clergyman is not new. It is a remoulding of the Protestant tradition, which was itself a conscious imitation of the life of the early Church.

From the first agonizings of the Genevan Academy onwards, Protestantism had considered the godly life and a good education to be of equal value in a minister. That was a way of recognizing that ministry was a vocation. It was a calling of God, and no mere career choice. Probing motivation demands real discernment – vocation and career are not easily prised apart, and in reality are blended in most people. The assumption that between around 1750 and 1850 the pastoral commitment of the clergy was vitiated by the glittering prizes and easy sinecures which flowed from agricultural improvement and an increase in the value of tithes and glebes needs to be treated with due caution. The proportion of sons of the gentry amongst the Anglican clergy rose steadily during this period, but even by 1830 only a fifth had any connection with either the gentry or the peerage. The Church might be an appropriate career for the high-born, but that does not mean that they were lacking in either vocation or pastoral diligence. What emerges clearly from a study of a sample of 25 per cent of the clergy of the diocese of London in 1714–1800 is that the Church actually recruited from all classes, from the gentry to the plebeian. It drew its workforce particularly from 'the sons of professional people – doctors, lawyers, merchants and traders, who lived in towns – sometimes called "pseudo-gentry", whose wealth and respectability earned them the status of gentlemen or even esquires, but who could not on any account be classified as country squires'.[9] Of the sample, 35.4 per cent were sons of the clergy, and although that proportion dropped to 19 per cent after 1781, it is a clear indication of the establishment of clerical 'dynasties'.

By 1850 the glittering prizes were looking tarnished, and Parson Woodforde decidedly less well-fed. The median income of a parish priest in 1830 was £275, and witnesses before a parliamentary commission in the mid-1850s considered £300–£500 to be a suitable income for an incumbent. Contemporary commentators assumed £100–£150 to be sufficient for a curate. That was wildly utopian in the 1850s and 1860s. In 1854 Conybeare discovered that only 1,174 livings were worth more than £500, and 8,000 were worth less than £300. The average salary of a curate was under £100. In other words, an upper-middle-class income was deemed appropriate for the clergy to do their work well and not to have to rely on other sources of income like teaching and farming. The Church provided a comfortable way of life for the fortunate, but it was scarcely a route to riches, and for many the poverty line was always in sight.[10] Clerical poverty was rightly perceived to be the enemy of pastoral efficiency, and Victorian politicians and church leaders were continually occupied in measures to redistribute the wealth of the Church that it might be assuaged.

Revisionist studies of the Georgian church suggest that, far from being idle time-servers, the parochial clergy strove to deliver a coherent pastoral service to their parishes. A reading of their Victorian critics reveals more about their expectations than the reality of life in the Georgian church – what had changed was the balance of expectation and response. The Georgian church was not 'worse' than the late-nineteenth-century church, it was different.[11] Charges of a decline in vocation are difficult to sustain within the Church of England, and even more so within the more straitened economic circumstances of the Dissenting communities.

Kenneth Brown's analysis of the social origins of the Nonconformist ministry between 1800 and 1930 shows that the bulk of its nineteenth-century ministry was predictably drawn from what Clyde Binfield termed families 'poised uncomfortably between the middle and lower classes' – white-collar workers, teachers, clerks and shop assistants. It is almost impossible to arrive at a mean figure for the income of Nonconformist ministers in the nineteenth century – the prescribed minimum for Wesleyans was £150 for a married man, but roughly a third of circuits were paying below that. Congregationalists and Baptists operated within a market economy. The great names in wealthy chapels commanded large stipends; their brothers in small congregations lived within continual sight of the poverty line. In 1830 the Congregationalists reckoned an average salary to be around £100 at a time when an Anglican median salary was £300. One point of striking similarity with Anglican figures is that a growing percentage were the sons of ministers.[12]

All professions in the nineteenth century showed a tendency to self-recruit from the sons of existing members. The clergy were no exception. The children of the clergy know better than most the financial and spiritual disciplines of vocational living, yet despite that they still offered themselves. Such evidence may, of course, be interpreted in many ways. It may show lack of imagination, or the attractions of a largely self-determined lifestyle. It may equally be evidence of vocation. What is surprising is not that the proportion of sons of the clergy within the workforce of all denominations showed a marked decline by the beginning of the twentieth century, but that it survived so long.

The classical Protestant dual requirement of godly lives and a solid theological education had not entirely disappeared during the eighteenth century, despite the much-vaunted shortcomings of the English universities which served as seminaries for the Church of England.[13] Anglican and Dissenting ordaining authorities still looked for evidence of godly lives. The proliferation of Dissenting academies, some of which were at the cutting edge of educational innovation, others of which were shoddy and poor affairs, is clear evidence of the value Dissenters placed on an educated ministry in the years following their exclusion from the universities.[14] The expansion of theological education and the 'new professionalism' of the Victorian Anglican and Dissenting clergy needs to be seen in a longer and broader context. Rosemary O'Day is surely correct when she argues that the clergy emerged as a professional group in the wake of the Reformation.[15] Indeed, one might go further and argue that they appeared as a professional group *because* of the Reformation. What changed in Victorian England was not the clergy's perception of their task – preaching, the conduct of worship, the exercise of pastoral discipline and pastoral care remain constant preoccupations in practical theological literature from Luther onwards. The legacy of the Reformation in pastoral care – preaching, education, discipline and guidance – began to be worked out in new forms.

Preaching ministry experienced a renaissance. The Victorian years were the golden age of the preacher. This was the era of words, of serial novels, of an endless procession of newspapers and journals, of educational explosion. The power of the pulpit reached new heights. Books of sermons poured from the presses – Joseph Parker of the City Temple once remarked that the back row of the City Temple reached to the Rockies. Published sermons were but the tip of an iceberg whose base was each church and chapel in the land. The territory of the preacher had shrunk.

As the liberal Anglican F. W. Robertson of Brighton protested, 'Once [the pulpit] was newspaper, schoolmaster, theological treatise, a stimulant to good works, historical lecture, metaphysics etc. all in one. Now they are portioned out to different officers, and the pulpit is no more the pulpit of three centuries back, than the authority of a master of a household is that of Abraham, who was soldier, butcher, sacrificer, shepherd and emir in one person.'[16] Active Victorian Christians (still some 40 per cent of the population) relished sermons. Sunday was not complete without at least one, and preferably two. Sermon-tasting was a delight as well as a duty, and in the large cities of the land the opportunity for 'sermon-tasting' was almost unlimited. Between 1855 and 1867 Edward Clodd, a Baptist bank clerk in London, recorded his impressions of preachers as varied as the Congregationalists Thomas Binney, Newman Hall, and Rowland Hill, and the Unitarian James Martineau. His diet was varied with sorties to hear F. D. Maurice at Lincoln's Inn, Dean Stanley at Westminster Abbey and Canon Liddon at St Paul's. Clearly the line between pulpit and theatre was a fine one, but that does not mean that preaching was not in essence a pastoral activity. Even in the great pulpits Victorian preachers are notable for their topicality, for their engagement with the flux of politics, the dilemmas of discipleship and the realities of doubt. That needs to be set against their unashamed play on the emotions which is so distasteful to modern ears yet so much in tune with the emotional register of a generation which wept at the death of Little Nell.

Victorian spirituality was formed in large measure by the sermon, and that was not limited to the worlds of Evangelicals and Dissenters. When he was vicar, Newman's sermons electrified the congregation of the University Church at Oxford, and in their published form were amongst the most widely read as well as being exquisite examples of Victorian prose. A glance at the sermons of Newman and Liddon shows that the Catholic revival in the Church of England was not carried out at the expense of the pulpit. Lay people were by no means limited to passive involvement. They read huge quantities on quiet sabbath afternoons, and they could be discerning critics. In 1844, 29 parishioners complained about the Calvinistic preaching of their vicar in High Wycombe – 'If you could my dear Sir, simply set forth the love of God instead of his election, how very acceptable it would be.'[17]

Fifty years later, as the sea of faith ebbed noisily on Dover beach, R. W. Dale, the great Birmingham Congregationalist, preached at the induction of a new minister at Chorlton Road Congregational Chapel in

Manchester on 3 November 1890. The published sermon was greatly extended, but it shows what Dale expected of the relationship between preacher and an able suburban congregation. He expected frank acknowledgement of intellectual revolution of the previous fifty years, and encouragement to draw new theological maps –

> To people who have never had, or who have lost, the faculty of clear thinking, and to people who will not take the trouble to think, an instructive preacher will sometimes be dull; let your minister know that you like him to be dull in that way – at least now and then. Encourage him to respect the rights of the intellect; do not ask him always to preach sermons which will be understood by everybody, and understood without effort. As long as men are unwilling to serve God with their understanding, they withhold from him half his claims.[18]

If he expected the minister to be honest and open about theological and biblical debate (and he did), he expected him also 'to speak of Christ that you may know for yourselves that He who died is alive again and liveth for evermore ... that you may be able to bear witness, on the strength of your own experience, that He has come to the Church, and that He abides with it for ever'. Most of all, however (and it is a recurrent them in Dale's writings), he expected minister and people to create a new way of civic discipleship. He threw down the gauntlet –

> The Christian ideal of life and conduct in this present century – what is it? The Christian ideal of the exchange, in the mill, in the workshop, in the counting-house, in Parliament, in the City Council, in the home – what is it? The Christian ideal for the employer, the Christian ideal for the employed – what is it? The old ways are out of repair, going to ruin; it is time to make straight paths for our feet.[19]

If the timbre of such a sermon typifies the Reformation heritage of a liberal Congregationalism tempered by the intellectual realities of a world post-Darwin and *Essays and Reviews*, its blend of theological thoughtfulness and social responsibility was echoed in the pastoral patterning of urban Anglicanism. William Cadman's managerial strategy for St George's Southwark, and his passion for sanitary improvement in its slum courts, and Harry Jones's poking into the drains, ashpits and water-tanks around St Luke's, Berwick Street, in the 1860s, exhibited the same perception that the gospel should actually change things.[20]

The ministry of the pulpit flowed naturally into education and instruction, in two ways. The work of Christian instruction within the Church remained a high priority. Victorian pastoral handbooks all stress the importance of preparing confirmands. Such work was time-consuming and demanding, yet essential, and it was done in parish churches and Dissenting chapels across the land. Public education also commanded the attention of Victorian clergy, from the work of Sunday Schools and the cascade of public lectures with lantern slides on every conceivable subject which was part of the armoury of every 'institutional' church to the national political battleground of the public provision of education. That was the site of the last great set-piece skirmish between the conflicting cultures of Establishment and Dissent in 1902, but it is evidence in itself of the enduring importance of the Reformation ideal of pastor as educator.

The exercise of discipline had largely fallen into disrepair by the beginning of the nineteenth century. The state church was viewed as a bulwark against subversion, and although the new 'professionalizing' of the clergy meant that an increasing number of clergy were reluctant to stand as county justices, the old spectre of social control still lurked in the shadows. The clergy, R. W. Evans, the vicar of Heversham in Westmorland, maintained in 1842, 'will be the mainspring of the police of his parish, but like the mainspring of a watch, it will not be seen'.[21] The maintenance of good order within the community remained a clerical responsibility, although by the end of the century when even bishops lent their weight to the London Dock Strike, stability and good order was no longer defined by siding with the establishment. Admonishing the faithful was transformed into urging them to create a just society. 'There may be morality where there is no religion', mused R. W. Dale in his Lyman Beecher lectures at Yale in 1878, 'but that there should be religion where there is no morality, is impossible. The moral law is the law of God. It is therefore just as much our duty to illustrate and enforce the obligations of morality as to insist on the necessity of believing the gospel.'[22]

Ministry to individuals remained a distinct part of a minister's life in the nineteenth century, and pastoral theologians show themselves to be consciously within the established tradition of 'soul-doctoring'. It was a part of pastoral care to which the Tractarians felt an especial attraction, but it was not absent from any tradition. An anonymous article in the High Church *Christian Remembrancer* in 1845 argued for a differentiation in pastoral care which would have been familiar to the great exponents of practical divinity of early ages. The clergyman should 'obtain the same intimate acquaintance with the souls of individuals which the physician obtains of their bodies'. Close attention to the detail of daily living, acute observation, a patient attitude, a knowledge of casuistry, as well as a good dose of Christian common sense, are the essentials of such a ministry. The pastor will only be truly effective once he 'knows' his parish intimately.[23] Systematic house-to-house visiting remained the basis of this part of the pastor's craft, even in large urban parishes where techniques of subdivision or multiple staffing were employed to enable it to happen. Care of the sick and preparation of the dying remained essential.

A comparison of two works of pastoral theology by English Presbyterian theologians, published in 1896 and 1908 respectively, shows how the old traditions of practical theology maintained their validity while being translated into a new, more scientific approach to the discipline. John Watson had a remarkable ministry at Sefton Park Presbyterian Church, Liverpool, distinguished both for the quality of his preaching and the texture of his pastoral care. Better known to contemporaries by his *nom de plume*, 'Ian MacLaren', he was the author of the surprise best-seller *Beside the Bonnie Briar Bush*, gentle tales of Scottish church life first published in the *British Weekly* under Robertson Nicholl's guidance in 1893. Three years later he gave the Lyman Beecher lectures on preaching at Yale. In his lecture on 'The work of a pastor' he extolled Baxter's *Reformed Pastor* and Herbert's *A priest to the Temple* for their 'depth of piety' and 'sweetness of spirit' and likened the work of the pastor to the physician's. He distinguished visitation from consultation. Visitation was empathetic attention to the ebb and flow of individual lives. 'Before evening [after a day's visiting] he has been a father, a mother, a husband, a wife, a child, a friend; he has been young, middle-aged, old, lifted up, cast down, a sinner, a saint, all sorts and conditions of life.'[24] It was structured, careful, meticulously recorded, exhausting work.[25] Consultation he regarded as a Presbyterian form of the confessional, initiated by the parishioner, and he urges care and discrimination in 'the diagnosis and treatment of spiritual diseases'. The 'honest sceptic' is not to be treated as one who rejects Christ out of 'intellectual pride'. The rich young man 'fighting the flesh with all his might' needs different counsel to the one who 'is feeding his imagination with evil books, and preparing for the sin into which he falls'. This is innate rather than scientific psychology, yet it stands in an honourable tradition which reaches back to Gregory the Great.

Watson would never have claimed to be a theologian, but his friend and colleague Oswald Dykes was. The first Principal of Westminster College in its Cambridge days, Dykes was a Presbyterian systematician of distinction. His *The Christian Minister and his Duties*, based on college lectures, shows how the pragmatic tradition of pastoral care which Watson exemplified was being transformed into a new theological discipline. He is acutely aware of the need for new patterns of pastoral visitation as ministers encounter a multiplying diversity of socio-cultural patterns, yet he remains convinced of the centrality of 'vigilant oversight, guidance in the Divine life, and brotherly counsel'. He traces its evolution from Gregory ('not even yet, I understand, antiquated in Roman Catholic seminaries') and through the literature of the Reformation. He notes that the care of souls became subsumed in Protestantism into 'pastoral theology', a subject dominated by preaching, before subdividing again in the last century. Now, 'continental authorities at least have agreed ... to restrict the name of Pastoral Theology to such functions as are not discharged in public assemblies nor designed for the congregation as a whole, but are directed to the individuals, whether singly or in groups, of whom it is composed'. His footnote recognizes Achelis' use of the name 'Poimenik' (the science of shepherding).[26]

The native British tradition of 'practical divinity' was at last feeling the effects of the weight of continental writings. Emerging social and psychological sciences were changing the nature of pastoral theology, and as they did so the tradition which can be traced from the Reformation through Perkins, Baxter, Burnet and the writers of early Victorian handbooks of pastoral theology was submerged. They still determined the actual practice of the clergy – Watson was typical, not unique – because the Reformation legacy had become the *modus vivendi* of the churches. It is interesting that the explosion of theological education in nineteenth-century England, driven by the need for more clergy and the 'professionalizing' agenda did not lead to a multiplication of posts in pastoral theology.

The universities took seriously pressure from the Church of England for reform. From 1842 Oxford had a Regius Professor of Pastoral Theology, charged with giving 'instruction in Ministerial duties, composition and the delivery of sermons, Knowledge of and History of the Liturgy, Rubrics and the like'. In Cambridge J. J. Blunt, the Lady

Margaret's Professor (1839–55) lectured on the theory of parish work, covering such subjects as clerical reading, sermons, school management, pastoral visiting and advice about rubrics and canons. Clement Rogers held a chair of liturgical and pastoral theology in the theology department of King's College, London, from 1854. This was the Reformation tradition turned into 'hints and tips' – and it was none the worse for that. Practical experience and the attaining of professional skills were insisted upon, but always as a secondary matter. The acquisition of technical theological competence took priority, even in non-graduate institutions which often simply tried to adopt the ways of the ancient universities.[27]

Elsewhere, as Dykes knew, things were different. Schleiermacher's *A Brief Outline of the Study of Theology* (1811) had attempted to place theology on a new scientific footing. His division of theological studies into three categories – the philosophical, the historical and the practical, 'root', 'body' and 'crown' was a departure from tradition. His insistence that the validity of theoretical understandings of Christianity stood or fell by Christian experience and living prepared the way for a new understanding of 'practical divinity' which was to bear fruit in America, and then in Britain.[28] The publication of an English translation of J. J. van Osterzee's *Practical Theology* in 1878 was a landmark, for it was the first attempt to treat pastoral theology as a science, acknowledging elementary pastoral psychology.[29]

Yet the new world which Dykes had discerned failed to make much impact on British pastoral theology and education in the early twentieth century.[30] The settlement movement made some theological teachers more aware of the need for a measure of sociology to be included in the syllabus. New College, Edinburgh, was one of the first to appreciate the value of supervised fieldwork and a constant dialogue between the social sciences and ministerial studies, formally adopting sociology into the curriculum in 1921. They were building on the pioneering work of A. H. Charteris, who in 1870 persuaded the presbytery of Edinburgh to let him take on the lapsed parish of the Tolbooth and run it with a succession of student assistants working under his guidance. The students involved were expected to keep detailed records and to meet with him fortnightly to discuss cases. He called it 'clinical divinity'.[31] This was distinctive and unusual, and it owes not a little to the fact that theology was a postgraduate subject in Scotland and constituted professional training in itself.

English theological education developed from different roots; from Oxbridge, the perception of bishops about the need for spiritual nurture and missionary engagement, and the traditions of the Dissenting academies. There was a serious continuity between the 'practical' theologies of Baxter and Burnet and the development of 'professional' clergy-training in the nineteenth century. Part of that continuity was a fierce resistance to specialization. Indeed, practical, applied, or pastoral theology arrived late on the scene, often seriously resisted, for the good, holistic reason that theology is theology, a unified rather than a divided discipline whose cutting-edge has to do with Christian experience. One of Dykes's successors as principal of Westminster was John Oman, the finest of British liberal theologians and a translator of Schleiermacher. Few have written of the relationship between the religious quest and the human personality with more insight and subtlety than Oman. Nonetheless, his one book on ministry, *Concerning the Ministry* (1936), a series of fireside talks to ordinands rather than a systematic treatise, is tellingly silent on the new sciences of sociology and psychology. It is hard to imagine the word 'poimenics' flowing from his pen.

Ministry to individuals still remains a fundamental part of the life of the Christian community, despite its contraction in the twentieth century. It was American pastoral theologians who first realized the potential of the new range of psychological and psychiatric disciplines that rose to prominence in Europe and America in the early twentieth century, and they sought to enter a constructive dialogue with these new disciplines. Working pastors quickly grasped the value of the insights of the social sciences for their work. The roll-call of networks and institutions devoted to exploring the relationship between theology and modern psychologies is impressive: the Emmanuel Movement in Boston in 1906, the religion and health movement in the USA, the development of Clinical Pastoral Education in the 1930s and the wholesale rise of counselling and Rogerian therapy in the 1940s.

That is not to suggest that it did not have an effect in England. It did, especially among the clergy. Geoffrey Studdert-Kennedy, First World War chaplain *par excellence*, caught the fascinations and limitations of the new discipline with characteristic wit:

> The manifold tempations,
> Wherewith the flesh can vex
> The saintly soul, are samples
> Of Oedipus complex.
> The subtle sex perversion,

> His eagle glance can tell.
> That makes their joyous heaven
> The horror of their hell.
> His reasoning is perfect,
> His proofs as plain as paint.
> He has but one small weakness.
> He cannot make a saint.[32]

The First World War heightened awareness of abnormal psychologies, and that in turn lent interest to the new discipline. Leslie Weatherhead's experiences as a chaplain deepened his interests in the subject. Like many Free-Church ministers he found the writings of the Congregationalist minister turned psychologist J. A. Hadfield particularly impressive. He applied his new knowledge to his pastorates in Manchester and Leeds; and during his famous ministry at the City Temple in the 1950s provided a model of how ministry and psychology might be integrated. His writings, particularly *Psychology, Religion and Healing*, were to have widespread influence and encouraged many to exploit the possibilities of psychology in ministry to individuals.[33]

It was, however, American theologians who most interested themselves in exploring the relationship between psychology and religion. Notable amongst them was Paul Tillich, whose interests in psychology and work with the New York Psychology Group led him to original and creative work at the interface between psychology and Protestant theology. Tillich always remained a theologian. Some question whether the conversation between theology and the human sciences was actually a conversation, or whether theology entered into a Babylonian captivity at the hands of the psychological disciplines. During the 1960s Evangelicals like Wayne Oates and Jay Adams, neo-orthodox Barthians like Eduard Thurneysen, and the founder of the Clinical Theology Association, Frank Lake, all in differing ways began to ask about the place of Scripture and tradition within the discipline. Thomas Oden's life and research are an interesting barometer of changing moods. From the 1950s to the 1970s he was at the forefront of the use of varying models of psychology and psychotherapy in pastoral care, but eventually disillusionment set in. Part of the cause was academic research in his own field, proving that psychotherapy's cure rate was about 65–70 per cent, which is roughly the same as that which appears through the normal passage of time.[34] Part was his lifelong passion for Kierkegaard, whose analytical insights he eventually considered to surpass those of Freud and the post-Freudians.[35] Part was his own reading of the Christian tradition and research into the way nineteenth- and twentieth-century pastoral theologians used the tradition. Cyprian, Tertullian, Chrysostom, Augustine, Gregory, Luther, Calvin, Baxter, Herbert and Taylor (his chosen sample) had simply disappeared from view in the works of Hiltner, Clinebell, Oates, Wise, Tournier, Stollenberg and Nuttin, whereas they had been abundantly present in his representative sample of nineteenth-century writers.

The subject, he suggested, had lost its identity. This was part of the Church's critical loss of confidence in its own insights. He quoted one therapist, Paul Pruyser, who had spent a lot of time in dialogue with clergy:

> 'I became aware that much of the instruction was one-sided, with the consent of both parties: the theologians sat at the feet of the psychiatric Gamaliels and seemed to like it. Pastors were eager to absorb as much psychological knowledge and skill as they could, without even thinking about instructional reciprocity ... I have learned that ministers would be hard put to know what to teach, from their own discipline, to members of the psychological professions even if they were specifically asked and salaried to do so.'[36]

Oden's intellectual journey exemplifies the dilemmas of the Protestant legacy of pastoral care. The combination of the centrality of preaching, the exercise of discipline and the pragmatic tradition of ministry to individuals determined the work of the clergy and the life of the laity well into the twentieth century, and in many congregations continues to do so.[37] Whatever the continuities of life at parochial level, however, the dislocations and uncertainties brought about by the collapse of the modernist synthesis, the crisis of confidence in science and the evolution of intellectual and ethical pluralism, have all taken their toll. The model of 'captivity' and 'liberation' is too simple to explain the complex history of pastoral care in the late twentieth century, and yet it contains an element of truth. Ministry to individuals would be much the poorer without the insights and resources of the range of psychological and psychiatric disciplines. Yet it would be equally impoverished without the resources of the Christian tradition, the sacraments of the Church and the healing presence of God known in Jesus Christ.

The 'science' of pastoral care which Dykes saw emerging in 1908, and which made such an impact in America, has only recently become part of the English theological spectrum. As Paul Ballard has pointed out, the growth of pastoral theology (in this specialized sense rather than in its more generalized nineteenth-century form) as a discipline in England was in large part a reaction to the growth of social sciences. The first university posts in the subject were not established until 1964.[38] The scope and methodologies appropriate to it are the subject of energetic debate.[39] Wesley Carr, although acutely aware of the difficulties of definition suggests that

> The concept of pastoral theology ... implies that its study encompasses normal human life, not simply crises or even abnormality. It links studies, such as counselling, with traditional skills, such as confession and absolution, spiritual direction, evangelism and sacramental theology.[40]

Luther would have recognized that starting-point, and rejoiced in it.

Notes

1. A point well made by Francis Knight, *The Nineteenth Century Church and English Society* (Cambridge, 1995), p. 24.
2. Michael MacDonald, 'Religion, social change and psychological healing in England 1600–1800' in W. J. Shiels (ed.), *The Church and Healing,* Studies in Church History, 19 (Oxford, 1982), pp. 101–25.
3. MacDonald, 'Religion'.
4. William A. Clebsch and Charles R. Jaeckle, *Pastoral Care in Historical Perspective* (New York, 1964), pp. 28–30.
5. E. G. Rupp, *Religion in England 1688–1791* (Oxford, 1986), pp. 389–91; Barrie Tabraham, *The Making of Methodism* (London, 1995), p. 47.
6. Knight, *Nineteenth Century Church,* pp. 201–3.
7. Brian Heeney, *A Different Kind of Gentleman: Parish Clergy as Professional Men in Early Victorian England* (Hamden, Conn., 1976), following Philip Elliott, *The Sociology of the Professions* (London, 1972).
8. Ibid., pp. 35–64
9. Viviane Barrie-Curien, 'The clergy in the diocese of London in the eighteenth century', in John Walsh, Stephen Taylor and Colin Haydon (eds), *The Church of England c.1689–c.1833: From Toleration to Tractarianism* (Cambridge, 1993), pp. 86–110, p. 89.
10. Rosemary O'Day, 'The clerical renaissance in Victorian England and Wales', in Gerald Parsons (ed.), *Religion in Victorian Britain,* vol. 1: *Traditions*

(Manchester, 1988), pp. 184–212, pp. 199–200; Heeney, *Different Kind of Gentleman*, p. 28.
11. See particularly Peter Virgin, *The Church in an Age of Negligence* (Cambridge, 1989), and Walsh *et al.*, *Church of England*.
12. Kenneth D. Brown, *A Social History of the Nonconformist Ministry in England and Wales 1800–1930* (Oxford, 1988), pp. 19–55, quotation from Binfield at p. 39.
13. Much vaunted, and possibly exaggerated – *see* Peter Searby, *A History of the University of Cambridge 1750–1870* (Cambridge, 1997), pp. 265–8 for at least one case where the 'unreformed' system worked admirably.
14. For the Dissenting academies see H. McLachlan, *English Education under the Test Acts* (Manchester, 1931); Michael Watts, *The Dissenters: From the Reformation to the French Revolution* (Oxford, 1978), pp. 366–71.
15. O'Day, 'Clerical renaissance', p. 187.
16. Quoted in Horton Davies, *Worship and Theology in England,* vol. 4: *From Newman to Martineau 1850–1900* (Princeton, 1962), p. 282.
17. Quoted in Knight, *Nineteenth Century Church,* p. 83.
18. R. W. Dale, 'The ministry required by the age', in *Fellowship with Christ* (London, 1891), pp. 247–77, p. 266.
19. Ibid., p. 276; for the context of such preaching see David M. Thompson, 'R. W. Dale and the "Civic Gospel"', in Alan Sell (ed.), *Protestant Nonconformity and the West Midlands of England* (Keele, 1996), pp. 99–119.
20. Heeney, *Different Kind of Gentleman,* p. 78.
21. Ibid., p. 66.
22. R. W. Dale, *Nine Lectures on Preaching* (London, 1878), p. 243.
23. Heeney, *Different Kind of Gentleman,* p. 49.
24. John Watson, *The Cure of Souls* (London, 1896), p. 183.
25. For his systematic approach to visiting, and examples of his counsel in letters, see W. Robertson Nicholl, *'Ian Maclaren' Life of the Rev John Wartson* D D (London, 1908), pp. 117–39.
26. J. Oswald Dykes, *The Christian Minister and his Duties* (Edinburgh, 1908), pp. 307–8.
27. David Dowland, *Nineteenth Century Anglican Theological Training: The Red-Brick Challenge* (Oxford, 1997), pp. 184–5.
28. Elaine Graham, *Transforming Practice* (London, 1996), p. 59–61.
29. Derek Tidball, *Skilful Shepherds: An Introduction to Pastoral Theology* (Leicester, 1986), pp. 214–19.
30. Ibid., p. 223.
31. David Lyall, 'Christian ethics and pastoral theology', in David Wright and Gary Baldock (eds), *Disruption and Diversity: Edinburgh Divinity 1846–1996* (Edinburgh, 1996), pp. 135–51.
32. G. A. Studdert-Kennedy, 'The psycholgist', in *The Unutterable Beauty* (London, 1927; pbk edn 1964), p. 107–8, quoted by Stuart Mews, 'The revival of spiritual healing in the Church of England 1920–26, in Shiels, *Church and Healing,* pp. 299–331.
33. Mews, 'Revival of spiritual healing', p. 318.

34. Thomas Oden, *Care of Souls in the Classical Tradition* (Philadelphia, 1984), p. 34.
35. Ibid., p. 24.
36. Ibid., p. 36.
37. For a telling example of the continuity of this tradition in a group of rural parishes, see Ronald Blythe, *Word from Wormingford* (London, 1997).
38. Paul Ballard, 'The emergence of pastoral studies', in Paul Ballard (ed.), *The Foundations of Pastoral Studies and Practical Theology* (*Holi* 4) (Cardiff, 1986), pp. 9–17.
39. See, for example, Wesley Carr, *Handbook of Pastoral Studies* (London, 1997); Graham, *Transforming Practice* for a feminist perspective, and the collected papers in Adrian M. Visscher (ed.), *Pastoral Studies in the University Setting* (Ottawa, 1988).
40. Carr, *Handbook of Pastoral Studies*, p. 21.

Bibliography

Paul Ballard, 'The emergence of pastoral studies', in Paul Ballard (ed.), *The Foundations of Pastoral Studies and Practical Theology* (*Holi* 4) (Cardiff, 1986), pp. 9–17

Kenneth Brown, *A Social History of the Nonconformist Ministry in England and Wales 1800–1930* (Oxford, 1988)

William A. Clebsch and Charles R. Jaeckle, *Pastoral Care in Historical Perspective* (New York, 1964)

Elaine Graham, *Transforming Practice* (London, 1996)

Brian Heeney, *A Different Kind of Gentleman: Parish Clergy as Professional Men in Early Victorian Britain* (Hamden, Conn., 1976)

Francis Knight, *The Nineteenth Century Church and English Society* (Cambridge, 1995)

J. T. McNeill, *A History of the Cure of Souls* (New York, 1951)

Thomas Oden, *Care of Souls in the Classical Tradition* (Philadelphia, 1984)

Derek Tidball, *Skilful Shepherds: An Introduction to Pastoral Theology* (Leicester, 1986)

PART V

The Modern World

19

Pastoral care at the end of the twentieth century

Ian Bunting

Pastoral care in the twentieth-century West has been an area in which the Church's ministry has been called into question by secular professionals. It has increasingly become a field for the exercise of professional expertise. The churches have struggled to respond appropriately.

Over the space of a hundred years, the secularization of institutional provision for care, schools and hospitals for instance, has led to a diminishing role for the churches. The explosion of knowledge about healthcare, and the widespread and popular dissemination of it, has enabled people to challenge established authorities, including the churches, for themselves. The decline in the number of professional clergy and the rapid increase of lay involvement in the Church's ministry has eroded confidence in traditional pastoral ministry of the authoritarian clerical sort, exercised in an amateur way. Above all, a greater understanding of the psychodynamics of both persons and groups has led to the development of the counselling movement.

In the mid-twentieth century, the theory and practice of pastoral counselling began to dominate the pastoral training of Christian clergy. However, the response to it was not uniform. We can trace two diverging paths. On the one hand, some pastors sought a greater knowledge of secular disciplines and skills for a therapeutic specialism which demanded recognized qualifications and professional accreditation. On the other hand, some became suspicious of disciplines which focused too much on the introspective tendencies of individuals in need. They affirmed a more societal approach to pastoral care. They believed the focus on the individual lacked a sharp theological critique and ran a further danger – it failed to recognize the long Christian tradition of care in the community, and the more managerial skills required to enable it to happen. Moreover, frequently they judged that pastoral counselling and its sister discipline, spiritual direction, did not adequately acknowledge those causes of pain which were closely associated with what were now being seen as oppressive structures in society at large. The gospel is liberating, and the freedom it brings is both individual and corporate. It affects people in their personal relationships, and together as communities of hope in the secular world as we experience it today.

In this chapter we shall look at three dimensions of the Church's pastoral care during the twentieth century: pastoral counselling, spiritual direction and 'care in the community'. It is not strictly a sequential survey. But, within each of these three movements, four tensions emerge and are critical for understanding the development of pastoral care in the modern period. The first tension lies in the focus on the individual on the one hand and the community on the other. The second lies between the directive and the non-directive approaches to pastoral care. The third lies between the contribution of professional expertise and the contribution of a lay church caring locally and mutually through the ministry of natural carers or amateurs. The fourth tension, linked with the other three, lies between the hierarchical and the companionship models of pastoral care in the Church. These four tensions run through the history of pastoral care in the twentieth century and the three principal movements. They are interwoven in what follows in this chapter.

It will become clear to the reader that this contributor locates innovative practice in pastoral care in the twentieth century largely within the United States. From the early years it was in America that psychological theories first captured ordinary people's imaginations in a new way, and most applications were developed. But that is not the whole story. Much of the theological inspiration for what happened in a Christian context came from theologians who were nurtured in a European climate, and therefore lived significantly near some of the traumatic sorrows which have afflicted the world, including two world wars, the fallout from ethnic cleansing and the use of weapons of mass destruction.

Towards the end of the century even more radical notes of protest, not least at the shortcomings of the Christian churches, began to make themselves heard. Movements among the poor, the oppressed, the overlooked and minorities who suffered from discrimination, usually in the developing world, gained sufficient confidence to make their voices heard further afield.

At the same time in the 'comfortable' world, the pain and frustrations of people in their search for relief from unbearable stress, and for meaning and happiness, has been undiminished and their needs met by a range of therapies and spiritualities. Some of these have posed questions about the nature of the gospel. Some present an ongoing challenge to a Christian approach to healing and wholeness.

The churches therefore find themselves facing a dilemma when it comes to discerning the way ahead in their continuing concern to provide Christian pastoral care. To that challenge we shall return below, after we have reviewed the three movements of the churches' pastoral care in the modern period and reflected on some of the lessons we may learn from the tensions within them.

Pastoral care

[Pastoral care is] any form of personal ministry to individuals and to family and community relationships by representative religious persons (ordained and lay) and by their communities of faith, who understand and guide their caring efforts out of a theological perspective rooted in a tradition of faith.[1]

Whether we believe the modern period began in the sixteenth or the eighteenth century it took many years for the distinctive field of study we know as pastoral theology to emerge. Following the Reformation, the old role of the priest in the Catholic tradition was taken over by the new role of the presbyter in the Protestant world. The old sacramental priestly task, individually applied in the confessional, led naturally into the new preaching task of the minister who was now seen as a master of the Word of God. He was public preacher to the flock of God and skilled shepherd to each member of it. George Herbert (1593–1633), who wrote *The Country Parson* (1632), and Richard Baxter (1615–91), who wrote *The Reformed Pastor* (1656), remain the model pastoral theologians of the post-Reformation period, and their books the classic texts.

However, the rate of change accelerated. The invention of printing, and the increasing dissemination of the Scriptures in the vernacular, led inevitably to a growing awareness of persons as individuals. They, for their part, saw themselves as complementing the revelation of God, objectively given in the written word, as they received the living Word for themselves personally and inwardly. The light and truth shone in their hearts and minds. The task of the preacher was therefore to enable this personal revelation to happen, not only by preaching publicly in church but also by visiting church members privately in their homes, to help them grown into spiritual maturity in the particular circumstances of their families, and as individuals.

For example, we can seen the change in pastoral practice in relation to death and dying in the modern period. In the mediaeval period the funeral rites, and the Masses which followed, were thought objectively to benefit the deceased in the afterlife. In the post-Reformation era the pastoral concern of the reformers tended to fall upon the need for the living survivors to 'die well'. A heated debate ensued about whether the funeral rites benefited the dead at all.

In short, the bond between Church, community and the faith of the individual within a coherent and general world-view, which accepted the close link between the worlds of the living and the dead, was more and more called into question. Pastors and their people interpreted the faith for themselves as individuals and groups, and gathered together in increasingly discrete communities with their own particular slant on the Christian story.

As a consequence, it is hardly surprising to find Friedrich Schleiermacher (1768–1834), with his strong emphasis upon feeling as the basis of religion, reacting to unifying orthodoxies, and rationalism, by advocating the study of the actual practice of the Christian faith. For him, practical theology was a particular discipline within the overall theological project or, as he put it, 'the method of the maintaining and perfecting of the church'.[2]

This view has until quite recently dominated the theory and practice of pastoral theology. It has been clergy oriented, church focused and within a pastoral mode which has tended to draw a line, for example, between the healing of the 'soul' and the more 'mechanical' concerns of the medical professions.

Pastoral care and counselling

[Pastoral Counselling is] 'a more specialised and structured form of religiously based care, distinguished by its degree of contractual formality (a helping contract or covenant between the parties) and by the special expertise of the helping person'.[3]

In the early part of the twentieth century the role of the pastor as shepherd began to yield its biblical underpinning, theological foundation and its developed church orientation to the more secular rationale of the psychological sciences. It was a critical period for the Church because an inherited theological framework of sin, judgement and redemption leading to salvation was influenced by humanistic concerns which required a diminished theological base and a different goal, not now of salvation from sin but of personal responsibility and self-actualization or self-fulfilment. This shift in emphasis resonated with the spirit of the age with which the century became increasingly familiar. For example, today most people tend to seek help not because they 'feel bad', but because they 'do not feel good'. Often, they are not so much feeling guilty as wounded. Whereas in the past a sin or misdemeanour would have led the culprit to seek a confessor or a spiritual director of the old school, more usually in our generation the resource to which they turn is a doctor, or a non-directive counsellor, or possibly to a spiritual director who acts like a soul friend, a companion on the road to recovery.

Perhaps the most important single theologian to contribute a theoretical underpinning to the pastoral counselling movement in the generation following the Second World War was Paul Tillich (1886–1965). He believed that it was important to correlate a modern philosophical and psychological analysis of existence with the Christian gospel. Having studied psychiatric theory, he recognized the coherence between psychological language and traditional theological concepts. Consequently, for example in his book *Courage to Be* (1952), he was able to relate the idea of unconditional acceptance with the doctrine of justification in such a way as to bring a liberating insight into human experiences of guilt, anxiety, freedom and courage.

Since then the therapeutic goal of wholeness, along with the secular practice of clinical care, has come to dominate the character of the Church's pastoral care for individuals, and groups. Today, in the developed world, when people are feeling distressed they will usually seek help from the doctor or therapist before the priest or church pastor. The source of the problem may well then be located in a hurt, perhaps in some abuse suffered in childhood or in another person injuring them. Moreover, if such persons do turn to the Church for help, in most cases it will be to meet an approach and skills which church workers, even the more conservative among them, have adapted or related to one or other of the contemporary schools of therapy or counselling.

In the twentieth century, the shepherding model of pastoral care with its focus on case study, clinical care and one-to-one counselling proved a particularly popular and useful way of looking at the task of helping the individual to face personal frustration, anger and disappointment, and to grow through it. However, some now believe the pastoral counselling movement has not always been able adequately to integrate the theology and practice of pastoral care so as to do justice both to Christian doctrine and to a psychological understanding of human beings.

It does nevertheless still have many proponents who look back with confidence to the biblical understanding of the living Christ who is the shepherd and guardian of our souls (1 Peter 2.25). So, for example, in Britain the Clinical Theology Association founded in 1962, although nowhere near as strong as it was, still found in 1997 the shepherd model of pastoral care a useful way of combining three ingredients of good pastoral practice; (1) a faith community that is rooted in traditional wisdom, but is enriched by the behavioural sciences; (2) pastoral practice whose context is ultimate meanings and values; (3) practitioners who as representative persons 'bring to bear upon human troubles the resources, the wisdom and the authority of Christian faith and life'. Pastoral carers are 'wounded healers' who, knowing themselves to be helped and inspired by the example of Jesus (Mark 1.32–4), help others on their journey to wholeness.

However, many others have come to feel that the 'shepherding' model of care, with its focus on directing and advising, is not in fact compatible with Tillich's insight into the human need to be 'accepted' or a non-directive approach to pastoral counselling, and is therefore regressive and open to challenge. Others again are equally convinced that the emphasis on the individual's search for 'acceptance' falls short of what is needed for true human wholeness, seen from a holistic and Christian perspective.

A brief and selective chronological history of the passage of counselling theory and practice in the churches may illuminate the rise of the movement and the subsequent questioning of its individualistic tendencies. It was in 1925 that Anton Boisen (1876–1965) introduced clinical pastoral training for American seminarians and ministers through the long-term supervised pastoral care of people in crisis in hospitals, prisons and other social institutions. For two decades, from the publication of

Boisen's book, *Counseling and Psychotherapy* (1942), the American psychologist Carl Rogers (b. 1902) strongly influenced the whole field of pastoral care with his emphasis upon an attitude of 'unconditional positive regard' and client-centred therapy. Seward Hiltner (1909–84) introduced this theme to American ministers in his work, *Preface to Pastoral Theology* (1958). He tried to emphasize the theological dimension of the task through the perspective of 'shepherding', which he took to mean the healing, sustaining and guiding activity of the Church. He thought it provided, for example in the ministry to a family in conflict, a possibly unrivalled window into the nature of the Christian gospel.

However, at the same time, the strong individualistic understanding of personal growth, together with the non-directive and unconditionally accepting method of pastoral counselling, was coming under criticism from four directions.

First, in the post-war period stories of the horrors of the Second World War slowly began to erode some of the confidence about human potential and the power of positive thinking which survived longer in the United States than it did in Europe. Reinhold Niebuhr (1892–1971), who wrote *The Nature and Destiny of Man* (1955), in particular brought a dose of Christian realism to the prevailing optimistic outlook on human beings. He managed to remind Christians in a psychologically convincing way of the seriousness of sin and human brokenness. His challenge enabled the pastoral counselling movement to become more theologically self-critical.

Second, within the counselling movement itself other therapists, Hobart Mowrer (1907–82) for instance, emphasized the importance of clients taking responsibility for their own difficulties. Pastoral counselling had become too non-directive and lacked a moral cutting edge. Don Browning, in *The Moral Context of Pastoral Care* (1976), more recently also acknowledged the need on occasions for moral confrontation in counselling relationships. He argues that too much attention has been paid to a therapeutic concern about what sort of person one should *be,* and insufficient attention has been given to what one should *do*. Consequently, he has struck a stronger ethical note. Recognizing the social and moral character of persons, and calling for confession and restitution as the way to relief, many counsellors have now begun to run counter to the popular and morally neutral approach of psychoanalysis.

A third and related critique has been offered by theologians and practitioners who are impatient with popular therapies and what they perceive to be a loss of contact with theology and the historical roots of Christian counselling. Thomas C. Oden, in *Care of Souls in the Classic Tradition* (1984), sees the need to recover historical wisdom as it may be seen, for instance, in the patristic and pre-modern ecumenical mode of which the work of Pope Gregory the Great is one example. He resists what he sees as the harmful individualism, narcissism and hedonism of the modern counselling movement.

A fourth criticism, and the one which has gained most force recently, has fastened upon the 'professionalization' of pastoral counselling which has threatened to remove it from the capability of the amateur – the one who literally does it out of love. For some, the fear of potential damage caused by untutored counsellors and the danger of abusing vulnerable people has led to a little-acknowledged 'de-skilling' or undervaluing of the natural carers people expect to find in their families and friendships. Many mediating institutions have tried to fill the gap. The Samaritans (founded 1953) is a good example of a voluntary organisation which has won respect as it has harnessed the listening skills of ordinary people in helping to support others in crisis.

In short, the increasing social mobility and the breakdown of the extended family has exacerbated the loss of confidence people have in the old sources of wisdom and help. Organizations like the Samaritans, and the provision of services such as parenting classes, bear witness both to a loss of esteem for formerly trusted resources and a popular demand for new skills to be provided and learned from qualified trainers.

This tendency to place one's trust in professionalized helpers could lead to a neglect of the corporate, social and political dimensions of local pastoral care and counselling, and an overemphasis upon the skills of service providers. We shall return to this below when we consider pastoral care in the community.

Pastoral care and spiritual direction

> [Spiritual Direction is] 'that form of pastoral counselling whose purpose is to help another to develop consciously his or her relationship with God and to live the consequence of that developing relationship'.[4]

We have seen above how one of the reactions of Thomas C. Oden to a perceived weakness in the counselling movement has been to search for the ancient paths trodden by those Fathers of the Church who had a clear theodicy, meaning literally, a view of the 'justice of God'. Classic theodicies held together God's goodwill and his power in the presence of evil and suffering, and applied them to the care of the sick, poor, dying and bereaved.

In the 1960s and 1970s, as we have seen, optimism about the human condition was flagging. People were hearing news of the 'death of God', 'religionless Christianity' and the coming 'secular city'. It prompted two reactions which could be broadly described as the *mystical* and the *militant*. The mystical response re-emphasized the importance of an interior life, not withdrawn from, but related to life in the world. The militant response pursued the social concerns and action prompted by a deeper appreciation of the demand for the justice of God to be established in the world.

Thomas Merton (1915–68) is one outstanding example of a Christian who combined a deep personal interior spiritual life with care for the common good. A Trappist monk, theologian and poet, he came to the point where he stressed the importance of experience rather than doctrine. When towards the end of his life he was drawn to the wisdom of Buddhist and Hindu spirituality he managed to couple his essentially Christian faith with the struggle against the war in Vietnam, the proliferation of nuclear weapons and the violation of the rights of African Americans.

Most Christians have been less successful than Thomas Merton in keeping the mystical and militant elements so creatively together. Consequently, it is helpful to consider each strand separately, and we shall return to the more militant below.

The last quarter of the 20th century saw spiritualities of all sorts flourish to the point where, speaking generally, books of spirituality sold widely, journals were well subscribed, retreat centres became popular, and spiritual directors became professionalized. Our concern here is with spiritual direction and its place within the overall framework of pastoral care. Spiritual direction is not the same as pastoral counselling.

Pastoral counselling aims to assist a person to become a more 'whole' human being through a practical application of insights derived from the Christian tradition on the one hand and theories of psychological development and the behavioural sciences on the other. It is an active, helping way within a highly organized field of study, programmes, skills and practices. The whole movement, as the illustrations in this chapter demonstrate, derives from the Protestant culture of pastoral care in general and in particular the clinical, therapeutic and psychological approach of professional practitioners of the twentieth century in the United States of America.

By contrast, one normally associates spiritual direction with the Orthodox, Catholic and Anglican traditions. Unlike the skilled counsellor, Thomas Merton believed that the spiritual director is essentially a charismatic figure, not someone to whom one turns because of his professional competence but a man to whom one has been drawn by his holiness. From the start, the ancient and modern goal of the spiritual director has been to bring people to the experimental knowledge of God. Essential to the director's understanding is the knowledge that God is both transcendent and immanent. The task is to accompany people who are 'on the look out for God', through their praying and their daily living, towards the mystery of God who is present in and through all creation. Therefore, in contrast to the counsellor, who helps a person towards a goal of self-actualization, the spiritual director accompanies the person in a journey of self-transcendence. If counselling is concerned with self-development and coping, spiritual direction is more likely to focus on self-surrender and abandonment to God.

Of course this distinction of pastoral caring roles is artificial because we cannot separate people simply on the basis of their psychological and spiritual needs. Both are important and, in the modern period, there has been a growth in the number of professionals in both fields. With regard to people's spiritual needs and in the face of an increasing diversity of spiritualities and the unresolved ache in the human spirit today, people turn more and more to spiritual guides for help. Spiritual directors, along with their counselling colleagues, therefore find themselves in a shared and ongoing work of relieving the anger, guilt, frustration and disappointment of human beings who feel unfulfilled both in their search for personal happiness and in their struggle with a sense of the absence of God in their religious lives.

Perhaps, latterly, we have witnessed a new convergence by which two ministries, which were often mutually ignorant of each other and sometimes still are, are learning to be thankful for the contribution they can now each make to Christian wholeness. One small visible sign of this convergence could be in the physical arrangements of the typical retreat-conductor's room. Where once there was a *prie-dieu* (prayer desk) for the penitent and one chair for the spiritual director, there are normally now two comfortable chairs opposite each other, and sometimes no prayer desk at all.

It is the spirituality of Ignatius of Loyola (1491–1556) which underlies much of the contemporary revival in spiritual direction. His *Spiritual Exercises* (1541) are based on a thirty-day retreat in which directors lead meditations on the life of Christ, explain different ways of praying, and help people discern true inspirations of God from those of the devil or human invention. The exercises take account of people's unique personalities and states of life, and draw on spiritual contributions through the use of a whole range of human faculties, including imagining, thinking, sensing, feeling and breathing. The purpose is to ensure that each person's journey constitutes a dynamic balance between subjectivity and objectivity. Holiness is both individual and social, and is the end of a journey which is both inward and outward. The way is contemplative and committed to God – who is both transcendent and immanent, other than creation yet present in and through the materiality of the created world, and active within it.

Karl Rahner (1904–84), brought up in the Jesuit tradition of Ignatian spirituality, and a Catholic theologian, wrote also about the spiritual life in a way which resonated with the practice of spiritual direction in the Ignatian mode. He believed grace to be present in human nature and therefore present in the transcendental experience of all human beings. Moreover, it can be realized without explicit faith in Christ and even without knowledge of the Christian revelation, by what he called 'anonymous Christians'. Not surprisingly, he also anticipated a de-clericalized Church with open doors and a spirituality to match. In *The Shape of the Church to Come* (1974) he looked forward to an ecumenical Church, with an institutional unity prior to a dogmatic unity, a Church from the roots, democratized and socio-critical. He therefore at one and the same time was laying a foundation for the broad development of spiritual direction in the Ignatian style, which has happened, and sowing the seeds of a critique both of it and of the individualistic and elitist character of the whole pastoral care movement in the modern period.

A critique of spiritual direction today must therefore fasten on some of the comments made earlier about pastoral counselling with which it has so much in common. For instance, although the number of paid full-time directors is small, at least in the United Kingdom, in the use of psychological insights and in practice both have been becoming increasingly professionalized. Thomas Merton would have criticized this shift on the basis of the tradition of spiritual direction as a spiritual charism. In the past people did not choose to become spiritual directors. It was a 'calling' discerned in the way that other people were drawn to seek their help, because of their perceived holiness. It was less a ministry which demanded certain specific skills and aptitudes than a ministry of example and discernment. Karl Rahner's suspicion of a hierarchical Church on the one hand and his awareness of the danger of the ghetto-like, 'little flock', mentality on the other was to be echoed in other theologians to whom we must now turn.

Pastoral care in the community

In a church or community where only ecclesiastical officials rather than all the members of the community are active, there is grave reason to wonder whether the Spirit has not been sacrificed along with the spiritual gifts ... With one another for one another: this is a principle of the charismatic ordering of the church.[5]

An increasing number of voices have been raised in criticism of the heavy emphasis on professionalized care for individuals in the fields of pastoral counselling and spiritual direction. It is not so much that the value of this form of care has been questioned. In fact it has been welcomed not least because it has helped Christians learn how to listen, to be less directive, less judgemental and more humble. Nevertheless, at the same time, professionalized care has been judged to undervalue the everyday care offered, for example, by family and well-meaning friends to people in pain. More significantly, it has proceeded from some theological presuppositions about interpersonal relationships based on a paradoxically hierarchical understanding of incarnation which is increasingly open to challenge and to which we shall return. In practice, the protest has taken three forms.

First, in Britain, Robert Lambourne (1917–72), a general practitioner, theologian and psychiatrist, wrote a book, *Community, Church and Healing* (1963), in which he argued that humankind is made up of social beings, and the healings of Jesus in the Gospels were community events as much as individual miracles. He was critical of the way that the Church had embraced psychotherapy. His concern was to challenge the modern pastoral care movement to become lay, voluntary and community-focused within a 'holistic' view of healing. In place of a problem-solving approach, like that of the professional counsellor, Lambourne understood the road to healing to be a mutual search. In similar vein, Alastair

Campbell has commented, 'In the last analysis, the difference may be seen as that between (one) who views care from the perspective of counselling and one who views counselling from the perspective of care.'[6]

Second, through a variety of practical pastoral initiatives Christians began once again to explore the idea of communities as the context for healing. Outstanding in this regard have been the L'Arche communities, founded and spread around the world by Jean Vanier (b. 1928), who wrote *Community and Growth* (1989). The L'Arche communities have offered a mutually caring ministry to people with learning difficulties (called 'core members') and their carers (called 'assistants'). But the idea of the healing community finds other much looser expressions of which some of the best-known in Europe are the Third Order of the Franciscans, the Iona Community in Scotland and, to a lesser extent, those who have shared in the Taizé experience in France. They do not offer 'belonging' in the sense of a shared community life, but they do appeal to people's longing to belong within a healthy open community which has a relevant modern form of Christian corporate spirituality. Also, many of the new churches, often evangelical and charismatic fellowships, may be regarded, certainly by their members, as healing communities. They hold a more interventionist awareness of God's healing power. They give a high profile to the healing ministry in their worship and recognize and use the spiritual gifts of individual members. Regarded as abusive by some, they are welcomed by others for the experience of a holistic salvation into which many of their members have entered.

Third, we have noted Karl Rahner's hope for a Church with a sociopolitical dimension to its life and mission. This displays the militant response, in parallel with the mystical, to which some of the deep questions raised by the theological scepticism of the 1960s and 1970s gave rise. We have come to associate this radical communitarian emphasis with the base-community movement, undergirded by the writings of mainly Catholic liberation theologians. Many of these were influenced by the writings of the Protestant theologian, Jürgen Moltmann (b. 1926). In his book, *The Church in the Power of the Spirit* (1977), Moltmann argues that the gospel always belongs within a community which, as an open society of friends, provides an alternative to the life of the world. The Church is a community of liberated disciples who, in the power of the Spirit, commit themselves to the poor and oppressed, not least because that is where Christ is to be found. The key principle is *ubi Christus: ibi ecclesia* – where Christ is, there is the Church.

In hindsight it has become clear that in the field of the Church's pastoral care the shift through various phases has reflected changing theological influences in the Church and changing social moods in the secular world. There has been a complex interplay. So, for example, while some have criticized the pastoral counselling movement, with other contemporary therapies, for being hierarchical, elitist and even oppressive, they recognize that paradoxically it has aimed to be non-directive. Again, many Christians have argued that it has helped to produce more skilful shepherds. However, the shepherding model upon which the Christian counselling movement has frequently depended, and which seems to give it a biblical foundation and theological credibility, has also been judged to be inadequate. Henri Nouwen (1932–96) commented: 'cure without care makes us into rulers, controllers, manipulators, and prevents a real community from taking shape'.[7]

We trace the same tension in the modern and still developing spiritual direction movement as it has adapted to some of the canons of counselling, its sister discipline. By doing so it has managed to escape some of the 'active-helping' pitfalls in some of its past practices. It has espoused a more kenotic (emptying) incarnational model of the director as companion. Such a model, however, reflecting the shepherd in Psalm 23, is still too individualistic in its understanding of incarnation. In its drift towards professionalization, spiritual direction may also run the risk of a hierarchical trinitarianism in relation to interpersonal pastoral care. A trinitarian approach which moves in a downward direction, albeit with a concern to listen before offering insight, faces the same dangers as the modern counselling movement.

The concept of care in the community, resonating with the dynamic New Testament models of the Church and the emphasis in Western society today upon participation and partnership, avoids these particular dangers. It relates to the age of the Spirit in which the Church has tended to locate itself at the end of the twentieth century. At the same time, a contemporary secular search is for wholeness within the community. For Christians, the vision is of a world which is moving towards the total harmony of the Body of Christ in obedience to God, and with gifted members giving to and receiving from each other, in mutual interdependence and self-giving love. Critics will suggest that this is more of a dream than a vision. They will defend the counselling and spiritual direction movements at least for their realism and orientation towards more achievable objectives.

Pastoral care – What comes next?

The twentieth century has been a turbulent and humbling one for the churches in the exercise of pastoral care. In particular, the pastoral counselling movement and its sister, spiritual direction, have brought a critique to bear on the churches' inherited attitudes and responses. These were often prescriptive, directive, patronizing, manipulative and male-dominant. The new insights into pastoral care in Christian ministry, as we have seen, often came from outside the churches and were addressed to the churches in the writings of secular prophets. If, sometimes, they were received too uncritically, they nevertheless challenged the churches in the way they addressed some of the complex emotional, social and moral problems – for example sexual relations and marriage – which today cause people so much pain and unease.

Finally, we return to the fascinating and difficult question with which we began. How are the churches of the future to offer Christian pastoral care in the climate and culture, frequently described as postmodern, which we have come to associate with the arrival of the new millennium?

We live in a day when many people want to tell their story. Others seem willing to listen, and there are therapists volunteering to provide answers to their expressed needs. The Oprah Winfrey television show, with its many imitators, thrived by highlighting the hurts of ordinary people and by introducing them to experts who offered self-help guides to relieve stress and achieve a happy and fulfilled life. Such presenters and experts have had the kind of appeal we tend to associate with the popular tele-evangelists in America. However, they fail to address the challenge of the Christian message to the comfortable world.

One of the emerging insights of the latter part of the twentieth century has been the recognition that the Church is the Church in mission and only in mission. That mission has as its motif the cross and resurrection of Jesus Christ. Christians are not here to be fulfilled so much as to be transformed and shaped for service and sacrifice. The question is not simply, Who and what are we? but, Who and what are we for? It is to see the vision for humankind in terms of fitness for purpose.

An understanding of human need outside a clear moral and social framework inevitably threatens the traditional theological and practical basis for pastoral care. The churches have been tempted to adopt and adapt, without sufficient critical rigour, the shepherd model of caring in a way which has owed more to secular psychological theories than biblical spiritual insights. Even in the Bible it was dangerously abused. The prophet Jeremiah castigated the shepherds (leaders) of Israel for guiding the sheep (people) astray, because they failed to consult the Lord (Jeremiah 10.21). The prophet Ezekiel in his day faced a similar situation where different shepherds led the sheep in diverse destructive paths, primarily for their own advantage (Ezekiel 34. 1–6). The Church dare not ignore the prophetic element within the shepherding role in the Bible and in the world of our day.

Nevertheless, in spite of the necessary critique, the shepherd model of pastoral care still has value. People need counselling help, spiritual discernment and Christian companionship in living and dying. Christians are convinced, along of course with those of many other faiths, that God has an ongoing and eternal concern for the wellbeing of the created order. For Christians, the shepherd – saviour, liberator, model and companion on the journey to healing and wholeness – is Jesus Christ, who, in his Spirit, is with us and among us to be known and made known.

The biggest task facing the Church today, therefore, is to recover confidence in that story which has been its inspiration and life-blood. The confidence is not simply that the story is valid for the individual Christian – which few will want to question that. The Church needs to recover the confidence that the story has the universal relevance the Bible and the fathers of the Church claimed for it. Much modern pastoral care has not had that confidence. The pastoral counselling movement in particular has tended to use the Bible as a contributor rather than as the foundation of its practice. Spiritual directors have valued the Church's tradition, but have tended latterly to concentrate on proven methods of using it, for example in the way of Ignatian spiritual direction. Likewise, the more communitarian approach to healing, as in the base communities of the developing world has expanded on the biblical story and used certain liberative themes, viewed from a modern radical perspective, to attack the oppressive socio-political forces. Today, therefore, there is not one method of counselling or spiritual direction, or one liberation theology. There is a wide variety of methods and theologies seeking Christian validation for convictions which owe more to a belief in individual, human and democratic rights than to the Bible or the tradition of the Church.

Of course the Christian comes to the task of pastoral care in the modern period no less prejudiced than anyone else. There is this difference, however: the preconceptions of the Christian in offering pastoral care must at some stage submit to the discipline of relating to the word of the Bible as it has been received in the Church. In the comfortable world of personal choice and the pursuit of attainable pleasure, the Christian story will stand as one among many stories, and one of the least attractive at that, because of the inescapable cost which is part of the message and the therapy. In an uncomfortable world, the story of God's love in creation, the passionate commitment of his incarnation, death and resurrection, the gift of his Spirit to restore and renew the world, in the light of the hope of his coming, still falls on receptive ears. This story may yet prove to be the healing story of immanence and transcendence that the world, as well as sinful and hurting individuals and communities, will want to welcome.

Notes

1. Rodney J. Hunter (ed.), *Dictionary of Pastoral Care and Counseling* (Nashville, 1990), p. xii.
2. F. D. E. Schleiermacher, *Die Praktische Theologie nach den Grundsatzeu der Evangelischen Kirche* (Berlin, 1850), p. 27.
3. Hunter, *Dictionary,* p. xii.
4. William A. Barry, in Francis Makower, *Call and Response* (London, 1994), p. 58.
5. Hans Küng, *The Church* (London, 1967), pp. 187, 189.
6. Alastair Campbell, *Professionalism and Pastoral Care* (Philadelphia, 1985), p. 47.
7. Henri Nouwen, *Out of Solitude* (Notre Dame, 1974), p. 37.

Bibliography

Alistair V. Campbell, *Rediscovering Pastoral Care* (London, 1981)
Alistair V. Campbell, *Paid to Care? The Limits of Professionalism in Pastoral Care* (London, 1985); published in USA: *Professionalism and Pastoral Care* (Philadelphia, 1985)
William A. Clebsch and Charles R. Jaeckle, *Pastoral Care in Historical Perspective* (New York, 1964)
Rodney J. Hunter (ed.), *Dictionary of Pastoral Care and Counseling* (Nashville, 1990)
John T. McNeill, *A History of the Cure of Souls* (London, 1952)
Stephen Pattison, *A Critique of Pastoral Care,* 2nd edn (London, 1993)

20

The sacraments of healing

Penance and anointing of the sick

Richard P. McBrien[1]

Introduction

We are initiated into the Christian community by baptism-confirmation and the Eucharist, but initiation is only the beginning of a process. We are not already fully mature in Christ by the mere fact of having been baptized, anointed and invited to share the Lord's Supper. We are human. Hence we are prone to sin and vulnerable to illness, physical incapacity, and finally death. And yet the call to Christian existence is a call to perfection: 'Be perfect, therefore, as your heavenly Father is perfect' (Matthew 5.48). It is God's will that we be sanctified (1 Thessalonians 4.3; Ephesians 1.4), that we become as saints (Ephesians 5.3). We are to love God with all our mind and all our strength, and our neighbour as ourselves (Mark 12.30). Jesus' proclamation of the Kingdom of God, which shaped his own ministry as well as the mission of the Church, is a call to conversion: 'The time is fulfilled, and the Kingdom of God has come near; repent, and believe in the good news' (Mark 1.15).

Two sacraments are celebrated by the Church as a sign and instrument of God's and of Christ's abiding healing power. The sacrament of *penance*

---

1. This essay should be read in conjunction with the study of the early penitentials by Thomas O'Loughlin (see pp. 93–111).

or *reconciliation,* is for those whose bond with the Church, and ultimately with God and Christ, has been weakened or even severed by sin. The sacrament of the *anointing of the sick* (formerly called *extreme unction*) is for those whose bond with God and the Church has been weakened by illness or physical incapacity. In either case, the purpose of the sacrament is to heal and to restore the morally and/or physically sick member to full communion with the Church so that once again he or she can participate in its life and mission.

Beyond that, Jesus is disclosed in these sacraments as one who heals and forgives, and the Church is disclosed as a healing and forgiving community, as the sacrament of the healing and forgiving Lord. The Church is also the penitent Church, ever bathing the feet of Christ with its tears and hearing his words, 'Neither do I condemn you' (John 8.11). And because of its unshakable confidence in the triumph of God's mercy and grace in Christ, when night falls the Church holds high the lamp of hope and reveals itself as the universal sacrament of salvation, the community which gives up on no one and no situation, no matter how seemingly hopeless.

Penance/Reconciliation

History

New Testament period

The text to which Catholic doctrine has traditionally appealed in asserting the sacramentality and divine origin of penance is John 20.22–3, which records one of Jesus' post-resurrection appearances: 'Receive the Holy Spirit. If you forgive the sins of any, they are forgiven them; if you retain the sins of any, they are retained' (see also Matthew 16.9; 18.18). By itself, the text does not 'prove' that Jesus instituted the sacrament of penance as we know it today or that he conferred the power to forgive sins only on the Apostles, their successors and their chosen delegates. We have no basis even for concluding that these are the 'very words' of Jesus, given the different approach to history in the Fourth Gospel, over against the Synoptics.

On the other hand, the text *is* entirely consistent with Jesus' abiding concern about sin and his readiness to forgive and to heal (e.g. Matthew 9.2–8; Mark 2.5–12; Luke 5.20–6). In all three reports of Jesus' cure of the paralytic at Capernaum there is mention of the forgiveness of sins. The forgiveness of sins is also prominent in the preaching of the Apostles (Acts 2.38; 5.31; 10.43; 13.38; 26.18). Accordingly, even though John does not tell us how or by whom this power was exercised in the community for whom he wrote, the very fact that he mentions it shows that it was exercised.

The pastoral strategy of the New Testament churches seems to have been one of compassion, correction and challenge. Mutual correction and forgiveness form part of the fabric of community life (Matthew 5.23–4; James 5.16), but compassion is balanced against an awareness of the effect of sin on the life and mission of the Church itself. In some few cases, a form of excommunication seems to have been practised (1 Corinthians 5.3–5; 1 Timothy 1.19–20).

Second and third centuries

The material for this period is scant. What evidence there is suggests that penance was available for the baptized. *The Shepherd of Hermas* (*c*.150), an important para-scriptural document, takes for granted the practice of post-baptismal forgiveness, but only once in a lifetime. The community would pray at the deathbed of one who fell into a publicly known serious sin a second time, but the sinner would be denied the sacraments. The first to deny the Church's and the bishop's right to forgive those guilty of serious sins were the *Montanists* and the *Novatians,* both arguing that certain sins (e.g. apostasy, murder, adultery) were outside the Church's powers.

Fourth, fifth and sixth centuries

The rigorists were condemned by the Council of Nicea (325), which explicitly directed that the dying are to be reconciled and given *Viaticum* (the term used for Holy Communion for those at the point of death – i.e. 'on the way', *via,* to heaven).

During this period, penance was public in character and came to be known as 'canonical penance' because local councils devoted a number of canons, or juridical decisions, to regulating its practice. Canonical penance was administered only once in a lifetime, since baptism was normally received late in life and was seen as calling for a deep conversion, neither easily nor frequently set aside. The Church demanded proof of reconversion before restoring the grace of baptism through penance.

Canonical penance was always reserved for serious sins, e.g. apostasy, murder, heresy, adultery. These were matters of common public knowledge. The offender would receive a form of liturgical excommunication and was forced to leave the celebration of the Eucharist at the Offertory, along with the catechumens. For less serious offences there were other forms of penance: almsgiving, fasts, charity to the poor and the sick, and prayers.

Public penance required the sinner's demonstrating a change of heart, presenting himself or herself before the bishop and the local community, and joining the local group of penitents. Then, after a suitable period of probation (the length of which varied substantially from region to region and from sin to sin), he or she would be readmitted to the Christian community by a rite known as the 'reconciliation of the penitent'. In the West, more often than in the East, an additional penance was sometimes imposed, namely, lifelong celibacy. This led to the break-up of marriages and provoked intense resistance from the laity, who began to postpone the sacrament until they were near death. It became effectively the sacrament of the dying.

As the needs of the people and the circumstances of the Church changed, private penance became more the rule and so, too, the actual 'confession' of sins. By the end of the sixth century, canonical penance came to be known simply as *Confession*. (The once-in-a-lifetime, public rite of penance officially ended in the West with the Fourth Lateran Council's decree in 1215 that all the baptized must confess their sins and receive Holy Communion at least once a year.)

Seventh to eleventh centuries

This period if marked by a pronounced Celtic influence as the missionary efforts of the Church reached into the British Isles, far removed from the influence of Rome and from all of Europe. (The Irish monks themselves were to bring this Celtic influence to bear upon the Continent in the late sixth and early seventh centuries.) Since the liturgical life of the Celtic church was monastically oriented, private penance became normative for priests and religious, and under their direction it spread among the laity as well. It was imposed even for trivial offences and became increasingly divorced from the larger community of faith. In fact, a person could be restored to the Eucharist even before completing the penance. If the penance were deemed too onerous, the penitent could ask for a commutation to a lighter penalty. It was also possible to substitute the payment of a sum of money instead of performing the actual penance. This practice was known as *redemption*.

Furthermore, penance was administered by priests as well as the bishop. In order to help the priests in the selection of appropriate penances, a codification of penitential practices was developed, the so-called penitential books (*libri poenitentiales*). These were lists of every kind of sin, with the exact type of penance attached. The minister of the sacrament was no longer the healer and the reconciler. He was now the judge. A formula of absolution was also developed at this time.

Eleventh to fourteenth centuries

Four principal changes occur in this period. Penance becomes satisfaction, confession, contrition and absolution. In the ancient Church the emphasis was on the reconciliation of the sinner with the Church and ultimately with God. Now the emphasis shifts to the doing of a penance, or the making of satisfaction, for sin. When this became too strenuous, the practices of commutation and redemption were introduced.

Second, confession of sins originally served the purpose of ensuring that adequate satisfaction was being imposed, but gradually confession came to be considered as having its own efficacy, its own power to reconcile the sinner. Thus, we find at this time the development of arguments urging the necessity of confessing to a priest.

Third, in the writings of Abelard (d. 1142) and Peter Lombard there was a shift to contrition, i.e. the conversion of heart. The sinner, if truly contrite, was already forgiven even before confession. So pronounced was this new stress on contrition that the purist Albigensians and Waldensians denied any efficacy whatsoever to confession to a priest, a view condemned by the Fourth Lateran Council in 1215.

All orthodox theologians and canonists came to the defence of the role of the priest, and this led to a fourth shift: to absolution by a priest. Since absolution was *not* part of the practice and teaching of penance in the early Church, there was some dispute among the mediaeval authors about its place in the sacrament. By the time of Thomas Aquinas, however, absolution came to be regarded as essential, along with confession and contrition.

From the Middle Ages to Vatican II

Thomas's theology was endorsed in the Council of Florence's *Decree for the Armenians* (1439):

(1) Penance is a sacrament;
(2) It consists of contrition of the heart (including the resolution not to sin in the future), oral confession to the priest, satisfaction (e.g. prayer, fasting, almsgiving), and absolution by the priest; and
(3) The effect of the sacrament is the forgiveness of sins.

The Reformers, and Luther in particular, rejected this teaching. Although Luther accepted the sacramentality of penance, he believed there was an abiding danger of regarding the works of the penitent as more important than faith in God's mercy. He also rejected the reservation of the power of forgiveness to priests. The first official reaction to Luther's views came in a bull of Pope Leo X (d. 1521), *Exsurge Domine* (1520). Calvin also accepted private confession and absolution as a means of arousing faith and confidence in God's mercy, but he denied its sacramentality.

The definitive response to the Reformers came from the Council of Trent (*Doctrine on the Sacrament of Penance,* Session XIV, 1551). It taught that penance is a sacrament instituted by Christ; that it is distinct from baptism; that the three acts of the penitent are contrition, confession of all serious sins in number and kind, and satisfaction; that absolution is reserved to priests alone; and that the priest must have jurisdiction, since absolution is a juridical act.

However, in the Council's earlier *Decree on Justification* (1547) it taught that God's grace is absolutely gratuitous, that we do nothing to gain it. Good works, including the act of contrition, the confession of sins, priestly absolution, and penance after confession, are to be viewed within this framework.

Vatican II

The Second Vatican Council called for a revision of the rite and formulae for the sacrament of penance 'so that they more clearly express both the nature and effect of the sacrament' (*Constitution on the Sacred Liturgy,* n. 72). The sacrament's purpose, the council's *Dogmatic Constitution on the Church* declares, is to 'obtain pardon from the mercy of God' and to be 'reconciled with the Church whom [sinners] have wounded by their sin, and who, by its charity, its example and its prayer, collaborates in their conversion' (n. 11).

The New Rite of penance

The new rite of penance was based on criteria proposed by Vatican II's *Constitution on the Sacred Liturgy:*

(1) The rite should clearly express both the nature and the effect of the sacrament;
(2) The role of the church community must be emphasized;
(3) The reading of the Word of God should be central;
(4) A public form of worship should predominate over a private form; and
(5) The rite should be short and clear, free from useless repetitions and not requiring extensive explanation.

There are four forms of the new rite: individual; communal with individual confession and absolution; communal with general absolution; and an abbreviated emergency ritual when death is imminent. The rite for the first three forms includes the following: a prayer of welcome; a reading of sacred Scripture (which is optional); a reflection on the Word of God; confession of sins with an expression of sorrow; a prayer of absolution; and a prayer of praise and dismissal.

Although not on a par with the new rite of christian initiation of adults, the new rite of peace does bring out the ecclesial dimension of the sacrament more fully than does the traditional (i.e. post-Tridentine) practice of private confession. In the new rite, the effect of the sacrament is identified as reconciliation with God and with the Church. The minister functions more as a healer than as a judge. Emphasis is placed on conversion inspired by the Church's proclamation of God's word. And communal celebration of the sacrament is provided for and encouraged.

Contemporary theological and pastoral issues

Theologians, religious educators, liturgists and other pastoral ministers continue to discuss several issues: the frequency of confession; the age of first confession; the use of general absolution; and the need to confess privately to a priest. Because the new rite takes more time and care, many believe that an emphasis on frequent confession might encourage a curtailing of key prayer-elements in the new rite. They are also sceptical about the pastoral wisdom of requiring very young children to receive the sacrament of penance before they are ready and also to make it a precondition for the reception of first Eucharist, as required by present church discipline. Third, various episcopal conferences differ regarding the use of general absolution, and some church leaders, contrary to the spirit of the new rite and the intention of the council, seem to want to make the first form of penance (individual-to-priest) normative. Finally, pastoral ministers and others wonder why, if general absolution is conferred and one's mortal sins are already forgiven, one should still have to confess privately to a priest.

Jesus, the Church, and penance

In its celebration of the sacrament of penance, the Church reveals itself as the sacrament of God's mercy in the world, but also as a sinful community, still 'on the way' to the perfection of the Kingdom. Those who sin and who must avail themselves of the sacrament are just as much 'the Church' as are those who, in the name of the Church, act to reconcile the sinner with God and the Church. The Church knows what it is both to forgive and to be forgiven, mindful always of the Lord's own prayer: 'And forgive us our sins, for we ourselves forgive everyone indebted to us' (Luke 11.4).

A Church which cannot admit its sin is not the Church of Christ. A Church which cannot forgive the sins of others against itself is not the Church of Christ. How the liturgical process of conversion, repentance and forgiveness is to be structured is always of less importance than the fact that it goes on continually within the Church.

And it goes on continually within the Church because the Church's model is always Jesus himself, who is the reconciler, the healer and the forgiver of sins *par excellence*. The sacrament of reconciliation does what Jesus does.

Anointing of the sick

History

New Testament

Apart from James 5.14 there is no mention of anointing as a sacred rite in the New Testament. The pertinent text is as follows: 'Are any among you sick? They should call for the elders of the church and have them pray over them, anointing them with oil in the name of the Lord.' It continues: 'The prayer of faith will save the sick, and the Lord will raise them up; and anyone who has committed sins will be forgiven. Therefore, confess your sins to one another, and pray for one another, so that you may be healed' (5.15–16).

The 'elders' or 'presbyters' are those appointed and ordained by apostles or disciples of Apostles (Acts 14.23; Titus 1.5). The presbyters are described by James as having extraordinary spiritual gifts which enable them to heal the sick. Sickness, it must be noted, was attributed to sin, as in the Old Testament and contemporary Judaism, and so it posed a problem for the early Church. At the sickbed it is the task of the presbyter to pray for the sick person and to anoint him or her with oil in the name of the Lord. The oil is regarded as a vital substance, a restorative. There is nothing magical implied, however. It is not the oil but the prayers to the Lord which provide the hope of recovery and the forgiveness of sins. (The recommendation that Christians declare their sins 'to one another' is not without relevance to our previous discussion of the sacrament of penance.)

Although James 5.14 by itself does not 'prove' the sacramentality of the anointing of the sick, it does indicate that there was such a practice in the early Church, that it required the presence of some leader of the community, that it involved prayers, anointing and the forgiveness of sins, and that its purpose was the restoration of the sick member not only to physical health but also to spiritual health within the community of faith.

Second century to the Middle Ages

There is, for all practical purposes, no evidence in the early centuries for the actual rite of anointing. Since it was not a public liturgical act like the rite of initiation, it was passed over in the liturgical books. Just as lay Christians brought home the Eucharist from the Sunday celebration for Communion during the week, so they also brought home blessed oil for use as needed. The bishop or other members of the local clergy undoubtedly visited the sick and may well have been the ministers of anointing. For the most part, however, the laity seem to have been the ordinary ministers of the sacrament. As penance was delayed until the imminence of death, the anointing, too, was delayed, since it was reserved to those in full communion with the Church. As anointing was delayed, it became part of a continuous rite alongside penance and *Viaticum* – all administered by a priest.

The first documentary item for the sacrament is provided by a letter of Pope Innocent I (d. 417) to Decentius, bishop of Gubbio, in which certain practical points are clarified regarding the administration of the rite of anointing. It links the anointing with the text of James and notes that the oil is blessed by the bishop and applied to the sick person by the bishop or a priest. This letter became a basic source for the late Roman and early mediaeval period, inasmuch as it was incorporated into the most important canonical collections and thus became the starting point for theological discussion of the sacrament.

In the first part of the eighth century, Bede the Venerable (d. 735), author of the earliest extant commentary on the Epistle of James, states that it has been the custom of the Church from apostolic times for presbyters to anoint the sick with consecrated oil and to pray for their healing. Nowhere in the early tradition does one find mention of the Anointing as a sacrament of preparation for death. Where mention *is* made of a 'sacrament of the dying', the reference is always to the Eucharist, administered as *Viaticum*.

The early mediaeval period

With the Carolingian reform at the beginning of the ninth century – i.e. the effort guided by the emperor Charlemagne to impose Roman liturgy and Roman disciplinary practices throughout his new Holy Roman Empire – anointing becomes established among the 'last rites'. By the middle of the twelfth century the association between anointing and dying was so taken for granted that it came to be called *sacramentum exeuntium* ('the sacrament of the departing') or in the words of Peter Lomard, *extrema unctio* ('last anointing').

By the close of the twelfth century, extreme unction was in fact appropriating to itself the function and effects previously associated with *Viaticum*. Thus, anointing became more and more a sacrament of the dying, although its original purpose was to be a remedy against sickness, with the real hope of recovery. Even in the early mediaeval period, the Church did not require that a sickness be terminal before the sacrament could be administered.

Thirteenth and fourteenth centuries

In this period the doctrine of the seven sacraments came to its full development, and anointing of the sick was counted among them. It was understood as the sacrament of spiritual help for the time of grave illness unto death. Restoration to bodily health was regarded as a subordinate and conditional effect only. Theologians began to exaggerate the sacrament's spiritual powers: The Franciscan school argued that all venial (i.e. non-serious) sins were forgiven as well as serious sins, and the Dominican school argued that the sacrament removed even the consequences of sin and anything which lessened a soul's capacity for the life of glory in heaven. To die immediately after extreme unction, in other words, guaranteed an unimpeded journey to God.

Fifteenth and sixteenth centuries

This theological understanding of the sacrament as a sacrament for the dying was endorsed by the Council of Florence's *Decree for the Armenians* (1439), which declared that the sacrament could 'not be given except to a sick person whose life is feared for'. The Council of Trent's *Doctrine on the Sacrament of Extreme Unction* (1551) was formulated as a complement to the council's teaching on the sacrament of penance. It defined the anointing of the sick as a true sacrament.

The first draft of its doctrinal formation, however, had directed that the sacrament be given 'only to those who are in their final struggle and who have come to grips with death and who are about to go forth to the Lord'. The final draft introduced important modifications, declaring that 'this anointing is to be used for the sick, particularly for those who are so dangerously ill as to seem at the point of departing this life'. It speaks of the sacrament's effects as purification from sin as well as from the effects of sin, comfort and strength of soul, the arousal of confidence in God's mercy, readiness to bear the difficulties and trials of illness, and even health of body, where expedient for the welfare of the soul.

Trent's teaching is remarkable not only for what it contains about the spiritual, psychological and bodily effects of the sacrament but also for what it omits about the sacrament as a last rite. The Council thereby struck at the root of a growing abuse which delayed the sacrament until the very last moment of life.

Twentieth century

The Tridentine doctrine shaped the theological, canonical and pastoral understanding and practice of this sacrament for centuries thereafter. In the twentieth century some tentative advances were suggested. Theologians and liturgists alike suggested that, insofar as this is a sacrament of the dying, it is essentially an 'anointing for glory'. Others, however, pointed out that the prayers of the ritual made no mention of death, and that the sacrament was really a sacrament of the sick. The 'last sacrament' is not the anointing, but *Viaticum*. Indeed, it was only in the middle of the twelfth century, these theologians argued, that the stress on preparation for death had emerged.

Vatican II

The Second Vatican Council endorsed this second line of thought, recommending that the sacrament be called the anointing of the sick rather than extreme unction and noting explicitly that it 'is not a sacrament reserved for those who are at the point of death', but for those who begin to be in some danger of death 'from sickness or old age' (*Constitution on the Sacred Liturgy,* n. 73). Indeed, the *last* sacrament to be administered to the dying is *Viaticum* (n. 68). The *Dogmatic Constitution on the Church* places the sacrament in its larger ecclesial context:

> In the holy anointing of the sick with the prayer of the priest, the whole church recommends the sick to the Lord, who suffered and has been glorified, asking him to give them relief and salvation. It goes further and calls upon them to associate themselves freely with the passion and death of Christ, and in this way to make their contribution to the good of God's people' (n. 11).

The new rite of anointing and pastoral care of the sick

The new rite acknowledges that sickness prevents us from fulfilling our role in human society and in the Church. On the other hand, the sick person participates in the redemptive sufferings of Christ and provides the Church with a reminder of higher things and of the limitations of human life. Indeed, Pope Paul VI's apostolic constitution promulgating the new rite in 1972 pointed out that the sick are also anointed for ministry: to become models of faithful and hope-filled association with Christ in his passion and death.

The ritual elements include a greeting, words to those present, a penitential rite (Scripture, litany), the priest's laying on of hands, blessing of oil, prayer of thanksgiving and the anointing of the forehead and hands with oil with the words, 'Through this holy anointing may the Lord in his love and mercy help you with the grace of the Holy Spirit' and 'May the Lord who frees you from sin save you and raise you up.' There is a prayer after anointing, the Lord's Prayer, communion and a blessing.

The rite presupposes earlier visits to the sick person, including communion calls, and some direct dealing with the sick person's sense of isolation and with the concerns of family and others intimately affected by the illness.

Jesus, the Church, and the anointing of the sick

The Church's concern for the sick is in fidelity to Christ's command to visit the sick and is consistent with a holistic understanding of salvation as reaching the total person. The Church discloses itself in this sacrament as the community of those who are on pilgrimage to the Kingdom of God, with eschatological faith and hope. The Church is a sacrament of Christ the healer, the one who saves us in our human wholeness, body as well as soul. It is at the same time a community always in need of healing, a community subject to physical as well as spiritual reverses.

A Church which is not interested in healing, and in the total health of the whole human person and of the human community at large, is not the Church of Christ. A Church which abandons those who, by certain of the world's standards, are no longer of practical use, is not the Church of Christ. Nor is that Church truly the Church of Christ if it turns its back on the sick whom society scorns or rejects: the drug addict, the alcoholic, the victim of AIDS. The Church which anoints the sick is the Church of the 'Lord Jesus Christ, [who] shared in our human nature to heal the sick and save all humankind' (Prayer After Anointing).

As in all the sacraments, it is Jesus who is revealed and who ministers. In the anointing of the sick he is revealed as a healer of body as well as of soul, and as one who ministers to the sick and the dying and who energizes their faith in the Kingdom of God and stirs their hope in eternal life.

Bibliography

Michael Ahlstrom, Peter Gilmour and Robert Tuzik, *A Companion to Pastoral Care of the Sick* (Chicago: Liturgy Training Publications, 1990)

James Dallen, *The Reconciling Community: The Rite of Penance (*New York: Pueblo Publishing Co., 1986)

Regis Duffy, *A Roman Catholic Theology of Pastoral Care* (Philadelphia: Fortress Press, 1983)
Joseph A. Favazza, *The Order of Penitents: Historical Roots and Pastoral Future* (Collegeville, Minn.: Liturgical Press, 1988)
Peter Fink (ed.), *Anointing of the Sick*. Vol. 7 of *Alternative Futures for Worship* (Collegeville, Minn.: Liturgical Press, 1987)
Richard Gula, *To Walk Together Again: The Sacrament of Reconciliation* (New York: Paulist Press, 1984).
Charles Gusmer, *And You Visited Me: Sacramental Ministry to the Sick and Dying* (New York: Puebloe Publishing Co., 1984)
Pope John Paul II, *Reconciliatio et Poenitentia* (Apostolic Exhortation on Reconciliation and Penance). *Origins* 14/27 (December 20, 1984)
Robert J. Kennedy (ed.), *Reconciliation: The Continuing Agenda* (Collegeville, Minn.: Liturgical Press, 1987)
Kenan Osborne, *Reconciliation and Justification* (New York: Paulist Press, 1990).
Bernard Poschmann, *Penance and the Anointing of the Sick* (New York: Herder and Herder, 1964)
Karl Rahner, 'Penance' in *Encylopedia of Theology: The Concise Sacramentum Mundi* (New York: Seabury Press, 1975) pp. 1187–1204
Karl Rahner, *On the Theology of Death* (New York: Herder & Herder, 1961)

21

Justice

Pastoral care and the ecclesiastical law

Rupert Bursell

Pastoral and judicial: healing and punishment

Talking to someone else is therapeutic. That is recognized in the early penitential system in the theme of 'healing', and the tendency to describe the confessor as medicus or physician. The practice of gaining a healing self-understanding from talking about one's sins to a sympathetic spiritual friend has warrant in James 5.16: 'Confess your faults to one another, and pray for one another, that ye may be healed. The effectual fervent prayer of a righteous man availeth much.'

But alongside the merciful or 'healing' ministry has always run a ministry of justice. God is just as well as merciful, and sin and offences against the law (of the state as well as of the Church) have, down the centuries, been deemed to be errors for which the Christian may properly be punished. This responsibility falls in part within the pastoral ministry of the Church.

To that end the Church in the East and West alike drew up codes of canon law. Especially in the West, this owed a great deal to the late-Roman codification of the Emperor Justinian. To that were added collections of papal letters and decrees, some spurious, but increasingly brought together in lists of rules, until Gratian created the definitive collection in the mid-twelfth century.

In the East there evolved the device of 'economy' or oikonomia. That allowed an offence to be set right by special allowance so long as the result did not disrupt the orderliness of the Church's conduct of its affairs. In the West the equivalent was dispensation, which let someone off adherence to canon law in an emergency situation, but again without it being deemed to alter the law.

The Middle Ages was much preoccupied with problems of overlap, especially between the jurisdiction of the Church and that of the state. Pastorally this was important because the way an offender was treated depended upon where he was tried. The Church's courts could not exact the death penalty. But perhaps more common than problems of the conduct of individuals were problems affecting property and property-rights.

In Rupert Bursell's description of the Church of England's present day canon law system the pastoral consequences of such issues emerge sharply.

G. R. Evans

Introduction

On 9 August, 1994, Euan Lloyd visited the ancient graveyard at Sept-Saulx near Reims to pay his respects to seven airmen of the Royal Air Force who had been shot down in 1943; they were aged between 21 and 30 years. They share a communal grave where a propeller blade, embedded in stone, carries their names and ranks; on the reverse is welded a primitive 'V for victory' sign. On the seven white markers installed by the Commonwealth War Graves Commission are messages from the stricken families: four out of seven include tender messages of love from Mum, Dad, Grandad and variations thereof. On his return to England that same day Mr Lloyd was so shocked by what he heard on the radio in relation to the ecclesiastical case of *Re Holy Trinity, Freckleton*[1] that he promptly wrote to *The Times* newspaper.[2] He said:

> To the survivors of those seven gallant RAF men their lost ones were indeed pets and their terms of endearment wholly appropriate. Higher authority in the Church of England should overturn the consistory court's ruling.

In the *Freckleton* case the local incumbent had refused the son and daughter-in-law of a deceased permission to erect a memorial with an inscription including the words 'a devoted and much loved husband, dad and grandad' because the Anglican incumbent felt that the words were unsuitable for a permanent memorial in a churchyard. Such descriptions had been allowed in the churchyard until three years before, although in the intervening years a number of other bereaved had agreed 'willingly and not so willingly'[3] to abide by the incumbent's ruling. In such a case the incumbent is only exercising an authority delegated by the diocesan chancellor, and the son and daughter-in-law therefore petitioned the chancellor in the consistory court for permission to erect the memorial; the incumbent and two members of the parochial church council opposed the petition. The petitioners pointed out that the diocesan regulations as to churchyard memorials were still not being implemented to their full extent in the particular churchyard; in addition reference was made to *The Churchyards Handbook*,[4] the authors of which were of the view that:

> An epitaph is a public document, and not a cosy one at that. Nicknames or pet names ('Mum', 'Dad', 'Ginger') inscribed in stone, would carry overtones of the dog-cemetery unsuitable for the resting place of Christian men and women.

In argument, other possibilities in other cases were mooted, such as abbreviations (Bill, Jack or Stan[5]), terms of endearment (Cuddles or Squidgy). What, too, of dialectical usages[6] such as granny, mom or nanna or, indeed, colloquialisms (hubby, blossom or mate)?

In his judgment the chancellor refused the petition on the grounds *inter alia* that familiar terms were unnecessary on a memorial and that to overrule the incumbent in the instant case would destroy the policy that the incumbent had followed in recent years; moreover, it would cause further pastoral problems with other parishioners. He nevertheless stressed that his ruling was not a precedent in other Anglican dioceses[7] or, indeed, binding on other incumbents within that diocese.[8]

In fact the only 'higher authority' that had any jurisdiction to interfere was the appellate court (the Chancery Court of York), and no appeal was made to it by the unsuccessful petitioners, perhaps because of the aspect of parochial policy. They had, however, already indicated that if they did not succeed they would apply for exhumation, although in his judgment the chancellor made it clear that in his view such exhumation could not be permitted in the light of legal precedents. When a petition for exhumation was thereafter lodged the chancellor felt that he should not himself adjudicate on the matter. His deputy, nevertheless, permitted the exhumation;[9] in his view in the particular circumstances the court should attempt to correct or mitigate the pastoral results of the situation.

In the *Freckleton* cases various pastoral problems clearly arose: there was the effect of the bereavement on the relatives; the tensions caused between them and the incumbent when he refused to permit the inscription that they felt reflected their familial grief and love, coupled with the effect of that refusal on their own grieving processes; the tensions caused within the parish because of past refusals and the possibility of a perceived difference in treatment if the initial petition were granted; the stressful effect of the consistory court case itself on the petitioners and of the confirmed refusal; the further application for an exhumation in the face of the chancellor's intimation that it was likely to be refused, although the intimation was no doubt made with the intention of preventing the pain of further disappointment; and the tensions caused by the actual exhumation of the loved one's body. Moreover, in part because of media attention it is likely that additional tensions[10] were also created, for example, in the minds of other people in other parts of the country as to their own situations. Whether one rule being applied throughout the country would in the long run cause less pastoral upset than individual uncertainty or different results in different areas, it is impossible to judge. No human law can hope to attain perfection.

General

All law, of course, is involved with human beings, directly or indirectly, and therefore pastoral situations inevitably arise. As a result it is imperative for any successful system of law to be able to adapt to different social and human conditions. What is acceptable in one century or social milieu is not necessarily appropriate in another. Even when the law permits flexibility, that flexibility itself causes tensions. To be just, law must be predictable and not open to the whim of the individual judge; on the other hand a rigid insistence on consistency may bring about injustice in particular cases.

Even if individual judges tend to reach similar conclusions in similar cases, it is inevitable that different judges interpret the same law on occasions differently. Moreover, in early English church law apparently different results might be occasioned merely because the law was particularly concerned with the salvation of the soul (*pro salute animae*):

results that might at first sight be seen as individually conflicting were inevitable when the individual was the prime (if not the only) concern. Moreover, the canon law recognized other ways of mitigating the rigours of the letter of the law, namely, local contrary custom,[11] a wider concept of necessity than that in the common law and dispensation. Only in the nineteenth century, when the influence grew in the ecclesiastical law of practitioners trained in the tradition of the common law at the expense of those trained in the civil[12] and canon law (coupled with other factors), did the binding force of precedent come to be fully accepted in the ecclesiastical courts of the Church of England.[13] Of course, even precedent can be distinguished in particular circumstances, but the doctrine that precedent must be followed creates a much greater consistency. The greater use of statute law, too, inevitably brought further consistency within the law, especially as it tends to militate against exceptions being made in individual cases.

Ecclesiastical law in particular is often concerned with situations where human beings are deeply involved emotionally, even before the intervention of the law or lawyers. Against this background how far then does modern Anglican church law match up to the pastoral challenge?

The law's view of the pastoral duties of the clergy

Canon C 24[14] sets out certain general duties on any priest having a cure of souls.[15] It provides:

> He shall be diligent in visiting his parishioners, particularly those who are sick and infirm;[16] and shall provide opportunities whereby any of his parishioners may resort unto him for spiritual counsel and advice.

Such visiting, therefore, is not purely social visiting but is aimed at the pastoral wellbeing of the parishioner; moreover, pastoral wellbeing embraces the spiritual wellbeing of the person concerned. The same point, in fact, is made in the services of Ordination of Priests:[17]

> You are to be messengers, watchmen, and stewards of the Lord; you are to teach and admonish, to feed and to provide for the Lord's family, to search for his children in the wilderness of this world's temptations and to guide them through its confusions, so that they may be saved through Christ for ever.

Thus in the field of ecclesiastical law the more immediately spiritual duties of a priest having a cure of souls are also part and parcel of his broad obligation of pastoral care: to take services, especially Holy Communion; to preach sermons; to instruct children, or to cause them to be instructed, in the Christian faith;[18] and to prepare persons for confirmation.[19] If at any time he cannot discharge these duties he must provide for another priest to do so.[20]

In particular, granting absolution from sin after due confession is an essential part of a priest's pastoral duties, whether generally as part of a church service or privately in auricular confession; indeed, in this regard the law imposes a strict duty of confidentiality on the priest.[21] Moreover, Canon B 29 provides:

> No priest shall exercise the ministry of absolution in any place without permission of the minister having the cure of souls thereof, unless he is by law authorised to exercise his ministry in that place without being subject to the minister having the general cure of souls of the parish or district in which it is situated: Provided always that, notwithstanding the foregoing provisions of the Canon, a priest may exercise the ministry of absolution anywhere in respect of any person who is in danger of death or if there is some other urgent or weighty cause.

Indeed, this latter exception from the general jurisdictional approach in relation to clerical duties underlines the importance placed on this pastoral duty. In addition, Canon B 37, para. 1, provides:

> The minister shall use his best endeavours to ensure that he be speedily informed when any person is sick or in danger of death in the parish, and shall as soon as possible resort unto him to exhort, instruct, and comfort him in his distress in such manner as he shall think most needful and convenient.[22]

The pastoral care of the sick and dying therefore has a special place within the ecclesiastical law; indeed, special services are provided for the ministry to the sick.[23] Furthermore, although it is unclear whether the wider canonical doctrine of necessity survived the Reformation,[24] necessity certainly permits, for example, reception of the sacramental elements in one kind by an alcoholic or of gluten free bread by a sufferer from coeliac disease.[25]

Baptism

The pastoral concern of the Church begins with the preparations for birth. Baptism is a 'legal and valid initiation into the Christian Church'[26] but, in the view of at least some, it was also the necessary prerequisite to salvation.[27] The Church therefore insisted that the laity should be instructed in the essentials of emergency baptism and that women should have water at hand for baptism at the time of their confinement.[28] In practice such instruction is probably never now given, but Canon B 22, para. 6, still provides:

> No minister being informed of the weakness or danger of any infant within his cure and therefore desired to go to baptise the same shall either refuse or delay to do so.

The occasion of an infant death is, of course, particularly traumatic. *The Alternative Service Book 1980* therefore goes out of its way to spell out a less rigorous theology and to insist on pastoral sensitivity towards the parents if the child dies:

> [The parents] should be assured that questions of ultimate salvation or of the provision of a Christian funeral for an infant who dies do not depend upon whether or not *he* had been baptized.[29]

Thus the pastoral problems consequent upon a salvationist view of the theology of baptism have now been mitigated; moreover, the theology of baptism must be the same whether or not the deceased is an infant.

In addition it should be noted that Canon B 22, para. 6, does not specify by whom the notification to the minister should be given. No doubt this is deliberate as the notification may come from anyone (for example, a nurse) but it can nevertheless cause its own pastoral problems. This is especially so when one or both of the child's parents may be of a non-Christian faith. In law the parents' consent is not required for baptism even though such parents might well object to baptism. When Anglican doctrine might have been seen as demanding baptism as a prerequisite to salvation, a minister would have declined to baptize at his peril: the refusal, after all, could be seen as jeopardizing the child's ultimate salvation.

However, now that a less rigorous theology prevails, the pastoral sensitivities of the parents should be taken into consideration. For this reason the Legal Advisory Commission of the General Synod of the Church of England has advised[30] that, although the canon imposes an absolute duty to attend on the child, there is nonetheless an implied duty on the minister, having attended, not to baptize 'where it is evident that, if the child lives, it is unlikely he or she will be brought up in the Christian faith'.

Equally, even when there is no emergency, one parent may object to a baptism sought by the other. In these circumstances the minister should apply to the diocesan bishop for guidance and directions.[31]

Marriage

When a couple wishes to be married in church, they must comply with ecclesiastical law, even when they have the legal right to marry in their parish church. That law imposes a duty on the minister of that church to explain to the couple, not only the Church's doctrine of marriage, but also the need for God's grace so that they may discharge aright their matrimonial obligations; the minister should also tell them that the good offices of the clergy are always available.[32] This is particularly important as the expressed view of the Anglican Church is that divorce cannot theologically end a marriage.[33] That view, however, has no more than 'moral authority'[34] and ecclesiastical law acknowledges the legal validity of marriages of divorced persons. This is not only because national marriage law takes precedence over any denominational view but also because the law specifies[35] that no Anglican clergyman is compelled to solemnize the marriage of 'any person whose former marriage has been dissolved and whose former spouse is still living'.

Originally this provision was necessary by reason of the legal duty upon incumbents to marry parishioners on the one hand and on the other the conscientious objections of those clergy whose doctrinal beliefs accord with the general view of the Church against remarriage. In fact the provision has also provided a legal way forward for those who do not share those objections and who wish to alleviate the pastoral problems consequent upon them. These clerics see the statutory provision as an implicit acknowledgement that their own doctrinal views are nevertheless acceptable. Nonetheless, for those divorced persons who cannot, or feel they should not, avail themselves of this way out of their individual pastoral dilemma the Church provides an episcopally supervised dispensation for divorced persons who have remarried in relation both to their undergoing baptism and their reception of holy communion.[36]

In practice, however, the tensions created by the unresolved conflict of clerical views are not entirely alleviated by any of these provisions. This is the more so as reported differences in the treatment of different divorced persons – a fundamental problem where there is the exercise of individual discretion – themselves create pastoral problems. Yet another approach to the pastoral situation, therefore, has been the creation by individual ministers of forms of service specially designed to be used after a civil divorce,[37] although these forms of service face the danger of making doctrinal statements that may be contrary to the already noted general view of the Anglican Church that divorce cannot theologically end the marriage.[38] In such forms of service, therefore, there is a difficult path to tread between an insensitive insistence on the one hand that an earlier marriage still subsists (with the concomitant insistence that any different sexual union is adulterous) and a bland declaration on the other that in the eyes of the Church the earlier marriage can be ignored.

Burial

In the ordinary course of events a parishioner is entitled to be buried in the Anglican churchyard of his parish[39] but the rubric at the commencement of the Order for the Burial of the Dead in the Book of Common Prayer forbade the use of the burial service '... for any that die unbaptized, or excommunicate, or having laid violent hands upon themselves'.

Moreover, originally ecclesiastical law did not permit a burial without an accompanying form of service.[40] Thus burial with the usual offices was denied to such persons; this was because they were regarded as no longer Christians.[41] In fact Canon B 38, para. 2, still embodies a very similar exception:

> ... except the person deceased have died unbaptised, or being of unsound mind have laid violent hands upon himself, or have been declared excommunicate for some grievous and notorious crime and no man to testify to his repentance ...

It is immediately apparent, however, that the additional words tend to mitigate the severity of the exception. In particular, although the question of excommunication will extremely rarely (if ever) now arise,[42] the possibility of repentance is introduced. Moreover, the exception only applies to suicides if of 'unsound mind'. In this regard not only must the suicide have reached the age of discretion but the minister's opinion cannot override a coroner's verdict.[43] Indeed, in practice most (if not all) ministers will use the authorized burial service without themselves raising the spectre of suicide; only if there has been a coroner's verdict to the contrary will they feel constrained to implement the exception. Even then, since the Burial Laws Amendment Act, 1980,[44] the bishop has the legal authority to authorize a special form of service for any persons falling within the exception,[45] so greatly mitigating the anguish of the relatives of the deceased.

Most deaths, but more particularly that of a child, are a time of sorrow, and the Church is now more apt to recognize the pastoral needs thereby engendered within the scope of its liturgies.[46] Moreover, in addition to the usual funeral services in the Book of Common Prayer and the Alternative Service Book, there are special services provided for funerals of children as well as one for those dying near the time of birth.[47]

Memorials

As has already been seen, the memorials placed to mark the place of interment themselves give rise to pastoral problems. In particular the bereaved do not necessarily understand that, although there is a right of burial, there is no specific right to mark the grave at all; indeed, in gardens of remembrance individual memorials (and even flower containers) are often not permitted. There may, therefore, be a tension between the wishes of the bereaved and the wishes of the church authorities to retain a specially perceived character to a particular burial ground. In addition, what is acceptable in a municipal cemetery may not be regarded as acceptable in, for example, a mediaeval Cotswold churchyard; indeed, the pastoral position may be aggravated when such memorials occur in the consecrated parts of municipal cemeteries which (being consecrated) also fall within the faculty jurisdiction of the ecclesiastical courts.[48] Moreover, the problem is made worse by the fact that more people now travel abroad and are attracted by customs and designs more traditional to the mainland of Europe than to England and Wales; what is more, continental stone is apparently often more accessible to monumental masons than those stones traditionally used in some parts of Great

Britain. The bereaved tend to choose a memorial with the mason before approaching the local incumbent as to the marking of the grave.

Most dioceses have churchyard rules which permit the incumbent, or rural dean, to authorize memorials within specific limits as to size, design, stone and inscription. Although in practice anyone may petition the relevant diocesan chancellor for a faculty outside these rules, such petitions tend to occur only in a small number of cases, probably because of the cost. Even then different chancellors may reach different conclusions, although in part this is explained by the different circumstances of the petitioners and the relevant churchyards.

One of the particular problems in recent years[49] has been the wish of some relatives to place photographs or photoplaques on such churchyard memorials. The first occasion when this was considered by the courts was in *In re St Mark's, Haydock*,[50] where Chancellor Hamilton said:[51]

> [T]he photographs were not special portrait photographs; they are ordinary, informal snapshots. There is a great deal of difference between their nature and quality and that of the rest of the stone. I was considerably worried about the quality of the photographs as such. One knows that photographs can fade, so that in 10 or 20 years time the photographs could be a smudgy blur, while the rest of the stone remains as it is now. Mr Rigby tells me the photographs are transferred to porcelain by a special process which is permanent, so that this problem does not arise. Even so, the photographs do not of their very nature harmonise with the rest of the stone.

The chancellor did, however, permit an etching of a replica of the deceased's car on the memorial as it would 'provide a pleasing and personal touch to the stone'. In spite of this, however, it is clear that the chancellor was concerned with the aesthetics of the memorial as a whole and in the particular churchyard.

In the same year in *In re St Mary's, Fawkham*[52] Chancellor Goodman felt it inappropriate to permit a memorial with a tile, on which a photograph of the deceased was transposed by heat treatment, to be erected in what was best described as an English country churchyard. On this occasion a faculty was refused as the memorial was likely to weather while the phototile would then stand out,[53]

> remaining clear, compelling and an attraction, which is not

appropriate in the case of a country churchyard. Sometimes described as 'God's acre', the churchyard and its stones are part of the English scene. They form a setting for the church and reflect it in all its periods and time.

On appeal the Dean of the Arches stressed the different interests of the individual petitioner, of the whole Church and of the public generally. Having pointed out that[54] 'Memorials which would have been considered appropriate 100 years ago may well be inappropriate today and vice versa', he continued:[55]

> I have clearly come to the view that memorials such as those [sic] sought ... would be so alien in an English country churchyard, and especially an ancient country churchyard, that they should not be allowed. My decision is based on aesthetic grounds.

Thereafter, in 1990 Chancellor Coningsby dismissed a petition for a porcelain photographic plaque on a gravestone on the grounds that[56]

> such plaques are, in principle, inconsistent with the type of memorial which ought to be allowed in a church burial ground, and could only be permitted if the petitioners were able to show exceptional grounds.

Nonetheless, it is difficult to know what such 'exceptional grounds' might be and there is a sneaking suspicion that people from different social and educational backgrounds might reach different conclusions on such aesthetic questions. In *In re St Mary's, Clifton*,[57] however, Chancellor Spafford in addition paid regard to theological questions:

> The introduction of a [porcelain] portrait would create an unfortunate precedent, as well as seeming unfair to others who had made similar unsuccessful requests. A proper understanding of Christian doctrines of death, resurrection and hope did not accord easily with the provision of a portrait.

It is, of course, difficult from a pastoral perspective to argue against theological questions but in *In re St Mary, Coxhoe*[58] the chancellor, having considered various theological arguments, stated:

> I am quite sure that the provision of a portrait or statue of a deceased person on a memorial purports to do no more than provide a picture of the deceased when alive for the comfort of the bereaved and the interest of posterity. As such it is saying nothing whatsoever about doctrine. If it were otherwise, a vast majority of memorials in Westminster Abbey ... would be entirely illegal. Indeed, the same would have to be said of the kneeling effigy of Bishop Shute Barrington in the south transept of Durham Cathedral.

In fact, Coxhoe churchyard was far from being either an ancient or country churchyard, but the photoplaque originally petitioned for was of plastic. In the absence of evidence as to durability the petition was refused: any memorial ought to weather as a whole or its eventual look will inevitably be displeasing. However, the chancellor gave leave for further evidence as to durability to be put forward or for the consideration of a representation of the deceased to be incised, mechanically or otherwise, directly into the stone. In the event the petitioner did not proceed further with her application.

Pastoral problems are bound to arise in relation to memorials, even though in most dioceses a period must pass for the ground to settle before a memorial may be erected. It is also clear that there are tensions between perceived aesthetic questions and the private wishes of the bereaved. However, as Chancellor Farrant said in *In re Edward Charles Lee, deceased*:[59]

> [N]othing could be more unfortunate than wrangling over matters of taste at the very graveside when the purpose of the enterprise is consolation.

Chancellors are certainly aware of these tensions and are concerned as to the effects of a refusal upon bereaved persons[60] but, as tastes change and language usages alter, it is possible that greater sensitivity should be shown towards a local community's own feelings as to what is appropriate. In this regard there is a further difficulty in that the views of the worshipping congregation may differ from that of the parishioners at large who nonetheless have a legal right to burial in the churchyard.

Exhumation

Finally, as has been seen, pastoral problems arise even when the deceased is buried and a memorial erected. Indeed, exhumation itself may cause distress not only to those intimately involved but to others with an interest in the churchyard, for example, someone living next to, or overlooking, it.[61] However, the prime cause of pastoral distress in such cases at the present arises when someone petitions for an exhumation so that the remains or ashes may be buried in a different churchyard or country, usually because the petitioner has to move and wishes still to be able to tend the grave.[62] Such cases are particularly distressing when there has been an infant death, often many years before, and the parents have to move away because of their own old age; in these cases there is often a pathological problem in relation to grieving.

At least in the nineteenth century permission for exhumation was not too difficult to obtain. Indeed, in *In re Sarah Pope*[63] Dr Lushington stated that

> Faculties for the removal of bodies are of very frequent occurrence, and are decreed to gratify the wishes of relations.

However, in *In re Church Norton Churchyard*,[64] Chancellor Quentin Edwards, QC, said:[65]

> The discretion has undoubtedly been expressed to be quite unfettered. It is to be exercised reasonably, according to the circumstances of the case, taking into account changes in human affairs and ways of thought but always mindful that consecrated ground and human remains committed to it should, in principle, remain undisturbed.

Thus a burden of proof was introduced which a petitioner had to displace in order to obtain permission for the exhumation which in the instant case was not displaced, even though there was no opposition to the petition. The chancellor commented:[66]

> The court should resist a possible trend towards regarding the remains of loved relatives and spouses as portable; to be taken from place to place so that the grave or place of interment of ashes may be the more easily visited.

Indeed, in such cases support for the burden of proof militating against exhumation is often gained from the wording of the burial services themselves.[67] Even in *In re Holy Trinity, Freckleton*,[68] already referred to, Deputy Chancellor Spafford spoke of 'a strong presumption' against exhumation. In practice, however, some chancellors have seemed more ready to find the burden of proof displaced on the ground of pastoral reasons than have others, although there is a danger in drawing conclusions only from the limited number of reported cases. In *In re Ryles, deceased*[69] the husband's ashes had been buried in 1985; when the wife died ten years later, it had been her wish not to be buried in the same cemetery because of its state. A faculty was refused to move the husband's ashes from one Rotherham cemetery to another, although the family longed to see them together. Chancellor McClean commented:

> In the absence of any mistake and of other special circumstances, the petitioner's wishes cannot prevail over the principle that remains committed to consecrated ground should rest undisturbed.

On the other hand Chancellor Goodman granted a faculty permitting exhumation in *Watling Street Cemetery Re Huntington, deceased*[70] so that after a family rift there would be no doubt that the widow might be able to be buried with her husband. He said:

> In the knowledge that my decision will give peace of mind to the petitioner and, I hope, lead to some reconciliation between different members of the family, I am willing to grant a faculty in this particular case, making it clear my decision in no way constitutes a precedent so far as petitions for exhumation in this diocese is concerned. The general principle must remain unaffected.

Of course, not only do the facts of cases differ but different chancellors might within the law reach different conclusions on the same facts; on the other hand it is clearly preferable if some form of consistency can be reached throughout the dioceses. In this regard it may be noted that two exhumation cases may shortly reach the appellate courts.[71] If so, it may be hoped that greater guidance may be forthcoming.

Conclusion

Unfortunately, perhaps, the ecclesiastical law no longer has the flexibility of the old canon law. Nevertheless, the law is concerned to impose duties on the clergy to meet the pastoral needs of their congregations. In addition, although pastoral questions are not at present given as much consideration in exhumation cases as they used to be, there are indications that in some dioceses at least such considerations are given particular weight. As to churchyard memorials there may be tensions between perceived aesthetic demands and the bereaved's wishes but, once again, there are indications that greater flexibility is permitted in some dioceses rather than others.

Notes

1. [1994] 1 WLR 1588; 3 Ecc. LJ 429.
2. The letter was published on 11 August 1994.
3. [1994] 1 WLR 1588 at p. 1596H.
4. Peter Burman and Henry Stapleton, *The Churchyards Handbook*, 3rd edn. (London, 1988), p. 106. This handbook has gained an impressive reputation although it in fact has no official status. Nonetheless in the instant case (at p. 1595G) the chancellor stated that the *Handbook* '*firmly prohibits* the use of nicknames or pet names' (emphasis supplied); this seems to imply some sort of unofficial authority. The next edition is eagerly awaited, especially to see how it will now treat this topic. The quotation in the text is preceded in the third edition by the statement: 'A few other points must command general agreement.' Presumably this rather tendentious statement will be amended.
5. In *In re Edward Charles Lee, deceased* (1995) 4 Ecc. LJ 763 Chancellor Farrant, having considered the *Freckleton* case, permitted the words 'Dad, Grandad and Ted' on a memorial in a municipal cemetery.
6. See Clive Upton and J.D.A. Widdowson, *An Atlas of English Dialects* (Oxford, 1996), p. 77. See, too, *In re St Mary, Hayton* (1990) 2 Ecc. LJ 227.
7. Even if not decided on its own particular facts, the decision of one consistory court is of no more than persuasive force in other dioceses. In fact private communication suggests that many chancellors do not object to the use of words such as Mum or Dad and, indeed, that such words are permitted in their dioceses.
8. See [1994] 1 WLR 1588 at pp. 1591C–D and 1598H.
9. *See In re Holy Trinity, Freckleton* (1995) 3 Ecc. LJ 429. In the deputy chancellor's view the petitioners had been inadvertently misled as to the wording of the proposed memorial and had accordingly acted to their detriment in the choice of the place of burial. Moreover, the incumbent did not object to the exhumation and it was unlikely that 'pastoral damage' would be caused thereby.

10. No doubt other pastoral problems can be postulated, for example, possible tensions between the chancellor and his deputy when the latter reached a different conclusion as to the law from that intimated by the former!
11. The Sacrament Act 1547 (1 Edw. 6, c. 1), s. 8, for example, recognized the situation that usually prevailed, when it went out of its way to state: '... any law, statute, ordinance, or custom contrary thereunto in no wise notwithstanding ...'
12. That is, the civilian system of law.
13. 14 *Halsbury's Laws of England*, 4th edn. (London, 1975), para. 1271.
14. A 'canon' is an ecclesiastical regulation binding on persons in holy orders. It may found a prosecution in the ecclesiastical courts for a 'serious, persistent or continuous neglect of duty': Ecclesiastical Jurisdiction Measure, 1963, s. 14(b).
15. In certain circumstances a deacon may have a cure of souls and it seems likely in such circumstances that the word 'priest' would then be interpreted to embrace a 'deacon'.
16. In this respect the canon reflects the general pre-Reformation canon law: see Lyndwood, *Provinciale Angliae* (Oxford, 1679), pp. 63–4.
17. *The Alternative Service Book 1980*, pp. 356–7. The Ordering of Priests in *The Book of Common Prayer* is to like effect.
18. He must also 'use such opportunities of teaching or visiting in the schools within his cure as are open to him': Canon C 24, para. 4.
19. Canon C 24.
20. Canon C 24, para. 8.
21. Rupert D. H. Bursell, *Liturgy, Order and the Law* (Oxford, 1996), p. 227, esp. n. 129.
22. Particular provision is made for the provision of Holy Communion to the sick: Canon B 37, para. 2.
23. See Bursell, *Liturgy, Order, Law*, pp. 225–6.
24. *Ibid.,* p. 42, n. 86.
25. *Ibid.,* pp. 108–9, 116–17. See, too, the Sacrament Act, 1547, s. 8, and the authorized service book *Ministry to the Sick*, p. 4 n. 7.
26. *Kemp v. Wickes* (1809) 3 Phillim. 264 at p. 275 *per* Sir John Nicholl.
27. See Bursell, *Liturgy, Order, Law,* p. 131, n. 8.
28. See ibid., pp. 140–1.
29. *The Alternative Service Book 1980*, p. 280 n. 106.
30. *Legal Opinions concerning the Church of England* (London, 1994), pp. 16d–e.
31. *Ibid.,* p. 16c. Incidentally, confirmation technically provides the only legally valid manner, short of an Act of Parliament, for changing an unwanted baptismal name: see *In re Parrott. Cox v. Parrott* [1946] Ch. 183 at pp. 186–7 *per* Vaisey, J; Canon B 27, para. 6; Bursell, *Liturgy, Order, Law,* p. 156.
32. Canon B 30, para. 3; Bursell, *Liturgy, Order, Law,* pp. 157–8.
33. *Acts of The Convocations* (London, 1961), pp. 90–3; see, too, Norman Doe, *The Legal Framework of the Church of England* (Oxford, 1996), pp. 376–7. Ecclesiastical law nonetheless recognizes that a marriage never existed if it is null and void: *ibid.,* p. 375.

34. *Bland v. Archdeacon of Cheltenham* [1972] Fam. 157 at p. 166D.
35. Matrimonial Causes Act, 1965, s. 8(2); see, too, the Marriage Act, 1949, s. 5A.
36. See Doe, *Legal Framework*, pp. 376–7.
37. Such services may, for example, be made by the minister having the cure of souls: Canon B 5, para. 2. The more widely accepted approach of blessing the civil marriage of a couple one or both of whom has been divorced also raises theological questions as to marriage itself: what is a church marriage other than the blessing of a couple who have reciprocally agreed to live together in a sexual union for life? Is it solely the pronouncement by the minister that they are man and wife? In fact, a blessing is not a legal essential to the validity of a marriage: see Bursell, *Liturgy, Order, Law,* p. 185.
38. For example, *A Form of Service Following a Civil Divorce* was printed in *The Church Times* on 19 April 1996. During the service the priest says: ' ... you are legally divorced ... You are no longer married ... ' The latter statement is, of course, legally accurate but may nevertheless be unacceptable as a theological statement.
39. Bursell, *Liturgy, Order, Law,* p. 301. This is so whether a non-Anglican service is to be used or no service at all: see the Burial Laws Amendment Act, 1880, and Bursell, ibid., p. 202 n. 33.
40. *Kemp v. Wickes* (1809) 3 Phillim. 264 at p. 295 *per* Sir John Nicholl.
41. *Kemp v. Wickes* (1809) 3 Phillim. 264 at p. 273 *per* Sir John Nicholl.
42. Bursell, *Liturgy, Order, Law,* p. 85 n. 253, and p. 213.
43. *Clift v. Schwabe* (1846) 3 CB 437 at pp. 472–6 *per* Pollock CB; *Dufaur v. Professional Life Assurance Co.* (1858) 25 Beav. 599 at p. 602; *Cooper v. Dodd* (1850) 2 Rob. Eccl. 270.
44. Section 13, now amended by the Prayer Book (Further Provisions) Measure, 1968, s. 6, and the Church of England (Worship and Doctrine) Measure, 1974, s. 6(2), Sch. I, para. 1.
45. Bursell, *Liturgy, Order, Law,* pp. 213, 219–20. The minister having the cure of souls cannot create such a service: *ibid.*, p. 222.
46. Indeed, *The Alternative Service Book 1980*, p. 306, n. 7, now reads: 'If pastoral needs require, additional material ... may be used at the Committal and the Interment of the Ashes.'
47. See Bursell, *Liturgy, Order, Law,* p. 212.
48. See, for example, *In re Edward Charles Lee, deceased* (1995) 4 Ecc. LJ 763.
49. I understand that there are even some Victorian examples in one of the London municipal cemeteries.
50. [1981] 1 WLR 1164.
51. At p. 1166A–C.
52. [1981] 1 WLR 1171.
53. At p. 1174A–B.
54. [1981] 1 WLR 1174 at p. 1175E–F. See, too, *In re Little Gaddesdon Churchyard, ex parte Cuthbertson* (1933) P 150 at p. 153 *per* Sir Lewis Dibdin on fashion and white marble.
55. At p. 1175G–H.

56. (1990) 2 Ecc. LJ 64.
57. (1993) 3 Ecc. LJ 117.
58. (1996) 4 Ecc. LJ 686 (Chancellor Bursell). See, too, *In re St Peter, Oundle* (1996) 4 Ecc. LJ 764 (Chancellor Coningsby) concerning carved caricatures of living persons at the top of columns in a church nave.
59. (1995) 4 Ecc. LJ 763.
60. There are other problems. What weight should be given to the wishes of a first wife? What standing, if any, should be accorded to a mistress of long standing?
61. It is, therefore, surprising that general citation, by which the parishioners may come to learn of the petition, may in certain circumstances be dispensed with: Faculty Jurisdiction Rules 1993 (1992 No. 2820), r. 12(9). Indeed, on occasion the actual hearing may be heard in private: see, for example, *In re Church of St Paul, Hanging Heaton* (1994) 3 Ecc. LJ 261.
62. On occasions, the wish is to keep the exhumed ashes unburied, for example, on the mantelpiece. In *In re Stokes, deceased* (1995) 4 Ecc. LJ 527 (*The Times*, 5 September 1995), the wish was that the exhumed ashes should be scattered in the Derbyshire hills.
63. (1857) 15 Jurist 614; see, too, *In re Dixon* (1892) P 386. In *In re Matheson* (1958) 1 WLR 246 at p. 248 Chancellor Steel said: '... each case must be considered on its merits and the Chancellor must decide as a matter of judicial discretion whether a particular application should be granted or refused'.
64. [1989] Fam. 37, otherwise reported *sub nom. Re Atkins* [1898] 1 All ER 14.
65. At p. 43E.
66. *In re Church Norton Churchyard* [1898] Fam. 37 at p. 43H. See, too, *In re St Mary Magdalen, Lyminster* (1990) 2 Ecc. LJ 127.
67. See *In re St Peter's Churchyard, Oughtrington* [1993] 1 WLR 1440, otherwise reported *sub nom. Re Smith* [1994] 1 All ER 90.
68. (1995) 3 Ecc. LJ 429.
69. 24 October 1995 (unreported).
70. 8 October 1996 (unreported).
71. See *Re Christ Church, Alsager* [1999] 1 All ER 117.

Bibliography

Bursell, *Liturgy, Order and the Law* (Oxford, 1996)
Doe, *Canon Law in the Anglican Communion: A Worldwide Perspective* (Oxford, 1998)
Halsbury's Laws of England, 4th edn. (London, 1975)

22

Ecumenism and ecclesial and pastoral proclamation

Jeffrey Gros, Eamon McManus and Ann Riggs[1]

> O God of unchangeable power and eternal light,
> look favorably upon thy whole Church,
> that wonderful and sacred mystery;
> and by the tranquil operation of thy perpetual providence
> carry out the work of human salvation;
> and let the whole world feel and see
> that things which were cast down are being raised up;
> that those which had grown old are being made new;
> and that all things are returning into unity
> through him by whom all things were made,
> even thy Son Jesus Christ our Lord.
>
> *Gelasian Sacramentary*

Cardinal Joseph Ratzinger has spoken of the Church as 'a company in constant renewal'. The ecumenical movement is a common pilgrimage of Christians in spiritual renewal who aspire to attain a more intimate relationship to Christ in the Trinitarian life, and hence draw closer to one another. Here, we will address the future of ecumenism and its implications for Catholic ecclesial and pastoral proclamation. Three themes will chart its progression:

---

1. First published in *Introduction to Ecumenism* (Paulist Press, 1998), pp. 234-49.

(1) the present ecumenical agenda of the Church,
(2) the ecclesiology of *koinonia,* and
(3) the importance of a spirituality of ecumenism.

The ecumenical pilgrimage, so central to Christian identity and the pastoral priorities of the Catholic Church, is rooted in faith in Jesus Christ and zeal for the Church and its unity. This faith and zeal have a specific history, content and set of spiritual resources which nourish the Christian along the way and enrich the Christian life, even before the goal of full communion is achieved. At this moment in the journey, the challenge of education is a major priority. The publication of the *Catechism of the Catholic Church,* the encyclical *Ut Unum Sint* and *The Directory for the Application of Principles and Norms on Ecumenism* should challenge educators, catechists and preachers at every level of church life to work with their ecumenical colleagues to integrate the results of the decades of dialogues, and the hopes of an ecumenical future, into the consciousness and experience of Christian life.

All the churches are faced with a variety of pastoral challenges which require them to take account of their own internal struggles. Yet these are shared challenges even when they appear with more urgency in another church than our own. For example, if we are searching for a common ground on an ethical issue, such as sexuality or concern for the poor, the debates are common even when they are articulated in only one church. When it is a question of catechetical or sacramental renewal, our ecumenical urgency toward the common faith and our quest for full Eucharistic communion should lead us toward common and complementary educational and liturgical approaches.

Three stages in the ecumenical movement

In preparation for the celebration of the 2,000th anniversary of the birth of Christ in the great Jubilee, the churches pray that they come closer to the prayer of Christ for full communion. As we survey the situation of the churches during the last few decades we can note a development from the initial contacts of collaboration and tolerance to a serious engagement in dialogue of charity and truth, progressing in our own day into decisions for deeper bonds of communion among the churches. While the pilgrimage moves forward, these stages overlap, and participation varies from one culture and church to another. The work of one stage continues as the others develop.

Moving from the Chicago–Lambeth Quadrilateral in 1888, through the Edinburgh Conference of 1910, the founding of the World Council in 1948, and the emergence of the Catholic Church into the ecumenical movement in 1961, foundations were laid for the ecumenical movement as we understand it today. Contact exists among evangelicals and is emerging with other Christian communities. Earlier models of the restoration of the New Testament Church, of a non-denominational Christianity, or of return to a static Orthodoxy or Roman Catholicism, have been replaced by a more sophisticated vision.

A second major stage was initiated by the intensive dialogue that engaged the churches to move beyond comparison of their differences and merely collaborative relationship in mission. The Christological methodology of the Faith and Order movement, its success after the Montreal 1963 World Conference, including *Scripture, Tradition and the Traditions,* as well as massive bilateral and church union developments introduced an immensely productive stage of the ecumenical movement which is continuing at present.

This stage has had a significant impact and has changed the way in which scripture studies and theology are now carried out. The Catholic Church has been an ardent supporter of these World Council bilateral and multilateral dialogues. Most dramatically in the 1980s, the ARCIC *Final Report,* the World Council's *Baptism, Eucharist and Ministry,* and the Lutheran-Catholic work *Justification by Faith* stimulated the Church to begin to re-evaluate the theological basis for unity for the first time since the Council of Florence (1439).

A third stage has begun, with a series of concrete proposals which bring the churches to authoritative decision. Common Declarations with the Eastern churches, some of which enable Eucharistic sharing; unions of churches, of which there have been five major examples in the last few decades in the United States alone; and a variety of proposals before the churches in these years on the threshold of the great Jubilee 2000 illustrate the vibrant tenor of this stage of development.

The concept of a united Church as an institutional merger bringing together the corporate structures of the various bodies has largely been put aside in recent decades. The perspective of this third stage envisions unity by stages, with phases of shared life over a reasonable space of time. An early sketch of this vision of Conciliar Fellowship was articulated in 1975 by the World Council. A more descriptive statement was the Lutheran-Catholic *Facing Unity* of 1980. It proposes multiple phases.

Two are particularly important: the re-evaluation and resolution of mutual condemnations and a transition from the collaborative exercise of *episcopé* to collegial exercise of episcopacy, with joint ordinations and community participation in the selection and affirmation of episcopal leadership. This vision of conciliar union by mutuality and by stages seeks to honour and receive the gifts of each community while advancing toward full communion.

The proposal for *Churches in Covenant Communion: The Church of Christ Uniting,* under consideration by the Episcopal, Presbyterian, Disciples of Christ, African Methodist Episcopal, Christian Methodist Episcopal, United Methodist, and African Methodist Episcopal Zion Churches, the United Church of Christ, and the International Council of Community Churches, envisions a phased union which will entail a service of recognition and reconciliation to be celebrated the first Sunday in Advent 2000 for those churches which have taken positive action by that time. The Catholic Church, though not a member of this essentially American union proposal, has been represented by canon lawyers, liturgists and theologians working with these churches on their pilgrimage toward full communion.

In 1997 the Episcopal and Evangelical Lutheran churches considered a *Concordat,* which would enable not only common work in mission, but also common episcopal ordinations in the future and full interchangeability or ordained ministers. This phased unity, while somewhat different from the *Facing Unity* and *Covenant Communion* proposals, is designed in light of the ecclesiology developed in these and articulated in *Toward Full Communion* (1991). The *Concordat* proposes that the Lutherans would suspend the requirement of subscription to the Augsburg Confession by Episcopal priests acting in their churches, while the Episcopalians would suspend the requirement in the preface to the Anglican *Ordinal,* which stipulates that all pastors be ordained by bishops in the apostolic succession. Eventually, all ordinations would entail bishops in the apostolic succession. This proposal for Anglican-Lutheran reconciliation is somewhat different from, but is complementary to, that approved by the Baltic, British and Scandinavian churches.

On the basis of *A Common Calling: The Witness of Our Reformation Churches in North America Today* (1993), Evangelical Lutheran, Presbyterian, Reformed and United Church of Christ Churches have approved a *Formula of Agreement* overcoming the mutual condemnations on Eucharist, Christology and predestination of the Reformation period and initiating full communion among them. Since there were never differences over the ordained ministry among these churches, this was not an issue that needed to be resolved among them, as it will be with Anglican, Catholic or Orthodox partners. The proposal, Joint Declaration on the Doctrine of Justification, will provide a first stage of putting aside mutual condemnations between Lutherans and Catholics.

Whether any or all of these proposals will have institutional success at this time is merely a footnote to the bigger issue in this third stage of ecumenical development. All of the churches will have been transformed by the dialogue and approach to decision making. Undoubtedly, the unsuccessful proposals will lead us to discern how, in the Lord's good time, more adequate formulations can be designed to serve that goal. All these considerations, however, evidence the quality of education and spiritual formation that is so urgently needed at this stage in the ecumenical movement to afford all of us the patience and zeal to continue the pilgrimage to which we are called and upon which we are embarked.

The Canberra Assembly encouraged the movement from dialogue to decision when it articulated these concrete challenges for the churches:

> The challenge at this moment in the ecumenical movement as a reconciling and renewing movement towards full visible unity is for the seventh assembly of the WCC to call all churches:
> - to recognize each other's baptism on the basis of the BEM document;
> - to move towards the recognition of the apostolic faith as expressed through the Nicene-Constantinopolitan Creed in the life and witness of one another;
> - on the basis of convergence in faith in baptism, eucharist and ministry to consider, wherever appropriate, forms of eucharistic hospitality; we gladly acknowledge that some who do not observe these rites share in the spiritual experience of life in Christ;
> - to move towards a mutual recognition of ministries;
> - to endeavor in word and deed to give common witness to the gospel as a whole;
> - to recommit themselves to work for justice, peace and the integrity of creation, linking more closely the search for the sacramental communion of the church with the struggles for justice and peace;
> - to help parishes and communities express in appropriate ways locally the degree of communion that already exists.
>
> (3.2)

This third period has also been characterized by the expansion and deepening of the universality of the churches in the ecumenical movement. The post-colonial period and the subsidiarity and collegiality articulated in the Second Vatican Council have begun to decrease the Eurocentric character of both the theology and the vision of the unity of the Church. New diversities have been introduced with the inculturation of the gospel in Asia and Africa and appreciation of the five-hundred-year contributions of Latin American Christian experience. Likewise, the voices of women, and an appreciation of the Church's responsibility in the world and for creation, have both enhanced and deepened the complexity of the ecumenical journey. The three stages of the ecumenical movement chart an ecumenical future that is both challenging and promising.

Koinonia *and the Ecumenical Future*

Perhaps one of the most unexpected fruits of the founding of the World Council and the meeting of the Second Vatican Council was the manner in which the ecclesiology of *koinonia* took root, not only in World Council relations but also in the Catholic Church. In 1948 the World Council used the category in its constitution, 'a fellowship of churches', and it became a key ecclesiological theme in Vatican II, was reaffirmed in the Extraordinary Roman Synod in 1985, and matured in a variety of ecumenical dialogues emerging from the second stage of ecumenical discussion.

Several international Catholic dialogues with Eastern Orthodox, Oriental Orthodox, Anglican, Lutheran and Methodist partners have articulated explicitly the vision of the communion we seek and have resolved some of the most intractable obstacles to full *koinonia*. Other international dialogues between the Catholic Church and the Disciples and Reformed are aimed toward the same full communion, but have moved toward it with more measured steps. Even dialogues between the Catholic Church and Pentecostal and Baptist groups, which have not formulated a goal of fully visible unity, have founded their work of promoting mutual understanding in communion ecclesiology.

The Catholic Church has come to see the importance of the local church or diocese as an important dimension of *koinonia*, where the bishop is its sacramental representative and expression, in union with the college of bishops and its centre, the bishop of Rome. The dual focus of the bishop as centre of unity in the local church and in *koinonia* with the worldwide communion of churches is further witness to the unity modelled on the divine Trinity.

The Catholic understanding of *koinonia* is exemplified by the active participation of the laity as the people of God, which contrasts with a merely secular democratic understanding of the Church. Communion is grounded in the common mission of all Christians, received in baptism and preceding the differentiations of functions, charisms or ministries. While there are tensions among members of the Church as there are between divided Christians, the theology of *koinonia* provides a solid basis for securing unity in Christ. The understanding of the Church as a *koinonia* and of the real, if imperfect, *koinonia* that exists among the still divided churches, will require the spiritual and ascetic qualities such as a deep sense of caring and openness, a commitment to dialogue, and a total reliance upon God. As Theresa of Jesus reminds us:

> Let nothing trouble you
> Let nothing frighten you
> Everything passes
> God never changes
> Patience obtains all.

All of this development of the theology of communion, vertical and horizontal, with the triune God and with the communion of Christian believers, occurs within the shared context of the World Council vision of the Faith and Order Commission and the Joint Working Group between the WCC and the Vatican. The 1991 World Council enumeration of elements necessary for full communion is helpful in delineating where the issues that still divide the churches are under discussion toward resolution:

ELEMENTS OF FULL COMMUNION FOLLOWING THE OUTLINES OF THE CANBERRA TEXT 2.1

1. **The common confession of the apostolic faith:**

   Confessional Character of the Church
   Creedal and non-creedal churches
   Christology
   Chalcedonian and non-Chalcedonian churches
   Assyrian Church of the East and Churches which accept Ephesus (431)
   Lutheran and Reformed churches

Pneumatology
Eastern and Oriental Orthodox and Western churches
Trinity
Oneness Pentecostals and Trinitarian churches
Justification
Roman Catholic Church and Reformation churches
Peace Witness
Anabaptist, Quaker and Just War churches
Racial Witness
African American and churches that tolerated slavery and racism

2. **A common sacramental life entered by the one baptism and celebrated together in one eucharistic fellowship:**

    Lutheran and Reformed churches
    Episcopally ordered and non-episcopal churches
    Roman Catholic, Orthodox churches and Reformation churches
    Believers' baptist and paedobaptist churches

3. **A common life in which members and ministries are mutually recognized and reconciled:**

    Episcopally ordered and non-episcopal churches

4. **And a common mission witnessing to the gospel of God's grace to all people and serving the whole of creation. The goal of the search for full communion is realized when all the churches are able to recognize in one another the one, holy, catholic and apostolic church in its fullness:**

    Denominational and 'churchly' ecclesiological understandings of the gospel
    Spiritual ecumenism and visible unity as a goal

5. **This full communion will be expressed on the local level and the universal levels through conciliar forms of life and action:**

    Congregational and catholic ecclesiologies
    Episcopal and non-episcopal churches

6. **In such communion churches are bound in all aspects of life together at all levels in confessing the one faith and engaging in worship and witness, deliberation and action:**

    Congregational churches and conciliar churches
    Global and national churches
    The Catholic Church (and its papal claims) and other churches

The vision of the Church as communion has not as yet developed to full fruition in the comprehension of the nature of grace and of the bonds of communion between Christ and believers in the Incarnation and Redemption. It has, however, reversed the complete identification of the Church and Christ, the subsequent equation of the Church as the prolongation of the incarnation, and a triumphalistic ecclesiology in Orthodox and Catholic theology. It accentuates the Trinitarian and sacramental character of the *koinonia* of Christ to Church and believers, thus recapturing many elements of the more ancient 'mystical body' ecclesiology and maintaining the identification of the Church as the body of Christ while preserving its differentiation.

The understanding of the doctrine of *koinonia* in terms of 'divinization' from the Eastern tradition and of grace rather than a mere 'participation' or 'sharing' in Trinitarian life, should lead the Christian churches to the Trinitarian centre of the Christian faith, recognizing the Holy Spirit as the source of our baptismal and Eucharistic life in Christ and as uniting the community mystically in Christ. Such a vision should situate all the Christian churches on an authentic ecumenical course.

The development of the implications of this communion with the Trinity in Christ will entail serious horizontal developments as well, if the third stage of ecumenism is to bear its full fruit in the life of the Church. This includes common affirmation of the apostolic faith; deepening a common sense of tradition; renewing the relationship between Scripture, tradition and the teaching office of the churches; developing a hermeneutic that sees the faith in the light of the hierarchy of truths; being nourished by the spiritual traditions of other churches as well as sharing one's own; bringing alive the conscious faith implicit in the baptism of all; internalizing the central role of the Bible in all areas of life; recognizing the convergences that have already occurred in liturgical life; and developing structures of accountability within the Church that hold all of us to our ecumenical commitment.

The future will call forth deepened work on the role of Mary. The US Lutheran-Catholic Dialogue VIII, *The One Mediator, The Saints, and Mary* (1983–1990), has been pioneering in this field. Because dialogues proceed from the most firm common ground to the more difficult issues, other dialogues have only begun discussion of the place of Mary in the Church's life that this more developed dialogue has been able to engage. Much work will be needed to develop an ecumenical interpretation of one's own and one another's approaches to popular devotion and piety.

The renewal of Marian theology and practice in the Catholic Church has been encouraged by *Lumen Gentium* and *Marialis Cultus* of Pope Paul VI, in particular. These offer hermeneutical guidelines to prevent abuses and to contribute to a genuine Mariology. Devotion to Mary derives from the understanding of Christ and his saving role. Renewal in Marian theology and practice is a parallel to the ecumenical contact and biblical devotion that have developed since the Council. There has been a significant contribution from the international Ecumenical Society for the Blessed Virgin Mary.

Spiritual ecumenism

Finally, pilgrimage toward unity and living in the tension between the divine imperative toward unity and the human experience of separation is nourished and sustained by the Holy Spirit with the help of concrete spiritual resources. The presupposition that the pursuit of ecumenism is fundamentally an exercise in spiritual theology, and 'Spiritual Ecumenism' remains the raison d'être of its development. It is well to concentrate upon this question in reference to ecclesial and pastoral proclamation.

There are several elements to emphasize. The necessity of Christian conversion emanates from the Gospel injunction, 'The kingdom of God is at hand. Repent, and believe in the gospel' (Mark 1.15). Conversion takes different forms: some occur very suddenly, while others are more gradual. Ecclesial conversion entails understanding and affirming Christ's essential call to his community in history. Conversion to one's own particular confessional tradition consists in a deeper attachment to the Triune God, to the overcoming of the sinfulness which impedes an enduring fidelity to the gospel, and to an effort to seek 'full communion' among the churches. Conversion on the part of churches requires them to acknowledge the sin of division and to renew themselves in their ecumenical commitment. It includes a willingness to reform their own structures in the light of the gospel.

A collective identity of any kind, and especially among churches, is always a paradoxical phenomenon that involves a tension among the forces of unification, integration, harmonization and social interaction. As a living reality, conversion alone can provide simultaneously for reception of new insights and fidelity to the tradition. Living in the tension of a pilgrimage in fidelity to both our call to an uncharted future and continuity with the apostolic heritage demands prayer, openness and continual conversion of spirit. In the ecclesiastical sphere, conversion alone can provide the essential ingredients needed for the Church to remain vital and true to itself.

Christian identity, founded as it is on Scripture and living tradition, upon the confession of the faith, and articulated in post-apostolic witnesses, in liturgy and in the creeds, is a dynamic and radical process. It includes a secure grounding in one's own community and an openness to the eschatological 'beyond' which constantly summons it forward. The Church as a 'mystery' is required to strive to become more 'catholic' and 'reformed' in the sense of always moving to reclaim its spiritual reality, and to overcome any contradictory attitude to the Christian gospel.

Symbolic gestures are an integral part of the process of turning to conversion, particularly on the part of separated churches. In this regard, one must admire the abilities of the recent Popes to employ symbolic gestures in the service of ecumenical rapprochement (UUS 71–3).

Movement into the third stage of ecumenism requires conversion, not only of theological formulations, but also of the hearts and minds of believers and of the institutional structures by which the Church lives. The decisions which authorities have already taken evidence a spirit of forgiveness and humility which is a necessary element of the Christian conversion process. The spiritual disciplines which serve an ecumenical spiritual life include, in addition to prayer for ecumenism, prayer with other Christians, participation in and appreciation of the variety of worship styles and spiritual traditions, reading the biographies and spiritual resources of other traditions, developing friends in other traditions, cultivating a style of personal and ecclesial hospitality and finding experiences of dialogue to nourish one's own ecumenical zeal and to expand one's ecclesial horizons.

Finally, an ecumenical spirituality entails attention and prayerful assessment of the classical marks of the Church to deepen our commitment together to unity; to recognize the holiness at work in separated fellow Christians; to expand our understanding of catholicity in order to incorporate the variety of cultures, races and traditions that Christ has given the churches; and to deepen and expand the understanding of apostolicity to encompass the modes of continuity testified to in the ecumenical results.

The ecumenical documents should not be seen as only theological resources for church leaders and academics. Rather, they should be read in a spirit of prayer and wonder at the *magnalia Dei* occurring in our midst and as written testimonies to the movement of the Spirit among us. They should call the Church to conversion and become occasions to deepen faith and renew worship and church life. The New Evangelization articulated by Pope John Paul, with its new ardour, methods and vision, is inherently ecumenical, as he noted in Germany, 1996:

> The new evangelization is therefore the order of the day. This does not mean the 'restoration' of a past age. Rather it is necessary to risk taking new steps. Together we must again proclaim the joyful and liberating message of the Gospel to the people of Europe ... The task of evangelization involves moving toward each other and moving together as Christians, and it must begin from within; evangelization and unity, evangelization and ecumenism are indissoluby linked with each other ... Because the question of the new evangelization is very close to my heart, as bishop of Rome I consider overcoming the divisions of Christianity 'one of the pastoral priorities'.
> (*L'Osservatore Romano*, English ed., 27/5 (3 July 1996] nos. 3, 5)

Conclusion

The ecumenical task takes place in a variety of cultures, in a variety of churches, and with the various gifts the baptized bring to their pilgrimage. However, the faith of the Church and of the churches together in this pilgrimage finally sustains them in this work of the Holy Spirit. As the stages of the ecumenical movement move forward, as the elements of communion between the churches deepen, the spirituality of all is enriched by fidelity to God's call and the eschatological hope of the reconciliation for which we pray.

In addressing the June 1994 extraordinary consistory of cardinals, Pope John Paul entrusted the care of ecumenism to the intercession of the Blessed Virgin and expressed his own hopes for the future of the Church thus:

> In view of the year 2000, this is perhaps the greatest task. *We cannot come before Christ, the Lord of history, as divided as we have unfortunately been during the second millennium.* These divisions must give way to *rapprochement* and harmony; the wounds on the path of Christian unity must be healed. As she faces this Great

Jubilee, the Church needs *'metanoia'*, *that is, the discernment of her children's historical shortcomings and negligence* with regard to the demands of the Gospel. Only the courageous acknowledgement of faults and omissions for which Christians have in some way been responsible, as well as the generous intention to remedy them with the help of God, can given an effective impetus to the new evangelization and make the path to unity easier. Here indeed is the essential core of our mission according to the explicit words of the divine Master, as he was about to face the dramatic events of his passion: 'That they all may be one, even as you, Father, are in me, and I in you, that they may also be one in us, so that the world may believe that you have sent me.' (Jn. 17.21) (IS no. 87 [1994], 218)

Selected readings

Ion Bria and Dagmar Heller (eds.), *Ecumenical Pilgrims: Profiles of Pioneers in Christian Reconciliation* (Geneva: World Council of Churches, 1995)

Gillian Evans, Lorelei Fuchs and Dianne Kessler, *Encounters for Unity: Sharing Faith, Prayer and Life* (Norwich: Canterbury Press, 1995)

Group des Dombes, *For the Conversion of the Churches,* James Greig, trans. (Geneva: World Council of Churches, 1993)

E. Glenn Hinson, (ed.), *Spirituality in Ecumenical Perspective* (Louisville: Westminster/John Knox Press, 1993)

Michael Kinnamon and Brian E. Cope, (eds.), *The Ecumenical Movement: An Anthology of Basic Texts and Voices* (Grand Rapids: Eerdmans, 1997), pp. 497–525.

Joan O. S. F. Puls, *Every Bush is Burning: A Spirituality for Our Times* (Geneva: World Council of Churches, 1985)

23

Sects and new religious movements

Martyn Percy

Why do people belong to cults, sects, new religious movements or churches? Strangely, the reasons often overlap with why those same people might belong to biological or adoptive families. As Rabuzzi notes ('Family', in Eliade, *Encyclopaedia of Religion*), families offer 'a universal symbol of ultimacy', in which 'various ritual processes' are enacted that help sustain meaning. Families – and there are many types – are basic collective or group forms of human existence which encourage growth, individuation, sociality and communal life. Yet what actually constitutes 'a family' is not always clear, an identity problem shared with bodies that are variously identified as 'cults' or 'sects'.

Nuclear families, extended families, ties of kinship, breakdown, divorce and marriage have morphological similarities with the operation of small religious groups. And where cults, families and sects coincide, there can be reinforcement of identity that is mutually beneficial, competition between units and individuals, or compensation when a unit fails in its filial or religious obligations to members.

Correspondingly, there are organizations which claim that cults and sects break up families, with some going further and offering to rescue individuals from allegedly oppressive or manipulative groups, and 'de-programme' them (involving allegations of 'brainwashing'), restoring them to 'normal' family relations. With no less justification, there are cults and sects who claim to rescue individuals from dysfunctional communities, and offer an alternative form of 'family' that is in the best interests of its members. In the course of my research, I have often met people of all ages who have freely chosen to live in exclusivist religious communities, regarding their lifestyle (including imposed constraints on freedom of choice and basic rights) as a better or higher form of family life than the biological one they may have abandoned. Such claims are not the exclusive provenance of cults or sects – 'Closed Brethren' and some modern House Churches are morphologically indistinguishable. Indeed, any mainstream religious order (e.g. Christian or Buddhist monks and nuns) could be seen in a similar light. Religious groups can provide levels of kinship, intimacy, control and relationality that may appear oppressive to some, but are experienced as liberation by others.

In effect, all forms of family are in some competition with religions that claim to offer alternative forms of 'family' relationality. As a number of scholars note, the problematic interaction between the two is generally encountered in the areas of growth, expansion and individuation. A helpful approach to this double-bind comes from J. Gordon Melton, in his *Encyclopaedia of American Religion* (1978), who categorizes all expressions of American religious life according to 'families'. In choosing to adopt the metaphor 'family' to describe expressions of religion, Melton is arguing for a structural understanding of religion that achieves two goals: (1) it permits him to reject the simplistic European-centred distinctions of Troeltsch between 'church', 'sect' and 'cult', which are potentially clumsy; (2) it allows religious expressions to be grouped together according to their ecclesial, social and doctrinal similarity, not according to size or social impact. But as fundamentalists have known for nearly a century, many of their 'family members' often do not recognize each other, let alone talk to one another. The reason for the proliferation and fragmentation of 'family members' in ecclesiastical history is not usually expansion, nor the indigenous enculturation of imported or exported religious tradition. Critically, it is much more likely to occur because of a breakdown in relationships. It is not faith that is usually rejected, but custodians of it. Personality clashes, charisma and authority disputes all play a part in sects and schisms.

Understanding cults, sects and new religious movements

Classifying religious groups as 'cults', 'sects' or even as 'new religious movements' is highly problematic. Rather like the word 'heretic', common usage of such terms is tainted by its doctrinal associations: history is written by the winners or the majority. The word 'cult' is now so pejorative as almost to have lost its meaning. Originally, it simply meant 'worship' or 'ritual' (Latin, *cultus*). Equally, 'sect' is etymologically related to the Latin *secare* ('to cut'), implying schism. Yet every religion owns its own sects or cults: Hare Krishna is a Hindu cult; the Mormons are a Christian sect. Religious families are broken up by doctrine and allegiance as much as biological families are, and the pain and the problems are no easier to bear.

In terms of understanding biological families and their relationships to sects, cults and new religious movements, some of the best introductions are not 'academic', but either fictional or semi-autobiographical. Jeanette Winterson's *Oranges Are Not the Only Fruit* (1985) is a gripping account of a young woman's struggle to come to terms with a strict Pentecostal sect and her own family, who are suffocatingly enmeshed in its worldviews. *The Handmaid's Tale* (1985) by Margaret Atwood is a futuristically based novel that explores the subjugation of women in a post-apocalypse America, where individual states have become like Old Testament tribes, and members of mainstream religious groups (e.g. Baptists) are hunted as heretics. Garrison Keillor's *Lake Woebegon Days* (1985) writes a deeply personal but ironic account of the problems of being brought up within the Brethren. *Knowledge of Angels* (1995), Jill Paton Walsh's award-winning novel, imagines a pre-modern world in which the spirit of humanism is crushed by a form of fundamentalism that bears a close relationship to the Spanish Inquisition. Iain Banks's *Whit* (1995) is a humorous, ironic novel that traces the genesis of a new religious movement through a narration that also charts the break-up of the leading cult family.

Such studies of religions and family life are often insightful, and helpful to have in mind before turning to the more academic responses. These can be divided into three groups, and each has its limitations:

Theological: helpful for understanding the doctrinal basis of a movement, but can be prone to being dogmatic, even 'anti-cult';
Psychological: useful for articulating the psycho-social features of a group, but prone to focus on 'mind control';
Sociological: usually even-handed or 'neutral', but prone to focus on structure as expression of value.

More formally, Bryan Wilson's sociology, in *Religious Sects* (1970), still offers a useful taxonomy for understanding cults, sects and new religious movements. His categorization has implications for a study of these groups in relation to families. Wilson identifies seven types: conversionist, revolutionist, manipulationist, thaumaturgical, introversionist, reformist and utopian.

Sects may be derived from schisms, and there have been a growing number of neo-conservative movements towards the end of the millennium: Opus Dei, Focolare and several Anglican-based groups. Some 'House Churches' are neo-radical, and can become 'cultish'. Yet considerable caution should be exercised in using these terms: arguably, Christianity was once a Jewish sect. More recently, Ray Wallis, *The Elementary Forms of New Religious Life* (1984), describes three kinds of group: those that engage, respectively, in Accommodation, Rejection and Affirmation of the world. Charisma is seen by Wallis to be vital in the maintenance of such groups, but it is a 'precarious commodity'.

Many scholars now agree that the partial secularization of society, coupled with the fragmentation of corporate or established religious life in the West, creates a 'free spiritual market' in which new religious movements can thrive. This process is accelerating. Moreover, such movements are often innovative in their beliefs and practice, including the development of 'alternative' forms of kinship. In other words, if 'families are failing' in the West (and this is a widely held assumption, although highly contestable), alternative forms of family are well-placed to fill the gap.

The characteristic response of pro-family and pro-mainstream religious lobbies is to 'demonize' the new religions for either causing, accelerating, or profiting from the fragmentation. Occasionally, some more 'right wing' groups have launched 'cult rescue' initiatives, or even attempted 'deprogramming' of allegedly vulnerable members. But this is probably an unfair overreaction to a common phenomenon. Sects, cults, new movements and alternative forms of family life have had their followers in every era of history. However, the conditions of postmodernity mean that followers are more choosy about what they believe: 'à la carte Catholics' are an instructive example. People seem increasingly content to believe yet not belong, which means that 'niche religious groups' can target specific audiences and thrive. The notion that new religious movements and sects 'brainwash' their followers has largely been discounted, but it may be true that 'horizons' of belief and rationality are more obviously narrowed and controlled in such groups.

The contours of concern

According to J. Saliba, *Perspectives on New Religious Movements* (1995), there are positives and negatives to be derived from membership of cults, sects or new religious movements. On the minus side, there may be demands for total allegiance to a leader or a creed that infringe the rights or freedom of an individual. Furthermore, rational thought may be 'discouraged', perhaps because it is portrayed as a barrier to 'faith' or religious experience (e.g. healing, deliverance, encounter, etc.). Features of groups can include tyrannical leadership, offensive or destructive proselytizing, and a rigid, all-embracing ideology that abrogates previous relationships or personal responsibility. That said, it is still important to remember that a number of 'mainstream' religious groups and orders are morphologically similar.

On the positive side, new religions, cults and sects can offer liberation from destructive or suffocating patterns of social life, including those which may be encountered in families. The alternative form of kinship offered may be attractive because of its immediacy, intimacy and identity, which is more fulfilling for an individual. In my research, I have met members of the Jesus Army, the Family of God, Community House Churches, Closed Brethren and others who voluntarily choose to lose their individual rights in favour of a being adopted by a new kind of kinship that they claim is superior to the families they have effectively left. Such people are not 'brainwashed', even though their original family members speak of 'losing' the individual, and of their personalities being 'altered' by the religious group. Alternative religious groups often offer a mixture of enthusiastic, experiential, disciplined and communal faith that creates new relationships.

That said, scholars also note that the optimum age for joining such a group is often in the late teens or early twenties. Frequently, in this normal era of experimentation in early adult life, religion is also something that will be explored. Yet as E. Barker, J. Saliba and others note, well over 90 per cent of those who join a new religion during this time will have left it within two years. Experimental religion, for many, is simply a phase.

Nonetheless, there are psychological characteristics that might indicate the type of individuals who may be likely to be attracted to a new religion. Some studies show that disaffected youths who are (a) deprived, (b) alienated, (c) religiously inclined/extreme, (d) experiencing some identity crisis or loss may be especially vulnerable. But this criterion encompasses almost all young people at some stage of their lives, and so its value as an indicator is rather limited. Moreover, it is important to stress that members of alternative religious groups may be: (a) normal, (b) not brainwashed, (c) often needy. People who join these groups may be converted, or may simply drift in (and eventually out): but they are not normally forced in against their will.

New religious movements are not necessarily destructive. They can be therapeutic, and provide helpful accounts of life for people. It is increasingly normal to see joining cults or new religious movements as a kind of rite of passage. This does not pose a drastic threat to family life; it simply highlights its limitations in a postmodern age. Protecting families against allegedly predatory cults – by offering rescue, de-programming and the like – is usually an overreaction to a situation, if not an outright mistake.

The form of family life is invariably inculcated into religious values and structures, and vice versa, that make the study of alternative religions in postmodern society all the richer. 'Fathers', 'Mothers', 'Child', 'Brother', 'Sister' and 'Member' are all terms that occur with frequency in most religions and most families. The conflation of terminology and identity, which in turn is linked to perceptions of what is divine, godly, authoritative or moral, can have the capacity to be either liberating or enslaving. The judgement of this depends on a complex equation, weighing the individual, group and context, situation and issue, the past, present and future.

For example, some families have used violent or illegal methods to 'rescue' or recapture one of their members. Equally, some cults have resorted to 'love-bombing' (letters, harassment, etc.) to pressurise ex-cult members to leave their families and rejoin the group. The metaphors and actuality of domestic/religious violence demonstrate that competition between families and alternative religions is high, and is an emotive issue. What is clear from this is that alternative religious groups will continue to provide alternative patterns of kinship that will closely resemble both the best and worst of family life. Family life, in turn, cannot prevent individuation and experimentation among its members, which may well include a religious dimension or phase. In such circumstances, understanding, empathy, dialogue and patience may be more valuable than any attempt forcibly to terminate what might turn out to be a tenuous and passing affiliation.

Conclusion: pastoral considerations

A movement by an individual towards a 'new' religious movement or a 'cult' often poses more of a problem for the family and friends who are left behind than it does for the initiate or convert. Very few religious groups can be deemed to be abusive, manipulative or dangerous. However, what they often have in common is that they bind people together in a new form of community. Inevitably, those who do join change their ideals, goals, lifestyle and relations. It is worth remembering that Jesus was no less demanding of his disciples: they were required to abandon their familes, jobs – and even the dead – to embrace the coming kingdom. Religions, by definition, upset existing social order and offer alternatives that are either competitive or complementary. Inevitably, religion reshapes minds and hearts.

One of the major pastoral considerations in addressing families, cults and new religious movements is keeping a sense of proportion. Those who are concerned about a 'sudden change' in someone – of lifestyle, character or behaviour – may find that the adjustment is akin to a kind of temporary bereavement. However, it must be remembered that for the convert who embraces a new faith, the trauma can be as great as for those who feel they have in this way 'lost' someone. In such circumstances, support is vital. The fact that a person embraces a new faith need not be read as a definitive rejection of their past, even though, in the early stages, it may appear to be so. Dialogue remains a vital key to fostering empathy and understanding, so that channels are kept as open as possible. From here, 'enabling' perspectives can grow that will lay the foundation for new relationships, irrespective of whether the choice to join a new faith turns out to be a passing phase or a decision that lasts a lifetime.

Bibliography

E. Barker, *New Religious Movements: A Practical Introduction* (London, 1989)
A. Brockway and J. Rajashekar, *New Religious Movements and the Churches* (Geneva, 1987)
M. Hamilton, *The Sociology of Religion: Theoretical and Comparative Perspectives* (London, 1995), ch. 17
M. McGuire, *Religion: The Social Context* (Belmont, Calif., 1992)
J. Melton, *Encylopaedia of American Religion* (Charlotte, NC, 1978)
J. Melton, *Encylopaedic Handbook of Cults in America* (New York, 1992)

K. Rabuzzi, 'Family', in M. Eliade, *Encyclopaedia of Religion* (New York, 1987)
J. Saliba, *Perspectives on New Religious Movements* (London, 1995)
R. Wallis, *The Elementary Forms of New Religious Life* (London, 1984)
B. Wilson, *Religious Sects* (London, 1970)

24

The pastoral care of people of other faiths

Christopher Lamb

Large issues

Who were the 'sheep' Peter was instructed to feed by the risen Lord? (John 21.17; cf. 10.16). Did they exclude those committed to other understandings of faith and religion? Is it conceivable that Christ's followers were intended to care only for those of their own 'household of faith' (Galatians 6.10)? If not, it is clear that pastoral care has an ineradicable missionary dimension. But how is that mission to be carried out? The question of the pastoral care of those outside the Christian community (however that is defined) thus raises large issues about the nature and purpose of pastoral care.

The pastor can normally rely on some sharing of the common inheritance of Christian assumptions and explicit teaching when in contact with the baptized. With those whose inheritance is Buddhist, Hindu, Muslim or Sikh there may be a lively spirituality, but there are likely to be problems other than a simple ignorance of Christian teaching. There may also be a residual antagonism to the Christian Church left over from the experience of colonialism. In the case of Jews, the antagonism may rise from centuries of what has been called the Church's 'teaching of contempt' about Judaism and the Jews. In many cases there will be a nervousness that the Christian pastor's ultimate intention is to convert, to 'missionize'. A party of Indian visitors from a British city came to Coventry Cathedral, but insisted that they did not need a guide. I chatted informally with them, and quickly discovered that they were deeply interested in the story and details of the building, but anxious lest an official guide would sit them down and preach Christianity at them. They felt that while they were standing they were safe.

Purity of motive

Anyone who aims to offer pastoral care to those of other faiths will rapidly encounter suspicion of his or her motives. Missionaries have long endured the accusation that their medical, education and social work is not done for its own sake, but simply as a means of exploiting vulnerable and disadvantaged people, and enticing them away from their traditional faith to accept Christianity. The term 'rice Christians' has been widely employed as a disparagement of the Asian churches, many of whose members came out of extreme poverty. Yet these churches are themselves now sending missionaries to other countries, and in some cases enduring not merely insulting comments on the authenticity of their faith but active persecution, for example in Pakistan and North Korea. In Pakistan and India, however, there is widespread admiration of the 'missionary zeal' which founded hospitals, schools, social institutions and other building-blocks of these modern nations.

At the personal level it can be difficult for the Christian pastor to reassure someone of another faith that what is offered in simple friendship, counsel or practical assistance has no strings attached, is unconditional goodwill, has its own authenticity. Help is being offered whether or not the recipient comes to faith in Christ, simply because it is Christ's example which is being followed. As Jesus pictures him, God cares for every last sparrow, and how much more for those made in his image.

Religiously plural societies

We have seen how pastoral care evolved over many centuries within the Christian churches. For most of this time the relationship between Christians and those of the major faith traditions in Europe was one of hostility or studied neglect. In Eastern Europe a genuinely pluralist society developed in only a few cities like Sarajevo and Odessa towards the modern period. In the Middle East the *millet* system created self-contained and, to some extent, self-governing communities based on religious adherence. Since these religiously based communities provided society, welfare, a system of personal and family law, and important elements of culture, very few ever ventured to take the unthinkable step of changing their community. A similar situation obtained further east for other reasons, of caste, or ethnicity. Consequently, though Christians have lived side by side with people of different faiths for many hundreds of years in places like Egypt and Sri Lanka, it is only recently, and in the West, that there has been any expectation that Christians might offer pastoral care to those of other faiths, or indeed receive it from them.

A new responsibility for the churches

Such a new situation has arisen from the unprecedented migration of peoples into Western European and North American cities since 1945, creating multi-ethnic and multi-religious populations where previously there had been relative homogeneity. Since many of those migrants and their families have found themselves in unfamiliar and difficult situations it is understandable that they have at times turned to the recognized religious functionaries of their new homeland for help. Religion in almost every land is associated with help to those in distress. Perhaps the parochial system also had a positive influence at this point. In the parish system the Church's responsibility for its 'cure of souls' is quantified by the total population of a geographically defined area rather than by the number of committed worshipping or donating families. Though this cannot increase the absolute responsibility of the Church to minister to all-comers, it is likely to engender a desire, at least, to be universally available for advice and care to those who live in the parish. This is likely to become known even to those who are unfamiliar with the new culture, if they are in acute need.

It has to be admitted with shame that black Christians from the West Indies were sometimes turned away from 'white' churches with the advice that 'you would be happier worshipping in one of your own churches', and the assumption has to be that 'we would be happier too'. But it is also true that British churches did much to assist Muslims, Hindus and Sikhs to find property and negotiate the bewildering maze of local authority regulations in the early decades of post-war migration. Since then many churches in British inner cities have pioneered advice centres and offered free legal and other information, initiated English-language classes and provided day centres for the elderly, and playgroups and nursery care for toddlers. Although this provision is for all-comers, and of course heavily dependent on local authority finance, it is significant that it consistently brings people of other faiths on to church premises, and into contact with worshipping Christians. Dr Ata'ullah Siddiqui, author of *Christian–Muslim Dialogue in the Twentieth Century* (1997), has written that in the early days of Muslim settlement in Britain

> their 'religious needs' were marginalised. The only sympathetic ear was from the churches ... (Their) response ... was primarily governed by the human concerns and plight of the immigrants. Basic needs, such as housing, jobs and even language interpretations, were taken up by them; Friday congregational facilities were made available for Muslims in some church premises. (*World Faiths Encounter* (November 1996), 14f.)

Engagement and advocacy

There are many other forms of what might be called the 'pastoral care' of an entire community. While one would not want to claim too much for the importance of the churches' activity, it is probably true, at least in the UK, both that communities of other faiths came to expect the assistance and advocacy of the churches at various points in their struggle to establish themselves in an alien environment, and also that the churches responded to those needs. The first needs were for adequate housing, employment and such benefits as the newcomers were entitled to. Later, especially when wives and families began to settle with their menfolk, a whole range of cultural and educational needs became apparent. Many worshipping groups of Muslims, Hindus and Sikhs used ordinary houses as mosques and temples initially, and had to find guidance through the local planning regulations, which had not been drawn up with such situations in mind. Some groups depended on the use of churches or, more often, church halls. As the communities became established, their presence began to be felt in schools, hospitals and soon prisons. In each place it could no longer be presumed that children, patients or prisoners would generally be some variety of Christian or 'post-Christian' or occasionally Jewish. If they were without commitment to religion, it was not necessarily the church they stayed away from. Now it might be the mosque or the temple. It is still noticeable in Britain, however, that religion remains much more important to families of Hindu, Muslim or Sikh origin than it does to the earlier indigenous population.

The vital ladder

Education was seen as the vital ladder for the next generation to leave the hardships of the first-comers behind, and to advance into financial security and acceptance in the wider society. Perhaps the most extensive contact of the families of other faiths with worshipping Christians came through the church schools. Many new citizens who were parents of another faith were uneasy about education which lacked a religious foundation, and they took pains to place their children in the Church of England and Roman Catholic schools in preference to the secular county schools. Some had been aware of, or had personally experienced, the high quality, disciplined education offered in India and Pakistan and elsewhere through schools founded by missionaries. They trusted a religious foundation even though it was not of their own faith, and looked for tight discipline and academic excellence from such schools.

Religious education

Britain is unusual in insisting on the inclusion of religious education among the statutory subjects to be taught in school, though parents have long had the right to withdraw their children from such lessons. The same obligation and concession applies to 'collective worship', in which the school gathers as a worshipping community. These provisions date from the Education Act of 1944, and were not fundamentally altered by the new Act of 1988, despite the decline in church attendance and the arrival of Hindu, Muslim and Sikh schoolchildren in the interim. Though many areas have remained entirely unaffected by such changes, because of 'white flight', there are schools, including church schools, in certain cities where a very high proportion, 90 per cent or even 100 per cent, of the pupils are Hindu, Muslim or Sikh in faith.

Access to public life

In Britain, naturalization has always been encouraged on terms which are generous compared with some other countries, and the legacy of empire has meant that many migrants have expected to exercise citizenship and take their part in British public life. In the nature of things the political parties have had much more to do with enabling that process than the churches. The creation of the Inner Cities Religious Council in 1993, however, demonstrates a partnership between government and the Church of England in particular which is aimed at engaging the religious leaders and networks of all faiths in the task of the economic regeneration of the inner cities, where so many members of minority ethnic communities live. Besides national leaders of the Hindu, Jewish, Muslim and Sikh communities the Council includes a Church of England and a Roman Catholic bishop and representatives of the black majority churches. Its secretary is a priest seconded from the Church of England, who is responsible to the government Department of Transport, Environment and the Regions.

Personal pastoral care among people of other faiths

It is appropriate to have begun with the community aspect of pastoral care in relation to Hindus, Muslims and Sikhs, since they are much less affected as yet by the individualism of Western life, and live communally in a way which has not been experienced by most Westerners for many decades. Even so, the term 'community' can be very misleading when applied to, for example, the Muslims of Britain, whose origins may lie in Pakistan, India, Bangladesh, Kenya, Uganda, Nigeria, Somalia, Turkey, Egypt or a dozen other countries, with no common linguistic or cultural bond between them except Islam and their residence in Britain. Even the mosque has been a source of ethnic division, since complaints are heard that particular mosques are dominated by one or other language group, and even at times by the sources of finance, from Saudi-Arabia, Iran or Libya. British Hindus too may originate from the Indian Punjab, Gujarat or East Africa, again worshipping according to those traditions, and being further divided by caste loyalties.

One consequence of this fragmentation is the confusion of young people from such backgrounds as to what exactly their faith requires of them. Young Muslims in particular may grow up with a set of ideas and practices inculcated from a home where the parents have tried to preserve in their new surroundings the customs and convictions of rural Pakistan. A sense of alienation from the dominant culture and its apparent obsession with sex, and customs forbidding things like alcohol and gambling, may reinforce a determination that their children shall not succumb to the prevailing decadence. Discipline may be harsh. On encountering other young Muslims from a different background, moulded perhaps by the Middle East rather than rural Pakistan or

Bangladesh, the young people begin to ask more seriously what Islam is and stands for, stripped of its cultural variations. Here is an opening for Christian teachers, social workers and pastors to offer a listening ear and a sensitive mind and judgement to young people struggling for an authentic faith. There is no way of knowing how often or how successfully that has been achieved, but any Christian adult in frequent contact with young people of another faith in Britain is likely to have registered the opportunity, and made at least a tentative effort to help. Even older people are often grateful for a conversation with a Christian who is at home in Western culture, who has maintained faith, and so may be a source of wisdom for those struggling on a path the Westerner is presumed to have travelled earlier.

It goes without saying that such exchanges require a level of trust and even intimacy which is not built up overnight, but is the result of long-term, unconditional friendship and mutual understanding. In the last ten years an increasing number of Christians have been employed by local churches in certain cities, aiming at just such friendships in the area served by the churches. Some would see that hope totally vitiated by the aim of evangelism and conversion which often goes with it, but most of the Christian activists are well aware of the potential for disillusionment in such friendships. Sally Sutcliffe, in *Aisha My Sister* (1997), quotes the question of a Muslim woman to her Christian woman friend: 'Do you love me because you want me to follow Christ, or do you want me to follow Christ because you love me?'

Arranged and unarranged marriages

It is no accident that the last example features the friendships of women. It is common experience that women reach a level of intimacy across cultural frontiers more quickly than men, whose conversations often stay with 'safe' subjects of political and economic questions. Women frequently and naturally discuss marriage and marriage prospects, and so it happens that a Christian can be drawn into discussion of an arranged marriage. In India and Pakistan arranged marriages are the norm for most people of all faiths, including Christians, but particular problems can arise in some recently settled families in Britain. Girls can be the source of much anxiety for such parents in case their virtue is questioned, which brings shame on the whole family. There is in consequence a sense of urgency about settling their marriage. But this is often resisted by a girl who sees the opportunity of higher education slipping away from her. More problematic still is the determination of some families to arrange a marriage with a bride or bridegroom from the homeland in India or Pakistan. Many young people from such families, especially girls, do not object to an arranged marriage in principle but want to stipulate that it should be with someone who has also been through the British educational experience. Some boys, however, claim to prefer a 'traditionally-minded' bride from the subcontinent, probably on the assumption that she will be more submissive to male authority. There are even reports of some vigilante activity on the part of young Muslim males, who track down and forcibly return to their homes girls who have run away from parental discipline felt to be intolerably restrictive.

Recent developments in the patterns of employment have brought about a quite new situation in the relationships of the sexes, because women have been able to find employment more readily than men. This has led to some serious difficulties for Asian women in the search for a suitable marriage partner, and even the rejection of marriage as an option for women. This is likely to exacerbate what is probably the sharpest conflict between the generations of Asian families in Britain, which concerns the proper role of women. Christian women can help to hold out the possibility, by precept and example, of female independence and self-fulfilment which has not sacrificed modesty, morality or faith.

Mixed-faith marriages

Christian clergy are likely to be directly involved when an 'unarranged' marriage is proposed between two young people of different faiths. Despite the desires and intentions of parents as noted above, young adult life, especially in college and university, brings together men and women who never imagined that they would marry outside their faith and culture. It is important to recognize that virtually no-one sets out to marry a person from another faith. It simply happens that they fall in love. But the consequences are often not thought through or even foreseen. Most faith communities firmly discourage mixed-faith marriages on the unassailable ground that it is better for married partners and their resulting families to have fundamental beliefs and practices in common. Immediate complications arise over the wedding ceremony, but there are long-term issues which can be causes of conflict for years, like the mundane ones of family custom over food and dress and festival, and the critical one of the religious identity and nurture of the children. Will it be Christmas or Hanukah? Baptism or circumcision? Both or neither? Kosher, halal, vegetarian or 'Western' food? What about alcohol? And in the end will it be burial or cremation?

Little solid research has yet been done on the incidence or character of mixed-faith marriages, but anecdotal evidence suggests that they may be more susceptible to divorce even than other marriages in the Western world. It is not the case that the partners are necessarily indifferent to their faith, at least initially. As noted above, people do not plan to fall in love across the faith divide. But the couple in which both partners retain a lively commitment each to their own faith would appear to be rare, and a common result of mixed-faith marriage seems to be either the dominance of one of the faiths or eventual indifference to all religion. It just creates too many problems.

One world people

One of the features of international migration has been the growing number of families which are split between three and even four continents. It is not uncommon for professional people in Britain whose families' origins lie in South Asia or East Africa to travel regularly to, say, India, Kenya and Canada, visiting close family members. This gives added significance in the context of pastoral care to international gatherings of churches, such as the ten-yearly Lambeth Conference of bishops of the Anglican Communion. In the 1998 Conference much greater attention was paid to the interfaith dimension of the Church's life than in any previous Conference, and Islam in particular was much discussed. It was clear that relationships between Christians and Muslims vary hugely across the globe, but also that the sustained attempts to create mutual trust in places like Bradford could have a beneficial effect on the very difficult situation of Christians in Pakistan. Conversely, British church leaders have consistently refused to hold Muslims in Britain accountable for what their co-religionists are reported to do to Christians in other countries. The advocacy of human rights, now seen as an integral part of pastoral care, has to be promoted indiscriminately for all.

Bibliography

James Beckford and Sophie Gilliat, *Religion in Prison: Equal Rites in a Multi-Faith Society* (Cambridge, 1998)

Communities and Buildings: Church of England Premises and other Faiths (Church House Publishing, 1996)

Roger Hooker and Christopher Lamb, *Love the Stranger: Ministry in Multi-faith Areas* 2nd edn (London, 1993)

Inter-Faith Consultative Group, *'Multi-Faith Worship'?: Questions and Suggestions from the Church of England's Board of Mission* (Church House Publishing, 1992)

The Marriage of Adherents of Other Faiths in Anglican Churches: A Report from the Inter-Faith Consultative Group to the House of Bishops, Church of England Board of Mission Occasional Paper No. 1

Marriages Between Christians and Muslims, ed. Christopher Lamb (Conference of European Churches, and European Catholic Bishops Conferences, 1998)

Religions in the UK: A Multi-Faith Directory, 2nd edn (Derby University and the Inter-Faith Network, 1997)

Rabbi Jonathan Romain, *Till Faith Us Do Part: Couples Who Fall in Love Across the Religious Divide* (HarperCollins, 1996)

Conclusion

This book tells a lengthy story and the reader who begins at the beginning and reads straight through must be left with the question whether it is a single story, or whether the history of Christian pastoral care has become so fragmented, has gone down so many by-ways, that it is now not one but several. For an answer one must go back to the New Testament and the early Church, for it is there that the ground-rules are laid.

Something bearing the distinctive marks of Jesus' teaching is described in all the chapters, but it is sometimes apparent that here, in orthopraxis (the orthodox living of the Christian life) there have been the same strains of inculturation as in orthodoxy (the maintenance of the faith century by century in culture after culture).

The book holds in balance and in tension not only the changes of the centuries but also a mixture of different 'churchmanships' and of ecumenical stances. Richard O'Brien writes about the sacramentality of penance and the anointing of the sick, from a Roman Catholic point of view; Rupert Bursell about canon law from the vantage-point of an English Anglican member of the judiciary. It is the more remarkable that that same inner core of consistency about the priorities of pastoral care is noticeable in so varied a list of contributions.

Inevitably there are gaps, even in so lengthy a volume, but we hope that the reader will be stimulated, as the contributors often remarked that they themselves had been, by the perception of cross-references, links and comparisons between the various accounts. These point to the deeper reaches of what is, in the end, the fulfilment of the law of the love of neighbour and God.

Index

abbot 77
Abelard, Peter 101ff, 404
Abraham 16, 45, 156, 368
absolution 67, 85, 109, 181, 227, 404, 406
abuse 388, 452
  child 271
acceptance, human need for 388
accommodation 254ff
  sleeping rough 336
acolyte 186
Acts, Book of 35
Adam and Eve 259
adaptability 307
Adderley, James 328, 330, 331, 332ff
adultery 93, 238, 402
Aesop 215ff
Africa 63
  East 462
African Americans 440
Albigensians 127, 404
alcoholics 419
Alexandria 71, 79, 116
Alfred, King 216
alienation 450
almsgiving 40, 66, 79, 121, 265, 403
altar 225
amateurs 384
Ambrose of Milan 7, 71, 95, 205, 206, 238
amendment of life 238
America 456
American clinical pastoral training 389
Anabaptists 235, 440
angels 66
Anglicans 214, 367, 392, 434, 438

Anglo-Saxons 94
anointing of the sick 401, 407ff
antinomianism 45
Antioch 31, 71, 79, 116
apocalyptic 53, 69
apostasy 53, 64, 95, 238, 402
apostolates 329
apostolic life 126
Aquinas, Thomas 123, 209, 404
Aramaic 31
architecture 298
  Church 225
ARCIC 435
Arminianism 314, 321
arts, the 257
asceticism 35, 36, 48, 68, 93, 94
Asia 455
  South 462
astrology 118
atheism 320
atonement 51
Augustine, Rule of 68, 151
Augustine of Hippo 7, 8, 61ff, 65, 69, 71, 95,
    205, 209, 270
Augustinians 117, 123
Austen, Jane 4

Babylon 24
Bangladesh 459
baptism 56–63, 70, 72, 202ff, 273ff, 316,
    352ff, 358, 420ff
  of desire 353
  of Jesus 36
  effect of 354

efficacy of 278
emergency 179, 268, 420
infant 3, 61, 203, 264, 266
sin after 93ff
Baptists 2, 368
barbarians 69
Basil, St 68, 79
Baxter, Richard 313, 314, 315, 316ff, 320, 363, 385
Bedlam 363
behavioural sciences 388, 392
Benedict, Rule of St 68
benefices 186
bereavement 417, 423
Bernard of Clairvaux 7
Bethlehem 24
Beza, Theodore 245
Bible 211, 398, *passim*
Bible study 8, 133
Biel, Gabriel 228
'binding and loosing' 38, 67, 233, 236
bishops 49, 71, 72, 73, 119, 128, 174, 404
Black Death 169ff, 171, 175
body, care of 237
Body of Christ 1, 396
Boethius 70
Boisen, Anton 388
Bonaventure 66
Bonhoeffer, Dietrich 15
Boniface VIII 173
Book of Common Prayer 272ff, 299
brainwashing 450
Brazil 54
bride of Christ 3
brokenness 87
Browning, Don 389
Bucer, Martin 231, 237–40, 363
Buddhism 391, 392, 454, 459
Bullinger 245
burial 422–3
Burnet, Gilbert 319, 362, 363, 313, 319ff
Byzantium 115

Caesarius of Arles 95, 97
Calvin; Calvinism 62, 63, 212, 240–7, 285, 295, 314, 315, 319, 321, 323, 363, 368, 405
campaigning 343
Canberra 437, 439
canon law 105, 116, 119
'care in the community' 384ff, 394ff, 396

carers 384, 395
Carmelites 117, 123, 334
Carolingians 409
Carthusians 118
Cassian, John 95ff
casuistry 316
catechesis 201ff, 316, 257, 209ff, 299, 301, 365
catechumens 61, 62, 403
Catharism 113
Catholic 392, *passim*
catholica 63
causation 169
celibacy 73, 264, 271, 403
Celsus 62, 64
Chalcedon, Council of 451
chantries 188
charism 49, 51, 70, 117, 392
charismatic figures 392
charity 403
Charlemagne 205, 409
chastity 208
Chaucer 121
children 214ff, 263–4, 266ff, 275, 347
abandoned 154ff
abused 271
children in the faith 203
China 140
Christine de Pisan 207, 208
Church 63, 80, 229, 351, 352, 407, 433
attendance 283
early 365
marks of 233
as mother 6
churchmanship 39
churchyards 414–15, 424
Cicero 205, 206
circumcelliones 64
circumcision 45
Cistercians 127, 335
City of God 204
Clare of Assisi 123
class meeting 364
Clement V, Pope 148
Clement VI, Pope 182
Clement of Alexandria 67, 203
clergy
shortage of 185
social origins 365ff
clinical care 387
Clinical Theology Association 388

codes   414
collegiality   70
Columbanus   103
Commandments, Ten   211, 227, 268, 276, 315
commerce   135
community   339, 384ff, 394ff
companionship   384ff
completeness   307–8
compunction   101
conferences, episcopal   407
confession   181, 223, 224, 227ff, 236ff, 241, 254, 267, 276, 389, 403, 419
  annual   117
  auricular   288
  of sins   162
confessor   77
confessor's manuals   227
confidentiality   419
confirmation   179, 266, 274
confraternities   255ff, 267
Congregationalism   39, 319, 440
consanguinity   120
conscience   314, 315
Constantine   59
Constantinople   71, 116, *see also* Byzantium
contemplative communities   329
continence   73
contrition   172, 404
Corpus Christi   228
correction   271
Cosin, John   285
cosmic order   225
counselling   84, 85, 260, 283, 363, 383ff, 386, 397, 398
Coventry   454
Cowley Fathers   336
Cranmer, Thomas   225, 228, 275, 299
creation   113, 202
creativity   115
Creed   113, 211, 243, 276
  Nicene   437
crime and punishment   98–9
Cross, sign of the   234, 277
Crusade; crusaders   114, 126, 149
cults   42, 446ff
cure of souls   418ff
Cyprian   95
Cyril of Alexandria   64
Cyril of Jerusalem   202

Dante   134
David   25
de-skilling   390
deacons   6, 38, 49, 71, 74, 100, 242, 351
Dead Sea scrolls   39
deadly sins, seven   227
death   267, 365, 386, 400, 406
  of God   392
debate, theological   368
deification   209
demons   66
Desert Fathers   7, 68 , 77ff
devil   79
devotional tracts   210
diaries   288
diaspora   52
dignity of labour   335
Diognetus   59
Disciples of Christ   436
discipline   254, 233, 362
  Church   323
discrimination   385
dispensation   414
disputes   15
dissent   318ff, 324, 325, 363, 367ff
divine guidance   349
divorce   422
doctors   365
Dominic   126, 127
Dominicans   117, 118, 252
Donatism   63, 95
Donne, John   286
dress   208
dualism   113

Eastern Orthodox   438, 440
eccentricity   4
ecclesial context   301
ecclesiology   241, 351, 440, 441
ecumenism   433ff
education   245, 253, 309, 322ff, 434, 458
  adult   258
  of clergy   190ff, 246ff, 321ff
  higher   461
  religious   458
Egypt   18, 78
elders   38, 49
election   314
Elijah   17, 19
Elisha   19
engagement   456

Ephesus, Council of   64
Erasmus   256
eschatology   37, 41, 43, 48, 134
eternal life   362
ethics   44, 46, 51
ethnic cleansing   384
Eucharist   78, 79, 85, 113, 180, 182, 223, 224, 225ff, 403, 435, 408
Eusebius of Caesarea   31, 321
evangelicals   8, 319, 346, 435
evangelism   325, 342
evil spirits   36
excommunication   73, 325, 236
exempla   132
exhumation   416, 427ff
exorcism   36
experience   303, 363
experts   85
extreme unction   400–1, 409

Faith
  and order   435, 439
  and works   50, 62
family   5, 16, 31, 262ff, 446
Family of God   450
fasting   36, 37, 40, 66, 69, 172, 228, 403
fatherhood   77
Fathers, the   30, 35, 302, 324
Ferrar, Nicholas   297
fines   98, 101
Finnian   101ff
First Mover   209
First World War   336
Florence, Council of, 1439   404, 410
folk elements   211
foot-washing   80ff
forgiveness   93ff, 401
fornication   95, 99
Francis, St   123, 126
Franciscan Third Order   331–2, 395
Franciscans   117, 252, 410
  Anglican   328ff
Franks   94
fratricide   16
Freckleton   415
free will   202
freedom   315
  of choice   447
friars   77, 126ff, 252ff, 330ff
Friends *see* Quakers
funeral sermons   284–6

funerals   180

gentry   365
Germany   230ff
Gerson, Jean   206, 207
gifts, diversity of   79
gifts of the Spirit   227
Gildas   99
God, will of   315
  word of   404, 406
godparents   265
good life   206
Good Shepherd   5
goodness   359
Gospel   31ff, 228, 384, 385
Gower, John   190
grace   41, 61, 63, 99, 208, 229, 266, 349, 351, 359
Gratian   106
Greece   43
Gregory of Rimini   228
Gregory the Great   7, 71, 72, 68, 75, 96, 223, 318, 390
guilt   61, 387, 392

hagiography   6
handbooks   364ff
healing   1, 307, 363, 383ff, 386, 387, 395, 407ff
  professions   386
healthcare   384
hearers   62
heart, change of   403
heathen   2
heaven   8
hedonism   390
Helena   59
Hellenism   51
Herbert, George   286–7, 294ff, 385
heresy   47, 49, 50, 53, 64, 126, 447
Hermas   93
hermetic tradition   351
hermits   68, 78ff
hierarchy   70
Hindus   391, 448, 454, 456, 458, 459
holiness   62, 302, 303, 345, 443
'holistic healing'   394
Holy Land   113, 122, 128, 138
holy man   68
holy places   66
Holy Spirit   34, 37, 69, 71, 72, 75, 209, 441

Index

homily 49, 278
hospital
  beds 154
  women's 164
hospitality 82, 148ff
Hospitallers 148ff
house-to-house visiting 381
House Churches 450
household 282–3, 302, 309
  godly 288
human rights 462
humanism 234
Humbert of Romans 130
humility 81ff
hymnography 204
hypocrites 185

iconography 210, 211
identity crisis 451
ideology 450
idolatry 317
Ignatius of Loyola 252ff
illegitimacy 276
images 211, 226
immanence 399
Incarnation 51, 441
income, clerical 366
India 140, 340, 460
individuals 16ff, 82, 384
  ministry to 370ff
individualism 3, 4
indulgences 181, 210, 121, 229
Industrial Revolution 329
industrialization 364
Inner Cities Religious Council 1993 458
Innocent I, Pope 409
Innocent III, Pope 113, 126ff
instruction 268, 276
  religious 270
instrument 400
intolerance 115
Iona Community 395
Ireland 94
Irenaeus 35
Isidore of Seville 97
Islam 114, 115
Israel 17
itineracy 330, 336

Jeremiah 398
Jerome 69, 75, 95, 205, 206

Jerusalem 25, 71, 116, 149, 150
Jesuits 252ff
Jesus Army 450
Jews 59, 113, 121
Joachim of Fiore 114
Job 20
John of Salisbury 206
John the Baptist 35, 41
Josephus 321
Judah 24ff
Judaism 31ff, 449, 457
judgement 83, 84, 362, 387
judicial arrangements 16
jurisdiction 252, 419
just war 440
justice 414
justification by faith 61, 227ff, 314, 346
Justin Martyr 67
Justinian 414

Kant, Immanuel 363
'keys' saying 38
Kierkegaard, Søren 375
kin-groups 22
Kingsley, Charles 345ff
koinonia 71, 438ff
kosher 462

La Fontaine 215ff
l'Arche 395
laity 64, 74, 78, 117, 133, 224, 225, 230, 233, 268ff, 286, 384ff, 403
Lambeth Conference 462
Lambourne, Robert 394ff
Langland, William 190
Languedoc 138
lapsed Christians 64, 65
Lateran III, Council 116
Lateran IV, Council 113, 126, 172, 192, 210, 223, 227, 403
law 98
  lawyers 365
lay ministry 363
Lazarus 156
learning difficulties 395
legal cases 45
Leiden 146
letters of commendation 74
libri poenitentiales 404
light 41, 42, 46, 202
literacy 269

Little Gidding 297
liturgy 79, 231, 203, 295ff, 299ff, 321, 406
liturgists 406
local communities 343
Lollards 6
Lombard, Peter 404
Lord's Prayer 205, 211, 243, 276
Lord's Supper 43, 70
'love-bombing' 451
loyalty 341
Loyola, Ignatius 306, 393, 398
Luther, Martin 61, 211, 212, 228ff, 241, 271, 363, 377, 405
Lutheran-Catholic dialogue 441
Lutherans 435, 438, 440
Lyons, Council of 115
Lyons, Second Council of 1274 140, 148

Magdeburg, Mechtild of 123
magic 118, 362
Malachi 7
managerial skills 384,
manners 207, 323
manual labour 74
Margery Kempe 8
Marie de France 216
marriage 4, 120, 178, 262ff, 316, 421
  arranged 469
  banns of 265
  clerical 272
  mixed faith 461, 462
Martha 78
martyrs 67
Mary, Virgin 269, 441, 444
Masses, private intercessory 267–8
masturbation 206
maturity 400
Maurice, F.D. 330
medical roles 159
medicine 17, 34, 36, 87, 118, 170, 246, 307, 315, 322
meekness 37, 72
melancholy 317
Melanchthon 229ff
membership 3, 56, 353
memorials 416, 423
mendicants 9
menstruation 270
mercy 106, 238, 357, 414
  works of 173
Merton, Thomas 391, 392, 393

Messiah 38
'Messianic secret' 33
Methodists 7, 363, 436, 438
Middle East 455
midwives 179
militancy 392
military orders 148
military roles 159
millennium 434
Milton, John 224
ministry 232, 234, 252ff, 257, 314, 322
minorities 385
miracles 33, 36, 225, 394
mirror of princes 215
mission 137, 253ff, 374, 397, 436
missionaries 455
missions 126
mob violence 52
monasticism 39, 77ff, 328ff
monks 100, 117, 252
Montanists 69, 402
moral authority 421
Moral Rearmament 340–1
moral training 209
Moravians 364
Mormons 448
Morocco 138
Moses 16, 49
mothers 211
Motlman, Jürgen 395
Mowrer, Hobart 389
murder 95, 238, 402
Muslims 454, 456, 457, 458–9
mystery 201
mysticism 8, 391

narcissism 390
naturalizations 458
nature, study of 345–6
Nazianzen, Gregory 96, 97
neighbour 1, 66, 77, 351
Nestorius 64
new creature 203
New Testament 1, 3, 402
Nicaea, Council of 64, 65, 64, 73, 74, 402
Niebuhr, Reinhold 389
nonconformist ministry 366
non-residence 322
North Korea 455
Nouwen, Henry 396
Novatians 402

noviciate   334
nuns   77
nuptial Mass   265
nursing   154

obedience   262ff, 269, 270, 280
Oden, Thomas C.   390, 391
oikonomia   414
oppression   385
order   70, 230ff, 239, 348ff, 415
ordination   72, 194, 316
  candidates for   174
    examination of   174
Oriental Orthodox   438, 440
Origen   64, 74, 75
original sin   2, 9, 61, 352
Orthodox   201ff, 441
other faiths   454ff
outcasts   10, 34, 335–9
outsiders   32, 53, 252ff

Padua, Anthony of   135
paganism   44, 59
pain   384
Pakistan   455, 459ff
palliative care   331
Papias of Hierapolis   31, 33
'papistry'   328
parental responsibility   262ff
parenting classes   390
Paris, Mathew   131, 134
parish   118, 131, 140, 253, 332, 437
  churches   117
  life   175ff
  priest   294ff
  registers   275
parousia   48
pastoral care   385ff *passim*
pastors   5, 454
patriarchate   71
patriarchs   115
Patrick   97, 98
Paul, St   4, 34, 42, 71, 253
peace-makers   86
Pelagius   61
penance   66, 170, 172, 223, 227ff, 236, 267, 355, 360, 400ff
  public   94, 99, 106, 402
  repetition of   95
penitential cycle   224
penitential manuals   106

'penitentials', Celtic   94
penitents   67, 392
Pentecostalism   69, 448
Perkins, William   313ff
persecution   52
Peter, St   33, 38, 71
pilgrimage   363, 443
pilgrims   148ff, 157ff, 224
plague, 'Children's'   184
Plato   49
pluralism, religious   455
poor   172, 328ff, 385, 434
Poor Law   3
Poor Men of Lyons   6
Popes   122, 126ff, 137ff, 444
popular piety   224
post-Christian   362, 457
poverty   34, 67, 126, 188, 189, 328ff
  clerical   366
  evangelical   134
  spiritual   34
power   342
  divine   433
powerlessness   38
prayer   34, 40, 66, 71, 78, 85, 87, 228, 301, 302, 328ff, 335, 403
  as witness   343
  corporate   299
preaching   70, 72, 116, 128ff, 140, 172, 231ff, 235ff, 240ff, 253, 268, 278, 300ff, 315, 321ff, 364–5, 367ff
  sermon-tasting   368
  topical   368
predestination   62, 296
pregnancy   276, 270
Presbyterianism   39
Presbyterians   319, 323, 325, 371, 436
presbyters   100, 408
prie-dieu   392
priesthood of all believers   232, 233–6
priests   6, 71, 72, 73, 128, 404
printing   385
prison   66, 159ff
private judgement   386
problem-solving   395
processions   183, 227, 258
professional accreditation   384
professionalism   364, 390
professionalization   390
prophecy   42, 50
prophets   17

prostitutes 207
providence 348ff
prudence 207
psalms 16, 78
psychiatry 394
psychology 392
psychotherapy 394
punishment 347, 356
  condign 356
  corporal 347
purification 172, 267, 274, 353
Puritanism 296
Puritans 318ff
purity 38
  laws of 16

Quadrilateral, Chicago–Lambeth 434
Quakers 288, 440
quasi-judicial sacrament 94

Rahner, Karl 393, 394, 395
rape 16
Ratzinger, Joseph 433
Real Presence 226
realism 389
reason 362
rebirth 358
reception (Eucharistic) 225
reconciliation 37–8, 238, 362, 400, 404
rectors 319
redemption 79, 387
Reformation 224, 419
reformers 405
relationships 31
relics 121, 224
Renaissance 207, 256
repentance 81, 96, 128, 358
  public 324
reputation 207
responsibility 387
restitution 389
restoration 1
resurrection 40
retreat 259, 393
retribution 356, 357
revelation 386
revival 258, 340–1
Rhodes 162
righteousness 40
rigorism 64, 356, 402
ring, wedding 269

Rite of Peace 406
ritual 16
Rogers, Carl 389
Roman Catholics 440
Roman Curia 122
Rome 4, 33, 43, 69, 228
Rufinus 97
rules 348
rural life 175
Russia 2, 9

Sabbath 37, 38
sacramental ministry 172
sacraments 61, 78, 85, 94, 178, 179, 181, 233, 271, 400
saints 65, 284
salvation 113, 172, 226, 228, 278, 315, 360, 387, 417
  religion of 15
Samaritans, the 390
Samuel 17
sanctification 209, 346, 350ff
Satan 38
satisfaction 227
Saul 17
Saxony, Jordan of 131
schism 63, 448, 449
Schleiermacher, Freidrich 363, 374, 386
scholasticism 230
schoolmasters 252ff
schools 133, 256ff, 331
  cathedral 192
science 362ff
Scotus, Duns 123
Scripture 78, *passim*; *see also* Bible
Second Coming 69
 sects 42, 51, 446ff
secular guidance 17
secular learning 256ff
secularism 383
secularization 364
self-fulfilment 387
Seneca 206
seniority 49
sensuality 316, 317
Sermon on the Mount 40
sermons *see* preaching
sex 276, 341, 374, 397
sexual sins 103, 324
sexuality 434
shepherd 18, 72, 387, 388, 398

sickness   270, 277, 307
sign   400
Sikhs   454, 456, 458, 459
silence   85
Simon   121
simony   73
sin   1ff, 15, 17, 84 , 93ff, 170, 172, 305, 347,
       348, 358, 387, 401
singing   215
Sisters of the Love of God   334
slavery   47, 316
sobriety   208
social conscience   347
social control   224
social hierarchy   309
social injustice   342
social mobility   390
society   25
solitude   85
Son of God   37
soothsayers   25
soul   3, 223, 386
   doctor   318
   friend   387
Spain   34, 114
Spirit, Holy   395
spiritual
   autobiography   315
   direction   260, 384ff, 384, 387, 390ff, 397
   ecumenism   440
   exercises   254
   friendship   340
   growth   36
   guidance   305
   sickness   170
   welfare   169
spirituality   294ff
St Cher, Hugh of   133
state religion   2
stewards   418
Strasbourg   237
sub-deacons   264
suffering   67
Sunday   368
   'best'   317
   Schools   10
superstition   65, 224
Switzerland   234
swords   119
syncretism   59, 65
Syria   33

Taizé   395
taxes   119
Taylor, Jeremy   306, 313, 316
teaching   238, 331, 298ff
Templars   148ff
Temple   42
temptation of Jesus   36
Tertullian   356
Tetzel, John   121
Thatcher, Margaret   48
theatre   66, 203, 257
Theodore of Canterbury   104
Theodulf of Orléans   104
theology
   academic   314
therapist   388
Thompson, Francis   11
Tillich, Paul   375, 387, 388
tithes   120
transcendence   399
Trappists   391
treasury of merits   66
Trent, Council of   231, 254, 406, 410
Trinity   113, 209, 434, 441, 442
Troelsch   447
Trollope, Anthony   4
Tyre, William of   151

Unitarians   368
United States of America   2, 384
universities   138, 232, 314, 321, 372ff
urbanization   364
   urban life   204
   urban problems   134ff
usury   135, 136, 137

Vanier, Jean   395
Vatican II Council   405, 406, 411
vernacular   211, 212, 217, 268, 385
vice   113, 205–6, 208
virtue   205–6, 208
visitation   277
visitation of the sick   267, 274ff
vocation   236, 303, 304, 365

Waldensians   404
Walton, Isaac   298ff
wayfarers   335
wealth   34, 67
weapons, mass destruction of   384
weddings   215, *see also* marriage

Wesley, John 363
West Indies 456
wholeness 387, 391, 392
Wilberforce, William 4
wills 267
Winfrey, Oprah 397
Wisdom 41
witchcraft 363
wizards 25

women 211, 257ff
  religious 329
Woodforde, Parson 365
worship 299, 302, 443
'wound healers' 388

York 416

Zwingli, Huldrych 234–6, 242